Tapping State Government Information Sources

Tapping State Government Information Sources

Lori L. Smith, Daniel C. Barkley,
Daniel D. Cornwall, Eric W. Johnson,
and J. Louise Malcomb

GREENWOOD PRESS
Westport, Connecticut • London

Library of Congress Cataloging-in-Publication Data

Tapping state government information sources / Lori L. Smith . . . [et al.].
    p. cm.
   Includes bibliographical references and index.
   ISBN 1–57356–387–0 (alk. paper)
   1. State government publications—United States—Bibliography.   2. State
governments—United States—Information resources.   I. Smith, Lori L.
Z1223.5.A1T36   2003
015.73053—dc21   2002044846

British Library Cataloguing in Publication Data is available.

Library of Congress Catalog Card Number: 2002044846
ISBN: 1–57356–387–0

First published in 2003

Greenwood Press, 88 Post Road West, Westport, CT 06881
An imprint of Greenwood Publishing Group, Inc.
www.greenwood.com

Printed in the United States of America

The paper used in this book complies with the
Permanent Paper Standard issued by the National
Information Standards Organization (Z39.48–1984).

10 9 8 7 6 5 4 3 2 1

This book is dedicated to Margaret T. Lane.

Her career has inspired us all.

Contents

Preface

Anyone who lives in the United States knows that Americans are not just Americans. They are also residents of the Granite State, the Lone Star State, the Hoosier State, the Beehive State, or one of the forty-six other political entities that joined together long ago to become the United States of America. Each of these states has its own unique culture and its own government. Each state government collects and publishes its own print and electronic information, and most have established some system for making this information available to their citizens. This book will serve as an introduction to the information that is produced by and about states, and as a guide for those who wish to gain access to it.

Although many of the sources described in this book include information about U.S. territories such as Guam and Puerto Rico, the publications of those governments will not be discussed here.

This book will be of use to persons planning to move to another state, to businesses that are considering expanding to another state, to librarians who wish to collect publications issued in other states, and to anyone with a curiosity about the unique nature of state governments and their information policies. It will also serve as a valuable source for state and local information resources, which are often difficult to find.

For each state, the most important state government–produced publications are listed, as well as some commercial publications. Publications and web sites are listed under these categories:

- Government Publishing and the Depository System
- Useful Addresses and Telephone Numbers
- Indexes to State Publications
- Essential State Publications
    Directories
    Financial/Budgetary Resources

  Legal Resources
  Statistical Resources
  Other Resources
- World Wide Web Home Page
- Commercial Publications and Web Sites

Much of the information in this book was obtained from the Internet. As most users of the Internet know, web addresses tend to change from time to time. The addresses given here for specific resources were correct at the time the writing of this book was completed. If any of the addresses are no longer correct, look at the home page of the agency or institution given as the producer of the resource to see if a link to the title can be located.

Every effort has been made to identify and describe the most important or useful titles issued by each state. If the reader feels an important title has been missed, he or she is encouraged to notify the publisher so that it can be added to a future edition of this book.

Acknowledgments

General:

The authors of this book would like to thank the librarians, library staff, and state government employees who have, over the years, strived to provide a bibliographic record of the publications of state governments.

Lori L. Smith:

I'd first like to thank my co-authors. When I realized this project was beyond my ability to complete alone, they all said yes when I asked for their help. Lou Malcomb taught the government publications course I took in library school. In that class she warned us that people who work with government publications often get inspired and feel compelled to "spread the documents gospel" to those who are unaware of how useful government information can be. The existence of this book proves that statement to be true. Eric Johnson is my supervisor at Sims Memorial Library. When I harassed him about getting his chapters completed by our deadline, he very kindly resisted the temptation to harass me about deadlines I was missing. Dan Barkley made time to help with this book despite being involved in several other writing projects and serving as a member of the Depository Library Council. Daniel Cornwall agreed to help with the book despite the fact that he and I have never actually met in person. For those reasons, and many others, I'm deeply grateful to my co-authors.

I am equally grateful to every person who took the time and effort to complete the survey I distributed when I began my research for this book in early 2000. The information they provided was extremely helpful. Those people are credited at the end of each state chapter. My deepest apologies go out to anyone who has been inadvertently omitted.

I am indebted to Henry Rasof, formerly with Oryx Press, who originally contacted me in 1999 to ask if I would like to submit a proposal for a book on state documents. Henry provided excellent advice and guidance as I created the outline for the book and the standard format for the chapters. My thanks also to Anne Thompson who helped me carry the project through to completion.

For the moral support and encouragement they provided, I'd like to thank my family, my colleagues at Sims Library, and every member of the depository library community in Louisiana. Special thanks go to Georgia Chadwick from the Law Library of Louisiana, who shared with me her research on state depository laws, and to Pattie Steib from my university's Center for Faculty Excellence, who assisted me with "capturing" the illustrations used in the book. I'd also like to thank Tom Jones, Gino Vannelli, Eddie Izzard, and the good folks at the Hershey Foods Corporation, all of whom helped to keep me sane during the writing of this book.

Finally, I'd like to thank Margaret Lane. The first book I ever bought as a professional librarian was Margaret's *Selecting and Organizing State Government Publications*. When I moved to Louisiana in 1991 I met the lady in person. She has been a friend and mentor to me ever since. This book is built on the foundation that she laid.

Daniel C. Barkley:

I would like to express my gratitude to the following for their support and guidance during the process of research and writing for this book: the University of New Mexico, Zimmerman Library, Faculty Promotion and Tenure Committee; Barbara Gienger, Monica Dorame, Clark McLean, and Stephanie West of the Zimmerman Library Government Information Department, University of New Mexico; Robert Wiberg, Library Information Technology, Zimmerman Library, University of New Mexico; my parents Donald and Lois Barkley; Nikki and Sam; and most certainly to Lori Smith for her leadership, editorial wizardry, and her patience.

Daniel D. Cornwall:

Thanks to my spouse, Louise, who was incredibly supportive, kind, and encouraging. Thanks to my supervisor, Mike Mitchell, who "nudged" me into filling out the state survey for Alaska and so started me on the path to being published.

Eric W. Johnson:

Thanks to Bette Siegel from the Massachusetts State Library, Leonard Adams from the University of Massachusetts at Amherst Library, Steve Newton from the Delaware Division of Libraries, and Al Palko from the Connecticut State Library.

J. Louise Malcomb:

I would like to acknowledge Mary Krutulis, librarian emeriti and former Director of Admissions at the IUB School of Library and Information Science. Mary spent hours reviewing the chapters for the Midwest and checking web sites. Her excellent editorial skills and diligent efforts made the completion of the chapters possible. I would also like to acknowledge the work of the students enrolled in L628, the government information course at the School of Library and Information Science at Indiana University–Bloomington, during the summer of 2001. They completed much of the initial exploration for the chapters.

Part I

General Sources Covering All Fifty States

Lori L. Smith

FINDING STATE INFORMATION

There are many sources published by the federal government and by commercial publishers that provide information about all fifty states. These sources provide facts about the history of each state, or statistical data, or directory-style listings of phone numbers and addresses, or dozens of other types of information. If one wishes to make comparisons among states, these sources will be the most useful.

Federal and commercial sources sometimes provide breakdowns of statistical information at the county/borough/parish, metropolitan statistical area, or city level. Publications issued by state government agencies will commonly provide much more detailed information for these lower governmental subdivisions. Therefore, those who wish to find comprehensive data about cities or small towns in a given state would be wise to seek out state publications.

AVAILABILITY

The commercially published sources mentioned in this chapter can often be found at large public or university libraries. Those who wish to purchase copies of titles still in print should be able to find them in bookstores, obtain them from online booksellers, or order them directly from the publishers. Federal government publications may be found at over 1,200 depository libraries around the country. One can determine the nearest Federal Depository Library by checking the U.S. Government Printing Office (GPO) web site at http:// www.gpo.gov/libraries. In fact, a great deal of state information that has been collected and published by the federal government is available on the web via the *GPO Access* page at http://www.gpoaccess.gov. GPO also sells copies of many government publications. Those who wish to purchase publications can check the Online Bookstore on the *GPO Access* page to see which titles are available. Some federal agencies, such as the Census Bureau, sell their own publications directly.

State government publications are rarely available in libraries outside the state in which they were published. Some very large research libraries, such as the Library of Congress, actively collect government publications from other states, but in general, one must contact a library within the state about which information is being sought.

Information posted on the Internet is, of course, available to anyone with access to the necessary computer equipment and software.

COMMERCIALLY PUBLISHED PRINT RESOURCES

The following sources, and perhaps others, may be located within libraries that hold them by searching the catalog for the titles listed, or by searching the following subject headings: "state governments," "U.S. states—statistics," "United States—statistics."

Almanac of the 50 States: Basic Data Profiles with Comparative Tables (Information Publications, annual)—The *Almanac* has separate chapters focusing on each state which provide information on geography, environment, demographics, vital statistics, education, housing, crime, labor force, economy, and additional topics. A section of U.S. summary information on the same topics is also provided. Another section in the *Almanac* contains tables that focus on one topic and provide comparative statistics for each state.

The Book of the States (Council of State Governments, biennial)—This title, first published in 1935, includes chapters on state constitutions, executive branches, legislatures, judiciary branches, elections and campaign issues, state finances, management and personnel issues, state programs, intergovernmental affairs, and additional topics. A chapter of "State Pages" provides basic information about each state such as the capital city, the date the state was admitted to the Union, population, land area, state motto, state flower, and so on. The "State Government in Review" chapter summarizes the priorities of the governor in each state and describes state initiatives in specific areas such as gaming or health care. It has a highly detailed table of contents and an index. The major drawback of this otherwise excellent publication is the incredibly small print in which the information is presented. Persons with less-than-perfect vision may need to use a magnifying glass.

Congressional Quarterly's State Information Directory (CQ Press)—The first edition of this title was published in 2000. Information provided for each state includes the name, address, phone number, fax number, and e-mail address for key officeholders in all three branches of government. When available, web page addresses are provided as well. Throughout each state listing, information on special topics is highlighted in a series of boxes. The first page of each listing includes a box with facts such as the state's population, number of counties/boroughs/parishes, state motto, state bird, and traditional date and location of the state fair. Another box provides names, web addresses, mailing addresses, and phone numbers for the state's institutions of higher education. A third box provides frequently called agency phone numbers, such as the number for tourism information. A box in the legislature section summarizes legal information such as the state's sales tax, marriage age, driving age, and speed limit.

CQ's State Fact Finder: Rankings Across America (CQ Press, annual)—Recent editions of this publication have been compiled by Kendra A. Hovey of the State Policy Research organization. The main offering in this source is tables of statistics for specific topics that first list the states alphabetically and then list the states in order by rank. Subjects covered include economics, recreational opportunities, education, health, crime, and transportation. A unique feature of this book is a section entitled "Finding Information Users Want to Know." This section lists reasons people may be seeking information about states and recommends tables in the book that address their needs, and often recommends other sources. Some of the reasons for seeking information that are discussed are deciding where to live or visit, and deciding where to locate a business.

Facts About the States (H.W. Wilson, irregular)—The second edition of this title was published in 1994. The book was edited by Joseph Nathan Kane, Janet Podell, and Steven Anzovin. Like the *Almanac of the 50 States* mentioned above, this book has a separate chapter for each state, and a section of comparative tables focused on particular subjects. This source, however, does not focus on statistics. The information provided for each state includes the correct name for an inhabitant, the date it was admitted to the Union, a short history of the capital city, the state motto and song, the state symbols, a description of the geography and climate, a list of historic sites, a chronology of historical events, basic demographic information, political information, a description of the cultural resources available, a listing of unusual state facts, and a bibliography of fiction and non-fiction books about the state.

Gale State Rankings Reporter (Gale Research Inc., biennial)—The title page of the 1995 edition summarizes this source very well when it says it has "about 3,000 rankings of the 50 states on a variety of topics, including Arts and Leisure, Demographics, Education, Government Expenditures, Taxes, etc., from Government, Business, and General Interest Sources." Most of the information included comes from federal government sources, which are listed at the end of the book. The *Reporter* has a location index, which is arranged by state, and a keyword index.

State and Local Statistics Sources (Gale Research Inc., irregular)—M. and S. Balachandran edited this massive volume, the second edition of which was released in 1993. The book provides a subject-divided listing of publications that include state-level statistical information. Each state chapter lists hundreds of statistical publications arranged by fifty-two different subject headings. The sources covered include those issued by commercial publishers, universities, state agencies, and other types of organizations.

State Document Checklists: A Historical Bibliography (William S. Hein & Co., Inc., irregular)—Most states produce some sort of bibliographical listing or checklist of publications that have been issued by state government agencies. Susan L. Dow compiled this listing of those bibliographical tools. For each state she provides a comprehensive list of each retrospective checklist that has been issued, as well as information about any checklist that is being issued on an ongoing basis. An excellent introduction provides a detailed history of national efforts to improve bibliographic access to state publications. The first edition of this title was published in 1990, and the most recent edition in 2000.

State Legislative Sourcebook: A Resource Guide to Legislative Information in the Fifty States (Government Research Service, annual)—In the introduction to the 1998 edition of this book, the author, Lynn Hellebust, says it is "designed for those who want to study, observe or lobby one or more of the state legislatures." For each state, Hellebust gives a basic description of the procedures followed by the legislature and the session calendar, and provides the names of persons to contact. She gives a biographical profile for each legislator, which includes financial information. She provides a section of detailed information on bills and other documents produced in the legislative process, sources of data for tracking the status of legislation, and publications that summarize actions taken during a given legislative session. Hellebust also includes sections of information on how to register as a lobbyist, and general information about state government. Appendices to the *Sourcebook* provide a list of telephone numbers for checking the status of bills, a list of telephone numbers for obtaining copies of bills, and an annotated bibliography of titles on how to influence state legislatures.

State Rankings: A Statistical View of the 50 United States (Morgan Quitno Press, annual)—The main offering of this publication is statistical information about each state arranged by topic. However, a section of "State Fast Facts" gives, among other things, the official song, flower, tree, bird, and nickname of each state. The topics covered in the statistical section include agriculture, crime, defense, economy, education, employment, energy, environment, geography, government finances, health, housing, population, social welfare, and transportation. Footnotes on each table cite the original source(s) from which the information was obtained. A unique feature of this publication is that each edition announces the winner of the year's "Most Livable State Award." The award is granted based on an analysis of several key statistics for each state. The 2002 winner was Minnesota. Morgan Quitno Press also publishes *Crime State Rankings* and *Health Care State Rankings*.

State Yellow Book (Leadership Directories, Inc., quarterly)—This source is subtitled *Who's Who in the Executive and Legislative Branches of the 50 State Governments*. The book provides names, addresses, phone numbers, fax numbers, and some e-mail and web site addresses for persons in state government. It includes photographs of some. Introductory chapters in the book discuss recent elections, legislative calendars, and political affiliations of government officials. The official mottoes, flowers, and other symbols adopted by each state are presented in a section of state profiles. A listing of the addresses, phone numbers, and web addresses of several intergovernmental organizations is given. Many of these organizations are professional associations for persons holding specific government positions in each state; for instance, the Conference of State Bank Supervisors. A subject index and a personnel index are provided.

Taylor's Encyclopedia of Government Officials, Federal and State (Political Research, Inc., biennial)—John Clements has compiled this source since 1967. A new edition is released in odd-numbered years and it is updated by quarterly supplements. This encyclopedia provides photographs of each state's top officials, including U.S. senators and congresspersons, lists the names of state senators and representatives, and gives statistical tables on education and the state budget. A unique feature of this source is the "Political Viewing Charts" given for states and counties/boroughs/parishes. The state political viewing chart is a map of the state that indicates the U.S. congressional district, state senatorial district, and state representative district to which each county/ borough/parish belongs. Shading on the map indicates whether the area voted Democratic or Republican in the most recent election for U.S. representatives. The county/borough/parish political viewing chart lists the counties alphabetically within U.S. congressional district and indicates the state districts to which the county belongs, as well as whether the county voted Democratic or Republican in the most recent U.S. representative election.

Worldmark Encyclopedia of the States (Gale Research Inc., irregular)—The fifth edition of this source was published in 2001. Information in each entry is extensive and includes the state's seal and flag, the origin of the state's name, the official symbols of the state (tree, stone, bird, motto, etc.), the location and size of the state, the topography of the land, the climate, the demographics and ethnicity of the population, the history of the state, a description of state and local governments, economic and industrial information, and a listing of famous persons born in the state. Each entry also includes a map of the state and a bibliography of sources consulted. In addition to entries for each state, and for U.S. dependencies, a final entry provides similar information for the United States as a whole. A useful glossary of terms such as "blue laws" and "sunbelt" is also included.

FEDERAL GOVERNMENT PUBLICATIONS

The official index to federal publications is the *Monthly Catalog of United States Government Publications*. This is a print or CD-ROM resource that should be available at all Federal Depository Libraries. A web-based, and more frequently updated version of the catalog is available on the *GPO Access* web site at http://www.gpoaccess.gov/cgp/. This electronic catalog is a searchable database of bibliographic information about publications issued by federal agencies since 1994. Most Federal Depository Libraries provide access to a commercially published electronic index that includes information about federal publications issued since 1976. Many federal depositories have also added records for their documents collections to their libraries' online catalogs. Again, the following subject headings will be useful in locating within a library those federal publications that include information about specific states: "state governments," "U.S. states—statistics," "United States—statistics." It can also be fruitful to simply search the name of the state about which information is being sought.

The following are just a few of the most popular and heavily used titles issued by federal government agencies that provide information for individual states. Most of the titles listed contain statistical information, but many other types of information about states are available in federal government publications.

Census of Population and Housing (U.S. Census Bureau, decennial)—The U.S. Census Bureau performs an official count of the U.S. population every ten years. A survey form is sent to each household that asks for information about the residents at that address, and about the residence itself. State-level statistics are reported in a wide variety of publications after each census. These statistics reveal the total number of persons living in the state, their ages, races, ancestries, incomes, education levels, marital status, and many other topics. Information from the decennial census, as well as from other surveys performed by the Census Bureau, is available on the web at http://www.census.gov/main/www/access.html.

County Business Patterns (U.S. Census Bureau, annual)—This is one of the many business-related sources issued by the Census Bureau. A volume for each state is published each year. It provides statistics on the number and types of business establishments in the state, their total payroll, and the number of people they employ. The same statistics are also presented for each county/borough/parish within the state. This title is available on the web at http://www.census.gov/epcd/cbp/view/cbpview.html.

Crime in the Unites States (Uniform Crime Reports) (Federal Bureau of Investigation, annual)—This publication provides detailed national statistics on the number and types of crimes committed, and also gives some crime totals by state. This title is available on the web at http://www.fbi.gov/ucr/ucr.htm.

Digest of Education Statistics (National Center for Education Statistics, annual)—This source contains a wealth of statistical information on elementary, secondary, and post-secondary schools. It gives predominantly national information. However, many tables do offer statistics by state. Topics covered include number of students enrolled, salaries of teachers, sources of school revenue, and educational achievement levels. This title is available on the web at http://nces.ed.gov/pubsearch/majorpub.asp.

Federal Depository Library Directory (U.S. Government Printing Office, irregular)—Arranged by state, and then by city, this directory provides the address and phone number of every Federal Depository Library in the country. Fax numbers and web addresses are also given. It is available on the web as a clickable map at http://www.gpoaccess.gov/libraries.html.

State and Metropolitan Area Data Book (U.S. Census Bureau, irregular)—This title is a supplement to the *Statistical Abstract of the United States*. It includes statistics broken down by state, metropolitan area, metropolitan county, and central city. Topics covered include population, birth rates, hospitals, schools, law enforcement, labor force, utilities, farms, retail trade, and others. This title is available on the web at http://www.census.gov/statab/www/smadb.html.

Statistical Abstract of the United States (U.S. Census Bureau, annual)—The subtitle of this source is *The National Data Book*, and it lives up to that name. This book includes statistics from many different federal agencies, as well as from some unpublished sources. It covers a wide variety of topics, and provides state-level statistics for most. Another valuable feature of this source is an appendix that provides information about similar statistical abstracts that have been issued for each state. The appendix provides the address and phone number of the agency or university that produces the state statistical abstract, and gives web addresses for those that are available online. This title is available on the web at http://www.census.gov/statab/www/.

STATE GOVERNMENT PUBLICATIONS

There is currently no comprehensive resource that indexes publications from all fifty states. The online catalog of the Library of Congress, however, does include a multitude of state publications. It may be searched on the web at http://catalog.loc.gov/.

A commercial database called *WorldCat* is available in many libraries. It contains bibliographic records that represent all types of materials held in libraries all across the country. It is another excellent source of information about state publications.

Following this chapter are chapters that discuss each state individually. These will reveal how and where to gain access to publications from each state.

INTERNET SITES

Each state has its own home page or "web portal" on the Internet. Links to all branches of state government are usually provided, and a search feature is sometimes available which allows one to search all state web pages for a particular piece of information. Several sites are listed below that offer links to all fifty state home pages.

Some libraries, professional organizations, or companies have created pages that provide links to the home page of the agency or department in each state that is responsible for regulating a particular area, such as education, or the environment; or to state web pages that provide information on a particular topic. A selection of these sites arranged by topic appears below.

Sites Providing Links to the Fifty State Home Pages

The following pages each provide links to all fifty state home pages. Some offer a textual list of states from which a selection may be made, and others utilize a clickable map of the United States.

http://www.statelocalgov.net/—Maintained by Piper Resources.

http://www.globalcomputing.com/states.html—Maintained by Global Computing.

http://www.state.sc.us/states/—Maintained by the state of South Carolina.

http://iridium.nttc.edu/resources/government/us_states.asp—Maintained by the National Technology Transfer Center.

http://www.pueblo.gsa.gov/call/state.htm—Maintained by the Federal Consumer Information Center.

Those interested in all fifty state home pages might also be interested in a report published in January 2002, entitled *State Web Portals: Delivering and Financing E-Service*. This report, written by Diana Burley Gant, Jon P. Gant, and Craig L. Johnson of Indiana University in Bloomington, discusses the effectiveness and financing of state web portals. It is available online at http://www.myscgov.com/SCSGPortal/johnsonreport.pdf.

Sites Providing Topical Links for All Fifty States

Multiple Topics

http://www.50states.com—As a source of basic information about each state, this site, maintained by Pike Street Industries, Inc., is unparalleled. It is very easy to navigate and provides access to an amazing quantity of information. Facts given for each state include date of admission to statehood, land area, telephone area codes, state bird, state flag, state flower, highest point, largest cities, and state motto. Links are provided to other web sites that provide information on famous people from each state, demographic statistics, and lists of museums, newspapers, state parks, and sports teams.

http://www.firstgov.gov—This is the federal government's official search engine, but it also provides access to a wealth of state government information. The "State, Local, Tribal and U.S. Territory Resources" page provides links to all fifty state pages and offers the user options to "Locate In-Person Service Centers in Your State and Community," or "Browse State Services by Topic." A search box on the site allows users to limit their search to state-level information from all states, or to one specific state (see Figure 1).

http://www.lib.umich.edu/govdocs/state.html—This site is an excellent place to begin any search for state government information on the Internet. It was compiled and is maintained by the Documents Center of the library at the University of Michigan. The site is divided into five sections: State Governments, State Legislatures, Public Policy, Special Subjects, and Local Government. The sections include not only links to information available on the web, but also give titles of print resources and electronic indexes available to those at the University of Michigan. These same print and electronic sources are also available at many other libraries throughout the country.

https://www.nascio.org/stateSearch/index.cfm—The National Association of State Chief Information Officers maintains this site, which is another good place to begin a search for state government information on the web. The page offers a list of thirty-two subject categories that link to state sites on those topics. Subjects available include agriculture, criminal justice, education, tourism, and transportation.

http://lcweb.loc.gov/global/state/stategov.html—The *State and Local Governments* page is maintained by the Library of Congress. It offers links to a number of meta-indexes that may be used for locating state information on the web. (Many of those indexes are mentioned in this chapter.) It also offers a selection of links for each state. These usually include the state's home page, the legislature, the State Library, the state Census Data Center, and other sources of statistical data.

http://www.statelocalgov.net—Piper Resources sponsors this site, which provides direct links to the home page of each state and to numerous other government pages in each state. The links listed include the governor, lieutenant governor, cabinet-level officials, the state telephone directory, the legislature, the Supreme Court, the major state departments, the State Library, and a selection of city and county-/borough-/parish-level pages.

http://www.umr.edu/~library/gov/statabl.html—This site, maintained by

FIRSTGOV
Your First Click to the U.S. Government

Search Federal/State   Citizen Gateway | Business Gateway | Government Gateway

○ Federal ○ State ○ Both   August 30, 2002

Search a State

[   ] Go

Advanced Search

Agencies
- The White House
- Federal
- State, Local & Tribal
- International

Reference
- News Releases
- Federal Forms
- Laws & Regulations
- Phone Directories
- Questions About Government?
- More

Select a Topic ▾ Go

America Responds to Terrorism

Comment to Government

Customer Survey

Free E-mail Newsletters

State, Local, Tribal and U.S. Territory Resources

State Government Home Pages
Visit a state government homepage by clicking on a state.

Alabama	Illinois	Montana	Rhode Island
Alaska	Indiana	Nebraska	South Carolina
Arizona	Iowa	Nevada	South Dakota
Arkansas	Kansas	New Hampshire	Tennessee
California	Kentucky	New Jersey	Texas
Colorado	Louisiana	New Mexico	Utah
Connecticut	Maine	New York	Vermont
D.C.	Maryland	North Carolina	Virginia
Delaware	Massachusetts	North Dakota	Washington
Florida	Michigan	Ohio	West Virginia
Georgia	Minnesota	Oklahoma	Wisconsin
Hawaii	Mississippi	Oregon	Wyoming
Idaho	Missouri	Pennsylvania	

Additional State, County and City Government Websites
Piper Resources' offers a frequently updated directory to additional state, county and city government websites.

State Sites for Kids
Visit these fun sites to learn about the history, state symbols, government and much more in your state.

Tribal Government Websites
Link to tribal government websites, from the Blackfeet Nation in Montana to the Wyandot Nation in Kansas and many more.

U.S. Territories and Outlying Areas
Link to the official government websites of U.S. Territories and outlying areas.

Locate In-Person Service Centers in Your State and Community
Locate government offices and services in your local community, region or state, such as social security offices, post offices, police departments, veterans facilities and much more.

Browse State Services by Topic
The National Association of State Chief Information Officers provides a topical clearinghouse to state government information on the Internet.

Contact State Governors
Do you have questions or comments about the services in your state? Get information about how to e-mail, fax or write to each State governor, including some who provide online feedback forms.

Statistics at the State and Local Levels
Get the latest statistics for your state or county. Find out what your state exports to other countries. Check out the State of the Cities.

FirstGov ™ is the U.S. government's official web portal.
Office of Citizen Services and Communications, U.S. General Services Administration
1800 F Street, NW, Washington, DC 20405
Have any questions about the federal government? Call 1-800-FED-INFO (1-800-333-4636)

Figure 1. A wealth of state information is accessible through the federal government's web portal, *FirstGov. Source*: http://www.firstgov.gov/Agencies/State_and_Tribal.shtml.

the Curtis Laws Wilson Library at the University of Missouri-Rolla, provides links to state home pages, and to topical sites covering state tax forms, flags and maps, statistical sources, and legal resources.

http://www.politicalindex.com/sect17.htm—This page, *Contacting State & Local Gov't Agencies*, is section seventeen of the *National Political Index*. It offers an alphabetical list of links to state home pages, legislatures, courts, elections offices, and other agencies.

http://www-libraries.colorado.edu/ps/gov/st/allstate.htm—The Library of the University of Colorado at Boulder maintains this page that provides links to statistical information, election results, labor market information, tax forms, flags, firearms laws, state publications, and other topics for all fifty states.

http://www.capitolimpact.com/gw/index_states.html—*The Gateway to the States* page offers extensive political and demographic information about each state. Information or links are provided on the state's congressional delegation, state government, county/borough/parish governments, city/town governments, law enforcement agencies, post-secondary schools, and media resources. A feature of the site allows the searcher to see campaign contributions made to political candidates within a given zip code.

http://www.stateline.org/—The Pew Center on the States, which is administered by the University of Richmond and funded by the Pew Charitable Trusts, created this site to "help journalists, policy makers, and engaged citizens become better informed about innovative public policies." For each state, a page of "news and background information" is provided. These state-specific pages give links to the state's home page, and to the pages of the legislature and the governor. The state pages also give biographical information about the governor, and session information about the legislature. A search feature on each state page allows keyword searching of news stories that have appeared on the site. Links to some statistical data are given, and the user has the option to compare statistics between states.

http://www.searchsystems.net—Pacific Information Resources, Inc., DBA Search Systems is the name of the company that maintains this site. It provides links to searchable databases of public records. The user may select a listing for individual states, for the United States as a whole, for U.S. territories, for Canada as a whole, for specific Canadian provinces, for Europe, for Asia, for the world, or even for Outer Space. While the tongue-in-cheek Outer Space option leads only to some information from NASA, the listings for individual states can be fairly extensive. These lists include links to searchable editions of state legal resources, directories of persons licensed to practice various professions within the state, and a variety of other sources. Although most of the databases listed are free, a "$" indicates those for which a fee is charged.

Counties

http://www.naco.org—The National Association of Counties (NACo) maintains a page which provides links to the county government association web site of each state. Many of these associations provide links on their web sites to the home pages of individual counties. From the NACo home page select "About NACo," then "Affiliates and Partnerships," then "State Associations."

Education

http://www.negp.gov/page13-1.htm—The National Education Goals Panel, an independent agency of the federal government, maintains this page of links to the state departments of education. The user may select a state from a drop-down menu, or may click the appropriate state on a national map.

Environment

http://www.clay.net/statag.html—This page is sponsored by Environmental Opportunities Inc., and is a link on the *Environmental Professional's Homepage*. The site provides links to environmental agency pages in each state.

Jobs

http://thejobpage.gov/statelocal.htm—In addition to providing links to state civil service pages, this site provides links to other state and local government employment information.

http://www.ajb.dni.us/—*America's Job Bank* is one of many sites maintained by the U.S. Department of Labor. It allows job seekers to search a database of job openings from all over the country and to post copies of their resumes. It allows employers to post job openings and search the resumes posted by job seekers. In the "State Gateway" section of the page there is a pull-down menu from which a specific state can be selected. The employment site of the state selected will pop up in a new window.

Laws and Legislation

http://www.law.indiana.edu/v-lib/—This address leads to the *WWW Virtual Law Library*, which is sponsored by the Indiana University School of Law Library and the World Wide Web Virtual Library. One of the options on this page is "Browse the Virtual Library by Information Source." "State Government" is one of the options in this section. Selecting this option leads to an alphabetical list of legal links for each state. The links include bar associations, state courts, state constitutions, state statutes, and so on. The links database is searchable, which allows the creation of topic-specific lists of links for each state.

http://www.llsdc.org/sourcebook/state-leg.htm—The Law Librarians' Society of Washington, D.C., Inc., maintains this excellent site. Links are provided to each state's legislature, laws, and regulations. Phone numbers are provided for the state government operator, the House, the Senate, the legislative information desk (or equivalent), and the state law library.

http://www.priweb.com/internetlawlib/17.htm—Pritchard Law Webs created and maintains this page. It's part of their *Internet Law Library* site. It offers a selection of links for each state that includes both governmental and nongovernmental sites. The governmental sites provide, among other things, statutes, constitutions, codes and regulations, and tax forms. The nongovernmental sites offer lists of law-related books from commercial publishers and articles on the state's laws from private authors.

http://www.alllaw.com/state_resources—The *All Law* page, copyrighted by AllLaw.com, provides links to state government sites, bar association sites, state court sites, sites with legal forms, and other law-related information on the web for each state. One nice feature of *All Law* is its "State Law Search" feature. It leads the user to state legal publications, such as codes and regulations, which are searchable on the web. Another feature on the site allows the user to find names and addresses of lawyers by geography and area of practice.

http://www.lawresearch.com/v2/state/cstate7.htm—This is the *U.S. Law & Government by State* page of the *Law Research* site. It offers topical links to state constitutions, state case law, state legislatures, and state governors. It also offers a long list of links for each state. These links are to legal sources, and to a wide variety of other information about population, state administration, and local governments.

http://www.legalethics.com/index.law—This site is maintained by Internet Legal Services. The home page asks the user to "Choose a Category," and provides a list of choices that includes "States." The user must then select a topic. Once "States" has been selected as the category, the list of topics from which the user may select is an alphabetical list of states, plus a "States (misc.)" option. The links for each state include administrative codes, constitutions, court rules, executive orders, legislation, tax forms, and tourist information. The miscellaneous option leads to a table of links to census information, and to pages maintained by various professional associations whose members are persons employed in local, county, or state governments.

http://www.findlaw.com/11stategov/index.html—The *FindLaw* site has links leading to state statutes, constitutions, directories, tax information, business information, and attorneys general. The site also includes information about the courts, law schools, and bar associations in each state. A search feature allows users to locate the address and phone number of an attorney or law firm with a particular type of specialty within a specific city.

http://www.lawsource.com/also/index.htm—The *American Law Sources On-Line (ALSO)* site has links leading to information on state courts and court decisions, constitutions, bills and resolutions, statutes, codes and regulations, forms, bar associations, and law schools. A unique feature of the site is a listing of law reviews and periodicals for each state. Another nice feature is a listing of uniform laws that indicates which states have passed a version of that law, and provides links to the versions available on the web.

http://www.law.cornell.edu/index.html—The Legal Information Institute at the Cornell Law School maintains this site. The main menu lists categories such as "Constitutions & Codes," "Court Opinions," and "Law by Source or Jurisdiction." Pop-up menus for each category allow the searcher to specify state-level information. A nice feature of this site is a topical listing of links to state law sources. Topics available for browsing include Agriculture, Corrections, Education, Elections, Family Law, and Health.

http://www.ncsl.org/public/leglinks.cfm—This site provides links to the home page(s) of the legislature in each state, including links to live audio and video feeds from those bodies that make such feeds available, and to the home pages of individual legislators. Links are also provided to legislative press rooms and to educational sites created by legislatures for children. The site is maintained by the National Conference of State Legislatures.

http://www.vote-smart.org/—Project Vote Smart is a non-profit, non-partisan venture. Their site provides an enormous amount of information about the president, the U.S. Congress, the state governors, and the fifty state legislatures. In addition to information about legislation, the site allows searchers to find out who their congresspersons and legislators are, and how they have voted on various issues. A wealth of information about elections is also provided.

Maps

http://www.nationalatlas.gov—The U.S. Department of the Interior maintains this site. Users can create digital maps that reflect a wide variety of information collected by federal government agencies. These maps can show the nation as a whole, individual states, or smaller geographic areas. Surface features such as roads and waterways, as well as political boundaries such as county lines or congressional districts can also be shown.

Publications Lists

http://www.library.uiuc.edu/doc/StateList/check/check.htm — *StateList: The Electronic Source for State Publication Lists* is a joint project of librarians at the University of Illinois at Urbana-Champaign, the University of Colorado Law Library, and Kenyon College. The site provides links to the official lists of state government publications that are currently available on the web. Some states do not yet have their publication lists online. The librarians in charge of the project are attempting to create a searchable database of these lists.

State Libraries

http://www.dpi.state.wi.us/dpi/dlcl/pld/statelib.html—This list of links to the web sites of state libraries is maintained by Wisconsin's Department of Public Instruction. Most state libraries have excellent collections of state publications, and many have online catalogs of their holdings that may be searched via their web sites. However, not every state has a state library.

Statistical Information

http://factfinder.census.gov/—The *American Factfinder* is part of the U.S. Census Bureau site. It is the bureau's main distribution point for statistics from the 2000 census of population and housing. The user has a choice of seeing the information presented in tables or displayed via maps. Statistics from the 1990 census of population and housing and from a series of business and industry censuses are also available. Totals may be requested for the United States as a whole, or for specific states, counties/boroughs/parishes, or cities.

http://www.census.gov/statab/www/stateabs.html—This page is also maintained by the U.S. Census Bureau and has links to the statistical abstract sites of each of the fifty states. These sources contain statistical information on a wide variety of subjects. Addresses and phone numbers for obtaining print copies of the abstracts are also provided.

http://www.census.gov/sdc/www/—Another Census Bureau page, this provides links to the web sites of the bureau's State Data Centers. These geographically distributed centers assist in making Census Bureau information available throughout the country. The site for each state will likely include a variety of demographic and social statistics about residents of that state, and may include links to other state-level statistical agencies.

Tax Forms

http://www.lib.lsu.edu/govdocs/taxes.html—This list of links to state and federal tax form sites is maintained by the Middleton Library at Louisiana State University.

Transportation

http://www4.trb.org/trb/homepage.nsf/web/state_sponsors—This list of links to state departments of transportation is maintained by the National Academy of Sciences' Transportation Research Board. Each link includes a picture of the state's flag.

http://www.aamva.org/links/mnu_linkJurisdictions.asp—This page presents a clickable map of the nation that leads to regional lists of links to the sites of state motor vehicle agencies. The page is maintained by the American Association of Motor Vehicle Administrators.

http://www.transportation.org/community/committees.nsf/allpages/direc torsmembership—The American Association of State Highway and Transportation Officials maintains this list of the members of its board of directors. The list provides the name, mailing address, and phone number for the head of each state transportation department, as well as a link to the department's web page.

Unclaimed Property

http://www.unclaimed.org—This site provides links to state unclaimed property offices. Select "Owners enter here" and then "Find Property."

Part II

State Government Information Sources

Alabama

Lori L. Smith

GOVERNMENT PUBLISHING AND THE DEPOSITORY SYSTEM

An act was passed in 1993 that laid the groundwork for the establishment of a depository system for Alabama state publications. According to section 41-8-40 of the *Alabama Code*, the intent of the legislature was that: "(1) State publications of public interest be made available to the public. (2) An efficient distribution and depository system of state publications be established. (3) The preservation of all state publications having historical value be ensured." A state publication is defined in section 41-8-41 of the *Alabama Code* as

any document issued by a state agency which the agency may legally release for public distribution, but does not include any of the following: 1. Code of Alabama. 2. Bound volumes of the Acts of Alabama. 3. Legislative bills, journals, and slip laws. 4. The Alabama Digest. 5. Alabama Reporter. 6. Any other items prepared for commercial sales. 7. Correspondence, interoffice or intraoffice memoranda, routine forms, other internal records, or any other item of a strictly administrative nature. 8. Any document published pursuant to the Administrative Procedure Act. 9. Indices prepared by the Legislative Reference Service.

Each state agency, or the state printer, is charged with sending nine copies of every state publication to the Alabama Clearinghouse for State Publications, which is part of the Alabama Public Library Service. The clearinghouse is charged with distributing two copies to the State Archives and two to the Library of Congress. The clearinghouse retains one copy for reference purposes, two for circulation, and uses the remaining two to reproduce additional copies for distribution to the libraries that have signed depository contracts.

At least that's how it is supposed to work. The fly in the ointment, however, is that the program has never been funded, and hence, has never been implemented. In the absence of an active depository program, each library in the state that wishes to collect Alabama publications must contact agencies individually to request copies.

Efforts to implement the depository legislation may have been hampered by the fact that Alabama does not have a state library. In many other states it is the state library that coordinates the depository system. However, efforts to improve the distribution and availability of Alabama state publications and information do continue. A task force was appointed by the Alabama Public Library Service and the Government Documents Round Table of the Alabama Library Association to examine the distribution of state information in paper and via the web. Their draft report, issued in March 2000, made several recommendations. Among these was the creation of an "Alabama Information Technology Commission" which would establish and oversee information technology policy in the state. Another was the use of the *Alabama Virtual Library* web site as a centralized finding aid for state publications. The report of the task force is available on the web at http://www.dpo.uab.edu/ ~dweather/ASPTFReport.html.

USEFUL ADDRESSES AND TELEPHONE NUMBERS

Since Alabama has no centralized state library, the best collections of Alabama state publications will likely be found at the state's two main library agencies:

Alabama Public Library Service
6030 Monticello Drive
Montgomery, AL 36130
Phone Number for Alabama Reference Questions: (334) 213-3900
E-Mail Address for Alabama Reference Questions: vthacker@apls.state.al.us
APLS Home Page: http://www.apls.state.al.us/

Alabama Department of Archives and History
P.O. Box 300100
Montgomery, AL 36130-0100
Phone Number for Alabama Reference Questions: (334) 242-4435
E-Mail Address for Alabama Reference Questions: nkerr@archives.state.al.us
Department of Archives and History Home Page: http://www.archives.state.al.us/

INDEXES TO ALABAMA STATE PUBLICATIONS

If the depository program is ever funded, one of the roles of the clearinghouse will be to compile and distribute periodically a list of state publications. At this stage, though, there is no comprehensive index to Alabama state publications. However, the Auburn University Libraries, in cooperation with the Alabama State Publications Task Force, maintain a comprehensive list of agencies, boards, commissions, and other state government organizations, with links to those that have web sites. The page is entitled *Electronic Resources for Alabama State Publications* and may be found at http://www.lib.auburn.edu/ madd/statepubs/. A similar listing of agencies, with both web links and contact information may be found on the state's official web site at http:// alabama.gov/2k3_directory.aspx.

ESSENTIAL STATE PUBLICATIONS

Directories

Alabama Industrial Directory (Alabama Development Office, Alabama Center for Commerce)—This source includes addresses, phone numbers, and contact names for mining and manufacturing companies in the state. It also gives the SIC codes for these companies and brief descriptions of their product lines. Some very basic information, including details about ordering a print copy, is available on the web at http://www.ado.state.al.us/direct1.htm. Those with questions can write to Alabama Development Office, Alabama Industrial Directory, Alabama Center for Commerce, 401 Adams Avenue, Suite 670, Montgomery, AL 36130-4106, or call (334) 242-0400, or (800) 248-0033.

Directory of Colleges and Universities in Alabama (Alabama Commission on Higher Education)—This source provides addresses, phone numbers, and web links for Alabama's institutions of higher education. It includes both two-year and four-year public and private colleges/universities. The directory is available on the web at http://www.ache.state.al.us/Institutional%20Directory/Inst.htm. Those with questions can write to Alabama Commission on Higher Education, 100 North Union Street, P.O. Box 302000, Montgomery, AL 36130-2000, or call (334) 242-1998.

State Employee Phone Directory (Department of Finance, Information Services Division)—This directory provides the names, phone numbers, and e-mail addresses of state employees. It can be searched by first name or last name, or a department can be selected from a pull-down menu. It is available on the web at http://www.alabama.gov/2k3_employee_form.aspx.

Financial/Budgetary Resources

Alabama Wage Survey (Department of Industrial Relations, Labor Market Information Division)—Hourly wage rates for hundreds of occupations are given in this source. It provides alphabetical breakdowns, as well as tables arranged by SIC code, Occupational Employment Statistics (OES) code, and metropolitan area. The most recent editions are available on the web by selecting "Information" and then "Publications" on the Labor Market Information Division web site at http://209.192.62.235/default.HTM. Those who wish to enquire about the availability of print copies can call (334) 242-8872, or e-mail LMI@dir.state.al.us.

State of Alabama Comprehensive Annual Financial Report (CAFR) (Comptroller's Office, Financial Reporting Section)—Detailed balance sheets and fund statements are presented in this report. A section of statistics gives a ten-year snapshot of state revenues and expenditures, demographic trends, and the state's general economic condition. The most recent editions of the report are available on the web at http://www.comptroller.state.al.us/. Print copies may be requested from the Comptroller's Office by calling (334) 242-2193, or by e-mailing a request to Mike Hudson at mhudson@comptroller.state.al.us.

State of Alabama, State Government Finances (Executive Budget Office)—A number of budgetary reports are available on this web page at http://www

.budget.state.al.us/stgovfin.html. Information is presented on appropriations for the state general fund and the education trust fund, as well as on revenues, operating funds, and the general budget cycle. Those with questions can write to Executive Budget Office, P.O. Box 302610, Montgomery, AL 36130-2610, or call (334) 242-7230.

Legal Resources

Alabama Administrative Code (Legislative Reference Service)—This source compiles the rules of all state agencies that are covered by the Alabama Administrative Procedure Act. Rules are presented in alphabetical order by agency. The title is available in both print and on the web, with the print edition being the official version. The web edition may be found at http://www.lrs.state.al.us/. Select "Links" from the menu. Those who wish to begin a subscription can write to Legislative Reference Service, Administrative Procedure Division, 435 Alabama State House, Montgomery, AL 36130, or call (334) 242-7560. In 2002, a one-year subscription was $720.

Alabama Administrative Monthly (Legislative Reference Service)—In this publication, state agencies announce their intent to adopt, amend, or repeal a rule. Brief descriptions of the proposed action and the rule to be affected are given, but the text of the rules is not included. Those wishing to see the proposed rules or amendments must request the text directly from the appropriate agency. The official version of this title is the print edition, but an unofficial version is available on the web at http://www.lrs.state.al.us/. Select "Links" from the menu and then select *Alabama Administrative Code*. The button to link to the *Administrative Monthly* appears on the *Administrative Code* page. Those who wish to begin a subscription can write to Legislative Reference Service, Administrative Procedure Division, 435 Alabama State House, Montgomery, AL 36130, or call (334) 242-7560. In 2002 a one-year subscription was $60.

Code of Alabama 1975 (Legislature)—This is the codified version of the state's current laws. The official, print edition of this title is listed below in the section on commercial publications. An unofficial edition is available on the web through the legislature's *ALISON* (Alabama Legislative Information System Online) site at http://alisdb.legislature.state.al.us/acas/alisonstart.asp. The site allows both browsing of the *Code*, and searching by keyword.

Constitution of Alabama—1901 (Legislature)—The basic rights and privileges of the state's citizens, and the basic structure of the state's government are outlined in this document. The original text, ratified in 1901, has been amended over 600 times. The original text and all the amendments are available on the web via the legislature's *ALISON* (Alabama Legislative Information System Online) site at http://alisdb.legislature.state.al.us/acas/alison start.asp.

Statistical Resources

Alabama Agricultural Statistics Annual Bulletin (Alabama Agricultural Statistics Service; Alabama Department of Agriculture and Industries)—This annual publication is produced jointly by the Agricultural Statistics Service, which is a field office of the U.S. Department of Agriculture, and the state's agriculture department. The *Bulletin* is available on the web at http://www.aces.edu/department/nass/. It includes statistics on numbers and acreage of farms, quantity and value of crops and livestock produced, cash receipts, and a basic summary of climatic conditions. Those with questions can write to Alabama Agricultural Statistics Service, 4121 Carmichael Road, Suite 200, Montgomery, AL 36105, or call (334) 279-3555. Questions can be e-mailed to nass-al@nass.usda.gov.

Alabama Vital Events (Department of Public Health, Center for Health Statistics)—Statistics on births, deaths, marriages, and divorces are reported in this publication. Some tables are available by selecting "Vital Statistics at a Glance" from the "Health Statistics" page at http://ph.state.al.us/chs/HealthStatistics/HEALTHSTATISTICS.HTM. Those with questions can write to Alabama Department of Public Health, Center for Health Statistics, RSA Tower, 201 Monroe Street, Suite 1150, P.O. Box 5625, Montgomery, AL 36103-5625, or call (334) 206-5426.

Crime in Alabama (Alabama Criminal Justice Information Center, Statistical Analysis Center)—This annual publication includes statistics on the number and types of crimes committed, the number of law enforcement personnel employed, the number of officers killed and assaulted, and so on. Several issues are available on the web at http://acjic.state.al.us/. Those who wish to enquire about the availability of print copies can write to Alabama Criminal Justice Information Center, 770 Washington Avenue, Montgomery, AL 36130-0660, or call (334) 242-4900.

Statistical Abstract: Higher Education in Alabama (Alabama Commission on Higher Education)—An annual publication, the *Statistical Abstract* provides statistics on Alabama's institutions of higher education including enrollment, degrees conferred, tuition and fees, income and expenditures, faculty salaries, and other topics. The most recent editions are available on the commission's "publications" web page at http://www.ache.state.al.us/publicat.htm. Those who wish to enquire about the availability of print copies can write to Alabama Commission on Higher Education, 100 North Union Street, P.O. Box 302000, Montgomery, AL 36130-2000, or call (334) 242-1998.

Other Resources

Alabama Virtual Library (Department of Education et al.)—The *Alabama Virtual Library (AVL)* is a collection of library catalogs and databases that is available to the citizens of Alabama in public, school, and university libraries across the state, and also from their homes. The main address for *AVL* is http://www.avl.lib.al.us/. The databases available in *AVL* are password protected and include a number of periodical indexes catering to different academic levels, as well as standard reference resources such as encyclopedias and dictionaries. Although this collection does not include state-published information, it is provided with state funds.

Official Alabama Vacation Guide (Bureau of Tourism and Travel)—This annual publication describes various historic and natural sites around the state that are popular tourist destinations. A free copy of this publication may be re-

Figure 2. Alabama's web portal uses a unique, graphic approach to presenting information. *Source*: http://www.alabama.gov/.

quested by calling (800)-ALABAMA, or by visiting the bureau's web site at http://www.touralabama.org.

Related Alabama History Links (Department of Archives and History)—This web page can be found at http://www.archives.state.al.us/related.html. The page includes links to sites that provide information about the state as a whole, or which focus on topics such as genealogy, state history, state government, local government, politics, newspapers, libraries and archives within the state, statistics, and organizations (such as the Alabama Library Association). Many of the sites with links on the *Related Links* page are non-governmental or commercial sites.

ALABAMA'S WORLD WIDE WEB HOME PAGE

Alabama's official home page is located at http://www.alabama.gov/. It is maintained by the Information Services Division of the Department of Finance.

The home page uses a unique, graphic image with four major sections: A-Z Directory; Alabama Travel and State Facts; User Help; and Services (see Figure 2). Each selection leads to a page with eight or fewer additional selections divided by subject or function. All pages on the site, subsequent to the home page, offer four options in a graphic at the top of the screen that cor-

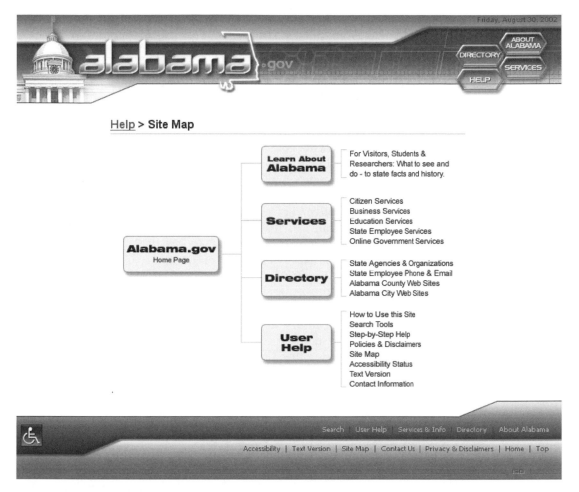

Figure 3. The site map for Alabama's web portal also makes good use of graphics. *Source*: http://www.alabama.gov/help_site_map.aspx.

respond to the four categories on the home page. Clicking on the *alabama.gov* icon returns the user to the home page. All screens are clear, concise, and very easy to navigate.

Selecting "Search" from the bottom of the home page leads to a page offering the user the option to search all state agency sites, or to limit the search to the *alabama.gov* site. The site map demonstrates yet another effective use of graphics (see Figure 3). A flowchart shows what type of information appears in each section.

COMMERCIAL PUBLICATIONS AND WEB SITES

Alabama Government Manual (Alabama Law Institute, P.O. Box 861425, Tuscaloosa, AL 35486-0013)—This quadrennial source describes the subdivisions of all three branches of state government. It provides a citation to the section of the *Alabama Code* in which the agency is established and given its charge.

Those who wish to purchase copies can call (205) 348-7411, or e-mail Linda Wilson at lwilson@ali.state.al.us. The web site for the Alabama Law Institute is http://ali.state.al.us.

Alabama Source Book (Litho-Media Co., Birmingham, AL)—This is an annual directory of personnel in state agencies, members of the legislature, officials at the county and city levels, and other governmental, political, or administrative officeholders. Those who wish to purchase copies of the *Alabama Source Book* can call (800) 917-9508, fax (205) 933-6331, or check the Litho-Media web site at http://www.lithomedia.com.

Michie's Alabama Code (LexisNexis/Michie Co., Charlottesville, VA)—This is the official edition of the state's laws. In 2002, the 34-volume set sold for $375. Current pricing and ordering information can be found on the LexisNexis Bookstore web site at http://bookstore.lexis.com/bookstore/catalog. Those with general questions can call the LexisNexis Bookstore at (888) 223-6337. Those who wish to place an order can call (800) 223-1940.

Economic Abstract of Alabama (University of Alabama, Center for Business and Economic Research, Box 870221, Tuscaloosa, AL 35487-0221)—Available in print or on CD-ROM, this source provides economic and demographic statistics for the state. Subjects covered include employment, income, retail sales, education funding, health care, and manufacturing. Statistics are presented at the state, county, city, and metropolitan statistical area (MSA) level. Information about how to order this title, and other publications issued by the Center for Business and Economic Research, is available online at http://cber.cba.ua.edu/publi.html.

SOURCES CONSULTED

Code of Alabama, 1975 online via the legislature web site, http://alisdb.legislature.state.al.us/acas/alisonstart.asp.

Numerous departmental web pages via *alabama.gov*, http://www.alabama.gov.

OCLC (Online Computer Library Center). *OCLC WorldCat*. Dublin, OH: OCLC.

Report of the Alabama State Publications Task Force, Draft, March 21, 2000, http://www.dpo.uab.edu/~dweather/ASPTFReport.html.

Survey response from C. Diann Weatherly, University of Alabama at Birmingham, 2000.

Alaska

Daniel D. Cornwall

GOVERNMENT PUBLISHING AND THE DEPOSITORY SYSTEM

The Alaska state publications depository program was started in 1970. It is administered by the State Library, and the laws governing the program are outlined in title 14 of the *Alaska Statutes*. Section 14.56.90 of the law establishes the State Library Distribution and Data Access Center, which is charged in section 14.56.100 with promoting "the establishment of an orderly depository library and data index distribution and access system." The center is popularly known as the "Alaska State Publications Program," since that name is easier to remember than "State Library Distribution and Data Access Center." State agencies are charged with depositing at least four copies of each of their publications with the center, and with supplying additional copies if necessary to meet the demands of the depository libraries. There are currently six Alaska depositories, and the center asks state agencies to submit eight copies of each of their publications. The Alaska State Library and the Elmer E. Rasmuson Library each receive two copies.

State publications are defined in section 14.56.180 of the law as including "any official document, compilation, journal, bill, law, resolution, bluebook, statute, code, register, pamphlet, list, book, report, study, hearing transcript, leaflet, order, regulation, directory, periodical, or magazine issued or contracted for by a state agency determined by the state librarian to be appropriate for retention in the center."

A unique feature of the Alaska depository system is that the publications of municipalities, federal agencies, and private companies are included in the program on a voluntary basis. These entities are given the option of depositing at least one copy of each publication and/or notifying the center about the creation of publications or databases. Provided that the publication is Alaska-related, it is accepted for the depository system. This is done to facilitate the Alaska State Library's mission to have a comprehensive collection of Alaskana.

Another unique feature of the system is that research reports done at the request of private individuals by state agencies, municipalities, or regional educational attendance areas will be included in the program, if the person for whom the report is being done gives permission.

USEFUL ADDRESSES AND TELEPHONE NUMBERS

The most complete collections of Alaska state publications may be found at the following libraries:

Alaska State Library
Government Publications
P.O. Box 110571
Juneau, AK 99811-0571
Phone Number for Alaska Reference Questions: (907) 465-2927
E-Mail Address for Alaska Reference Questions: asl@eed.state.ak.us
Alaska State Library's Home Page: http://library.state.ak.us
Depository Program Home Page: http://library.state.ak.us/asp/asp.html

University of Alaska Fairbanks
E. E. Rasmuson Library
P.O. Box 756800
Fairbanks, AK 99755-1010
Phone Number for Alaska Reference Questions: (907) 474-7261
E-Mail Address for Alaska Reference Questions: fyapr@uaf.edu
E. E. Rasmuson Library Home Page: http://www.uaf.edu/library

Those with questions about Alaska's depository library system may contact the State Library's Government Publications Librarian at the address, phone number, or e-mail address given above for the State Library.

INDEXES TO ALASKA STATE PUBLICATIONS

Each state depository receives a paper copy of the *Monthly Checklist* to assist them in processing the documents they receive. The *Checklist* is arranged alphabetically by issuing agency. The most recent *Monthly Checklist* is available on the web via the Alaska State Publications Program site at http://library .state.ak.us/asp/asp.html. From 1997 to date, an annual *Cumulative Monthly Checklist* of state publications is also available at that site. For access to information about publications issued prior to 1997, the site provides links to the online catalogs of various Alaska depository libraries. The site also has a link to a *Core List of Alaska State Publications* that was compiled by Patience Fredericksen and Rebecca Orford of the Alaska State Library.

There is no unique system of call numbers used for Alaska state publications. They are assigned Library of Congress call numbers.

ESSENTIAL STATE PUBLICATIONS

Directories

Alaska Directory of Banks and Financial Institutions (Department of Community and Economic Development, Division of Banking, Securities, and Corporations)—This directory provides addresses, phone and fax numbers, e-mail addresses, and web site addresses for the banks, credit unions, trust companies, and other financial institutions that are chartered by the state. This source is available only on the web and may be found at http://www.dced.state.ak .us/bsc/banking.htm.

Alaska Directory of State Officials (Alaska State Legislature, Legislative Affairs Agency, semi-annual)—Contact information is provided for all persons holding offices in all three branches of government. Contact information is also given for the state's U.S. congressional delegation. The title was first published in 1959, the year in which Alaska was granted statehood. The most recent edition is available on the web at http://w3.legis.state.ak.us/doso/dosotable .htm.

Alaska Education Directory (Department of Education and Early Development)—This directory is a valuable resource for finding information about Alaska school districts, individual schools, colleges and universities, education organizations, and other education-related groups. Included are names, addresses, phone numbers, fax numbers, e-mail addresses, and more. It is available on the web at http://www.eed.state.ak.us/Alaskan_Schools/, or you can order a printed directory by sending a check for $15 made out to the State of Alaska to: EED, Attn: Education Directory, 801 W. 10th Street, Juneau, AK 99801-1894, or call (907) 465-2800.

Financial/Budgetary Resources

Alaska Economic Information System (Department of Community and Economic Development)—Launched in 2002, this Internet-only resource draws information from several different departments to provide an economic snapshot of each of Alaska's boroughs. Each borough (county equivalent) entry contains the following sections: at-a-glance (quick numbers), overview narrative with basic industry information, population, personal income, unemployment, subsistence, per capita wealth, capital improvement projects, and detailed industry discussion. This rich and growing resource is located at http://www.dced.state.ak.us/cbd/AEIS/AEIS_Home.htm.

Comprehensive Annual Financial Report (Department of Administration, Division of Finance, annual)—Statistical information about the revenues and expenditures of the state within a given fiscal year are reported. Detailed data are provided for specific funds and accounts. Editions issued since 1997 are available on the web at http://fin.admin.state.ak.us/dof/financial_reports/ cafr_toc.jsp. That page also provides information about ordering a print copy of the report.

Swiss Army Knife of Budget Workbooks (Alaska State Legislature, Legislative Finance Division)—This is an essential guide to the Alaska appropriations process and to the various documents produced during the budget process. Illustrations make it easy to distinguish the different budget documents. The guide is available only on the web at http://www.legfin.state.ak.us/ SwissArmy/swissarmy.html.

Legal Resources

Alaska Administrative Code (Alaska State Legislature, Legislative Affairs Agency)—This source presents the regulations in force in the state arranged into sections by subject. A commercial edition is available in print from LexisNexis/Michie Co., but a free version is available online at http://www .legis.state.ak.us/folhome.htm.

Alaska Public Notices Home Page (Lieutenant Governor's Office)—This web site replaced the *Alaska Administrative Journal*. It includes notices about regulations that have been adopted or proposed, Attorney General opinions, requests for proposals, and announcements of upcoming agency meetings. The address of the page is http://notes3.state.ak.us/pn/pubnotic.nsf.

Alaska Statutes (Alaska State Legislature, Legislative Affairs Agency, annual)—This publication contains the state laws currently in force, arranged by subject. Like the *Code*, a commercial version is available in print from LexisNexis/Michie Co., and a free version is available on the web at http:// www.legis.state.ak.us/folhome.htm. The print version is published biennially.

The Constitution of the State of Alaska (Alaska State Legislature, Legislative Affairs Agency)—This title describes the basic structure of Alaska's state and local governments, and outlines procedures to be used for holding elections, introducing and passing legislation, and amending the Constitution itself. It is available online at http://www.legis.state.ak.us/folhome.htm.

Final Status of Bills and Resolutions (Alaska State Legislature, Legislative Affairs Agency, annual)—This source provides a summary of the status of bills and resolutions introduced in the legislature during that year. The summary is available only in paper. A copy may be requested from the Juneau Legislative Information Office at (907) 465-4648. Similar information is available on the web at http://www.legis.state.ak.us/folhome.htm.

Session Laws of Alaska [Slip Laws] (Alaska State Legislature, Legislative Affairs Agency)—Each law that is passed by the legislature is printed as an individual booklet. These slip laws, going back to 1981, are also available on the web at http://www.legis.state.ak.us/folhome.htm.

Sexual Offender Registration Central Registry (Department of Public Safety, Alaska State Troopers)—This is a searchable database of the sex offenders required to register under AS 12.63.010. It makes available the following information about those offenders: name, address, photograph, place of employment, date of birth, crime for which convicted, date of conviction, and place and court of conviction. The *Registry* is available on the web at http:// www.dps.state.ak.us/nSorcr/asp/.

Statistical Resources

Alaska Agricultural Statistics (Department of Natural Resources, Division of Agriculture, annual)—This source is published each fall and includes numerous statistics on agriculture in Alaska. It is available only in paper. Those who wish to enquire about the availability of copies can write to Division of Agriculture, 1800 Glenn Highway, Suite 12, Palmer, AK 99645-6736, or call (907) 745-7200.

Alaska Bureau of Vital Statistics Annual Report (Department of Health and Social Services, Division of Public Health, Bureau of Vital Statistics, annual)— This provides detailed statistics on births, deaths, marriages, divorces, and adoptions in the state. Recent editions are available on the web at http://www.hss.state.ak.us/dph/bvs/statistics/pubs.htm.

Alaska Statistics Index (Alaska State Library)—Located on the web at http://library.state.ak.us/asp/statestatistics.html, this resource attempts to link to all state agency web publications and pages known to have statistical information. This page offers a plain "back of the book" style subject index drawn both from words found on the indexed pages and likely search terms. Although this page takes a while to download, it is a good first stop to finding state-issued statistical information about Alaska. Users who prefer to browse statistical links by issuing agency should point their browsers to http://library.state.ak.us/asp/statisticsbyagency.html.

Crime Reported in Alaska (Department of Public Safety, Division of Administrative Services, annual) This presents statistical information about crimes committed in the state. Recent editions are available on the web at http://www.dps.state.ak.us/UCR/.

Research and Analysis Home Page (Department of Labor and Workforce Development, Research and Analysis Division)—This resource is absolutely the first stop for demographic information about Alaska. Population estimates and projections, employment trends, and wage formation are just a few of the items that can be found here. Much of the information provided here is also available in paper, but all of it is a click away at http://almis.labor.state.ak.us/.

Other Resources

Alaska Community Database (Department of Community and Economic Development, Research and Analysis Section)—The amount of data available from this web site is phenomenal. For each city and town in the state, information is provided on location and climate, history and culture, taxes, demographics, schools, health care facilities, utilities, economy, and transportation. Contact information is given for key agencies and organizations located in the community, including the newspapers, and radio and television stations. Photographs of local events and native wildlife are available. The address for the site is http://www.dced.state.ak.us/cbd/commdb/CF_COMDB.htm.

Relocating to Alaska (Department of Labor and Workforce Development)— In response to the torrents of people who dream about living in "The Last Frontier," the Department of Labor and Workforce Development put together a web site that answers questions about where jobs are, where housing is, and how much groceries cost. Alaska is unique in that much of its relocation information is aimed at *discouraging* people from moving to the state! Under "Finding work in Alaska," it says, "Before you come to Alaska: You should have a round trip ticket and cash or credit card resources ($2,000 for temporary and $3,000 for permanent work) to live on while looking for work. Many who arrived short of cash encountered serious hardship and shattered dreams. Public assistance programs cannot be counted on by persons relocating to

Alaska without adequate funds." The relocation guide is available only through the web at http://www.labor.state.ak.us/research/relocate/reloc map.htm.

Student Information Guide (Department of Community and Economic Development, Division of Tourism)—This web site provides links to information on Alaska's state symbols and song, as well as to information about the state's history, economy, geography, time zones, governmental structure ("Boroughs, Not Counties!"), wildlife, famous natives, and the Aurora Borealis. The page may be found at http://www.dced.state.ak.us/tourism/student.htm.

Handbook of Alaska State Government (Alaska State Legislature, Legislative Affairs Agency, biennial)—This handbook describes the role and purpose of each state agency. It is one of many publications available on the legislature's "Legislative Information Documents" page at http://www.legis.state.ak.us/infodocs/infodocs.htm.

ALASKA'S WORLD WIDE WEB HOME PAGE

As can be seen from the number of web addresses presented earlier in this chapter, Alaska has a wealth of excellent information on the web. The starting point to access this information is the state's home page at http://www.state .ak.us. The page has direct links to sites for the governor, lieutenant governor, legislature, courts, state budget, and an employee directory. Other links lead to a list of departmental home pages, and to information about business, services, communities, and technology training available to state employees. The home page has a small section of news headlines that link to further information. It has a section of links to facts about the state, instructions for obtaining hunting and fishing licenses, a listing of employment opportunities, legal notices, and an activity page for kids. The home page is searchable by keyword, and is available in a text-only version.

As of 2003, the Governor's Office was responsible for maintaining the Alaska state home page. The webmaster may be reached at webmaster@ state.ak.us.

COMMERCIAL PUBLICATIONS AND WEB SITES

Alaska Budget Report (Capital Information Group, Juneau, AK)—The *Alaska Budget Report* is published every week when the Alaska legislature is in session and irregularly during the rest of the year. At approximately $2,220 for a year's subscription, this is an expensive but essential publication for anyone needing in-depth analysis of Alaska's budget process. The editors often do extensive financial analysis on budget numbers provided by the executive and legislative branches, often finding fault with both. Lengthy interviews with state leaders are often featured. A staff transitions section is also included in nearly every issue. Subscriptions can be ordered from Capital Information Group, P.O. Box 21804, Juneau, AK 99802. The publisher may also be contacted by phone at (907) 586-3118, by fax at (907) 586-1987, or by e-mail at gerickso@alaska.com.

Alaska Media Directory (Alaska Media Directory, Anchorage, AK)—This annual looseleaf volume lists Alaska newspapers, radio stations, and television stations, as well as media-related companies. Each entry contains full contact information, including e-mail and web addresses, if available, a description of the media company's offerings, and deadlines for news and advertising. The publisher of *Alaska Media Directory* also offers mailing labels for a nominal fee. Questions about subscriptions, contents, or mailing labels should be directed to Alaska Media Directory, 6828 Cape Lisburne Loop, Anchorage, AK 99504-3958. The publisher may also be contacted by phone at (907) 338-7288, by fax at (907) 338-8339, or by e-mail at akmedia@ak.net.

West's Alaska Reporter (West Group, Eagan, MN)—This series, part of the *Pacific Reporter*, has been the official reporter for the appellate courts in the state of Alaska since 1960. Each volume lists the justices and judges for the Alaska Supreme Court, the Court of Appeals, the Superior Court, and all District Courts. In addition to the court opinions in each issue, there is a table of cases, a list of words and phrases, and the copyrighted Key Number digest. Subscriptions for this series may be ordered from the publisher's web site at http://west.thomson.com.

SOURCES CONSULTED

Alaska Statutes 1999. Juneau: Alaska State Legislature, 1999. (Via the web at http://www.legis.state.ak.us/folhome.htm.)

Frederiksen, Patience, and Orford, Rebecca. *Core List of Alaska State Publications*. Juneau: Alaska State Library, 1999.

Numerous departmental web pages via the state's home page, http://www.state.ak.us/.

Arizona

Daniel C. Barkley

GOVERNMENT PUBLISHING AND THE DEPOSITORY SYSTEM

In Arizona, the depository system is administered by the Director of the Department of Library, Archives and Public Records (Director). Any public or university library in Arizona may contract with the Director to become an Arizona depository. Research libraries in other states may also contract with the Director to become exchange partners. Those libraries must agree to send publications from their state in exchange for Arizona publications. Title 41, Section 1335, B., 1 of the *Arizona Revised Statutes* states that "except for statutes and official supplements of the statutes which shall be purchased directly by the department and distributed, the department shall make requisition upon the secretary of state, the heads of departments and all officers and agents of the state for the number of copies of official publications the department needs for the depository system and any exchange programs established pursuant to this subsection, and it shall be the duty of the officers to supply them." The law does not define "official publications."

USEFUL ADDRESSES AND TELEPHONE NUMBERS

The most complete collections of Arizona state publications may be found at the following libraries:

Arizona State Library, Archives and Public Records
Research Division
1700 West Washington
Phoenix, AZ 85007
Phone Number for Arizona Reference Questions: (602) 542-3701 or (800) 228-4710
  (toll-free in Arizona only); fax (602) 542-4400
E-Mail Address for Arizona Reference Questions: research@dlapr.lib.az.us
Reference Desk E-Mail: rerefde@lib.az.us
Arizona State Library's Home Page: http://www.lib.az.us/is/index.html
Research Division Home Page: http://www.lib.az.us/research/index.html
Archives & Public Records Online Catalog Home Page: http://aslaprcat.lib.az.us/

Arizona State University
Hayden Library
Government Documents Service
Box 871006
Tempe, AZ 85287-1006
Phone Number for Arizona Reference Questions: (480) 965-3390
E-Mail Address for Arizona Reference Questions: http://www.asu.edu/lib/help/
    askalib.htm
Hayden Library's Home Page: http://www.asu.edu/lib/hayden/
Government Documents Services Home Page: http://www.asu.edu/lib/hayden/
    govdocs/

Northern Arizona University
Cline Library
Box 6022
South San Francisco Street
Flagstaff, AZ 86011-6022
Phone Number for the Cline Library Reference Questions: (520) 523-6805; fax (520)
    523-6860
E-Mail Address for Arizona Reference Questions: http://www4.nau.edu/library/
    reference/aal/askalibrarian.html
Cline Library's Home Page: http://www.nau.edu/cline/

University of Arizona
Main Library
Government Documents Department
P.O. Box 210055
Tucson, AZ 85720-0055
Phone Number for Arizona Reference Questions: (520) 621-6441
E-Mail Address for Arizona Reference Questions: http://dizzy.library.arizona.edu/
    library/type1/libraryservices/data/emailref.html
Main Library's Home Page: http://dizzy.library.arizona.edu/aboutlib/aboutlib.shtml

INDEXES TO ARIZONA STATE PUBLICATIONS

Until 1990, the Government Documents Service at Arizona State University's Hayden Library produced a computer-generated "key-word-out-of-context" index to state publications called the *Arizona Governmental Publications KWOC Index*. An electronic list of the Arizona "core collection" with web links is still available online via the Hayden Library site at http://www.asu.edu/lib/hayden/govdocs/onlinepubs/statedocscore.htm. Materials published after 1990 may be found by searching the online catalogs of the Hayden Library or the State Library.

The Hayden Library many years ago created a system of call numbers to be assigned to Arizona publications that was based on the Superintendent of Documents classification system used with U.S. government documents. Like Superintendent of Documents numbers, Arizona documents call numbers arrange the collection by issuing agency rather than subject. This numbering system is still used to classify Arizona state publications.

New Arizona state agency publications received by the State Library each month are flagged in the catalog and can be located by searching the catalog using the phrase:

Checklist m/yyyy

where m is the month and yyyy is the year

e.g., Checklist 3/2000

If a state agency supplied distribution copies of a publication, there is a notation in the record and depository libraries can request a copy while the supply lasts. Otherwise, the issuing agency must be contacted directly for publications.

ESSENTIAL STATE PUBLICATIONS

Directories

Arizona Department of Education Educational Directory (Department of Education)—An online comprehensive resource for education in Arizona, this directory is divided into education agency, public and private educational institutions, school districts, school boards, and other entities involved in the educational process in Arizona. Copies may be obtained from the Arizona Department of Education, 1535 West Jefferson Street, Phoenix, AZ 85007, or call (602) 542-3088. It may be found online at http://www.ade.state.az.us/schools/directory.

Arizona Library Directory (Department of Library, Archives and Public Records)—This annual publication (1985–) provides contact information on individuals associated with the operations of the State Library. Copies are available from the state depository program or by contacting the Arizona State Library, Archives, and Public Records, 1700 West Washington Street, State Capitol Room 300, Phoenix, AZ 85007, or call (602) 542-3701.

Arizona Criminal Justice Commission Directory (Criminal Justice Commission)—An online directory that provides links to the various law enforcement agencies within Arizona, the information includes the name of the agency (in alphabetical arrangement), name, title, address, phone and fax numbers, and an e-mail address. A copy may be obtained from the Arizona Criminal Justice Commission, 3737 North 7th Street, Suite 260, Phoenix, AZ 85014, or call (602) 230-0252. It can be viewed at http://www.acjc.state.az.us/resources/cj_directory.asp.

Directory of the [No.] Legislature of the State of Arizona (Secretary of State)—An online directory that lists all federal and state legislators and judicial officials in Arizona, this source also includes staff of the Arizona House and Senate and a seating arrangement of each chamber. It is available in a PDF format, on the web at http://www.sos.state.az.us/publications.htm. Copies may be obtained by contacting the Office of the Secretary of State, 1700 West Washington Street, 7th Floor, Phoenix, AZ 85007, or call (602) 542-4086.

State Agency Contact Information (Office of the Governor)—This web site is a part of the *Arizona @ Your Service* portal maintained by the state of Arizona.

As such, this directory provides links to all state agency web sites. Each agency web site provides further contact information including name, address, phone number, and e-mail. The directory can be viewed at http://www.az.gov/webapp/portal/alpha.jsp?name=agency.

[Year] State of Arizona Telephone Directory (Department of Telecommunications)—This annual publication provides telephone information on every Arizona agency, board, commission and council, and is divided into four sections: Agency Abbreviations; Agencies, Boards, Commissions and Councils Listings; Legislative Listings; and Arizona State Senate and Representatives. Also included is a searchable database available to the public. Go to http://azdirect.state.az.us/ for further information.

Financial/Budgetary Resources

Arizona Department of Economic Security, Comprehensive Annual Financial Report for the Fiscal Year Ended . . . (Division of Business and Finance)—The Department of Economic Security is a human services agency that oversees programs related to job placement, food stamps, child protective services, domestic violence, and services for the elderly and the developmentally disabled. The department's annual report provides statistics on these services, plus a general economic forecast for the state. Recent annual reports as well as many other DES reports are available online at http://www.de.state.az.us/links/reports/index.html. Some paper copies may be available. Contact the Arizona Department of Economic Security, 1717 West Jefferson Street, Phoenix, AZ 85005, or call (602) 542-5678.

Arizona Financial Highlights: A Report to the Citizens of the State for Fiscal Year [Year–Year] (Department of Administration, General Accounting Office)—This report presents basic information regarding the financial condition of the state of Arizona. While it is not intended to replace the more detailed financial reports issued by this department or other state agencies, this report is prepared for citizens in an easy-to-understand format. Contact the Arizona Department of Administration, General Accounting Office, 100 North 15th Avenue, #302, Phoenix, AZ 85007, or call (602) 542-5405, or see http://www.gao.state.az.us.

The Executive Budget, Fiscal Years . . . (Office of the Governor, Office of Strategic Planning and Budgeting)—This annual title reports in detail the revenues and expenditures of the state. It outlines the funding received by each state agency, plus money spent for capital improvement projects and specific programs. It outlines the governor's recommendations for future funding. The most recent edition of the *Executive Budget* is available on the governor's web site at http://www.state.az.us/ospb/budgeting.cfm.

Financial Institutions Reports (Arizona State Banking Department)—Currently there are only a few financial reports available on the Department's web page at http://www.azbanking.com/Reports.htm. The long-range plan is to include as many financial reports as required by Arizona state law. They are available in a PDF format.

State of Arizona Comprehensive Annual Financial Report for the Fiscal Year Ended . . . (Department of Administration, General Accounting Office)—This annual report is prepared in accordance with generally accepted accounting principles and is the report relied upon by those who seek to buy or sell bonds or other obligations of the state. It provides a more detailed and complex accounting report than others heretofore mentioned. Recent reports are available on the web at http://www.gao.state.az.us/financials/.

Legal Resources

ALIS (Arizona Legislative Information System) Online (Arizona Legislative Council)—*ALIS*, the official web site of the Arizona legislature, is at http://www.azleg.state.az.us/. Via this site one can search the online versions of the *Arizona Revised Statutes*, the *Arizona Constitution*, the bills introduced in the legislature since 1995, the floor calendar, and a wealth of additional information about the legislative process. All of the state legislative manuals are also available at this web site. These include the House and Senate rules, the *Legislative Bill Draft Manual* and the *Legislative Manual*. All of the online manuals are also available in a paper format for a small fee. Contact the Arizona Legislative Council, Suite 100, Legislative Services Wing, State Capitol, Phoenix, AZ 85007, or call (602) 542-4236.

Arizona Administrative Code (Secretary of State)—This title compiles all the rules and regulations that have been promulgated by state agencies, in a nine-volume set composed of twenty subject titles. The set is updated by a quarterly supplement. Some information from the *Code* is available online through the secretary of state's web site at http://www.sosaz.com/Rules_and_Regulations.htm. The entire *Code* is available in paper format for $450.00 per year. Supplements to the *Code* are available for $120.00 per year. Go to http://www.sos.state.az.us/public_services/orderform.htm for further information.

Arizona Administrative Register (Secretary of State)—This weekly source contains the rules and regulations that have been proposed by state agencies, and which have recently been finalized or eliminated. It also includes the Executive Orders and Proclamations of the Governor, summary opinions of the attorney general, and notices about the appointment of various state officials. The *Register* is available on the web at http://www.sosaz.com/aar/. The *Register* is available in paper for $276.00; there are a limited number of back issues available for $7.00 per issue. Go to http://www.sos.state.az.us/public_services/orderform.htm for further information.

Arizona Agency Handbook (Attorney General's Office)—The 2001 edition, recently revised from the original publication issued in 1993, is used to provide guidance and directions to state officers, state employees, and lawyers who represent the state or appear before its boards and agencies. It is intended to be used as a reference source on laws that have been created by statute, regulation, or the state or federal constitution rather than as a source to create legal rights or obligations. Currently available online at http://www.attorneygeneral.state.az.us/Agency_Handbook/Agency_Handbook.html, individual chapters will be updated periodically to reflect significant changes in Arizona law. Contact the Solicitor General's Office, Office of the Attorney General, 1275 West Washington Street, Phoenix, AZ 85007, or call (602) 542-5025 for comments, suggestions, or to obtain a paper copy.

The Arizona Judiciary (Office of the Administrative Director of Courts)—This publication provides brief biographical and historic information on the court systems in Arizona, and includes a glossary and a chart. It can be purchased for $5.00 from the Arizona Supreme Court, Office of the Administrative Director of the Courts, 1501 West Washington Street, Phoenix, AZ 85007, or call (602) 542-9300. It is also available at the Arizona State Library and Archives as well as many other Arizona state depository libraries.

Arizona Revised Statutes (Arizona Legislative Council)—Arizona's current laws are presented in this source. The laws are divided by subject into forty-nine separate sections, or "titles." The statutes may be searched online via *ALIS* at http://www.azleg.state.az.us/ars/ars.htm. A CD-ROM version of this title may be purchased from the Legislative Council. Call (602) 542-4236 to request a copy. A commercial version of the title, published by the West Publishing Company, is available in paper.

Arizona Rulemaking Manual (Secretary of State's Office)—This manual was "developed in 1995 as a guide for state agencies when making, amending, or repealing rules." Developed in conjunction with the State Agency Rulewriters' Consortium, the updated (2001) manual reflects all changes to Arizona statutes, rules, and writing style since 1995. Both the 1995 and 2001 manuals are available at http://www.sos.state.az.us/public_services/rulemakingmanual/2001/manual.htm. As changes occur, paper copies will be made available from the Office of the Secretary of State, 1700 West Washington Street, 7th Floor, Phoenix, AZ 85007, or call (602) 542-4751.

Arizona State Constitution & Enabling Act (Arizona Legislative Council)—This keyword searchable database is maintained by the *ALIS*. It provides the ability to search the entire constitution or a particular section. It also provides a direct link to the full text of the constitution. See http://www.azleg.state.az.us/const/const.htm.

Arizona Uniform Commercial Code (Secretary of State's Office)—Part of the *Arizona Revised Statutes* (Title 47), a copy is available for $17.00 from the Arizona Secretary of State's Office, 1700 West Washington Street, 7th Floor, Phoenix, AZ 85007-2888, or call (602) 542-7386. It is available online at http://www.sos.state.az.us/business_services/ucc.htm.

Bills of Arizona (Arizona Legislative Council)—This is a keyword-searchable database that provides links to all Arizona legislative bills that have been introduced since 1995. See http://www.azleg.state.az.us/legtext/bills.htm.

Statistical Resources

Arizona Community, County, State and Indian Land Profiles (Department of Commerce)—This web portal provides access to a variety of statistical information in both text and table format on Arizona communities. Each profile is usually one or two pages in length and contains information on the population, principal economic activities, labor force, and scenic attractions. Each database is keyword searchable and all the information can be downloaded. There are also additional links to Arizona businesses, commerce, and community services. See http://www.azcommerce.com/Communities/default

.asp. Contact the Arizona Department of Commerce, 3800 North Central Avenue, Suite 1500, Phoenix, AZ 85012, or call (602) 280-1300.

Arizona Facts and Figures (Arizona State Library and Archives)—This web site provides links to a variety of subject-oriented web pages containing statistical information. Statistics range from agriculture to weather. Go to http://www.lib.az.us/links/factsAZ.htm.

Arizona Vital Statistics (Bureau of Public Health Statistics)—This is an annual report on health and vital statistics in Arizona. This web site provides statistics on natality, morbidity, mortality, and the health status of Arizona residents. Data can be chosen from a menu of subject terms or by the title of a specific report. Data range from the mid-1980s until present. Additional tables present birth, death, and marriage statistics from 1950 through 1987. The geographic coverage varies from state down to census tract level. The site is located at http://www.hs.state.az.us/plan/ohpes.htm. Contact the Office of Epidemiology and Statistics, Bureau of Public Health Statistics, Arizona Department of Health Services, 1740 West Adams Street, Phoenix, AZ 85007, or call (602) 542-1216.

Crime in Arizona, [Year]: An Annual Report Compiled by Access Integrity Unit of the Arizona Department of Public Safety (Department of Public Safety, Access Integrity Unit)—This annual report mirrors the *Uniform Crime Report* produced by the Federal Bureau of Investigation. It contains detailed statistics on crimes and criminal activity in Arizona. Reports have been generated since 1993 and are available at most of the state depository libraries. See http://www.dps.state.az.us/welcome2.htm for more information.

Motor Vehicle Crash Facts for Arizona (Department of Transportation, Traffic Engineering Group, Traffic Records Section)—This annual report, produced since 1997, is a statistical review of motor vehicle crashes occurring in Arizona each year. In some instances, some preliminary statistics may be used. The information is gathered from traffic reports submitted to the Department of Transportation by state, county, city, tribal, and other law enforcement agencies. It is available on the web at http://www.dot.state.az.us/ROADS/rdfway.htm. Paper copies may be obtained by contacting the Arizona Department of Transportation, Traffic Engineering Group, Traffic Records Section, 2828 North Central Avenue, Suite 880, Phoenix, AZ 85004, or call (602) 712-6968, 6687; e-mail azcrashfacts@dot.state.az.us.

Other Resources

Arizona (Georgetown University, E. B. Williams Law Library)—This is a very good source of state and local government information including the state constitution. Executive, legal, judicial, and other information can be found at http://www.ll.georgetown.edu/states/arizona.cfm. This site contains electronic links to numerous state and local information sites.

Arizona Blue Book, [Years] (Secretary of State's Office)—This biennial publication presents current and historical information and facts on Arizona. Categories include information on the Arizona and U.S. Constitutions, the three branches of Arizona government, Native American nations and tribes, elections, and more. The current edition is Arizona's "Millennium Edition" and is available for $25.00 for the hardcover, $15.00 for the softcover. It is available on the web at http://www.sos.state.az.us/Publications.htm. An order can also be placed with the Secretary of State, 1700 West Washington Street, 7th Floor, Phoenix, AZ 85007, or call (602) 542-4086.

Arizona Code of Judicial Administration (Arizona Supreme Court)—This web site contains the policies and procedures that guide Arizona municipal courts, justices of the peace, superior courts, and appellate courts in conducting their administrative functions. These policies are developed by the Arizona State Supreme Court as mandated by the state constitution. See http://www .supreme.state.az.us/orders/admcode for the *Code.*

Arizona Governor's Community Policy Office Home Page (Governor's Community Policy Office)—The focus of the page is on public policy and its development and effect on the citizens of Arizona. Many of the divisions in this office focus on topical issues facing citizens of Arizona (e.g., domestic violence, education, children). There is also a link to the *GCPO Grant Brochure* that provides information on grants administered in Arizona. See http://www .governor.state.az.us/cfpo/cfpo.cfm for more information.

Arizona Highways Magazine (Arizona Department of Transportation)—Each issue includes articles and photographs of different sights and highlights of the Arizona scenic highway system. A yearly subscription is available for $21.00 from the Department of Transportation. Order online at http://www .arizonahighways.com/newFiles/subs.html, or call (800) 543-5432 for further information.

Arizona State Tax Forms and Tax Information (Department of Revenue)—This is a web site that provides information and forms on all types of taxes imposed in Arizona. Links are provided to state tax forms along with an electronic filing capability, information on income and corporate taxes, professional licensing, tax credits, and other tax information. There are additional links to Arizona statutes and codes, the Department of Revenue's annual report, and phone numbers for tax assistance. See http://www.revenue.state.az.us/ for further information.

Full-Text Legislative Study Committee Report Online (Arizona State Library)—From 1999 to the present, these reports, available by subject or committee, are the results of studies commissioned by Legislative Study Committees or Interim Committees of the Arizona legislature, and are maintained by the Arizona State Library, Archives and Public Records, Law and Research Library Division. Go to http://www.lib.az.us/is/lsc/index.html to view all the available reports.

A Guide to Arizona Courts (Arizona Supreme Court)—The booklet is designed to help one become more familiar with the Arizona judicial system. Information presented includes how the courts are organized, the special functions of the courts, how cases are processed, the role of people involved in the court systems, judge selection, and court and judge evaluation processes. The site is maintained by the Arizona Supreme Court and can be found at http://www.supreme.state.az.us/guide/.

Labor Shortages and Illegal Immigration: Arizona's Three-Pronged Strategy (Arizona-Mexico Commission)—This 2001 report highlights some of the critical issues facing Arizona and its relationship with Mexico. The Arizona-

Mexico Commission (AMC), formed in 1959, is a non-profit corporation consisting of ten working committees that formulate programs and action items relating to issues that impact Arizona and Mexico. The AMC works in collaboration with public and private sector groups in promoting "goodwill, understanding and the overall development of the Arizona-Mexico region by utilizing cultural, economic, human, natural and technical resources." This report is available at http://www.azmc.org/index.asp. Select "Studies" from the menu. For more information contact the Arizona-Mexico Commission, 1700 West Washington Street, Suite 180, Phoenix, AZ 85007, or call (602) 542-1327.

Master List of State Government Programs, [Years] (Governor's Office of Strategic Planning and Budgeting)—Published every even-numbered year, this list contains state agency–level operational plans and a comprehensive inventory of all state government programs and subprograms. The list provides users with the opportunity to view an agency's mission, description, strategic issues, goals, and key performance measures. The list can be viewed at http://www.state.az.us/ospb/master.cfm. For further information contact the Office of Strategic Planning and Budgeting, 1700 West Washington Street, Suite 500, Phoenix, AZ 85007, or call (602) 542-5381.

The New Deal in Arizona (State Parks Board)—Written by William S. Collins, this book presents the programs and policies of the Franklin D. Roosevelt administration from 1933 to 1939 and the impact of the New Deal in Arizona. Of particular note is the chapter on the Indian New Deal, a set of policies that had a tremendous impact on the large Native American populations in Arizona. Other chapters focus on the copper mining industry, the economy, and the vast amount of land owned by the federal government. It is available from Arizona State Parks, State Parks Board, Attention: Business Services, 1300 West Washington Street, Phoenix, AZ 85007.

State of the State (Office of the Governor)—This is the governor's assessment of Arizona state affairs, similar in nature to the U.S. president's address to the nation on the affairs of the United States. The assessment includes matters on social and economic policies, health care, education and other pertinent issues facing the state. Speeches from 1998 to date are available at http://www.governor.state.az.us/sos/index.cfm.

ARIZONA'S WORLD WIDE WEB HOME PAGE

Arizona @ Your Service (http://www.az.gov/webapp/portal/) is the official web site for the state of Arizona. Like many other states Arizona's web page has been designed as a portal to provide citizens, government officials, and visitors with quick and easy access points to a variety of information sources and services. Designed to find information by category, quick link, or topical information of the day, *Arizona @ Your Service* is a very useful and functional information resource.

There are nine main categories on the web page. Each category, or subject-specific area, provides links to a variety of informational resources or government services for that subject. Running the gamut from business services to government employees, information can be located to satisfy one's curiosity or questions on Arizona. Whether one is relocating to Arizona and requires information on education, health, or licensing and permits, or just passing through and looking for places to visit or stay, this page provides that information.

Additionally, there are quick links to specific services such as tourism, Arizona courts, employee benefits, and taxes. The latest news pertaining to Arizona can also be found here. As well, there are several links that connect one to topical points of interest such as fire conditions, homeland security, the state legislator, or state facts.

A keyword search can be conducted from the initial page. Utilizing the "More Search Options" button will link one to three search engines for legislative bills, state agency web pages, or *Arizona @ Your Service*. Each of these search engines can be utilized with common language terms, Boolean operators, or specific phrases. There are also links provided to a state agency directory, cities, counties, news, Arizona events, and a services directory. Links are provided from these to more specific types of information.

The web page is maintained by *Arizona @ Your Service*, 411 North Central Avenue, Suite 770, Phoenix, AZ 85004.

COMMERCIAL PUBLICATIONS AND WEB SITES

Arizona Business Directory (American Business Directories Staff, 5711 South 86th Circle, Omaha, NE 68127)—This directory contains up-to-date information on Arizona businesses, including phone numbers, addresses, e-mail, and web pages. It is an annual publication and is available for $595.00. Contact American Business Directories Staff at the address above or call (877) 708-3844 or go to http://www.directoriesUSA.com.

Arizona High Tech Directory (Jean Wendelboe, ed.) (Keiland Corporation, P.O. Box 12742, Scottsdale, AZ 85267)—This is an annual publication available for $65.00. It contains the latest information on high-tech companies in Arizona, and is available from Keiland Corporation at (602) 502-1194.

Arizona State Map (Arizona Maps, 1861 East Indian Wells Drive, Chandler, AZ 85249)—For the price of $2.95 the 2001 "millennium" edition of the Arizona state map can be obtained. Contact Arizona Maps at the address above or call (877) 438-2627. A web page order form can be found at http://www.azmaps.com/Order.htm.

The Great Arizona Almanac: Facts about Arizona (Dean Smith, ed.) (Graphic Arts Center Publishing Company, P.O. Box 10306, Portland, OR 97296-0306)—This is a one-stop resource for a variety of facts and figures on Arizona. The price for the 2000 edition is $12.95. Contact Graphic Arts Center Publishing Company at the address above or call (503) 226-2402.

SOURCES CONSULTED

AllLaw.com, http://www.alllaw.com/state_law_search/arizona/.
Departmental web pages via the state's home page, http://www.az.gov/webapp/portal.
Government Documents Round Table, American Library Association. *Directory of Gov-*

ernment Document Collections & Librarians, 7th ed. Bethesda, MD: Congressional Information Service, 1997.

Jobe, Janita. "State Publications." *Journal of Government Information*, 27 (2000): 733–768.

Maxymuk, John, ed. *Government Online: One-Click Access to 3,400 Federal and State Websites*. New York: Neal-Schuman Publishers, 2001.

Notess, Greg R. *Government Information on the Internet*, 3rd ed. Lanham, MD: Bernan Press, 2000.

State Governments and Politics, http://www.lib.umich.edu/govdocs/state.html.

State Legal Resources on the Web, http://www.lib.umich.edu/govdocs/statelaw .html#A.

Statehouse Reports: Internet Resource Guide, http://www.stateline.org.

U.S. State & Local Gateway, http://www.statelocal.gov/.

Arkansas

Lori L. Smith

GOVERNMENT PUBLISHING AND THE DEPOSITORY SYSTEM

The first depository system for Arkansas state publications was established in 1947. In Act Number 170 passed that year, the Mullins Library at the University of Arkansas was selected to become the official depository for state public documents, and for the publications of cities and counties as well. In 1971 the depository system was expanded to include all state colleges and universities. The Arkansas State Library in that year was charged with compiling and publishing a checklist of state, county, and city publications. The State Library sent the checklist to the libraries of the state's colleges and universities, who requested copies of the publications they wished to include in their collections. Act Number 489 of 1979, which is still in effect today, established the Arkansas State Library as the official depository for state, city, and county publications, and charged the State Library with creating a State and Local Government Publications Clearinghouse. Each state and local agency was directed to send up to fifty copies of each publication to the clearinghouse. Agencies who did not have sufficient funding to supply fifty copies were directed to send no less than three copies. The 1979 law also gave the Arkansas State Library the authority to set up depository agreements with any public, school, or academic library in the state.

State and local publications are defined in section 13-2-201 (a) of the *Arkansas Code of 1987* as including

any document issued or printed by any state agency or local government which may be released for distribution, but these terms do not include: (1) The bound volumes of the printed acts of each of the sessions of the General Assembly of the State of Arkansas; (2) The bound volumes of the Arkansas Supreme Court Reports; (3) Printed copies of the Arkansas Statutes Annotated of 1947 or pocket part supplements thereto; (4) Any other printed document which may be obtained from the Office of the Secretary of State upon the payment of a charge or fee therefor; (5) Correspondence and intraoffice or interoffice or agency communications or documents which are not of vital interest to the public; (6) (A) Publications of state or local agencies intended or designed to be of limited distribution to meet the requirements of educational, cultural, scientific, professional, or similar use of a limited or restricted purpose and which are not designed for general distribution. (B) Similarly, other publications or printed documents which are prepared to meet the limited distribution requirements of a governmental grant or use, which are not intended for general distribution, shall also be deemed exempt from the provisions of this subchapter unless funds have been provided for printing of a quantity of such publications sufficient for distribution.

USEFUL ADDRESSES AND TELEPHONE NUMBERS

The most complete collections of Arkansas state publications may be found at the following libraries:

Special Collections (David W. Mullins Library)
University Libraries
University of Arkansas
Fayetteville, AR 72701-1201
Phone Number for Arkansas Reference Questions: (479) 575-5577
E-Mail Address for Arkansas Reference Questions: refer@uark.edu
University Libraries' Home Page: http://libinfo.uark.edu/
Special Collections Division Home Page: http://libinfo.uark.edu/specialcollections/

Arkansas State Library
One Capitol Mall
Little Rock, AR 72201
Phone Number for Arkansas Reference Questions: (501) 682-2053
E-Mail Address for Arkansas Reference Questions: aslref@asl.lib.ar.us
Web Form for Arkansas Reference Questions: http://www.asl.lib.ar.us/asl_reference
    _form.asp
Arkansas State Library's Homepage: http://www.asl.lib.ar.us/

Those with questions about the depository program in Arkansas may contact the State Library's Coordinator of Documents Services at (501) 682-2326.

INDEXES TO ARKANSAS STATE PUBLICATIONS

Arkansas Documents, the official index to state publications, was first issued by the Arkansas State Library in 1980. A cumulative edition, covering 1980 through 1994, was published in 1995. New issues continue to be published monthly.

Arkansas state publications are assigned call numbers using a system which is based on the Superintendent of Documents numbering system used with federal publications. The call number assigned to *Arkansas Documents* is ED 1.36:A 7/years.

Although the index is not available on the web, the online catalog of the Arkansas State Library is searchable via the web, and it does include thousands of records for state publications. The catalog may be accessed from the State Library's home page at http://www.asl.lib.ar.us/.

ESSENTIAL STATE PUBLICATIONS

Directories

Arkansas Education Directory (Department of Education, Division of Communication and Dissemination)—Arkansas Documents Call Number—ED 1.5: A 7/year. Names, addresses, and phone numbers for elementary and secondary schools, and for school system personnel are given in this source. An excerpt from this directory, in addition to other searchable files of school information, is available on the *AS-IS (Arkansas School Information Site)* web page at http://www.as-is.org/directory/index.php. The *AS-IS* page is maintained by the department's Information and Research Division. Those interested in enquiring about the availability of print copies of the directory can write to Arkansas Department of Education, #4 Capitol Mall, Little Rock, AR 72201, or call (501) 682-4475.

Directory of Arkansas Higher Education Personnel (Department of Higher Education, annual)—Arkansas Documents Call Number—HI 1.5:D 5/year. This publication provides the mailing address, phone number, fax number, and e-mail address of personnel in the Department of Higher Education and in each college and university in the state. It also lists the names and addresses of the members of the Arkansas Higher Education Coordinating Board, and lists which members belong to the committees of the board. Those who wish to enquire about the availability of print copies can write to Arkansas Department of Higher Education, 114 East Capitol Avenue, Little Rock, AR 72201, or call (501) 371-2000. The most recent edition is available on the web at http://www.arkansashighered.com/publications.html.

State of Arkansas Telephone Directory (Department of Information Systems, annual)—Arkansas Documents Call Number—INS 1.7:S 7/year. This directory includes a map of Arkansas area codes; a national list of area codes by state; a guide to the location of state offices by building for use by messenger services; a list of services which indicates the agency responsible for providing the service and the phone number to call; a list of agencies with mailing addresses, phone numbers, and web site addresses; a list of boards and commissions with phone numbers; and a list of state personnel which gives agency affiliation, e-mail addresses, and phone numbers. A searchable version, as well as a printable version which may be downloaded, are available on the web at http://www.accessarkansas.org/directory/. Those with questions can e-mail info@ark.org, or call (501) 324-8900.

Financial/Budgetary Resources

Arkansas Comprehensive Annual Financial Report for the Fiscal Year Ended June 30, . . . (Department of Finance and Administration, Office of Accounting, annual)—Arkansas Documents Call Number—FI 22.3:year. An introductory section, a financial section, and a statistical section are the component parts of this report. The first section provides a list of the state's principal officials, and an organization chart for the state government. The financial section includes detailed statements of revenues, expenditures, cash flows, and fund balance changes. The statistical section presents summary tables of expenditures by function and revenues by source, as well as a selection of general demographic and economic statistics. A list of the twenty-five largest employers in the state's private sector is also included. The report is available on the web at http://www.accessarkansas.org/dfa/accounting/cafr.html. Those with questions about the report can write to Arkansas Department of Finance and Administration, Office of Accounting, P.O. Box 3278, Room 403, DFA Building, Little Rock, AR 72203, or call (501) 682-2583.

State of Arkansas [Years] Biennial Budget (Department of Finance and Administration, biennial)—Arkansas Documents Call Number—FI 39.7:A 7/year. Appropriations for state agencies and allocations to specific funds and programs are reported in this publication. Expected revenues are projected. Statistics are also provided on the number of persons employed by each agency, and on the overall pay plan for state employees. Excerpts from the report are available on the web at http://www.state.ar.us/dfa/budget/book.html. Those with questions about this publication can write to Arkansas Department of Finance and Administration, Office of Budget, DFA Building, Room 402, 1509 W. 7th Street, Little Rock, AR 72203, or call (501) 682-1941.

Legal Resources

Arkansas Code of 1987 Annotated (General Assembly)—Arkansas Documents Call Number—GE 1.4:A 73/volume/year. This source contains the laws of the state organized by subject. The laws are divided into twenty-nine sections, or titles. The last major revision of the *Code* was done in 1987, but it is updated regularly as new laws are passed. The official version of the *Code* is a commercial publication issued by the LexisNexis/Michie Company. An unofficial version is available on the web at http://www.arkleg.state.ar.us/data/resources.asp.

Arkansas Register (Secretary of State, monthly)—Arkansas Documents Call Number—ST 1.6:A 7/volume-issue. The *Register* includes the full text of Attorney General opinions, and lists the rules and regulations that have been adopted by the state's agencies and other administrative bodies. Each entry under "Adopted Rules and Regulations" includes the name of the agency, board, or commission that adopted the rule or regulation, as well as a docket number, an effective date, and the name and phone number of a contact person. Notices of legislative audit reports and insurance orders are also included. Issues from recent years are available on the web at http://www.sosweb .state.ar.us/ar_register.html. A subscription to the *Register* is available for $40 per year. Individual issues can be purchased for $3.50. Copies of rules from the *Register* can be requested for a $.25 per page fee. Those interested can write to Secretary of State's Office, Arkansas Register, 026 State Capitol, Little Rock, AR 72201, or call (501) 682-3527 or (800) 482-1127.

Constitution of the State of Arkansas of 1874 (Secretary of State, Elections Division)—Arkansas Documents Call Number—ST 1.4:C 66/year. The Constitution outlines the basic structure of state government in Arkansas. It describes the duties and powers of government officials, the election process, the process to be used in adopting legislation, and includes sections dealing with topics such as agriculture, education, and taxation. It has been amended more than seventy times since it was originally adopted. An online edition, provided by the Arkansas General Assembly, is available at http://www .arkleg.state.ar.us/data/resources.asp. The only edition available for purchase is sold by LexisNexis under its Michie imprint. The address of its online bookstore is http://bookstore.lexis.com/bookstore/catalog/.

Statistical Resources

Arkansas Maternal and Child Health Statistics (Department of Health, Center for Health Statistics)—Arkansas Documents Call Number—HE 208.7:M 37/ year. The first section of this publication provides statistics, in both tables and graphs, about live births and infant deaths in the state from 1965 to the present. The second section focuses on live births and includes statistics divided by the age, race, education level, and marital status of the mother. This section also reports on the trimester when prenatal care began, the sex of the child, and maternal usage of tobacco. The third section focuses on mortality and gives statistics for fetal, neonatal, perinatal, postneonatal, and infant deaths. It is available on the web via the Department of Health's "Data and Research" page at http://www.healthyarkansas.com/data/data.html. Those interested in enquiring about the availability of print copies can write to Arkansas Department of Health, Center for Health Statistics-Slot 19, 4815 West Markham Street, Little Rock, AR 72205-3867, or call (501) 661-2003.

Arkansas Vital Statistics (Department of Health, annual)—Arkansas Documents Call Number—HE 208.7:A 8/year. This report is divided into ten sections: General Summaries, Natality, Induced Abortions, Fetal Deaths, Spontaneous Abortions, Infant Mortality, Mortality, Marriages, Divorces and Annulments, and Maps and Figures. Statistics are presented for the state as a whole and for counties. Many tables give totals divided by age, race, and sex, and some tables include historic statistics going back as far as 1940. It is available on the web at http://www.healthyarkansas.com/data/data.html. Those interested in enquiring about the availability of print copies can write to Arkansas Department of Health, Center for Health Statistics-Slot 19, 4815 West Markham Street, Little Rock, AR 72205-3867, or call (501) 661-2003.

Census State Data Center (University of Arkansas at Little Rock, Institute for Economic Advancement)—This is a web site that may be found at http:// www.aiea.ualr.edu/census/default.html. As an affiliate of the U.S. Census Bureau, the Census State Data Center houses, disseminates, and analyzes census data about Arkansas. Statistics from the 1980, 1990, and 2000 censuses are available from this site, as are historic statistics, population estimates, school district data, and downloadable maps of the state.

Crime in Arkansas (Arkansas Crime Information Center)—Arkansas Documents Call Number—YA.C 929/7:C 6/year. Summary statistics from police departments, sheriffs' offices, and university police departments are presented in this report. The major crimes included are murder, rape, robbery, aggravated assault, burglary, theft, motor vehicle theft, and arson. In addition to giving the number of these crimes that were committed, statistics are also given on the number of law enforcement officers who were assaulted or killed, the value of property that was stolen and recovered, and on the persons who were arrested. The most recent editions of the report are available on the web at http://www.acic.org/statistics/stats.htm. Those who wish to enquire about the availability of print copies can write to Arkansas Crime Information Center, One Capitol Mall, Little Rock, AR 72201, call (501) 682-2222, or e-mail acic@acic.org.

Hometown Health Factbook, Arkansas (Department of Health, Center for Health Statistics and Division of Vital Records)—Arkansas Documents Call Number—HE 208.7:H 65/year. The focus of this publication is on the need for, and the availability of, health services in each county. Statistics are given by county and by health management area, and include basic demographic information about the population, data on births and deaths, numbers of health care professionals in the area, and a listing of community health centers and local health units. The *Factbook* is available on the web via the Department of Health's "Data and Research" page at http://www.healthyarkansas.com/data/data.html. Those interested in enquiring about the availability of print copies can write to Arkansas Department of Health, Center for Health Statistics-Slot 19, 4815 West Markham Street, Little Rock, AR 72205-3867, or call (501) 280-4067.

Rape in Arkansas (Arkansas Crime Information Center)—Arkansas Documents Call Number—YA.C 929/7:R 3/year. This publication begins by presenting the legal definition of "rape" in Arkansas state law and in the Uniform Crime Reporting System. Statistics are provided on the total number of rapes committed and attempted, with a chart reflecting the trend over the last ten years. Statistics are also given on the number of rapes by time of day, day of the week, the relationship of the offender to the victim, weapons used, and other topics. This title may have ceased or been absorbed by *Crime in Arkansas*. The most recent edition is the 1997 edition, which was issued in 1998.

Other Resources

Arkansas Fishing Guide (Arkansas Game and Fish Commission, annual)—Arkansas Documents Call Number—PA 1.8:A 744/year. This publication provides information about places to fish in Arkansas. It is available free of charge and may be requested by calling (800) NATURAL or by filling out a form on the web at http://www.arkansas.com/vacation_kit/.

Arkansas Resources (University of Arkansas Libraries, Fayetteville)—This web site may be found at http://libinfo.uark.edu/specialcollections/arkansaslinks.asp. The site provides a subject-divided list of links to other sites that provide information about Arkansas. The subject sections include Business, Cities and Towns, Government and Politics, Maps, Media, Miscellaneous, Northwest Arkansas, and University of Arkansas.

Arkansas Tour Guide (Department of Parks and Tourism)—Arkansas Documents Call Number—PA 1.7:A 7/year. This guide to cultural resources and recreational opportunities throughout the state is available free of charge and may be requested by calling (800) NATURAL, or by filling out a form on the web at http://www.arkansas.com/vacation_kit/.

ARKANSAS' WORLD WIDE WEB HOME PAGE

Arkansas' official home page may be found at http://www.state.ar.us or at http://www.accessArkansas.org. A box in the center of the page presents announcements and a link to the governor's page. There are lists of recent and upcoming additions to the site, and selections leading to information on these topics: Arkansas Government, e-Government Online Services, Children and Education, Community and Civic Info, Tourism and State Parks, Business and Employment, Living in Arkansas, Working in Arkansas, and Visitor's Guide to Arkansas. The site is searchable, and a site map is available. A very small link near the bottom right corner of the page leads to an "overview" of the site that describes the types of information that are available in each section.

One noteworthy selection in the "Arkansas Government" section is the "State Directory." This is a searchable directory of state agencies and personnel. Each agency listing includes a brief summary of its mission, an address, telephone, and fax number, and in most cases a link to the agency web site, a listing of the divisions of the agency, and statistics on the number of personnel employed in that agency.

The site is maintained and copyrighted by the Information Network of Arkansas.

Information Network of Arkansas

The Information Network of Arkansas, or INA, is an instrumentality of the state that was established by the passage of a law in 1995. This law now appears as title 25, section 27-101 of the *Arkansas Code*. The INA maintains the state's home page, but its larger purpose, as stated in sections 27-104(4) and (5) of that title is, "To explore ways of expanding the amount and kind of public information provided, increasing the utility and form of the public information provided, and implement such changes as required to be consistent with the provisions of this chapter; To explore ways of improving citizen and business access to public information, and, where appropriate, implementing such changes." Public information is defined in section 25-102(5) of that title as meaning

any information stored, gathered, or generated in electronic or magnetic form by an agency, its agencies, or instrumentalities, which is included within the information deemed to be public pursuant to the Freedom of Information Act of 1967, § 25-19-101 et seq., and other provisions of the *Arkansas Code* providing for release of information to the public at large to specified groups or recipients.

Thus, the INA is somewhat like a depository program for electronic state information. One major difference is that the INA is a fee-supported agency, and it charges an annual subscription fee for access to specific "premium services." The fee schedule and list of premium services is available from INA's home page at http://www.ark.org/ina.html. Those with questions about INA may call (501) 324-8900 or (877) 727-3468.

COMMERCIAL PUBLICATIONS AND WEB SITES

Arkansas Code of 1987 Annotated (LexisNexis/Michie Co., Charlottesville, VA)—As described above under "Legal Resources," this source contains the laws of the state arranged by subject. This is the official printed version of the *Code*. The Michie Company is part of the LexisNexis publishing empire. A searchable catalog of LexisNexis' legal publications may be found on the web at http://bookstore.lexis.com/bookstore/catalog/. In 2002, the most recent edition of the *Code* was a 55-volume set that sold for $990.

Arkansas Statistical Abstract (University of Arkansas at Little Rock, Institute for Economic Advancement)—This publication includes statistics on population, law enforcement, health, education, elections, agriculture, banking, labor force, and a wide variety of other topics. Those interested in ordering a copy can write to Census State Data Center, Ottenheimer Library 508A, University of Arkansas at Little Rock, Little Rock, AR 72204-1099. The center's phone number is (501) 569-8530, and its web site is http://www.aiea.ualr.edu/census/default.html. The price for the 2000 edition was $48, including shipping and handling.

SOURCES CONSULTED

Arkansas Code of 1987 Annotated, online via the General Assembly web site, http://www.arkleg.state.ar.us/data/resources.asp.

Numerous departmental web pages via the state's home page, http://www.state.ar.us/.

OCLC (Online Computer Library Center). *OCLC WorldCat*. Dublin, OH: OCLC.

Online Catalog of the Arkansas State Library via its home page, http://www.asl.lib.ar.us/.

Survey response from Frances Hager, Arkansas Tech University, 2000.

California

Daniel C. Barkley

GOVERNMENT PUBLISHING AND THE DEPOSITORY SYSTEM

The California state depository system, established in 1945 by the Library Distribution Act (*California Government Code*, Sections 14900–14912, as amended), currently contains 137 depository libraries. As determined by the State Librarian, the State Printer "shall print a sufficient number of copies of each state publication" in order to "meet the requirements for deposit in a 'library stockroom' for distribution to libraries as hereinafter provided" (*California Government Code*, Section 14901). If a state agency performs the printing, a sufficient number of copies are required in order for the publication to be placed in state depository libraries as well as made freely available to other requestors. Two additional copies are to be printed and made available to the State Archivist. "The cost of printing, publishing, and distributing such copies shall be fixed and charged pursuant to Section 14866."

State publications are

to include any document, compilation, journal, law, resolution, Blue Book, statute, code, register, pamphlet, list, book, report, memorandum, hearing, legislative bill, leaflet, order, regulation, directory, periodical or magazine issued by the state, the Legislature, constitutional officers, or any department, commission or other agency thereof or prepared for the state by private individual or organization and issued in print. (*California Government Code*, Section 14902)

Accordingly, print is defined as: "to include all forms of duplicating other than by the use of carbon paper" (*California Government Code*, Section 14902).

Once a sufficient number of copies have been placed in the stockroom, the State Printer forwards fifty copies of each publication to the State Library in Sacramento. Twenty-five copies are sent to the University of California libraries at Berkeley and Los Angeles, and fifty copies are sent to the California State University to be further allocated among libraries as directed by the Trustees of the California State University (*California Government Code*, Section

14903). Remaining copies are then distributed as determined by a mailing list composed of complete and selective depository libraries.

In order for a library to become a state depository library, certain guidelines must be met. Each library contracts with the Department of General Services and agrees to provide an adequate facility for storage and use of depository materials. Further, each depository must provide a "reasonable service without charge to qualified patrons in the use of publications" (*California Government Code*, Section 14905). A full depository receives one copy of every state publication. Selective libraries receive materials based on their individual needs and selections.

In 1984, an amendment to the law placed new restrictions on the distribution of state publications. "No state agency shall distribute a state publication, as defined in Section 14902, except in response to a specific request therefor, or to the subjects of a mailing list or distribution list" (*California Government Code*, Section 11094[a]). Additionally, the law requires that state agencies include in their fiscal year budget requests a list of all state publications added in the previous fiscal year. These amendments also have placed other restrictions or guidelines on distribution, or printing of state publications (see *California Government Code*, Sections 11097–11099).

USEFUL ADDRESSES AND TELEPHONE NUMBERS

The most complete collections of California state publications may be found at the following libraries:

California State Library
Government Publications Section
Room 304
Sacramento, CA 95814
Phone Number for California Reference Questions: (916) 654-0069
E-Mail Address for California Reference Questions: cslgps@library.ca.gov
Library Home Page: http://www.library.ca.gov
Government Publications Section Home Page: http//www.library.ca.gov/html/gps
   .cfm

California State University, Long Beach
University Library and Learning Resource
1250 Bellflower Boulevard
Long Beach, CA 90840-1901
Phone Number for California Reference Questions: (562) 985-4029
Library Home Page: http://www.csulb.edu/library

San Francisco Public Library
Main Library
Government Information Center
100 Larkin Street
San Francisco, CA 94102-4796
Phone Number for California Reference Questions: (415) 557-4400
Library Home Page: http://sfpl.lib.ca.us/

University of California, Berkeley
Government and Social Science Information Service
2nd Floor, DOE Library
Berkeley, CA 94720-6000
Phone Number for California Reference Questions: (510) 642-2569
Government and Social Science Information Service Home Page: http://www.lib
    .berkeley.edu/gssi

University of California, Los Angeles
Young Research Library
Reference and Instructional Services
Box 95157
Los Angeles, CA 90095-1575
Phone Number for California Reference Questions: (310) 825-1201
E-Mail Link for California Reference Questions: http://www.library.ucla.edu/
    libraries/yrl/reference/emailref.htm
Library Home Page: http://www.library.ucla.edu

INDEXES TO CALIFORNIA STATE PUBLICATIONS

California state law requires the State Library to issue on a monthly or quarterly basis a "complete list of state publications issued during the immediately preceding month or quarter, such lists to be cumulated and printed at the end of each calendar year" (*California Government Code*, Section 14910). The *California State Publications* list began in 1949 and is available both in paper and on the web. (See http://www.lib.state.ca.us. Click on the link to "New State Documents.") Additionally, each state agency, department, commission, or other government entity is required, upon request, to furnish information to the State Library regarding its publications that have been made available to the depository libraries in the state.

A call numbering system has been developed for use within the state depository system (CalDoc). Similar to the classification system developed at the federal level (SuDoc), publications are classified according to issuing agency, subagency, department, or office within each state executive-level agency. Full depository and many selective depository libraries adhere to this classification system

ESSENTIAL STATE PUBLICATIONS

Directories

California Library Directory (California State Library)—This is an annual listing of libraries, their staff, and the types of operations each library engages in. The information contained in this publication is culled from annual reports from California academic, special, state agency, and county law libraries. Available from the Library Development Services Bureau, California State Library, Sacramento, CA 95814, or call (916) 654-0183. The online version is available at http://ferguson.library.ca.gov/html/main.cfm.

California On-Line Directory (Department of General Services, Telecommunications Division)—This directory is a service provided by the Telecommunications Division of the Department of General Services and is designed to improve access to government information and services for state employees, local governments, and the general public. Its services include White Pages, Yellow Pages, and State Government Organization Charts, as well as a keyword search. The Yellow Pages allow the user to locate information for a specific state agency. After selecting an agency, organizational structure and pertinent contact information are provided. The White Pages allow searching by employee name. The State Government Organization Charts had not yet been implemented at the time of this writing. Contact the Department of General Services, Telecommunications Division, 601 Sequoia Pacific Boulevard, Sacramento, CA 95814-0282, or call (916) 657-9900 for further assistance. This directory is available online at http://www.cold.ca.gov/index.asp.

California Public School Directory (Department of Education)—This annual publication provides a directory of administrative and supervisory personnel within the California public school system, and is available from the California Department of Education, Sales Unit, Bureau of Publications, Sacramento, CA 95802-0271, or call (800) 995-4099. It can be viewed online at http://www.cde.ca.gov/schooldir/.

Narcotic Treatment Program Directory (California Department of Alcohol and Drug Programs, Narcotic Treatment Licensing Branch)—The 2002 directory provides extensive information on all drug treatment programs available in California. The online version is available at http://www.adp.ca.gov/help/aod_help.shtml in the "Program Directories" section. Contact the California Department of Alcohol and Drug Programs, Narcotic Treatment Licensing Branch, 1700 K Street, 3rd Floor, Sacramento, CA 95814-4037, or call (916) 322-6882 for further information.

Roster, California State, County, City and Township Officials (Secretary of State)—This is an annual publication that lists all pertinent government officials operating from local through U.S. Congress levels. To enquire about print copies, contact Secretary of State, Attention: California Roster, 1500 11th Street, 6th Floor, Sacramento, CA 95814, or call (916) 653-7244. Recent editions of the publication can be viewed online at http://www.ss.ca.gov/executive/ca_roster/ca_roster.htm.

Financial/Budgetary Resources

Budgetary/Legal Basis Annual Report (State Controller's Office)—This report, prepared by the controller of the state of California, shows the financial condition of all funds and operations for the end of the fiscal year. Prepared in conjunction with the *Comprehensive Annual Financial Report*, each report is reflective of budget allocations, spending, and reserve funds as mandated by the California legislature. Copies are available from the State Controller's Office, Division of Accounting and Reporting, Budgetary/Legal Reporting Section, P.O. Box 942850, Sacramento, CA 94250, or call (916) 445-2636. The cost is $45.00 per copy. It is available online at http://www.sco.ca.gov/pubs/index.shtml#stagovrep.

California Economic Indicators (Department of Finance, Budget Division)—

This is a bimonthly publication that summarizes economic trends and data in California. Recent economic trends are reviewed and summarized in text and tables. Data have been seasonally adjusted. It is not available in paper. This source was developed by the Department of Finance, Budget Division, 915 L Street, Sacramento, CA 95814. Call (916) 445-3878. The most recent data are available online at http://www.dof.ca.gov/html/fs_data/indicatr/ei_home .htm. The data can be retrieved in a PDF format and are available from 1998 to the present.

Financing California's Statewide Ballot Measures (Secretary of State, Political Reform Division)—This publication reports on money raised and expended to support or defeat measures placed on a General Election ballot. Several issues of the report are available online at http://www.ss.ca.gov/prd/ campaign_info/financing_analyses/list_camp_rpts.htm. More recent information of a similar type is available through the *Cal-Access* database described below in "Other Resources." For more information, write to California Secretary of State, Political Reform Division, 1500 11th Street, Room 495, Sacramento, CA 95814, or call (916) 653-6224.

Governor's Budget (Department of General Services)—Submitted by the governor to the California legislature, this annual report provides detailed financial operating data by all bureaus, divisions, and programs in California state agencies, departments, boards, and commissions. It also contains statistical information on annual expenditures and staffing by civil service classification. The full report is available for $100.00 from the Department of General Services, Office of State Publishing, 344 N. 7th Street, Sacramento, CA 95814, or call (916) 445-5386. A summary of the report is available for $20.00. The online report can be found at http://www.dof.ca.gov/html/bud_docs/bud_link.htm.

Major Features of the [Year] California Budget (California State Assembly, Joint Legislative Budget Committee)—This report highlights the major features of each California legislative fiscal year budget. By no means an in-depth review of the state's budget, it does provide highlights of funding and spending initiatives. The report is available for $2.00 from the California State Assembly, Joint Legislative Budget Committee, Legislative Analyst's Office, Suite 1000, 925 L Street, Sacramento, CA 95814, or call (916) 445-4656. An online version of several recent issues is available from LAO's publications web site at http://www.lao.ca.gov/frmpub_index_subject_text_date.asp. Search for the word "Features" to pull up a list of available issues.

Legal Resources

California's Legislature (Office of the Assembly Chief Clerk)—This is the most authoritative and detailed source on California's legislative branch. It is a rich source of information for scholars, elected officials, and the general public. A paper copy can be obtained for $5.00 from the California Legislature, Office of the Assembly Chief Clerk, Legislative Bill Room, 712 R Street, Sacramento, CA 95814, or call (916) 445-2645. It can be found online at http://www .leginfo.ca.gov/califleg.html.

California Regulatory Notice Register (Office of Administrative Law)—This is a weekly publication of changes to the California codes and laws including proposed changes, notices of state agency meetings, and other pertinent state business. It is similar to the *Federal Register*. The Internet version is available from July 7, 2000 forward. See http://www.oal.ca.gov/notice.htm. A paper subscription can also be obtained for $302.00 from the Office of Administrative Law, 300 Capitol Mall, Suite 1250, Sacramento, CA 95814-4602, or call (916) 445-5391.

California State Assembly (Office of the Chief Clerk)—This, the home page of the California State Assembly, provides a wealth of information, including a member and staff directory, organization charts of the legislature, a mechanism for the public to provide comments to their legislators on introduced bills and party and ethnic caucuses, and other pertinent resources. See http://www.assembly.ca.gov/defaulttext.asp for further information.

California State Assembly Journals (California State Assembly)—Although still published in paper (an annual subscription is $380.00), the *Journals* are now also available in CD-ROM or online formats. See the link on the Office of the Chief Clerk's home page at http://www.assembly.ca.gov/clerk/. The *CSAJ* provides an account of each day's California House and Senate assembly sessions. The *Journals* are similar in style and content to the U.S. Congress' *Congressional Record*. The CD-ROM is available from the California State Assembly, Office of the Chief Clerk, State Capitol, Room 3196, Sacramento, CA 95814, or call (916) 445-2323.

California State Senate (Office of Legislative Counsel)—This, the home page of the Senate, provides links to various functions and aspects of the state Senate. Included are the new Senate districts, schedules, committee and member information, and information on how to view the Senate sessions on television or listen to them on the radio. It is available online at http://www.sen.ca.gov/.

The *State Administrative Manual* (Office of State Publishing)—The manual is a reference resource for statewide policies, procedures, regulations, and information that have been developed and issued by various authoring agencies such as the Governor's Office, the Department of General Services, the Department of Finance, the Department of Information Technology, and the Department of Personnel Administration. The manual has been developed to provide a uniform approach to statewide management policy. The contents of the manual have the approval of and are published by the authority of the Department of Finance Director and the Department of General Services Director. The manual can be obtained for $257.00 from the Accounting Office, Office of State Publishing, 344 North 7th Street, Sacramento, CA 95814-0212, or call (916) 327-8908. The web version is available at http://sam.dgs.ca.gov/default.htm and provides links to order forms.

There is a host of other legally oriented resources available online. Most often, the commercially published editions of California's legal and regulatory resources are "official"; therefore, many of the resources listed below are "unofficial" and caution should be used when utilizing a resource for citation purposes. It is most advisable to check the legal status of each web page prior to use in a research or other legal document.

California Bills, http://www.leginfo.ca.gov/bilinfo.html

California Code of Regulations, http://www.calregs.com/

California Courts, http://www.courtinfo.ca.gov/

California Courts, Self Help Center, http://www.courtinfo.ca.gov/selfhelp/

California Department of Justice/Office of Attorney General, http://caag.state.ca.us/

California Law, http://www.leginfo.ca.gov/calaw.html

California State Constitution, http://www.leginfo.ca.gov/const.html

California Statutes, http://www.leginfo.ca.gov/statute.html

Official California Legislative Information, http://www.Leginfo.ca.gov/

Statistical Resources

California County Profiles (Department of Finance)—This annual publication is a compilation of selected economic, social, and demographic data for the fifty-eight California counties. Information includes demographics of each county and the largest cities, educational enrollment and spending, labor force characteristics, business, housing, manufacturing, agriculture, roads, highways, and local government tax collections and expenditures. The data are available in PDF, Zip, and Excel formats either as a whole or by county. Paper copies may be obtained from the California Department of Finance, Demographic Research Unit, 915 L Street, Sacramento, CA 95814, or call (916) 445-3878. The web page for this resource is located at http://www.dof.ca.gov/html/fs_data/profiles/pf_home.htm.

California Statistical Abstract (Department of Finance, Economic Research Unit)—This annual abstract provides a compilation of data on social, economic, and physical aspects of California. It also contains comparison data on past, current, and projected demographic and economic statistics for California. The data are available in PDF, Zip, and Excel formats. The print edition can be requested from California Department of Finance, Economic Research Unit, 915 L Street, 8th Floor, Sacramento, CA 95814-3701, or call (916) 445-3878; e-mail ficpalad@dof.ca.gov. The web page can be viewed at http://www.dof.ca.gov/html/fs_data/stat-abs/sa_home.htm.

Crime and Delinquency in California (Department of Justice, Criminal Justice Statistics Center)—An annual publication containing data sets on California crimes, arrests, and other types of criminal justice action, the report also provides statistics on the amount and types of offenses known to public authorities, criminal justice expenditures for all levels of crime and enforcement, citizens' complaints against police officers, and domestic violence cases reported. Paper copies are available by contacting the California Department of Justice, Criminal Justice Statistics Center, Special Request Unit, P.O. Box 903427, Sacramento, CA 94203-4270, or call (916) 277-3509. The web page can be viewed at http://caag.state.ca.us/cjsc/pubs.htm. Data are available from 1996 to the present.

Information Bulletin (Department of Justice)—The *Bulletin* is published periodically and provides updates to the annually published *Crime and Delin-*

quency in California, a statistical compilation of crime. Paper copies can be obtained from the California Department of Justice, Public Inquiry Unit, P.O. Box 944255, Sacramento, CA 94244-2550, or call (916) 322-3360, or toll-free inside California (800) 952-5225.

Other Resources

California Blue Book: An Official Directory of the Judicial, Executive and Legislative Departments of the California State Government (Secretary of State)—This title was published regularly between 1850 and 1976, when it ceased. It listed all officials occupying each of the three branches of state government. A special sesquicentennial edition was published in 2000 that featured 150 years of information on California officials, including bibliographical references and index. Copies of the 2000 edition were sold for $100.00. To enquire if copies are still available, write to Legislative Bill Room, State Capitol, Sacramento, CA 95814, or call (916) 445-2323.

Ballot Pamphlets On-line (Secretary of State)—This source provides texts, summaries, and arguments for the past few elections (1996–). Also available from this online resource is the University of California Hastings College of the Law's comprehensive, searchable database of California ballot measures from 1911. To view, go to http://www.ss.ca.gov/elections/elections_i.htm.

Borderbase (San Diego Association of Governments)—This database is available online at http://www.borderbase.org/Welcome.asp. This is a keyword-searchable, bilingual directory of California state government organizations, agencies, and non-profit institutions that conduct their affairs along the California-Baja border. *Borderbase* strives to promote cross-border collaboration between Mexican and Californian entities. The database also provides contact information, project descriptions, and links to the aforementioned agencies.

Cal-Access (Secretary of State, Political Reform Division)—This database is another valuable electronic resource that provides financial information supplied by state candidates, donors, lobbyists, and others. *Cal-Access* stands for "California Automated Lobbying and Campaign Contribution and Expenditure Search System." One begins a search by selecting either "Campaign Finance Activity" or "Lobbying Activity." Guides and help screens are provided. *Cal-Access* also contains links to elected officials, propositions, ballot measures, PACs, political parties, major donations, daily filings, and late contributions, as well as to the secretary of state's home page, the California Business Portal, and other political reform information. View the database at http://cal-access.ss.ca.gov/.

The 1851 Directory and History of Sacramento (California State Library Foundation)—This is a facsimile edition of Sacramento's First Book, which was edited by Mead B. Kibbey. This edition of J. Horace Culver's *Sacramento Directory for the Year 1851* now makes available one of the rarest and most important books concerning Sacramento and the Gold Rush, which contains a history of Sacramento to 1851, biographical sketches, and informative appendices. The original edition was published two years after the founding of Sacramento. It came out at a time when the future state capitol had been ravaged by floods, pestilence, financial panics, and riots, and consequently provides a unique record of the Gold Rush city. It is an essential work for those interested in California's local history. The publication includes five appendices with a directory arranged by modern street addresses. Twenty-nine illustrations, a ten-page table converting old to modern addresses, and a map further enrich this important contribution to California history. It is available for $40.00 from the California State Library Foundation. See the "Publications" page at http://www.cslfdn.org/, or write to California State Library Foundation, 1225 8th Street, Suite 345, Sacramento, CA 95814-4809, or call (916) 447-6331.

Strategic Plan: A Vision for the Future/State Water Resources, Regional Water Quality Control Boards (State Water Resources Control Board)—This is a recent report detailing the current and future aspects of water, water quality, and water resources for California. It is available from the California State Water Resources Control Board, P.O. Box 100, Sacramento, CA 95812-0100; call (916) 341-5240; or online at http://www.swrcb.ca.gov/strategicplan/index.html. E-mail vreeves@exec.swrcb.ca.gov for information about acquiring a paper copy.

CALIFORNIA'S WORLD WIDE WEB HOME PAGE

As California seems to be the leader in the development of new technologies, it should come as no surprise that California's home page at http://www.ca.gov/state/portal/myca_homepage.jsp, also known as *My California*, is a portal that provides links to valuable information regarding state offices and agencies, business, tourism, and education. The page is user-friendly and provides a powerful search mechanism to find practically anything of interest about California. It was created as an information portal in 2001 by Governor Grey Davis.

As such, the home page provides interconnectivity to sites that offer sound and video capabilities. There are virtual tours available that include the State Capitol, many state agency buildings and, of course, Hollywood. One may activate a service that provides notifications via e-mail, pager, or cell phone. You can schedule an appointment with the DMV, file your state income tax, obtain a professional license, and even play the state lottery. The California Home Page has it all.

My California was recently voted as the "best of the web" in a contest sponsored by the Center for Digital Government and *Government Technology Magazine*, and it has won for seven consecutive years.

COMMERCIAL PUBLICATIONS AND WEB SITES

Barclay's Official California Code of Regulations (Eagan, MN: West Group)—This is a 35-volume looseleaf set of publications containing all of the *California Administrative Code* and the *Code of Regulations*. The cost of a print set in 2003 was approximately $4,000.00. The set is also available on CD-ROM. Some individual titles from the set can be purchased separately on CD-ROM. For more information see the publisher's web site at http://west.thomson.com, or call (800) 328-4880.

California Cities, Towns, & Counties: Basic Data Profiles for all Municipalities & Counties (Palo Alto, CA: Information Publications, 1998)—This contains basic data profiles on all municipalities and counties in California. Each data profile is a one-page statistical sheet on all incorporated cities, towns, and counties in California. It is available for $84.00. See http://www.informationpublications.com for further information.

California Communities (Walnut Creek, CA: California State Association of Counties and League of California Cities)—California Statewide Communities Development Authority ("California Communities") is a government agency established in 1988 under the *California Government Code* as a statewide Joint Powers Authority. This agency provides local governments and private industry with access to low-cost, tax-exempt financing for projects that employ local people and help communities improve. Currently, more than 340 local public agencies are members, and more than $12 billion in tax-exempt financing has been issued. See http://www.cacommunities.com/ for further information.

California County Data Book (Oakland, CA: Children Now)—This provides detailed information on children by county, and includes information on children's well-being, family economics, health, education, and safety. It also contains information focusing on factors that contribute to a child's success. A one-county data set is available free of charge. The cost of the publication is $13.00. Contact Children Now, 1212 Broadway, 5th Floor, Oakland, CA 94612, or call (510) 763-2444; fax (510) 763-1974. Other publications centering on children are also available from this non-profit organization. See its web site at http://www.childrennow.org.

California Courts and Judges Handbook: 2000 Edition (Santa Ana, CA: James Publishing)—The eighth edition contains valuable information on the California court system and the judges that administer California law. The price of the publication is $175.00. Contact James Publishing, Inc., P.O. Box 25202, Santa Ana, CA 92799, or call (714) 755-5450 or (800) 440-4780.

The California Handbook: A Comprehensive Guide to Sources of Current Information and Action, with Selected Background Material (Ted Trzyna and Julie Didion, eds.) (Claremont, CA: California Institute of Public Affairs, 1999)—This $40.00 publication compiles a wealth of information on current public affairs within California. The California Institute of Public Affairs is affiliated with the Claremont Graduate University. See http://www.interenvironment.org/cipa/publications.htm for further information and other publications.

California Political Almanac (Sacramento, CA: California Journal Press)—This provides information on California government and politics including state legislators and lobbyists. The latest edition is available for $34.95. See http://www.statenet.com for more information on this and other publications.

The California State Constitution: A Reference Guide (Joseph R. Grodin, Calvin R. Massey, and Richard B. Cunningham, eds.) (Westport, CT: Greenwood Press, 1993)—This contains the history of the California State Constitution, and also provides bibliographic references and citations. The price is $92.50.

Index of Economic Material in Documents of the States of the United States— California, 1849–1904 (Washington, DC: Carnegie Institution of Washington, 1908)—This is a subject index to most California state documents from the nineteenth century. It is now out of print but available in many state depository libraries.

State of Health Insurance in California (Los Angeles, CA: UCLA Center for Health Policy Research and School for Public Health, University of California, Berkeley)—This seminal publication provides an overview of health insurance in California. Containing a mixture of text and statistics, it outlines the problems facing California health insurers including cost, cost recovery, providing indigent care, and other relevant social topics. It has been updated since originally issued in 1996 and is available online at http://chpps.berkeley.edu/publications/thanks99.htm.

Statewide Database (Berkeley, CA: University of California, Berkely, Institute of Government Studies)—Originally created in 1982 by the California State Assembly to gather and collect data for state and federal redistricting purposes, the California Assembly voted in 1993 to permanently locate this database at Berkeley's Institute of Government Studies. See http://swdb.berkeley.edu/ for more information and access to this database.

SOURCES CONSULTED

AllLaw.com, http://www.alllaw.com/state_law_search/california/.
Bowker's *Books in Print*. New York: R.R. Bowker, 2000/2001.
Correspondence with Brent Miller, California State Library.
Google, http://www.google.com.
Government Documents Round Table, American Library Association. *Directory of Government Document Collections & Librarians*, 7th ed. Bethesda, MD: Congressional Information Service, 1997.
Jobe, Janita. "State Publications." *Journal of Government Information*, 27 (2000): 733-768.
Numerous departmental web pages via the state's home page, http://www.state.ca.us/.
State Government and Politics, http://www.lib.umich.edu/govdocs/state.html.
State Legal Resources on the Web, http://www.lib.umich.edu/govdocs/statelaw.html#A.
State Web Locator, http://www.infoctr.edu/swl.
Survey response from Marianne Leach, California State Library, 2000.
U.S. State and Local Gateway, http://www.statelocal.gov.

Colorado

Daniel C. Barkley

GOVERNMENT PUBLISHING AND THE DEPOSITORY SYSTEM

The Colorado State Depository system was created in 1980 by *Colorado Revised Statutes* (CRS) 24-90-201 mandating that a "state publications depository and distribution center" be established. The center is currently located at the Colorado State Library and is administered by the State Librarian. CRS 24-90-202 provides definitions as to what a center, depository, library, state agency, and state publication are.

Accordingly, a state publication is defined as

any printed or duplicated material, regardless of format or purpose, which is produced, purchased for distribution, or authorized by any state agency, including any document, compilation, journal, law, resolution, bluebook, statute, code, register, contract and grant report, pamphlet, list, microphotographic form, audiovisual material, book, proceedings, report, public memorandum, hearing, legislative bill, leaflet, order, rule, regulation, directory, periodical, magazine, or newsletter with the exception of correspondence, interoffice memoranda, and those items detailed by section 24-72-204. (CRS 24-90-202-4)

There are currently nineteen state depository libraries. See http://www.cde.state.co.us/stateinfo/sldepsit.htm for a complete list. Colorado state law permits up to thirty libraries the ability to participate in the depository program. Only four are considered to be "full" depositories: the University of Colorado, Boulder (UCB), the Colorado State University (CSU), the Denver Public Library (DPL), and the State Publications Library (SPL). The University of Colorado, Boulder is the backup archive to the State Publications Library.

Every state agency has a publications office and officer that has responsibility for ensuring that copies of all agency publications are deposited with the State Publications Library. Additionally, the SPL obtains publications from the Colorado General Assembly, the Colorado Governor's Office, the Colorado Supreme Court, boards and commissions, and state colleges and universities.

A minimum of four copies must be deposited with the SPL by the afore-mentioned bodies (CRS 24-90-204). Upon request from the State Librarian, each state agency shall also furnish a complete list of its current publications (CRS 24-90-205). The SPL retains two copies, one copy is sent to UCB, and one copy to the Library of Congress. CSU and DPL receive copies if a sufficient number are made available. The remaining state depositories receive a core set of documents such as annual reports of agencies.

The SPL classifies each document received using a classification system based on the hierarchy of the Colorado state government. The classification system is updated on a regular basis and published. Cataloging for materials is done by OCLC (Online Computer Library Center), a vendor well versed in the creation of cataloging and bibliographic control records.

The SPL's catalog is available on its home page at http://www.cde.state .co.us/stateinfo, or through the Colorado Alliance of Research Libraries page at http://set.coalliance.org/. It can also be accessed from the ACLIN (Access Colorado Library and Information Network) Colorado Virtual Library home page at http://www.aclin.org. All publications in the SPL are available for use in the library as well as for Interlibrary Loan.

USEFUL ADDRESSES AND TELEPHONE NUMBERS

The best collections of Colorado state publications can be located at the following libraries:

Colorado State Library
State Publications Library
201 E. Colfax
Room 314
Denver, CO 80203
Phone Number for Colorado Reference Questions: (303) 866-6725
E-Mail Address for Colorado Reference Questions: crocker_m@cde.state.co.us
State Library Home Page: http://www.cde.state.co.us/index_library.htm
State Publications Library Home Page: http://www.cde.state.co.us/stateinfo/index
.htm

Morgan Library
Colorado State University
501 University Avenue
1019 Campus Delivery
Fort Collins, CO 80523-1019
Phone Number for Colorado Reference Questions: (970) 491-1841
E-Mail Link for Colorado Reference Questions: http://lib.colostate.edu/reference/
emailref.html
Library Home Page: http://lib.colostate.edu/

Denver Public Library
Government Publications and Business Reference
10 West 14th Avenue Parkway

Denver, CO 80204-2731
Phone Number for Colorado Reference Questions: (720) 865-1711
E-Mail Link for Colorado Reference Questions: http://www.denver.lib.co.us/ask_us/
ask_us.html
Library Home Page: http://www.denver.lib.co.us/
Government Publications Home Page: http://www.denver.lib.co.us/govpubs/
govpubs.html

University of Colorado, Boulder
Government Publications
Campus Box 184
Boulder, CO 80309-0184
Phone Number for Colorado Reference Questions: (303) 492-8834
E-Mail Address for Colorado Reference Questions: govpubs@colorado.edu
Government Publications Library Home Page: http://www-libraries.colorado.edu/
ps/gov/frontpage.htm

INDEX TO COLORADO STATE PUBLICATIONS

CRS 24-90-207 mandated that a quarterly index of state publications be published and distributed to all depository libraries and others as designated by the State Librarian. From 1989 through 1999, the SPL issued in a paper format a monthly checklist of state publications. The *Accessions Checklist: Colorado State Publications* was culled from cataloging records received from OCLC. The cataloging records were created the previous month from all publications received by the SPL. Beginning in January 2000, the checklist was sent via e-mail to all state depository libraries. The SPL also made this list available online at http://www.cde.state.co.us/stateinfo/slstpnewt.htm.

ESSENTIAL STATE PUBLICATIONS

Directories

Colorado Education and Library Directory (Department of Education)—This annual compilation provides names and numbers of personnel working in the state public education sector, broken into sections such as the state Department of Education, school districts/buildings and personnel, charter schools, academic and public libraries. It is produced and maintained by the Colorado Department of Education, 201 E. Colfax Avenue, Denver, CO 80203-1799, or call (303) 866-6600. The directory can be viewed at http://www.cde.state.co.us/edulibdir/directory.htm. The files are in PDF and can be viewed or downloaded.

Colorado Higher Education Directory (Colorado Commission on Higher Education)—This annual publication presents information on Colorado's higher education system. This web-based searchable index provides links to the Colorado Commission on Higher Education, private and public schools and universities, governing education boards, vocational and technical schools, and other organizations affiliated with higher education. Contact the Colorado Commission on Higher Education, 1380 Lawrence Street, Suite 1200, Denver,

CO 80204, or call (303) 866-2723; fax (303) 866-4266. This directory is located at http://www.state.co.us/cche/direct/higher.html.

A Directory of Colorado State Government (Colorado Legislative Council)—This annual directory includes information on the Colorado executive, legislative, and judicial branches of the state government. Also included are organizational charts, and brief programmatic and budgetary overviews. It is published by the Colorado Legislative Council, Room 029, State Capitol Building, Denver, CO 80203, or call (303) 866-3521. A link to the directory is available on the General Assembly's "General Legislative Resources" page at http://www.state.co.us/gov_dir/leg_dir/geninfo.htm.

Legislative Directory House and Senate (Colorado Legislative Council)—This source is commonly referred to as the "Pink Book." It is now available solely online. The directory provides current information on both chambers of the Colorado state legislature. Included are office numbers and phone numbers for staff, committees, and others involved in the day-to-day operation of the state government. Contact the Colorado Legislative Council, Room 029, State Capitol Building, Denver, CO 80203, or call (303) 866-3521. A link to the directory can be found in the "Contact Information" section of the General Assembly's home page at http://www.state.co.us/gov_dir/stateleg.html (see Figure 4).

State of Colorado Telephone Directory (Personnel and Administration Department)—The directory is updated periodically but does not include all state employees. Contains contact information on Colorado higher education personnel, an organizational telephone listing of state government personnel, and an e-mail address and phone number to request information on the Colorado state government. The database is searchable by employee name as well. Additionally, there are links from this page to the Commission on Higher Education phone listings, and the Colorado Organization telephone listings. It is produced by the Department of Personnel and Administration, General Support Services, Division of Central Services, 1120 Lincoln, Suite 1420, Denver, CO 80203, or call (303) 894-2136. The directory's web page is located at http://www.state.co.us/test9/telemp/telemp_search.cfm. A paper copy is available from the Colorado State Forms and Publications Department, 4200 Garfield Avenue, Denver, CO 80203, or call (303) 321-4164.

Financial/Budgetary Resources

Comprehensive Annual Financial Report for the year ended June 30th . . . (Department of Personnel and Administration, State Controller's Office)—This report has been issued annually from 1988 to the present. It reviews all financial operations at the state government level, and is produced by the Colorado Department of Personnel and Administration, State Controller's Office, Division of Finance and Procurement, 1525 Sherman Street, Suite 250, Denver, CO 80203, or call (303) 866-3281. The online report can also be found at http://www.sco.state.co.us/cafr/cafr.htm and is available in a PDF format.

County and Municipal Financial Compendium (Division of Local Government)—This annual compendium has been compiled since 1975. Part of the CEDIS (Colorado Economic and Demographic Information System), the da-

| Current Year | Contact | Staff | General Resources | Intranet |

Welcome!

Audio Broadcasts of Current Legislative Proceedings

Ballot Issues

Current Special Session Information

Reapportionment

Commission on Taxation

HOUSE - Current Special Session
Bills, Calendar, Journals, Resolutions/Memorials, Status, Fiscal Notes

Prior Session
Information

SENATE - Current Special Session
Bills, Calendar, Journals, Resolutions/Memorials, Status, Fiscal Notes

Colorado Revised
Statutes

Current Regular Session Information

Session Laws

HOUSE - Current Regular Session
Bills, Calendar, Journals, Resolutions/Memorials, Status, Fiscal Notes

Bill Digest

SENATE - Current Regular Session
Bills, Calendar, Journals, Resolutions/Memorials, Status, Fiscal Notes

Rules & Regulations
of Executive Agencies

Contact Information

Legislative Social
Calendar

Available options (phone, fax, e-mail) for constituent correspondence with individual legislative members can be found in these directories.

Interim Information
Activities having taken place
between legislative sessions.

Legislative Directory (Pink Book)
HOUSE -   Directory, Legislator Home Pages
SENATE -   Directory, Legislator Home Pages

Who are my elected
officials ?

Service Agencies

Contact information for legislative staff agencies can be found here.

Legislative Council, Legislative Legal Services, Office of the State Auditor, Joint Budget Committee

Capitol Tour

Disclaimer

General Legislative Resources

Colorado Revised Statutes, Research and Publications, Ballot Issues/Initiatives, Legislative Rules, Frequently Asked Questions

To Purchase an Official Set of Colorado Revised Statutes, Contact Bradford Publishing

[State Home | Colorado
Legislature | Top]

This page last updated on
08/27/2002 11:17:05

Thank you for Visiting the Colorado Legislative Website!
Your comments on the layout and organization of our Web page are appreciated. **Correspondence intended for legislative members sent to this address will not be forwarded.** For information about how to contact legislative members, see the "Contact Information" link above. Due to the large volume of comments we receive, we are unable to respond to each one individually.

Comments to: Comments.GA@state.co.us

Welcome graphic created by **Central Services - Design Center**
Department of Personnel/General Support Services
Colorado State Government

Figure 4. Colorado's "Pink Book" is accessible from the "Contact Information" section of this page. The "Pink Book" is no longer a book, but the online version does use a pink screen background. *Source*: http://www.state.co.us/gov_dir/stateleg.html.

tabase contains time-series and cross-section financial data on local and municipal government operations. Culled from each local government's annual financial statement, the data represent revenues and expenditures during the past fiscal year. For further information contact the Colorado Division of Local Government, 1313 Sherman Street, Room 521, Denver, CO 80203, or call (303) 866-4987. The web page can be located at http://www.dola.state.co.us/lgs/ta/compendium.htm.

Economics (Governor's Office of State Planning and Budgeting)—This online database provides a variety of economic information, including recent forecasts on the Colorado economy. The database also includes special reports that have been generated, a monthly update on economic activity, and other related economic links. It is produced by the Governor's Office of State Planning and Budgeting, 200 E. Colfax, Room 111, Denver, CO 80203, or call (303) 866-3317; e-mail ospb@state.co.us. The database can be located at http://www.state.co.us/gov_dir/govnr_dir/ospb/econ.html.

Governor's Budget (Governor's Office of State Planning and Budgeting)—This report contains the current fiscal year budget submitted by the governor to the Colorado state legislature. It provides a narrative and statistical summary of the past fiscal year and financial needs and assessments for the new fiscal year. It ceased being issued in paper with the 1994/1995 year. It is produced by the Governor's Office of State Planning and Budgeting, 200 East Colfax, Room 111, Denver, CO 80203, or call (303) 866-3317; e-mail ospb@state.co.us. The report can be located at http://www.state.co.us/gov_dir/govnr_dir/ospb/budget.html.

Legal Resources

Analysis of Ballot Proposals (Colorado Legislative Council)—This publication provides a summary of all ballot proposals that will appear during an election cycle. Particularly important are the pro and con arguments that are presented in this publication. It is produced by the Colorado Legislative Council, Room 029, State Capitol Building, Denver, CO 80203, or call (303) 866-3521. The web page is located at http://www.state.co.us/gov_dir/leg_dir/lcsstaff/balpage.htm.

Colorado Constitution (State Archives)—The text of the Constitution is available online at http://www.archives.state.co.us/constitution/index.html.

Colorado General Assembly Home Page (General Assembly)—The page provides links to information from the current legislative session including bills, calendars, journals, resolutions, memorials, and fiscal notes to both chambers. The *Legislative Directory* (aka the "Pink Book") can also be found here. Constituents can contact their legislators, find out who their elected officials are, and review ballot issues, reapportionment, and other matters before the General Assembly. Go to http://www.state.co.us/gov_dir/stateleg.html to view this web page.

Colorado Judicial Branch (State Court Administrator's Office)—This web site provides access to all courts that are part of the Colorado judicial branch. Access includes the state Supreme Court, the Court of Appeals, and all district and county courts; the exception being Denver County. This site does not

provide links to municipal courts. The site is available at http://www.courts
.state.co.us/.

Colorado Revised Statutes (Office of Legislative Legal Services)—The statutes
are a result of editing, collating, and revisions as provided by the Office of
Legislative Legal Services. Since 1997 the "official" set of statutes has been
published by Bradford Publishing. However, the office is responsible for the
distribution of the statutes to all state government agencies. The Committee
on Legal Services has responsibility for assuring the accuracy of all reprints
of the statutes, and the office administers the contracts entered into by the
committee. For more information, or to search the statutes online, go to the
Office of Legislative Legal Service's web page at http://www.state.co.us/
gov_dir/leg_dir/olls/HTML/colorado_revised_statutes.htm.

Digest of Bills (Colorado General Assembly)—This online database provides
summaries of all bills and concurrent resolutions enacted by the General Assembly. Although publication occurs several months following the end of each
regular legislative session, this publication is mandated by CRS 2-3-504. The
Digest is not a substitute for the text of bills or the revisions that occur to the
Colorado Revised Statutes. The *Digest* is meant to provide users with a summary
of changes that have occurred to the statutes during a particular legislative
session. For further information, go to http://www.state.co.us/gov_dir/leg
_dir/olls/HTML/digest_of_bills.htm.

Long Bill Narrative (Joint Budget Committee)—This publication usually accompanies the House bill submitted for the coming fiscal year budget consideration by the Colorado House and Senate. The bill (in the 2002/03 FY is H.B.
02-1420) and the narrative accompanying it contain an analysis of the past
year's economic picture as well as an analysis of the next year's fiscal needs.
It is produced by the Joint Budget Committee, 200 E. 14th Avenue, 3rd Floor,
Legislative Services Building, Denver, CO 80203, or call (303) 866-2061. The
Narrative is available from the Joint Budget Committee's "Staff Documents"
page at http://www.state.co.us/gov_dir/leg_dir/jbc/jbcstaffdocs.htm.

Research Publications (Colorado Legislative Council)—These research publications provide valuable background information on bills introduced into the
Colorado General Assembly. One of the CLC's functions "is to be a research
service for the Colorado General Assembly." Because no currently published
information exists on the legislative history of Colorado bills passed, these
publications provide crucial background information for state legislators and
their staff. This is compiled by the Colorado Legislative Council, Room 029,
State Capitol Building, Denver, CO 80203, or call (303) 866-3521. Go to http://
www.state.co.us/gov_dir/leg_dir/lcsstaff/research.htm to review the current
research papers.

Rules and Regulations Promulgated by Executive Departments (Office of Legislative Legal Services)—This is a web page providing links to Internet sites
maintained by specific Colorado state agencies for their rules and regulations.
The page was developed as mandated by House Bill 98-1401, part of the general appropriations bill. See http://www.state.co.us/gov_dir/leg_dir/olls/
HTML/rules.htm for further information.

Session Laws of Colorado (Office of Legislative Legal Services)—This online
database contains enacted bills for a session of the Colorado legislature. The

database, dating back to 1993, can be searched by chapter number, enacted House or Senate bill, or by statute number. The Colorado General Assembly, Office of Legislative Legal Services maintains the database. The address for the database is http://www.state.co.us/gov_dir/leg_dir/olls/HTML/ses sion_laws_of_colorado.htm.

Statistical Resources

Colorado by the Numbers (State Library of Colorado)—This page, the result of a grant-funded project, is an online, linked, statistical abstract of Colorado. The links are divided into subject categories ranging from agriculture to water. Each page provides links to statistics on that subject. Files are in a download-able text format. The page is available at http://www.colorado.edu/ libraries/govpubs/online.htm.

Colorado Demography Section (State Demographer)—This is an online re-source that provides demographic information culled from a number of fed-eral and state sources. Each subject has its own method of information provision ranging from complete reports to statistical tables. Population esti-mates and projects, economic data, county profiles, and census data can be found here. It is compiled by the State Demographer, Colorado Department of Local Affairs, 1313 Sherman Street, Room 521, Denver, CO 80203, or call (303) 866-4147. The statistical information can be found at http://www.dola .state.co.us/demog/demog.htm.

Colorado Economic and Demographic Information System [CEDIS] (Local Affairs Department)—*CEDIS* is a subscription database that provides a wealth of demographic, financial, and occupational information on Colorado local gov-ernments. Data can be downloaded into spreadsheet applications for further manipulation. This is produced by the Department of Local Affairs, 1313 Sher-man Street, Room 500, Denver, CO 80203, or call (303) 866-2771; e-mail ddola .helpdesk@state.co.us.

Colorado Education Statistics (Department of Education)—This online data-base provides information on the education system in Colorado. Enrollment, dropout, and graduation rates, district-by-district comparisons, teacher sala-ries, and other useful information can be found here. There are also links to staff directories, state and federal grant availability, charter schools, and many other important topics. It is available from the Colorado Department of Ed-ucation, 201 Colfax Avenue, Denver, CO 80203-1799, or call (303) 866-6600. Go to http://www.cde.state.co.us/index_stats.htm to access the information.

Colorado Employment and Wages (Department of Labor and Employment, La-bor Market Information)—This quarterly and annual publication provides em-ployment and wage data arranged by county and industry for both private business and government employers. The data go back to 1994 and are avail-able in a PDF format. The information is gathered by the Colorado Depart-ment of Labor and Employment, Labor Market Information-ES 202, 1515 Arapahoe, Tower 2, Suite 300, Denver, CO 80202, or call (303) 318-8000. A link to the publication can be found on the Labor Market Information page at http://www.coworkforce.com/LMI/. The material is in the public domain.

The department requests that all who use this resource provide appropriate citations and credit where applicable.

Colorado Vital Statistics (Department of Health)—This annual report on demographic, economic, health, education, and other statistical categories regarding Colorado has been available since 1993. It is produced by the Colorado Department of Health, Health Statistics Section, CHEIS-HS-A1, 4300 Cherry Creek Drive South, Denver, CO 80246-1530, or call (303) 692-2160; e-mail health.statistics@state.co.us. The report can be found online at http://www.cdphe.state.co.us/hs/hsshom.asp.

Other Resources

Colorado Business Resource Guide (Office of Economic Development and International Trade et al.)—This guide is an online resource that was created to provide information to assist new start-ups and small businesses. It provides a collection of tools and references to help businesses succeed in today's environment, and is a joint effort by the Colorado Small Business Development Center, the U.S. Small Business Administration, and the Colorado Service Corps of Retired Executives. For more information contact the Colorado Business Assistance Center, 2413 Washington Street, Denver, CO 80203, or call (303) 592-5920. For online assistance and information go to http://www.state.co.us/oed/guide/index.html.

Colorado Outdoors (Department of Natural Resources, Division of Wildlife)—This is a bimonthly magazine containing a variety of articles on conservation and the enjoyment of outdoor life in Colorado. Many articles contain color illustrations and photographs. It is produced by the Colorado Department of Natural Resources, Division of Wildlife, 1313 Sherman Street, Room 718, Denver, CO 80203, or call (303) 866-3311. A yearly subscription is available for $10.50. For more information go to the Division of Wildlife page at http://wildlife.state.co.us/ and look for the *Colorado Outdoors* link.

Colorado School Violence Prevention and Student Discipline Manual (Attorney General's Office)—This 2000 revised manual is designed for school administrators, attorneys, principals, teachers, safety personnel, and parents on the laws that cover student discipline, school-zone crimes, and school searches. The manual is available from the Colorado Attorney General's Office, 1525 Sherman Street, 7th Floor, Denver, CO 80203-1712, or call (303) 866-4500. It is also available online at http://www.ago.state.co.us/cssm/cssm.htm.

Corporate Master File (Colorado Secretary of State)—This microfiche publication contains all corporation filings registered with the secretary of state during each fiscal year. Contact the Colorado Secretary of State, 1560 Broadway, Suite 200, Denver, CO 80203, or call (303) 894-2200. A searchable database of filings is also available online at http://www.sos.state.co.us/pubs/business/main.htm.

Resources to Help Children and Adults Cope (Colorado State Library)—This online bibliography was produced by the Colorado State Library in conjunction with the Colorado Department of Education. The bibliography contains resources to assist adults, teachers, and others that provide care to children to help them cope with recent terrorist attacks. Included are web sites and books of fiction and non-fiction. The web sites are culled from a number of federal, state, local, and private sources. Books are drawn from the American Library Association's Booklist and from contributions from Colorado librarians. The bibliography can be found at http://www.cde.state.co.us/cdelib/resources _cope.htm.

Special Report from the Summit on School Safety and the Prevention of Youth Violence (Office of the Governor)—Governor Bill Owens and Attorney General Ken Salazar are the authors. Drawn from the *Summit on School Safety and the Prevention of Youth Violence,* a report that was generated from the tragedy at Columbine High School, this report focuses on ways to recognize and prevent another such event from occurring. Several recommendations were made in this report, including parents looking for changes in their children's behavior at home, ways to promote safer schools, combating gang violence, promoting more after-school events, and providing for more parental participation. A copy of the report is available from the Office of the Governor, State Capitol, 200 East Colfax, Room 136, Denver, CO 80203-1792, (303) 866-6312. The report can also be found at http://www.state.co.us/gov_dir/govnr_dir/reader .html.

Trade Name Search System (Colorado Department of Revenue)—This microfiche publication contains an alphabetical listing of trade names that have been registered with the department. The online database can be searched by industry codes, business registration numbers, or zip codes. There is no fee to use the database. Contact the Colorado Department of Revenue, 1375 Sherman Street, Denver, CO 80261, or call (303) 866-3091. Many of the state depository libraries have copies of the microfiche set. See http://itapsrv1.dor.state.co .us:7777/tradenames/ for the online database.

COLORADO'S WORLD WIDE WEB HOME PAGE

Located at http://www.colorado.gov/, *Discover Colorado* is the official Colorado state web site. This portal provides links to all aspects of life in Colorado. Easy to follow and use, this simple yet nicely designed web page expedites searches though keyword and browseable indexes and provides direct links to important operations of government, business, employment, recreation, law, transportation, and the environment. One may also find fire bans and restrictions, real-time road and weather information, telephone directories, and other pertinent information.

The portal also has multiple "featured" sites that change on an irregular basis. These links are topical in nature and usually focus on a variety of forms (e.g., tax, driver's licenses), education, family, and employment. There is also a "current events" section that will focus on a major event occurring in Colorado.

COMMERCIAL PUBLICATIONS AND WEB SITES

Colorado Atlas and Gazetteer: Topo Maps of the Entire State: Public Lands, Back Roads, 4th ed. (Yarmouth, ME: DeLorme Mapping Company, 2000)—This provides topographical maps of popular recreational areas in Colorado, and also includes scenic features and wildlife areas. It is available for $19.95. Go to http://www.delorme.com for more information.

Colorado Business Review (Boulder, CO: Business Research Division)—The *Review* is published bimonthly by the University of Colorado, Boulder Leeds School of Business, Business Research Division. It is a four-page newsletter devoted to business topics and research. Subscriptions are free to Colorado residents. Go to http://leeds.colorado.edu/interactive/brd/cbr for further information.

Colorado's Government: Structure, Politics, Administration and Policy, 6th ed. (Robert S. Lorch) (Boulder, CO: University Press of Colorado, 1997)—This is a detailed review of the political history of Colorado. Included in the book are breakdowns of the major aspects of government in Colorado, a detailed analysis of all three branches of state government, political parties, interest groups, and fiscal matters. It also provides noteworthy explanations of city, county, and other governmental entities. The current edition is available for $29.95. Contact the University Press of Colorado, 5589 Arapahoe Avenue, Suite 206C, Boulder, CO 80303, or call (720) 406-8849. You can also find information online at http://www.upcolorado.com.

Colorado Grants Guide (Denver, CO: Community Resource Center)—This biennial publication is arranged by type of funding available and funding source. It also includes a number of useful grant indexes, by topic, geographic location, type of grant, funding organization, and foundation trustees. For further information contact the Colorado Community Resource Center, 1245 East Colfax Avenue, Suite 205, Denver, CO 80218, or call (303) 860-7711.

Colorado Legislative Directory (Denver, CO: Colorado Press Association)—This is a complete guide to each session of the Colorado legislature that has been published since 1962. It contains biographies of key state officials, and includes photographs. Contact the Colorado Press Association, 1336 Glenarm Place, Denver, CO 80204, for more information, or call (303) 571-5117. Its web site is located at http://newmedia.Colorado.EDU/cpa/online.

Colorado Newspaper Directory (Denver, CO: Colorado Press Association)—This is a complete source for information on Colorado newspapers. Directory information includes key department heads, addresses, contact information, format, publication frequency, and circulation. There are also lists of associate members, newspapers by ownership group, college journalism contacts, and other press associations. For more information, contact the Colorado Press Association, 1336 Glenarm Place, Denver, CO 80204, or call (303) 571-5117.

Colorado Revised Statutes (Denver, CO: Bradford Publishing Company)—For over 100 years, Bradford has been the official printer and distributor for the Colorado statutes. The 2002, 14-volume edition was available in either paper or CD-ROM. The paper was $99.00, the CD-ROM was $150.00 or both could be purchased for $225.00. Contact the Bradford Publishing Company, 1743 Wazee Street, Denver, CO 80202, or call (303) 292-2500. You can also visit its home page at http://www.bradfordpublishing.com/index.cfm.

Directory of Colorado Manufacturers (Boulder, CO: Bureau of Business Research, University of Colorado, Boulder)—The 2002 edition was published in cooperation with the Colorado Development Council. This biennial directory contains contact and product information on over 6,000 manufacturing firms in Colorado. Arranged in alphabetical and geographical sections, as well as by product, it includes firm names, addresses, telephone numbers, contact persons, NAICS codes, products, employees and sales ranges, and years of incorporation. It is available from the Business Research Division, University of Colorado, Boulder, CB 419, Boulder, CO 80309-0419 or call (303) 492-8227. The paper copy is available for $100.00, the CD-ROM for $250.00, or both can be purchased for $300.00. Go to http://leeds.colorado.edu/brd/publica tions/dcm for further information.

Hiking Colorado, Vol. 2 (Caryn Boddie and Peter Boddie) (Helena, MT: Falcon Publishing, 1999)—This is one of the most popular hiking guides to Colorado. It is available for $15.95 from Falcon Publishing, Inc., 48 Last Chance Gulch, Helena, MT 59601, or call (800) 582-2665.

SOURCES CONSULTED

Correspondence with Tim Byrne and Susan Xue, University of Colorado, Boulder.

Government Documents Round Table, American Library Association. *Directory of Government Document Collections & Librarians*, 7th ed. Bethesda, MD: Congressional Information Service, 1997.

Jobe, Janita. "State Publications." *Journal of Government Information*, 27 (2000): 733–768.

Notess, Greg R. *Government Information on the Internet*, 3rd ed. Lanham, MD: Bernan Press, 2000.

Numerous department web pages via the state's home page, http://www.colorado.gov.

State Legal Resources on the Web, http://www.lib.umich.edu/govdocs/statelaw.html#A.

State Web Locator, http://www.infoctr.edu/swl.

Survey response from Leanne Walther, Colorado State Library, 2000.

Connecticut

Eric W. Johnson

GOVERNMENT PUBLISHING AND THE DEPOSITORY SYSTEM

The Connecticut State Documents Depository Program was first established by Connecticut Public Act 77-561 (*General Statutes of Connecticut*, 11 CGS 9b-9d) in 1977. Since that time, the program has grown to the point where it handles approximately 25,000 pieces per year. State publications are defined in Section 11-9b as "all publications printed or published by or under the direction of the state or any officer thereof, or any other agency supported wholly or in part by state funds."

The State Library has the responsibility of administering a Connecticut state publications collection and a depository library system; establishing and administering, with the approval of the State Library Board, the necessary rules and regulations, and developing and maintaining standards for depository libraries. The State Library must receive and retain sufficient copies of state publications for "preservation, reference and interlibrary loan purposes." Although no set number of required items from each agency is specified, the State Library must distribute two copies of each publication to the Library of Congress and one copy to an additional national or regional research library, as well as copies to depository libraries within the state.

In addition to the Connecticut State Library, twelve other libraries—eight public and four academic—maintain collections of state documents.

USEFUL ADDRESSES AND TELEPHONE NUMBERS

The most complete collections of Connecticut state publications may be found at the following libraries:

Connecticut State Library
231 Capitol Avenue
Hartford, CT 06106

Phone Number for Connecticut Reference Questions: (860) 757-6570
E-Mail Link for Connecticut Reference Questions: http://www.cslib.org/asklib.htm
State Library's Home Page: http://www.cslib.org
Government Information Services Home Page: http://www.cslib.org/gis.htm

Homer Babbidge Library, Research and Information Services
University of Connecticut
369 Fairfield Road
Storrs, CT 06269
Phone Number for Connecticut Reference Questions: (860) 486-2513
E-Mail Link for Connecticut Reference Questions: http://norman.lib.uconn.edu/
    askHomer/AskQuestion.cfm
University of Connecticut Library's Home Page: http://norman.lib.uconn.edu/
    NewSpirit/Redesign/

Bridgeport Public Library
Reference/Information Department
925 Broad Street
Bridgeport, CT 06604
Phone Number for Connecticut Reference Questions: (203) 576-7403
E-Mail Link for Connecticut Reference Questions: http://kiwi.futuris.net/bpl/mail2
    .htm
Bridgeport Public Library's Home Page: http://kiwi.futuris.net/bpl/

A listing of additional libraries designated as state document depositories may be found at http://www.cslib.org/deposits.htm. Questions about the state's depository library system may be directed to the Government Information Unit Head at the State Library address noted above, at (860) 757-6576, or via e-mail at jschwartz@cslib.org. In addition, the State Library's web site features an "About Connecticut" FAQ page at http://www.cslib.org/faq .htm, with quick answers to common questions about the state.

INDEXES TO CONNECTICUT STATE PUBLICATIONS

The quarterly *Checklist of State Publications* is prepared by the Connecticut State Library, and lists state documents cataloged by the Library. The *Checklist* is available on the web as part of CONSULS—the Connecticut State University Library System—at http://csulib.ctstateu.edu/search~/.

The State Library performs original cataloging on each document, using its own locational, rather than descriptive, classification scheme, which is patterned after the Superintendent of Documents system. Subject, author, and title indexing is provided, as well as the state document's call number and location. Depository libraries are provided with catalog copy via the state's online catalog, and records are entered into both that catalog and OCLC's *WorldCat*.

A useful index of full-text Connecticut documents that are available on the Internet is maintained by the University of Connecticut's Library on its web site at http://www.lib.uconn.edu/ConnState/CTDocalph.htm. The list is arranged by title, with hyperlinks to the state documents.

While a selection of the most important Connecticut state documents may be found on the State of Connecticut web site at http://www.ct.gov/, the State Library provides a more detailed index via a link on its *Government Information Services* page at http://www.cslib.org/gis.htm. Select "Connecticut Government Resources."

ESSENTIAL STATE PUBLICATIONS

Directories

Connecticut State Register and Manual (Secretary of State)—This annual fact-book of state information, widely known as "The Blue Book," is arranged by broad topics: Historical; Biographies and Photographs; State Government (Legislative, Executive and Administrative, and Judicial); Counties; Local Government; and Political. It also includes some U.S. government information. Cities and towns are listed alphabetically, with information on state officials, tax rates, town associations, regional agencies, distances, and post offices. Some census information is included. An interactive version is available on the web at http://www.sots.state.ct.us/RegisterManual/regman.htm. A paper copy of the *State Register and Manual* may be obtained by e-mailing the Management and Support Services Division at mss@po.state.ct.us. For more information, contact the Office of the Secretary of State, 30 Trinity Street, Hartford, CT 06106.

Connecticut Education Directory (State Department of Education)—This comprehensive annual is an overview of education in the state. It includes lists of public schools and academies by type and level, regional education centers, non-public schools, colleges and universities, and education-related organizations. It is available on the web at http://www.csde.state.ct.us/public/der/directory/index.htm. Requests for print copies may be made to the Office of Public Information, Connecticut State Department of Education, P.O. Box 2219, Hartford, CT 06145, or call (800) 713-6548.

Connecticut Telephone Directory (Department of Administrative Services)—This web-only telephone and e-mail directory contains most state employee telephone and e-mail listings, and provides links to other similar online directories, as well as the state agencies' Blue Pages. It is available at http://www.ct.gov/phone/. For more information or to enquire about a print version, contact the Department of Administrative Services, 165 Capitol Avenue, Room 491, Hartford, CT 06106, or call (860) 713-5100; e-mail das.webmaster @po.state.ct.us.

Financial/Budgetary Resources

Comprehensive Annual Financial Report (Office of the State Comptroller, Budget and Financial Analysis Division)—Prepared in accordance with Generally Accepted Accounting Principles, this annual report analyzes the state's overall fiscal position and provides audited financial statements for state and state-supported fiscal activities. Reports from 1995 to the present are available online at http://www.osc.state.ct.us/reports/. For more information, contact the Office of the State Comptroller, 55 Elm Street, Hartford, CT 06106, or call (860) 702-3330.

Governor's Budget for the Biennium [Year–Year] (Governor)—The governor's annual budget proposal to the legislature includes the Budget-in-Brief, the Budget-in-Detail (Operating Budget and Capital Program), and Proposed Appropriations. The document is available on the web from a link at http://www.opm.state.ct.us/publicat.htm.

Governor's Budget Summary, FY [Year]–FY [Year] Biennium (Governor)—This summary of the annual budget provides a thorough overview of financial and budgetary information, proposed appropriations, capital program, and municipal aid. It includes a town listing and an agency index. The document is available on the web from a link at http://www.opm.state.ct.us/publicat.htm.

Governor's Midterm Budget Adjustments (Governor)—This addendum to the *Governor's Budget* notes updates and changes for the interim years between the official biennium budgets. It is available on the web from a link at http://www.opm.state.ct.us/publicat.htm.

Economic Report of the Governor (Governor)—This annual consists of "the recommendations of the Governor concerning the economy, and includes an analysis of the impact of both proposed spending and proposed revenue programs on the employment, production and purchasing power of the people and industries of Connecticut" (*General Statutes*, Section 4-74a). It provides a brief profile of the state and its economy, revenues and economic assumptions supporting the *Governor's Budget*, an employment profile, an in-depth analysis of important Connecticut sectors, performance indicators, and revenue forecasts. The document is available on the web from a link at http://www.opm.state.ct.us/publicat.htm.

Paper copies of all budget documents may be obtained from the Office of Policy and Management, 450 Capitol Avenue, Hartford, CT 06106, or call (860) 418-6200.

Legal Resources

Connecticut General Statutes (Office of the Legislative Commissioners)—Published every other year, this set contains the law of the state of Connecticut, divided into thirteen volumes. The online version, which began in 2001, corresponds to the printed *General Statutes*, and may be searched by chapter or section, or browsed in its entirety. It is available on the web at http://www.cga.state.ct.us/lco/Statute_Web_Site_LCO.htm.

Public and Special Acts (Office of the Legislative Commissioners)—Published twice yearly, this compilation includes the text of all acts passed during the January and June legislative sessions of the General Assembly, printed in numerical order. The Public and Special Acts are available on the web at http://www.cslib.org/psaindex.htm.

Print copies of the *General Statutes* and *Public and Special Acts* may be obtained from the Office of the Legislative Commissioners, Suite 5500, Legislative Office Building, Hartford, CT 06106-1591, or by calling (860) 240-8410.

Statistical Resources

The Connecticut Economic Digest (Department of Labor, Office of Research and Department of Economic and Community Development, Public and Government Relations Division)—This monthly is a comprehensive source for current information on the workforce and economy, within perspectives of the region and nation. Included are statistics on economic activity and employment, tables of current economic indicators, a leading economic index for the state, and a feature article analyzing an aspect of the Connecticut economy. A topic index to the *Digest* can be found on the web at http://www.ctdol .state.ct.us/lmi/misc/digindex.htm. The *Digest* itself is available on the web at http://www.ctdol.state.ct.us/lmi/misc/ctdigest.htm. A free print subscription is available by calling the Office of Research at (860) 263-6290 or requesting one via e-mail at dol.econdigest@po.state.ct.us.

Profiles of Our Schools; the Condition of Education in Connecticut (Department of Education)—This annual provides demographic data and information on enrollment statistics, class size, hours of instruction, staffing, attendance, expenditures, and indicators of education progress related to the State Board of Education's *Comprehensive Plan*. The latest edition is available on the web at http://www.csde.state.ct.us/public/der/coe/index.htm.

Strategic School Profiles (Department of Education)—The K–12 *Strategic School Profiles* database contains over 1,000 regular education statistics that are updated annually. These statistics include disaggregated student data, teacher data, financial data, and information regarding school programs and student outcomes. It is available on the web at http://www.csde.state.ct.us/public/der/ssp/index.htm. Requests for print copies may be made to the Office of Public Information, Connecticut State Department of Education, P.O. Box 2219, Hartford, CT 06145, or by calling (800) 713-6548.

Connecticut Market Data (Department of Economic and Community Development)—This biennial (but somewhat irregular) publication is a summary of Connecticut economic and demographic statistics and comparative features, and includes information on labor force, markets, business, education, housing, income, exports, foreign direct investments, and other topics. Both the current and past issues are available online at http://www.ct.gov/ecd/. A CD-ROM version is available from the Connecticut Economic Resource Center, Research Department, 805 Brook Street, Building 4, Rocky Hill, CT 06067-3405, or by calling (800) 392-2122.

Connecticut Town Profiles (Department of Economic and Community Development, Public Affairs and Strategies Division)—This biennial compilation of current statistics describing the state's 169 towns includes demographics, economics, education, housing, labor force, government, and quality of life. It is available on the web at http://www.ct.gov/ecd/. More information about *Connecticut Town Profiles* may be obtained by calling the Department of Economic and Community Development's Research Division at (860) 270-8021.

Labor Force Characteristics for Connecticut Labor Market Areas and 169 Towns (Department of Labor, Employment Security Division)—This monthly statistical report provides figures on employment and unemployment, and compares them to national averages. It is available on the web (as *Labor Force Data by Town*) at http://www.ctdol.state.ct.us/lmi/laus/lmlftown.htm. A print copy may be requested from the Department of Labor, 200 Folly Brook Boulevard, Wethersfield, CT 06109, or by calling (860) 263-6000.

Registration Report of Births, Marriages, Divorces, and Deaths for the Year Ended December 31, [Year] (Department of Public Health)—This annual report provides vital statistics from the state. Reports from 1992 to the present are available on the web through the department's publications/statistics page at http://www.dph.state.ct.us/Publications/publications.htm. A print copy may be obtained from the Office of Policy, Planning, and Evaluation's Division of Policy, Planning, and Analysis by calling (860) 509-7120.

Other Resources

The Connecticut Economy: A University of Connecticut Quarterly Review (University of Connecticut)—This quarterly journal, published by the Connecticut Center for Economic Analysis, provides ongoing analysis and evaluations of data, condition, issues, and development of the Connecticut economy, including a consumer price index, a confidence index, up-to-date estimates and forecasts of gross state product, as well as other indicators for travel and tourism, housing affordability, and employment trends by industry. The journal is available on the web at http://www.lib.uconn.edu/ccea/quarterly.htm. A paid subscription can be obtained using the form at that URL or through the Connecticut Center for Economic Analysis, University of Connecticut, 341 Mansfield Road, Unit 1240, Storrs, CT 06269-1240.

Connecticut Official State Tourism Map (Department of Transportation, GIS Development Section, Bureau of Policy and Planning)—In addition to providing a detailed map of the state, this annual tourism map includes general travel information (driving tips, public recreational facilities, public transit services, ferries, and state police). Contact the Office of Tourism, 505 Hudson Street, Hartford, CT 06106, or call (800) 282-6863 for a copy.

Connecticut Vacation Guide (Office of Tourism)—This annual travel guide divides the state into eleven sectors and lists tourist information, attractions, accommodations, and special events. A free *Vacation Guide* may be obtained by filling out the electronic form at http://www.tourism.state.ct.us/Order VacationGuide.asp.

Digest of Administrative Reports to the Governor (Department of Administrative Services)—This is an annual compendium of abstracted versions of annual reports of Connecticut state agencies to the governor (and/or General Assembly). The reports of most small agencies are generally reproduced in their entirety. The *Digest* is available from the Department of Administrative Services Communications Office, 165 Capitol Avenue, Room 516, Hartford, CT 06106, or by calling (860) 713-5195.

FAQs About Connecticut (Connecticut State Library)—This is a web-only guide to information resources about the history, genealogy, and government of the state. Links from this site bring the user to a page with many "where can I find" questions and answers. The URL for this web site is http://www.cslib.org/faq.htm.

CONNECTICUT'S WORLD WIDE WEB HOME PAGE

The state of Connecticut has an excellent, user-friendly, and colorful home page, located at http://www.ct.gov/. This portal site was unveiled in December 2002, and replaced the previous web site, *ConneCT*.

The major divisions of the page are Working, Doing Business, Living, Learning, Visiting, and Government. "About Connecticut" links to state facts and figures, and a "Latest News" section provides links to general state news items.

The Government section details the executive, judicial, and legislative branches of the state government with hyperlinks to agencies, officials, and the state telephone directory. A link to the Connecticut Licensing Information Center (located on the web at http://www.ct-clic.com/) provides information on obtaining licenses and consumer and business permits. A "ConneCT Kids" section, at http://www.kids.state.ct.us/, aimed at younger users of the site, provides information on state history, symbols, government, schools, and libraries, and includes puzzles and games.

The web site is managed by the Connecticut Department of Information Technology, 101 East River Drive, East Hartford, CT 06108-3274. The webmaster may be reached through a link on the home page, by e-mailing webmaster@ct.gov, or by calling (860) 622-2200.

COMMERCIAL PUBLICATIONS AND WEB SITES

The Connecticut Atlas: A Graphic Guide to the Lands, People, and History of Connecticut, 3rd ed. (Thomas E. Sherer, Jr.) (Kilderatlas Publishing Company, 262 Mile Creek Road, Old Lyme, CT 06371)—This collection of maps details a range of Connecticut history, resources, and demographics, and also includes uncopyrighted outline maps and bibliographic references.

Connecticut Magazine (35 Nutmeg Drive, Trumbull, CT 06601)—This is a monthly magazine with feature articles about Connecticut life, as well as general information about restaurants, theatre, and events. Subscription information, highlights of the current issue, and selected full-text articles from back issues may be found at http://www.zwire.com/site/News.cfm?brd=2329. For more information call (203) 380-6600.

SOURCES CONSULTED

Connecticut State Library's web site, http://www.cslib.org/.
Numerous departmental web pages via the state's web site, http://www.ct.gov/.
Survey response from Al Palko, Connecticut State Library, 2000.

Delaware

Eric W. Johnson

GOVERNMENT PUBLISHING AND THE DEPOSITORY SYSTEM

Delaware has no formal state documents depository system. However, according to Title 29, Part VIII, Chapter 87, Section 8731 of the *Delaware Code Annotated* (DCA), the State Librarian, who is the Administrator of the Department of Libraries, shall "provide access to a complete collection of current documents published by state government and a comprehensive collection of current local, state and federal documents of interest to the state." Section 8731 also says, "every state agency shall provide and deposit with the Department sufficient copies of all publications issued by such agencies for the purpose of making accessible to Delaware and other citizens resource materials published at the expense of the State." The State Librarian is charged with recommending the number of copies required for deposit, consistent with state interests.

The Delaware Public Archives also functions as a depository library in some ways, collecting state documents along with other types of state records. In addition, the Delaware Public Archives creates and distributes an annual microfiche collection entitled *Delaware Documentation* that contains the full text of many, but not all, documents published by the state. More information can be found on its web site at http://www.state.de.us/sos/dpa/. The Delaware Government Information Center is attempting to capture web pages and electronic state documents; its web site is located at http://www.state.de.us/sos/gic.

USEFUL ADDRESSES AND TELEPHONE NUMBERS

The most complete collections of Delaware state publications can be found at the following libraries:

The State Library of Delaware
Delaware Division of Libraries

43 S. Dupont Highway
Dover, DE 19901-7430
Phone Number for Delaware Reference Questions: (302) 739-4748
Library's Home Page: http://www.lib.de.us

University of Delaware
Morris Library
181 South College Avenue
Newark, DE 19717-5267
Phone Number for Delaware Reference Questions: (302) 831-2965
E-Mail Address for Delaware Reference Questions: http://www2.lib.udel.edu/ref/
    askalib/
Library's Home Page: http://www.lib.udel.edu/

Delaware Public Archives
121 Duke of York Street
Dover, DE 19901
Phone Number for Delaware Reference Questions: (302) 744-5000
E-Mail Address for Delaware Reference Questions: archives@state.de.us
Archives' Home Page: http://www.state.de.us/sos/dpa/

INDEXES TO DELAWARE STATE PUBLICATIONS

Although the *Delaware Statutes Annotated* states that "from time to time a listing of [agency publications] received [by the Division of Libraries] under the terms of this section shall be published" (DSA, Title 29, Part VIII, Chapter 87, Section 8731), there is no regular list of state publications. The State Library Commission issued a *Checklist of Official Delaware Publications* for 1968–1969, but it does not appear to have been continued. In 1971, the Delaware State Planning Office issued a *Bibliography of Delaware State Agency Publications*. The annual microfiche collection issued by the Delaware Public Archives, *Delaware Documentation*, includes an index by agency of the documents in the collection. This is not an exhaustive list of all Delaware documents, however.

State publications are listed in DELCAT, the online catalog of the University of Delaware's Libraries, accessed at http://www.lib.udel.edu/. The State Library does not have an online catalog.

ESSENTIAL STATE PUBLICATIONS

Directories

Delaware Educational Directory (Department of Education)—This is an annual listing of Delaware's public and non-public schools, school districts, colleges, educational organizations, and state agencies. School entries provide school code, grade level, address, telephone and fax numbers, principal and assistant principal(s), and e-mail address. This directory is available online at http://www.doe.state.de.us/EduDir/EduDirStart.asp, and is searchable by school district. A print version may be requested from the Department of Education, P.O. Box 1402, Townsend Building, 401 Federal Street, Dover, DE 19903-1402, or by calling (302) 739-4601, or online at http://www.doe.state.de.us/Edu DirCode/OrderForm.pdf.

Directory of Delaware Arts and Cultural Resources (Division of the Arts)—This is an online directory of art and cultural organizations, listing names and contact information, web sites, and a brief description of the association. It is available online at http://www.artsdel.org/organizations/directoryofdel.htm. For more information, contact the Division of the Arts, a branch of the Department of State, at Carvel State Office Building, 820 North French Street, Wilmington, DE 19801, or call (302) 577-8278, or via e-mail at delarts@state .de.us.

State Telephone Directory (Department of Technology and Information)—This online version of the state's *Yellow Book* includes names, titles, and telephone numbers of state employees by department; boards, councils, committees, and commissions; a fax directory; emergency numbers; and toll-free numbers. It is available online at http://www.state.de.us/ois/telecom/phonelist/index .htm. For more information, contact the Department of Technology and Information at the William Penn Building, 801 Silver Lake Boulevard, Dover, DE 19904, or call (302) 739-9500.

Financial/Budgetary Resources

FY__ Governor's Recommended Operating Budget (Office of the Budget)— The state operating budget, available online via a link at http://www.state .de.us/budget/index.html, includes a financial overview; the governor's policy overview; a financial summary, charts, and schedules; and a summary and detail report by department. Highlights of the governor's budget may also be found online at http://www.state.de.us/governor/budget.htm. For more detailed information, contact the Office of the Budget, 540 S. DuPont Highway, Thomas Collins Building, Suite 5, Dover, DE 19901, or call (302) 739-4206.

Legal Resources

Delaware Code Annotated (Delaware Code Revisors)—The official laws of the state of Delaware are divided into thirty-one titles. A browseable and searchable online version is available at the LexisNexis Group's web site at http:// 198.187.128.12/delaware/lpext.dll?f=templates&fn=fs-main.htm&2.0. For information about the print version, published by the Michie Company, Charlottesville, VA, contact LexisNexis at (800) 223-1940.

State of Delaware Constitution, as Adopted in Convention, June 4, 1897, with Amendments Made Subsequently thereto through August 1995 (Legislative Council)—This provides the text of the state Constitution, comprised of a Preamble and 17 Articles, the first of which is a Bill of Rights. The Constitution is available online at http://www.state.de.us/facts/constit/de_const.htm. Inquiries about a print version may be made to the Legislative Council, Legislative Hall, 411 Legislative Avenue, Dover, DE 19901, or call (302) 744-4200.

Statistical Resources

Delaware Vital Statistics Annual Report (Health and Social Services, Division of Public Health, Office of Vital Statistics)—This is an annual report of population, marriages and divorces, live births, reported pregnancies, infant mortality, and general mortality in the state. The latest edition can be accessed at http://www.dehealthdata.org/Publications.html. For information on obtaining a print copy, contact the Office of Vital Statistics, P.O. Box 637, Dover, DE 19903.

Report of Educational Statistics [Year]–[Year] (Department of Education)—This online listing of state educational statistics includes figures on numbers of students enrolled in public and non-public schools, attendance rate, finances (pupil expenditures, teacher salaries, etc.), teachers, and more. It is available online through a link at http://www.doe.state.de.us/reports/School_Reports .htm. More detailed information is available in the print version, which may be obtained by contacting the Technology Management and Design Group at the Department of Education at (302) 739-4583.

The Delaware Economic Development web site, http://www.state.de.us/ dedo/new_web_site/frame_data_center.html, provides links to a number of statistical resources on demographics (population estimates, housing units and data), community profiles, quality of life (cost of living, housing costs, and climate), business (the top 50 Delaware employers), labor (employment and unemployment by state and county), and education. For more information, contact the Delaware Economic Development Office at the address above.

Other Resources

Delaware Facts and Symbols (Government Information Center)—This brief online compendium of basic state facts and figures includes information on state area, population, government, climate, elevation, products, and symbols. It may be found at http://www.state.de.us/gic/facts/history/delfact.htm. For more information, contact the Government Information Center, 121 Duke of York Street, Dover, DE 19901, or call (302) 739-4111; e-mail gic@state.de.us.

Delaware Official Transportation Map (Delaware Tourism Office)—The state's annual roap map includes a mileage chart, driving regulations, information on state parks, and small maps of major cities.

Experience Delaware; Official State Travel Guide (Delaware Tourism Office)— This is the state's official annual travel guide with subject articles (the 2001–2002 edition focused on art museums, history, outdoors, and other topics) as well as information on attractions and accommodations by region and city. Detailed itineraries help travelers plan day trips to historic areas and attractions in the same region.

The guide and map are available free of charge from the Tourism Office, 99 Kings Highway, Dover, DE 19901-7305, or call (866) 284-7483. They also may be ordered online at http://www.visitdelaware.com/publications.asp.

DELAWARE'S WORLD WIDE WEB HOME PAGE

In April 2001, the state of Delaware unveiled its new portal-approach web site, *Delaware.gov*. The streamlined site, located at http://delaware.gov, has links to the governor, state agencies, e-Government information, and "Hot Topics," as well as buttons labeled "Resident," "Visitor," "State Employee," "Business," and "Government," each button linking to a host of informative web pages. The use of Yahoo! software allows users to personalize the portal.

The web site was developed by a joint effort between an e-Government Steering Committee headed by the State Treasurer and Accenture, a web design company. For more information on the web site, contact the Delaware Government Information Center, 121 Duke of York Avenue, Dover, DE 19901, or call (302) 739-4111; or via e-mail at gic@state.de.us.

COMMERCIAL PUBLICATIONS AND WEB SITES

Delaware Almanac (*The News Journal*, P.O. Box 15505, Wilmington, DE 19850)—This is an annual online almanac of Delaware facts, figures, and information, with expanded information on sports and leisure activities. The 2002 edition is available on the web at http://www.delawareonline.com/newsjournal/almanac/2002/index.html. For more information on the *Almanac*, contact *The News Journal* at the address above, or call (302) 324-2500 or (800) 235-9100.

Delaware Government (League of Women Voters of Delaware, 2400 W. 17th Street, Clash Wing, Wilmington, DE 19806)—This is an encyclopedic factbook of state information, including maps, a state overview, the Constitution, and information on the legislative, executive, and judiciary branches; elections; state finance; education; local governments; and citizen opportunities. Originally published in 1976, the fourth updated edition appeared in 1999. It may be ordered from the league at the address above, or online at http://www.de.lwv.org/delgovbook.htm. An online version, published by the Delaware Government Information Center, 121 Duke of York Street, Dover, DE 19901, is available at http://www.state.de.us/sos/gic/lwv/.

Delaware League of Local Governments On-Line Directory—The Delaware League of Local Governments is a statewide, non-profit, non-partisan association of city, town, and county governments established in 1963 to improve and assist local governments through legislative advocacy at the state and federal levels. The league also serves as a clearinghouse for important governmental and business-oriented information. This online directory, available at http://www.ipa.udel.edu/localgovt/dllg/, provides links to lists of mayors/managers; fax numbers for municipalities; municipal pages and web sites; county, statewide, and national elected officials; and state senators and representatives. The municipality pages, accessed through http://www.ipa.udel.edu/localgovt/dllg/municipalities/index.html, include handy general facts about Delaware's cities and towns (populations, officials, events, telephone and fax numbers). The web site is maintained by the Institute for Public

Administration, 180 Graham Hall, University of Delaware, Newark, DE 19716; for information call (302) 831-8971, or e-mail the institute at ipa@udel.edu.

SOURCES CONSULTED

Correspondence with Steve Newton, Delaware Division of Libraries.

Delaware Division of Libraries web site, http://www.lib.de.us/.

Numerous departmental web pages via the state's official web site, http://www.delaware.gov/.

University of Delaware Library web site, http://www.lib.udel.edu/.

Florida

Lori L. Smith

GOVERNMENT PUBLISHING AND THE DEPOSITORY SYSTEM

Florida's public documents depository system was established with the passage of legislation in 1967. The system is administered by the State Library, which is a component of the Division of Library and Information Services (DLIS) of the Department of State. Twenty-four libraries around Florida, as well as the Library of Congress, receive the publications distributed through the program. Six of these, including the State Library, are considered "lending depositories," and as such they receive two copies of each publication distributed.

Section 257.05(1) of the *Florida Statutes* defines a public document as

any document, report, directory, bibliography, rule, newsletter, pamphlet, brochure, periodical, or other publication, whether in print or nonprint format, that is paid for in whole or in part by funds appropriated by the Legislature and may be subject to distribution to the public; however, the term excludes publications for internal use by an executive agency as defined in s. 283.30.

The law requires state agencies and officials to furnish the Division of Library and Information Services with thirty-five copies of each public document they produce. The DLIS is empowered to request fifteen copies beyond the original thirty-five. However, if an agency or official has fewer than forty copies of a document, they are required to supply at least two copies to be deposited in the State Library.

The DLIS is charged with designating depository libraries, distributing publications to them, and publishing a bibliography of state publications. The libraries that receive depository publications are required to make them accessible to the public.

USEFUL ADDRESSES AND TELEPHONE NUMBERS

The most comprehensive collections of Florida state publications can be found in the following libraries:

State Library of Florida
Florida Collection
R.A. Gray Building
500 S. Bronough Street
Tallahassee, FL 32399-0250
Phone Number for Florida Reference Questions: (850) 245-6600
E-Mail Link for Florida Reference Questions: http://dlis.dos.state.fl.us/stlib/help
  .html
Library's Home Page: http://dlis.dos.state.fl.us/stlib/
Florida Collection Home Page: http://dlis.dos.state.fl.us/stlib/flcoll.html

George A. Smathers Libraries
University of Florida
Government Documents Department
P.O. Box 117001
Gainesville, FL 32611-7001
Phone Number for Florida Reference Questions: (352) 392-0367
E-Mail Link for Florida Reference Questions: http://web.uflib.ufl.edu/docs/refmail
  .html
Government Documents Department's Home Page: http://web.uflib.ufl.edu/docs/

Government Documents Department
S.E. Wimberly Library
Florida Atlantic University
Boca Raton, FL 33431
Phone Number for Florida Reference Questions: (561) 297-3788 or (561) 297-3785
Government Documents Department's Home Page: http://www.library.fau.edu/
  depts/govdocs/govdoc.htm

INDEXES TO FLORIDA STATE PUBLICATIONS

Florida Public Documents, the official bibliography of state publications, has been published by the State Library since 1968. It is not available online, but the State Library's collection of Florida documents is included in its online catalog, which can be accessed from the library's home page at http://dlis .dos.state.fl.us/stlib/. In addition to providing details about the library's collection, the catalog includes hot-linked web addresses that allow the searcher to access those publications that are available online. A retrospective bibliography, entitled *Short-title Checklist of Official Publications of Florida, 1900–1945*, was compiled by James A. Servies and published in 2000.

The State Library assigns Dewey Decimal numbers to Florida documents. However, Florida Atlantic University (FAU) in 1969 devised and began using a classification scheme similar to the SuDoc system used with federal documents. This scheme, the KWIC index, is still used by many Florida depositories. Catalogers at FAU assign KWIC classification numbers and forward them to the State Library. Catalogers at the State Library add the KWIC numbers to the records in the national bibliographic database, OCLC.

FAU also compiles and makes available online its *Florida Documents Index*. It can be accessed from its "State and Local Government" web page at http://www.library.fau.edu/depts/govdocs/state.htm, or from Florida International University's "Florida and South Florida Government" web page at http://library.fiu.edu/subjects/florida.html. The index includes information about the Florida publications collected by FAU since 1966.

An index that is particularly useful for finding government publications on the web is the *Florida Government Information Locator*. This site, maintained by the State Library, can be found on the web at http://dlis.dos.state.fl.us/fgils/. The site provides links to information sources by subject. The subjects available are Government, Education, Business, Tourism, Consumer, History/Culture, Working, and Libraries. The site also offers an A to Z directory of links to information on topics from "Abandoned Property" to "Workplace Safety."

ESSENTIAL STATE PUBLICATIONS

Directories

411 (State Technology Office)—This is the online version of the state telephone directory. It provides addresses and phone numbers for state government employees and is available at http://www.myflorida.com/myflorida/411/index.html. The directory can be searched by employee name, agency, city, university, and a variety of other methods. A printable list of phone numbers can be created as a PDF file.

Florida Agricultural Export Directory (Department of Agriculture and Consumer Services, Division of Marketing and Development)—Contact information is given in this directory for firms in Florida that are seeking opportunities to export agricultural products. Information is also provided to assist those firms in making international contacts, and to assist companies outside the United States who wish to do business with the firms listed. The directory is available online at http://www.fl-ag.com/export/welcome.htm. A free copy of the directory, among other agriculture-related publications, can be requested by completing the web form at http://www.florida-agriculture.com/pubs/pubform.htm. Those with questions about the directory can contact the Division of Marketing and Development at (850) 487-8000.

Florida Government Information Resources (University of Florida, George A. Smathers Libraries, Government Documents Department)—This source, located on the web at http://www.uflib.ufl.edu/fefdl/florida/florida.html, is part of the larger *Florida Electronic Federal Depository Library* site. The *Florida Government Information Resources* page is a directory of links to many state and local government web sites. It provides lists of links in the following categories: Florida Main Homepages, Census, County Business Patterns, Crime Statistics, Florida Departments and Agencies, Local Resources, General Information Resources, and Florida Freenet System, among others. The General Information Sources section includes links to the online version of the *Florida*

Administrative Code and other titles discussed in this chapter. Those with questions about the page can contact the Government Documents Department at (352) 392-0367.

Financial/Budgetary Resources

Comprehensive Annual Financial Report (Department of Banking and Finance, Office of Comptroller)—The revenues and expenditures of the state are reported in great detail each year in this publication. The introductory section of the report includes a state government organizational chart and an overview of revenues and expenditures. The second section presents detailed financial statements for departments and programs. The final section provides general economic and demographic statistics. Several recent editions of the report are available on the web at http://www.dbf.state.fl.us/aadir/cafrlist.html. A shorter, more easily readable version of the report is issued as the *State of Florida's Citizens Report*. That version is available online at http://www.dbf.state.fl.us/aadir/cafrgateway.html. Those who wish to enquire about the availability of print copies of either report may write to Florida Department of Banking and Finance, Office of Comptroller, 101 E. Gaines Street, Tallahassee, FL 32399-0350, or call (850) 410-9286. There is also a toll-free consumer hotline number, (800) 848-3792. Questions can be sent via e-mail to dbf@mail.dbf.state.fl.us.

Executive Budget (Governor)—Florida's governor submits a proposed budget to the legislature each year. After a long process of discussion and debate, the revised version of the budget is passed by the legislature as a General Appropriations Act. Links to various versions of the budget are available on the governor's "Laws, Executive Orders and Legislative Actions" web page at http://www.myflorida.com/myflorida/government/laws/index.html. Persons with questions about the budget can contact the Governor's Office of Policy and Budget at (850) 488-7810.

Legal Resources

Florida Administrative Code (Department of State, Division of Elections)—This publication includes all the rules and regulations that have been adopted by state departments and agencies. An unofficial version is available online at http://election.dos.state.fl.us/fac/index.shtml. Those with questions about the publication can contact the Bureau of Administrative Code and Weekly at (850) 245-6270. The official version, *Florida Administrative Code Annotated*, is a commercial publication described below.

Florida Administrative Weekly (Department of State, Division of Elections)—Proposed rules and regulations, as well as bid announcements and general public notices appear in this weekly publication. Current issues are released online at http://faw.dos.state.fl.us/index.html. Previous issues are made available online as space allows. Those with questions about the publication can write to Bureau of Administrative Code and Weekly, 107 West Gaines Street, The Collins Building, Room L43, Tallahassee, FL 32399, or call (850) 245-6270.

Florida Statutes (Legislature)—This official codified version of the state's laws is published each year. The six-volume hardbound set, which also includes the text of the state's Constitution, is usually available in late September. The 2001 edition sold for $235, including shipping and handling. The set can be ordered from the legislature's Law Book Services Office at (850) 488-2323, or via e-mail to lawbook.services@leg.state.fl.us. The print edition can also be ordered online with a credit card at the legislature's "Legistore," which can be accessed from the legislature's home page at http://www.leg.state.fl.us. An unofficial version of the *Statutes* can be viewed or searched online at http://www.flsenate.gov/Statutes/index.cfm.

Statistical Resources

Florida School Indicators Report (Department of Education, Bureau of Education Information and Accountability Services)—This source provides information about dropouts, graduation rates, average class sizes, numbers of students with disabilities, and other figures for individual schools, or aggregated at the school district or state level. Several editions of the report are available online at http://info.doe.state.fl.us/fsir/. Those who wish to enquire about the availability of print copies can write to Florida Department of Education, Bureau of Education Information and Accountability Services, 852 Turlington Building, 352 West Gaines Street, Tallahassee, FL 32399-0400, or call (850) 487-2280.

Florida Statistical Abstract (University of Florida, Bureau of Economic and Business Research)—Produced annually, this publication includes statistics on a wide variety of topics gathered largely from government sources. The original sources of the statistical information are cited, so it also functions as a guide to those publications. The 2001 edition of the *Statistical Abstract* sold for $46 in paper or $90 as a CD-ROM. Editions from some previous years are available for sale as well. Those interested in obtaining copies can write to Bureau of Economic and Business Research, University of Florida, P.O. Box 117145, Gainesville, FL 32611-7145, or call (352) 392-0171, extension 219. Orders or requests for information can be sent via e-mail to info@BEBR.ufl.edu. An order form can be downloaded from the bureau's web site at http://www.bebr.ufl.edu.

Florida Statistical Sources (University of Florida, George A. Smathers Libraries, Government Documents Department)—This wonderful web page can be found at http://www.uflib.ufl.edu/fefdl/florida/fl_statistics.html. It provides a very comprehensive list of links to web sources arranged by topic, and includes links to many of the titles described in this chapter. Those with questions about the page can contact the Government Documents Department at (352) 392-0367.

Florida Vital Statistics Annual Report (Department of Health, Office of Vital Statistics)—Statistics on live births, fetal and infant deaths, abortions, adult deaths, marriages, and divorces are given in this report. Totals for the United States, Florida, and counties within Florida are reported for most statistics. Several recent editions of the report are available on the web at http://www9.myflorida.com/planning_eval/vital_statistics/statistical_report.htm.

Those who wish to enquire about the availability of print copies can write to Florida Department of Health, Office of Vital Statistics, Public Health Statistics Section, P.O. Box 210, Jacksonville, FL 32231-0042, or call (904) 359-6900. Questions can be sent via e-mail to VitalStats@doh.state.fl.us.

State University System Factbook (Board of Education, Division of Colleges and Universities)—This annual publication allows the user to compare standard statistics for all of Florida's public universities. Statistics presented include the physical size of the campus, the number of enrolled students, average age of the students, and the number of volumes in the university library. Facts about degree programs available and fees charged are also given. Several recent editions of the report are available online at http://www.fldcu.org/factbook. Those who would like to enquire about the availability of print copies can write to Florida Board of Education, Division of Colleges and Universities, Office of Information Resource Management, 325 West Gaines Street, Florida Education Center, Suite 1420, Tallahassee, FL 32399-1950, or call (850) 201-7270.

Uniform Crime Reports (Department of Law Enforcement)—Several different statistical reports are available on this web page at http://www.fdle.state.fl.us/fsac/UCR/index.asp. Some of the titles available are *Annual Crime in Florida*, *Annual Arrest Totals by Age and Sex*, *Annual County and Municipal Offense Data*, and *Annual Statewide County Report*. Those who wish to enquire about the availability of print copies can write to Florida Department of Law Enforcement, P.O. Box 1489, Tallahassee, FL 32302-1489, or call (850) 410-7000. Many other statistical reports regarding crime and law enforcement are available from the Florida Statistical Analysis Center web page at http://www.fdle.state.fl.us/FSAC/index.asp.

Other Resources

Florida Government Accountability Report (Legislature, Office of Program Policy Analysis and Government Accountability)—Provided as a service to legislators and the public, this web site compiles information about the purpose, funding, and performance of each state government agency. By using links to other resources on the web, each agency description refers to the legislation that established the agency, the issues and challenges currently being faced by the agency, and the reports and statistics that demonstrate how effectively the agency is performing its duties. The site can be searched by keyword, topic, or agency, and a site map is also provided. The address of the site is http://www.oppaga.state.fl.us/government/. Those with questions can contact the Office of Program Policy Analysis and Government Accountability at (800) 531-2477 or (850) 488-0021.

Sunbiz (Department of State, Division of Corporations)—The *Sunbiz* web site, at http://www.sunbiz.org, is described in its welcome information as "the Florida Division of Corporations' online information, research, and electronic processing service center." The site provides a searchable database of corporations that have registered to do business in the state, as well as lien information and images of actual documents filed. Those with questions about the database can call (850) 488-9000 or e-mail corphelp@mail.dos.state.fl.us.

FLORIDA'S WORLD WIDE WEB HOME PAGE

Florida's home page is found at http://www.myflorida.com. The page was designed with the assistance of Yahoo!, and a note at the bottom claims the site is "Fortified with Yahoo!" Because of this partnership, the site offers many features that will be familiar to users of Yahoo! The site can be browsed, searched, or even personalized.

The home page offers four categories—Visitor, Floridian, Business, Government—which the user can select to begin browsing information. Each category leads to more specific topics from which the user can select. A trail of "breadcrumbs" near the top of the screen will show users the selections they have made and will allow them to return to any stage of their browsing history. To search rather than browse, there is a box on the home page that allows the user to enter keywords to be searched on the site. The "My Page" option allows the user to create a personalized version of the page.

Near the top of the page there is a "First Time User" selection that leads to a detailed description of ways the site can be navigated and the types of information that can be located.

Other major sections on the page provide "Florida's Latest News," "Florida Government Headlines," "e-Government Service," "Hot Topics," and information about the "Florida Lottery."

COMMERCIAL PUBLICATIONS AND WEB SITES

Florida Administrative Code Annotated (Darby Printing Company, 6215 Purdue Drive, Atlanta, GA 30336)—This is the official version of the rules and regulations adopted by state agencies and departments. It is issued in a looseleaf format and includes detailed annotations and a variety of indexes. It can be ordered by writing to Darby Printing Company at the address given, or by calling (800) 241-5292. A catalog of Darby's products is available on their web site at http://www.darbyprinting.com/.

The Florida Almanac (Pelican Publishing Company, P.O. Box 3110, Gretna, LA 70054)—This almanac provides information on Florida's history, landmarks, schools, taxes, festivals and fairs, rivers and waterways, and a multitude of other topics. It includes several maps and charts. The hardback version of the 2002–2003 edition was sold for $23.00, and the paperback version for $15.95. It is widely available, but it can be ordered directly from the publisher at the address above, or by calling (800) 843-1724 or (888) 5-PELICAN. There is also an online order form available on the Pelican Publishing web site at http://www.pelicanpub.com/home.asp.

The Florida Handbook (Peninsular Publishing Company, 2503 Jackson Bluff Road, Tallahassee, FL 32304)—The twenty-eighth edition of this biennial publication was issued in 2001. The *Handbook* contains nearly encyclopedic information on Florida's history, population, geography, government, businesses, and many other topics. One of the *Handbook*'s long-time compilers, Dr. Allen Morris, passed away in 2002. He was the Clerk-Emeritus and Historian of Florida's House of Representatives. Copies of the book can be ordered from many sources. Those with questions can contact the publisher at the address given above, or at (850) 576-4151.

SOURCES CONSULTED

Florida Statistical Sources, University of Florida, George A. Smathers Libraries, http://www.uflib.ufl.edu/fefdl/florida/fl_statistics.html.

Florida Statutes, online via the legislature web site, http://www.flsenate.gov/Statutes/index.cfm.

Numerous departmental web pages via *MyFlorida.com*, http://www.myflorida.com.

OCLC (Online Computer Library Center). *OCLC WorldCat*. Dublin, OH: OCLC.

Survey response from Cherie McCraw and Cay Hohmeister, State Library of Florida, 2000.

Georgia

Lori L. Smith

GOVERNMENT PUBLISHING AND THE DEPOSITORY SYSTEM

Georgia has one of the most unique and progressive depository systems in the country. The current system was established in 1993 when title 20, chapter 5, section 2 of the *Official Code of Georgia Annotated* was amended to require executive branch departments and institutions to submit to the director of the University of Georgia Libraries at least five copies of any public documents they issue. The director was empowered to request up to sixty copies and to distribute these copies to any library affiliated with an educational institution.

Subsection (e) of 20-5-2 defines public documents as

books, magazines, journals, pamphlets, reports, bulletins, and other publications of any agency, department, board, bureau, commission, or other institution of the executive branch of state government but specifically shall not include the reports of the Supreme Court and the Court of Appeals, the journals of the House and the Senate, or the session laws enacted by the General Assembly and shall not include forms published by any agency, department, board, bureau, commission, or other institution of the executive branch of state government.

Although it is somewhat unique that the depository program is restricted to the publications of the executive branch, and it is also slightly unusual that the program is administered by a university, the truly unique aspect of the Georgia depository system is that public documents are distributed mainly by technology rather than by transportation. In addition to the University of Georgia Libraries, only the Odum Library at Valdosta State University and the Henderson Library at Georgia Southern University receive physical copies of depository publications. To offer access to others, the program uses a high-tech approach. Documents are scanned into a digital format by the University of Georgia Libraries and made universally accessible via the *Georgia Government Publications Database (GGPD)* (see Figure 5). The database currently includes publications from 1994 to date. *GGPD* is one of many databases

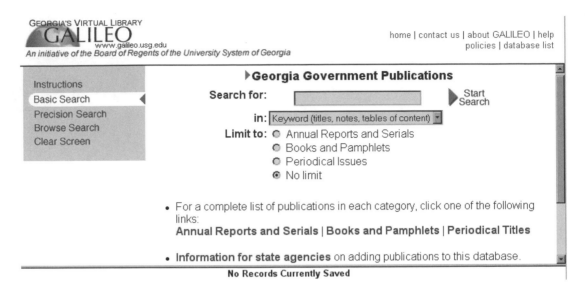

Figure 5. The *Georgia Government Publications* database not only provides bibliographic information about state publications, but often includes the full text of publications as PDF files. *Source*: http://www.galileo.usg.edu. © Board of Regents, University System of Georgia.

available through Georgia's *GALILEO* system. To access the *GGPD*, go to the *GALILEO* site at http://www.galileo.usg.edu and select the "Georgia" tab. From the drop-down menu, select "Government Information and Publications." If you get a screen that requests a password, select the "public databases" button near the bottom of the screen, then select "Georgia Government Publications."

To assist with the University of Georgia Libraries' efforts to distribute and preserve state documents in an electronic format, the law was amended in 2000 and a new subsection (m) was added to 20-5-2. It states that "any person or agency required by the provisions of this Code section to submit to the director of the University of Georgia Libraries copies of documents shall also submit such documents in such electronic form as the director shall specify, if such electronic form is readily available."

USEFUL ADDRESSES AND TELEPHONE NUMBERS

The most complete collection of Georgia publications can be found at the following library:

Government Documents Department
University of Georgia Libraries
Athens, GA 30602-1645
Phone Number for Georgia Reference Questions: (706) 542-3251
E-Mail Address for Georgia Reference Questions: mainref@arches.uga.edu
State of Georgia Publications Home Page: http://www.libs.uga.edu/govdocs/
    collections/georgia.html
Georgia Government Publications Database (via *GALILEO*): http://www.galileo.usg.edu

INDEXES TO GEORGIA STATE PUBLICATIONS

Prior to the University of Georgia Libraries being designated to coordinate the depository program, there was a Georgia State Library that did so for many years. The Georgia State Library no longer exists as a single institution, but during the time that it did, it compiled and published two indexes to state publications. From the early 1900s until January 1954, the *Checklist of Georgia Documents Entered at the Georgia State Library* was published irregularly. According to the national bibliographic database, OCLC, the only library in the country that holds a copy of that earliest index is the New York State Library. From February 1954 until June 1989, the Georgia State Library published the *Checklist of Official Publications of the State of Georgia*. In 1990, the Government Documents Department of the University of Georgia Libraries began publishing the *Georgia Doclist: A Monthly Bibliography of Georgia State Documents*. That title continued in print until 1999. For titles issued from 1994 to date, the *Georgia Government Publications Database* mentioned above can be searched.

ESSENTIAL STATE PUBLICATIONS

Directories

Georgia Infosource (Department of Industry, Trade and Tourism, Economic Development Division)—This web site can be accessed from a link on the Economic Development Division page, located at http://www.georgia.org/economic/index.asp, or directly at http://www.georgiainfosource.com. It provides a database of available buildings that can be searched by size limitations and location. The description of each building includes an address, details about square footage, expansion potential, and special features. The *Infosource* also provides a directory of manufacturers and a directory of facilities that are owned in part or in full by foreign companies.

Georgia Public Education Directory (Department of Education)—GA Docs. Call Number—GA E300 .S1 D5. Names, addresses, phone numbers, fax numbers, and e-mail addresses are given in this source. The first section provides information about the State Superintendent of Schools and other persons in state-level offices. The second section gives a county-by-county listing for persons working at the county level and for the principal of each school. A variety of indexes are provided at the end. The directory is available online via the *Georgia Government Publications Database*, and via the Department of Education web site at http://www.doe.k12.ga.us/. Those who wish to enquire about the availability of print copies can write to Georgia Department of Education, 2054 Twin Towers East, Atlanta, GA 30334, or call (404) 656-2446. Persons in Georgia can call (800) 311-3627.

Historical Organizations and Resources Directory (Secretary of State, State Archives)—GA Docs. Call Number—GA S700 .A7 S1 D5. The Georgia Historical Records Advisory Board maintains this directory. It is no longer issued in print, but can be found online at http://www.sos.state.ga.us/archives/ghrab/dir/dir.htm. Each listing includes the name, address, and telephone number of an organization, along with some or all of the following:

fax number, e-mail address, web site address, program description, collections description, year founded, number of members, director's name, hours of operation, parent institution, contact names, and the last date the entry was updated. Those with questions about the directory can write Georgia Historical Records Advisory Board, State Archives of Georgia, 330 Capitol Avenue SE, Atlanta, GA 30334, or call (404) 656-2362.

Official Directory of U.S. Congressmen, State and County Officers (Secretary of State)—This web site, http://www.sos.state.ga.us/cgi-bin/OfficialDirectory Index.asp, provides information about Georgia's government officials from U.S. senators and representatives down to county coroners and sheriffs. Information provided about each includes name, mailing address, phone number, fax number, and when available, web site address.

State of Georgia [Year] Telephone Directory (Georgia Technology Authority)— GA Docs. Call Number—GA A300 .S1 T4. The directory provides addresses and phone numbers for state employees, departments/agencies, colleges/universities, and elected officials. The Department of Administration formerly released a print edition, but the Georgia Technology Authority recently assumed responsibility for issuing the directory and it is now available only on the web at http://gist.gagta.com. Those with questions about the directory can write to Georgia Technology Authority, 100 Peachtree Street, Suite 2300, Atlanta, GA 30303-3404, or call (404) 463-2300.

Financial/Budgetary Resources

Comparative Summary of SFY [Year] General Appropriations Act, H.B. [Bill #] (Legislative Budget Office)—GA Docs. Call Number—GA L400 .B8 S1 A7. The Legislative Budget Office advises both the House and the Senate on budgetary matters. After the General Assembly passes the general appropriations act for a given fiscal year, the Legislative Budget Office publishes on its web site a report for each department/agency that shows the budget amount originally recommended by the governor, the amounts included in the House and Senate bills, and the amount in the Conference Committee version of the bill. A link to the final text of the act is also provided. The address of the page is http://www.legis.state.ga.us/legis/budget/documents.html. Those with questions about the summary can write to Georgia Legislative Budget Office, 142 State Capitol, Atlanta, GA 30334, or call (404) 656-5050.

Comprehensive Annual Financial Report (Department of Audits and Accounts)—GA Docs. Call Number—GA A800 .A12. This report provides a detailed picture of the state's revenues, expenditures, and fund balances. The introductory section contains the letter of transmittal from the State Auditor, an organizational chart for the state government, and a listing of the state's officials. The second section of the report contains the audited financial statements of the various departments/agencies and funds. The final section provides statistics on government expenditures by function, revenues by source, a selection of demographic statistics, and other miscellaneous statistical information. The report is included in the *GGPD*, and the three most recent editions are also available on the Department of Audits and Accounts site at http://www2.state.ga.us/Departments/AUDIT/ppd/cafr_main.htm. Those who wish to enquire about the availability of print copies can write to Department of Audits and Accounts, State Government Division, 254 Washington Street SW, Suite 214, Atlanta, GA 30334-8400, or call (404) 656-2180.

The Governor's Budget Report, Fiscal Year [Year] (Governor, Office of Planning and Budget)—GA Docs. Call Number—GA G620 .S1 B8. The governor's budget recommendations to the legislature for the upcoming fiscal year are detailed in this annual report. In addition to recommended appropriations for specific departments/agencies and initiatives, the report includes information about the state's projected revenues and about past budgets and expenditures. The introduction to the report presents an overview of the governor's recommendations and includes a "Reader's Guide" section that describes the various budgetary documents issued by the governor. The detailed departmental summaries in the report usually include an organizational chart, a financial summary, a budget summary, a functional budget summary, a description of the department's legal responsibilities, a discussion of major projects being undertaken by the department, a summary of capital outlay projects, and a results-based budgeting section. The report is available online through the *GGPD*, or via a link from the Office of Planning and Budget's web site at http://www.opb.state.ga.us/Budget%20Information.htm. That page also includes a link to an online "Budget Document Request Order Form." Those with questions can contact the Office of Planning and Budget at 270 Washington Street SW, Atlanta, GA 30334, or call (404) 656-3820.

Legal Resources

Georgia Code Unannotated (General Assembly)—This unofficial version of the state's codified laws is available online via a link at http://www.legis.state.ga.us/. It contains laws of the state arranged by subject. The site allows searching of the *Code* by keyword or by code number, and it can also be browsed by title. The *Official Code of Georgia Annotated* is a commercial publication issued by LexisNexis/Michie Co.

Rules and Regulations of the State of Georgia (Secretary of State)—The rules and regulations adopted by state government departments/agencies are collected and published in this serial. It is available online at http://www.ganet.org/rules/ and can be searched by keyword or section number. The online edition is updated by the departments/agencies themselves, so some sections may be more current than others. A full 18-volume print edition is available for $300. That fee includes one year of monthly updates. A subscription to the monthly updates can be renewed at the end of the calendar year for $45. Those interested in obtaining the print edition can write to Office of Secretary of State, Administrative Procedure Division, Attention: Janice Gilley, 2 MLK Jr. Drive, Atlanta, GA 30334, or call (404) 656-2865. Prepayment is required.

Summary of General Statutes Enacted at the [Year–Year] Session of the General Assembly of Georgia (General Assembly)—GA Docs. Call Number—GA L400 .L4 S1 S7. Issued annually, this publication contains a summary of all the generally applicable statutes that were passed in one session of the General Assembly. Resolutions, local acts, and other types of legislation that will not be included in the *Official Code of Georgia Annotated* are not provided. A table in the publication tells which sections of the *Code* were amended by the newly passed legislation. It is available online in the *GGPD*, and via the Georgia General Assembly's "Previous Sessions" page at http://www.legis.state.ga.us/links/Prev.htm. Those with questions can contact the House Public Information Office at (404) 656-5082, or the Senate Information Office at (404) 656-0028.

Statistical Resources

Georgia Vital Statistics Report (Department of Human Resources, Division of Public Health)—GA Docs. Call Number—GA H800 .P8 S1 S7. This annual report presents statistics on births and deaths, including fetal deaths and induced terminations of pregnancy. General demographic statistics and information on the most popular first names for infants are also included. Summaries are given for the state as a whole, for the nineteen public health districts, for metropolitan statistical areas, and for counties. Some editions of the report are available in the *GGPD*, and some are available on the Division of Public Health's web site at http://www.ph.dhr.state.ga.us/healthdata/vital.shtml. Those with questions about the report can write to Division of Public Health, Office of Health Information and Policy, Two Peachtree Street, NW, Room 15-212, Atlanta, GA 30303-3186, or call (404) 657-6320. Questions can be sent via e-mail to gdphinfo@dhr.state.ga.us.

[Years] Report Card (Office of Education Accountability)—Georgia's Office of Education Accountability was established in 2000. Its online *Report Card* for K–12 schools can be found at http://www.ga-oea.org/report_card.html. This annual publication presents statistical information in four major areas: student performance on Georgia state tests, school performance indicators, school demographic information, and student performance on national tests. Those with questions about the *Report Card* can write to Office of Education Accountability, 101 Marietta Street, NW, Suite 2500, Atlanta, GA 30303, or call (404) 463-1150. Similar information from earlier years can be found on the Department of Education's "Report Card" page at http://techservices.doe.k12.ga.us/reportcard/.

Statistical Data on Georgia (University of Georgia, Carl Vinson Institute of Government)—This web page is part of the *GeorgiaInfo* web site discussed below in the "Other Resources" section. The address for the page is http://www.cviog.uga.edu/Projects/gainfo/gastat.htm. The page provides links to many other web sites, such as the *Georgia Statistics System* and *FEDSTATS*, and to specific files housed on other sites, such as the *Map of 50 States Showing Numeric Change: 1990–2000* and *Georgia Local Government Employment Data*.

[Year] Summary Report: Uniform Crime Reporting (URC) Program (Georgia Bureau of Investigation, Crime Information Center)—GA Docs. Call Number—GA I675 .C7 S1 C75. Since 1975, Georgia has participated in the Federal Bureau of Investigation's Uniform Crime Reporting program. This annual report provides statistics on UCR "Part 1" offenses—which include murder, non-negligent manslaughter, forcible rape, robbery, aggravated assault, burglary, larceny, motor vehicle theft, and arson—and on "Part 2" offenses, for which

less detailed statistics are given. Georgia also collects and reports statistics on family violence. Editions of the report are available in *GGPD*, and on the Georgia Bureau of Investigation's web site at http://www.ganet.org/gbi/disclucr.html. Those with questions about the report can write to Georgia Bureau of Investigation, P.O. Box 370808, Decatur, GA 30037-0808, or call (404) 244-2501.

Other Resources

Georgia Official and Statistical Register (Secretary of State, Department of Archives and History)—This publication was issued biennially from the early 1920s until the early 1990s. There were a few minor title changes during that period. The *Register* included mostly directory-type information for state officials, but also included the state's Constitution, some historical lists, and a variety of statistical information. It is unlikely that there are still print copies available for sale, but those who wish to enquire can write to State Archives of Georgia, Box RPM, 330 Capitol Avenue SE, Atlanta, GA 30334, or call (404) 656-2393.

GeorgiaInfo (University of Georgia, Carl Vinson Institute of Government)—The table of contents for this excellent web site includes entries for: General Information, Georgia Maps, Voter Information, Georgia Government, Georgia Counties, Georgia Cities, Special-Purpose Governments, and U.S. Government. The headings of pages within each section are given on the table of contents as well. For instance, the General Information section includes Georgia in the news, Georgia history, geography, demographic statistics, Georgia's economy, directories, and other. The address for the site's home page is http://www.cviog.uga.edu/Projects/gainfo/. Those with questions about the site can write to Carl Vinson Institute of Government, University of Georgia, 201 North Milledge Avenue, Athens, GA 30602-5482, or call (706) 542-2736.

Picture Georgia (Department of Industry, Trade and Tourism)—A selection of digital photographs depicting various activities and locations around the state of Georgia is available at http://www.georgia.org/images/picture georgia/index.asp. The database of pictures can be searched by location, by activity, or by keyword.

GEORGIA'S WORLD WIDE WEB HOME PAGE

Georgia's home page can be found on the web at http://www.georgia .gov/. It is maintained by the Georgia Technology Authority.

The left side of the screen offers links to information on the following subjects: Transportation, Family and Health, Education and Training, Tourism and Recreation, Business Services and Employment, Government, and Legal and Public Safety. Links near the center of the screen lead to a site map, a list of frequently asked questions, a list of state agencies and organizations, and a list of county and city web sites. The right side of the screen has a box in which the user can enter terms to be searched on the site, and boxes leading to information on "I want to . . ." and "How do I . . .". The bottom of the screen features links to information on the Georgia Lottery, a short list of headlines, and a section titled "At Your Service" which links to information on various elected officials.

The government link on the home page leads to links on state government, municipal government, county government, federal government, citizen involvement, and laws and regulations. The agencies and organizations link leads to a page with an alphabetical list of links to agencies, bureaus, commissions, and other units of state government. That page also offers an option to sort the list by acronym.

As links are followed through the site, a history is maintained at the top of the screen that documents the path followed. The user can return to any step in the path by clicking a link in that list. Each page beyond the home page offers direct links back to the home page, to the site map, and to the agencies and organizations page. Each page also provides a search box.

COMMERCIAL PUBLICATIONS AND WEB SITES

Georgia Statistical Abstract (University of Georgia, Selig Center for Economic Growth, Terry College of Business, The University of Georgia, Athens, GA 30602-6269)—One of the many publications issued by the Selig Center for Economic Growth, the *Georgia Statistical Abstract* compiles statistics from a wide variety of state and federal sources. Economic statistics are emphasized, but more general statistics are presented as well. The 2000–2001 edition of this title was available in print or on a CD-ROM that included additional data. Those who wish to purchase a copy can find ordering information in the "Publications" section on the Selig Center's web site at http://www.selig.uga.edu. Ordering information can also be obtained by writing to the address above, or by calling (706) 542-4085. Questions can be sent via e-mail to SeligCenter@terry.uga.edu.

Official Code of Georgia Annotated (LexisNexis/Michie Co., Charlottesville, VA)—As described above under "Legal Resources," this source contains the laws of the state arranged by subject. This is the official printed version of the *Code*. The Michie Company is part of the LexisNexis publishing empire. A searchable of catalog of LexisNexis' legal publications may be found on the web at http://bookstore.lexis.com/bookstore/catalog/. The most recent edition of the *Code* was issued in forty-five volumes and sold for $826. Those with general questions can call the LexisNexis Bookstore at (888) 223-6337. Those who wish to place an order can call (800) 223-1940.

SOURCES CONSULTED

Georgia Code Unannotated, via the General Assembly site, http://www.legis.state.ga.us/.

Numerous web pages via the Georgia home page, http://www.georgia.gov.

OCLC (Online Computer Library Center). *OCLC WorldCat*. Dublin, OH: OCLC.

Survey response from Susan Tuggle, University of Georgia Libraries, 2000.

Hawaii

Daniel C. Barkley

GOVERNMENT PUBLISHING AND THE DEPOSITORY SYSTEM

The Hawaii state depository system was established in 1965 under the *Hawaii Revised Statutes* (HRS) 93-1. The law set forth the establishment of a state publications distribution center (known as the Hawaii Documents Center—HDC) within the public library system and under the direction of the State Librarian. The law also sets forth that each of Hawaii's counties shall have a minimum of one depository library. The center is responsible for "depositing and distributing government publications and for promoting an orderly depository library system for state and county publications."

Under HRS 93-3, each state and county agency must send fifteen copies of each publication to the distribution center and one copy to the University of Hawaii. Additional copies of state or county publications may also be deposited with the center upon request from the State Librarian. The State Librarian is empowered to enter into depository agreements "with private and public or public educational, historical, or scientific institutions or other libraries, within or without the State in order to achieve the objectives sought under this part." The State Librarian will also designate one depository library in every county as well as distribute one state or county publication to each depository. For a list of all the public libraries in Hawaii, see http://www.hcc.hawaii.edu/library/hawaiilibs.html.

HRS 93-2 defines "publication" to include "any document, compilation, journal, report, statute, regulation, ordinance issued in print by any state or county agency." Confidential publications may be deposited following security regulations that have been determined by the issuing agency. HRS 93-2 also defines print as including "all forms of printing and duplications, except administrative forms." A state or county agency is defined as including "every state, city and county and county office, officer, department, board, commission, and agency, whether in the legislative, executive, or judicial branch."

Currently there are eight participating depository libraries. All but one of the current depositories resides within the Hawaii State Public Library System (HSPLS), the exception being the University of Hawaii, which is named separately in HRS 93-3 as a recipient of state and county government publications.

USEFUL ADDRESSES AND TELEPHONE NUMBERS

The most complete collections of Hawaii's state government publications can be found at the following libraries:

Hawaii State Archives
Historical Records Branch
Kekauluohi Building
Iolani Palace Grounds
Honolulu, HI 96813
Phone Number for Hawaii Reference Questions: (808) 586-0329
Hawaii State Archives Home Page: http://www.state.hi.us/dags/archives/welcome
  .html

Hawaii State Library
Hawaii and Pacific Section
478 South King Street
Honolulu, HI 96813-2901
Phone Number for Hawaii Reference Questions: (808) 586-3535
E-Mail Address for Hawaii Reference Questions: hslfed@lib.state.hi.us
Hawaii and Pacific Section Home Page: http://www.hawaii.gov/hidocs/hp_main
  .html

University of Hawaii Hilo
200 West Kawili Street
Hilo, HI 96720-4091
Phone Number for Hawaii Reference Questions: (808) 974-7346
E-Mail Link for Hawaii Reference Questions: http://library.uhh.hawaii.edu/ask
  _librarian.htm
Hawaiian Collection Home Page: http://library.uhh.hawaii.edu/hawaiian_collection
  .htm

University of Hawaii at Manoa
Hamilton Library
2550 McCarthy Mall
Honolulu, HI 96822
Phone Number for Hawaii Reference Questions: (808) 956-8264
E-Mail Address for Hawaii Reference Questions: speccoll@hawaii.edu
Hawaiian Collection Home Page: http://www2.hawaii.edu/~speccoll/hawaii.html

INDEXES TO HAWAII STATE PUBLICATIONS

The Hawaii Documents Center (HDC) at the Hawaii State Library and the State Librarian have responsibilities in procuring, listing, indexing, microfilming, and distributing to state depository libraries all publications produced by state agencies at state expense. Much of the monographic material received by the HDC is also cataloged into the Hawaii and Pacific collection at the Hawaii State Library and available from its online catalog.

Because of the relatively small number of depository libraries no formal list of publications issued is compiled or made readily available. The HDC uses the Jackson Classification System, which classifies publications by issuing agency. The HDC assigns a classification number to each publication received. The HDC also includes bibliographic and document handling information (e.g., date the publication is received, number of copies, distribution locations). This information is compiled into a monthly Hawaii documents list. This list is printed and distributed to all public and selected government and academic libraries.

Many of the depositories receive, on an annual basis, microfiche copies of materials from the HDC. This ensures that all depositories eventually receive copies of state agency publications that have been deposited with the HDC. This provides continuity and equal access to state agency publications across all parts of Hawaii.

Because the number of state agency publications received by the HDC may vary, and in a situation where less than fifteen copies of a publication are received, there is a hierarchy of depository recipients. When this scenario happens the main branch depository, Neighbor Island depositories, other Oahu depositories, and the remaining branch libraries receive publications. With this type of situation occurring, there are no standard depository shipments sent on a regular basis nor is a shipping list compiled.

ESSENTIAL STATE PUBLICATIONS

Directories

Government in the State of Hawaii: State Contact Information (eHawaiiGov)—This web site is part of the Hawaii information portal. This service provides phone and e-mail directories for all state employees. It was designed as part of the state's overall initiative to provide citizens of Hawaii with access to more information electronically. This directory can be found online at http://www.ehawaiigov.org/government/html/contactinfo.html. The directory is maintained by eHawaiiGov, 220 South King Street, Suite 2190, Honolulu, HI 96813, or call (808) 587-4220.

Hawaii Directory of State, County and Federal Officials (Legislative Reference Bureau)—This web site provides complete contact information for all branches of state government, county officials, and members of the Hawaiian congressional delegation. Divided into nine PDF-formatted sections, the directory provides an alphabetically arranged index of all employees involved in government operations. A paper copy is produced every February. The directory can be accessed online from the "Hawaii State Directory and Guide" page at http://www.state.hi.us/lrb/capitoli/dirguide/. To obtain a paper copy contact the Hawaii Legislative Reference Bureau Library, State Capitol, Room 005, Honolulu, HI 96813, or call (808) 587-0690.

Hawaii Education Directory (Department of Education)—This online directory provides contact information on educational institutions and those involved in education in Hawaii. Searches can be performed by first or last name, by institution, by school, or phonetically. Each person's name, institution, phone number, and e-mail address will be provided via the search. Go to http://165.248.6.166/employees/Default.asp to review this directory. For more information contact the Hawaii Department of Education, P.O. Box 2360, Honolulu, HI 96804, or call (808) 586-3230.

Financial/Budgetary Resources

Budget in Brief: Executive Supplemental Budget, FY [Year] (Department of Budget and Finance)—This report accompanies the governor's more detailed report listed below. It is prepared as an adjunct budget document that the governor may submit in even-numbered years to the state legislature in order to adjust that fiscal year's budgetary needs. This document is submitted as a bill that the legislature must approve before any budgetary adjustments can be made. During the bill's consideration no other bills may be introduced that pertain to the state budget. For more information contact the State of Hawaii, Department of Budget and Finance, P.O. Box 150, Honolulu, HI 96810, or call (808) 586-1530. This document can be found online at http://www.state.hi.us/budget/statefin/statefin.htm.

The Multi-Year Program and Financial Plan and Executive Budget (Department of Budget and Finance)—This report provides detailed financial information on state government operations. It is a combined report featuring the governor's budget report for the current budget period (a two-year period) and a report on anticipated budget revenues and receipts for a six-year period. It is available online at http://www.state.hi.us/budget/statefin/Executive%20Budget.htm. For more information contact the State of Hawaii, Department of Budget and Finance, P.O. Box 150, Honolulu, HI 96810, or call (808) 586-1530.

Statement of Total Outstanding Indebtedness of the State of Hawaii (Department of Budget and Finance)—This report, prepared annually, provides concise information on the debt of the Hawaiian state government. The publication supports "schedules of the total principal amount of bonds issued and outstanding by type of bond and a listing of special purpose revenue bonds authorized by the [state] Legislature." The most recent editions are available online at http://www.state.hi.us/budget/statefin/debtoutindex.htm. The web site is maintained by the State of Hawaii, Department of Budget and Finance, P.O. Box 150, Honolulu, HI 96810, or call (808) 586-1530.

Legal Resources

Hawaii Administrative Rules Directory (Legislative Reference Bureau)—The 2001 cumulative edition is a listing of all rules Hawaii state government agencies had filed with the Office of the Lieutenant Governor prior to May 1, 2001. This directory replaces the 1995 edition. The directory provides a detailed table of contents of the state's administrative rules but lists only the rules that conform to the uniform format for state agencies mandated by HRS 91-4.2.

The directory does not provide a history of rule amendments nor does it provide a table of statutory rules or sections affected. The online version can be located at http://www.state.hi.us/lrb/reports/. A copy may be obtained from the Hawaii Legislative Reference Bureau, State Capitol, Honolulu, HI 96813, or call (808) 587-0690.

Hawaii Legislative Drafting Manual (Legislative Reference Bureau)—This publication provides guidelines to state agencies and individuals who prepare bills for introduction into the Hawaii legislature. The latest edition reflects changes in legislative drafting procedures and practices as well as including suggestions from those who use this reference guide on a daily basis. The manual is specifically designed for new legislators and their staffs but is useful for anyone associated with the legislative drafting process. It can be found online at http://www.state.hi.us/lrb/reports/pams.html. A copy may be obtained from the Hawaii Legislative Reference Bureau, State Capitol, Honolulu, HI 96813, or call (808) 587-0690.

Hawaii Legislators' Handbook (Legislative Reference Bureau)—This source provides a comprehensive reference book for legislators and their staffs regarding the basic information on the legislative process. The 1997 edition includes changes in laws and procedures that have impacted the legislative process since the last edition was published in 1990. The *Handbook* is available section by section for easy review and retrieval, and can be found at http://www.state.hi.us/lrb/reports/pams.html. A copy may be obtained from the Hawaii Legislative Reference Bureau, State Capitol, Honolulu, HI 96813, or call (808) 587-0690.

Hawaii Revised Statutes (State Legislature)—A searchable version of the Statutes is available in the "Status and Documents" section of the legislature's site at http://www.capitol.hawaii.gov/.

Hawaii State Legislature (State Legislature)—This online resource provides links to a variety of information generated by or about the Hawaii state legislature. Access is provided to information on each legislative chamber, directories, definitions, new releases, committee reports, and other useful resources. Additionally, in the "Status and Documents" section, a search can be performed to find information on bills, hearings, and action sheets generated from the latest legislative session. The site is available at http://www.capitol.hawaii.gov/.

The Virtual Rules (Office of the Lieutenant Governor)—This web site is part of SWAT (Slice Waste and Tape) which is a multiyear project concerning rules and regulations that the Hawaii business community must abide by. SWAT has so far identified nearly sixty chapters of administrative rules that have been slated for revision or elimination through recent legislative action. Additionally, SWAT is working toward making the *Hawaii Administrative Rules* 100 percent electronically available, eliminating rules no longer needed; revising rules that have been updated; and creating a feedback mechanism for the business community, the general public, and state employees. The *Virtual Rules* supplies links to each state agency and the administrative rules that govern that agency. The web site can be found at http://swat.state.hi.us/VRC.htm. The site is designed and maintained by the Lieutenant Governor's Office, State Capitol, 5th Floor, Honolulu, HI 96813, or call (808) 586-0252.

Statistical Resources

Annual Visitor Research Report (Department of Business, Economic Development and Tourism)—This annual report reflects Hawaii's largest import—tourists. This is a statistical compendium reflecting various aspects of the economic impact of the tourist trade in Hawaii. Major categories include visitor characteristics by major market area, by accommodation, by category, and by first or repeat visitor status. The web site also provides links to the latest monthly report as well as historical data. Recent issues of the report are available online at http://www.hawaii.gov/dbedt/stats.html. A copy might be available from the State of Hawaii, Department of Business, Economic Development and Tourism, P.O. Box 2359, Honolulu, HI 96840, or call (808) 586-2423.

Crime in Hawaii—A Review of Uniform Crime Reports (Office of the Attorney General, Crime Prevention and Justice Assistance Division)—This is a statistical compendium of crimes committed in the past year in Hawaii. Statistics reflect the FBI's Hierarchy Rule that limits a crime involving multiple offenses to counting only the most serious offense committed. Arrest counts may also be affected by this rule. Statistics include type of offense committed, arrest, age, race, and gender. Statistics were culled from the four county police departments in Hawaii. The latest year can be found at http://www.cpja.ag .state.hi.us/rs/index.shtml. The report has been prepared by the Research and Statistics Branch, Crime Prevention and Justice Assistance Division, Department of the Attorney General, 235 South Beretania Street, Suite 401, Honolulu, HI 96813, or call (808) 586-1150.

DBEDT Statistical Report Series (Department of Business, Economic Development and Tourism)—This online resource provides links to a number of statistical reports generated by the DBEDT. Statistical resources include housing unit estimates, county district trends, population, land ownership, military personnel and their dependents, and a host of other useful reports. Some of these reports may be available in state depository libraries. To review the reports go to http://www.hawaii.gov/dbedt/sr.html.

Labor and Occupational Information Hawaii (LO'IHI) (Department of Labor and Industrial Relations, Research and Statistics Office)—This online resource provides a wealth of information on wages, employment, unemployment, and work injuries and illnesses. Other links provide occupational information, a search mechanism for employment seekers, the latest job market information, career information, and education and training. Each major category includes several links to specific text or statistics. To review the web site go to http:// www.state.hi.us/dlir/rs/loihi/. This site is maintained by the State Department of Labor and Industrial Relations, Research and Statistics Office, P.O. Box 3680, Honolulu, HI 96811-3860, or call (808) 586-8999.

[Year] State of Hawaii Data Book (DBEDT, Research and Economic Analysis Division)—This publication, now in its 33rd edition, reflects the structure and format of its counterpart, the *Statistical Abstract of the United States*. The arrangement is done in order to make comparisons between state and national data easier to find and use. The emphasis is on statewide data rather than on counties, islands, urban, or small places. Reference sources are provided with

each table or headnote to provide information for correct interpretation of the data presented. There are twenty-four major subject arrangements, an index, bibliography, and section downloads. Links are also provided to other DBEDT statistics and publications and its home page. Several editions of the *Data Book* can be found at http://www.hawaii.gov/dbedt/stats.html. An order form with price information is provided at http://www.hawaii.gov/dbedt/dborder.html. Contact the Department of Business, Economic Development and Tourism, Research and Economic Analysis Division, ATTN: Data Book Request, P.O. Box 2359, Honolulu, HI 96804, or call (808) 586-2423.

State of Hawaii Facts and Figures (Department of Business, Economic Development and Tourism)—This is a brief guide to facts and figures on the state and its four counties. Some historical as well as current information is available and reflects social and economic trends. The latest information is available at http://www.hawaii.gov/dbedt/facts/index.html. The file is available in a PDF format for easy review and downloading (see Figure 6). It is maintained by the Department of Business, Economic Development and Tourism, P.O. Box 2359, Honolulu, HI 96804, or call (808) 286-2423.

Other Resources

[Year] Annual Report to the Hawaii State Legislature (Hawaii Tourism Authority)—This annual report is prepared by the Hawaii Tourism Authority and provided to the state legislature on the tourism industry in Hawaii. It reflects the tourism industry from facts and figures to accomplishments by those in the public and private sector that are in charge of various tourist activities. The report also contains a narrative summary of tourist activities for the past year as well as the Authority's plans and goals for the coming year. To review the latest year's activities go to http://www.state.hi.us/tourism. For a copy, contact the Hawaii Tourism Authority, Hawaii Convention Center, 1801 Kalakaua Avenue, Honolulu, HI 96815, or call (808) 973-2255.

The Arts Resource Directory (Committee for Arts and Culture)—This directory is an online version of the paper *Hawaii Arts Resource*. The directory provides contact information such as telephone and fax numbers, and e-mail addresses for a number of arts and culture groups on Oahu. There are twelve sections, each focused on a particular art form (dance, music) or genre (museums, galleries). Also included are public agencies and educational institutions involved in the promotion of art and culture. The directory is located at http://www.hcc.hawaii.edu/artweb/directory.html.

Guide to Government in Hawaii (Legislative Reference Bureau)—This guide is the companion volume to the *Directory of State, County and Federal Officials*. Last revised in 2002 (12th edition), the guide provides discussion on state and county departments, their organization, and federal agencies that have offices in Hawaii. Organizational charts of county and state government agencies are included. The guide can be found at http://www.state.hi.us/lrb/capitoli/dirguide/. For a paper copy, contact the Legislative Reference Bureau, State Capitol, Honolulu, HI 96813, or call (808) 587-0690.

How to Research Constitutional, Legislative, and Statutory History in Hawaii (Legislative Reference Bureau)—The third edition, published in 2001, updates

----DBEDT-

State of Hawai'i
FACTS & FIGURES

State of Hawaii
Facts & Figures
Social & Economic Trends

Kauai County
Facts & Figures
Social & Economic Trends

City & County of Honolulu
Facts & Figures
Social & Economic Trends

Maui County
Facts & Figures
Social & Economic Trends

Hawaii County
Facts & Figures
Social & Economic Trends

 2000 State of Hawaii Facts & Figures

Statistics & Publications | DBEDT Home Page

Figure 6. Many sites that present information as PDF files offer a link to the Adobe site where the Acrobat Reader software necessary to view the files can be downloaded free of charge. *Source*: http://www.hawaii.gov/dbedt/facts/index.html.

the editions published in 1983 and 1984. Much of the guide is similar to the early editions with the exception that now many of the references are to web sites rather than computer systems. Session law references found in statutory source notes were also updated. A new chapter was added to discuss the repeal and reenactment process as well as how to find temporary session law materials. Otherwise this guide provides tips, shortcuts, and other mechanisms used to perform historical research on the state constitution, bills, and laws. The guide can be found at http://www.state.hi.us/lrb/reports/pams .html. For a paper copy contact the Legislative Reference Bureau, State Capitol, Honolulu, HI 96813, or call (808) 587-0690.

Inventory of Historic Properties (Department of Land and Natural Resources, State Historic Preservation Division)—This listing provides information on approximately 38,000 properties of historical significance in Hawaii. The list expands by close to 1,000 properties per year. Included in the list are over 3,500 properties that are of an archaeological significance. Also included on this web page are links to a geographic information system, now under development, which will take the researcher to an exact location electronically. There are also links to the Hawaii and National Register of Historic Places, the Hawaii Historical Places Review Board, and the administrative rules governing this agency. The web site is located at http://www.state.hi.us/dlnr/hpd/hpinvntory.htm. It is maintained by the Department of Land and Natural Resources, State Historic Preservation Division, Kakuhikewa Building, 601 Kamokila Boulevard, Suite 555, Kapolei, HI 96707, or call (808) 692-8015.

HAWAII'S WORLD WIDE WEB HOME PAGE

The official name of Hawaii's home page, found at http://www.state.hi.us, is *eHawaiiGov*. Like many other state home pages, Hawaii's home page is an information portal that leads one to subject-oriented links for more information. There are seven main subjects ranging from "Government in Hawaii" to "About eHawaiiGov." Each of these main links provides further detail on that subject. Hawaii's home page motto is "get online rather than in-line."

One can locate information on the Hawaiian state government, on working, living, or visiting Hawaii, on education in Hawaii, and various facts and figures on Hawaii. There are also "spotlight" services highlighted. These include various online government services that can be conducted (such as paying taxes, applying for professional licenses, etc.). One can also order a certified copy of a birth or marriage certificate, view and download a GIS state map, and link to other services offered by the state agencies.

The page is useful, easy to navigate, and informative. The page is well maintained, updated frequently, and is not overly cluttered. For those who wish to visit, practically every question one might have regarding sites, hotels, beaches, surfing, and so on, can be answered from this page. Those who are relocating to Hawaii will find all the information necessary to ease the move and transition.

The page is produced in conjunction with the Hawaiian Information Consortium. For more information contact eHawaiiGov, 220 South King Street, Suite 2190, Honolulu, HI 96813, or call (808) 587-4220.

COMMERCIAL PUBLICATIONS AND WEB SITES

Bank of Hawai'i Pacific Islands Reports (Honolulu, HI: Bank of Hawaii)—This is a series of reports compiled by the Economics Research Center at the Bank of Hawaii on the economies of the various Pacific Islands. The reports provide a detailed insight into the economic activity of each island. Many have had recent revisions, although a few of the reports date back to 1995. The data presented are useful, especially to those wishing to engage in business transactions, or for research purposes. The reports are available online at http://www.boh.com/econ/pacific/index.asp.

Hawaii Annual Economic Report (Honolulu, HI: Bank of Hawaii, 1999)—This report reflects the fiftieth anniversary of economic research at the Bank of

Hawaii. The report reflects the Hawaiian economy at all levels and includes a narrative introduction along with a vast amount of statistical data on all aspects of economic activity. Also included are economic forecasts and predictions for the coming calendar year. To view recent editions of the report, go to http://www.boh.com/econ/.

Hawaii Atlas and Gazetteer: Topographical Maps of the Entire State, Public Lands, and Back Roads (Yarmouth, ME: DeLorme Mapping Company, 2000, $19.95)—This atlas provides detailed topographic information on Hawaii. The information includes details on hiking on public lands, travelling around the back roads and country, and other information useful for those interested in outdoor activities in Hawaii. For purchase or more information contact the DeLorme Mapping Company, Two DeLorme Drive, P.O. Box 298, Yarmouth, ME 04096, or call (800) 581-5105.

Hawaii Business Directory (Omaha, NE: American Business Directories, 2001)—The cost is $375.00 for a paper or CD-ROM edition. This directory contains information on over 3,600 businesses in Hawaii. The arrangement is alphabetical by name of business in each county. There is also a subject index at the end of each county section. Information on businesses includes company name and address, telephone and fax numbers, officers and board of directors, number of employees, date business was established, a brief description of each business, and the gross annual sales volume. For more information contact American Business Directories, 5711 South 86th Circle, Omaha, NE 68127, or call (402) 596-4600; e-mail directory@infoUSA.com.

Hawaiian Journal of History (Honolulu, HI: Hawaiian Historical Society)—First published in 1967, the *Journal* contains a series of scholarly articles on the history of Hawaii, Polynesia, and the Pacific area. Each quarterly publication contains articles on a variety of subjects, including illustrations, book reviews, and a bibliography of Hawaiiana titles of historical significance. Members of the Hawaiian Historical Society receive this publication free; subscriptions are available for $40.00 per year. Printed indexes are available for volumes 1 through 25; indexes for more recent volumes are available online at http://www.hawaiianhistory.org/pubs/hjhmain.html. For more information on subscriptions contact the Hawaiian Historical Society, 560 Kawaiahao Street, Honolulu, HI 96813, or call (808) 537-6271.

Hawaii Manufacturers Directory (Evanston, IL: Manufacturers' News Inc., 2001, $58.00)—This directory provides contact information on manufacturers in Hawaii. Divided into sections, it contains an alphabetical list of businesses, businesses by type of product, businesses by city or town, by SIC code, and by parent company. It should be noted that this directory is not comprehensive and other directories may need to be consulted in order to ensure comprehensive coverage. For purchase or more information contact the Manufacturers' News Inc., 1633 Central Street, Evanston, IL 60201, or call (847) 864-7000; e-mail info@manufacturersnews.com.

Native Hawaiian Data Book (Honolulu, HI: Office of Hawaiian Affairs, 2002)—This publication provides valuable demographic information on native Hawaiians (defined as those with 50 percent or more Hawaiian blood). The data book "reports descriptive statistics and cogent information strictly on the Native Hawaiians in Hawaii." For more information contact the Office of Hawaiian Affairs, Planning and Research Office, 711 Kapi 'Olani Boulevard, Suite 500, Honolulu, HI 96813, or call (808) 594-1888; e-mail oha2002@aloha.net. The latest data book is not yet available on the web, but is available free of charge by contacting the Office of Hawaiian Affairs.

SOURCES CONSULTED

Correspondence with Patrick McNally, Hawaii State Library; Noella Kong, Office of Hawaiian Affairs.

Google, http://www.google.com.

Government Documents Round Table, American Library Association. *Directory of Government Document Collections & Librarians*, 7th ed. Bethesda, MD: Congressional Information Service, 1997.

Jobe, Janita. "State Publications." *Journal of Government Information*, 27 (2000): 733–768.

Numerous departmental web pages via the state's home page, http://www.state.hi.us.

State and Local Government on the Net, http://www.piperinfo.com/state/index.cfm.

State Web Locator, http://www.infoctr.edu/swl/.

Idaho

Daniel D. Cornwall

GOVERNMENT PUBLISHING AND THE DEPOSITORY SYSTEM

The Idaho state publications depository program was started in 1972. The State Library is responsible for the depository system and the laws governing the program are outlined in Title 33, Section 2505 of the *Idaho Statutes*. According to the law, each state agency is required to deposit "all documents, reports, surveys, monographs, serial publications, compilations, pamphlets, bulletins, leaflets, circulars, maps, charts, or broadsides of a public nature which it produces for public distribution." The law itself does not give a definition for either "document" or "public distribution," but the State Library has published some guidelines at http://www.lili.org/statedocs/what-is .htm. A document is any publication produced by a state agency or at state government expense and distributed outside the agency. To illustrate, an internal newsletter for agency employees would not be deposited in the program, but a newsletter that went out to a limited list of program clients would be. The web page that explains what a state document is also invites agency publication producers to call the library with questions. There are currently nineteen Idaho depository libraries and the State Library asks agencies to submit twenty copies of their publications. Two copies are kept by the State Library—one to preserve and one to loan to patrons—one copy is sent to the Library of Congress, and seventeen are sent to the remaining Idaho depository libraries. At an absolute minimum, agencies are required to deposit three copies, two for the State Library, and one for library at the University of Idaho. Unlike many states, depository libraries in Idaho have complete discretion to keep or discard Idaho state publications as they see fit. They are also totally responsible for any steps in making material supplied by the State Library available to their patrons.

USEFUL ADDRESSES AND TELEPHONE NUMBERS

The most complete collections of Idaho state publications may be found at the following libraries:

Idaho State Library
State Documents
325 W. State Street
Boise, ID 83702
Phone Number for Idaho Reference Questions: (208) 334-2150
E-Mail Address for Idaho Reference Questions: govinfo@isl.state.id.us
Idaho State Library's Home Page: http://www.lili.org/
Depository Program Home Page: http://www.lili.org/statedocs/

University of Idaho Library
P.O. Box 442350
Moscow, ID 83844-2350
Phone Number for Idaho Reference Questions: (208) 885-7951
E-Mail Link for Idaho Reference Questions: http://drseuss.lib.uidaho.edu/reference/
    ask_a_librarian.htm
Library Home Page: http://drseuss.lib.uidaho.edu/
Special Collections Department Page: http://www.lib.uidaho.edu/special-collections/
    sc-intro.htm

Those with questions about Idaho's depository library system may contact
the State Documents Coordinator at the address, phone number, or e-mail
address given above for the State Library.

INDEXES TO IDAHO STATE PUBLICATIONS

Until September 2002, the *Checklist of Idaho Government Publications* was updated monthly on the Internet at http://www.lili.org/statedocs/#checklist
and published annually in paper. The paper version was distributed to public,
academic, and secondary school libraries in Idaho, usually in April or May.
A few editions of the *Checklist* can still be obtained at the *Checklist* web site.
The *Checklist* began publication in 1989. It is arranged first by keyword of the
publishing agency, then by agency divisions, then alphabetically by title. The
Checklist does not contain each agency's complete hierarchy, but does offer
agency mailing addresses and links to agency home pages. To find information about Idaho government publications issued since October 2002, users
can search the State Library's online catalog at http://catalyst.boisestate
.edu/.

Idaho state publications are classified according to a system similar to Superintendent of Documents numbers.

ESSENTIAL STATE PUBLICATIONS

Directories

Idaho State Government Telephone Directory (Department of Administration)—
Idaho Documents Call Number—A1000.10 STA01 years. This provides contact
information for persons in the state government, and is published annually in
paper and available on the Internet at http://www.accessidaho.org/govern
ment/gov_phone.html. The paper edition is available from Marcum and Associates, 110 E. Woodvine Street, Boise, ID 83706, or call (208) 344-2866. The

directory is $18.00, including shipping and handling, and is free to Idaho public libraries and state agencies.

[Number]th Idaho Legislature: [Years] Regular Session: Directory (Legislature, Legislative Services)—Idaho Documents Call Number—L4000.10 years. Each session published is in paper. Free copies are available from Legislative Services Office, State Capitol, Room 108, P.O. Box 83720, Boise, ID 83720-0054. Similar information can be found on the legislature's web site at http://www2.state.id.us/legislat/legislat.html. The web site includes legislators' occupations and lists the names of their spouses, if there is one.

Idaho Educational Directory (Department of Education)—Idaho Documents Call Number—E2100.10 years. This is an annual directory of public, private, and charter K–12 institutions. To ask about print copies, contact the Idaho Department of Education, (208) 332-6840. A downloadable version is available on the Internet as a PDF file at http://www.sde.state.id.us/admin/eddirectory/.

Financial/Budgetary Resources

Legislative Budget Book (Legislature, Legislative Services)—Idaho Documents Call Number—L4000.28 years. This annual publication contains the budget requests from state agencies and includes recommendations from the governor. It is prepared for the Joint Finance-Appropriations Committee of the legislature, and the latest issue is available on its web site at http://www.jfac.state.id.us/publications.htm.

Fiscal Facts (Legislature, Legislative Services)—Idaho Documents Call Number—L4000.16 FIS01 years. Published annually, this is a pocket reference to facts, figures, and trends on Idaho's state budget. It includes current and historical budget information for all state agencies as categorized into six functional areas. Each functional area is presented in a ten-year historical perspective. Also included are charts, graphs, and narrative sections that interpret the numbers. It is available on the web at http://www.jfac.state.id.us/publications.htm.

Fiscal Source Book (Legislature, Legislative Services)—Idaho Documents Call Number—L4000.02 SOU01 year. Last published in 2001, this book details the sources and uses of funds for state agencies. It is arranged by the name of the agency that administers or has spending authority for the listed funds. The book also provides descriptions of fund sources and uses. There is also a helpful section explaining Idaho fund codes. The introduction states this book is an "ongoing project" which will be updated as new funds are added. It is available on the web at http://www.jfac.state.id.us/publications.htm.

Legal Resources

Idaho State Constitution (Secretary of State, Election Division)—Idaho Documents Call Number—S2000.05 CON01 year. The most recent revision of the Constitution is available on the Election Division's "Publications and Document Links" page at http://www.idsos.state.id.us/elect/publindx.htm.

Statutes of the State of Idaho (Legislature)—The statutes are available on the web at http://www3.state.id.us/idstat/TOC/idstTOC.html. The online version may be browsed by title, then by chapter. A search engine for both the statutes and the Constitution is available at http://www3.state.id.us/legislat/idstat.html.

Current Legislation/Previous Legislation (Legislature)—The legislature provides searchable/browseable databases of current legislation and legislation from the previous session. Each bill record includes Daily Data Tracking History, Bill Text, and Statement of Purpose/Fiscal Impact. This last feature should be extremely valuable to people doing legislative history. The current legislation is available at http://www3.state.id.us/legislat/legtrack.html. Legislation for the immediate prior legislative session can be searched at http://www3.state.id.us/legislat/oldtrack.html. It does seem unfortunate that prior years are not available.

Idaho Administrative Bulletin (Department of Administration, Office of Administrative Rules)—Notices of proposed, temporary, and final rules promulgated by state agencies are published in the *Bulletin*. It is available on the Internet at http://www2.state.id.us/adm/adminrules/bulletin/mstrtoc.htm.

Idaho Administrative Code (Department of Administration, Office of Administrative Rules)—This title is an annual compilation of all administrative rules in effect as of July 1 of the current year. It is available on the Internet at http://www2.state.id.us/adm/adminrules/agyindex.htm. Those interested in subscribing to the *Administrative Bulletin* or the *Administrative Code* can write to Department of Administration, Office of Administrative Rules, P.O. Box 83720, Boise, ID 83720-0306, or call (208) 332-1820.

Statistical Resources

2000 Census Data (Department of Commerce)—This site is the best place to start a search for state- and county-level data. Located at http://www.idoc.state.id.us/data/census/index.html, this site contains spreadsheet format files on population and housing data by age, ethnicity, and race. In addition, it has a link to business data such as a downloadable file of Idaho's largest employers and a listing of total business revenue in Idaho.

County Profiles of Idaho (Department of Commerce)—Idaho Documents Call Number—C6000.16 COU02 year. The last paper edition came out in 1999, but current, individual county profiles are available on the web at http://www.idoc.state.id.us/idcomm/profiles/index.html. These profiles are gold mines, plain and simple (see Figure 7). Each eight-page PDF file gives you statistics on population, housing, employment, local government revenues, income, business and farms, education, welfare rolls, crime rates, marriage and divorce, land ownership and utilization, motor vehicle registrations, and population trends for each of Idaho's counties. Some selected historical statistics are also provided in these profiles.

Idaho Vital Statistics Annual Report (Department of Health and Welfare)—Idaho Documents Call Number—H2500.16 VIT01. This annual publication is released in December in paper and on the Internet at http://www2.state.id.us/dhw/vital_stats/vsarmenu.html. The web site offers the *Vital Statistics Annual Report* from 1994 onwards, except for 1996 and 1997, for which sum-

COUNTY PROFILES OF IDAHO **Adams**

COUNTY SEAT: COUNCIL

I. PEOPLE

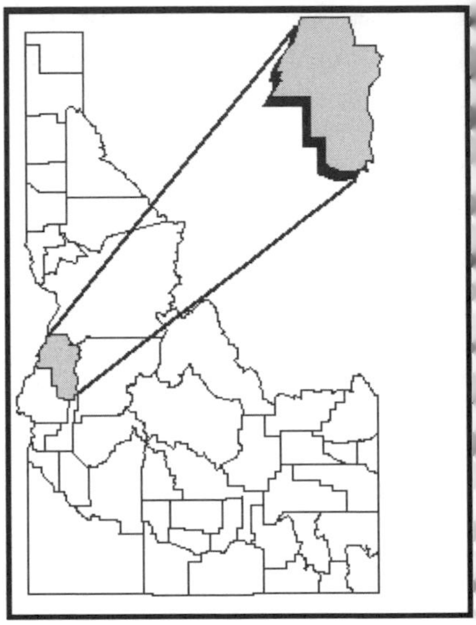

Population

	1970	1980	1990	2000
Total	2,877	3,347	3,254	3,476
Per sq. mi.	2.1	2.5	2.4	2.5

	70-80	80-90	90-00
Population Change (%)	16.3	-2.8	6.8

	1980	1990	2000
Percent Rural	100.0	100.0	100.0
Percent Urban	0.0	0.0	0.0

Demographic Component Changes

	1970-1980	1980-1990	1990-2000
Births	500	494	371
Deaths	200	264	312
Net Migration	200	-324	163
Percent Migration	6.7	-9.7	5.0

	1980	1990	1999
Birth Rate	15.8	15.4	6.9
Fertility Rate	85.5	77.9	37.4

	1980	1990	2000
Median Age	31.2	36.2	44.4
Under 18 Years (%)	31.6	28.4	23.9
18 to 64 Years (%)	56.0	57.0	60.0
65+ Years (%)	12.4	14.6	16.1
Persons Per Household	2.75	2.59	2.42

Geographic Mobility: 1990

Persons 5 Years and Older Living in a Different State in 1985 (%)	12.6
Persons 5 Years and Older Living in a Different County in 1985 (%)	13.4

Figure 7. This is the first page of the *County Profile* for Adams County from Idaho's Department o Commerce. *Source*: http://www.idoc.state.id.us/idcomm/profiles/pdfs/Adams.pdf.

mary data are given. Each annual report contains chapters on Population, Trends and Summary, Natality, Mortality, Induced Abortion, and Marriage and Divorce. Among the more interesting divorce statistics is the number of times a husband and wife have been married at the time of their latest divorce. Printed copies of the *Vital Statistics Annual Report* may be obtained by writing the Bureau of Vital Records and Health Statistics at Idaho Department of Health and Welfare, P.O. Box 83720, Boise, ID 83720-0036, or by calling (208) 334-5992; or you may e-mail your request to vitalstatistics@idhw.state.id.us.

Profiles: Idaho School Districts (Department of Education)—Idaho Documents Call Number—E2100.16 PRO01. This source provides statistics on all of Idaho's school districts. It is available on the web at http://www.sde.state.id.us/Dept/. Select "Statistical Data" from the menu. A paper version is available from the Department of Education, by writing 650 W. State Street, P.O. Box 83720, Boise, ID 83720-0027, or by calling (208) 332-6800.

Crime in Idaho (Idaho State Police, Bureau of Criminal Identification, Uniform Crime Reporting Unit)—Idaho Documents Call Number—L3000.25. This is an annual compilation of crime statistics statewide and by local jurisdiction. Each volume contains the following sections: Offense Profile, Crimes Against Persons, Crimes Against Property, Crimes Against Society, Arrest Profile, Hate Crime, Officers Assaulted, Agency Crime, Law Officers Employed. The section on "Agency Crime" is a report on all crimes reported and cleared by each Idaho law enforcement agency. All editions since 1999 are available on the web at http://www.isp.state.id.us/identification/ucr/crime_idaho.html. Paper copies may be requested by writing Idaho State Police, Uniform Crime Reporting Unit, P.O. Box 700, Meridian, ID 83680-0700, or by calling (208) 884-7155.

Other Resources

Starting a Business in Idaho: Idaho Works (Department of Commerce)—Idaho Documents Call Number—C6000.08 BUS01 years. This source tells you all you need to know about starting your own business in the state. This biennial publication walks you through the procedures and forms needed to comply with Idaho law. Notable features include sample business plans and a one-stop order form for state *and* federal forms, posters, and so on. This thirty-eight page booklet is available on the web at http://www.idoc.state.id.us/business/idahoworks/substartbusiness.htm. Paper copies can be requested by writing the Department of Commerce at 700 West State Street, P.O. Box 83720, Boise, ID 83720-0093, or by calling (800) 842-5858.

Idaho Blue Book (Secretary of State, Election Division)—Idaho Documents Call Number—S2000.25 year. Published annually in paper, this resource provides constitutional, historical, and statistical facts about Idaho. Copies may be ordered by writing to Secretary of State's Office, Attn: Marilyn Johnson, P.O. Box 83720, Boise, ID 83720-0080, or by calling (208) 334-2852. The cost of the *Blue Book* is $10.00 (postage and handling included). A few excerpts from the *Blue Book* are available on the web at http://www.idsos.state.id.us/elect/bluebook.htm. These excerpts include historical rosters of elected officials. This item is distributed free to all Idaho schools and libraries.

Inside Idaho: Interactive Numeric & Spatial Information (University of Idaho, Boise)—This is a library of digital geospatial and numeric data for the state of Idaho. The site allows access to a number of data sources in various formats that are housed in individual agencies and libraries around the state. Compiled at the University of Idaho under the direction of Lily Wai, it is available on the web at http://inside.uidaho.edu/.

IDAHO'S WORLD WIDE WEB HOME PAGE

The official web site of the State of Idaho is called *Access Idaho* and is found at http://www.accessidaho.org. *Access Idaho* lives up to its name and is definitely citizen-friendly. The left-hand side of the page has a menu with entries for: About Idaho; Education; Government; Health and Safety; Laws and Rules; Tourism and Transportation; and Working. Each of these options has a pop-up menu to directly access a subcategory. For example, "Education" has a subcategory "K–12 Schools."

On the right side of the screen are listed several "Top Picks." These include: Fish and Game, Idaho Maps, Motor Vehicles, Parks and Recreation, and Visit Idaho. The center of the screen offers direct links to the governor, legislature, and judiciary, as well as state government news headlines.

Another outstanding feature of *Access Idaho* is its search feature. Its main search page offers direct links to the most popular items in several categories. For example, under "Employment" is a link to an online job search database, and under "Legal" are links to "Constitution Search" and "Searchable *Idaho Code*." The screen also offers a search box that allows keyword searching.

Idaho's excellent web site is maintained by a private contractor called Idaho Information Consortium (IIC). It has been managing *Access Idaho* since December 1999. Although IIC has day-to-day management of the web site, the state of Idaho maintains oversight through the *Access Idaho* Committee, which oversees network operations, sets policies, and approves portal services. The seven-member committee is composed of state officials and the *Access Idaho* general manager. The webmaster may be contacted using a form at http://www.accessidaho.org/contact.html. Like much of the *Access Idaho* web site, this page contains helpful links like "Ask a Librarian" and "Idaho Law Search."

COMMERCIAL PUBLICATIONS AND WEB SITES

Directory of Idaho Foundations (Caldwell Public Library, Caldwell, ID)—This is a directory of Idaho endowment foundations.

Idaho Business Directory (American Directory Publishing Company, Omaha, NE)—This is a compilation of Idaho phone directory Yellow Pages. The publisher's toll-free phone number is (800) 555-6124; web address: http://www.directoriesUSA.com.

Idaho's Citizen's Guide: The Insider's Handbook to Getting Things Done in the Gem State (Ridenbaugh Press, 1429 Shenadoah Drive, Boise, ID 83712)—This guide covers contact information and "how-to" on politics, government, and the economy. The publisher's phone number is (208) 338-9700.

Idaho Place Names: A Geographical Dictionary (Lalia Phipps Boone) (University of Idaho Press, P.O. Box 1107, Moscow, ID 83844-1107)—This contains histories of Idaho place names. The publisher's toll-free phone number is (800) 847-7377.

Idaho Yearbook and Directory (Ridenbaugh Press, 1429 Shenadoah Drive, Boise, ID 83712)—This directory deals with libraries, government, recreation, and so on, in Idaho, and is a political almanac. The publisher's phone number is (208) 338-9700.

Roadside Geology of Idaho (David A. Alt) (Mountain Press Publishing Company, P.O. Box 2399, Missoula, MT 59806-2399)—This is a guide to interesting and unique geological features in the state which are either next to or near major highways. The publisher's toll-free phone number is (800) 234-5308.

SOURCES CONSULTED

Booksinprint.com. New Providence, NJ: R.R. Bowker, 2002.

Idaho State Publications home page, http://www.lili.org/isl/statedocs/.

Idaho Statutes 2000. Boise, ID: Idaho State Legislature, 2000. (Via the web at http://www3.state.id.us/idstat/TOC/idstTOC.html).

Numerous departmental web pages via the state's home page, http://www.accessidaho.org/.

Survey response from Danna Angevine, Idaho State Library, 2000.

Illinois

J. Louise Malcomb

GOVERNMENT PUBLISHING AND THE DEPOSITORY SYSTEM

In 1967, the General Assembly of Illinois passed legislation requiring each state agency to deposit copies of publications with the Illinois State Library for collection and exchange purposes. Documents received for the collection are published in paper, microform, maps, sound recordings, and electronically. According to 23 IAC 3020.100 of the *Illinois Administrative Code*, the Illinois state depository library program is an agreement between a library and the secretary of state, whereby the library agrees to make Illinois publications deposited in its collection available to citizens.

Publications are defined as "all forms of media, including microforms, recordings, and other printed material paid for in whole or in part by funds appropriated by the General Assembly or issued at the request of a state agency, excepting however, correspondence, interoffice memoranda and confidential publications." New rules adopted and effective January 1, 2003, 27 Ill. Reg. 209, update the definitions to include additional electronic information requiring state agencies to notify the State Library of electronic-only publications "by submitting the URL of the publication and metadata describing the publication." If the publication does not have a URL, the agency is to submit an electronic version to the State Library via FTP.

Depository libraries are designated according to 23 IAC 3020.200, which states that designation "shall be based on the institution's ability to provide access to the material to the public, the institution's interest in the publications of the State of Illinois, and the institution's geographic location." Depository libraries must make reference service available to all Illinois citizens, agree to catalog the materials, and retain documents for seven years. The Illinois State Library retains ownership of the documents and requires that depositories submit lists of unneeded documents so other depositories may review and select if needed. The Illinois State Library and other designated Reference and Research Centers, "shall keep all depository documents indefinitely, including ephemeral materials, except for superseded items." Depository libraries are routinely inspected to ensure that they are providing public access and adequately preserving the documents.

Twenty-six depository libraries have been designated in Illinois, with an additional thirty libraries receiving legislative materials on microfiche. A complete directory is available at http://www.cyberdriveillinois.com/library/isl/depos/dir_ill.html that provides basic information including hours, staff, and electronic access. Illinois Documents Depository Libraries are located at Augustana College (Rock Island, IL), Benedictine University (Lisle, IL), Bradley University (Peoria, IL), Chicago Public Library (Chicago, IL), Chicago State University (Chicago, IL), Eastern Illinois University (Charleston, IL), Governors State University (University Park, IL), Illinois State Library (Springfield, IL), Illinois State University (Normal, IL), Illinois Valley Community College (Oglesby, IL), Loyola University of Chicago (Chicago, IL), Northeastern Illinois University (Chicago, IL), Northern Illinois University (Dekalb, IL), Northwestern University Library (Evanston, IL), Poplar Creek Public Library (Streamwood, IL), Quincy Public Library (Quincy, IL), Rockford Public Library (Rockford, IL), Skokie Public Library (Skokie, IL), Southern Illinois University at Carbondale (Carbondale, IL), Southern Illinois University at Edwardsville (Edwardsville, IL), Southern Illinois University—Law (Carbondale, IL), University of Illinois at Chicago (Chicago, IL), University of Illinois at Springfield (Springfield, IL), University of Illinois at Urbana–Champaign (Urbana, IL), University of Illinois—Law (Champaign, IL), and Western Illinois University (Macomb, IL). Six other depositories are outside the state of Illinois: California, Colorado, District of Columbia, Kentucky, Massachusetts, and England.

USEFUL ADDRESSES AND TELEPHONE NUMBERS

The most complete collections of Illinois state documents can be found in the following libraries:

Illinois State Library
300 S. 2nd Street
Springfield, IL 62701-1796
(217) 785-5600
TDD (800) 655-5576
Phone Number for Illinois Reference Questions: (217) 782-7596; fax: (217) 524-0041
E-Mail Link for Illinois Reference Questions: http://www.cyberdriveillinois.com/library/forms/email_ref.html
State Library's Home Page: http://www.sos.state.il.us/library/isl/isl.html
Depository Program Home Page: http://www.sos.state.il.us/library/isl/depos/depos.html

Illinois State Archives
Norton Building
Capitol Complex
Springfield, IL 62756
Phone Number for Illinois Reference Questions: (217) 782-4682; fax: (217) 524-3930

State Archives Home Page: http://www.sos.state.il.us/departments/archives/
archives.html

University of Illinois at Urbana–Champaign
200-D Library
1408 W. Gregory
Urbana, IL 61801
Phone Number for Illinois Reference Questions: (217) 244-6445
E-Mail Link for Illinois Reference Questions: http://www.library.uiuc.edu/doc/email
-doc.asp
Government Documents Library Page: http://www.library.uiuc.edu/doc/illinois.htm

Legislative Reference Bureau
112 State House
Springfield, IL 62706
Phone Number for Illinois Reference Questions: (217) 782-6625
Legislative Reference Bureau Home Page: http://www.legis.state.il.us/commission/
lrb_home.html

INDEXES TO ILLINOIS STATE PUBLICATIONS

Since 1971, the Illinois Documents Center staff has compiled and issued the
Illinois Documents List, a monthly list of Illinois state documents. *Publications
of the State of Illinois* (Z1223.5.I3 P83) has been issued since 1961 (semi-annually
by the secretary of state, 1961–1970; triennially by the secretary of state and
State Librarian 1971–1974; by the Illinois State Library, 1975–1979; and by the
Library's Documents Section, 1980–1982 and annually since 1983). The latest
edition is available at http://www.cyberdriveillinois.com/library/isl/depos/
depos.html. It was preceded by *Illinois State Publications*, which was published
from 1950 to July 1960, and *Publications of the State of Illinois*, which was published from 1902 to 1950.

For historical documents, refer to John Moses' *Illinois, historical and statistical:
comprising the essential facts of its planting and growth as a province, county, territory, and state: derived from the most authentic sources, including original
documents and papers.* (Chicago: Fergus Printing Co., 1895.) Also refer to Bowker's *State Publications: a provisional list of the official publications of the several
states of the United States from their organization.* (New York: Office of the Publishers' Weekly, 1908.)

Abbreviated as IGI, the *Illinois Government Information* web site (Illinois Secretary of State and the Illinois State Library), http://199.15.3.6/Findit/start
.htm, provides access to Illinois state documents through the Internet, implementing the 1995 revision of the State Library Act. The site offers information
about its goals in the "What is IGI?" section. It states, in part, "Web-based
access to state documents is now required by law . . . IGI currently provides
access to State of Illinois Web pages. By offering word matching and subject
category browsing in the same search site, IGI will give patrons better results
in locating information." Through IGI, access to significant current and historic
government information, both state and local, is provided.

Descriptive Inventory of the Archives of the State of Illinois (Illinois State Archives, Second Edition, 1997) provides a description of the holdings of the Illinois State Archives that serves, by law, as the depository of public records of Illinois state and local governmental agencies. It is available on its web site at http://www.cyberdriveillinois.com/departments/archives/archives.html.

ESSENTIAL STATE PUBLICATIONS

Directories

Illinois Blue Book (Illinois Secretary of State)—This is published biennially and represents the primary reference source for information about Illinois state government. It contains biographical information about state officials; describes the function of each government agency including identification of staff; gives a historical overview of the state; lists counties and their officers; lists incorporated cities and villages; and lists state political parties, newspapers, radio and television stations, and cable television services. The *Blue Book* includes the text of the state and U.S. Constitutions. The 1999–2000 edition is available online at http://www.cyberdriveillinois.com/bb/toc.html.

Handbook of Illinois Government (Illinois Secretary of State)—This is a less detailed version of the *Illinois Blue Book*. The secretary of state maintains the gateway, the *CyberDriveIllinois* web site, http://www.cyberdriveillinois.com, where these publications may be ordered. See the "Publications" section of the site. *CyberDriveIllinois* also provides *Government Services Telephone Directory*, which lists phone numbers of the various state agencies and federal government toll-free numbers.

Financial/Budgetary Resources

Comprehensive Annual Financial Report (Illinois Office of the Comptroller, 1981–)—The CAFR is issued by the Office of the Comptroller, which makes it, as well as reports on appropriations and tax expenditures issued since 1999, available at http://www.ioc.state.il.us/Office/index.cfm.

Illinois State Budget (Illinois Office of the Governor, 1919/21–)—This contains detailed appropriations for funding state government programs and agencies. The latest edition is available online at http://www.state.il.us/budget/.

Quarterly Financial Report (Bureau of the Budget)—This report is available online at http://www.state.il.us/budget/.

Legal Resources

The Constitution of the State of Illinois (Illinois Legislative Reference Bureau)—Illinois' current Constitution was adopted at a special election on December 15, 1970. It is available online at http://www.legis.state.il.us/commission/lrb/conmain.htm, the web site of the Illinois Legislative Reference Bureau, whose primary responsibility is to draft and prepare legislation. The web site also provides information on researching legislative history and organization of Illinois law. For earlier editions of the Constitution, refer to the *Illinois Blue Book*, described above.

Legislation (Illinois General Assembly)—The full text and status of bills and resolutions within the Illinois General Assembly may be searched by selecting "Legislation—Status and Text" from the legislature's home page at http://www.legis.state.il.us/.

Laws of the State of Illinois and *Illinois Compiled Statutes* (Illinois General Assembly)—Both of these titles provide access to the laws of the state of Illinois. The online version of the Laws since 1999, *Public Acts*, is easily assessible from http://www.illinois.gov/government/gov_legislature.cfm, as is the *Illinois Compiled Statutes* (the codified edition). The web site is maintained by the Legislative Reference Bureau and also provides links to rules and General Assembly member biographies, journals, and schedules. These titles are also available on the General Assembly site at http://www.legis.state.il.us/.

Illinois Register (Secretary of State, Department of Index)—According to its web site, http://www.cyberdriveillinois.com/departments/index/division .html, the Administrative Code Division of the Department of Index "publishes proposed, adopted, emergency and other rulemaking activities weekly in the *Illinois Register*. A Cumulative Index and the Sections Affected Index are issued quarterly as a part of this publication. An annual subscription to the *Illinois Register* is $290." Department of Index, Springfield Office, 111 E. Monroe Street, Springfield, IL 62756, or call (217) 785-7538.

Illinois Administrative Code (Secretary of State, Department of Index)—Also published by the Department of Index's Administrative Code Division, the *Illinois Administrative Code* compiles regulations following their publication in the *Illinois Register*. The table of contents is available online at http://www .cyberdriveillinois.com/departments/index/division.html and specific sections may be ordered at fifty cents per page. The entire *Illinois Administrative Code* may be ordered on CD-ROM on an annual subscription for $290.00 per year. Department of Index, Springfield Office, 111 E. Monroe Street, Springfield, IL 62756, or call (217) 785-7538.

Illinois Reports (Illinois Supreme Court)—These are the official reports of the Illinois Supreme Court, which include a table of cases in each volume. Some Illinois Supreme Court documents are available online at http://www.state .il.us/court/Opinions/default.htm.

Illinois Appellate Court Reports (Illinois Courts)—This contains a syllabus of the cases and opinions of the court. Most information related to Illinois case law is available at http://www.state.il.us/court/Opinions/Search.htm. This includes the Illinois Supreme Court Rules, and the Illinois Supreme Court and Appellate Court Opinions. The Administrative Office of the Illinois Courts (AOIC) maintains a database of statistics and reports related to the courts at http://www.state.il.us/court/Administrative/default2.htm.

Statistical Resources

Illinois Statistical Abstract (University of Illinois, Bureau of Economic and Business Research, College of Commerce and Business Administration,

1973–)—Issued as the *State of Illinois Statistical Abstract* in 1973 by the bureau, the *Statistical Abstract* replaced *State of Illinois Statistical Report* (Office of Planning and Analysis: Department of Finance). It is the annual compilation of basic statistics about the state, including projections and some historical statistics. Most of the data are for the counties and cities of Illinois as well as state totals. Available for purchase from Office of Research, College of Commerce and Business Administration, University of Illinois at Urbana-Champaign, 430 Commerce W., 1206 S. Sixth Street, Champaign, IL 61820, or call (217) 333-2330; fax: (217) 333-7410. The price for the most recent edition in 2002: book $50.00; book and diskettes $90.00; book and CD-ROM $100.00; book, diskettes, and CD-ROM $125.00; plus $4.00 postage and handling (waived for prepaid orders).

Illinois Vital Statistics (Illinois Department of Public Health, 1900–)—This annual statistical volume gives detailed statistics on births, deaths, marriages, and divorces. Some historic information is provided. Many statistics are available online at http://www.idph.state.il.us/health/statshome.htm.

Illinois Agricultural Statistics (Illinois Cooperative Crop Reporting Service, 1953–)—Several editions of this report are available online at http://www.agstats.state.il.us/website/reports.htm.

Illinois Crash Facts and Statistics (Illinois Department of Transportation, 1991–)—The Illinois Department of Transportation web site, at http://www.dot.state.il.us/tpublic.html, also provides an interactive roadmap, information about all forms of transportation, and road conditions.

Other Resources

Illinois Place Names (Illinois State Historical Society)—This is available for $21.25 from ISHS, 210 1/2 South Sixth Street, Suite 200, Springfield, IL 62701, or call (217) 525-2781. For other works on the history of Illinois, consult the ISHS web site at http://www.historyillinois.org/.

Illinois Libraries (Illinois State Library)—While of most interest to library staff, occasional issues focus on the state and state government publications. See the State Library home page at http://www.sos.state.il.us/library/isl/isl.html for more information.

Illinois Outdoors Magazine (Illinois Department of Natural Resources)—This is a monthly magazine on state parks, scenic drives, outdoor recreation, and natural resources issues in Illinois. It is available from the Department at 524 South Second, 5th Floor, Springfield, IL 62701, or call (800) 720-3249 toll-free in Illinois, (217) 782-7454, and the TTY# (217) 782-9175. An index of articles is available at the web site, http://dnr.state.il.us/OI/index.htm.

Environmental Progress (Illinois Environmental Protection Agency)—Available from 1021 North Grand Avenue East, Springfield, IL 62702, or call (217) 557-9069, this quarterly magazine reports on various environmental issues within Illinois. The Illinois EPA web site, http://www.epa.state.il.us/forms-publications.html, provides access to various other publications of interest in the field of the environment.

ILLINOIS' WORLD WIDE WEB HOME PAGE

Illinois Government (Illinois Technology Office)—Illinois' official state government web site is located at http://www100.state.il.us/government/. It is the "State Government" link from *Illinois First*, the portal to state information at http://www100.state.il.us/ilfirst/Illinois%20First.cfm. *Illinois Government* includes subject links to business, learning, and technology as well as links to city, county, and federal government sites. It includes a search engine and the official privacy policy statement. *Illinois Government* provides an excellent gateway to state agency web sites, the state legislature, and the state government employee directory. It links to *Illinois Gallery*, a cutting-edge web site that gives webcams, video postcards, and a virtual tour of the governor's mansion in both an HTML and a Flash version. *Illinois Gallery* also gives quick links to state parks, the Department of Natural Resources, and other tourist-oriented web sites.

COMMERCIAL PUBLICATIONS AND WEB SITES

Smith-Hurd Illinois Statutes (St. Paul, MN: West Publishing Co., 1992)—This set compiles the laws of Illinois by subject.

West's Illinois Digest (St. Paul, MN: West Publishing Co., 1992)—This digest serves as an index to Illinois Supreme Court and Appellate Court cases, covers cases decided since 1938, and is kept up-to-date with pocket parts and re-placements volumes.

More information about both titles above can be found on the Publisher's web site at http://west.thomson.com/store/.

SOURCES CONSULTED

Dow, Susan L. *State Document Checklists: A Historical Bibliography*. Buffalo, NY: William S. Hein & Co., 1990.

Lane, Margaret T. *State Publications and Depository Libraries: A Reference Handbook*. Westport, CT: Greenwood Press, 1981.

Manz, William H. *Guide to State Legislative and Administrative Materials*. Littleton, CO: Fred B. Rothman Publications, 2000.

Parrish, David W. *State Government Reference Publications: An Annotated Bibliography*, 2nd ed. Littleton, CO: Libraries Unlimited, 1981.

State Capital Universe. Bethesda, MD: LexisNexis, 2001; http://web.lexis-nexis.com/stcapuniv, September 10, 2001. (Available to subscribers only.)

Statistical Universe. Bethesda, MD: LexisNexis, 2001; http://web.lexis-nexis.com/statuniv. September 10, 2001. (Available to subscribers only.)

U.S. Census Bureau. *Statistical Abstract, 2000 Edition*. "Appendix 1: Guide to State Statistical Abstracts," December 4, 2001; http://www.census.gov.

Wendt, Laurel. *Illinois Legal Research Manual*. St. Paul, MN: Butterworth Legal Publishers, 1988.

WorldCat. Columbus, OH: OCLC; http://www.oclc.com, October 4, 2001. (Available to subscribers only.)

Indiana

J. Louise Malcomb

GOVERNMENT PUBLISHING AND THE DEPOSITORY SYSTEM

The Indiana General Assembly established the Indiana Document Depository Program with the passage of Public Law 27 in 1973. Bryan Swanson gave an excellent description of the history of the program in his article "Indiana State Documents: A History and a Critique" for *Indiana Libraries*, Volume 6, Number 1 (1986). "The basic framework of the depository program is based on the Indiana state agencies providing the State Library with two to fifty copies of publications. The State Library keeps two copies for its collections and distributes the others to secondary depository libraries." The documents, intended for distribution through the depository system, according to IC-4-23-7.1-26 of the *Indiana Code*, are publications of agencies "whether printed, mimeographed, or duplicated by them in any way, which are not issued solely for use within the issuing office." In subsequent sections of the law, specific documents, such as those of university presses, are excluded from the depository system. Agencies are required to submit only two copies of the types of publications that are exempted from distribution to the secondary depositories.

Section IC 4-23-7.1-25 of the *Indiana Code* says that the State Library's "collection shall be the official file of Indiana state documents." The Library of Congress and the four state university libraries are designated depositories as are other public and college libraries selected geographically by the State Library to receive copies of "documents that are of general interest." There are currently twelve depository libraries, in addition to the Library of Congress and the State Library. They are located in Bloomington, Columbus, Evansville, Fort Wayne, Kokomo, Muncie, New Albany, Richmond, South Bend, Terre Haute, Valparaiso, and West Lafayette.

The State Library is required to publish the *Checklist of Indiana State Documents* and to distribute it to interested libraries and institutions. Secondary depository libraries make the documents available to the public within their area and provide reference and interlibrary loan services. The law also requires the State Library to establish exchange programs with other states to acquire selected documents. For specifics, refer to the depository law, IC 4-23-7.1, at http://www.state.in.us/legislative/ic/code/title4/ar23/ch7.1.html or the regulations in the *Indiana Administrative Code*, 590 IAC 1-32-1 et seq., at http://www.state.in.us/legislative/iac/title590.html.

USEFUL ADDRESSES AND TELEPHONE NUMBERS

The most complete collections of Indiana state publications may be found at the following libraries:

Indiana Division, Indiana State Library
140 North Senate Avenue
Indianapolis, IN 46204
Phone Number for Indiana Reference Questions: (317) 232-3670
E-Mail Link for Indiana Reference Questions: http://www.statelib.lib.in.us/www/
    isl/ask/index.html
Indiana Division Web Site: http://www.statelib.lib.in.us/www/isl/whoweare/
    indiana.html
State Library's Home Page: http://www.statelib.lib.in.us/

Indiana University–Bloomington, Government Publications Department
C264 IUB Main Library
1320 E. 10th Street
Bloomington, IN 47405
Phone Number for Indiana Reference Questions: (812) 855-6924
Government Publications Department Home Page: http://www.indiana.edu/~libgpd

Those with questions about the state's depository library system may contact the State Documents Coordinator at (317) 232-5083. Address and web site information are listed above.

INDEXES TO INDIANA STATE PUBLICATIONS

The Indiana Division of the Indiana State Library prepares the *State Documents Checklist Database*, which provides a listing of state documents received at the Indiana State Library since 1996. It is available on the web at http://www.statelib.lib.in.us/www/isl/indiana/statedocs.html. Documents may be searched by Agency, Title, Subagency, Subject, OCLC Control Number, or ISL Location Call number.

The *Checklist of Indiana State Documents*, issued by the Indiana State Library between 1973 and 1995, preceded the database. The web site provides access to the *Checklist* for years between 1990 and 1995. The State Library included a list of state documents in its periodical, *Library Occurrent*, between 1906 and 1973. For earlier bibliographies of state documents, consult http://www.indiana.edu/~libgpd/findingindiana.html, which lists indexes from when Indiana was established as a Territory in 1800.

ESSENTIAL STATE PUBLICATIONS

Directories

Biographical Directory of the Indiana General Assembly, 1816–1984 (Indiana Historical Bureau; Committee on the Centennial History of the Indiana General Assembly)—Two agencies worked cooperatively to publish this two-volume set. It provides basic biographies for all who have served in the Indiana General Assembly since statehood.

Indiana School Directory (Indiana Department of Education)—This Directory is available on the Department of Education web site at http://www.doe .state.in.us/. It lists education-related state agencies, special schools and programs, institutions of higher education, vocational-technical schools, and public and non-public schools. Maps of state House and Senate districts and graphs of a variety of statistical information are also included.

Roster of State and Local Officials of the State of Indiana (State Board of Accounts)—Issued since 1857 by various agencies, the *Roster* serves as the official state directory. It provides names, addresses, and phone numbers for officials in departments at state, county, and city level, including county commissioners and city mayors. Several recent issues are available online at http://www.in.gov/sboa/publications/roster/.

State Agency Phonebook (Indiana State Information Center)—This source is available on the web at http://www.in.gov/sic/phonebook/index.html. It provides a list of toll-free numbers for agencies and a searchable database of phone numbers for state agency employees. Numbers can be searched by agency, or by the name of the individual being sought. A phone number can even be entered and searched to find the name and department of the person to whom it belongs.

Financial/Budgetary Resources

Budget Documents (General Assembly; Budget Agency; Governor)—The Indiana General Assembly establishes the state budget biennially. Indiana's Budget Agency oversees the publication of the state's budget documents, including the *Budget* (as submitted by the governor), *List of Appropriations* (as passed by the General Assembly), and *Revenue Forecast*. Titles and exact content have varied but budget documents have been issued since the 1940s. The Budget Agency's web site provides current budget documents, plus some historical information and related documents: http://www.in.gov/sba/.

Comprehensive Annual Financial Report (Indiana Auditor of the State)—The *Report*, issued since 1989, gives an overview of the state's financial situation. The Introductory Section provides the state's organization chart and a list of auditors of the state. The Financial Section reports the revenues, expenditures, and balance sheet. The Statistical Section provides a variety of current as well as historical data such as per capita income, taxable income, governmental revenues, largest Indiana public and private companies, property tax schedules, assessed value of property, and county facts. The "Publications" section of the State Auditor's web site, http://www.in.gov/auditor/publications/, provides copies of the report for the past several years.

Indiana Handbook of Taxes, Revenues and Appropriations (Legislative Services Agency, Office of Fiscal and Management Analysis)—This small volume reviews the tax structure for the state and local areas and includes a revenue summary. It is available in print from the Legislative Services Agency, Legislative Information Center, 200 W. Washington Street, Suite 301, Indianapolis, IN 46204-2789, or call (317) 232-9856. Requests can be made via e-mail to Webmaster@iga.state.in.us. It is available on the web at http://www.in.gov/legislative/publications/.

Legal Resources

Acts of the State of Indiana (Indiana General Assembly)—This publication is similar to the federal *United States Statutes at Large*. It includes the text of all acts as passed each year. The acts are printed in numerical order representing the order in which they are passed by the General Assembly. *BillWatch* permits users to track legislation through the current session of the Indiana General Assembly. It is, however, an exclusive service of *accessIndiana*, and therefore users must subscribe at http://www.in.gov/billwatch/.

Constitution of the State of Indiana (Indiana Legislative Services Agency)—Indiana's first Constitution, 1816, is available from the Indiana Historical Bureau site at http://www.statelib.lib.in.us/www/ihb/resources/constitutions.html. It was revised in 1850, ratified August 4, 1851, becoming effective November 1, 1851. According to *Here's Your Indiana Government*, it is the "seventh oldest and third shortest among the 50 states." With revisions, the Constitution is available from the Indiana Legislative Services Agency or at http://www.in.gov/legislative/ic_iac/. The Constitution outlines the basic structure of state and local governments in Indiana. It is composed of the following Articles: 1. Preamble, 2. Suffrage and Election, 3. Distribution of Powers, 4. Legislative, 5. Executive, 6. Administrative, 7. Judicial, 8. Education, 9. State Institutions, 10. Finance, 11. Corporations, 12. Militia, 13. Indebtedness, 14. Boundaries, 15. Miscellaneous, and 16. Amendments. A comprehensive summary of amendments and an index are also included.

Indiana Administrative Code (IAC) (Indiana General Assembly)—The *IAC* includes all the rules that have been officially adopted by state agencies. As the U.S. government's *Code of Federal Regulations* is updated with the *Federal Register*, the *IAC* is updated with the *Indiana Register* (see below). Titles within *IAC* are assigned numbers between 10 and 930. *IAC* is available on the Indiana General Assembly web site at http://www.in.gov/legislative/iac/.

Indiana Code (Office of Code Revision, Indiana Legislative Services Agency)—This is the codified version of the acts. The *Code* is available on the web at http://www.in.gov/legislative/ic/code/.

Indiana Register (Indiana General Assembly)—Published monthly, the *Register* reports the proposed and final rules being adopted by state regulatory agencies. The *Indiana Register* includes the following sections: State Agency List, Final Rules, Recall Notice, Emergency Rules, Executive Orders/Proclamations, Nonrule Policy Documents, Cumulative Table of Nonrule Policy

Documents, Cumulative Table of Executive Orders and Attorney General's Opinions, Rules Affected, Index, and Order Form. Recent issues are available online but with a disclaimer: "These documents were created from the files used to produce the official (printed) Indiana Register, however, these documents are unofficial." See http://www.in.gov/legislative/ic_iac/.

Statistical Resources

Education in Indiana: Facts and Statistics (Department of Education)—This new publication provides quick facts about the state of Indiana's education. It, along with easily accessed statistics for school districts and numerous other publications, is now available on *Ideanet*, the Indiana Department of Education's web site, which provides an interface for searching by students, teachers, and parents. See http://www.doe.state.in.us/publications/welcome.html.

Election Report, State of Indiana (Secretary of State, State Election Division)— Election results are maintained and reported by the Secretary of State Election Division and overseen by the Indiana Election commission. Recent results are available at the commission's web site at http://www.in.gov/sos/elections/.

Highlights (Department of Workforce Development)—A separate volume is issued for each county that provides statistics on employment, wages, and population. Recent statistics are also posted on the agency's web site at http://www.in.gov/dwd/lmi/index.html, along with information for job seekers and employers.

Indiana Natality/Induced Termination of Pregnancy/Marriage Report [New Combined Report] and *Indiana Mortality Report* (Department of Health)—Compiled and issued annually, this report provides statistics on births, deaths, marriages, and divorces. It includes a summary of vital events, such as the age of the oldest bride who was married and the weight of the largest baby who was born during the year. There is a section of general population information, and separate sections on live births, spontaneous fetal deaths, abortions, deaths, infant and maternal mortality, and marriage and divorce. A section of statistics at the end of the report focuses on progress made toward meeting the goals outlined in *Healthy People 2000*. Indiana's Department of Health also publishes the *Indiana Health Behavior Risk Factors*. These publications are generally available in print from the agency: Two N. Meridian Street, Indianapolis, IN 46204. Some are also available on the web at http://www.in.gov/isdh/.

Other Resources

Indiana Official Highway Map (Department of Transportation)—This is published annually. Call (800) 261-9144 to request a copy, or request one online at http://www.in.gov/dot/pubs/.

Outdoor Indiana (Department of Natural Resources)—This glossy magazine is published bi-monthly to assist in fulfilling the department's mission "to protect, enhance, preserve, and wisely use natural, cultural, and recreational resources for the benefit of Indiana's citizens through professional leadership, management, and education." Articles focus on the state's recreation, history, hunting, fishing, and environmental topics. For more information, see the "Publications" section of the DNR web site at http://www.in.gov/dnr/publications/.

Recreation Guide (Department of Natural Resources)—Issued annually, the *Guide* describes the different activities and scenic sites available in each area of the state. Call (800) 677-4082 to request a copy, or request one online at http://www.in.gov/dnr/.

State of the Environment (Indiana Department of Environmental Management)—Published annually, this report gives an overview of Indiana's environment, including water, air, chemicals, and land. Along with other statistical reports and fact sheets, copies of the report from 1998 to date are available on the IDEM web site at http://www.in.gov/idem/publications/.

Statewide Comprehensive Outdoor Recreation Plan: SCORP 2000–2004 A New Millennium, A New Tradition (Department of Natural Resources, Natural Resources Commission)—Federally mandated, *SCORP* is produced every five years to assist recreation providers and users. *SCORP 2000–2004* contains information about the status of outdoor recreation in Indiana and establishes priorities for recreation grant programs administered by the Indiana Department of Natural Resources, Division of Outdoor Recreation. *SCORP 2000–2004* also includes the Indiana trails plan, the *DNR Resources Manual*, and the *Environmental Yellow Pages*, available from DNR or online at http://www.in.gov/dnr/outdoor/planning/scorp/.

INDIANA'S WORLD WIDE WEB HOME PAGE

Access Indiana, http://www.state.in.us/, is an excellent source of information that provides links to pages for the governor, the lieutenant governor, the legislature, the judiciary, all state departments, and local governments. There are also direct links from *Access Indiana* to pages on tourism, business, education, jobs, government services, state employee information, and general information about the state. A site map is available, as is a search feature that allows one to perform a keyword search of all pages on the site. *Access Indiana* is maintained by a private web firm through a contract with the state of Indiana. Several agencies elect to maintain their own sites, so there is some difference in the functionality of various pages. Some of the most popular links are to the State Lottery Commission's web site, the *Driver License Manual* at the Bureau of Motor Vehicles, and the DNR pages noted above.

COMMERCIAL PUBLICATIONS AND WEB SITES

Burns Indiana Statutes Annotated, Revised Statutes (Charlottesville, VA: LexisNexis/Michie Co.)—This is the official edition of the *Revised Statues*. It contains the codified version of Indiana's laws, and is similar to the federal *United States Code*. More information can be found on the publisher's web site at http://bookstore.lexis.com/bookstore/catalog.

Here Is Your Indiana Government (Indianapolis: Indiana State Chamber of Commerce)—This source serves as an unofficial "government manual," providing a descriptive overview of state and local government, basic facts, lists of governors and symbols. It may be ordered online at http://www .indianachamber.com/publications.asp.

Indiana Factbook (Bloomington: Division of Research, Indiana University School of Business)—This title is issued irregularly, with the latest edition dated 1999. Like its federal counterpart, the *Statistical Abstract of the United States*, this source presents statistical information gathered by numerous agencies. *STATS Indiana*, http://www.stats.indiana.edu/, gives the most recent information in an interactive environment. There is emphasis on population and economic data.

The Indiana General Assembly Legislative Directory (Indianapolis: Indiana State Chamber of Commerce)—This directory provides a complete listing of General Assembly members with photographs, seating charts, and short biographies. It has been issued since 1943 and is available for purchase for $5.00. It may be ordered via the chamber's web site at http://www.indianachamber .com/publications.asp.

SOURCES CONSULTED

Constitution of the State of Indiana. Indianapolis: Indiana Legislative Services Agency, December 2000; http://www.in.gov/legislative/ic/code/const/, June 6, 2001.

Dow, Susan L. *State Document Checklists: A Historical Bibliography*. Buffalo, NY: William S. Hein & Co., 1990.

Here's Your Indiana Government. Indianapolis: Indiana State Chamber of Commerce, 2001.

Lane, Margaret T. *State Publications and Depository Libraries: A Reference Handbook*. Westport, CT: Greenwood Press, 1981.

Numerous departmental web pages via *Access Indiana*, http://www.state.in.us/.

Parrish, David W. *State Government Reference Publications: An Annotated Bibliography*, 2nd ed. Littleton, CO: Libraries Unlimited, 1981.

State Documents Checklist Database. Indianapolis: Indiana State Library, 1996–; http://www.statelib.lib.in.us/www/isl/indiana/statedocs.html, June 11, 2001.

Statistical Universe. Bethesda, MD: LexisNexis, 2001; http://web.lexis-nexis.com/statuniv, June 6, 2001. (Available to subscribers only.)

Iowa

J. Louise Malcomb

GOVERNMENT PUBLISHING AND THE DEPOSITORY SYSTEM

The public documents depository system was established by the 1978 act, "An act to the establishment of a depository center within the Iowa library department," by the Iowa Assembly. The original regulations, defined in *Iowa Annotated Code* 303A.21 to 303A.24, state that a depository library center would be created and the State Librarian would appoint a depository librarian. The depository system would have its own classification scheme for state publications. Later, *Iowa Administrative Code* 560 IAC 1.12 further explained the administration of the depository program. The depository library center would be the central agency for the collection and distribution of state publications to depository libraries. State agencies were required to provide seventy-five copies of their publications at no cost to the depository center for distribution.

The legislation defines state publications as "all multiply produced publications of state agencies regardless of format which are supported by public funds, except correspondence and memoranda intended solely for internal use within the agency or between agencies, and materials designated by law as being confidential" (560 IAC-1.12(2)).

Specifically noted in the *Code* to act as permanent depositories are the State Library and the University of Iowa Library, but other libraries can be added. Depository libraries are selected according to geographic location, federal depository status, and ability to successfully manage a collection. Depositories are required to hold publications for three years and to make documents freely available to the public. The withdrawal method from the program is described in the *Code*. There are currently forty-five depository libraries in Iowa including the two permanent sites.

The State Library of Iowa does not maintain collections of local Iowan historical information. Patrons are directed to the State Historical Society of Iowa library to obtain materials on genealogy, county and city histories, historical census records, newspapers, photographs, and manuscripts.

USEFUL ADDRESSES AND TELEPHONE NUMBERS

The most complete collections of Iowa state documents can be found in the following libraries:

State Library of Iowa
State Documents Center
1112 East Grand Avenue
Des Moines, IA 50319
Phone Number for Iowa Reference Questions: (515) 281-4102
E-Mail Link for Iowa Reference Questions: http://www.silo.lib.ia.us/for-state-govt/
  reference-questions/index.html
Library Home Page: http://www.silo.lib.ia.us/
State Documents Center Home Page: http://www.silo.lib.ia.us/for-state-govt/state
  -documents-center/index.html

University of Iowa Library
100 Main Library
Iowa City, IA 52242-1420
Phone Number for Iowa Reference Questions: (319) 335-5927
E-Mail Address for Iowa Reference Questions: lib-govpub@uiowa.edu
Government Publications Department Home Page: http://www.lib.uiowa.edu/
  govpubs/index.html

Questions about the Iowa depository program can be directed to the State Library at (515) 281-4352 or at the address given above.

INDEXES TO IOWA STATE PUBLICATIONS

According to the *Iowa Annotated Code* and regulations in the *Iowa Administrative Code*, the depository library center is required to compile a core list of Iowa state documents that is defined in section 1.12(10) as "a selected list intended to meet the basic document needs of libraries." The list is currently known as the *Core Documents List*. This list is published in a print format but it is now available at the Iowa State Library web site at http://www.silo .lib.ia.us/for-state-govt/state-documents-center/index.html. This publication lists the document numbers and titles of the core documents, the retention period, and in many cases also provides a link directly to the online versions.

The list of official state publications has changed format and name over the years. A *Checklist of Iowa State Documents (1938–1955)* was published in 1977. The next incarnation was titled *Iowa Documents*, published 1956–1979 by the University of Iowa Libraries. In 1979, the State Documents Center took over the publication. These publications represent the holdings of the State Library and the University of Iowa Library.

Using a variety of bibliographies by various agencies and individuals, Helen Stewart compiled *Iowa State Publications* as a cumulative listing for 1838–1937 as her L.S. Thesis in 1937 at the Graduate School of Library Science at the University of Illinois. For specific lists published prior to that time, consult the references in Dow's *State Document Checklists: A Historical Bibliography*.

Additionally, Bowker's *State Publications: A Provisional List of the Official Publications of the Several States of the United States from their Organization* can be consulted for historical publications, pages 301–312.

ESSENTIAL STATE PUBLICATIONS

Directories

Iowa Official Register (Iowa Secretary of State)—Produced annually since 1886, the *Iowa Official Register* provides a thorough overview of the state's government officials, agencies, and their responsibilities, including photographs and charts. It is indexed, and produced in print, in limited supply, by the office of the secretary of state. The *Register* is available online at http://www.sos.state.ia.us under "Publications" and is referred to as the "Redbook."

Iowa Official Directory of State and County Officers (Iowa Secretary of State)—Issued biennially, this lists state officers, U.S. senators and representatives, judges of the Supreme Court and the Court of Appeals, and county officers.

Official Directory of the Legislature, State of Iowa (Iowa Secretary of State)—Issued annually since 1980, the current edition is available through the web site at http://www.legis.state.ia.us/Members/79GA-members.html.

Iowa Educational Directory (Iowa Department of Education, Division of Financial and Information Services)—Providing information about the educational institutions, agencies, and organizations in the state as well as state licensing requirements, the directory is available both in a print format and online at http://www.state.ia.us/educate/directory.html. The online format has information in both HTML and PDF formats and allows the user to build custom reports of selected information. The print version of this directory can be ordered from the Iowa Department of General Services, Hoover Building, Level A, 1305 East Walnut, Des Moines, IA 50319, for $8.48. Prepayment is required.

DNR Program Directory (Iowa Department of Natural Resources)—Available online at http://www.iowadnr.com/, this directory provides an excellent overview of the state's natural resources including recreational and environmental resources. It provides telephone, fax, and other contact information about all programs. It is available free while supplies last from the department at Wallace State Office Building, 900 E. Grand Avenue, Des Moines, IA 50319-0034.

Directory of Services (Iowa Department of Public Health, Division of Health Promotion, Prevention and Addictive Behavior)—This directory provides information about agencies that work in substance abuse or gambling treatment and prevention. This online database, http://www.drugfreeinfo.org/lasso/srchdir.html, can be searched by agency name or location and allows limiting by type of service or type of patient. The directory lists the name, phone number, and address of each agency.

Financial/Budgetary Resources

Budget Report (Department of Management)—Iowa's budget has been available in print since 1917. It provides an overview of the state's budget that is arranged primarily by department. The Department of Management also publishes the *Budget Summary* on its web site at http://www.dom.state.ia.us/state/budget_proposals/index.html. Both of these documents include the governor's recommendations for spending by agency.

Comprehensive Annual Financial Report for the Fiscal Year Ended June 30, [Year] (Iowa Department of Revenue and Finance)—Copies of this annual publication are available at no cost while supplies last from its issuing agency, the Iowa Department of Revenue and Finance, Financial Management Division, located at Hoover State Office Building, 1305 E. Walnut Street, Des Moines, IA 50319. Several recent editions are available online on the "Publications and Classes" page at http://www.state.ia.us/tax/educate/educate.html; select "Statistical Reports."

Salary Book: List of Employees of the State of Iowa (Iowa Department of General Services)—Published annually, the *Salary Book* is available in print format (Call Number 17 G326P 5:S162) and online at http://www.dmregister.com/extras/salary. The paper version has been available since 1937 while the online version provides information only for the most recent year available. The publication contains the name, gender, county or city of residence, official title, and salary of the official. It is searchable online.

Legal Resources

1857 Constitution of the State of Iowa (Iowa Secretary of State)—The last print edition of the Constitution appears to be 1991. It is also available online, with all amendments passed previously to 1998, at http://www.legis.state.ia.us/Constitution.html. This site is sponsored by the General Assembly and provides the Constitution in a form that is easy to access. The Constitution has the following articles: I. Bill of Rights, II. Right of Suffrage, III. Of the Distribution of Powers, IV. Executive Department, V. Judicial Department, VI. Militia, VII. State Debts, VIII. Corporations, IX. Education and School Lands, X. Amendments to the Constitution, XI. Miscellaneous, and XII. Schedule.

Code of Iowa (Iowa General Assembly)—Published annually, the *Code* is available full-text online in HTML format at http://www.legis.state.ia.us/IowaLaw.html. The 1995, 1997, and 1999 editions are available with all supplements and amendments merged with the 2001 edition partially available at this writing. This can be searched for a particular chapter and section or browsed by table of contents. The 1999 and 2001 editions of the *Code of Iowa* are also available as hardbound volumes from the Legislative Service Bureau, Attn: Stephanie Cox, State Capitol, Des Moines, IA 50319. An order form can be printed from the web site mentioned above.

Iowa Court Rules and Supplements (Iowa Legislative Service Bureau)—It can be purchased in print format (Call Number 17 A39:C862) or on CD-ROM from the Legislative Service Bureau, or can be downloaded in PDF format from http://www.legis.state.ia.us/Rules2.html. The publication includes information about the reorganization of the Iowa courts, rules for the different types of courts, and information about court security and conduct. To order copies write to Legislative Service Bureau, Attn: Stephanie Cox, State Capitol, Des

Moines, IA 50319. An order form can be printed from the web site mentioned above.

Statistical Resources

Iowa Crash Facts: A Summary of Motor Vehicle Crash Statistics on Iowa Roadways (Iowa Department of Transportation, Motor Vehicle Division)—Issued annually, this report provides a statistical analysis on highway safety and accidents. The report is Internet-only, but for additional information contact the Iowa Department of Transportation, Motor Vehicle Division, Driver Services Office, Park Fair Mall, 100 Euclid, P.O. Box 9204, Des Moines, IA 50306-9204. See http://www.dot.state.ia.us/mvd/ods/index.htm.

Vital Statistics of Iowa (Iowa Department of Public Health)—Issued under various titles over the years, this report provides statistics on births, deaths, and marriages by county and city for Iowa. The print report costs $5.00 from the Iowa Department of Public Health, State Center for Health Statistics, 321 East 12th, Des Moines, IA 50319-0075. For other reports on health-related issues, including the state's legislatively mandated reports, see the department's web site at http://www.idph.state.ia.us/admin/health_statistics.asp.

Iowa Election Results (Iowa Secretary of State)—This biennial publication of the Iowa Office of the Secretary of State, Elections Division is now provided only online at http://www.sos.state.ia.us/. Earlier editions were issued in print. Some election statistics are provided in the *Iowa Official Register* (or Redbook) but because of printing costs, these are now limited.

Iowa Agricultural Statistics (Iowa Department of Agriculture and Land Stewardship)—Critical for tracing the overall impact of agriculture on the state's economy and development, this annual report is issued by the Department of Agriculture and Land Stewardship. Print copies may be purchased for $10.00 from the Iowa Agricultural Statistics, 210 Walnut Street, Room 833, Des Moines, IA 50309-2195. For current statistics, directories of agricultural markets, and related information, consult the department's web site at http://www.agriculture.state.ia.us/.

Other Resources

Iowa Conservationist Magazine (Iowa Department of Natural Resources)—Subscribe at the DNR's Publications web site for the following costs: 1 year (6 issues) $12.00, 2 years (12 issues) $18.00, or 3 years (18 issues) $24.00. See http://www.iowadnr.com/pub.html. The web site also lists other publications such as *Bats of Iowa, Statewide Comprehensive Outdoor Recreation Plan, Forest Resources Fact Book, Iowa Fishing Guide*, and many more.

IOWA'S WORLD WIDE WEB HOME PAGE

The Iowa state official web site can be accessed through two different addresses: http://www.state.ia.us, or http://www.iowaccess.org. Links to the governor, lieutenant governor, the Assembly, and county and city governments are listed. The site organizes the links to the various agencies both by subject and alphabetically and provides access to information about moving to Iowa, finding a job, or tourism. Online services such as tax forms, paying parking tickets, and the sex offender registry are accessible online. Translations of the site are available in a variety of languages and a site map and search engine allow easy access to information. The site is maintained by the state's Information Technology Department, a group that facilitates information flow for all state agencies.

COMMERCIAL PUBLICATIONS AND WEB SITES

State Government in Iowa (Iowa City: University of Iowa, Institute of Public Affairs)—This guide to Iowa state government was produced by Brian Carter. The latest edition seems to be 1990. For more information write to the Institute at 100 Oakdale, Campus #N310 OH, Iowa City, IA 52242-5000, or call (319) 335-4520.

Iowa Atlas and Gazetteer (Yarmouth, ME: DeLorme)—This print map resource provides not only maps but also sections about places to visit and things to do in the state. The map section is fifty-one pages of highway maps, topographical maps, and GPS grid maps. The Gazetteer section includes rivers, lakes, covered bridges, camping areas, geological features, scenic drives, and historic homes. For more information see the publisher's web site at http://www.delorme.com/.

The State Historical Society of Iowa is an organization that fills a need in the library system in Iowa. The society maintains two libraries, one in Des Moines and the other in Iowa City. Information about library services and collections can be accessed on the web site http://www.iowahistory.org/library/index.html. These research library collections include books, periodicals, community newspapers, census materials dating back to 1840, archives, photographs, original manuscripts, and maps. Unfortunately, these collection catalogs are not available on the Internet, but the library does provide reference help by telephone and e-mail. In Des Moines call (515) 281-6200, and in Iowa City call (319) 335-3916.

SOURCES CONSULTED

Dow, Susan L. *State Document Checklists: A Historical Bibliography*. Buffalo, NY: William S. Hein & Co., 1990.

"Guides to Government Information." University of Iowa Library, Government Publication Department, http://www.lib.uiowa.edu/govpubs/guides.htm.

Lane, Margaret T. *State Publications and Depository Libraries: A Reference Handbook*. Westport, CT: Greenwood Press, 1981.

Parrish, David W. *State Government Reference Publications: An Annotated Bibliography*, 2nd ed. Littleton, CO: Libraries Unlimited, 1981.

Peters, John. A. "Government Publications: Only a Library Away." *Wisconsin Library Bulletin* (Fall 1983): 108–109.

State Capital Universe. Bethesda, MD: LexisNexis, 2001; http://web.lexis-nexis.com/stcapuniv, December 5, 2001. (Available to subscribers only.)

State Document Center Web site, http://www.silo.lib.ia.us/stdocsctr/statedocshome page.htm.

State Historical Society of Iowa Library Web site, http://www.iowahistory.org/#SHSI.

State of Iowa Official Home page, http://www.iowaccess.org.

Statistical Universe. Bethesda, MD: LexisNexis, 2001; http://web.lexis-nexis.com/stat univ, December 5, 2001. (Available to subscribers only.)

U.S. Census Bureau. "Appendix 1: Guide to State Statistical Abstracts." *Statistical Abstract of the United States 2000.* Washington, DC: Department of Commerce, 2000, 902–905.

WorldCat. Columbus, OH: OCLC; http://www.oclc.com, December 4, 2001. (Available to subscribers only.)

Kansas

Daniel C. Barkley

GOVERNMENT PUBLISHING AND THE DEPOSITORY SYSTEM

The Kansas state depository system was established in 1976 under *Kansas Statutes* (KS) 75-2566-a. The law directs the State Librarian to "establish, operate, and maintain a publication collection and depository system." This statute also mandates that each state agency deposit "with the Kansas state library and the state historical society one printed copy of any publication issued by such state agency." The statute allows the State Librarian to request additional copies as needed. Further, the statute directs that the State Librarian forward two copies to the Library of Congress, one copy to the Kansas State Historical Society, one copy to the Center for Research Libraries (though the Center no longer actively collects state documents), and one copy is permanently retained in the Kansas State Library.

Under KS 75-2565-a, an agency publication is defined as "any report, pamphlet, book or other materials provided by a state agency for use by the general public." KS 75-2565-b defines a state agency as "any state office or officer, department, board, commission, institution, bureau, society or any agency division or unit within any state office, department, board, commission or other state authority."

Any library in Kansas may become a full depository if certain conditions are met (KS 75-2567). That library must contract with the State Librarian to become a full depository and must "provide adequate facilities for the storage and use of any such publication and to render reasonable service without charge to qualified patrons in the use of such publication." Further, full depositories agree to maintain the full collection of publications distributed indefinitely unless the State Librarian issues a disposal order. Libraries may also be designated as selective depositories. These libraries receive publications through individual request. There are no statutes governing retention or disposal of state publications for selective depository libraries.

Printing of state agency publications is done under the direction of the Central Duplication Service (CDS), a division of the Department of Administration. Every state agency must utilize this service for its publication needs.

As more Kansas government information is being made available exclusively in an electronic format (e.g., CD-ROM, Internet), recent changes to KS 75-3048(a–c) reflect the requirements for dissemination and retention of these electronic publications. For example, if a state agency makes a publication available on the Internet for a period of twelve months, that agency is not required to print copies for further dissemination, as long as that agency retains an electronic copy in its archives for historical purposes.

If the issuing agency is required by law to provide a publication to another Kansas state agency or official, the issuing agency shall notify that agency or official that the publication in question is available via the Internet or by e-mail. In order for this requirement to be met, the publication must remain available for a period not less than twelve months in its electronic format. Additionally, the issuing agency may also comply by providing a print or CD-ROM copy.

KS 75-3048(b) requires that regardless of format chosen, the issuing agency is mandated to "notify and provide a printed copy to the Kansas state library and state historical society." KS 75-3048(c) requires the issuing agency to provide a print copy of each publication to the governor, state librarian, and the secretary of the state historical society if the publication has been issued in a print or CD-ROM format.

Print or CD-ROM copies are still required to be submitted to the legislature and its members per KS 46-1212(c). If a printed or CD-ROM copy is made available for sale to the general public, according to KS 75-3048(c), the "publication shall be sold at approximately the cost of printing the same." The only exception to this law is that "research, industrial, agricultural, and education matter of general concern to the people of Kansas may be distributed without charge."

There are currently twenty-six libraries in Kansas that participate in the depository program. Because this number is very close to the minimum number of publications mandated by statute, there are some inconsistencies in publication distribution and retention. Some libraries may have complete runs of annual reports and others may have gaps in their collections. It is best to contact the library nearest you before visiting.

USEFUL ADDRESSES AND TELEPHONE NUMBERS

The most complete collections of Kansas state documents can be found at the following libraries:

Emporia State University
William Allen White Library
1200 Commercial Street
Emporia, KS 66801
Phone Number for Kansas Reference Questions: (620) 341-5207
E-Mail Address for Kansas Reference Questions: libref01@esumail.emporia.edu

Government Documents Department Home Page: http://www.emporia.edu/libsv/
  gdfront.htm

Fort Hays State University
Forsyth Library
Government Documents Department
600 Park Street
Hays, KS 67601-4099
Phone Number for Kansas Reference Questions: (785) 628-4340
Government Documents Department Home Page: http://www.fhsu.edu/forsyth_lib/
  govdoc.shtml

Pittsburg State University
Leonard H. Axe Library
1605 South Joplin Street
Pittsburg, KS 66762-5589
Phone Number for Kansas Reference Questions: (620) 235-4889
E-Mail Link for Kansas Reference Questions: http://library.pittstate.edu/ref/services
  .html#emailref
Leonard H. Axe Library Home Page: http://library.pittstate.edu/

State Library of Kansas
300 SW 10th Avenue, Room 343-N
Topeka, KS 66612
Phone Number for Kansas Reference Questions: (785)-296-3296
E-Mail Address for Kansas Reference Questions: ksdocs@kslib.info
Reference Division Home Page: http://kslib.info/ref/
Library's Home Page: http://skyways.lib.ks.us/ksl/

University of Kansas
Kansas Collection
Spencer Research Library
Lawrence, KS 66045
Phone Number for Kansas Reference Questions: (785) 864-4334
E-Mail Address for Kansas Reference Questions: ksrlref@ku.edu
Kansas Collection Home Page: http://spencer.lib.ku.edu/kc/

INDEXES TO KANSAS STATE PUBLICATIONS

Under KS 75-2567 the State Librarian "shall periodically publish and distribute to complete depository libraries, selective depository libraries, state agencies, state officers, and members of the Kansas legislature, an official list of state publications with at least an annual cumulation." This is accomplished through the inclusion of a shipping list in each depository shipment received by a depository library. The list includes a record of each agency publication with the author, title, subject headings, and other necessary cataloging information. Each state agency, in turn, is required to provide the State Library with a complete list of its publications from the previous year to assist the State Librarian in maintaining a complete and permanent record of agency publications.

A cataloging librarian at the Kansas State Library catalogs each state publication using an in-house-developed cataloging classification that mirrors the hierarchical arrangement of the state agency. It is in many ways similar to the Federal Superintendent of Documents Classification System used by the Government Printing Office. An OCLC record is created for the purpose of providing bibliographic information for Kansas depository libraries should they choose to use the State Library classification system.

ESSENTIAL STATE PUBLICATIONS

Directories

Kansas Directory (Secretary of State)—This online directory contains PDF files of all state employees working in state or federal positions. Also included is information on the Kansas legislature (salaries and district maps), a review of state history and government, a listing of county officials, and more. Maintained and updated with some frequency by the Secretary of State, First Floor, Memorial Hall, 120 SW 10th Avenue, Topeka, KS 66612-1594, or call (785) 296-4564. The directory is available only at http://www.kssos.org/kansas/kansas_directory.html.

Kansas Legislative Directory (University of Kansas, Policy Research Institute)—This directory is designed to provide legislative contact information to the voters of Kansas. Conducting a productive search will yield the legislator's name, county and city of residence, district, political party affiliation, and a map. Also included is information on local and legislative contacts, committee membership, district statistical information, a photograph, and a map of the district represented with details to the street level. The directory was formerly maintained by the Kansas Legislative Administrative Service. The directory can be found at http://www.ku.edu/pri/ksdata/vote/. Additional information may be obtained from the Policy Research Institute, 1541 Lilac Lane, 607 Blake Hall, University of Kansas, Lawrence, KS 66044-3177, or call (785) 864-3701.

Kansas Library Directory (Kansas State Library)—This directory is divided into three sections. The "Library Directory" section contains contact and collection information, the "Staff Directory" contains contact information on all staff in Kansas libraries, and the "Interlibrary Loan Directory" contains information on interlibrary loan polices with participating Kansas libraries. Contact information includes the library name, street address, city, zip code, library type, phone number, and the library director's name. A search can be performed by person or by library. Although the information is public it is a violation of Kansas state law to give, sell, or use names from a public record for selling or offering for sale property or services. The directory is updated regularly. For more information contact the Kansas State Library, 300 SW 10th Avenue, Room 343-N, Topeka, KS 66612-1593, or call (785) 296-3296. The directory can be viewed at http://skyways2.lib.ks.us/kld/.

[Year–Year] Kansas Educational Directory (Department of Education)—This annual publication provides contact information for all personnel involved in education in Kansas, and is updated and published each fall. Entries contain

the names, addresses, and phone numbers of teachers, school administrators, and boards of directors. The files are available in text or PDF format. The directory is divided into alphabetical sections ranging from Administrators to Rural and Elementary schools. There are also links to assist one in printing mailing labels, statistics, and school district maps. The directory is no longer published in hard copy. It is maintained by the Kansas Department of Education, 120 SE 10th Avenue, Topeka, KS 66612-1182, or call (785) 296-3201. The directory can be found at http://www.ksde.org/eddir/eddir.html.

Online Communication Directory (Department of Administration)—This online directory provides contact information for state employees and agencies. The information was derived from the *State of Kansas Communications Directory*, published in 2000, and is updated on an annual basis. It should be noted that not all state employees will be found in the directory. A search for an individual can be done by either first or last name, or by agency. Also included on the web page are links to the governor's office, Kansas state and federal representatives, most requested numbers, lottery and tax refund numbers, and other useful information. A copy can be obtained for $2.00 in person or $5.00 by mail. To order, contact the Communications Service Directory, Division of Information Systems and Communications, 900 SW Jackson Street, Room 751S, Topeka, KS 66612-1275, or call (785) 296-2730. The online version can be found at http://da.state.ks.us/phonebook/.

Financial/Budgetary Resources

The FY [Year] Governor's Budget Report (Division of Budget)—This two-volume report provides a narrative and detailed budget for state agency fiscal operations. Volume 1 provides the budget narrative and schedules as developed by the governor and his budget office. Volume 2 contains detailed budgetary statistical information on all state agencies. The web site also provides budget amendments and memoranda. Other recent budget reports can also be found here. Go to http://da.state.ks.us/budget/gbr.htm to review these reports. The reports are available in a PDF format. A copy may also be obtained by contacting the Kansas Division of the Budget, 300 SW 10th Avenue, Room 152-E, Statehouse, Topeka, KS 66612, or call (785) 296-2436.

The Governor's Economic and Demographic Report (Division of Budget)—This annual report provides a summary of economic and demographic data in Kansas as compared to the United States. The report is published as a supplement to the *Governor's Budget Report*. There are four main chapters and eight appendices that provide detailed information on the U.S. economy, Kansas employment and income, local and regional employment and income, and Kansas demographic information. Earlier years (1998–2001) are available at http://da.state.ks.us/budget/ecodemo%20past.htm. The current year's report is located at http://da.state.ks.us/budget/ecodemo.htm.

Kansas Fiscal Facts (Legislative Research Department)—This document includes information on the Kansas state budget. The intent is to provide the state legislature, along with the general public, basic budgetary information. The report contains the latest expenditures that have been approved by the legislature. Time-line information is available for comparison purposes. Detailed information is provided including the approved budget, trends data, state personnel, and state revenues. Also found are levels of expenditures and staffing for each state agency. A glossary of selected budget terms and a list of legislative fiscal analyst assignments can be found at the end of the document. For more information or to obtain a copy of the document contact the Kansas Legislative Research Department, 300 SW 10th Avenue, Room 545-N, Statehouse, Topeka, KS 66612-1504, or call (785) 296-3181. An online version of this document is available at http://skyways.lib.ks.us/ksleg/KLRD/pubpage2.htm.

Kansas Legislature [Year–Year] Appropriations Report (Legislative Research Department)—This annual publication features detailed budgetary and financial information and statistics on state agency fiscal operations. Produced at the beginning of the new fiscal year (October), this publication assists state agencies as well as the general public on the financial aspects of government operations. A copy may be obtained from the Kansas Legislative Research Department, 300 SW 10th Avenue, Room 545-N, Statehouse, Topeka, KS 66612-1504, or call (785) 296-3181. The report can be found at http://skyways.lib.ks.us/ksleg/KLRD/pubpage2.htm.

Legal Resources

Kansas Attorney General Opinions (Attorney General's Office)—This web site provides all Kansas Attorney General opinions rendered from October 1995 through the present. Opinions can be located by number, or a search can be conducted by date, requestor, attorney general, author, topic, synopsis, or full text. The web site is maintained by the Office of the Kansas Attorney General, 120 SW 10th Avenue, Topeka, KS 66612, or call (785) 296-2215. The web site is located at http://www.kscourts.org/ksag/.

Kansas Legislature (Administrative Services Offices)—This web site provides one-stop shopping for many of the legislative needs a researcher may have. Bills, the *Kansas Statutes Annotated*, House and Senate Journals, Calendars, Committee Membership, and much more can be found here. Additionally, this web site is part of the *Information Network of Kansas* (INK), a fee-funded state agency that provides value-added services for interested parties. INK is cost-recovery service, which is why user fees are charged. For more information on subscriber services go to http://www.accesskansas.org/subscriber.html. To view the legislative web site go to http://www.kslegislature.org/help/subscriber.html. Although there are subscription services available at this web site, approximately 95 percent of the information found here is free.

Kansas Register (Secretary of State)—Published every Thursday, this title contains information ranging from new state laws enacted to various public notices. The *Register* contains newly adopted administrative regulations, legislative bills recently introduced, summary opinions of the Attorney General, RFPs, dockets of the Kansas Supreme Court and Court of Appeals, and other public notices. An archive is available from 1994. Part of INK, a subscriber service is available for $.25 per regulation viewed. A subscription can be obtained for $80.00 per year. An online form is available, or those interested can contact the Kansas Register, Secretary of State, First Floor, Memorial Hall, 120

SW 10th Avenue, Topeka, KS 66612-1594, or call (785) 296-3489. To view the *Register* or request a free sample go to http://www.kssos.org/resources/ resources_faq_kansas.html.

Kansas State Constitution (Legislative Administrative Services)—The state Constitution is one of many links found on the Kansas legislature home page. The Constitution is available in a PDF format that provides the fifteen articles contained in the document. Also available is the "Ordinance and Preamble" and the "Kansas Bill of Rights." The Constitution can also be found at http: // kslib.info/ref/constitution/index.html. Paper copies can be found in all the state depository libraries. A limited number of copies may be available from the Kansas Legislative Administrative Services, 300 SW 10th Avenue, Room 511-S, Statehouse, Topeka, KS 66612-1540, or call (785) 296-2391.

Legislative Procedure in Kansas (Legislative Research Department)—The eleventh edition of this manual, published in 2002, describes the lawmaking process in the Kansas legislature. The manual is "based on legislative rules, practices, statutes, constitutional provisions, and court decisions in effect prior to the 2003 legislative session." The manual is therefore not a complete "legislative manual" but is designed as a general reference guide for legislators and the public. The last edition was compiled by the Kansas Legislative Research Department, 300 SW 10th Avenue, Room 545-N, Statehouse, Topeka, KS 66612-1504, or call (785) 296-3181. An online version can be found at http://skyways.lib.ks.us/ksleg/KLRD/pubpage2.htm.

Statistical Resources

Annual Summary of Vital Statistics (Center for Health and Environmental Statistics)—This annual compilation provides summary information on a variety of vital statistics on citizens in Kansas. The information is compiled from vital events such as births, deaths, abortions, marriages, and divorces or dissolutions. In some of the counties, data are summarized by population "peer group." This category allows one to compare or contrast statistical information on counties of similar size, population, and density. The online edition can be found at http://www.kdhe.state.ks.us/hci/. For an alternative copy contact the Kansas Department of Health and Environment, Center for Health and Environmental Statistics, Office of Health Care Information, 1000 SW Jackson Street, Suite 130, Topeka, KS 66612-1354, or call (785) 296-8627.

Crime Statistics (Kansas Bureau of Investigation)—This web site provides a variety of statistics on criminal activity in Kansas. Included are the latest crime statistics, a ten-year trend analysis on arrests, Law Enforcement Officers Killed or Assaulted, and Meth statistics (on clandestine chemical laboratories) dating back to 1994. Each file is in a PDF format. A keyword search is also possible on the site. There are also links to missing persons, registered offenders, information about the KBI, and drug enforcement activities. The web site is located at http://www.accesskansas.org/kbi/stats.htm.

K–12 School Reports (Department of Education)—This web site provides statistical information on schools, students, staff, and school finances. Information can be accessed by county, by organization, by school, or state total. Information found includes school/district address, e-mail address, home page address, administrators, enrollment, dropouts, graduates, staff, vocational education enrollment, school violence, attendance rates, and other useful statistics. There are links provided to other related school data such as a building report card, the *Kansas Educational Directory*, School Nutrition Programs Reports, and a labeling program for label creation. The web site is located at http://www.ksde.org/k12/k12.html. The site is maintained by the Kansas Department of Education, 120 SE 10th Avenue, Topeka, KS 66612-1182, or call (785) 296-3201.

Kansas County Health Profiles, 1999 Index Page (Local and Rural Health Office)—This web site provides detailed statistics on demographic, economic, health, education, crime, death, and disease in each Kansas county. This is the second edition, which updates the first published in 1994. Access to the information can be gained through either a pull-down menu or by clicking on a county. All the files, including the User's Guide, are available in a PDF format. The User's Guide provides information regarding the source of data, complete definitions, technical notes, and notes regarding comparability between the 1999 and 1994 data. User's Guides for non-commercial purposes may be reproduced without first contacting the office. For paper copies of the county health profiles contact the Office of Local and Rural Health, 900 SW Jackson Street, Room 1051-S, Topeka, KS 66612-1364, or call (785) 296-1200. The web site can be found at http://www.kdhe.state.ks.us/olrh/index.html.

Kansas Health Statistics (Center for Health and Environmental Statistics)—This web site provides essential statistical information on public health in Kansas. Information found on this site includes births, deaths, fetal deaths, marriages, and divorces. An analysis of health care data is available. The Kansas Information for Communities (KIC) Interactive Data System can be accessed at this site. KIC provides a user the ability to tailor questions on events such as births and deaths. The data will then be reported by county, sex, race, age group, cause of death, or birth outcome. A considerable number of other health-related links are also included on this page. The site is maintained by the Kansas Department of Health and Environment, Center for Health and Environmental Statistics, 1000 SW Jackson Street, Suite 110, Topeka, KS 66612-2221, or call (785) 296-1414. The web site can be located at http://www.kdhe.state.ks.us/ches/.

Occupational Wage and Outlook Reports (Labor Market Information Services)—This online resource provides links to a variety of statistical data on wages, occupations, and an occupational outlook in Kansas. Wage surveys can be found for the years 1995/1996 to the present. Occupational outlooks for 2005 and 2006 can be located here. Go to http://laborstats.hr.state.ks.us/occupatn/occupatn.htm. This site is maintained and updated by the Kansas Labor Market Information Services, 401 SW Topeka Boulevard, Topeka, KS 66603, or call (785) 296-5058.

Selected Statistics (Department of Transportation)—This 1997 report provides information on the Kansas transportation system. The PDF document contains a wealth of statistical data on Kansas highways; public transit; and rail, air, and water transport. Also included in the report is information on federal and state financing; travel and mileage data for the state; and highway accident, fatality, and alcohol-related data. A copy of this report can be requested from the Kansas Department of Transportation, Division of Planning and Development, Docking State Office Building, 8th Floor, Topeka, KS 66612, or call (785) 296-2253; e-mail dtplan@ksdot.org. An online copy can be found at http://www.ink.org/public/kdot/divplanning/selstat/index.html.

Other Resources

Kansas Community Networks (Kansas Historical Society)—This "network" is actually a county and town research center. The goal of this network is to "help Kansas Communities establish a presence on the Web and establish an archive of Kansas history." Once known as the *Historical Directory of Kansas Towns*, the network contains an alphabetical county arrangement and a link to that county's seat. From there, historical information can be found on the area. The web page can be found at http://history.cc.ukans.edu/heritage/towns/countown.html.

Kansas Department of Commerce and Housing Home Page (Department of Commerce and Housing)—This home page provides a wealth of information on living, traveling, or conducting business in Kansas. It is divided into several sections, each covering a subject-specific topic. Using the various resources available, it is possible to plan a trip using the calendar of events; or find a list of business properties, community profiles or major businesses in Kansas, or Kansas "firsts." To view this web page go to http://kdoch.state.ks.us/ProgramApp/index_mm.jsp.

Kansas Environment (Department of Health and Environment)—This publication helps provide insight into the environmental issues and trends found in Kansas. The report includes useful maps, statistical tables, and graphs; and illustrations about air and water quality, waste management, and environmental remediation in Kansas. To review this publication, go to http://www.kdhe.state.ks.us/environment/index.html.

Steps to Success: A Resource Guide to Starting a Business in Kansas (Department of Commerce and Housing)—This resource provides a step-by-step guide on everything one needs to know when starting a business in Kansas. The five sections and chapters within each section provide insight and useful information on topics such as taxes, venture capital resources and other financial alternatives, contact information for state and federal offices, surcharges, disposal fees, and other information necessary to engage in proper and safe business practices. A copy of this guide may be obtained from the Kansas Department Commerce and Housing, 1000 SW Jackson Street, Suite 100, Topeka, KS 66612-1321, or call (785) 296-5298.

KANSAS' WORLD WIDE WEB HOME PAGE

There are two important and useful web pages available to browse and research information on Kansas. *AccessKansas*, http://www.accesskansas.org/, is the official web site for the state. *Blue Skyways*, http://www.skyways.org/index.html, is a web site developed by the Kansas State Library. Both provide easy access, useful information, and a variety of links to other web sites. Both are also designed with particular purposes and functions as well.

AccessKansas is a portal that provides its users broad subject access to eight categories. From online services to Kansas facts and history, this portal provides information on state and local government, the economy, and a variety of services for the citizens of Kansas. Typical services include links to state government agencies, online license applications, information about relocating to Kansas, and business opportunities, to name a few. The *State Phone Directory* can be accessed from this site, as can the governor's web page, and other timely and useful information regarding recreational and other activities being conducted in the state.

AccessKansas is a part of the Information Network of Kansas (INK). INK was created by an act of the Kansas legislature in 1990 (KSA 74-9302) with the intent to provide electronic services for Kansas' citizens. Designed to provide state, county, and local information, INK is a joint public/private venture. It is a government service with entrepreneurial designs. This is where subscription-based services to the *Kansas Register*, *Kansas Statutes Annotated*, and other fee-based services can be found. Although INK does provide a wide variety of informational services free of charge, due to the joint private/public venture, some of the information accessed will come with a price.

Blue Skyways, on the other hand, is a service-oriented web page developed for libraries and library patrons by the Kansas State Library. The links found on this site are there because they hold value to Kansas librarians and their clients, provide easy and quick access to library catalogs and Internet resources, support community networks, and promote partnerships with libraries across the state.

Blue Skyways provides access to thousands of web pages. There are links to community-based pages, education, government, and libraries. There are also links to the *KS GenWeb Project*, an online genealogy resource. The services offered are free and the site is supported financially through the Kansas state legislature.

For more information on *AccessKansas* contact AccessKansas, 534 South Kansas Avenue, Suite 1210, Topeka, KS 66603-3434, or call (785) 296-5059. For *Blue Skyways* contact the Kansas State Library, Information Technology Division, 300 SW 10th Avenue, Room 343-N, Topeka, KS 66612-1593, or call (785) 296-3154.

COMMERCIAL PUBLICATIONS AND WEB SITES

KLM Online (Topeka, KS: The League of Kansas Municipalities)—The League currently makes available several subscription-based services (as well as paper equivalents) that focus on supplying business operations in Kansas with information on conducting their affairs with municipalities and the people who have responsibility for their operations. There is a *Directory of Kansas Public Officials* ($50.00 for members, $75.00 for non-members) that provides contact information on individuals involved in municipal operations as well as within the Kansas legislature. Their *Business Links Online* provides a list of businesses that offer products and services to local governments. This service is arranged by broad category. The League also offers a variety of paper publications oriented toward those working in local government or doing business with local governments. For more information contact the League of Kansas Municipalities, 300 SW 8th Avenue, Topeka, KS 66603-3912, or call (785) 354-9565. Visit their web site at http://www.lkm.org/publications/.

Kansas Atlas and Gazetteer: Topo Maps of the Entire State, Public Lands, and Back Roads (Yarmouth, ME: DeLorme Mapping Company, 2000, $19.95)—This atlas provides detailed topographical maps of public lands and back roads of Kansas. DeLorme Mapping Company produces an atlas for practically every state in the United States. For purchasing information contact DeLorme Mapping Company, Two DeLorme Drive, P.O. Box 298, Yarmouth, ME 04096, or call (800) 581-5105.

Kansas Business and Economic Review (KBER) (Lawrence, KS: Policy Research Institute)—The KBER has recently undergone a format change and is now available for no charge at http://www.ku.edu/pri/publicat/kbr/kber.shtml. Published semi-annually, the KBER contains up-to-date information on the economic and business environment in Kansas and the Midwest. The KBER also includes research studies and reports in the fields of economics, business, and related public policy areas, and provides timely economic indicators and forecasts. For more information contact the Policy Research Institute, 1541 Lilac Lane, 607 Blake Hall, University of Kansas, Lawrence, KS 66044-3177, or call (785) 864-3701.

Kansas Calendar of Events (Clafin, KS: Tour Kansas Guide)—This is a monthly listing of events being hosted in and around Kansas. Each event is listed in chronological order with date(s) and location. There is also a very brief description provided with each event; phone numbers are included. As many of the events are becoming an annual occurrence, past months are included on the list. The calendar is compiled by the Tour Kansas Guide, P.O. Box 158, Claflin, KS 67525, or call (620) 587-3238. The calendar can be viewed at http://skyways.lib.ks.us/kansas/community/index.html/.

Kansas Information Express Disc (Manhattan, KS: Kansas State University, Cooperative Extension and Agricultural Research, 2001, $15.60)—This is a CD-ROM containing over 2,000 publications that have been issued by the KSU Cooperative Extension and Agricultural Research over the past few years. Subject areas range from agriculture to gardening. To purchase a copy go to http://www.oznet.ksu.edu/library/orders/orderform.htm. Many of the publications on the CD-ROM are also available at http://www.oznet.ksu.edu/library/. You may also contact the Kansas State Research and Extension Office, Production Services, Kansas State University, 24 Umberger Hall, Manhattan, KS 66506-3402, or call (785) 523-5830.

Kansas Statistical Abstract (Lawrence, KS: Policy Research Institute)—The *Abstract* contains the most recent state-, county-, and city-level data on the Kansas population, vital statistics, health, education, and a host of other pertinent statistical categories. Culled from numerous state and federal sources, the *Abstract* contains all the statistical information necessary for the researcher or novice. The thirty-fifth edition, published in 2000, was the last issued in print. The thirty-sixth edition is the first to be available exclusively online (http://www.ku.edu/pri/ksdata/ksah/). There is no paper equivalent, nor is one planned for dissemination. To order the thirty-fifth edition, go to http://www.ku.edu/pri/orderKSA.htm. For more information contact the Kansas Statistical Abstract, Policy Research Institute, 1541 Lilac Lane, 607 Blake Hall, University of Kansas, Lawrence, KS 66044-3177, or call (785) 864-3701.

SOURCES CONSULTED

Correspondence with Mac Reed, Ft. Hays State University; Nan Myers, Wichita State University.

Google, http://www.google.com.

Government Documents Round Table, American Library Association. *Directory of Government Document Collections & Librarians*, 7th ed. Bethesda, MD: Congressional Information Service, 1997.

Jobe, Janita. "State Publications." *Journal of Government Information*, 27 (2000): 733–768.

Maxymuk, John, ed. *Government Online: One-Click Access to 3,400 Federal and State Websites*. New York: Neal-Schuman Publishers, 2001.

Numerous state agency and department web pages via the Kansas home page, http://www.accesskansas.org/.

State Government and Politics, http://www.lib.umich.edu/govdocs/state.html.

Survey response from Bill Sowers, State Library of Kansas.

U.S. State and Local Gateway, http://www.statelocal.gov/.

Kentucky

J. Louise Malcomb

GOVERNMENT PUBLISHING AND THE DEPOSITORY SYSTEM

The Kentucky Department of Libraries and Archives oversees the "State Publications Program" and provides an overview, instructions for requesting publications, the monthly accessions list, and Internet databases linking to state publications on its web site at http://www.kdla.state.ky.us/arch/statpub .htm. Most revealing is the statement included with the *Monthly Accessions List*, "All publications listed in KSPA are filmed annually and available for purchase on microfiche. For assistance in locating or using Kentucky state publications or for interlibrary loan, contact the Public Records Division, State Publications Program at (502) 564-8300 ext. 248, or e-mail brichardson@ctr .kdla.state.ky.us."

Unlike many states, state publications of Kentucky are viewed as public records, deposited with the Department of Libraries and Archives, and microfilmed for distribution. Libraries and others may request copies of the publications from the agencies directly or rely on interlibrary loan from the Department of Libraries and Archives. Section 171.500 of the *Kentucky Revised Statutes* establishes the Department of Libraries and Archives (KDLA) as the central depository, requiring state agencies to supply copies of publications and authorizing the KDLA to distribute copies to other libraries that serve as depositories. Section 725 1:040 of the *Kentucky Administrative Regulations* further defines these responsibilities, requiring agencies to send three copies to the Department of Libraries and Archives. The regulations define state publications as

Reports and publications as used in this administrative regulation shall be construed in the broadest sense to include typed, printed, mimeographed, and multilithed publications. In case of doubt by any records officer as to whether a particular publication or report constitutes a publication or report, the records officer should consult with the Director, Public Records Division, and work out a mutual agreement.

While this section of the regulations does not speak directly to electronic re-cords, section 1 KAR 5:010 concerns "Accession of public records by means of electronic data processing procedures" and states: "Public records accession administrative regulations shall apply to all public agencies of government and budget units thereof, which utilize electronic data processing equipment and procedures to process public records."

The Kentucky Department for Libraries and Archives web site at http://www.kdla.state.ky.us/arch/core.htm provides lists of core documents (de-scribed further later) published by Kentucky, which serve as notification to libraries about their availability. The instructions infer that libraries should request needed publications, especially those noted as core, stating, "Original copies of these publications may be secured from the issuing agency; supplies however, will vary. Publications listed here are available for purchase on mi-crofiche either individually or as a set." The site further states that the bibli-ography of state publications is prepared by "KDLA's State Publications Program in cooperation with the Committee on State Publications, a standing committee of the Kentucky Library Association's Government Documents Roundtable." While not a "depository system" in the traditional sense, this is an excellent program with good focus on "preserving" state publications, yet clearly the system can distribute the documents to interested libraries. It does put the responsibility for acquiring the documents on libraries, unlike the traditional dissemination of documents to designated libraries.

USEFUL ADDRESSES AND TELEPHONE NUMBERS

The most complete collection of Kentucky state documents can be found at the following library:

State Publications Program
Department for Libraries and Archives
300 Coffee Tree Road
P.O. Box 537
Frankfort, KY 40602-0537
Phone Number for Kentucky Reference Questions: (502) 564-8300, ext. 248; fax: (502) 564-5773
E-Mail Address for Kentucky Reference Questions: KDLAStatePubs@kdla.state.ky.us
Department for Libraries and Archives Home Page: http://www.kdla.net
State Publications Program Home Page: http://www.kdla.net/arch/statpub.htm

INDEXES TO KENTUCKY STATE PUBLICATIONS

Kentucky State Publications Accessions (KSPA) (Kentucky Department of Li-braries and Archives)—KSPA is compiled bimonthly in an effort to assist those responsible for acquiring current Kentucky state agency publications.

Publications are listed alphabetically by issuing agency and include an agency address and telephone number for additional information. REQUESTS FOR PUBLICATIONS SHOULD BE SENT TO THE SMALLEST ADMINISTRATIVE UNIT OF THE ISSUING

AGENCY. Unless otherwise indicated, all telephone numbers are area code 502. The symbol (C) indicates publication is a CORE REFERENCE selection. The symbol $$$ indicates cost item. All publications listed in KSPA are filmed annually and available for purchase on microfiche. For assistance in locating or using Kentucky state publications or for interlibrary loan, contact the Public Records Division, State Publications Program at (502) 564-8300, ext. 248, or e-mail brichardson@ctr.kdla.state.ky.us.

Checklist of Kentucky Imprints, 1787–1810 (U.S. Historical Records Survey)— Authored by Douglas C. McMurtrie and Albert Henry Allen, the Historical Records Survey sponsored the preparation of the *Checklist* during the 1930s, and later the *Check List of Kentucky Imprints, 1811–1820* and the *Supplementary Check List of Kentucky Imprints, 1788–1820*. These list many early state documents.

Checklist of Kentucky State Publications (Kentucky State Archives and Records Service)—Under variant agency names and on an irregular basis, Kentucky has issued this list of state publications since 1962. From 1963 to 1969, it was entitled *Checklist of Kentucky State Publications and State Directory*. Between 1973 and 1981, it was entitled *Monthly Checklist of Kentucky State Publications*.

Core Collection of Kentucky Publications (Kentucky State Archives)—Very helpful are the core lists of state publications and other databases provided by the State Archives on its web site including:

- http://www.kdla.state.ky.us/arch/newcore.htm—core collection of Kentucky publications by agency;
- http://www.kdla.state.ky.us/arch/core.htm—core collection of Kentucky publications by keyword; and
- http://www.kdla.state.ky.us/arch/pubson.htm—"Kentucky State Archives"—a set of "state agency publications and databases available on the Internet."

ESSENTIAL STATE PUBLICATIONS

Directories

Directory of Kentucky Libraries and Archives (Kentucky Department of Libraries and Archives)—The current edition of this directory is available online as a PDF file at http://www.kdla.net/dir.htm. It can be viewed as a complete document, or in sections. It provides a detailed listing of offices and departments within the Kentucky Department of Libraries and Archives, as well as academic, public, and school libraries.

Kentucky State Telephone Directory (Commonwealth of Kentucky Governor's Office for Technology)—The directory is now available online at http://phone.state.ky.us/. For additional information contact the Office for Technology at 101 Cold Harbor Drive, Frankfort, KY 40601-3050, or call (502) 564-3130. The *Directory* includes a list of government agencies, but also the state government organization chart, an employee search, and maps of various Kentucky cities.

Kentucky General Assembly Directory (Legislative Research Commission)— This directory of current members of the General Assembly includes biographical information as well as photographs. To obtain copies of the above publication write to Legislative Research Commission Publications Room 78, Capitol Building, 700 Capitol Avenue, Frankfort, KY 40601, or call (502) 564-8100 ext. 884; or e-mail margaret.bingham@lrc.state.ky.us. The *Who's Who* web site, on the legislature's web site, also provides contact and biographical information to members of the Senate and House, along with a photograph. See http://www.lrc.state.ky.us/whoswho/whoswho.htm.

Kentucky Schools Directory (Kentucky Department of Education)—This is available in print from the department from the KDE Bookstore, located at: 500 Mero Street, 19th floor, Frankfort, KY 40601, or call (502) 564-3421; fax (502) 564-6470. The Bookstore is operated by the Kentucky Department of Education, Office of Communication Services. The latest edition is available online at http://www.kde.state.ky.us/KDE/About+Schools+and+Districts/default.htm. The directory lists public and non-public schools and school districts.

Financial/Budgetary Resources

Commonwealth of Kentucky Comprehensive Annual Financial Report for the Year (Kentucky Finance and Administration Cabinet, Office of the Controller)—This report provides an overview of the state's finances, including revenues, assets, and expenditures. It is available in print while supplies last from Finance and Administration Cabinet, Office of the Controller, Accounts Division, Room 484, Capitol Annex, 702 Capitol Avenue, Frankfort, KY 40601-3454, or call (502) 564-2210, but copies of 1996 to date are also available on the controller's web site at http://www.state.ky.us/agencies/finance/manuals/tax/cafr.htm.

Budget of the Commonwealth (Kentucky Office of State Budget Director)—With the 1996–1998 budget, the office has provided access to the full budget on its web site at http://www.osbd.state.ky.us/budgets_of_the_common wealth.htm. It is also available, if supplies exist, from the Office of the State Budget Director at 284 Capitol Annex, 700 Capitol Avenue, Frankfort, KY 40601, or call (502) 564-7300; fax (502) 564-2517.

Kentucky Deskbook of Economic Statistics (Economic Development Cabinet)—Available by section or complete in PDF form online at http://www.thinkkentucky.com/edis/deskbook/, the *Deskbook* provides basic demographic, labor force, and economic statistics for counties in Kentucky. For additional information, contact the Economic Development Representative at (502) 564-4886. The Cabinet for Economic Development's Research and Statistics web site also links to its other publications, including *Kentucky Facts, Fact Sheets on Doing Business in Kentucky*, and *Community Profiles*. See http://www.edc.state.ky.us/kyedc/resandstat.asp.

Legal Resources

While principal legal resources are explored here, Robin R. Harris provides an excellent overview of Kentucky's legal resources in the Summer 1989 article in *Kentucky Libraries*, "Kentucky Statutes and Regulations: A Basic Roadmap."

Additional information is also available at http://www.lrc.state.ky.us. This web site is comprehensive, providing excellent contact information and copies of the resources used in the legislative process in Kentucky. Kentucky's attorney general's web site, at http://www.law.state.ky.us/office/links.htm, also provides links to legal resources.

Constitution of the State of Kentucky (Kentucky Legislature)—Kentucky's current Constitution was adopted in 1891 with amendments as recent as 2000. It is available online at http://www.lrc.state.ky.us/legresou/constitu/intro.htm.

Kentucky Revised Statutes (Kentucky Legislative Research Commission)—The *Kentucky Revised Statutes* serve as the legal code for the state. They are provided in PDF on the legislature's web site at http://www.lrc.state.ky.us/statrev/frontpg.htm, which also indicates that the web version is "unofficial" and that "The certified versions of the *Kentucky Revised Statutes* should be consulted for all matters requiring reliance on the statutory text." The web site further stipulates:

Two printed editions of the *Kentucky Revised Statutes* have been designated as certified versions by action of the Kentucky Legislative Research Commission. The publishers of these two certified versions are: Lexis Law Publishing (formerly Michie Law Publishers), (800) 542-0957, and West Group (formerly Banks-Baldwin Law Publishing Company) (800) WESTLAW (800-937-8529).

Acts of the Kentucky General Assembly (Kentucky General Assembly)—Laws, as passed, are available on the legislature's web site in PDF from 1998 at http://www.lrc.state.ky.us/acts/mainacts.htm. Texts of bills and legislative action are also available at http://www.lrc.state.ky.us/Legislat/legislat.htm. Earlier legislation, Acts, and other reports are available at the Penny King Legislative Library, Room 27 of the Capitol Complex, Lexington, KY. Contact the Legislative Research Business Office for hard copies or for CD-ROM copies, available from 2000.

Kentucky Administrative Regulations (KAR) (Kentucky Legislative Research Commission)—Copies of specific regulations are available for 15 cents per single-sided copy or 20 cents per two-sided page from the Legislative Research Commission, Room 029, Capitol Annex, Frankfort, KY 40601, or call (502) 564-8100, ext. 312. Subscriptions to the complete service are also available from the commission for $150.00 per year. Unofficial copies are available on the web at http://www.lrc.state.ky.us/kar/frntpage.htm.

Kentucky Register (Kentucky Legislative Research Commission)—The *Register* updates the *Kentucky Administrative Regulations*. It is available from the Legislative Research Commission, Room 63 Capitol Annex, Frankfort, KY 40601, or call (502) 564-8100, ext. 564. A subscription is $48.00, or the subscription may be combined with one for the *Kentucky Administrative Regulations* for $175.00. For additional information, see the front page of the KAR web site at http://www.lrc.state.ky.us/kar/frntpage.htm.

LouisvilleLaw—http://www.louisvillelaw.com/. This large web site has a directory for finding lawyers; cases, code, statutes; also links to non-legal resources.

Statistical Resources

Annual Report of the Department of Mines and Minerals, Commonwealth of Kentucky, for the Year (Kentucky Department of Mines and Minerals)—Issued for over 100 years, the report presents statistics on coal mine production, employment, and safety, critical for a state rich in mineral resources. A print report is available for $15.00 from the Department of Mines and Minerals, 1025 Capital Center Drive, Suite 201, Frankfort, KY 40602-2244, or call (502) 573-0140; fax (502) 573-0152.

Crime in Kentucky (Kentucky State Police)—This is an annual report on crime in Kentucky, including incidence and arrests by offense and locale, and arrests by offender characteristics, 1998, with selected comparisons to 1997 and trends from 1988. State Police, Statistics Section, Information Services Branch, 1250 Louisville Road, Frankfort, KY 40601, or call (502) 695-6300. Print copies are free of charge from issuing source when available. It is available online at http://www.kentuckystatepolice.org/data.htm#ciky.

Kentucky Agricultural Statistics (Kentucky Department of Agriculture)—This is an annual report on Kentucky agricultural production, marketing, and finances, 1999, with some data for 2000, and selected trends from the mid-1990s or earlier. Data generally are shown by commodity and/or county and district, with some comparisons to other states, Appalachian and other regions, and the total United States. Kentucky Agricultural Statistics Service, P.O. Box 1120, Louisville, KY 40201-1120, or call (502) 564-4696. Print copies are generally available free of charge from issuing source while supplies last.

Kentucky Annual Vital Statistics Report (Kentucky Cabinet for Health Services, Department for Public Health)—Vital statistics, covering births, deaths by major cause, marriages and divorces, and population, by location and demographic characteristics with selected trends, are provided for the state. It is available on the web at http://publichealth.state.ky.us/data-warehouse.htm, but may be purchased for $10.00 plus $2.50 shipping and handling from the State Center for Health Statistics, Division of Health Planning and Epidemiology, Health Data Branch, Health Services Building, HS1E-C, 275 E. Main Street, Frankfort, KY 40621, or call (502) 564-2757; e-mail healthdata@mail.state.ky.us.

Kentucky Facts (Governor)—This web site, at http://gov.state.ky.us/kids page.htm, pulls together basic information and statistics about Kentucky, which would be great for someone just moving to Kentucky, and a good resource for student projects on Kentucky.

Kentucky State Data Center Home Page (University of Louisville)—State Data Centers are famous for their provision of statistical information and the Kentucky State Data Center is no exception. Its web site at http://ksdc.louisville.edu/ is produced by the University of Louisville, Urban Studies Institute, 426 W. Bloom Street, Louisville, KY 40208, or call (502) 852-7990; fax (502) 852-7386.

Kentucky Traffic Accident Facts (Justice Cabinet)—Fatalities, injuries, property damage, and number of persons killed and injured are detailed with various breakdowns. Includes heavily requested information about involvement of alcohol, drugs, and use of safety restraints. Free while available, request the

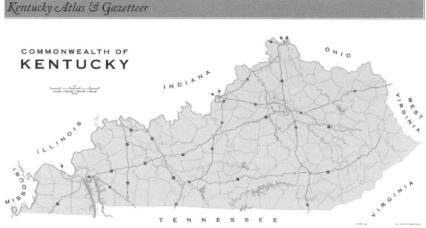

Kentucky Atlas & Gazetteer

COMMONWEALTH OF
KENTUCKY

Select a county from the map for more information or see the counties summary. Relief and physiographic maps are also available.

Kentucky is located in the central United States. In 1990 it had a population of 3,685,296 in an area of 40,395 square miles, an average of 91 people per square mile. The capital of Kentucky is Frankfort.

Search the Gazetteer by the name of a place or feature: [   ]   [Search]

More information about Kentucky is available.

Figure 8. Many states are providing cartographic information driven by web-based geographic information systems, such as this one from Kentucky. *Source*: http://www.uky.edu/KentuckyAtlas/.

report from the Kentucky State Police, Statistics Section, Information Services Branch, 1250 Louisville Road, Frankfort, KY 40601.

Official Primary and General Election Returns (Kentucky Office of the Secretary of State, State Board of Elections)—Results of voting at the Kentucky primary, general, and special elections are provided in this report, which includes breakdowns by party, voter characteristics, and precinct. It is available free from the Kentucky Office of the Secretary of State, State Board of Elections, 140 Walnut Street, Frankfort, KY 40601-3240, or call (502) 573-7100; fax (502) 573-4369. Many statistics also available from the office's web site at http://www.kysos.com/index/main/elecdiv.asp.

Other Resources

Kentucky Atlas and Gazetteer (University of Kentucky)—Located on the web at http://www.uky.edu/KentuckyAtlas/, this online atlas is one of the best to use Geographic Information System(s) (GIS) to provide citizens with various maps (see Figure 8).

Let's Talk Documents (Government Documents Round Table of the Kentucky

Library Association)—Once issued in print, *Let's Talk Documents* is now available only electronically via the Round Table's e-mail listserv. "To subscribe to the LTD list, simply send an e-mail message to listserv@lsv.uky.edu and put the following phrase in the body of your message (without quotation marks): 'subscribe ltd'." The newsletter discusses federal as well as state publications, but is a good connection for exploring Kentucky state documents. For additional information, consult the Kentucky GODORT web site at http://www .kylibasn.org/godort.htm.

KENTUCKY'S WORLD WIDE WEB HOME PAGE

Kentucky Direct (Commonwealth of Kentucky)—Kentucky's official web site, located at http://kentucky.gov/, provides an overview of its purpose, privacy policy, and search engine. It states: "Ensuring electronic access to state government information and services while maintaining privacy is a guiding principle of the state's *Strategic Information Technology Plan*." It is available at http://www.state.ky.us/kirm/sitp/sitp.htm. From a library perspective, the link for "Publications, Research, Maps" leads to the most relevant resources for state documents.

COMMERCIAL PUBLICATIONS AND WEB SITES

Kentucky Annual Economic Report, 2000 (CBER University of Kentucky)—The Center for Business and Economics Research produced the *Kentucky Statistical Abstract* in 1988, but most recently in 2000, it published the *Kentucky Annual Economic Report*. The report and additional information are available on its web site, http://www.gatton.uky.edu/CBER/cber.htm, or from the center at 335-BA Gatton College of Business and Economics, Lexington, KY 40506-0034, or call (859) 257-7675; fax (859) 257-7671; e-mail cber@uky.edu.

SOURCES CONSULTED

Dow, Susan L. *State Document Checklists: A Historical Bibliography.* Buffalo, NY: William S. Hein & Co., 1990.

Harris, Robin R. "Kentucky Statutes and Regulations: A Basic Roadmap." *Kentucky Libraries*, 53 (Summer 1989): 14–19.

Jones, Roxanna. "How to Find Kentucky Government Publication," http://www.uky .edu/Libraries/LI/kydocs.htm.

Lane, Margaret T. *State Publications and Depository Libraries: A Reference Handbook.* Westport, CT: Greenwood Press, 1981.

Parrish, David W. *State Government Reference Publications: An Annotated Bibliography,* 2nd ed. Littleton, CO: Libraries Unlimited, 1981.

State Capital Universe. Bethesda, MD: LexisNexis, 2001; http://web.lexis-nexis.com/ stcapuniv, December 15, 2001. (Available to subscribers only.)

Statistical Universe. Bethesda, MD: LexisNexis, 2001; http://web.lexis-nexis.com/ statuniv, December 15, 2001. (Available to subscribers only.)

U.S. Census Bureau. "Appendix 1: Guide to State Statistical Abstracts." *Statistical Ab-*

stract of the United States 2000. Washington, DC: Department of Commerce, 2000, 902–905.

WorldCat. Columbus, OH: OCLC; http://www.oclc.com, December 4, 2001. (Available to subscribers only.)

Louisiana

Lori L. Smith

GOVERNMENT PUBLISHING AND THE DEPOSITORY SYSTEM

The public documents depository system in Louisiana was established in 1948, and is outlined in Title 25 of the *Louisiana Revised Statutes*, sections 121 through 124.1. A public document is defined in section 121 as "any informational matter, for public distribution regardless of format, method of reproduction, source, or copyright, originating in or produced with the imprint of, by the authority of, or at the total or partial expense of, any state agency. Correspondence and inter-office or intra-office memoranda and records of an archival nature are excluded."

The State Librarian is charged with inaugurating and overseeing the depository system. The Recorder of Documents, who reports to the State Librarian, is charged with managing the system. State agencies are directed to appoint a liaison to the recorder's office, and to supply the recorder with copies of their publications for distribution to the depository libraries. The depositories are required to make the documents freely accessible, to assist the public in using the documents, and to abide by any directives from the recorder.

The rules governing the public document depository system are further fleshed out in Title 25, Volume 7, Part VII, Subpart 5 of the *Louisiana Administrative Code*.

The State Library of Louisiana and Louisiana State University's Hill Memorial Library are designated in the law as complete depositories. Other libraries that wish to become depositories must submit an application to the State Librarian, and, if granted depository status, sign a contract with the State Library. There are currently forty-three Louisiana public document depositories, one of which is the Library of Congress.

USEFUL ADDRESSES AND TELEPHONE NUMBERS

The most complete collections of Louisiana state publications may be found at the following libraries:

State Library of Louisiana
P.O. Box 131
Baton Rouge, LA 70821
Phone Number for Louisiana Reference Questions: (225) 342-4914
E-Mail Address for Louisiana Reference Questions: ladept@pelican.state.lib.la.us
State Library's Home Page: http://www.state.lib.la.us
Recorder of Documents' Home Page: http://www.state.lib.la.us/Dept/UserServ/
  recorder.html

Hill Memorial Library
LSU Libraries
Louisiana State University
Baton Rouge, LA 70803
Phone Number for Louisiana Reference Questions: (225) 578-6547
Web Form for Louisiana Reference Questions: http://www.lib.lsu.edu/special/
  frames/llmvc.html (click "Electronic Reference Request" at the bottom of the page)
Hill Memorial's Home Page: http://www.lib.lsu.edu/special/

Those with questions about the state's depository library system may contact the Recorder of Documents at the State Library address printed above, at (225) 342-4929, or via e-mail at docs@pelican.state.lib.la.us.

INDEXES TO LOUISIANA STATE PUBLICATIONS

The Recorder of Documents compiles, and the State Library publishes, two indexes to state publications—*Public Documents*, which is issued semi-annually, and *Official Publications*, issued every five years. Both sources provide subject, author, and title indexing of state publications, as well as a listing of publications. In *Public Documents*, the listing of publications is given in order by issuing agency. In *Official Publications*, the listing is given in order by Louisiana documents classification (LaDoc) number. In both indexes, a LaDoc number is given for each title. The LaDoc numbering scheme is based upon the Superintendent of Documents classification system commonly used with U.S. government publications, and it arranges documents by issuing agency rather than by subject. The Recorder of Documents is responsible for assigning LaDoc numbers to Louisiana state publications. The LaDoc number for *Public Documents* is Li 1.10:PD/issue #/year/months, and the number for *Official Publications* is Li 1.10:OP/vol. #/years.

Each issue of both titles also includes the text of the law governing the depository system, a list of historic state publication bibliographies, and a list of the current depository libraries.

Public Documents now provides addresses for many agency web sites. Although *Official Publications* is not yet available on the web, the most recent issues of *Public Documents* and a monthly list of publications which have been

received by the recorder's office for distribution are available at http://www
.state.lib.la.us/Publications/docs/index.htm.

ESSENTIAL STATE PUBLICATIONS

Directories

Louisiana School Directory: Bulletin 1462 (Department of Education, Office of
Communications and Legislative Services)—LaDoc Call Number—E 1.9:years.
First issued in 1940, this annual publication is divided into two sections. The
first section lists names, addresses, and phone numbers for staff and officials
within the state Department of Education. Separate listings, with breakdowns
by office and by function, are provided. This section also includes lists of adult
education programs by parish, proprietary schools by city, GED testing centers, and other education-related programs and organizations. The second
section of the *Directory* lists names, addresses, and phone numbers for parish-
level school superintendents and staff, as well as for each public school. A
separate listing for non-public schools is also included in this section. Those
interested in obtaining a print copy of the directory can write to Office of
Communications and Legislative Services, Louisiana Department of Education, P.O. Box 94064, Baton Rouge, LA 70804-9064, or call (225) 342-3773. It is
not available online.

Louisiana State Telephone Directory (Office of Telecommunications Management)—LaDoc Call Number—GO 100.9/2:year. Issued annually, this directory lists state employees by city and department. It is available online at
http://www.state.la.us/otm/listings/telefone.htm.

Roster of Officials (Secretary of State)—LaDoc Call Number—S 1.9:year. This
annual publication provides pictures, addresses, phone numbers, and biographical information on elected officials statewide. This includes U.S. senators and representatives, and state senators and representatives. Names,
addresses, and phone numbers are given for officials in state departments, for
state, parish, and city courts, for parish officials such as sheriffs and coroners,
and for city officials such as mayors and chiefs of police. A separate section
of the *Roster* provides a brief explanation of the duties and terms of office for
each type of official. A final section lists officeholders on state boards and
commissions. A limited number of copies are available for sale. Those interested in obtaining a copy can write to Louisiana Secretary of State, Commercial Division, Administrative and Legal Services Section, P.O. Box 94125, Baton
Rouge, LA 70804-9125, or call (225) 922-0415.

Financial/Budgetary Resources

Comprehensive Annual Financial Report (Governor's Office, Division of Administration, Office of Statewide Reporting and Accounting Policy)—LaDoc
Call Number—Go 100.6/1:years. The *Report*, issued annually, is divided into
three sections. An introductory section provides a textual overview of financial
activity of the state within the reported fiscal year. This section also includes
graphs, and a presentation of the state government's organizational chart. The

second section is composed of subsections headed: General Purpose Financial Statements, Notes to the Combined Financial Statements, Special Revenue Funds, Debt Service Funds, Capital Projects Funds, Proprietary Funds, Fiduciary Funds, General Fixed Assets Account Group, General Long-Term Debt Account Group, College and University Funds, and Discretely Reported Component Units. The third section of the *Report* gives a variety of statistics about the state's population and business environment, as well as some multiple-year summaries of revenues and expenditures. Several recent editions are available online at http://www.doa.state.la.us/osrap/CAFR-2.htm.

Executive Budget and Governor's Supplementary Budget Recommendations (Governor's Office, Office of Planning and Budget)—LaDoc Call Number—Go 100.6:years. This annual, multiple-volume set details the governor's recommended funding of each state agency and special program for a given fiscal year. Several recent editions are available on the web at http://www.doa .state.la.us/opb/pbb/ebsd.html.

Legal Resources

Acts of the Legislature (Legislature)—LaDoc Call Number—Y 1.1:year/regular or extraordinary. This publication is similar to the federal *United States Statutes at Large*. It includes the text of all acts passed during a given legislative session. The acts are printed in numerical order, representing the order in which they were signed by the governor. Similar information can be found in a searchable database on the legislature site at http://www.legis.state.la.us/; select "Session Info."

Constitution of the State of Louisiana of 1974 (House of Representatives)— LaDoc Call Number—Y 5.1:year. A revised edition is issued annually. The Constitution outlines the basic structure of state and local governments in Louisiana. A comprehensive summary of amendments and an index are also included. The Constitution is one of many legal resources that can be searched on the legislature's site at http://www.legis.state.la.us/; select "Louisiana Laws."

Environmental Regulatory Code (ERC) (Department of Environmental Quality)—LaDoc Call Number—NR 200.5:part #/year. Published annually, the ERC is essentially a reprint of Title 33 of the *Louisiana Administrative Code*. It provides the rules and regulations that have been adopted regarding solid waste, air quality, and other environmental issues. It is issued in the following parts: Office of the Secretary, Air, Hazardous Waste and Hazardous Materials, Inactive and Abandoned Hazardous Waste and Hazardous Substance Site Remediation, Solid Waste, Water Quality/Groundwater Protection, Underground Storage Tanks, and Radiation Protection. It is available on the web at http://www.deq.state.la.us/planning/regs/title33/index.htm.

Louisiana Administrative Code (LAC) (Governor's Office, Office of the State Register)—LaDoc Call Number—Go 50.5:vol. #/year. Issued annually, the LAC includes all the rules that have been officially adopted by state agencies. It is similar to the U.S. government's *Code of Federal Regulations*. Titles within the set are assigned numbers between 1 and 76, but there are only about thirty active titles. Most titles are available on the web at http://www.state.la.us/

osr/lac/lac.htm. Information about purchasing volumes of the *Code* is also available from that page.

Louisiana Register (Governor's Office, Office of the State Register)—LaDoc Call Number—Go 50.7:vol. #/issue #. Published monthly, the *Register* reports the proposed and final rules being adopted by state regulatory agencies. It is divided into seven different sections. These are: Executive Orders, Emergency Rules, Rules, Notices of Intent, Administrative Code Update, Potpourri, and Index. Many recent issues, along with information about beginning a subscription, are available on the web at http://www.state.la.us/osr/reg/register .htm.

Resume of Acts, Propositions, Vetoed Bills, Resolutions, and Study Requests (House of Representatives)—LaDoc Call Number—LL 1.8a:year. This annual publication reports on the disposition of all bills, resolutions, and so on, introduced into the legislature during the year. For each session, the *Resume* provides a description of the statutes that were enacted and explains how the new law differs from the prior law. It also includes a listing of proposed amendments to the Constitution, a description of bills which were vetoed, a description of simple and concurrent resolutions, and a listing of requests made by the House and Senate to specific committees to study and report on various issues. Similar information is available in the "Louisiana Laws" section of the legislature's web site at http://www.legis.state.la.us/.

Statistical Resources

District Composite Reports (Department of Education, Office of Management and Finance)—LaDoc Call Number—E 1.2:Pr/year. This statewide report of educational performance indicators is issued annually. The indicators include, among others, class size, faculty education level, student attendance, student dropouts, and student expulsions. Separate reports are produced for each parish, and statistics are given down to the individual school level. The most recent editions are available on CD-ROM and/or online at http://www.doe .state.la.us/DOE/asps/home.asp. Select "District Composite Reports" from the "Most Requested Info" pull-down menu. Those interested in obtaining a print or CD-ROM copy can write to Louisiana Department of Education, Office of Management and Finance, Division of Planning, Analysis and Information Resources, P.O. Box 94064, Baton Rouge, LA 70804-9064, or call (225) 342-3764, or (877) 453-2721.

LEAP (University of Louisiana-Monroe)—*LEAP* stands for Louisiana Electronic Assistance Program. This web site is maintained by the University of Louisiana–Monroe in a partnership with the U.S. Small Business Administration, and provides a wealth of demographic and business information. The address for the site is http://leap.ulm.edu/.

Louisiana Health Report Card (Department of Health and Hospitals, Office of Public Health)—LaDoc Call Number—H 1.1:RC/year. This publication has been issued annually since 1996. It is divided into six sections: Population and Vital Statistics, Morbidity, Health Assessment Programs, Preventative Health Outreach and Service Programs, Louisiana State Health Care System, and Recommendations for Improving Health Status. Numerous tables of statistics are provided in each section. The publication also includes a listing of telephone numbers for various divisions of the Department of Health and Hospitals, and an index. It is available online at http://oph.dhh.state.la.us/records statistics/statistics/index.html. Those interested in obtaining print copies can write to Public Health Statistics Section, 325 Loyola Avenue, Room 103, New Orleans, LA 70112, or call (504) 568-5337. Questions can be e-mailed to statsweb@dhh.state.la.us.

Louisiana Vital Statistics Report (Department of Health and Hospitals, Office of Public Health)—LaDoc Call Number—H 1.7/2a:year. Compiled and issued annually, this report provides statistics on births, deaths, marriages, and divorces. It includes a summary of vital events, such as the age of the oldest bride who was married and the weight of the largest baby who was born during the year. There is a section of general population information, and separate sections on live births, spontaneous fetal deaths, abortions, deaths, infant and maternal mortality, and marriage and divorce. A section of statistics at the end of the report focuses on progress made toward meeting the goals outlined in *Healthy People 2000*. Recent issues are available online at http://oph.dhh.state.la.us/recordsstatistics/statistics/index.html. Those interested in obtaining print copies can write to Public Health Statistics Section, 325 Loyola Avenue, Room 103, New Orleans, LA 70112, or call (504) 568-5337. Questions can be e-mailed to statsweb@dhh.state.la.us.

Other Resources

Louisiana Conservationist (Department of Wildlife and Fisheries, Information and Education Division)—LaDoc Call Number—CoW 1.7:vol. #/issue #/date. This glossy magazine is published bimonthly. The stated motto of the magazine is, "Dedicated to the conservation and restoration of Louisiana's natural resources." Articles focus on hunting, fishing, and environmental topics, and usually include one or more recipes. The table of contents of the most recent issue may be viewed by selecting the *Louisiana Conservationist* link on the Information and Education Division's home page at http://www.wlf.state.la .us/apps/netgear/page58.asp. Those with questions can call the Public Information Section at (225) 765-2925.

Louisiana Official Highway Map (Department of Transportation and Development and Department of Culture, Recreation and Tourism)—LaDoc Call Number—PWH 1.8m:year. This is published annually. Call (800) 261-9144 to request a copy, or request one online at http://www.louisianatravel.com/.

Louisiana Tour Guide (Department of Culture, Recreation and Tourism)—LaDoc Call Number—C 10.2:Gu/year. This is issued annually, and describes the many different activities and scenic sites available in each area of the state. Call (800) 677-4082 to request a copy, or request one online at http://www .louisianatravel.com/.

LOUISIANA'S WORLD WIDE WEB HOME PAGE

Those who do not have easy access to one of Louisiana's public documents depositories will find that the state's home page, *Info Louisiana*, is an excellent source of information. The page is located at http://www.state.la.us/.

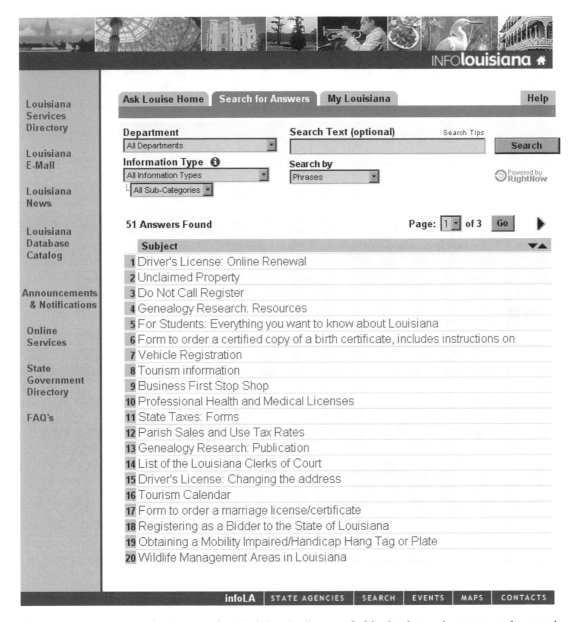

Figure 9. Louisiana's web site provides "Ask Louise," a searchable database of answers to frequently asked questions. *Source*: http://www.state.la.us.

Info Louisiana's main menu provides the following subject choices: Government, Louisiana Life, Business, Visit Louisiana, Education, Employment, About Louisiana, and Services. Each provides a pop-up menu of additional choices. The Government submenu provides, among other selections, a listing of state agencies, and a publications page that gives easy access to many of the titles mentioned in this chapter.

The center of the home page provides a brief listing of state government news headlines, and a listing of featured services and information sources. The right side of the page has options for Louisiana News, Louisiana Services Directory, Louisiana E-Mall, and Ask Louise. Ask Louise is a searchable version of the site's extensive collection of FAQs (see Figure 9).

A site search feature, accessible from a button on the toolbar at the bottom of the screen, allows one to perform a keyword search of all pages on the site.

The state's Division of Administration is responsible for maintaining the *Info Louisiana* site. The webmaster may be reached at (225) 219-4025, or at webmaster@doa.state.la.us.

COMMERCIAL PUBLICATIONS AND WEB SITES

Louisiana Almanac (Pelican Publishing Company, P.O. Box 3110, Gretna, LA 70054)—This source provides impressively comprehensive information on all things related to Louisiana—history, weather and climate, demographics, geology, agriculture, religion, vital statistics, and so on. See the publisher's web site at http://www.pelicanpub.com/ for more information.

Statistical Abstract of Louisiana (Division of Business and Economic Research, College of Business Administration, University of New Orleans, New Orleans, LA 70148-1536)—Like its federal counterpart, the *Statistical Abstract of the United States*, this source presents statistical information gathered by numerous different agencies. The 1997 edition is available online at http://leap .ulm.edu/STAAB.htm.

West's Louisiana Statutes Annotated, Revised Statutes (West Group, 610 Opperman Drive, Eagan, MN 55123)—This is the official edition of the *Revised Statutes*. It contains the codified version of Louisiana's laws, and is similar to the federal *United States Code*. For more information, see the publisher's web site at http://west.thomson.com/store/default.asp.

SOURCES CONSULTED

Calhoun, Milburn, ed. *Louisiana Almanac 1997–98 Edition*. Gretna, LA: Pelican Publishing Company, 1997.

Constitution of the State of Louisiana of 1974, Current Through November 1998. Baton Rouge: Louisiana House of Representatives, December 1998.

Numerous departmental web pages via *Info Louisiana*, http://www.state.la.us/.

Public Documents No. 97, January–June 1998. Baton Rouge: State Library of Louisiana, 1998.

Public Documents No. 98, July–December 1998. Baton Rouge: State Library of Louisiana, 1998.

Maine

Eric W. Johnson

GOVERNMENT PUBLISHING AND THE DEPOSITORY SYSTEM

Title 1, Section 501-A of the *Maine Revised Statutes* established in 1997 the requirement for all state agencies to deposit eighteen copies of their publications with the Maine State Library, which acts as the central depository in a multilibrary State Document Depository Program. According to the statute, the term "publications" includes

periodicals; newsletters; bulletins; pamphlets; leaflets; directories; bibliographies; statistical reports; brochures; plan drafts; planning documents; reports; special reports; committee and commission minutes; information handouts; and rules and compilations of rules, regardless of number of pages, number of copies ordered, physical size, publication medium or intended audience inside or outside the agency.

There are two exceptions to this rule. The State Library receives at least fifty-five copies of any annual or biennial report that is not included in the *Maine State Government Annual Report* for exchange and library use, and agencies or committees that electronically publish information are required to provide only one printed copy of an electronic publication. Publications that are designed to provide the public with current information and are subject to frequent additions and deletions (such as daily updates of weather conditions or job advertisements) are exempt from the electronic publications rule.

The Documents Office at the State Library keeps three copies of state publications—one as a non-circulating archival copy and the other two available for borrowing. Two additional copies are sent to the Library of Congress, and the remaining copies are distributed to the twelve libraries (ten academic, one public, and one legislative) in the depository program.

USEFUL ADDRESSES AND TELEPHONE NUMBERS

The most complete collections of Maine state publications may be found at the following libraries:

Maine State Library
Documents Office
State House Station #64
Augusta, ME 04333
Phone Number for Maine Reference Questions: (207) 287-5600
E-Mail Link for Maine Reference Questions: http://msl1.ursus.maine.edu/mslref/
   mslrq/mslrqref_entry.cfm
Documents Office Home Page: http://www.state.me.us/msl/about/msldocs.htm
Library's Home Page: http://www.state.me.us/msl/

Fogler Library
Special Collections
University of Maine
Orono, ME 04469-5729
Phone Number for Maine Reference Questions: (207) 581-1686
E-Mail Address for Maine Reference Questions: spc@umit.maine.edu
Special Collections Department's Home Page: http://www.library.umaine.edu/
   speccoll/statdocs.htm
Library's Home Page: http://www.library.umaine.edu/default.asp

INDEXES TO MAINE STATE PUBLICATIONS

Government Publications Checklist—Published since 1941 by the Maine State
Library, this is the official checklist for state publications. While the *Checklist*
is not available online, state publications may be found in the online catalog
URSUS, the shared catalog of the University of Maine System, Bangor Public
Library, the Maine State Library, and the Maine State Law and Legislative
Reference Library, at http://ursus.maine.edu/. They may also be located
through the *Maine Info Net Statewide Catalog*, which includes a number of on-
line catalogs for academic and public libraries, including *URSUS*. The *Maine
Info Net Statewide Catalog* may be found at http://130.111.64.9/.

ESSENTIAL STATE PUBLICATIONS

Directories

Directory of Maine Schools (Department of Education)—Known familiarly as
"The Moose Book," this directory contains contact and statistical data for the
school systems in Maine. Listings include alphabetical indexes for municipalities and schools and other reports which show name, location, mailing address, telephone, fax, school principal, grade span, school type, and e-mail
address. The online version allows searching of reports by name, municipality,
county, school administrative unit, and superintendent region. The directory
is available online at http://www.state.me.us/education/eddir/homepage
.htm. Inquiries about the print version may be directed to the Department of
Education, 23 State House Station, Augusta, ME 04333-0023, or call (207) 624-
6620.
Maine College/University Directory (Finance Authority of Maine)—This is an
online listing of public and private colleges, universities, technical schools,

hospitals, and cosmetology and barber schools, with telephone numbers. It may be found online at http://famemaine.com/html/education/directory.html.

Maine State Government Electronic Directory Listings (Bureau of Information Services)—This is an online telephone and address listing by department or bureau names, including the commissioner or director. A "white pages" listing by personnel is accessible only through Maine state government computers, but the "yellow pages" list information related to such subjects as fish, road, tax, or forest. This directory may be accessed online at http://www.state.me.us/bis/phone/phone.htm. For further information, contact the Bureau of Information Services, 145 State House Station, Augusta, ME 04333-0145, or call (207) 624-8800.

Financial/Budgetary Resources

Maine State Government Annual Report (Bureau of the Budget)—This is the annual report of the state's finances, mandated by federal law. It is available in paper from the Division of Purchases, Central Printing, 9 State House Station, Augusta, ME 04333-0009, or call (207) 624-7340.

State of Maine Budget Document (Bureau of the Budget)—This biennial publication includes an overview, the state budget and financial plan, and strategic operational plans. The budget message by the governor outlining financial policy precedes detailed estimates of expenditures and revenues, including statements of the state's bond indebtedness. The online version of the *Budget Document* may be found at the Bureau of the Budget's web site at http://www.state.me.us/budget/homepage.htm, and includes general summaries, departmental funding breakdowns, appropriations and revenues, and Highway Fund information. A paper copy of the document may be requested from the Bureau of the Budget, Burton M. Cross State Office Building, 109 Sewall Street, 3rd Floor, #58 State House Station, Augusta, ME 04333-0058, or call (207) 624-7810.

Legal Resources

Maine Revised Statutes (Legislature, Revisor of Statutes)—This title is maintained and updated each fall to incorporate changes made by the immediately preceding legislative session. The online version of the statutes contains historical references to changes made to the statutes since the last general revision in 1964, and may be browsed in its entirety, or by title, chapter, or section. The statutes are accessible online at http://janus.state.me.us/legis/statutes/. The statutes are also available as the *Maine Revised Statutes Annotated*, a commercial publication listed below.

Laws of the State of Maine (Legislature, Revisor of Statutes)—This biennial contains all Session Laws and related documents of each legislative session. Included are public laws, private and special laws, resolves, constitutional resolutions, joint study orders, and revisor's reports. The online version includes all laws since the 118th Legislature, from December 1996 to the present, and may be found at http://janus.state.me.us/legis/ros/lom/lomdirectory

.htm. More information about these publications may be obtained from the Office of the Revisor of Statutes, Room 108, State House, Augusta, ME 04333-0007, or call (207) 287-1650. The e-mail address for the revisor is revisor .office@state.me.us.

Statistical Resources

School Profiles; Maine's K–12 Schools (Department of Education)—This online directory provides school profiles for public and private schools, school administrative units, the Education of Unorganized Territories System, and state-operated and charter schools. In addition to the typical directory-type information (name, address, principal or superintendent), statistical information on background data, educational resources, and student outcomes is included. The *Profiles* may be found at http://www.state.me.us/education/profiles/profilehome.htm.

Annual Statistical Report for the Calendar Year [Year] (Bureau of Health)—This compilation of statistics on births, deaths, marriages, and divorces may be obtained from the Office of Data, Research and Vital Statistics, Department of Human Services, 11 State House Station, 161 Capitol Street, Augusta, ME 04333, or by calling (207) 287-5500.

Labor Market Digest (Department of Labor, Labor Market Information Services)—This monthly newsletter provides statistical information on gross state product, civilian labor force, wage and salary, unemployment compensation program indicators, earnings and hours, private employer costs, and other related labor topics. The newsletter may be found on the web at http://www.maine.gov/labor/lmis/index.html?pubs.html. A print subscription can be obtained through Labor Market Information Services, 20 Union Street, Augusta, ME 04330-6826, or call (207) 287-2271; or by e-mailing LMIS at lmi .me@state.me.us.

Other Resources

Maine Invites You (Office of Tourism)—This annual travel guide, "Maine's Official Travel Planner," inlcudes general tourist information, attractions, accommodations, and special events. A copy of the travel guide may be requested from the Office of Tourism's web site at http://www.visitmaine .com/home.php. The Office of Tourism can be contacted at 59 State House Station, Augusta, ME 04333-0059, or call (207) 287-5711

Facts about Maine—This is an online compilation of facts about Maine and its history, capitol, symbols, and products. "Fast facts" includes area, population, capital, date of statehood, and so on while "fun facts" links both to the "Kids' Page" and to general information for adults, covering everything from Maine firsts to license plates and Maine products. *Facts about Maine* is available online at http://www.maine.gov/portal/facts_history/facts.html.

MAINE'S WORLD WIDE WEB HOME PAGE

The official Maine state web site, http://www.Maine.gov/, was redesigned in 2002. At the top of the home page, users can link to sections on Government,

Living, Visiting, Working, Business, Education, and Facts and History, all of which provide either links to pertinent information or the information itself. There is a state agency index with hyperlinks to agency and departmental pages. A "Press Room" provides links to online news and press releases from the agencies. At the bottom of the page, links to the governor, the legislature, and the judicial branch are available. Special links include information on homeland security, Maine weather, and a "Kids' Page," where children can find facts, cartoons, schools, games, and homework helpers. Links to online services and answers to common questions, along with photographs of Maine, round out the page.

The "Facts and History" link connects the user to sections on Maine history as told by mariners, genealogical resources, geology, history, weather and climate, and maps, as well as an extensive statistics page with further links to such topics as demographics and population, crime, health, motor vehicles, taxes, and the *Maine Statistical Almanac*.

The state web site is managed by InforME, a public/private partnership created by the InforME Access to Public Information Act. The fifteen-member InforME Board combines government and private business interests, education, and association representation. Board members include representatives from state agencies that are major data custodians, the University of Maine System, a municipalities association, a non-profit organization advancing citizens' rights of access to information, and the libraries. For more information on the web site or InforME, contact Information Resource of Maine at (877) 212-6500 or e-mail the webmaster at webmaster@informe.org.

COMMERCIAL PUBLICATIONS AND WEB SITES

Maine Register (Tower Publishing Company, 588 Saco Road, Standish, ME 04084)—Maine's oldest and most respected business publication since 1820, the *Maine Register* is the most comprehensive, accurate, and complete single-volume source on the governmental, business, and professional community in Maine. The annual *Register* contains federal, state, and local government offices and officials; over 45,000 listings of Maine businesses, the judicial system, census data, tax valuations, law offices, libraries, chambers of commerce, and hundreds of professional and non-profit organizations. It can be ordered from the publisher at the above address or through the publisher's web site at http://www.towerpub.com/.

Maine Revised Statutes Annotated (West Group, 610 Opperman Drive, Eagan, MN 55123)—This annual compilation of Maine state law contains the full text of the Maine State Constitution, statutes, rules, session laws, and legislative history, as well as court orders and decision notes, including federal cases originating in Maine. It also includes extensive annotations and cross-references, as well as library references to other relevant material, such as *Maine Digest*. The 2002 edition sold for $840, and was available through the publisher's web site at http://west.thomson.com/store/default.asp, or by calling West Group's customer service at (800) 328-4880.

Maine Statistical Almanac (Publius Research, 2 Jays Ledge Lane, Harpswell, ME 04079)—The goal of this online almanac is "to provide basic, nontechnical, and easily accessible factual information" about the state of Maine. Information is searched through a listing of keywords, and includes facts and figures on government, budget, vital statistics, economy, and a host of other topics. It may be found on the web at http://www.maine.com/users/publius/masintro.htm.

Publius Research also publishes *Maine 2002: An Encyclopedia*, edited by James S. Henderson. This CD-ROM "encyclopedia of people, places, ideas, issues, fact, and fiction" includes more than 1,000 articles on Maine history, geography, biography, government, education, and high school sports, and over 1,000 photos, maps, and charts. It can be ordered through the address or web site listed above, or by calling the publisher at (207) 833-5911; or through e-mail at publius@maine.com.

The Fact Book 2001 (Mainebiz Publications, 413 Congress Street, Portland, ME 04101)—This compilation of demographic information and marketplace statistics for Maine was published by Mainebiz, which is also the name of the state's major business news publication. Information on ordering *The Fact Book* can be obtained on Mainebiz's web site at http://www.maine-biz.com/, or by calling (207) 761-8379.

SOURCES CONSULTED

Maine State Library's web site, http://www.state.me.us/msl/.
Numerous departmental web pages via *Maine.gov*, the state's official web site, http://www.maine.gov/.
Various publishers' web pages, noted above.

Maryland

Lori L. Smith

GOVERNMENT PUBLISHING AND THE DEPOSITORY SYSTEM

In 1982, legislation was passed to establish a depository program in Maryland. In early 1983, the State Publications Depository and Distribution Program began functioning as a unit within Maryland's State Library Resource Center. The State Library Resource Center is the Enoch Pratt Free Library, which reports to the Division of Library Development and Services of the Maryland State Department of Education.

The responsibilities of the program, as outlined in the law, are to collect state publications and distribute them to depository libraries, to determine which publications can be exempted from distribution, and to issue a monthly list of publications received. The director of the Resource Center is charged with appointing an administrator for the program. State agencies are required to appoint a person to supply the program with a sufficient number of their publications for the depository libraries. Bicounty agencies are also required to appoint a person to supply publications, but they have the choice to supply only one copy of each publication to the program and to distribute copies to all public libraries in their bicounty areas; or, to supply sufficient copies to the program for all depository libraries.

In title 23, section 301(1) of the *Maryland Code*, state publication is defined as

informational materials produced, regardless of format, by the authority of, or at the total or partial expense of any State agency. It includes a publication sponsored by a State agency, issued in conjunction with, or under contract with the federal government, local units of government, private individuals, institutions, corporations, research firms or other entities. "State publication" does not include correspondence, interoffice and intraoffice memoranda, routine forms or other internal records. It also does not include publications of bicounty agencies which comply with this program as required in §23–304 of this article and it does not include any informational listing which any State statute provides shall be sold to members of the public for a fee.

The definition of state agency includes state-supported institutions of higher education and units from all three branches of state government.

Funding for the program is designated in the law to come from the State Board of Education's budget. In a round of statewide budget cuts in 1991, funding for the program was eliminated. The Enoch Pratt Free Library continued to provide a more limited version of the depository program until 2002, when they ceased to distribute publications. The legislation that established the program is still in place, but without funding, the gears of the system ground to a halt. Many Maryland publications are now available on the web, and that fact may have contributed to the library's decision to cease distribution of print materials.

USEFUL ADDRESSES AND TELEPHONE NUMBERS

The best collections of Maryland publications can be found at the following libraries:

Enoch Pratt Free Library
400 Cathedral Street
Baltimore, MD 21201
Phone Number for Maryland Reference Questions: (410) 396-5430
Web Form for Maryland Reference Questions: http:www.epfl.net/ask/epfl_ask.html
Library's Home Page: http://www.epfl.net/index.html

Maryland State Law Library
Robert C. Murphy Courts of Appeal Building
361 Rowe Boulevard
Annapolis, MD 21401-1697
Phone Number for Maryland Reference Questions: (410) 260-1430, or toll-free in
    Maryland (888) 216-8156
E-Mail Address for Maryland Reference Questions: mdlaw.library@courts.state.md.us
Library's Home Page: http://www.lawlib.state.md.us

University of Maryland Libraries
Hornbake Library
Marylandia and Rare Books Department
College Park, MD 20742
Phone Number for Maryland Reference Questions: (301) 405-9210
Web Form for Maryland Reference Questions: http://www.lib.umd.edu/RARE/
    index/queries.html
Maryland Collection Home Page: http://www.lib.umd.edu/RARE/Maryland
    Collection/index.html

INDEXES TO MARYLAND STATE PUBLICATIONS

In the first few years of its existence, the State Publications Depository and Distribution Program issued a monthly bibliography entitled *Maryland State Publications: Documents Received by the State Publications Depository Distribution Program*. The Hall of Records Commission, an advisory body to the State Archives, for several years published *Maryland State Documents Received at the Hall of Records During the Month of . . .*, which was followed by the very similar title *Maryland State Publications Received at the Hall of Records During the Month of. . . .* The Maryland State Archives currently provides several searchable databases of government information. These can be accessed online from its "Search the Archives" page at http://www.mdarchives.state.md.us/msa/homepage/html/search.html.

The Library and Information Services Division of the General Assembly's Department of Legislative Services currently issues a monthly bibliography called *Maryland Documents*. As of this writing it is not yet available on the web. Those who wish to enquire about the availability of print copies can write to Department of Legislative Services, Library and Information Services, 90 State Circle, Annapolis, MD 21401. Persons in Maryland can call toll-free (800) 492-7122. Persons in Washington, DC, can call (301) 970-5400; others can call (410) 946-5400.

The Enoch Pratt Free Library's online catalog, which includes records for Maryland publications, can be accessed by clicking the "PRATTCAT" icon on the library's home page at http://www.epfl.net/index.html. State documents can most easily be located by selecting the "Power Search" option, then selecting "Government Document" from the pull-down menu for "type." A union catalog of publications held by the libraries in the University System of Maryland can be searched at http://catalog.umd.edu/.

No standard call numbers are assigned to Maryland documents, so each library assigns a number based on its own local practices.

ESSENTIAL STATE PUBLICATIONS

Directories

Directory of Maryland Public and Private Higher Education Institutions, Agencies and Boards (Maryland Higher Education Commission)—This directory provides contact information for all of Maryland's universities, and for education-related organizations. The directory is not available online, but links to university web sites and other information sources are provided on the commission's "Colleges and Universities" page at http://www.mhec.state.md.us/Colleges&Universities/colleges.htm. Those who wish to enquire about the availability of a print copy of the directory can write to Maryland Higher Education Commission, 839 Bestgate Road, Suite 400, Annapolis, MD 21401, or call (410) 260-4500. Persons in Maryland can call toll-free (800) 974-0203.

Maryland Directory of Public Education (Department of Education)—This directory lists members of the Maryland State Board of Education and gives the date each member's term on the board will end. For each county-level office, an address, phone number, fax number, and web site address are given. The members of the county's Board of Education are listed. Names, titles, and phone numbers are given for persons in the Office of the Superintendent, and the offices of Administration and Finance, Instruction and Staff Development, and Pupil Services and Special Education. For each school, the school's name, mailing address, principal's name, and phone number are provided. The directory also includes addresses for higher education organizations, and an alphabetical list of Department of Education employees with their phone numbers. The directory is available on the web at http://www.msde.state.md.us/directory_printed/toc.html. Those who wish to enquire about the availability of print copies can write to Maryland State Department of Education, 200 West Baltimore Street, Baltimore, MD 21201, or call (410) 767-0100.

Maryland Farmers' Market Directory (Department of Agriculture)—A county-by-county list of farmers' markets is available online at http://www.mda.state.md.us/market/fmd.htm. The location of the market is given along with the normal months and hours of operation. A contact person and phone number for additional information is provided for each.

Maryland State Government Telephone Directory (Department of Budget and Management, Office of Information Technology)—This directory can be accessed from the Maryland state portal by selecting "Statewide Telephone Directory" from the drop-down menu of online services, or directly at http://www.dbm.state.md.us/SearchUtility/default.htm. It provides names, position titles, phone numbers, and e-mail addresses for state government employees and for state agencies. The directory can be searched by name, position title, office/division, or department/agency. Options for sorting results are offered. A form can be printed from the web for use in ordering a print copy of the directory from the Department of General Services.

Roster and List of Committees of the General Assembly of Maryland (Department of Legislative Services, Library and Information Services)—A new edition of this title is issued for every session of the General Assembly. The publication provides lists of House and Senate members, lists of persons on House, Senate, and Joint committees, and includes biographical information about each legislator. Those who wish to enquire about the availability of print copies can write to Department of Legislative Services, Library and Information Services, 90 State Circle, Annapolis, MD 21401. Persons in Maryland can call toll-free (800) 492-7122. Persons in Washington, DC, can call (301) 970-5400; others can call (410) 946-5400. Questions or requests can also be e-mailed to libr@mlis.state.md.us.

Financial/Budgetary Resources

Analysis of the Maryland Executive Budget for the Fiscal Year Ending June 30, [Year] (Department of Legislative Services, Office of Policy Analysis)—As required by law, the Office of Policy Analysis reviews the budget recommendations submitted by the governor and prepares this report to advise the General Assembly on increases or reductions it might wish to consider based on agency performance and other factors. The report is distributed to members of the General Assembly before a vote is taken on bills related to appropriations. The most recent edition of the report is available on the General Assembly web site at http://mlis.state.md.us/. Those who wish to enquire about the availability of print copies can write to Department of Legislative Services, Library and Information Services, 90 State Circle, Annapolis, MD 21401. Persons in Maryland can call toll-free (800) 492-7122. Persons in Washington, DC, can call (301) 970-5400. Others can call (410) 946-5400. Questions or requests can also be e-mailed to libr@mlis.state.md.us.

Comprehensive Annual Financial Report for the Fiscal Year Ended June 30, [Year] (CAFR) (Comptroller of Maryland)—The revenues and expenditures of the state government are reported in detail in this publication. The introductory section lists state officials and provides an organizational chart for the state government. The financial section presents balance sheets and other general financial statements. The third section of the report contains required supplementary material on selected state pension systems. The fourth section, "Combining Financial Statements and Schedules," reports on special revenue funds, debt service funds, other funds, and account groups. The final section provides statistics on various topics. Many tables in that section include figures for the last ten fiscal years. The most recent edition of the CAFR can be found on the comptroller's "Fiscal Reports" web page at http://www.marylandtaxes.com/publications/fiscalrprts/default.asp.

FY [Year] Capital Budget as Enacted (Department of Budget and Management, Office of Capital Budgeting)—Maryland's *Capital Budget* covers capital improvements or projects such as building a new facility or renovating an old one. The amount awarded to each agency for such projects is reported each year in this publication. Funds allocated are reported as general obligation bonds, general funds, special funds, federal funds, and revenue bonds. Details about the projects being funded are supplied in the "Project Lists" section. Several recent editions of the publication are available on the department's web site at http://www.dbm.maryland.gov/. Those with questions can write to Department of Budget and Management, 45 Calvert Street, Annapolis, MD 21401, or e-mail marylandgov@dbm.state.md.us. Persons in Maryland can call toll-free (800) 705-3493.

FY [Year] Operating Budget Detail (Department of Budget and Management, Office of Budget Analysis)—The *Operating Budget* reports each agency's mission, vision, key goals, objectives, and performance measures. It provides detailed figures on agency expenditures in the previous fiscal year, appropriations for the current fiscal year, and their allowance for the next fiscal year. Recent issues are available on the department's web site at http://www.dbm.maryland.gov/. Select "Budget" from the top toolbar. Those with questions can write to Department of Budget and Management, Office of Budget Analysis, 45 Calvert Street, Annapolis, MD 21401, or call (401) 260-7271. Persons in Maryland can call toll-free (800) 705-3493.

Maryland Budget Priorities FY [Year] Budget (Governor)—In many other states this publication would be called the governor's executive budget. It outlines the amounts of money that the governor would like the General Assembly to allocate to state departments/agencies and for specific projects. Summaries for each agency describe the purpose of the agency, give highlights of projects the agency has planned, and provide a three-year table of appropriations, expenditures, positions, and performance measures. The most recent edition of the publication is available online from the Department of Budget and Management web site at http://www.dbm.maryland.gov/. Select "Budget" from the top toolbar. Those with questions can e-mail the governor at governor@

gov.state.md.us, or write to Maryland Governor, State House, Annapolis, MD 21401. Maryland residents can call toll-free (800) 811-8336.

Legal Resources

Code of Maryland Regulations (COMAR) (Office of the Secretary of State, Division of State Documents)—*COMAR* compiles the regulations promulgated by all state agencies and departments. Most of the thirty-three titles in the multiple-volume set relate to one agency or department. The set is issued in a looseleaf format for easy annual updating. Titles can be purchased individually, or an entire set can be ordered. The price for a complete set in 2002 was $975. Current pricing and ordering information can be found on the Division of State Documents' web site on the "*COMAR* Order Form." Both the online edition of *COMAR* and the order form can be accessed from http://www.sos.state.md.us/sos/dsd/comar/html/comar.html. The online edition of the publication can be searched by keyword, as a whole or limited to a specific title, or browsed by table of contents. Those with questions about obtaining print volumes can write to Division of State Documents, 1700 Margaret Avenue, Annapolis, MD 21401, or call the *COMAR* Subscription Manager at (410) 974-2486, extension 317. Persons in Maryland can call toll-free (800) 633-9657. Questions can be e-mailed to statedocs@dsd.state.md.us.

Maryland Register (Office of the Secretary of State, Division of State Documents)—This title is a biweekly supplement to *COMAR*. It contains proposed and adopted regulations, emergency regulations, the governor's executive orders, the Attorney General opinions, and a variety of public notices. The online edition of the *Register*, which includes only the six most recent issues, and a subscription form, can both be accessed from http://www.sos.state.md.us/sos/dsd/mdreg/html/mdreg.html. A subscription in 2002 was $190 for delivery by first-class mail, and $110 for delivery by second class. Individual issues can be requested for a fee of $5 plus $2 for postage and handling. Those with questions can write to Division of State Documents, 1700 Margaret Avenue, Annapolis, MD 21401, or call (410) 974-2486. Persons in Maryland can call toll-free (800) 633-9657. Questions can be e-mailed to statedocs@dsd.state.md.us.

Maryland Statutes (General Assembly)—The official version of Maryland's codified laws is a commercial publication called *Annotated Code of Maryland*. Since copyright restrictions prevent the General Assembly from providing free access to the *Annotated Code*, its web site at http://mlis.state.md.us provides two alternate ways to view Maryland's laws. The first is a cumulative database of statutes. To search this database, select the "Search Site" option from the General Assembly home page. The search page allows the user to do a keyword search, and to limit the search to statutes, or to other publications such as amendments, bill texts, chapters, or fiscal notes. The other method of viewing laws from the General Assembly site is to select *Maryland Code Online* from the home page. This leads to a free version of the *Code* provided by the publisher of the commercial edition. It does not provide all the features or information included in the official version, but it does provide the basic text of the laws.

Synopsis of Laws Enacted (Department of Legislative Services, Library and Information Services)—The laws enacted and joint resolutions passed during a session of the General Assembly are summarized in this publication. Bills that were vetoed are also summarized. A variety of indexes are provided, and sections of the *Annotated Code* that were amended or repealed are listed. Those who wish to enquire about the availability of print copies can write to Department of Legislative Services, Library and Information Services, 90 State Circle, Annapolis, MD 21401. Persons in Maryland can call toll-free (800) 492-7122. Persons in Washington, DC, can call (301) 970-5400. Others can call (410) 946-5400. Questions or requests can also be e-mailed to libr@mlis.state.md.us.

Statistical Resources

Data Book (Maryland Higher Education Commission, Office of Policy Analysis and Research)—This annual publication provides statistics on the universities, community colleges, and private career schools in Maryland. Statistics are presented in the following categories: Students, Retention and Graduation, Degrees, Faculty, Revenues and Expenditures, Tuition and Fees, Financial Aid, and Private Career Schools. The most recent edition of the report is available online at http://www.mhec.state.md.us/Research/Studies andReports/ResearchInformationPage.htm. Those who wish to enquire about the availability of print copies can write to Maryland Higher Education Commission, Office of Policy Analysis and Research, 839 Bestgate Road, Suite 400, Annapolis, MD 21401, or call (410) 260-4540. Persons in Maryland can call toll-free (800) 974-0203.

Data Center (Department of Business and Economic Development)—In an effort to encourage businesses to locate in Maryland, this department makes available a wide variety of statistical information about the state on its *Data Center* page at http://www.dbed.state.md.us/datacenter/index.asp. The original source of the statistics cited is usually mentioned and often a link is provided for those who need additional information.

Maryland Statistical Abstract (Towson University, Regional Economics Study Institute and Maryland Department of Business and Economic Development)—Produced biennially, this source provides statistics in categories such as: Demographics, Vital Statistics, Education, Manufacturing, Transportation, Government Finances, Elections, and Climate and Natural Resources. Totals are provided for the state, regions within the state, and other substate levels. Some national statistics are provided for comparison. The 2000 edition of the *Abstract* was sold in print and on a CD-ROM. The print was $75 plus $5 for shipping and handling, and the CD was $50 plus $5 for shipping and handling. A set of both formats was $100, plus $5 for shipping. An order form for the most recent edition is available at http://www.resiusa.org/statab.asp. Those with questions can write to Regional Economics Study Institute, Towson University, 8000 York Road, Towson, MD 21252-7097, or call (410) 704-7374.

Maryland Vital Statistics Annual Report (Department of Health and Mental Hygiene, Vital Statistics Administration, Division of Health Statistics)—Tables of statistics are presented in this publication in eight major sections: Population, Life Expectancy, Natality, Fetal and Infant Mortality, Mortality, Marriages, Divorces (which includes annulments), and Comparative Vital Statistics. Many tables give figures for the state as a whole, for regions such as the Northwest Area and the Baltimore Metro Area, and for counties within those regions. The comparative section provides statistics for Maryland and for the United States. Many statistics are also presented as charts. The 1999 edition is based on the tenth revision of *International Classification of Diseases* (ICD-10). The impact of this change on statistics reported is explained in detail. Recent editions of the report are available online at http://mdpublichealth .org/vsa/html/reports.html. Those who wish to enquire about the availability of print copies can write to Vital Statistics Administration, Division of Health Statistics, 201 West Preston Street, Baltimore, MD 21201, or call (410) 767-5950. Persons in Maryland can call toll-free (877) 4MD-DHMH (877-463-3464).

Other Resources

Maryland Electronic Capital (State Archives)—This web site is similar in scope to the state's official Internet portal, but it is somewhat easier to navigate. The address of the site is http://www.mec.state.md.us/. The home page provides a simple list of topics/links from which to select. The list includes Governor's Office, General Assembly, Judiciary, Tourism, State Tax Information, State Agencies/Boards/Commissions, and several others. Those with questions can e-mail mecweb@mdarchives.state.md.us.

Maryland Hospital Performance Evaluation Guide (Maryland Health Care Commission)—Available on the web at http://hospitalguide.mhcc.state.md.us/ index.htm, this guide provides information about how well Maryland's hospitals have performed in treating patients with specific conditions. A "Facility Profile Report" is given for each hospital that provides an address, phone number, and web site address, information about who owns and operates the hospital, number of beds available, and if the hospital has been accredited. A "Hospital Report by Diagnosis Related Group" provides statistics for each hospital on the number of cases of a specific condition they've treated, the average number of days that patients being treated stayed in the hospital, and the percentage of patients readmitted after treatment. A "Facility Diagnosis Related Group Report" gives statistics for one hospital's performance with a group of similar diseases, such as circulatory disorders. For each specific disorder within the group, statistics for the hospital are given on number of patients treated, length of stay, and readmissions. Those with questions about the guide can write to Maryland Health Care Commission, 4201 Patterson Avenue, 5th Floor, Baltimore, MD 21215, or call (410) 764-3460.

Maryland Manual (State Archives)—Each agency, department, division, and subdivision in Maryland state government is described in this source. Names, addresses, phone numbers, and e-mail addresses for officers are provided, as is information about the agency's origin and functions, historical evolution, organizational chart, organizational structure, budget, and the reports they issue. Print and/or CD-ROM copies of the manual can be ordered by sending a request to Maryland State Archives, 350 Rowe Boulevard, Annapolis, MD 21401, or by calling (410) 260-6429. Requests, or questions about pricing, can also be sent to ref@mdarchives.state.md.us. Ordering information for both the print and CD editions can be accessed from the *Maryland Manual On-Line* page at http://www.mdarchives.state.md.us/msa/mdmanual/html/mmtoc.html. The online edition, which is searchable by keyword, is updated regularly and is used to produce the quarterly CD-ROM editions. Questions about the contents of the manual can be sent to mdmanual@mdarchives.state.md.us.

SAILOR, Maryland's Public Information Network (SAILOR Operations Center, Enoch Pratt Free Library, State Library Resource Center)—This web site, at http://www.sailor.lib.md.us, provides access to a great deal of information about Maryland. Links on the home page lead to information on: Arts and Entertainment, Business/Employment, Education, Government and Law, Health, History, Kids' Pages, Libraries, Places and People, Science and Technology, and Society and Culture. The site is a joint project of public libraries in Maryland. In addition to web links, it also provides access for Maryland's residents to a selection of commercial databases. Those with questions can write to SAILOR Operations Center, 400 Cathedral Street, Baltimore, MD 21201, or call (401) 396-5551. Questions can be e-mailed to askus@sailor.lib .md.us.

MARYLAND'S WORLD WIDE WEB HOME PAGE

Maryland's Internet portal, or home page, is at http://maryland.gov. The site is maintained by the Department of Budget and Management. The toolbar section at the top of the page, which remains constant throughout the site, provides a search box and buttons leading to help, a FAQ, and back to the home page. There are also buttons for eight "virtual agencies" leading to information on: Education; Business; Travel and Recreation; Taxes; Family, Health and Safety; Motor Vehicles and Transportation; Career Opportunities and Development; and Government and Elections. The page provides a section of "Quick Links" to information on events, weather, traffic, and kids' pages. A section of "News and Alerts" is also provided. A section listing "Online Services" is offered that includes options like "file personal income tax," "find a state job," and "statewide telephone directory."

One of the most useful links, the "Agency Index," appears in the "Online Services" section and in small print at the bottom of the screen, along with links to the governor's office and information about the *Maryland.Gov* site. If the user attempts to find agency sites by selecting the "Government and Elections" button from the home page, then selecting "Maryland State Government," a list of agency types is retrieved, but the correct type must be selected to find the link to the agency itself. Since Maryland has Constitutional Offices, Governor's Coordinating Offices, Executive Departments, Independent Agencies, and Executive Commissions, Committees, Task Forces and Advisory Boards, it is difficult to know what category a specific agency might fall within. The "Agency Index" provides direct links to agency sites by listing the agencies in each category.

If any of the "virtual agency" buttons are selected, the next screen will provide a box that lists the most popular content from that subject area. Items can be selected from that list for direct access. Additional subject categories will also appear that can be selected to continue narrowing the search.

COMMERCIAL PUBLICATIONS AND WEB SITES

Maryland Report's Guidebook to Maryland Legislators (Bancroft Information Group, Inc., P.O. Box 65360, Baltimore, MD 21209)—This is a directory of the members of the Maryland General Assembly. It provides biographical information. Questions about this source can be directed to the editor, Bruce Bortz, at bruceb@bancroftpress.com, or at (410) 358-0658.

Michie's Annotated Code of Maryland (LexisNexis/Michie Co.)—This source contains the laws of the state arranged by subject. It is the official printed version of the *Code*. The Michie Company is part of the LexisNexis publishing empire. A searchable catalog of LexisNexis' legal publications may be found on the web at http://bookstore.lexis.com/bookstore/catalog/. The most recent edition of the *Code* was issued in forty volumes and sold for $1,636. Those with general questions can call the LexisNexis Bookstore at (888) 223-6337. Those who wish to place an order can call (800) 223-1940.

SOURCES CONSULTED

Commission on State Publications Depository and Distribution Program. *First Annual Report of the Commission on State Publications Depository and Distribution Program, F.Y. 1983, to His Excellency Harry R. Hughes, Governor.* Baltimore, MD: State of Maryland, 1984.

OCLC (Online Computer Library Center). *OCLC WorldCat.* Dublin, OH: OCLC.

Survey response from and correspondence with Carl Olson, Towson University, 2002.

Telephone interview with Lynda Cunningham, Maryland General Assembly, Department of Legislative Services, Library and Information Services, August 2002.

Massachusetts

Eric W. Johnson

GOVERNMENT PUBLISHING AND THE DEPOSITORY SYSTEM

Chapter 412 of the *Acts of 1984* (*General Laws of Massachusetts*, Chapter 6, Section 39B) created the state depository system for Massachusetts. Each state agency must furnish eight copies of its publications to the State Library of Massachusetts no later than five working days after they are received from the printer or contractor. Three of the eight copies are made "available for public consultation in the library and for permanent historic preservation by the library." Of these three, two are cataloged and added to the library's permanent collection, while the third is microfilmed. Additional copies are sent to the Library of Congress and to each of the state's depository libraries: the Boston Public Library, Springfield City Library, Worcester Public Library, and the University of Massachusetts/Amherst Library.

The definition of "publication" given in Chapter 6, Section 39 of the law is

any document, study, rule, regulation, report, directory, pamphlet, brochure, periodical, newsletter, bibliography, microphotographic form, tape or disc recording, annual, biennial or special report, statistical compendium, or other printed material regardless of its format or manner of duplication, issued in the name of or at the request of any agency of the commonwealth or produced or issued as part of a contract entered into by any agency of the commonwealth regardless of the source of funding, provided they constitute "public records" as defined in clause Twenty-six of section seven of chapter four, excepting correspondence, blank forms, and university press publications.

Clause Twenty-six exempts several types of publications that might be "made or received" by state government employees, such as personnel and medical files, scoring keys to tests, and trade secrets.

The collection of Massachusetts state publications at the State Library dates back to the beginning of the library in 1826. According to the library's web site, "Legislative, executive and judicial documents are part of the Library's collection as well as publications from commissions, authorities and other agencies of Massachusetts government."

The State Library is charged with establishing and maintaining a depository library system and with maintaining a complete collection of Massachusetts state publications, both current and historic. Each state publication is fully cataloged and entered into the OCLC database.

USEFUL ADDRESSES AND TELEPHONE NUMBERS

The most complete collections of Massachusetts state publications may be found at the following libraries:

George Fingold Library
State House, Room 341
Boston, MA 02133
Phone Number for Massachusetts Reference Questions: (617) 727-6279
E-Mail Link for Massachusetts Reference Questions: http://www.state.ma.us/lib/services/ask.htm
E-Mail Address for Massachusetts Reference Questions: reference.department@state.ma.us
State Library's Home Page: http://www.state.ma.us/lib/
Government Information Home Page: http://www.state.ma.us/lib/government/govt.htm

University of Massachusetts
W.E.B. Du Bois Library
Amherst, MA 01003
Phone Number for Massachusetts Reference Questions: (413) 545-2765
E-Mail Address for Massachusetts Reference Questions: len.adams@library.umass.edu
Du Bois Library's Home Page: http://www.library.umass.edu/libraries/dubois.html

Questions about the state's depository library system may be directed to the Government Documents Librarian at the State House address printed above, at (617) 727-6279, or via e-mail at Bette.Siegel@state.ma.us.

INDEXES TO MASSACHUSETTS STATE PUBLICATIONS

Two indexes to state publications are prepared by the State Library of Massachusetts and printed and distributed through the State Bookstore—the *Quarterly Checklist* and the annual *Massachusetts State Publications*, which began publication in 1962. The *Checklist* provides a listing of those publications received at the State Library during the period indicated. Newsletters and serials with a frequency greater than quarterly are not included in this list. Both indexes provide subject, author, and title indexing of state publications, as well as a listing of publications. Each document in the *Checklist* is microfilmed, and the entry for each document includes the list number and a microfilm number. The Massachusetts numbering scheme is similar to the Superintendent of Documents classification system used with U.S. government publications; the numbering system starts with MR and all state documents have M3 at the end of the first line. Original cataloging is done by the State Library for each state document.

The *Quarterly Checklist* and *Massachusetts State Publications* are not available on the web. The catalog of the State Library may be accessed through the C/W MARS (Central/Western Massachusetts Automated Resource Sharing) Network at the following address: http://cmars.cwmars.org/search~s54/.

ESSENTIAL STATE PUBLICATIONS

Many of the most important Massachusetts state documents may be found on the web at http://www.mass.gov/portal/index.jsp. Additionally, they are available for purchase at the State Bookstore in the State House. For availability, contact the State Bookstore at (617) 727-2834.

Directories

A Citizens' Guide to State Services; a Selective Listing of Governmental Agencies and Programs (Secretary of the Commonwealth, Citizen Information Service)—This annual comprehensive listing of state services and officials is arranged by subject. Areas covered include Business and Economic Development, Consumer Information, Education, Employment, Health, Public Safety, Transportation, and State Administration and Revenue. The publication is available on the web at http://www.state.ma.us/sec/cis/ciscig/guide.html. For more information, contact the Citizen Information Service, One Ashburton Place, Room 1611, Boston, MA 02108, or call (617) 727-7030; or via e-mail at cis@sec.state.ma.us. A print version is available for sale at the State Bookstore; for more information, contact the State Bookstore at (617) 727-2834.

Corporations Book (Department of Revenue, Division of Local Services)—This online-only annual list of Massachusetts' domestic and foreign corporations subject to an excise, while designed for Massachusetts' assessors, provides a comprehensive listing of almost 200,000 business corporations, limited liability companies, financial institutions, and insurance companies, and is searchable by keyword. The list is available at http://dorapps.dor.state.ma.us/corpbook/home/home.asp; an online tutorial can be found at http://dorapps.dor.state.ma.us/corpbook/home/tutorial.asp. For more information, contact the Division of Local Services, P.O. Box 55490, Boston, MA 02205-5490, or call (617) 626-2300.

Directory Profiles (Department of Education)—Located on the web at http://profiles.doe.mass.edu/, this directory contains basic information about Massachusetts elementary and secondary schools. Through the site can be found facts about enrollment, school spending, demographics, and test scores. The information is searchable by organization type (public school/district, private school, charter school, collaborative, and special education school) and area, and includes the names of superintendents and principals, services, number of schools by grade span, and relationships with other schools. For more information, consult the help page at http://profiles.doe.mass.edu/help.html; call the DOE at (781) 338-DATA; or send e-mail to data@doe.mass.edu.

School Directory: A Listing of All Public and Private Elementary, Middle and Secondary Schools in Massachusetts (Department of Education)—Published annually since 1990, this directory provides the addresses and names of key personnel in Massachusetts schools. For information on a print version, contact the Department of Education via e-mail at http://www.doe.mass.edu/contact/qanda.asp.

Financial/Budgetary Resources

Comprehensive Annual Financial Report (Office of the Comptroller)—Published each December, this is the comptroller's report of the state's finances, as audited in accordance with Generally Accepted Accounting Principles. All reports since 1994 are available online at http://www.state.ma.us/osc/Reports/cafr_about.html. For information about a print version, contact the Office of the Comptroller, One Ashburton Place, 9th Floor, Boston, MA 02108, or call (617) 727-5000.

Governor's Budget Recommendation. Fiscal Year [Year] (Governor, Fiscal Affairs Division)—The governor's annual budget proposal includes the governor's message, highlights of the budget, and sections on fiscal health, capital outlay, local aid/education, and appropriate changes to sections of the *General Laws of Massachusetts*. The most recent and previous budgets are available on the web at http://www.state.ma.us/bb/. For more information on a print version of the budget, contact the Fiscal Affairs Division, State House, Room 272, Boston, MA 02133, or call (617) 727-2081.

The Municipal Data Bank (Department of Revenue)—This source collects, analyzes, and distributes financial, demographic, and economic data on Massachusetts' cities and towns. Financial data are collected from reports submitted annually by municipalities, while demographic and economic data are collected from other state and federal agencies. Included are municipal spreadsheets containing current and historical socioeconomic, financial, budget, property tax, and assessment data for all cities and towns, as well as articles from *City and Town* analyzing the data. All spreadsheets may be downloaded. The document is available on the web at http://www.dls.state.ma.us/mdm.htm. For more information about the *Data Bank*, or for information about contacting the Department of Revenue, consult the contact page online at http://www.dls.state.ma.us/contact.htm.

Legal Resources

Acts of [Year] (Session Laws) (Legislature)—This annual listing includes the text of all acts passed during a given legislative session, printed in numerical order. The Acts are available on the web at http://www.state.ma.us/legis/. See the "Laws" section.

The Code of Massachusetts Regulations (CMR) (Secretary of the Commonwealth)—The *CMR* contains regulations promulgated by state agencies pursuant to the Administrative Procedures Act. Regulations set forth standards for public health and safety, licensing of professionals, consumer and environmental protection, among others. Some agencies, such as the Division of

Personnel Administration and the Civil Service Commission, are exempt from the publication requirement. The *CMR* is organized according to the cabinet structure of state government, with each agency assigned a three-digit number identifying the cabinet office involved and the specific agency. The regulations are further broken down by chapter numbers. The *CMR* in its current format was published in 1979 and reprinted in 1986, and contains twenty-five loose-leaf volumes. It is updated through the biweekly *Massachusetts Register*. Selective portions of the *CMR* are available on the web, and are indexed at http://www.lawlib.state.ma.us/cmr.html.

Massachusetts Register (Secretary of the Commonwealth)—The *Register* updates *The Code of Massachusetts Regulations*. It contains executive orders by the governor, Attorney General opinions, permanent and emergency regulations, notice of public hearings, the State Register of Historic Places, and a list of recently enacted legislation. For information about obtaining print versions of the *CMR* and the *Register*, contact State Publications and Regulations, One Ashburton Place, Room 1611, Boston, MA 02108, or call (617) 727-7030; or consult the information online at http://www.state.ma.us/sec/spr/sprinf/inforegi.htm.

The Constitution of the Commonwealth of Massachusetts (Legislature)—This publication outlines the basic structure of state government. It is divided into the following parts: Preamble; I. A Declaration of the Rights of the Inhabitants of the Commonwealth of Massachusetts; II. The Frame of Government: The Legislative Power; Executive Power; Judiciary Power; Delegates to Congress; The University at Cambridge, and Encouragement of Literature, etc.; Oaths and Subscriptions, etc.; III. Articles of Amendment; IV. Legislative Action on Proposed Constitutional Amendments. The Constitution is available on the web at http://www.state.ma.us/legis/. For availability of a print version, contact the State Bookstore at (617) 727-2834.

The General Laws of Massachusetts (MGL) (Legislature)—This publication contains the law of the Commonwealth of Massachusetts, divided into five parts: Administration of the Government; Real and Personal Property and Domestic Relations; Courts, Judicial Officers and Proceedings in Civil Cases; Crimes, Punishments and Proceedings in Criminal Cases; and The General Laws, and Express Repeal of Certain Acts and Resolutions. The online version of the *MGL*, available at http://www.state.ma.us/legis/ states emphatically that it is "not the official version of the *MGL*." A commercial version is available through the West Group; information is provided under "Commercial Publications and Web Sites" in this chapter.

Journal of the House of Representatives of the Commonwealth of Massachusetts (General Court, House of Representatives)—This title started regular publication in 1854. It is published daily while the House is in session, with an annual cumulation, and is the daily record of House proceedings. Uncorrected proofs of issues from January 24, 2001 to the present can be found on the web at http://www.state.ma.us/legis/. An official print copy of the *House Journal* is available from the Legislative Document Room, State House, Room 428, Boston, MA 02133, or call (617) 722-2860.

Journal of the Senate (General Court, Senate)—This title, which started publication in 1868, is issued daily while the Senate is in session and is cumulated annually. It can be found in uncorrected form from March 12, 1998 to the present at http://www.state.ma.us/legis/. An official print copy of the *Senate Journal* is available from the Legislative Document Room, State House, Room 428, Boston, MA 02133, or call (617) 722-2860.

Statistical Resources

Annual Report of Vital Statistics of Massachusetts (Department of Public Health, Registry of Vital Records and Statistics)—Also called Public Document No. 1, this is the state's primary statistical overview of births, deaths, marriages, and divorces. It also includes general population information. The report was first published in 1843 under a slightly different title. It has been published under this title since 1964. It is compiled and issued annually. Contact the State Bookstore at (617) 727-2834 for availability. The department's Bureau of Health Statistics, Research and Evaluation has birth, death, and population statistical reports on its web site at http://www.state.ma.us/dph/bhsre/resep/resep.htm#birth. For more information, contact BHSRE, 250 Washington Street, 6th Floor, Boston, MA 02108, or call (617) 624-5600.

Community Profiles (Department of Housing and Community Development)—This is an excellent source of general data on Massachusetts' cities and towns. Included for each are the municipal seal and a narrative history of the city or town, as well as information on geography, government, demographics, housing characteristics, education, economic development, transportation, culture and recreation, and finance. The *Profiles* are available online at http://www.state.ma.us/dhcd/iprofile/default.htm.

Other Resources

Massachusetts Facts (Secretary of the Commonwealth, Citizen Information Service)—Originally written and issued by the Division of Tourism of the Department of Commerce and Development (now the Office of Travel and Tourism), this "Review of the History, Government, and Symbols of the Commonwealth of Massachusetts" includes sections on symbols (state flower, bird, etc.), politics, statistics, and miscellaneous facts, as well as a historical sketch of the state, an overview of the New Massachusetts State House, and economic data and statistics. It can be found on the web at http://www.state.ma.us/sec/cis/cismaf/mafidx.htm.

Massachusetts Getaway Guide (Office of Travel and Tourism)—Published annually by Marblehead Communications Inc., on the behalf of the Office of Travel and Tourism, the *Guide* provides travel and tourist information. It includes lists of lodgings, and pull-out state and city maps. A copy may be requested via the web at http://www.massvacation.com/.

MASSACHUSETTS' WORLD WIDE WEB HOME PAGE

The Commonwealth of Massachusetts has provided seekers of state information with an easily navigable portal web site, *mass.gov*, located at http://www.mass.gov/portal/index.jsp.

The site's home page has six main sections: "Home and Health," linking to housing, family, consumer, health, safety, and community information; "Doing Business," designed with business owners and entrepreneurs in mind; "Work and Education," with information on education, child care, work, and taxes; "Having Fun," listing places to visit, outdoor activities, and arts and cultural attractions; "Getting Around," linking to information on cars and other vehicles, commuting and travel, and places to visit; and "Your Government," with links to state agencies and general information about elected officials and voting, cities and towns, working for the state, doing business with the government, an interactive tour of the State House, and fun facts.

Two more features, "Online Services" and "News and Updates," allow citizens to transact state business online and provide them with current information about the Commonwealth. A second link to online services, as well as links to agencies, elected officials, and help, appears along the top of the home page. The site is fully searchable from the page.

A "Kids' Page" can be accessed via the governor's page, but it merely links to the Citizen Information Service's "Massachusetts Facts" page.

The redesigned web site was launched in May 2002, the first step in the Commonwealth's vision for e-government, and was the result of a public/ private collaborative effort involving a seventy-five-member E-Government Task Force, comprised of state government officials and representatives from the private sector, academia, and municipal governments. Customer support is provided by the Executive Office for Administration and Finance's Information Technology Division, which also maintains the site. The division can be contacted at Mass.Gov Customer Support, Information Technology Division, One Ashburton Place, Room 1601, Boston, MA 02108, or call (866) 888-2808; or via e-mail at Mass.Gov@state.ma.us.

COMMERCIAL PUBLICATIONS AND WEB SITES

Historical Atlas of Massachusetts (University of Massachusetts Press, Amherst, MA)—Published in 1991, and edited by Richard W. Wilkie and Jack Tager, this collection of historical maps details the growth of the Commonwealth, economic and population changes, and specific historic events. (It is out of print.)

The Massachusetts Political Almanac (Center for Leadership Studies, P.O. Box 400, Centerville, MA 02632)—This annual is a "comprehensive directory of the legislative, executive and judicial branches of Massachusetts government," and includes detailed political and biographical profiles and photographs, election results, key roll call votes, committee assignments, campaign financing, a lobbyist roster, district profiles, independent agencies, boards appointed by the governor, organizational charts, and job descriptions. A pocket reference guide accompanies it, and the purchaser of the *Almanac* is given access to the searchable online version, which is updated throughout the year. The *Almanac* is available from the publisher via telephone at (800) 833-7600 or via the publisher's web site at http://www.elobbying-mass.com/order.shtml.

West's General Laws of Massachusetts (GLM) (West Group, 610 Opperman Drive, Eagan, MN 55123)—This paperback edition of the *GLM* is the official source of the state's laws. It is the only compilation recognized by the Massachusetts Supreme Court, and the only source from which the *General Laws* can be legally cited. For ordering information, contact West Group at (800) 328-4880 or via their web site at http://west.thomson.com/.

SOURCES CONSULTED

Citizens' Guide to State Services; a Selective Listing of Government Agencies and Programs, 6th ed., rev. Boston: Secretary of the Commonwealth, Citizen Information Service, 1996.

Correspondence with Leonard Adams, University of Massachusetts at Amherst.

The Massachusetts Political Almanac 2000. Centerville, MA: Center for Leadership Studies, 2000.

Massachusetts State Library's web site, http://www.state.ma.us/lib/.

Numerous departmental web pages via the Commonwealth's web site, http://www.mass.gov/portal/index.jsp.

Quarterly Checklist. Boston: State Bookstore.

Survey response from Bette Siegel, Massachusetts State Library, January 2001.

Telephone conversation with Leonard Adams, University of Massachusetts at Amherst, July 2001.

Michigan

J. Louise Malcomb

GOVERNMENT PUBLISHING AND THE DEPOSITORY SYSTEM

The history of Michigan government publishing and document distribution, given in the *Manual for Michigan State Documents Depository Libraries* (http://www.michigan.gov/documents/michdocmanual2002_46514_7.pdf), dates back to 1829. The current program stems from legislation passed in 1895, although the system was reviewed in the 1960s with changes made by Public Act 367 of 1976. The *Manual* states, "In 2001, the Legislature enacted Public Act 62 of 2001. This legislation moved the Library of Michigan from the legislative branch to the newly formed Department of History, Arts, and Libraries under the executive branch. Section 9, regarding the depository library program, remained largely untouched under this revision." Libraries already involved in the program retained their depository designation if they agreed to make the documents accessible to citizens of the state without charge. The law further required the State Library to keep one copy as a "permanent reference copy" and to continue to deposit one copy with the Library of Congress. The order of distribution to the depository libraries was also established at this time, based upon a priority ranking of those libraries able to provide the most service to the largest number of citizens.

State agencies are required to deposit copies (currently seventy-five) of state publications with the Library of Michigan whose staff also proactively solicit state agencies to meet this requirement. The Library of Michigan distributes these to state depositories and retains a non-circulating copy in its Official Collection as well as a circulating copy. The *Manual* stipulates "any publication printed in multiple copies by an agency that is intended for distribution beyond the issuing agency is covered by the depository requirement." For specific definition of what documents are included in the program, state agencies can refer to *Management and Preservation of Michigan Government Information*, at http://www.michigan.gov/documents/preservation_46540_7.pdf. The

Library of Michigan continues, according to the *Manual*, to investigate the distribution of electronic resources.

Although the Michigan Documents Classification Scheme was developed in 1967 and used to facilitate distribution of the documents, the Library of Michigan now uses the Library of Congress Classification System. It also includes records in its online catalog, *ANSWER*, and in OCLC.

Currently, there are fifty-two depository libraries including the Library of Congress, thirty-two public libraries, seventeen academic institutions, one law library, and one cooperative library. State depositories must be open to the public. The Library of Michigan provides a list of depository libraries, *Michigan State Documents Depository Libraries*, which is available at http://www .michigan.gov/hal/0,1607,7-160-17449_18637-57845--,00.html.

Both Act 540 of 1982, which established the Library of Michigan, and Public Act 62 of 2001, which moved the libraries to the jurisdiction of the Department of History, Arts and Libraries in the executive branch, retain the requirements for the document depository system. The Library of Michigan oversees the rules and regulations of the depository program. Its web site, http://www .michigan.gov/hal/0,1607,7-160-17449_18637-57845--,00.html, provides a PDF copy of the *Manual*, *Information for State Agencies*, the *Directory of State Documents Depository Libraries*, *Shipping Lists*, and *Michigan Documents*.

USEFUL ADDRESSES AND TELEPHONE NUMBERS

The most complete collections of Michigan publications can be found at the following libraries:

Library of Michigan
717 West Allegan Street
P.O. Box 30007
Lansing, MI 48909-7507
Phone Number for Michigan Reference Questions: (517) 373-1300
E-Mail Address for Michigan Reference Questions: librarian@libraryofmichigan.org
Live Reference Assistance is Available at: http://www.libofmich.lib.mi.us/services/ question.html
Library Home Page: http://www.michigan.gov/hal/0,1607,7-160-17445_19270---,00 .html
Depository Program Home Page: http://www.michigan.gov/hal/0,1607,7-160-17749 _18637-57845--,00.html

University of Michigan Documents Center
203 Hatcher North
Ann Arbor, MI 48109-1205
Phone Number for Michigan Reference Questions: (734) 764-0410
E-Mail Address for Michigan Reference Questions: govdocs@umich.edu
Documents Center Home Page: http://www.lib.umich.edu/govdocs/mich.html

Those with questions about the depository program can contact Christie Pearson Brandau, State Librarian, at (517) 373-1580, or by fax at (517) 373-5700.

INDEXES TO MICHIGAN STATE PUBLICATIONS

ANSWER Library of Michigan Online Catalog (Library of Michigan)—According to the *Michigan Documents Manual*, the most comprehensive source listing Michigan documents is the online catalog. It is available on the web at http://opac.libofmich.lib.mi.us/screens/opacmenu.html.

Michigan Bibliography: A Partial Catalogue of Books, Maps, Manuscripts and Miscellaneous Materials Relating to the Resources, Development and History of Michigan From Earliest Times to July 1, 1917: Together with Citation of Libraries in Which the Materials May be Consulted and a Complete Analytic Index by Subject and Author. (Floyd Benjamin Streeter) (Michigan Historical Commission)—"Streeter" is a two-volume bibliography on Michigan and includes many Michigan documents. It was published in 1921. The *Michigan Documents Manual* states that this is the "cornerstone" bibliography for identification of historical Michigan material. If not available, R.R. Bowker's *State Publications: A Provisional List of the Official Publications of the Several States of the United States from their Organization* can be consulted for historical publications.

Michigan Documents (Library of Michigan)—This publication has been issued in a variety of formats (print 1952–1978; microfiche 1966–1991; print 1991–1995; and online 1995–present at http://tree.libofmich.lib.mi.us/). The *Michigan Documents Manual* indicates that annual printed accumulations will be resumed for 1999 forward, and a single cumulated issue will be produced for 1995–1998, when resources permit.

Michigan Documents Backlog (Library of Michigan)—Produced on microfiche, this is a cumulative index of Michigan Documents dated from the early 1800s to 1965. There is a supplement published in 1984 that covers later years. Susan Dow also mentions the *Report of the State Librarian* (Michigan State Library), which lists Michigan Documents from 1860 to 1916, and *Michigan Library News* (Michigan State Library), that lists selected Michigan materials from 1916 to 1952.

ESSENTIAL STATE PUBLICATIONS

Michigan in Brief: Information About the State of Michigan (Library of Michigan)—This web site, http://www.michigan.gov/hal/0,1607,7-160-15481_20826_20829-56001--,00.html, provides basic information about Michigan and specifically the government of Michigan. It includes a section on Michigan facts that gives the nickname, state motto, state flower, but also has sections on Michigan history, government, and education. Links are included to relevant official web sites and a bibliography for further reading is provided.

Michigan Manual (Michigan Legislative Service Bureau)—Published biennially by the Legislative Service Bureau under the direction of the Legislative Council, the *Michigan Manual* provides comprehensive basic information about Michigan state government, including a copy of the state's Constitution, descriptions of the branches of government, an overview of the state's history, and general information and statistics. The latest edition is available from the legislature's web site at http://www.michigan.gov/emi/0,1303,7-102-116_355-2838--,00.html, with chapters in PDF. Contact the Legislative Services

Bureau for availability of print copies: P.O. Box 30036, Lansing, MI 48909-7536; Information (517) 373-0170; Document Room (517) 373-0169.

Directories

Government Address and Phone Directory (*Michigan.gov*)—This web site, http://www.michigan.gov/emi/1,1303,7-102--15554--,00.html, replaces the *State of Michigan Telephone Directory* previously produced by the Office Services Division, Office of Management and Budget.

Directory Senate and House of Representatives (Clerk of the House and Secretary of the Senate)—While the Michigan legislature's web site provides a search mechanism for current legislators, this source dates back to 1997: http://www.michiganlegislature.org/law/mileg.asp?page=SponsorSearch.

Michigan Public School Academy Directory (Michigan Department of Education)—The *Michigan Education Options* web site, http://www.michigan.gov/mde/1,1607,7-140-6525_6530_6558---,00.html, provides access to the directories for public school academies alphabetically or by city. It also gives information about home schools, non-public academies, and school choice.

Directory of Michigan Libraries (Library of Michigan)—The *Directory of Michigan Libraries* (http://envoy.libraryofmichigan.org/isapi/4disapi.dll/directory/search.html/) gives lists of all libraries with address information. It also lists services and regional cooperatives. A map is included. To order a paper copy of the *Directory of Michigan Libraries*, 2001–2002 edition, call (517) 373-9452; fax (517) 373-5815.

Financial/Budgetary Resources

State of Michigan Comprehensive Annual Financial Report (Michigan Department of Management and Budget, Office of the State Budget, Office of Financial Management)—This is an annual report on the financial condition of the Michigan state government, presenting assets and liabilities, revenues by source, expenditures by function and/or object, and fund balances; for general, special revenue, debt service, capital projects, enterprise, internal service, and trust and agency funds, and for component units (legally separate entities related to state government, including universities), FY2000, with trends from FY1991. It also includes data on budgeted versus actual revenues and expenditures; state investments by type; retirement system participation and finances; bonded debt and debt service requirements through 2030; and general state social and economic indicators. Data were compiled by the Department of Management and Budget. Recent years are available on the Internet at http://www.michigan.gov/budget, or print copies may be requested from the Michigan Department of Management and Budget, Office of Financial Management, 111 South Capitol Avenue, Lansing, MI 48913, or call (517) 373-1010.

State of Michigan 2000 Economic Report of the Governor: Progress in the 1990s (Michigan Department of Treasury, Revenue and Tax Analysis Office)—This recurring report, for 2000, analyzes recent developments in the Michigan economy. It includes data on employment, income, prices, population, major industries, property taxes, and other topics, primarily for the 1970s through 1999, with selected data for 2000 and some earlier trends from the 1950s or 1960s. It also includes selected comparisons to total U.S. figures. It is available on the Internet at http://www.michigan.gov/documents/2000ERG_3655_7 .pdf, with print copies generally available free from the Michigan Department of Treasury, Revenue and Tax Analysis Office, Treasury Building, P.O. Box 15128, Lansing, MI 48901, or call (517) 373-3200.

Legal Resources

Michigan Constitution of 1963 (Library of Michigan)—http://www .michigan.gov/hal/0,1607,7-160-15841_20826_20829---,00.html. The latest edition of the Michigan Constitution is available in several places including this version from the Library of Michigan. It is also reproduced and available in PDF format from the *Michigan Manual* (see above).

Citizen's Guide to State Government (Legislative Service Bureau)—Updated in April 2002, this guide focuses on a citizen's access to legal and official government information. It is available on the Internet at http://www .michiganlegislature.org/law/mileg.asp?page=publications, but may be requested from the Legislative Service Bureau in print. The Michigan legislature web site states

The Michigan Legislature Website is a free service of the Legislative Internet Technology Team in cooperation with the Michigan Legislative Council, the Michigan House of Representatives, and the Michigan Senate. The information obtained from this site is not intended to replace official versions of that information and is subject to revision. The Legislature presents this information, without warranties, express or implied, regarding the information's accuracy, timeliness, or completeness.

The Legislative Process in Michigan: A Student's Guide (Michigan Legislature)— This 42-page booklet was published in 2001 with the primary purpose of providing basic information about the legislature for students studying government.

Public Acts (Michigan Legislature)—For laws as enacted by the state of Michigan, the Michigan legislature provides this web site: http://www .michiganlegislature.org/law/mileg.asp?page=PublicActs. There is a good search engine, but a list of "Common Documents" is also provided, listing the most frequently requested acts. Links are provided to current legislation.

Michigan Compiled Laws (Michigan Legislative Council)—Michigan's laws are codified in this database, available at http://www.michiganlegislature .org/MILEG.asp?Page=LawInfo&userid. Both "basic" and "advanced" searching is provided at the web site, along with a listing of frequently requested laws, MCL Tables, historical documents, and copies of Michigan constitutions. Published since 1971, the *Michigan Compiled Laws* was preceded by *Compiled Laws of the State of Michigan*.

Michigan Register (Office of Regulatory Reform)—According to the office's web site, http://www.michigan.gov/orr/0,1607,7-142-5694_8363---,00.html, the Michigan Administrative Procedures Act (1969) established the current rule-making procedures. These are published in the *Michigan Register* and then entered in the *ORR's Michigan Administrative Code Database*. Links are provided to recent issues of the *Register*, to the *Administrative Code*, and to its annual supplement. The *Register* and the *Code* may be searched by department or keyword. The *Register* has been published since 1984 by the Legislative Council. The Legislative Council produces the *Administrative Code*, first published in 1944 under the authority of the secretary of state. To enquire about a subscription write to Office of Regulatory Reform, Department of Management and Budget, 1st Floor Ottawa Building, 611 West Ottawa, Lansing, MI 48909, or e-mail lancej@michigan.gov.

Michigan Legislative Handbook (Clerk of the House, Secretary of the Senate)— Published biennially from 1900 to 1998, this publication served as both a directory to members of Michigan's legislature and a basic guide to legislative actions. Information is now available through the legislature's web site at http://www.michiganlegislature.org/.

Statistical Resources

Michigan Agricultural Statistics (Michigan Department of Agriculture)—This annual report provides statistics on agricultural production, marketing, finances, and trends within the state of Michigan. The report gives statistics on farms, their production, prices, value, acreage, farm real estate value, and rent; farm income from government payments, cash receipts, and production expenses; agricultural labor, hours worked, and wages; fertilizer and pesticide use; grain facilities, capacity, and stocks; refrigerated warehouses and capacity; and trout, mink, and maple syrup production, among others. The data are prepared by the Michigan Agricultural Statistics Service in cooperation with USDA National Agricultural Statistics Service. Copies are available free of charge while supplies last from the Michigan Agricultural Statistics Service, P.O. Box 26248, Lansing, MI 48909-6248, or call (517) 324-5300.

Education in Michigan (Michigan Department of Education)—This PDF document provides basic statistics concerning educational achievements in the state. It is available at http://www.michigan.gov/documents/FastFacts2 _8395_7.pdf.

State of Michigan's Environment, 2001 (Michigan Department of Environmental Quality)—The department's web site states: "Since 1999, the Department of Environmental Quality (DEQ) has prepared two environmental quality reports (*Environmental Quality Report 1999* and *2000*) in order to provide a baseline from which future environmental protection progress could be measured." The Michigan legislature passed the Environmental Indicators Law in 1999 requiring that the Department of Environmental Quality and the Department of Natural Resources publish the information biennially. The report is available upon request from the department or at http://www.michigan .gov/deq/0,1607,7-135-3308_7255-11648--,00.html. The web site also provides links to other current statistical reports related to Michigan's environment, including relevant reports on the Great Lakes.

Michigan Election Results (Michigan Secretary of State, Elections Bureau)— This is a biennial report presenting results of the Michigan general elections.

It includes data on registered voters by county as well as votes cast for major offices and proposals/measures. Data are shown by county and/or district, and include most candidates' party affiliation.The report is available from the Michigan Secretary of State, Elections Bureau, P.O. Box 20126, Lansing, MI 48901-0726 for $2.50. It is also available from the Elections Bureau web site at http://www.michigan.gov/sos/1,1607,7-127-1633---,00.html.

Michigan Selected Health Statistics (Michigan Department of Community Health)—This annual compilation of Michigan vital statistics supersedes the annual print report, *Michigan Health Statistics*. Data include trends for many tables since 1900. It is available on the department's "Statistics and Reports" web site at http://www.michigan.gov/mdch/0,1607,7-132-2944---,00.html, which also provides many other health-related statistics. For more information write to Michigan Department of Community Health, Sixth Floor, Lewis Cass Building, 320 South Walnut Street, Lansing, MI 48913, or call (517) 373-3500.

Michigan Traffic Crash Facts (Michigan Department of State Police, Highway Safety Planning Office)—The Michigan Department of State Police compiles these data on Michigan traffic accidents involving fatalities, injuries, property damage, and number of persons killed and injured. The report includes trends and breakdowns by various victim and driver characteristics. While available on the Internet, http://www.michigan.gov/msp/0,1607,7-123-1645_3501---,00 .html, the report may be requested in print from the Michigan Resource Center, 111 W. Edgewood Boulevard, Suite 11, Lansing, MI 48911, or call (800) 626-4635, or (517) 882-9955; e-mail info@michiganresourcecenter.org.

Crime in Michigan, Uniform Crime Report (Michigan Department of State Police, Criminal Justice Information Center, UCR Section)—As with the FBI's annual uniform crime report, this report provides data on crimes and arrests tabulated by cities and counties within the state. It is available at http://www.michigan.gov/msp/0,1607,7-123-1645_3501---,00.html, or upon request from the Michigan Department of State Police, Criminal Justice Information Center, UCR Section, 7150 Harris Drive, Lansing, MI 48913, or call (517) 322-5385. The state police web site also provides many other interesting links, including Michigan's Most Wanted, Missing Persons, and additional publications which might be of interest.

Other Resources

Michigan Department of Transportation Map (Michigan Department of Transportation)—The department's web site provides information concerning Michigan's roads and a form for requesting a copy of the state's highway map: http://www.michigan.gov/mdot/0,1607,7-151--30026--,00.html.

MICHIGAN'S WORLD WIDE WEB HOME PAGE

Michigan.gov (Michigan Department of Information Technology)—The Michigan portal provides excellent access to all levels of state information. It includes links to its "Accessibility Policy" and "Privacy Policy." It provides a good search engine, a site map, quick links to most frequently visited sites, and a link to "State Web Sites." The "State Web Sites" link includes a link to

Michigan eLibrary, maintained by the Department of History, Arts and Libraries. Even so, the *Government Address and Phone Directory* mentioned earlier, http://www.michigan.gov/emi/1,1303,7-102--15554--,00.html, is most helpful in linking directly to agency information.

COMMERCIAL PUBLICATIONS AND WEB SITES

Michigan Facts (Clements Research II, Inc.)—This Michigan volume of the "Flying the Colors" series was first issued in 1990, with plans for a triennial update, but there is no evidence that any later editions have been published. The volume provides an overview of the state, as well as of each county. For more information write to Clements Research, 16850 Dallas Parkway, Dallas, TX 75248, or call (800) 782-9002. See the web site of Clements' parent company at http://www.politicalresearch.com/.

Michigan Statistical Abstract (Bureau of Business Research, School of Business Administration)—Issued biennially from 1955 to 1976 and annually from 1977 to 1987, the *Michigan Statistical Abstract* was compiled and published at Michigan State University and Wayne State University. It ceased with the twentieth edition, 1987. The 1987 volume appears to still be available on a limited basis from *Amazon.com*.

Michigan Statistical Abstract (University of Michigan Press, Michigan Employment Security Agency)—The preface from the 1996 edition states, "After nearly a decade without a standard Michigan statistical data book, the Michigan Employment Security Commission (M.E.S.C.) has produced a new edition of the *Michigan Statistical Abstract*." There is no indication that the volume has been issued since the 1996 edition, which is still in print and available for $55.00 from *Amazon.com*.

SOURCES CONSULTED

Dow, Susan L. *State Document Checklists: A Historical Bibliography*. Buffalo, NY: William S. Hein & Co., 1990.

Lane, Margaret T. *State Publications and Depository Libraries: A Reference Handbook*. Westport, CT: Greenwood Press, 1981.

Manual for Michigan State Documents Depository Libraries, 2nd ed. Lansing: Library of Michigan, 2002; http://www.michigan.gov/documents/michdocmanual2002_46514_7.pdf.

Parrish, David W. *State Government Reference Publications: An Annotated Bibliography*, 2nd ed. Littleton, CO: Libraries Unlimited, 1981.

Peters, John. A. "Government Publications: Only a Library Away." *Wisconsin Library Bulletin* (Fall 1983): 108-109.

State Capital Universe. Bethesda, MD: LexisNexis, 2002; http://web.lexis-nexis.com/stcapuniv, July 30, 2002. (Available to subscribers only.)

Statistical Universe. Bethesda, MD: LexisNexis, 2002; http://web.lexis-nexis.com/statuniv, August 15, 2002. (Available to subscribers only.)

U.S. Census Bureau. "Appendix 1: Guide to State Statistical Abstracts." *Statistical Abstract of the United States 2000*. Washington, DC: Department of Commerce, 2000, 902–905.

WorldCat. Columbus, OH: OCLC; http://www.oclc.com, August 18, 2002. (Available to subscribers only.)

Minnesota

Daniel D. Cornwall

GOVERNMENT PUBLISHING AND THE DEPOSITORY SYSTEM

The roots of Minnesota's depository program stretch back to 1905 when the University of Minnesota was designated a depository of all books, pamphlets, documents, maps, and other works published by or under the authority of the state of Minnesota. Retention and distribution of state documents did not really take off until 1973, when the Legislative Reference Library (LRL) was designated as a "depository of all documents published by the state." Agencies were then required to send the Legislative Reference Library ten copies of any reports required by the legislature. Other documents could be contributed at the agencies' discretion. Systematic distribution of most state documents received by the LRL did not begin until 1981, when depository libraries began receiving microfiche copies of all documents. Today, thirty-six libraries are designated as Minnesota state documents depositories.

Currently, all state agencies are required to send six copies of their documents to the Legislative Reference Library. The LRL sends reminder letters to a specified contact when the reports are due. One copy is cataloged into the LRL collection, one copy is sent to the Minnesota Department of Administration for microfilming and distribution to the state's thirty-six depository libraries, one copy is sent to the Library of Congress, and the remaining copies are given to interested legislators and staff. The microfiche is available to the public at the various depository libraries. In addition, the Legislative Reference Library is open to the general public, who can view the microfiche or print documents at the library. Any online versions of state documents are linked from the Legislative Reference Library's catalog, available through the PALS (Project for Automated Library Systems) site at http://www.pals.msus .edu/. Select "Search PALS," then select the Legislative Reference Library from the pull-down list of member libraries.

Not all documents received by the Legislative Reference Library are included in the depository system. The Minnesota microfiche distribution system depends on issuing agencies to pay for microfilming their documents. Items from agencies that refuse to pay for microfilming are not included in the depository system; neither are exclusively electronic items unless the Legislative Reference Library chooses to print them and arrange for microfilming. As a result, the LRL has the most comprehensive collection of Minnesota state documents.

Minnesota state documents are cataloged using the Library of Congress classification system and given a six-digit accession number when they are distributed in microfiche. Patrons will need this number, in the format YY-NNNN for monographs and PNN for periodicals, to retrieve documents at depository libraries. If the document is available on the Internet, the URL is recorded in the catalog record.

USEFUL ADDRESSES AND TELEPHONE NUMBERS

The most comprehensive collections of Minnesota state documents can be found at the following libraries:

Minnesota Legislative Reference Library
645 State Office Building
St. Paul, MN 55155-1050
Phone Number for Minnesota Reference Questions: (651) 296-8338
E-Mail Address for Minnesota Reference Questions: refdesk@library.leg.state.mn.us
Library's Home Page: http://www.leg.state.mn.us/lrl/
Minnesota State Documents Page: http://www.leg.state.mn.us/lrl/mndocs/mndocs
    .asp

Minneapolis Public Library and Information Center
300 Nicollet Mall
Minneapolis, MN 55401-1992
Phone Number for Minnesota Reference Questions: (612) 630-6120
Library's Home Page: http://www.mplib.org/

Another extremely useful, though non-library resource is Minnesota's Bookstore, located at http://www.comm.media.state.mn.us/bookstore/ (see Figure 10). Minnesota's Bookstore sells every published state agency publication and some Minnesota-related commercial publications as well. Visitors can search for publications by keyword or browse by a limited set of subjects. Each publication entry contains the document title, a short description, and a Minnesota Bookstore stock number. Items may be ordered online, or by phone at (800) 657-3757. Important pieces of information you will not find for publications listed in Minnesota's Bookstore include publishing agency name and Internet availability. These are weaknesses, but should not prevent Minnesota's Bookstore from being your first stop when looking for physical copies of Minnesota state documents.

INDEXES TO MINNESOTA STATE PUBLICATIONS

There are two Internet-only guides to Minnesota state publications. Both are available at http://www.leg.state.mn.us/lrl/mndocs/mndocs.asp. The *Min-*

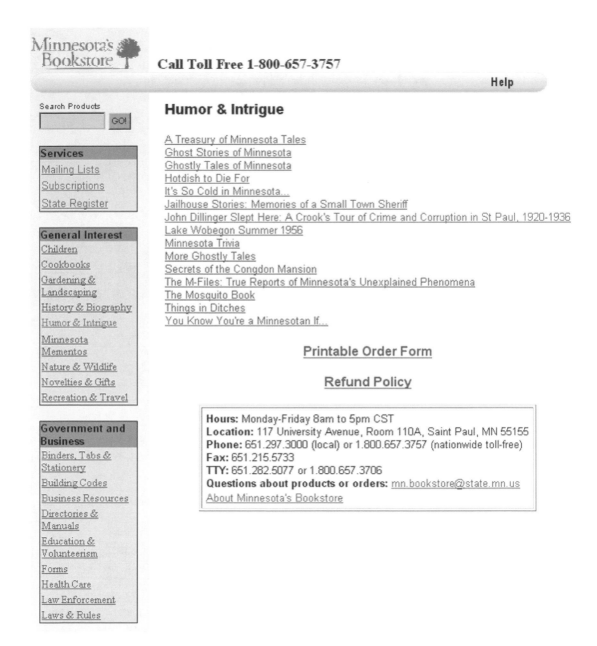

Figure 10. Some very intriguing state publications are sold through Minnesota's Bookstore. *Source*: http://www.comm.media.state.mn.us/bookstore/.

nesota State Documents Lists ("Docs on Fiche") are distributed monthly with the microfilmed documents sent to Minnesota document depositories. Each entry lists the Minnesota documents accession number, and the document's title, author, and publishing date. Microfiche copies of documents on "Docs on Fiche" can be purchased from Document Communications, Minnesota Department of Administration. Call (651) 779-5200 for specific price information.

Another resource is Minnesota *State Agency Periodicals*. This resource is divided into three parts: an alphabetical list by title, which contains an agency contact for each item; a publishing agency index list; and an alphabetical subject index.

ESSENTIAL STATE PUBLICATIONS

Directories

Annual Compilation and Statistical Report of Multi-Member Agencies (Secretary of State)—This is a review of current membership in state agency committees and councils, including appointing authority, address/phone for members, term length, and compensation. An index at the front of the book lists the current vacancies. According to the introduction to the statistical section of the report, it "contains information about vacancies and appointments by county, congressional district, legislative district, gender, political party, and race/national origin. Information about current membership is provided by congressional district, gender, political party, and race/national origin." You may browse the *Annual Compilation* on the web at http://www.sos.state.mn .us/openapp. Paper copies of this publication can be ordered online through Minnesota's Bookstore at http://www.comm.media.state.mn.us/bookstore/, or by phone at (800) 657-3757.

Education and Community Service Directory (Department of Children, Families and Learning)—The online version of this directory has seven sections: A. Staff Directory (for Minnesota Department of Children, Families and Learning), B. Services Delivered by County, C. School District and School Information, D. Community Services Programs, E. Miscellaneous, F. Education Statistic Summary, and G. Raw Data Available for Downloading. Section B, Services by County, provides a list of social services available in each county. Section D, Community Services, lists child care and child health resources; Section E, Miscellaneous, gives contact information for library consortia and state and national educational organizations. Section G, Raw Data Available for Downloading, provides most of the data in the directory as spreadsheet-friendly, tab-delimited files. The 400-page plus directory may be browsed on the web at http://children.state.mn.us/cfldirectory/directory.html, or order paper copies through Minnesota's Bookstore at http://www.comm.media .state.mn.us/bookstore/, or by phone at (800) 657-3757.

Licensed and Certified Health Care Facilities (Health)—Minnesota Documents Fiche Number—02-0362 (2002 edition). This is a comprehensive listing of hospitals, nursing homes, supervised living facilities, outpatient clinics, home health agencies, hospices, and so on within the state of Minnesota. Lists are organized by county and alphabetically. This nearly 400-page listing is available on the Internet at http://www.health.state.mn.us/divs/fpc/directory/ fpcdir.html. A print copy may be ordered from Minnesota's Bookstore at http://www.comm.media.state.mn.us/bookstore/ or by phone at (800) 657-3757. The 2002 edition costs $23.95.

Minnesota Grown Directory (Agriculture)—This is an annual consumer guide to food and ornamental products available direct from the farm. It lists over

500 pick-your-own berry farms, apple orchards, Christmas tree farms, nurseries, specialty meat providers, and many other places to find the freshest Minnesota-grown products. There is a searchable version of the *Minnesota Grown Directory* at http://www2.mda.state.mn.us/webapp/mngrown/mngrown_default.jsp. This version lets you search by product, region, county, city and farm/market name. From alpacas to wreaths, you can find it grown in Minnesota. Free copies of the *Minnesota Grown Directory* may be requested by filling out the form at http://www.mda.state.mn.us/scripts/polyform.dll/request.

Minnesota Guidebook to State Agency Services (Office of the State Registrar)—Minnesota Documents Fiche Number—01-0537 (2001/2003 edition). This biennial guide provides a concise review of the executive, judicial, and legislative branches of Minnesota state government. More than 300 agencies are catalogued. Each listing describes the agency's programs and services and provides specific contact persons, phone and fax numbers, mail and e-mail addresses, and opportunities for citizen involvement in policy making. An index is also provided. The *Guidebook* may be browsed, or paper copies obtained, online through Minnesota's Bookstore at http://www.comm.media.state.mn.us/bookstore/, or by phone at (800) 657-3757.

State of Minnesota Telephone Directory (Administration)—This directory provides alphabetical listings of all Minnesota state employees plus agency listings, including fax numbers, e-mail addresses, and TTY numbers. Paper copies may be ordered online through Minnesota's Bookstore at http://www.comm.media.state.mn.us/bookstore/ or by phone at (800) 657-3757. Similar information is available via Minnesota's web portal at http://www.state.mn.us. Select "Government" from the home page, then select "Government Directory" from the "Quick Links" section.

Financial/Budgetary Resources

Biennial Budget Home Page (Finance)—Located at http://www.budget.state.mn.us/budget/operating/index.html, the biennial budget includes expenditures for education, health care, public safety, housing, natural resources, agriculture, economic development, as well as dollars to state agencies and local units of government. In addition to the actual budget, citizens can also find profiles of state agencies, links to economic forecasts, and links to earlier years' budget information.

Capital Budget Home Page (Finance)—Located at http://www.budget.state.mn.us/budget/capital/index.html, this site provides links to the current capital budget, which funds land acquisitions, construction and repair of state buildings, state infrastructure, higher education facilities, and capital grants to schools and local governments. Other documents available through this site include a FAQ section on the capital budget, a chart showing the distribution of Minnesota state employees, and budget instructions to state and local agencies.

Comprehensive Annual Financial Report for the Year Ended June 30, [Year] (Finance)—Minnesota Documents Fiche Number—02-0007 (2001 edition and supplement). This annual report is divided into three sections: Introductory

Section; Financial Section, including the auditor's opinion and basic financial statements; and the Statistical Section, containing financial and other data for prior and current years. Some of the facts available from the Statistical Section include the Employment Mix in Minnesota, Minnesota-Based Companies Included in the *Fortune* 500, and the Average Daily Public School Membership. The current *Comprehensive Annual Financial Report* and prior editions back to 1997 are available on the Internet at http://www.finance.state.mn.us/cafr/. Alternative formats, including paper, may be obtained by contacting the Department of Finance at 400 Centennial Office Building., 658 Cedar Street, St. Paul, MN 55155-1603; by phone at (651) 296-5900; or by fax at (651) 296-8685.

Legal Resources

Attorney General Opinions (Attorney General)—Located at http://www.ag .state.mn.us/office/opinions/Default.htm, this site provides access to all published Attorney General opinions since 1993. Opinions may be browsed by date, subject, and entity requesting opinions. For published opinions prior to 1993, users can consult several resources including *Minnesota Statutes Annotated*, *Biennial Report of the Attorney General to the Governor of the State of Minnesota*, and the *Minnesota Legal Register*. Detailed instructions for using these resources can be found at the bottom of the *Opinions* page.

Minnesota State Register (Administration)—Minnesota Documents Fiche Number—P182. The *State Register* is published weekly and includes: Minnesota Rules—proposed, adopted, and exempt; Official Notices—including requests for outside opinions, revenue notices, executive orders, meetings, vacancies in agencies, and so on; Professional, Technical and Consulting Contracts; and State Grants and Loans. Issues of the *Register* dating back to March 1997 are available at http://www.comm.media.state.mn.us/bookstore/state _register_archives.asp. Paper subscriptions may be ordered through Minnesota's Bookstore at http://www.comm.media.state.mn.us/bookstore/, or by phone at (800) 657-3757.

Minnesota Rules (Office of the Revisor of Statutes)—The online version of this publication is located at http://www.revisor.leg.state.mn.us/arule/. Rules are usually grouped under the agency that administers them. Agencies may be assigned multiple chapters in *Minnesota Rules*. On the web site, the rules are arranged both alphabetically by agency and numerically by chapters. Each chapter is arranged in a decimal numbering system, with the last four digits designating the part number of the chapter. No part number is smaller than .0001 or larger than .9999. The web version is updated weekly, but does not have the graphs and charts contained in the printed edition. An official, hardbound edition of *Minnesota Rules* is published every odd-numbered year. Each edition is supplemented twice in even-numbered years with pocketpart supplements. Ordering information for *Minnesota Rules* publications may be obtained by calling the Office of the Revisor of Statutes at (651) 296-2868 or the Print Communications Division of the Department of Administration at (651) 297-3000.

Minnesota Statutes (Office of the Revisor of Statutes)—A user-friendly, online edition of the Statutes can be found on the Internet at http://www.leg.state

.mn.us/leg/statutes.asp. Users may retrieve statutes by citation, search by keywords or phrase, browse by table of contents, or use its exceptional index at http://www.revisor.leg.state.mn.us/stix/. This index relies on drop-down menus and is nearly as easy to use as a printed index. Ordering information for the official, printed edition of *Minnesota Statutes* may be obtained by calling the Office of the Revisor of Statutes at (651) 296-2868 or the Print Communications Division of the Department of Administration at (651) 297-3000. A CD-ROM version is also available.

Opinions of the Minnesota State Appellate Courts Archive (Minnesota State Law Library)—This web site, located at http://www.lawlibrary.state.mn.us/archive/, provides access to opinions and orders of the Minnesota Supreme Court and the Minnesota Court of Appeals. Coverage of opinions and orders goes back to May 1996. This archive is searchable by keyword and browseable by release date, docket number, and by the first party of case name. Opinions and orders are available as Rich Text Format and MS Word files. An explanation of the various opinions and orders issued by Minnesota courts appears at http://www.lawlibrary.state.mn.us/opinio.html. For paper copies of all published Minnesota appellate opinions, see the *North Western Reporter*, available from West Publishing at http://west.thomson.com.

Statistical Resources

Compare Minnesota (Trade and Economic Development)—Think of this Internet-only publication as the *Statistical Abstract of the United States* for Minnesota. This biennial publication has dozens of tables arranged in the following ten sections: Demographics; Economic Diversity; Minnesota's Key Industries; Government; Labor; Education; Capital Resources; Energy, Transportation and Telecommunications; Construction and Real Estate; and Quality of Life. A few tables of special interest are: The 10 Largest Population Centers (Table 1.1), The 25 Largest Electronic Equipment and Computer Manufacturers Operating in Minnesota (Table 2.10), and Research and Development, Fiscal Year [year] and Average Number of Patents Per 10,000 People [year] (Table 6.5). *Compare Minnesota*'s tables are drawn from many sources and the original source of information in each table is cited below the table, along with notes on definitions and clarifications of methodology, when appropriate. *Compare Minnesota*, along with other statistical publications, may be viewed at http://www.dted.state.mn.us/00x04-f.asp.

Health Statistics (Health)—The official annual report on Minnesota's health statistics is divided into eight chapters: Live Births, Induced Abortions, Fertility, Infant Mortality and Fetal Deaths, General Mortality, Marriage, Divorce, and Population. Each 100-plus-page issue may be ordered online through Minnesota's Bookstore at http://www.comm.media.state.mn.us/bookstore/ or by phone at (800) 657-3757. This report, along with many other health-related statistical publications, can be browsed at http://www.health.state.mn.us/stats.html.

Minnesota Crime Information (Public Safety)—Minnesota Documents Fiche Number—02-0142 (2000 edition). This is an annual report on crime and arrests in Minnesota. The report contains statistics on violent crimes and crimes against property. Statistics are available for the state as a whole, by county, and by arresting agency. *Minnesota Crime Information* also contains sections on hate crimes, missing children, and police chases. This report may be viewed at the Criminal Justice Information System web site at http://www.dps.state .mn.us/bca/CJIS/Documents/cjis-intro.html. Paper copies of this report may be ordered through Minnesota's Bookstore at http://www.comm.media.state .mn.us/bookstore/ or by phone at (800) 657-3757.

Minnesota School District Profiles (Department of Children, Families and Learning)—Minnesota Documents Fiche Number—01-0244 (1999/2000 edition). This annual report is available online at http://cfl.state.mn.us/ PUBRES.html. It can be ordered in paper through Minnesota's Bookstore at http://www.comm.media.state.mn.us/bookstore/ or by phone at (800) 657-3757. The online version offers all tables in Excel format on the following topics: Pupils, Staff, Districts, Taxes, and Expenditures. A school district listing is also included.

Other Resources

Minnesota Level 3 Predatory Offender Information (Corrections)—Located at http://www.doc.state.mn.us/level3/level3.asp, this resource contains information mandated by Minnesota's Community Notification Law (*Minnesota Statutes* 244.052) that permitted the release of information about sex offenders judged to be at highest risk for reoffending. The database can be searched by offender name, city, county, and zip code. Each listing contains mug shots of the offender, current address, information about the offense, and the date the offender was released from prison.

Offender Locator (Corrections)—Located at http://info.doc.state.mn.us/ publicviewer/, this site can be used to retrieve public information about adult offenders who have been committed to the Commissioner of Corrections, and who are still under the department's jurisdiction. This includes people in prison or on probation. Adult offenders can be located using offender name, date of birth, or a Minnesota-issued offender ID. Each record retrieved includes a description and photos of the offender, a description of the prisoner's offense, his or her current location, and, if incarcerated, the expected release date.

MINNESOTA'S WORLD WIDE WEB HOME PAGE

North Star, Minnesota's official web portal, is located at http://www.state .mn.us. There is a navigation bar at the top of every page with seven buttons: Business, Travel and Leisure, Health and Safety, Environment, Government, Learning and Education, and Living and Working. The left-hand portion of the home page has a handy list of online government services. Options offered include registering a car, getting a business license, and applying for unemployment. The middle section of the page contains announcements and web links of current interest. The right-hand side of the page presents a list of "Quick Links" to popular pages on the site. As the user explores *North Star*, the "Quick Links" being offered often change to a listing appropriate to the portion of the site being explored.

In the future, Minnesota citizens will be able to personalize their *North Star* experience and use electronic signatures for state services.

COMMERCIAL PUBLICATIONS AND WEB SITES

25 Bicycle Tours in the Twin Cities and Southeastern Minnesota (Countryman Press, Woodstock, VT)—This guide describes bike routes in the metro area and southeastern Minnesota. These tours range from ten to sixty miles in length and include both urban and rural settings. Each tour includes a detailed map, total mileage, complete mile-by-mile directions, and points of interest. This book may be ordered from the publisher's web site at http://www.countrymanpress.com/.

A Citizen's Guide to State Finance: An Overview of Minnesota Government Revenue and Expenditures (Minnesota League of Women Voters)—Last published in 1994, this volume reviews the state budget process, expenditures, property and income tax, and the fiscal relationships between state and local governments. At sixty pages, this title informs without overwhelming the citizen. The *Citizen's Guide* can be ordered through Minnesota's Bookstore at http://www.comm.media.state.mn.us/bookstore/ or by phone at (800) 657-3757.

Death Certificate Index (Minnesota Historical Society, St. Paul, MN)—This index, available at http://people.mnhs.org/dci/Search.cfm, covers Minnesota death certificates from 1908 to 1996. It was in 1908 that the state became the custodian of the official record of deaths. The index can be searched by last name, first name, and mother's maiden name. Names can be searched by exact spelling, or by the U.S. Census Bureau's Soundex code. Results can be sorted by last name, first name, year of death, or county of death. Each record contains the deceased's name, certificate number, place of birth, mother's maiden name, and date and county of death. Visitors can place orders for unofficial copies of actual death certificates, which are stored on microfilm in the society's library. For more information, write to Minnesota Historical Society, 345 W. Kellogg Boulevard, St. Paul, MN 55102-1906, or call (651) 296-6126.

Harris Minnesota Directory of Manufacturers (HarrisInfoSource, Twinsburg, OH)—Published since 1998, this annual publication lists companies alphabetically by community, and by type of product manufactured. Each entry has the company name, address, phone and fax number, sales volume, market products, area sales, and marketing and purchasing data. The 2002 edition was over 900 pages long and sold for $135.00. This publication may be ordered from either the publisher's web site at http://www.harrisinfo.com/, or through the state-run Minnesota's Bookstore at http://www.comm.media.state.mn.us/bookstore/ or by phone at (800) 657-3757.

Minnesota Place Names (Minnesota Historical Society, St. Paul, MN)—Located at http://mnplaces.mnhs.org/upham/, this online version of the locally well-known book *Minnesota Geographic Names*, by Warren Upham, provides access to the history of more than 10,000 place names. Visitors will find the history behind the names and links to census information, photos, and maps.

A visitor can search by name, or browse by county, towns, lakes and streams, people, other English names, and names from other languages.

SOURCES CONSULTED

Depository program home page, http://www.leg.state.mn.us/lrl/mndocs/mndocs .asp.

Minnesota State Documents: A Guide for Depository Libraries. St. Paul: Government Documents Round Table, Minnesota Library Association, 1984.

Minnesota's Bookstore, http://www.comm.media.state.mn.us/bookstore/.

Numerous departmental pages via the state's home page, http://www.state.mn.us.

Survey response from David Schmidtke, Minnesota Legislative Reference Library, 2000.

Mississippi

Lori L. Smith

GOVERNMENT PUBLISHING AND THE DEPOSITORY SYSTEM

A depository program was first established in Mississippi in 1966. The Recorder of Public Documents, then in the Office of the Secretary of State, coordinated the program. In 1975 a revision to the legislation transferred the program and the Recorder of Public Documents to the Mississippi Library Commission.

In title 25, chapter 51, section 3 of the *Mississippi Code of 1972 Annotated* it says,

> All agencies of state government shall furnish to the director of the Mississippi Library Commission sufficient copies of each public document printed, and the director of the Mississippi Library Commission shall deliver to each depository as many as two (2) copies of each document requested. These records shall be made accessible by the depository receiving them to any person desiring to examine the same.

The law itself doesn't supply a definition of "public document," but a note in title 25, chapter 51, section 1 of the *Code* refers to Attorney General Opinion #95-0686. The note says, "Under Section 25-51-1, a document issued for public distribution is a document created by a state agency for the general public, as opposed to internal memos, attorney work product, or records created in the course of business."

Another definition of "public document" is provided on the *State Depository Program* page on the Mississippi Library Commission's web site. It defines a state document as "Any item published by the state government, for the state government, or at state government expense, and which would be available without charge upon request from any person other than employees of the producing agency and bears the imprint of the producing agency." That page is at http://www.mlc.lib.ms.us/reference/state-docs/state-deposit-prog.htm.

There are twenty-eight depository libraries participating in the program, including the Mississippi Library Commission, and agencies are asked to provide thirty copies of their publications whenever possible. The commission keeps two copies for archival storage and distributes the remainder to the depositories.

In addition to gathering and distributing documents, the Recorder of Public Documents assigns classification numbers to the publications and produces the *Mississippi State Government Publications Index*, which is described in more detail below.

USEFUL ADDRESSES AND TELEPHONE NUMBERS

The most complete collections of Mississippi state documents can be found at the following libraries:

Mississippi Library Commission
Government Services Department
1221 Ellis Avenue
Jackson, MS 39209-7328
Phone Number for Mississippi Reference Questions: (601) 961-4111 or 1-877-KWIK-
   REF (toll-free for in-state residents)
E-Mail Address for Mississippi Reference Questions: mlcref@mlc.lib.ms.us
Library's Home Page: http://www.mlc.lib.ms.us
State Documents Home Page: http://www.mlc.lib.ms.us/reference/state-docs/index
   .htm

Government Information Services
J. D. Williams Library
University of Mississippi
University, MS 38677
Phone Number for Mississippi Reference Questions: (662) 915-5865
Web Form for Mississippi Reference Questions: http://www.olemiss.edu/depts/
   general_library/files/ref/ask.html
Library's Home Page: http://www.olemiss.edu/depts/general_library/

INDEXES TO MISSISSIPPI STATE PUBLICATIONS

From 1966 to 1975 the Office of the Secretary of State issued a semi-annual index entitled *Public Documents of the State of Mississippi*. When the depository program was transferred to the Mississippi Library Commission (MLC) in 1975, that agency began issuing a cumulative index entitled *Mississippi State Government Publications*. Only four volumes of that title were issued: Retro 1 (1966-1970), Retro 2 (1971–1975), Volume 1 (July 1975–June 1980), and Volume 2 (July 1980–June 1985). Since 1985 the MLC has published the *Mississippi State Government Publications Index*. It was issued on a monthly basis for some time and is now issued quarterly. The most recent editions of the index are available online at http://www.mlc.lib.ms.us/reference/state-docs/indexes/index .html.

The Recorder of Public Documents assigns state publications a classification number using the *Mississippi State Documents (MsDocs) Classification Scheme*.

The second edition of a publication outlining this scheme was issued by the MLC in 1985. The classification system has features similar to both Dewey Decimal numbers and to the Superintendent of Documents numbers assigned to federal publications.

ESSENTIAL STATE PUBLICATIONS

Directories

Educational Directory of Mississippi Schools (Department of Education)—MsDocs Call Number—205.1:DI. The introduction to the 1997–1998 edition of this source called it a "detailed overview of all schools and school-related organizations in the state." Contact information is provided for personnel in the Department of Education, for school district superintendents and school principals, and for various other educational organizations. Similar information is available online from the Department of Education's web site at http://www.mde.k12.ms.us/districts/msmap2.htm. Those who wish to enquire about print copies of the directory can write to Mississippi Department of Education, Central High School, P.O. Box 771, 359 North West Street, Jackson, MS 39205, or call (601) 359-3513.

Mississippi Official and Statistical Register (Secretary of State)—MsDocs Call Number—111.1:SR. This is the state's comprehensive government manual, or "Blue Book." It is published every four years and gives a description of each department, agency, and elected office in all three branches of the state's government. In addition to contact information for current personnel or officeholders, the Blue Book provides facts about the legislation that established the agency and a summary of the purpose for which it was established. Information about federal, county, and municipal government officials is provided as well. The symbols of the state, such as state flower or song, are listed, and statistics are given on a number of different topics. The most recent edition of the Blue Book is available online in the "Education and Publications" section of the secretary of state's home page at http://www.sos.state.ms.us. A limited number of print copies are available free of charge until the supply is exhausted. E-mail a request along with your name, address, and telephone number to publications@sos.state.ms.us.

Mississippi State Government Telephone Directory (Department of Information Technology Services)—MsDocs Call Number—601.5:DI. This directory provides phone numbers, fax numbers, e-mail addresses, and basic mailing addresses for state government personnel. Print copies can be ordered by sending a check for $5.00, along with shipping information, to MS Department of ITS, 301 N. Lamar Street, Suite 508, Jackson, MS 39201-1495, ATTN: Voice Services, or call (601) 359-1359. The directory is available online at http://dsitspe01.its.state.ms.us/its/webphone.nsf/home.

Financial/Budgetary Resources

Audited Financial Statements for the Year Ended . . . (Office of the State Auditor)—MsDocs Call Number—151.1:AF. Financial statements from Mississippi's counties, school districts, and universities are audited by the state and the results of those audits are reported in this series. Each report includes a summary of the finances of the entity that was audited and a statement from the auditor regarding compliance with the state's laws and regulations. If areas of non-compliance are found, the "auditee's corrective action plan" will also be reported. Copies of many reports from recent years can be found on the web at http://www.osa.state.ms.us/. Those who wish to enquire about print copies can write to Office of the State Auditor, 501 North West Street, Suite 801, Woolfolk Building, Jackson, MS 39201, or call (601) 576-2800 or (800) 321-1275.

MERLIN (Mississippi Executive Resource Library and Information Network) (Department of Finance and Administration, Mississippi Management and Reporting System)—This searchable database is one of three maintained by the Mississippi Management and Reporting System (MMRS). It is available on the web at http://merlin.state.ms.us. The other two databases maintained by MMRS are the *Statewide Automated Accounting System* (SAAS) and the *State Payroll and Human Resource System* (SPAHRS). *MERLIN* obtains most of the information it reports from the other two databases. There are five basic sections on the *MERLIN* site: Budget, Revenue, Vendor, Workforce, and Dictionary. The Budget section provides figures for agency appropriations, expenditures, and encumbrances as reported in the SAAS. Budgetary information can be searched by agency, by type of expense, by government function, or by type of fund. The totals for the current fiscal year are updated daily. Totals are also available for previous fiscal years back to 1998. The Revenue section of the site also utilizes SAAS data to provide figures on the state's general fund tax revenues. The Vendor and Workforce sections of *MERLIN* report on vendors doing business with the state and on the state's payroll and number of employees. The Dictionary section simply provides definitions of terms used in *MERLIN*. Those with questions about the database can write to MMRS at 501 North West Street, 1201A Woolfolk Building, Jackson, MS 39201, or call (601) 359-6570. Questions can also be e-mailed to mmrs@mmrs.state.ms.us.

Mississippi, Comprehensive Annual Financial Report (CAFR) (Department of Finance and Administration, Office of Fiscal Management, Bureau of Financial Reporting)—MsDocs Call Number—160.1:FR. As the title indicates, this annual report summarizes the overall financial situation of the state. The introductory section provides a table of contents, a textual summary of the state's financial performance for the fiscal year, a listing of state officials, and an organization chart for the state government. The financial section gives detailed tables of the state's revenues, expenditures, and changes in various fund balances. The third section of the report provides statistics that demonstrate economic trends and other factors related to the state's financial performance. The most recent editions of the *CAFR* are available online at http://www.dfa.state.ms.us/resources.html. Those who wish to enquire about the availability of print copies can contact the Bureau of Financial Reporting at (601) 359-3538, or write to Office of Fiscal Management, Woolfolk State Office Building, P.O. Box 1060 (39215-1060), 501 North West Street, Suite 1101-B, Jackson, MS 39201-1113.

Legal Resources

Mississippi Gaming Commission Regulations (Mississippi Gaming Commission)—MsDocs Call Number—185.4:199102. Mississippi's laws have empowered various boards and commissions to create and enforce regulations. These regulations have not been compiled into a comprehensive set, but are published independently by each regulatory body. *Mississippi Gaming Commission Regulations* is only one example of these publications. It describes the powers and duties of the commission and the rules and procedures that persons in the gaming industry must follow in Mississippi. It is available online at http://www.mgc.state.ms.us. Those who wish to find regulations for other industries or professions in Mississippi can browse the list of agencies available from the state's home page at http://www.ms.gov and then check the appropriate agency page to see if regulations are available. If it isn't obvious which agency would regulate the area in question, the *Mississippi Code*, discussed below, can be searched.

Mississippi Unannotated Code (Secretary of State, Publications and Administration)—This unofficial version of the *Mississippi Code of 1972 Annotated* is available from a link on the secretary of state's site at http://www.sos.state.ms.us/pubs/MSCode/. The link on that page takes you to a site maintained by LexisNexis Publishing, which is the company that publishes the official edition of the *Code*. This edition, which does not include the historical and explanatory notes contained in the official edition, is available free of charge and may be searched by keyword or browsed by title.

Statistical Resources

Community Profiles (Mississippi Development Authority)—In order to assist businesses that wish to locate in the state, the Mississippi Development Authority provides a large series of *Community Profiles*. Each city/town profile provides statistical information in the following categories: Population, Location, Labor Unions, Wages, Labor Force, Retail Sales, Income, Assessed Value, Financial Institutions, Education, Transportation, Health Care, Utilities and Services, County Features, Fire Insurance Rating, Cost of Housing, Property Tax, and Construction Costs. A list of the largest manufacturers in the county is provided, as are a selection of maps. The profiles can be searched to find cities or counties with a specified number of residents. The address to access the profiles is http://www.mississippi.org/doing_busn/site_selectors/comm_profiles.htm. A series of county-level *Education Profiles* is also available from the Mississippi Development Authority site. Those with questions about the *Profiles* can contact the Mississippi Development Authority at (601) 359-3449, or write to P.O. Box 849, Jackson, MS 39205.

Mississippi Economic Review and Outlook (Mississippi Institutions of Higher Learning, University Research Center)—MsDocs Call Number—251 RP.1:ER. Each issue of this semi-annual publication includes an overview of the economic outlook for the state and for the United States as a whole. Articles in each issue focus on different economic or business-related topics. Most articles include tables of statistics. A one-year subscription to the publication costs individuals $10 and institutions $20. A two-year subscription is $15 for individuals and $30 for institutions. Persons who work for state government agencies or libraries in Mississippi may be able to begin a subscription free of charge. To subscribe or to enquire about a free subscription, write to Mississippi Institutions of Higher Learning, Center for Policy Research and Planning, 3825 Ridgewood Road, 4th Floor Tower, Attention: Deborah Bridges, Jackson, MS 39211, or call (601) 432-6742. Recent issues are also available online from a link at http://www.ihl.state.ms.us/URC.html.

Vital Statistics, Mississippi (Department of Health, Office of Community Health Services, Bureau of Public Health Statistics)—MsDocs Call Number—301.1:VS. Issued annually, this report provides statistics on live births, fetal deaths, induced terminations of pregnancy, deaths, marriages, and divorces. Summaries are given at the state, county, and place level. Several "time series" are included that give summary statistics for years from the early 1900s to the present. The most recent editions of the report are available online at http://www.msdh.state.ms.us/phs/statisti.htm. The report does not appear to be offered for sale, but those interested in obtaining a copy could contact the Bureau of Public Health Statistics at (601) 576-7960, or write to them at P.O. Box 1700, Jackson, MS 39215-1700. The Department of Health also has a web form for questions and requests that might prove to be useful. It is available at http://www.msdh.state.ms.us/board/inforq.htm.

Other Resources

MARIS (Mississippi Automated Resource Information System) (Mississippi Institutions of Higher Learning)—Although this database of geographic information is administered by the Technical Center at the Mississippi Institutions of Higher Learning, it is actually a joint project of many different state agencies. State legislation established the project in 1986. A task force of state agency technical personnel and program managers meets monthly to discuss and coordinate projects that utilize the geo-spatial data available in *MARIS*. The task force also coordinates its efforts with key people from federal agencies, local governments, and the private sector. Most of the data on the site are available as Arc/Info export files or ArcView shape files. Types of data available include county borders, bodies of water, railroads, public school districts, primary roads, secondary roads, and catfish ponds, among many others. The address of the site is http://www.maris.state.ms.us/index.html. Those with questions about the database can call (601) 432-6128.

Mississippi Government Publications Online (University of Mississippi Libraries)—Arranged alphabetically by agency/department, this web page provides links to specific state publications that are available online, or to agency sites that list multiple publications. Many of the titles mentioned in this chapter are included and may be accessed from this page. The address is http://www.olemiss.edu/govinfo/ulgbis/miss_st/mspubs.html.

MISSISSIPPI'S WORLD WIDE WEB HOME PAGE

Mississippi's home page may be found on the web at http://www.ms.gov. The site is maintained and copyrighted by the Mississippi Department of Information Technology Services.

There are seven basic navigation buttons on the left side of the page: Mississippi Government, Working in Mississippi, Learning in Mississippi, Living in Mississippi, Visiting Mississippi, Healthcare in Mississippi, and Online Services. Each of those buttons leads to a page with additional links to resources related to that topic. The center of the page lists featured sites and provides links to tourist information, to selected online services, and to the pages of the governor and lieutenant governor. The right side of the page, in a section headed "How Do I . . .", lists frequently asked questions which link to answers. Below that section is a short list of "Quick Links" to external pages that provide information about businesses in the state, jobs available in the state, weather conditions, and other topics. Small buttons in a toolbar at the top of the page lead to the home page itself, to basic information about the state, to the site index, to a list of state agencies, and to contact information. The list of state agencies provides a choice of arrangement by agency name or by topic.

The site is searchable. Search terms can be entered into a box on the upper right corner of the page. Advice on how to perform a more sophisticated search is available via a "Help?" button near the search box.

COMMERCIAL PUBLICATIONS AND WEB SITES

Mississippi Almanac: The Ultimate Reference on the State of Mississippi (Computer Search and Research, 340 North Street, Yazoo City, MS 39194-4245)— James L. Cox compiles and writes this biennial publication. A wide variety of topics are covered in the *Almanac*. Section headings include, among others: Geography of Mississippi; Weather in Mississippi; Most Common Surnames in Mississippi; Movies Filmed in Mississippi; Mississippi Superlatives and Trivia; Government of Mississippi; Health in Mississippi; Crime in Mississippi; Tree Species of Mississippi; Tourist Attractions in Mississippi; Places in Mississippi with Indian Names; How Mississippi Ranks Among All Southern States. It includes a geographic index, an index of people, and a general index. Tables of statistics include a source note, but in some cases the note refers to a state or federal agency rather than a specific publication. Requests for copies can be sent to the address above or made via phone to (601) 746-1919.

Mississippi Code of 1972 Annotated (LexisNexis/Michie Co., Charlottesville, VA)—LexisNexis contracts with the Mississippi Joint Legislative Committee on Compilation, Revision and Publication of Legislation to produce this official version of the state's codified laws. It is issued with the imprint of the Michie subdivision of LexisNexis, but the copyright for the publication rests with the state of Mississippi. The 1999 edition was thirty-two volumes and sold for $825. Those interested in purchasing a print copy can call (800) 424-4200. It is available online through the *Academic Universe* database, which can be accessed in many university libraries. Information about publications issued by LexisNexis and its many subdivisions is available from its bookstore web site at http://bookstore.lexis.com/bookstore/catalog.

Mississippi Statistical Abstract (Mississippi State University, College of Business and Industry, Office of Business Research and Services, Box 5288, Mississippi State, MS 39762-5288)—MsDocs Call Number—254BI.1:SA. The thirty-fourth annual edition of this title was published in 2002. It includes statistics, and some non-statistical data, in the following subject areas: Mississippi Tax Structure; Population; Health and Vital Statistics; Education; Labor Force, Employment and Earnings; Manufacturing and Trade; Transportation; Communications; Banking, Finance and Insurance; Law Enforcement, Courts and Crime; Forest and Mineral Products; Public Finance and Tax Revenue; Social Insurance and Welfare Service; Government and Politics; Construction, Housing and Public Utilities; Agriculture; Recreation, Gaming, Geography, and Climate. Each section has its own table of contents and there is a general index at the end. The original source of statistical data is cited at the bottom of each table. Non-statistical data provided include such things as lists of newspapers published within each city/county and lists of senators and representatives. The 2002 edition was made available both in paper and on CD-ROM. The paper edition was $40 plus $3.95 for shipping, and the CD-ROM was $50 plus $1.30 for shipping. Copies can be requested via phone at (662) 325-8475, or via e-mail to the editor, Janis Bryant, at janbryant@cobilan.msstate.edu.

SOURCES CONSULTED

Mississippi Code of 1972 Annotated, via LexisNexis' *Academic Universe* database.

Mississippi Unannotated Code, online via the secretary of state's link to the LexisNexis web site, http://www.sos.state.ms.us/pubs/MSCode/.

Numerous web pages via the state's home page, http://www.ms.gov.

Survey response from Mary Chrestman, University of Mississippi, 2000.

Survey response from Phoebe Terry, Mississippi Library Commission, 2000.

Missouri

J. Louise Malcomb

GOVERNMENT PUBLISHING AND THE DEPOSITORY SYSTEM

Established in 1977, the Missouri State Documents Depository Program is described in Sections 181.100–181.130 of the *Missouri Revised Statutes*. "State Publications" include all multiple-produced publications of state agencies, regardless of format or purpose, with the exception of correspondence and interoffice memoranda. A "report" refers to a state publication which is either a printed statement by a state agency issued at specific intervals, that describes its operations and progress and possibly contains a statement of future plans; or a formal, written account of an investigation given by a person or group delegated to make the investigation.

Forty-two libraries participate in the Missouri depository program, including three statutory (the Missouri State Library, the State Archives, and the State Historical Society), one special library (the Library of Congress), ten full depositories (including Cape Girardeau, Columbia, Kansas City, Kirksville, Maryville, St. Joseph, St. Louis), and twenty-eight partial depositories. All depositories are listed with address and contact information at http://www.sos.mo.gov/library/reference/statedocs/sdeplib.asp.

Each state agency that issues annual, biannual, or periodical reports is required to provide forty-five copies of each document free of charge to the Missouri State Library. In addition, two copies of all reports are to be provided to the legislative library, one copy to the chief clerk of the Missouri House of Representatives, one copy to the secretary of the Missouri Senate, one copy to the Supreme Court Library, and one copy to Missouri's governor's office. The State Library distributes two copies to the State Archives and two copies to the State Historical Society for preservation. The State Library is responsible for entering into depository agreements with public, college, and university libraries that meet standards for depository eligibility.

Section 181.110 of the *Missouri Revised Statutes* indicates that designated state publications are "core documents" and should be distributed to all full and partial depositories, to provide a group of basic publications that can answer general questions about state government and Missouri. Librarians and state agencies review the list periodically and are encouraged to suggest additions to the list. A copy of the core list is available in the "Depository Materials" section at http://www.sos.mo.gov/library/reference/statedocs/stdocs.asp.

The statutes also require the Missouri State Library to publish *Missouri State Government Publications* for distribution to all depository libraries. An annual list of periodicals, irregular serials, and annuals is also published, entitled *Missouri State Government Serial Publications*. Both lists are in MoDoc Number (Missouri State Documents classification number) order and provide agency, title, cost, and basic bibliographic information.

USEFUL ADDRESSES AND TELEPHONE NUMBERS

The most complete collections of Missouri state publications may be found at the following libraries:

Missouri State Library
P.O. Box 387 or 600 N. Main
Jefferson City, MO 65102-0387
Phone Number for Missouri Reference Questions: (573) 751-3615
E-Mail Address for Missouri Reference Questions: libref@sosmail.state.mo.us
Depository Program Home Page: http://www.sos.mo.gov/library/reference/
    statedocs/stdocs.asp
Library's Home Page: http://www.sos.mo.gov/library/

University of Missouri-Columbia
Government Documents Collection
106B Ellis Library
Columbia, MO 65201-5149
Phone Number for Missouri Reference Questions: (573) 822-6733
Government Documents Collection Home Page: http://web.missouri.edu/~govdocs/
    mobasic.htm

Those with questions about the depository program can contact the State Documents Librarian, Bryan Dunlap, at the address given above for the State Library, by phone at (573) 751-3075, or by e-mail at dunlab@sosmail.state.mo.us.

INDEXES TO MISSOURI STATE PUBLICATIONS

Currently known as *Missouri State Government Publications* (Missouri State Library), this list of publications has been issued under various titles since 1962, with 1997 to present available online at http://www.sos.mo.gov/library/reference/chcklist/default.asp. The State Library also publishes an annual list of serials, entitled *Missouri State Serial Publications*. The *Cumulative Index to Missouri Government Publications* was published for 1972–1978; 1979–1982; 1983–1985; and 1986–1987. Earlier indexes include: F. A. Sampson's *Bib-*

liography of Missouri State Official Publications covering 1905–1909, Cerilla Elizabeth Saylor's *Official Publications of the State of Missouri* covering 1805–1940, and the *Checklist of Official Publications of the State of Missouri* for 1951–1963 by the Missouri State Library.

Additionally, Bowker's *State Publications: A Provisional List of the Official Publications of the Several States of the United States from their Organization* can be consulted for historical publications, pages 313–356.

ESSENTIAL STATE PUBLICATIONS

Directories

Official Manual for the State of Missouri (Missouri Office of the Secretary of State)—Commonly called the "Blue Book" or Missouri Manual, the *Official Manual* is published biennially. It includes descriptions of state agencies and their responsibilities, biographies with photographs of state officials and legislators, lists of county officials and state employees, and contact information for various state agencies. The volume also contains some statistics, such as election returns, census statistics, and information about political parties. It has been published since 1887 with the most recent edition available free, online at http://www.sos.mo.gov/BlueBook/default.asp.

Missouri Roster: A Directory of State, District, and County Officials (Missouri Office of the Secretary of State)—Issued biennially, this directory includes anticipated contact information but also statistical data about elections, voter registration, and population. Some print copies available while supplies last from Missouri Office of the Secretary of State, 600 West Main Street, P.O. Box 778, Jefferson City, MO 65102-0778, or call (573) 751-4936. The earlier title was *Roster of State, District and County Officers of the State of Missouri* (1893–1986).

State of Missouri Telephone Directory (Missouri Office of Administration)—The Division of Information Services issues this directory annually to list work-related telephone numbers for all state employees. The online edition, available at http://www.oa.state.mo.us/cgi-bin/teledir/directory/teledir.htm, is searchable by name, agency function, or department. An e-mail directory is also available at this web site and is searchable by last name or department.

General Assembly Roster (Missouri Office of the Secretary of State)—This is published biennially to correspond with the bicameral sessions of the Missouri General Assembly. Information on the state's senators and representatives is given here as well as in the *Official Manual of the State of Missouri* (described above). Additionally, a list of the members of the General Assembly is provided on the Missouri General Assembly web site, http://www.moga.state.mo.us/, or from the respective pages for the House, http://www.house.state.mo.us, or Senate, http://www.senate.state.mo.us, with a link under "Who Is My Representative/Senator," which permits a zip code search.

Missouri School Directory (Missouri Department of Elementary and Secondary Education)—This directory is an annual publication providing an alphabetical listing of elementary, middle, junior high, secondary, vocation/technical, charter, and private/parochial schools with descriptive information about school districts. It is available online at http://www.dese.state.mo.us/directory/, where links to individual school web sites are provided. The Missouri Department of Elementary and Secondary Education also includes information about school laws and legislation on its web site. Information about how to order a printed copy of the directory can be found at http://www.dese.state.mo.us/directory/order.html.

Directory of Missouri Libraries (Missouri State Library)—This provides basic information about Missouri's public, special, institutional, college, and university libraries. Similar listings are available online at http://www.sos.mo.gov/library/libdir.asp.

Financial/Budgetary Resources

Missouri Executive Budget (Missouri Office of Administration)—The Division of Budget and Planning within the Office of Administration produces the state's budget, which includes an analysis of budget policy issues and provides the fiscal information to the Budget Commissioner, the Governor's Office, and the General Assembly. Issued annually, the budget is also available online at http://www.oa.state.mo.us/bp/execsum.htm. For more information, write to Office of Administration, Division of Budget and Planning, Capitol Building, Rooms 124/129, Jefferson City, MO 65101, or call (573) 751-2345.

Comprehensive Annual Financial Report (CAFR) (Missouri Department of Revenue)—This annual report presents the financial position and results of operations performed by the department as measured by the financial activity of various state funds. The CAFR is divided into three sections: Introductory, Financial, and Statistical (see Figure 11). The Financial section includes descriptions of special revenue funds, agency funds, fixed asset accounts, and long-term debt accounts. The Statistical section is divided into expenditures, taxes administered, fees administered, non-appropriated fund sources, and the State Treasurer's report. The current report is online at the Department of Revenue's web site at http://www.dor.state.mo.us/cafr.

Legal Resources

Missouri Constitution (Missouri Office of the Secretary of State)—Missouri has had four constitutions: 1820, 1865, 1875, and 1945. Printed copies of the current Constitution may be requested from the Office of the Secretary of State, P.O. Box 778, Jefferson City, MO 65102, ATTN: Publications Division, or call (573) 751-4218, and is available online at http://www.moga.state.mo.us/homecon.asp. It is composed of the following Articles: 1. Bill of Rights, 2. The Distribution of Powers, 3. Legislative Department, 4. Executive Department, 5. Judicial Department, 6. Local Government, 7. Public Officers, 8. Suffrage and Elections, 9. Education, 10. Taxation, 11. Corporations, 12. Amending the Constitution, and 13. Public Employees. Past versions of the Missouri Constitution can be located through the *Missouri Revised Statutes* or the *Official Manual*.

Laws of Missouri (Missouri General Assembly)—Laws passed during individual sessions of the Missouri General Assembly are published in these

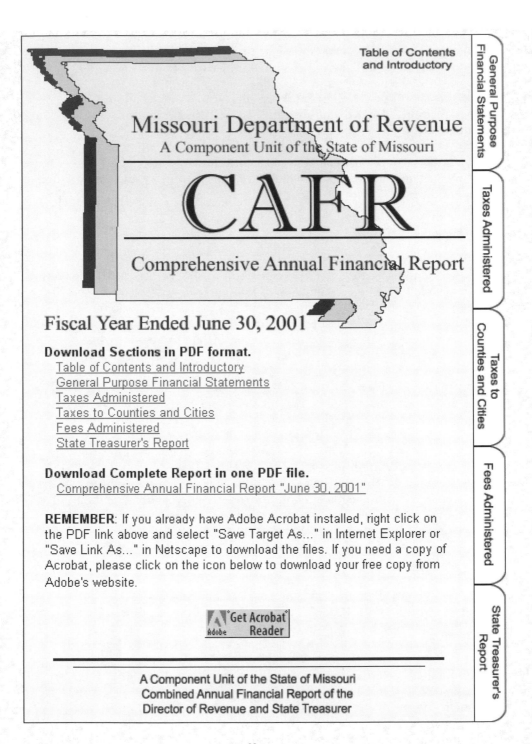

Table of Contents
and Introductory

Missouri Department of Revenue
A Component Unit of the State of Missouri

CAFR

Comprehensive Annual Financial Report

Fiscal Year Ended June 30, 2001

Download Sections in PDF format.
Table of Contents and Introductory
General Purpose Financial Statements
Taxes Administered
Taxes to Counties and Cities
Fees Administered
State Treasurer's Report

Download Complete Report in one PDF file.
Comprehensive Annual Financial Report "June 30, 2001"

REMEMBER: If you already have Adobe Acrobat installed, right click on the PDF link above and select "Save Target As..." in Internet Explorer or "Save Link As..." in Netscape to download the files. If you need a copy of Acrobat, please click on the icon below to download your free copy from Adobe's website.

Get Acrobat
Adobe Reader

A Component Unit of the State of Missouri
Combined Annual Financial Report of the
Director of Revenue and State Treasurer

General Purpose Financial Statements

Taxes Administered

Taxes to Counties and Cities

Fees Administered

State Treasurer's Report

Home

Figure 11. The online version of Missouri's CAFR is presented with informational tabs along the side, much as the print version would be. The tabs can be clicked to access that section of the report. *Source*: http://www.dor.state.mo.us/cafr/.

annual volumes, along with referendum bills, vetoed bills, proposed constitutional amendments, and concurrent resolutions. Not yet available online, *Laws of Missouri* is available at various Missouri depository libraries. James S. Garland compiled *An Index to the State Laws of Missouri*, covering 1804–1868.

Missouri Revised Statutes (Missouri General Assembly)—The codified edition of Missouri laws is issued every ten years, updated annually with the *Supplement to the Revised Statutes*. A print copy of the *Revised Statutes* can be ordered for $300.00 (20 volumes hardbound) from the Revisor of Statutes, State Capitol Building, Room 117A, Jefferson City, MO 65101-1556, or call (573) 526-1288. The statutes are also available on a CD-ROM. Information about ordering the CD is available at http://www.moga.state.mo.us/rsmocons.htm. The *Revised Statutes* are available online at http://www.moga.state.mo.us/homestat.htm and are searchable by keyword or statute citation, with a Popular Name Table also included.

Governor's Executive Orders (Missouri Office of the Secretary of State)—Executive orders are issued to direct the offices of the executive branch and are contained in this annual register. It is available online at http://www.sos.mo.gov/library/reference/orders/orders.asp. The web site contains executive orders since 1984 and includes a keyword index, but is not the "official" version of the *Executive Orders*. The official version can be obtained through the Office of the Secretary of State, Commissions, 600 W. Main, Jefferson City, MO 65101, or call (573) 751-4936.

Code of State Regulations (Missouri Office of the Secretary of State)—This publication is arranged by "titles" according to state agencies and compiles rules and regulations of the state government. It is updated biweekly by the *Missouri Register*. An unofficial version is available online at http://www.sos.mo.gov/adrules/csr/csr.asp. For more information about obtaining a copy, contact the Office of the Secretary of State, Administrative Rules, P.O. Box 1767, Jefferson City, MO 65102, or call (573) 751-4015.

Missouri Register (Missouri Secretary of State)—This contains proposed rules for review by the citizens, public comments, and revisions in these proposed rules. Final versions of the rules are codified and printed in the *Code of State Regulations*. Issues from October 1, 1999 to the present are available online at http://www.sos.mo.gov/adrules/moreg/moreg.asp.

Reports of Cases Determined by the Supreme Court of the State of Missouri (Missouri Supreme Court)—Judicial opinions from the Missouri Supreme Court and Court of Appeals are available online at the Missouri judiciary web site at http://www.osca.state.mo.us/index.nsf. Opinions are listed in reverse chronological order from the present back to March 3, 1997. The web site also includes contact information and a description of the courts. For earlier reports, consult *Reports of Cases Determined by the Supreme Court of the State of Missouri* (Missouri Supreme Court), published under various titles by various publishers since 1821 and available at many Missouri depository libraries.

Statistical Resources

Missouri Vital Statistics (Missouri Department of Health)—The Center for Health Information Management and Evaluation issues this annual compilation of basic health statistics. Copies are usually free while supplies last from Missouri Department of Health, Center for Health Information Management and Evaluation, 920 Wildwood, P.O. Box 570, Jefferson City, MO 65102-0570, or call (573) 751-6272. The Department of Health's web site includes PDF files of the most recent editions. See http://www.health.state.mo.us/GLRequest/Data.html.

Missouri Farm Facts (Missouri Department of Agriculture)—Available while supplies last from Missouri Agricultural Statistics Service, P.O. Box L, Columbia, MO 65205, this annual volume reports statistics about farms and farm production. The most recent edition is available online at http://agebb.missouri.edu/mass/farmfact/index.htm from the Agricultural Statistics Service. The Missouri Department of Agriculture's web site is located at http://www.mda.state.mo.us. For more information call (800) 551-1014 or (573) 876-0950.

Missouri Economic Overview (Missouri Department of Economic Development)—Available from the Missouri Economic Research and Information Center's web site, the report provides all of the basic economic indicators for the state. See http://www.ded.state.mo.us/business/researchandplanning/.

Traffic Accident Statistics (Missouri Department of Transportation)—This annual report provides statistics about traffic accidents that occurred on Missouri state highways. It is available on the web at http://www.modot.state.mo.us/newsandinfo/trafficaccidentstatistics.htm. For more information contact the department at (888) ASK-MODOT or (573) 751-2551.

Other Resources

Lottery Fact Book (Missouri Department of Revenue)—Irregularly issued by the Lottery Commission, the *Fact Book* provides a history of the Missouri lottery and statistics about the lottery's proceeds. It is available online as the "Media Factbook" at http://www.molottery.state.mo.us/learnaboutus/mediacenter/mediacenter.shtm.

Missouri Resources (Missouri Department of Natural Resources)—This magazine, issued three times each year, informs readers of important natural resource issues within the state. It is available free to Missouri residents upon request but there is a $6.00 annual charge for out-of-state subscriptions. It is also available online at http://www.dnr.state.mo.us/magazine/index.html. Missouri residents can request a subscription by completing a form on the web site. Persons out-of-state can call (800) 334-6946.

Missouri State Parks and Historic Sites (Missouri Department of Natural Resources)—Basically a manual about the state's resources, *Missouri State Parks and Historic Sites* includes information on camping, lodging, concessions, employment opportunities, and historic preservation. It is available online at http://www.mostateparks.com.

Missouri Official Highway Map (Missouri Department of Transportation)—The official highway map may be requested free from the department's web site at http://www.modot.state.mo.us/, which also includes access to a variety of reports and the *Long-Range Transportation Plan* for the state.

MISSOURI'S WORLD WIDE WEB HOME PAGE

The Missouri state government web page, *Show Me Missouri*, is located at http://www.state.mo.us and provides free access to most of the state's essential publications. It has four pull-down menus with links to Executive, Judicial, and Legislative Branches with a separate one for State Departments. The "Show me how to . . ." section offers quick links to frequently requested information. There is a keyword search allowed.

COMMERCIAL PUBLICATIONS AND WEB SITES

Statistical Abstract for Missouri (University of Missouri)—This includes basic statistical, socioeconomic, demographic, and governmental data for the state with selected data going back to the 1950s. Issued biennially, the 1999 edition is the tenth edition. To acquire, contact the University of Missouri, College of Business and Public Administration, B & PA Research Center, Ten Professional Building, Columbia, MO 65211. The price for the 1999 edition was $30.00.

Vernon's Annotated Missouri Statutes (West Group, Eagan, MN)—This is the print copy of the Missouri *Code*, updated with pocket parts, also available on CD-ROM. For more information see the publisher's web site at http://west .thomson.com/, or call (800) 328-4880.

SOURCES CONSULTED

Dow, Susan L. *State Document Checklists: A Historical Bibliography.* Buffalo, NY: William S. Hein & Co., 1990.

Lane, Margaret T. *State Publications and Depository Libraries: A Reference Handbook.* Westport, CT: Greenwood Press, 1981, 553–554.

Manz, William H. *Guide to State Legislative and Administrative Materials.* Littleton, CO: Fred B. Rothman Publications, 2000.

Missouri State Government web site, http://www.state.mo.us, October 3, 2001.

Parrish, David W. *State Government Reference Publications: An Annotated* Bibliography, 2nd ed. Littleton, CO: Libraries Unlimited, 1981.

State Capital Universe. Bethesda, MD: LexisNexis, 2001; http://web.lexis-nexis.com/ stcapuniv, October 5, 2001. (Available to subscribers only.)

Statistical Universe. Bethesda, MD: LexisNexis, 2001; http://web.lexis-nexis.com/ statuniv, October 5, 2001. (Available to subscribers only.)

United States. Census Bureau. *Statistical Abstract, 2000 Edition.* "Appendix 1: Guide to State Statistical Abstracts." August 4, 2001, http://www.census.gov.

University of Missouri–Columbia Government Documents web site at http://www .missouri.edu/~govdocs, October 1, 2001.

WashLaw. Washburn University School of Law, http://www.washlaw.edu, October 4, 2001.

WorldCat. Columbus, OH: OCLC; http://www.oclc.com, October 4, 2001. (Available to subscribers only.)

Montana

Daniel D. Cornwall

GOVERNMENT PUBLISHING AND THE DEPOSITORY SYSTEM

The Montana State Publication Center was established in 1967 under sections 22-1-211 to 22-1-218 of the *Montana Code Annotated* (MCA). Currently, there are fourteen participating state depository libraries, not including the Montana State Library. In 2002, five were full depositories and nine were selective depositories. Depository libraries are chosen by geography and a commitment to allow public access to state publications. The selective libraries choose agencies whose documents they are willing to house.

The depository law requires that state agencies deposit a minimum of four copies of their publications with the State Library. Depending on supplies and the requirements of selective depositories, the State Library will receive and distribute more copies. Two copies of state publications are added to the State Library's collection and one is sent to the Montana Historical Society Library. The remaining copies are distributed through the depository system.

A state publication is defined by MCA 22-1-211 as

any document, compilation, journal, law, resolution, bluebook, statute, code, register, pamphlet, list, book, proceedings, report, memorandum, hearing, legislative bill, leaflet, order, regulation, directory, periodical, or magazine issued in print or purchased for distribution by the state, the legislature, constitutional officers, any state department, committee, or other state agency supported wholly or in part by state funds.

The depository law's definition of "print," also found in MCA 22-1-111, is explicitly format-independent, despite having been written in 1967. Only correspondence and interoffice memoranda are explicitly excluded from the state depository program. Thus, Montana has, at least in theory, one of the most inclusive systems for providing state government information to the public.

USEFUL ADDRESSES AND TELEPHONE NUMBERS

The most complete collections of Montana publications may be found at the following libraries:

State Publications Center
Montana State Library
1515 East 6th Avenue
P.O. Box 20180
Helena, MT 59620-1800
Phone Number for Montana State Reference Questions: (406) 444-5351
E-Mail Address for Montana State Reference Questions: MSLReference@state.mt.us
Montana State Library Home Page: http://msl.state.mt.us
State Publications Center Home Page: http://msl.state.mt.us/lisd/spc/index.htm

Montana Historical Society Library and Archives
P.O. Box 201201
Helena, MT 59620-1201
Phone Number for Montana Reference Questions: (406) 444-2681
E-Mail Address for Montana Reference Questions: MHSLibrary@state.mt.us
Library's Home Page: http://www.his.state.mt.us/departments/Library-Archives/
   index.html

Maureen and Mike Mansfield Library
University of Montana
32 Campus Drive #9936
Missoula, MT 59812-9936
Phone Number for Montana Reference Questions: (406) 243-6700
E-Mail Address for Montana Reference Questions: ml_dir@selway.umt.edu
Library's Home Page: http://www.lib.umt.edu/

Those with questions about the depository program can contact the State Publications Center Coordinator at the address given above for the State Library, at (406) 444-5432, or via e-mail to jkammerer@state.mt.us.

INDEXES TO MONTANA STATE PUBLICATIONS

The main index to current Montana state publications is the monthly *Shipping List*. The *Shipping List* is distributed in paper to Montana state depository libraries and is available on the web at http://msl.state.mt.us/lisd/spc/pub-lists.htm. Lists are available from August 2000 until the present.

The *Shipping List* is arranged alphabetically by agency, then by division, and finally by title. Each entry has a document title, a date published, and a web address if the document is available on the Internet. An entry will have an OCLC number the first time a title has been cataloged.

ESSENTIAL STATE PUBLICATIONS

Directories

Directory of Montana Schools (Office of Public Instruction)—This directory lists Montana's schools and education associations, along with the names, addresses, phone and fax numbers for OPI staff, school superintendents, clerks, principals, and board chairs from all of Montana's school districts. In addition, it has listings for public and private colleges, as well as a listing of bonded firms licensed to sell textbooks in Montana. The *Directory of Montana Schools* is available online at http://www.opi.state.mt.us/Directory/ as either a large PDF file, or as individual dBase files suitable for printing mailing labels. Printed copies may be obtained for a fee by writing to Advanced Litho Printing, 226 9th Avenue S., Great Falls, MT 59405-4034, or call (406) 453-0393.

Montana Agricultural Buyers Directory (Agriculture)—Located at http://agr.state.mt.us/programs/add/buyerdir.shtml, this directory lists agricultural producers and processors across Montana. From alfalfa to wool, you should be able to find a Montana supplier using the directory. You can get a free print copy of the *Montana Agricultural Buyers Directory* by contacting the Montana Department of Agriculture Marketing Office at (406) 444-2402, or by writing Department of Agriculture, P.O. Box 200201, Helena, MT 59620, or by e-mailing them at agr@mt.gov.

Montana Library Directory (Montana State Library)—The paper edition of this directory is distributed to Montana libraries. The web version, located at http://montanalibraries.org/Directory/mldHome.asp, is updated continuously by individual libraries and presented as either a browseable database or as a PDF file. The PDF file is updated once yearly in February and is identical to the printed version. Each library entry contains contact information, library hours, and OCLC symbol. The directory also contains listings for consortia and state and federal document depositories. The paper edition is not available for purchase.

Montana State Government Telephone Directory (Administration)—This is available in paper and online at http://www.state.mt.us/css/govt/statedir.asp. The Internet version is divided into three sections: Agency Listings, City Listings, and Toll-Free Government Telephone Numbers. The print version includes the e-mail addresses of employees, organizational charts, a map of the Capitol complex, universities and colleges, and Montana zip codes. The state agency listings include agency subdivisions and addresses, telephone and fax numbers, and home pages when available. Paper copies can by obtained by calling the Department of Administration at (406) 444-2586 or by writing them at Department of Administration, Information Technology Services Division, Room 21, Sam W. Mitchell Building, Helena, MT 59620-0113.

Financial/Budgetary Resources

Executive Budget of the State of Montana (Office of Budget and Program Planning)—Located at http://www.state.mt.us/budget/css/budget/budget.asp, the *Executive Budget* is split into five online volumes. Most of the budget is a list of proposed spending divided into the broad subject areas of General Government and Transportation, Public Health and Human Services, Natural Resources and Commerce, Public Safety and Justice, Education, Long-Range Planning, and a Unified Information Technology Summary. Budget documents are in Word and Excel formats. Other useful features of the *Executive Budget* are a state government organizational chart and a tourism tax report.

Legislative Fiscal Report (Legislature)—The Legislative Fiscal Division prepares the report of the budget as adopted by the legislature. According to the introduction for the 2003 Biennium edition, the four-volume *Legislative Fiscal Report*

was designed to report to the 2001 legislature and all interested parties on the fiscal actions of the 2001 legislature (including both legislation passed and stated legislative intent related to fiscal issues) and the fiscal status of state government through the 2003 biennium. It accomplishes its purpose by: 1) reporting on appropriations to and revenues of state government as determined by the legislature; and 2) discussing other fiscal issues pertaining to the state's fiscal status.

The report is available on the Internet at http://leg.state.mt.us/css/fiscal/2003_biennium/fiscal_report.asp and all budget documents are in PDF format.

Montana Comprehensive Annual Financial Report (Administration)—The *Comprehensive Annual Financial Report* (CAFR) is divided into three sections, an Introductory section with a state government organizational chart, a Financial section, and a Statistical section. The Statistical section includes data for the prior ten fiscal years on state income and expenditures, personal income, private employment, and enrollment at Montana state colleges. Users can find issues of this report back to 1999 on the Internet at http://www.discoveringmontana.com/doa/adm/Cafr/CAFR.htm.

Legal Resources

Administrative Rules of Montana (Secretary of State)—The *Administrative Rules of Montana (ARM)* is not available on the Internet except through various fee-based services such as *State Capital Universe* from LexisNexis. The *ARM* is available as a 23-volume looseleaf binder set housing state agencies' effective rules. Rules are found using a simplified three-part rule numbering system. The set contains a cross-reference table from *Montana Code Annotated* (MCA) citations to *ARM* rules at end of each title. There is also an index of all titles prepared by the Office of the Secretary of State. The *Administrative Rules of Montana* are updated quarterly. As of 2002, the *Administrative Rules of Montana* cost $350 for the initial set, with an annual update fee of $250. Prepaid orders should be sent to Secretary of State, Administrative Rules Bureau, P.O. Box 202801, Helena, MT 59620-2801. If you have questions about *ARM*, please call the Administrative Rules Bureau at (406) 444-2055.

Montana Administrative Register (MAR) (Secretary of State)—This twice-monthly publication contains all proposed new, amended, repealed rules, adopted rule changes, notification of hearing dates and address for written comments, Attorney General's opinions, and state declaratory rulings. Each issue has a "How to Use Guide" for both the *MAR* and the *ARM*. Each register has a cumulative table listing all rule-making actions since the last update of the *Administrative Rules of Montana*. Other features of the *Register* include a list of appointees to and vacancies on boards and councils published once a month, and a twice-yearly cross-reference table listing MCA citations to *ARM* rules. The *Montana Administrative Register* is available free on the Internet at http://sos.state.mt.us/css/ARM/ARM.asp. A paper subscription is available for $300 annually for twenty-four issues. Prepaid orders should be sent to Secretary of State, Administrative Rules Bureau, P.O. Box 202801, Helena, MT 59620-2801. If you have questions about *ARM*, please call the Administrative Rules Bureau at (406) 444-2055.

Montana Code Annotated (Legislature)—The *Montana Code Annotated* (MCA) is published in odd-numbered years incorporating changes made by the legislature of that year. The MCA is available in both web and paper format. The web version of the MCA is located at http://leg.state.mt.us/css/mtcode _const/default.asp and contains only the basic text of the Constitution and the laws of Montana—there are no annotations. The web version is keyword searchable and supports "any" and "all" searches. One can also search phonetically if an exact spelling is unknown. Previous versions of the MCA are available back to 1995 on this web site. The MCA is also available as a 12-volume set in paper or as a CD-ROM. For the 2001 *Code*, the paper set sold for $325 and the CD-ROM sold for $315. Both items may be obtained by using the order form available at http://leg.state.mt.us/css/publications/purchase .asp.

Although the *Montana Code Annotated*'s title suggests it includes annotations, it does not. A separate set, entitled *Annotations to the Montana Code Annotated*, is available for $320 per year. Published in even-numbered years, it includes annotations to applicable court decisions, Montana Attorney General's opinion, the *Administrative Rules of Montana*, law review articles, and legal encyclopedia references. There is no similar service available on the Internet.

Montana Supreme Court Opinions/Orders (Judicial Branch)—Opinions and orders of the Montana Supreme Court since 1986 are available at http://www .lawlibrary.state.mt.us/dscgi/ds.py/View/Collection-36. Opinions are listed by year, month, docket number, and case name and are fully searchable. This site also contains the appellate briefs that have been filed with the Supreme Court. Jury instructions, court rules, opinions of the Montana Attorney General, Constitutional Convention Proceedings, and other legal materials are available at http://www.lawlibrary.state.mt.us.

Statistical Resources

Census and Economic Information Center Home Page (Commerce)—The Census and Economic Information Center (CEIC) is a unit of the Business Resources Division (BRD) in the Department of Commerce and provides a central, comprehensive economic and demographic information resource on the web at http://ceic.commerce.state.mt.us. Included are data giving detailed population and housing characteristics; income and employment; agriculture; retail and wholesale trade; manufacturing; mining, foreign trade; construction; small area market data; government finances; and so on. CEIC is the state of Montana's lead agency in the U.S. Census Bureau's federal–state cooperative State Data Center (SDC) and Business/Industry Data Center (BIDC) programs. For data requests or for more information, call (406) 841-2740 or e-mail ceic@state.mt.us.

Montana Agricultural Statistics (Montana Agricultural Statistics Service)—This report is divided into eight chapters: General, Economic, Rank, State Estimates—Crops, County Estimates—Crops, State Estimates—Livestock, County Estimates—Livestock, and Agricultural Exports. In this volume you can find the number of Montana farms, see maps of sheep production, and see the major causes of sheep loss. A print copy can be ordered by using a form available at http://www.nass.usda.gov/mt/general/subscrp.htm. For more information write to Montana Agricultural Statistics Service, 10 W. 15th Street, Suite 3100, Helena, MT 59626, or call (406) 441-1240 or (800) 835-2612.

Montana Vital Statistics (Public Health and Human Services)—This annual publication is available in paper and on the Internet at http://www.dphhs.state.mt.us/services / statistical_information / vital / statistical _tables.htm. From this site you can also access prior years' reports back to 1999, as well as selected vital statistics back to 1910. *Montana Vital Statistics* is divided into several major sections: Natality (births), Mortality, Cancer, Induced Abortions, Marriage, and Marriage Termination. One unusual set of statistics concerns births outside hospitals. Free paper copies of this publication are available by writing the Office of Vital Statistics, Montana Department of Public Health and Human Services, DPHHS Building, Room 205, P.O. Box 4210, Helena, MT 59604-4210. Copies may also be requested by phone at (406) 444-4228, by fax at (406) 444-1803, or by e-mail at bschwartz@state.mt.us.

Other Resources

Montana Natural Resource Information System (Montana State Library)—A clearinghouse of information about Montana's natural resources is available at http://nris.state.mt.us/. Programs include the Natural Heritage Program, the Water Information System, and the Geographic Information System.

Montana Outdoors (Fish, Wildlife and Parks)—*Montana Outdoors* is the official publication of the Department of Fish, Wildlife and Parks. Published six times a year, it has information on Montana's wildlife, natural resources, and outdoor opportunities. It is not available on the web, but you can sign up for a subscription at https://commerce.cdsfulfillment.com/MOD/subscriptions .cgi. A year's subscription is currently $9.

Montana Election Information Web Site (Secretary of State)—Located at http://sos.state.mt.us/css/ELB/Contents.asp, this is the place to get information on candidates, their finances, and their term limits. Visitors can also view turnout figures, election results back to 1992, and order a copy of Montana's registered voters list.

MONTANA'S WORLD WIDE WEB HOME PAGE

The official home page of Montana is *Discovering Montana*, accessible at both http://www.state.mt.us and http://www.discoveringmontana.com. As with many other state home pages, with an 800 × 600 screen resolution you will need to scroll down the screen to see the whole page. This is not obvious because the page is set up with a menu on the left and a beautiful photograph on the right that takes up the entire first screen. Only a touch of blue at the bottom alerts you to extra content. This extra content includes links to the governor's web site and featured state agency sites as well as a search box for Montana's web pages.

The heart of *Discovering Montana* is the left-hand menu, which has seven options: About Montana, Tourism and Recreation, Working and Living Here, Online Services, Doing Business, Government, and Education. Mousing over any of these options reveals submenus. If your browser does not support javascript, there is a "text only" link in the top right-hand corner of the page. The *About Montana* menu contains more serious information than similar menus from other states. In addition to the kids' info and state symbols you would expect to find here, *About Montana* provides links to census information, road conditions, and Native American resources. The "Tourism and Recreation" menu provides useful information for all interested tourists, from listings of museums to information on obtaining fishing licenses. The "Working and Living Here" menu provides links to several resources including a "Newcomer's Guide" and links to Montana newspapers. The "Online Services" menu provides links to dozens of e-services available to Montanans, including business entity searches, paying income taxes, and freeway cameras. The "Doing Business" menu allows current and prospective business people to discover how to sell to state government, obtain permits, and participate in the state's "Made in Montana" program. The "Government" menu provides links to federal, state, local, and tribal officials, as well as a link to Montana's Constitution and Laws. The "Education" menu not only provides links to schools, colleges, and libraries, but to day care resources as well.

Several features of *Discovering Montana* make it straightforward to search. First, if you are looking for something transaction related, start with the Services menu. On the state home page, there is a link to a browseable and searchable subject index of pages. The browse feature lists subject pages along with the agencies that published them. Many people will find this convenient. There is a simple keyword search box on the home page. The home page also features a link to an advanced search page where you can narrow your search by agency and whether the page you are looking for has been modified in the past week, month, or year. The presence of "week" suggests that *Discovering Montana* has a fresh index, which is a boon for people looking for the latest Montana information. The text of the latest year's legislative bills can also be searched from the advanced search page.

COMMERCIAL PUBLICATIONS AND WEB SITES

Montana Almanac (Falcon Publishing, Helena, MT)—This publication was issued in 1997 and contains nearly 500 pages. The *Montana Almanac* has hundreds of tables, graphs, maps, and photographs, in addition to seventy-seven biographical sketches of notable Montanans. It is not available through the publisher's web site at http://www.globe-pequot.com/falcon.cfm. However, it can be ordered from Amazon.com or other booksellers.

Names on the Face of Montana: The Story of Montana's Place Names (Mountain Press Publishing, Missoula, MT)—Arranged alphabetically, this book contains entries on how Montana places got their names. It is available through the publisher's web site at http://www.mountain-press.com.

SOURCES CONSULTED

Montana Core Collection 2002. Compiled by Montana State Library Staff.
Montana State Publications Center web page, http://msl.state.mt.us/lisd/spc/index.htm.
Montana State Publications Lists, http://msl.state.mt.us/lisd/spc/pub-lists.htm.
Numerous departmental pages accessed via the state's home page, http://www.state.mt.us.
Survey response from Jim Kammerer, Montana State Library, 2000.

Nebraska

Daniel D. Cornwall

GOVERNMENT PUBLISHING AND THE DEPOSITORY SYSTEM

The Nebraska Publications Clearinghouse Service was established in 1972 by *Nebraska Revised Statutes* 55-411 to 51-418. The clearinghouse's mission is to collect the publications of all branches of state government and state-funded educational institutions to ensure that state government information is made available to a wide audience. Other aims of the depository program are to ensure that valuable records are preserved for future generations and to reduce publication and distribution costs for state agencies who can refer individuals to the clearinghouse. The clearinghouse is run by Nebraska's State Library Commission.

Currently, there are three complete state depository libraries that receive their materials in paper and fourteen selective depository libraries that receive microfiched materials. The Nebraska depository program requires state agencies to send the clearinghouse four copies of all state publications intended for public distribution. The clearinghouse catalogs and retains one copy for loan to the public. It also forwards a copy to the Nebraska State Historical Society and another to the Library of Congress. Selected copies are dismantled and microfiched. The microfiche is then sent to the selective state document depository libraries across the state, based on the *Core List of State Publications and Criteria for Preservation of Nebraska State Documents in Microfiche*. The Library Commission currently houses over 100,000 state documents and microfiche.

The depository program has started to make some government resources available electronically. *State Government Publications Online*, http://www.nlc.state.ne.us/docs/pilot/pilot.html, includes both links to full-text state publications posted on agency servers and a selection of state publications in PDF format posted on the Library Commission server.

Nebraska state documents are classified according to a Superintendent of Documents–like system called Nedocs. The Nedocs classification system is based on agency name and type of publication (e.g., H6000A001 means Historical Society Annual Report).

USEFUL ADDRESSES AND TELEPHONE NUMBERS

The most complete collections of Nebraska state publications may be found at the following libraries:

Nebraska Library Commission
The Atrium
1200 N. Street, Suite 120
Lincoln, NE 68508-2023
Phone Number for Nebraska Reference Questions: (402) 471-4016
E-Mail Address for Nebraska Reference Questions: govref@neon.nlc.state.ne.us
Library Home Page: http://www.nlc.state.ne.us/
Depository Program Home Page: http://www.nlc.state.ne.us/docs/stclear.html

University of Nebraska at Lincoln
Love Memorial Library
Documents Department
State Documents Office Room 213
Lincoln, NE 68858-0410
Phone Number for Nebraska Reference Questions: (402) 472-2562 or 6663
E-Mail Address for Nebraska Reference Questions: jerryf@unllib.unl.edu
Library Home Page: http://www.unl.edu/libr/libs/love/love.html
Government Resources Home Page: http://www.unl.edu/libr/govdocs/docs1.htm

INDEXES TO NEBRASKA STATE PUBLICATIONS

Current Nebraska documents can be found in *What's Up Doc*, the depository program's newsletter. This bimonthly newsletter lists all new state publications received. Issues and annual cumulations are available at http://www.nlc.state.ne.us/docs/docpubs.html. Older documents can be found through the *Nebraska Publications Checklist* (issued to depositories on microfiche) for documents issued from 1972 to 1992.

ESSENTIAL STATE PUBLICATIONS

Directories

Nebraska Criminal Justice Directory (Commission on Law Enforcement and Criminal Justice)—Nebraska Documents Call Number—L2500D001 YEAR. This annual publication includes names and contact information for law enforcement officials down to the local level; correctional facilities, courts, and judges to the county level; legislators and congressional representatives; victim and domestic violence assistance personnel; and criminal justice organizations. It is not available on the Internet, but copies may be obtained by writing the Nebraska Commission on Law Enforcement and Criminal Justice, P.O. Box 94946, Lincoln, NE 68509-4946, or call (402) 471-2194.

Nebraska Education Directory (Education)—Nebraska Documents Call Number—E2200 D001. This annual publication is available on the Internet at http://ess.nde.state.ne.us/DataCenter/EducationDirectory/EdDirectory.htm, and contains a "Teacher Locator System" and statistical data on Nebraska school districts. The Teacher Locator System allows one to find a single school district employee or a list of employees for a district. The statistical data include enrollment and funding figures for each school in Nebraska. A printed copy of the 2001–2002 *Nebraska Education Directory* is available by writing Nebraska Department of Education, Education Support Services, Data Administration and Support, P.O. Box 9498, 301 Centennial Mall South, Lincoln, NE 68509-4987, or by calling (402) 471-2367 or (402) 471-2486. The printed copy of the 2001–2002 *Education Directory* is $23.00 (includes $3.00 for shipping), prepaid to the address provided. For the same price you may buy the directory on disk in a spreadsheet-friendly format. Beginning with the 2002–2003 edition, the directory will be exclusively published on the Internet and will no longer be available in print.

Nebraska Manufacturers Directory (Economic Development)—Nebraska State Documents Call Number—E1400D001. Located at http://pio.neded.org/ManDir02.htm, this directory offers listing by business name, by product type, and by city of business. Each entry contains the business' name, its type of business, contact information, chief officer, and number of employees. For more information call the department's nationwide toll-free number, (800) 426-6505.

Nebraska State Government Directory (Department of Administrative Services, Communications Division)—Nebraska State Documents Call Number—A2600D001 YEAR. Each year, the Department of Administrative Services Division of Communications publishes and distributes the *Nebraska State Government Directory*. Available as a link from the Communications Division page at http://www.doc.state.ne.us/, the directory provides names, addresses and telephone numbers for state agencies, as well as a listing of state employees. It is available in hard copy for a nominal fee. You can purchase a copy of the most recent directory by calling (402) 471-2761.

Financial/Budgetary Resources

State of Nebraska Annual Budgetary Report (Administrative Services)—Nebraska Documents Call Number—A2100A002. The current year's report is located at http://www.das.state.ne.us/accounting/budrept/contents.htm and contains statements of actual revenues and expenditures. The report also includes information on major aid payments and a listing of taxes by revenue source. Data for years back to 1999 are available by selecting the appropriate year from the bottom of the page. For more information write Department of Administrative Services, State Accounting Division, State Capitol Room 1309, Lincoln, NE 68509, or call (402) 471-2581.

State of Nebraska Comprehensive Annual Financial Report (Administrative Services)—Nebraska Documents Call Number—A2100A001. In addition to the state government financial information you would expect to find in this report, there are some interesting statistics about the state. Some available statistics are the ten largest private employers, enrollment figures for pre-K–12 schools as well as Nebraska universities, and transportation-related statistics. Reports from 1999 onward are available at http://www.das.state.ne.us/accounting/cafr/cafrcon.htm. For more information contact the State Accounting Division at the address or phone number given above.

Legal Resources

Citizen's Guide to Nebraska's Courts (Supreme Court)—Nebraska Documents Call Number—S3000H001 YEAR. The *Guide* describes the basic structure of the Nebraska court system and describes the responsibilities of each court level. In addition, the Internet version provides court addresses with maps, and links to judicial biographies, with photographs, and recent court opinions for the Supreme Court and Court of Appeals. Only the past ninety days' worth of opinions are available on this site. Paper subscriptions to slip opinions and requests for bound volumes of opinions should be directed to the court's publications office. The publications office can be contacted by e-mail at ppolacek@nsc.state.ne.us or by regular mail at Publications Office, P.O. Box 98910, Lincoln, NE 68509-8910. Court calendars are also available for the Supreme Court and Court of Appeals. This guide is available on the Internet at http://court.nol.org/publications/citizenGuide.htm. For paper copies of the *Citizen's Guide*, please contact the publications office at the addresses above.

Revised Statutes of Nebraska (Legislature)—Nebraska Documents Call Number—L3500 Q001. This has been revised and edited under the authority and supervision of the 1943 Statute Commission, with reissued volumes published by the Revisor of Statutes. The *Revised Statutes* comprise all the statutory laws of a general nature in force at the date of publication. They are kept up-to-date by "reissue" volumes, added volumes, and softbound supplements. The *Revised Statutes* are available on the Internet at http://statutes.unicam.state.ne.us/. The web version has an obvious keyword search. An undocumented feature is the ability to browse the statutes, along with the Constitution, UCC, and the statute appendices. Clicking on the folders next to the search box will eventually lead you to specific sections of the law. Clicking on a folder will also allow you to narrow your search to a particular section of the law.

Statistical Resources

Nebraska Agricultural Statistics (Agriculture)—Nebraska Documents Call Number—A5100A002 YEAR. This publication is available on the Internet at http://www.nass.usda.gov/ne/nebrpubs.htm in PDF and text formats for each table. *Nebraska Agricultural Statistics* is divided into five broad chapters: General, Weather and Crop Progress, Crops, Livestock and Products, and Prices and Economic Data. Some of the specific topics included in this annual report include number of farms, number of days over 95 degrees Fahrenheit, acres of crops harvested, livestock inventory, and prices received for crops and livestock. To request a copy, write to Nebraska Agricultural Statistics Service, P.O. Box 81069, Lincoln, NE 68501, or call (402) 437-5541.

Nebraska Databook (Department of Economic Development)—Nebraska Doc-

uments Call Number—E1500 S002. Available at http://info.neded.org/
stathand/contents.htm, the *Databook* provides tables and graphs in the following areas: Population, Agriculture, Education, Tourism and Recreation, Geography, Income, Government, Labor Force, Finance and Insurance,
Manufacture and Business, Energy, Health and Welfare, Transportation and
Communications, Construction and Housing, Gross State Product, Law Enforcement, People, Places, History, and Maps. Some of the questions that can
be answered by the *Databook* include: "Tell me how the population of Nebraska's towns has changed since 1860"; "How many people visit Nebraska
state parks each year?"; and, "Where can I find a map of historical earthquakes
in Nebraska?" While the *Databook* is not sold to the public in hard copy, the
Department of Economic Development will periodically produce a paper version of the *Nebraska Databook* for archival purposes. The paper version is sent
to the Nebraska Library Commission for reproduction on microfiche and for
addition to the print collection of Nebraska state documents.

Statistical Report of Abortions (Health and Human Services)—Nebraska Documents Call Number—H8320 S001. This annual report presents tabulations of
statistical information reported on records of induced abortions performed in
Nebraska during the prior calendar year. The department is required by *Nebraska Statutes* sections 28-343 through 28-346 to collect this information. The
result is a set of twenty tables describing who is having abortions in Nebraska
and why. Tables 11 through 20 are not very meaningful because their data
are based on optional questions which were mostly ignored by the recording
institutions. The remaining tables have useful information such as the age of
women seeking abortions (Table 3), the reasons given (Table 4), and the number of prior abortions a patient has had (Table 6). This publication is available
on the Internet at http://www.hhs.state.ne.us/srd/srdindex.htm.

Statistics and Facts about Nebraska Schools (Education)—Nebraska Documents
Call Number—E2500S001 YEAR. This biennial publication includes enrollment in public and nonpublic schools by grade, race and sex, ranking of
schools by size of enrollment, number of graduates, and dropouts by race and
sex. Several recent editions are available on the web via the Education Support
Services home page at http://ess.nde.state.ne.us/. It is no longer issued in
print.

Vital Statistics Report (Health and Human Services)—Nebraska Documents
Call Number—H8610S001 YEAR. This annual report provides information on
births, deaths, marriages, and divorces. Some of the specific topics covered by
this report are number of teen births, method of delivery, cancer deaths by
selected sites and sex, Alzheimer's Disease deaths by Nebraska county of residence, number of marriages, and divorces by duration of marriage. Some
historical information going back to 1940 is also available in this report (see
Figure 12). Most of the information contained in this report is also available
on the Internet at http://www.hhs.state.ne.us/ced/vs.htm. For more information contact HHS Finance and Support, Communications and Legislative
Services Division, P.O. Box 95026, Lincoln, NE 68509-5026, or call (402) 471-
3996.

Nebraska Health and Human Services System

Vital Statistics

This is the most current information that's available.

Birth Summary	Birth Tables
Death Summary	Death Tables
Marriage & Divorce Summary	Marriage & Divorce Tables

2001 Statistical Report of Abortions

**Documents in PDF format require the use of Adobe Acrobat Reader
which can be downloaded for free from** Adobe Systems, Inc.

1940-2001 Births, Deaths, Marriages and Divorces by Number and Rate per 1,000 Estimated Population

1960-2001 Population by County

2001 Summary of Vital Statistics

Births

1999-2001 Births by Place of Occurrence and by Usual Residence of the Mother

2001 Births by Sex, Race and Hispanic Origin by Place of Residence

2001 Birth Order by Age of Mother

2001 and 1997-2001 Teen Births by Place of Residence

2001 Births by Trimester Prenatal Care Began

2001 Births by Number of Prenatal Visits (Percent) by Age of Mother

2001 Births by Number of Prenatal Visits (Percent) by Education of Mother

2001 Births by Number of Prenatal Visits (Percent) by Birth Weight of Child

2001 Births by Number of Prenatal Visits (Percent) by Race/Hispanic Origin of Mother

2001 Births by Trimester Prenatal Care began and Percent Receiving Inadequate Care

2001 Births by Weight Groups

2001 Very Low and Low Birth Weight Births by Place of Residence

2001 Births - Medical History Factors of the Mother

2001 Nebraska Obstetric Procedures

2001 Births - Events of Labor and/or Delivery

2001 Births - Method of Delivery

2001 Births - Conditions of the Newborn

2001 Births - Drugs Used During Pregnancy

2001 and 1997-2001 Births to Unmarried Women by Place of Residence

1997-2001 Births to Unmarried Women by Age of Mother

2001 Births to Unmarried Women by Age and Race/Hispanic Origin of Mother

1980-2001 Births - Percent of Race/Hispanic Origin Births to Unmarried Women

1980-2001 Births - Percent of Age Group Births to Unmarried Women

Figure 12. Some reports, like this one from Nebraska, provide historical statistics. *Source*: http://www.hhs.state.ne.us/ced/vs.htm.

Other Resources

Nebraska Blue Book (Nebraska Legislative Council)—Nebraska Documents Call Number—L3000 D001. Published since 1922, this biennial publication is now available on the Internet at http://www.unicam.state.ne.us/bluebook/index.htm. This 1000-plus-page publication is divided into six chapters: Nebraska, U.S. Government in Nebraska, Nebraska State Government, Local Government in Nebraska, Nebraska Education and Information Resources, and Nebraska Political Parties and Elections. The U.S., state, and local government chapters provide contact information for the agencies at every governmental level in Nebraska. The chapter on education and information resources includes listings of libraries and schools, and radio and television stations. Print copies can be ordered from the Clerk of the Legislature's Office, Room 2018, State Capitol, P.O. Box 94604, Lincoln, NE 68509-4604, or call (402) 471-2271; or e-mail bluebook@unicam.state.ne.us.

NEBRASKA'S WORLD WIDE WEB HOME PAGE

The home page for the state of Nebraska is called *Nebraska Online* and is located at http://www.nol.org. *Nebraska Online* has been operating since 1996. The web site is administered by the Nebraska State Records Board, which contracts with a private company for the actual design and maintenance of the site. The result is a clean, user-friendly interface packed with information for citizens, businesses, and visitors.

The left-hand side of the screen offers a link to the text version of the page and a search box. The top right-hand side of the screen offers three other alternate navigation functions—a business portal, a site map, and to the credit of our profession, a tab marked "Ask a Librarian!" The bottom of the screen has eight shortcut buttons to very helpful items such as road conditions, weather, and a public meetings calendar.

The middle of the screen, quite appropriately, is taken up with the main menu to *Nebraska Online*. The options offered are: Ag and Natural Resources, Business and Employment, Citizen Services, Education in Nebraska, Facts about Nebraska, Health and Safety, Moving to Nebraska, Visiting Nebraska, and Your Government. Mousing over any of these entries brings up a pop-up menu if your browser is javascript enabled. If not, you can access the submenus directly from the text version of the home page.

Some highlights of each menu are worth noting. "Ag and Natural Resources" includes links to agricultural statistics and to the state's cooperative extension service, a rich resource for farmers, gardeners, and 4-H participants alike. "Business and Employment" is the place to go for business forms and information on professional licensing. This section also houses a "Business Toolkit" that has information on starting a business in Nebraska, links to a manufacturers' directory, and to relevant state and federal laws. "Citizen Services" is a listing of popular topics, such as where to obtain birth certificates, where to find child care, or to find information about the Nebraska lottery. People can also use this link to find out if they have unclaimed property in Nebraska. "Education" takes you to information on both public and private schools and colleges in Nebraska. "Facts about Nebraska" includes the information a student would expect to find, such as state symbols, notable Nebraskans, and a Nebraska FAQ. In addition, this section points you to two extremely helpful publications, the *Nebraska Databook* and the *Nebraska Blue Book*, described above under essential publications. "Health and Safety" is where you can find out how to get a birth certificate or locate a health care facility. "Moving to Nebraska" provides links to salary calculators and other relocation information. "Visiting Nebraska" is the place to look for highway conditions and current cultural events in the state. "Your Government," as you might expect, provides links to federal, state, and local offices. Unexpectedly, it also provides links to libraries in Nebraska.

As noted above, an exciting feature of the Nebraska home page is a prominent link to an "Ask a Librarian" service. Choosing this link sends you to a page that provides e-mail and phone contact information for the Nebraska Library Commission reference section and also provides links to a Nebraska FAQ, a subject guide to state information, and a listing of state publications available on the Internet.

COMMERCIAL PUBLICATIONS AND WEB SITES

Directory of County Officials in Nebraska (Nebraska Association of County Officials, Lincoln, NE)—An alphabetical listing by county of names and addresses for elected and appointed county officials in the state, this directory can be ordered through the association's web site at http://www.nacone .org/.

Nebraska Business-to-Business Sales and Marketing Directory (American Business Directories, Omaha, NE)—This is the Nebraska volume of the series published by the directory arm of InfoUSA, the company that produces many business data products in print, on CD, and online for subscribers. This publication can be ordered through the publisher's web site at http://www .infousa.com/.

Nebraska Directory of Municipal Officials (League of Nebraska Municipalities, Lincoln, NE)—This is an annual alphabetical listing by town of names, addresses, and phone numbers of elected and appointed officials in all Nebraska municipalities. It also lists the tax rate, assessed valuation, population, class designation, and meeting schedule for each municipality. Addresses and phone numbers of Nebraska state senators and congressional representatives are also included. This item may be ordered from the publisher's web site at http://www.lonm.org/.

SOURCES CONSULTED

Nebraska Publications Clearinghouse home page, http://www.nlc.state.ne.us/docs/ stclear.html.
Numerous departmental web pages via the state's home page, http://www.nol.org.
Survey response from Beth Goble, Nebraska Library Commission, 2000.

Nevada

Daniel C. Barkley

GOVERNMENT PUBLISHING AND THE DEPOSITORY SYSTEM

The Nevada state depository system was established in 1971 under *Nevada Revised Statutes* (NRS) 378.170. That statute created the State Publications Distribution Center that is currently under the direction of the State Library and Archives Administrator. The State Library and Archives Administrator has, under this statute, the ability to make regulations as necessary to fulfill the obligations of the Distribution Center. The administrator "shall establish standards for eligibility as a depository library" (NRS 378.190), enter into depository library agreements with any city, county, district, regional, town, or university library in Nevada, and distribute to each depository library copies of state publications. Currently, there are nine participating libraries in the state depository program. For a list of participating state depository libraries go to http://www.library.unr.edu/depts/bgic/guides/government/nevada/nevada.html#depos.

Under NRS 378.150, the intent of the depository legislation is that "all state and local government publications be distributed to designated depository libraries for use by all inhabitants of the state and designated depository libraries assume the responsibility for keeping such publications readily accessible for use and rendering assistance, without charge, to patrons using them." As defined under NRS 378.160, a state publication is "any document that is issued in print by any state agency and has been legally released for public distribution." The few exceptions under this statute include the *Nevada Revised Statutes with Annotations*; the *Nevada Reports*; bound volumes of the *Statutes of Nevada*; press releases of the university and community college systems that are not, by nature, public; office communications that are not of vital public interest; and publications from state agencies that are required by federal and state law to be distributed to depository libraries and which duplicate those publications that fall under NRS 378.200.

NRS 378.160 defines print as "all forms of printing and duplicating other than by use of carbon paper." A state agency is defined as "the legislature, constitutional officers or any department, division, bureau, board, commission or agency of the State of Nevada." Each state agency must deposit with the administrator twelve copies of each state publication that was not printed by the state printing division. Further, every state agency must deposit with the administrator twelve additional copies that have been printed by the state printing division for depository libraries, public libraries, and university and community college system libraries distribution. As well, every city, county, and regional agency and every school district and special district shall deposit with the administrator six copies of each of its publications.

Under NRS 378.200, after receipt of an agency publication, the administrator distributes one copy to the Legislative Counsel Bureau, two copies to the Library of Congress, and two copies to each depository library in Nevada. The administrator must also retain sufficient copies for preservation and use by the general public. Any remaining copies are distributed to other states for exchange purposes or for interlibrary loan.

USEFUL ADDRESSES AND TELEPHONE NUMBERS

The most complete collections of Nevada state publications are at the following locations:

Business and Government Information Center
Getchell Library
University of Nevada, Reno
Reno, NV 89557-0044
Phone Number for Nevada Reference Questions: (775) 784-6500, x257
E-Mail Link for Nevada Reference Questions: http://www.library.unr.edu/depts/
    reference/askalibrarian.html
Getchell Library Home Page: http://www.library.unr.edu/geninfo.html
Business and Government Information Center Home Page: http://www.library.unr
    .edu/depts/bgic/Default.htm

Lied Library
University of Nevada, Las Vegas
4505 Maryland Parkway
Las Vegas, NV 89154-7001
Phone Number for Nevada Reference Questions: (702) 895-2220
E-Mail Link for Nevada Reference Questions: http://www.library.unlv.edu/ref/
    refquestion.html
Government Publications Home Page: http://www.library.unlv.edu/govpub/index
    .html

Nevada Legislative Counsel Bureau
Research Library
401 South Carson Street
Carson City, NV 89701-4747
Phone Number for Nevada Reference Questions: (775) 684-6827
E-Mail Address for Nevada Reference Questions: admin@lcb.state.nv.us

Nevada Legislative Counsel Bureau Library Home Page: http://leg.state.nv.us/lcb/research/library/index.cfm

Nevada State Library and Archives
100 North Stewart Street
Carson City, NV 89701-4285
Phone Number for Nevada Reference Questions: (775) 684-3320
E-Mail Link for Nevada Reference Questions: http://dmla.clan.lib.nv.us/docs/email/nslaform.htm
Nevada State Library and Archives Home Page: http://dmla.clan.lib.nv.us/docs/nsla
State Publications Distribution Center Home Page: http://dmla.clan.lib.nv.us/docs/nsla/stpubs/stpubs.htm

INDEXES TO NEVADA STATE PUBLICATIONS

Under NRS 378.210, the State Publications Distribution Center issues a list of state publications periodically. The Nevada State Publications Distribution Center published a sequentially numbered *Nevada Official Publications List* of state publications received from the State Printer from 1953 through 1991. In 1999 a publication entitled *State of Nevada Publications Index, 1993–1998* was published in cooperation with Catamount Fund Ltd., and included state publications received by the State Publications Distribution Center during that period. A *Nevada Official Publications List* covering the period 1999–2002 will be completed in early 2003 and will cover publications received by the distribution center during that period of time. For further information contact the Nevada State Library and Archives, State Publications Distribution Center, 100 North Stewart Street, Carson City, NV 89701-4285, or call (775) 684-3320; fax (775) 684-3330; e-mail ejkessle@clan.lib.nv.us.

A *Nevada State Publications Shelf List Catalog* on microfiche contains cataloging for Nevada state publications received by the Nevada State Library spanning the period from Territorial time through October 1993. The State Library Public Access Catalog, through Cooperative Libraries Automated Network (CLAN), contains the majority of these records as well as many state publications published since 1993. Go to http://www.clan.lib.nv.us/Polaris.

The University of Nevada, Reno, provides a searchable database of state publications that is available at http://www.library.unr.edu/depts/bgic/guides/government/nevada/nevada.html. It includes state and local publications distributed to Nevada depositories since 1995.

The State classifies archives state agency publications in a modified SWANK classification system. Depositories may or may not use this classification system, depending on their local policies and procedures.

ESSENTIAL STATE PUBLICATIONS

Directories

Nevada Department of Education School List (Education Department)—This online list provides contact information on Nevada public, private, and charter schools. Information includes the school district, address, phone and fax numbers, school and enrollment for all educators, and school superintendents and administrators. The public school list is available in a PDF format and the private and charter school lists are available in HTML. There are also links from this page to standards, licensing, and other educational information. The page can be viewed at http://www.nde.state.nv.us/admin/deptsuper/fiscal/nvschools.html. For more information contact the Nevada Department of Education, 700 East 5th Street, Carson City, NV 89701, or call (775) 687-9200.

Nevada Library Directory and Statistics [Year] (Nevada State Library and Archives)—This directory provides contact information on all public, academic, special, and school libraries in Nevada. Library statistics are also available from this page. The page provides the directory as a Word file, and includes information on personal e-mail addresses, statistics from 1996 to the present, and a form to request changes in the directory. The page can be found at http://dmla.clan.lib.nv.us/docs/nsla/directory/. The site is updated and maintained by the Department of Cultural Affairs, Nevada State Library and Archives, 100 North Stewart Street, Carson City, NV 89701-4285; call (775) 684-3360.

State of Nevada Telephone Directory (Department of Information Technology)—This online directory provides basic contact information on state employees. Contact information includes employee names and departments. Utilizing a search engine by employee name, one can locate address, department, phone, and fax numbers. There are two listings available by employee or department and the capability exists to print either listing in Word. The directory is available online at http://telephone.state.nv.us/directory/syncrosplash/dir.htm. For more information contact the Department of Information Technology, 505 East King Street, Room 403, Carson City, NV 89701, or call (775) 684-7342.

[Year] Directory of State and Local Government (Legislative Counsel Bureau)— The 2001 edition of this directory provides contact information for all employees working in state, county, or city government in Nevada. There are links to individual government operations (e.g., constitutional officials, county offices) as well as the ability to view the entire directory. Depending on the link used, contact information includes the office with the address, phone, and fax numbers, and the *Nevada Revised Statute* that created the office. The directory can be viewed at http://www.leg.state.nv.us/lcb/research/sandlgov .cfm. A copy may be available from the Nevada Legislature, Legislative Counsel Bureau, 401 South Carson Street, Carson City, NV 89701-4747, or call (775) 684-6825.

Financial/Budgetary Resources

Citizen's Assets: An Annual Report on State Government to the Citizens of Nevada (State Controller's Office)—This annual report is a condensed version of the *Comprehensive Annual Financial Report* (CAFR). It presents a synopsis of fiscal activity in Nevada for the past fiscal year. It is designed as a supplement to the CAFR with the intent of providing the citizens of Nevada an easy-to-understand format on the state's financial condition. The online report includes text and statistics covering subjects ranging from new initiatives to the economic impacts of mining, tourism, and gaming. The report is available at http://www.state.nv.us/controller/; select "Popular Report." This report is the first of its kind released by the Nevada State Controller, 101 North Carson Street, Suite 5, Carson City, NV 89701-4786; call (775) 684-5777.

Comprehensive Annual Financial Report (State Controller's Office)—This annual report presents to the governor, legislators, and citizens of Nevada a detailed financial report on fiscal activities during the past year. The report contains four sections, a state organizational chart, major initiatives, and an economic outlook. There is also trend information on fiscal, social, and demographic activities. Recent editions of the report can be found online at http://www.state.nv.us/controller/CAFR_Download_Page.htm. For more information contact the Nevada State Controller, 101 North Carson Street, Suite 5, Carson City, NV 89701-4786, or call (775) 684-5777.

Executive Budget in Brief (Administration Department)—This biennial publication presents the governor's budget figures and highlights for the next two fiscal years. This report provides readers with a more efficient and streamlined report that includes some duplicative materials, simplified tabular presentations, and a more detailed "highlight" section. This is also the first time this report has appeared online. It includes an economic overview, fund balances, sources of revenue, budget highlights, future challenges, and contacts. It can be seen at http://www.budget.state.nv.us/index.htm; select "Publications." A copy may be obtained by contacting the State of Nevada, Department of Administration, 209 East Musser Street, Room 200, Carson City, NV 89701-4298, or call (775) 684-0222.

Gaming Revenue Report (Gaming Control Board)—This annual report provides a detailed summary of gaming revenue information on non-restricted activity for the past month, quarter, or calendar year. This is one of many gaming-related reports available from the board. Because gaming is the largest source of state revenue, the board produces numerous reports on the various types of gaming activity conducted in Nevada, as well as publications on where to obtain legal chips and tokens, manufacturers/distributors, and restricted locations. All of these reports are available for sale. Contact the Gaming Control Board, P.O. Box 8003, Carson City, NV 89702-8003, or call (775) 684-7700. An order form is available at http://gaming.state.nv.us/agency _forms.htm. Select "List of Publications" in the Administration Division section. The form includes prices for each publication produced. Visit the board's web page at http://gaming.state.nv.us.

Legal Resources

Nevada Law Library (Legislative Counsel Bureau)—This online resource provides links to many of the important legal resources pertaining to Nevada law. This one-stop resource has links to the *Nevada Revised Statutes*, the *Nevada Constitution*, *City Charters*, the *Nevada Administrative Code*, the *Nevada Register*, the *Nevada Supreme Court Opinions*, and *Legislative Measures* for the past three legislative sessions. Clicking on one of the links takes you to that particular law resource. From there, a table of contents and index are offered for browsing, or a keyword search can be performed. Most of these resources are available in paper and can be purchased (see the "Commercial Publications" section below for more information on purchasing these resources). This most useful site can be found at http://www.leg.state.nv.us/law1.cfm. It should be noted that this site is for informational purposes and is not to be viewed as the official record of action. Only the printed versions of these publications are considered legally binding resources. The site is maintained by Nevada Legislative Publications, Legislative Building, Room 1189, 401 South Carson Street, Carson City, NV 89701-4747, or call (775) 684-6825.

Register of Administrative Regulations (Legal Division)—This is the official online site to view state agency–proposed or adopted administrative regulations. Published monthly, the *Register* contains the state agency's request, proposed and adopted text of the regulation, notice of intent, a written notice of adoption, an informational statement, and a date as to when that regulation becomes effective. A search engine provides the capability to use either a free-text or queried search. The online site, located at http://leg.state.nv.us/register/, has links to regulations and proposed regulations from 1999 to the present. Volumes 1 through 68 can also be viewed and searched at this web site. A paper copy is also available on a subscription basis. For more information contact the Nevada Legislature, Legislature Counsel Bureau, Legal Division, 401 South Carson Street, Carson City, NV 89701-4747, or call (775) 684-6830.

Selected Nevada Revised Statutes Relating to Criminal Law [Criminal Law Manual] (Legislative Publications)—This manual contains Nevada statutes relating to specific crimes, punishments, criminal case procedures, traffic laws, and related law issues pertaining to evidence and witnesses. The table of contents can be viewed online at http://www.nevadalegislature.com/publications/Print/criminallaw.htm. The paper edition is a biennial publication that is available either in an annotated or unannotated version. The unannotated version, a two-volume set, is available for $30.00 for the biennial pages-only edition, or for $45.00 for a new set of pages, binder, and divider tabs. The annotated version is a four-volume set that is available for $52.50 for the pages-only, and $77.50 for a new set of pages, binder, and divider tabs. To order, or for more information, contact Nevada Legislative Publications, Legislative Building, Room 1189, 401 South Carson Street, Carson City, NV 89701-4747, or call (775) 684-6835.

[Year] Legislative Manual (Legislative Counsel Bureau)—This annual publication provides guidelines to members of the Nevada legislature and their staff. Designed to ensure accurate and complete bills or proposals for introduction onto the House or Senate floor, the *Manual* is updated regularly to reflect changes in the law or parliamentary procedures in the legislature. It can be viewed online at http://www.leg.state.nv.us/lcb/research/publications.cfm. A paper copy is available for purchase for $18.00. To purchase a subscription contact the Nevada Legislature, Legislative Counsel Bureau, 401 South Carson Street, Carson City, NV 89701-4747, or call (775) 684-6825.

Statistical Resources

Labor Market Information (Employment Training and Rehabilitation Department)—This is a virtual one-stop resource providing labor, wage, demographic, and economic statistical information on a state and local basis. Also included is the *Nevada Career Information System* that provides comprehensive career guidance. A wealth of statistical and summary information can be found at this web site (see http://detr.state.nv.us/lmi/index.htm), separated by major subject category (e.g., Employment/Unemployment, Economic Indicators). Other links direct one to affirmative action reports, publications available free or for purchase, area profiles, and career information. The web site is maintained by the Nevada Department of Employment Training and Rehabilitation, Information Development and Processing Division, Research and Analysis Bureau, 500 East 3rd Street, Carson City, NV 89713. Call (775) 684-0450.

Nevada Central Cancer Registry (State Health Department)—This online database provides statistical information on cancer occurrences in Nevada. Data are gathered from hospitals and pathology laboratories participating in this program. These facilities have internal cancer registries from which aggregate data are withdrawn. The information collected is used to track cancer incidence and other related information appropriate in conducting epidemiological studies of cancer and related diseases. This resource can be found at http://health2k.state.nv.us/cancer/. A biannually published report is generated along with special reports on a periodic basis. The *Registry* is maintained by the Nevada State Health Department, Cancer Registry, 620 Belrose Street, Las Vegas, NV 89158. Call (702) 486-5065.

Nevada Interactive Health Databases (Bureau of Health Planning and Statistics)—This Internet query database provides statistics on birth, death, hospitalization, and population. The query search allows one to search for birth, cancer, death, population, or hospital discharges. Search results can be either copied or downloaded. There are also links to reports from the Nevada Center for Health Data and Research, population estimates and projections, and the *Nevada Statistical Abstract*. This online resource can be found at http://health2k.state.nv.us/matchiim/. The site is maintained by the Nevada State Health Division, Bureau of Health Planning and Statistics, 505 East King Street, Room 102, Carson City, NV 89701-4749. Call (775) 684-4218.

Nevada's Vital Statistics (Office of Vital Records)—This online resource provides data that have been compiled from original birth, death, stillbirth, induced abortion, marriage, and divorce records that have been filed with the Office of Vital Records. Data are gathered via standardized forms completed by appropriate hospital personnel, funeral directors, county recorders, county clerks, physicians, or medical attendants. For more information contact the Nevada State Health Division, Bureau of Health Planning and Statistics, Office of Vital Records, 505 East King Street, Room 102, Carson City, NV 89701-4749, or call (775) 684-4242.

[Year] Nevada Statistical Abstract (Department of Administration)—This online annual report provides statistical data on a myriad of subjects ranging from crime to voting trends in Nevada. Compiled and arranged in a manner

that is consistent with the *Statistical Abstract of the United States*, Nevada's *Abstract* is arranged by subject, provides brief statistical information on that subject, and gives sources of data for more information. The *Abstract* is a fluid document that will have sections added as they are compiled. It is available at http://budget.state.nv.us/sa01Index.htm. For further information, contact the Nevada Department of Administration, Budget and Planning Division, 209 East Musser Street, Room 200, Carson City, NV 89701-4298, or call (775) 684-0222.

Other Resources

Domestic Violence and Children: A Report to the Nevada State Legislature (Task Force on Family Violence)—This report, issued in 1999, provides recommendations to meet the needs of children exposed to domestic violence. The task force identified several major areas of concern that it felt needed to be addressed immediately. Those areas included law enforcement, prosecution, and victims' services. The report includes a copy of the bill creating the task force, a bibliography, and a survey used to question the Child and Family Services' caseworkers. The report is available from the Division of Child and Family Services, Task Force on Family Violence, 711 East 5th Street, Carson City, NV 89701, or call (775) 684-4400.

Historical Documents of Nevada (Legislative Counsel Bureau)—This web site offers five links to historical legal documents pertaining to Nevada. Court rules, the Nevada admission acts, the Nevada Constitution, city charters, and selected special and local acts are available from this web page, which is located at http://www.leg.state.nv.us/other. It is maintained by the Nevada Legislature, Legislative Counsel Bureau, Legal Division, 401 South Carson Street, Carson City, NV 89701-4747. Call (775) 684-6830.

Major Mines of Nevada, [Year]: Mineral Industries in Nevada's Economy (Division of Minerals)—This annual report provides summary information on mining activity in Nevada. Produced in cooperation with the Mackay School of Mines, University of Nevada–Reno, this report demonstrates the importance of mining activity in Nevada, which is probably the third leading economic activity conducted in the state, behind gaming and tourism. Figures include employment, tons mined, minerals mined, and production. Sand and gravel operations are not included in this report. The report can be viewed at http://minerals.state.nv.us/forms/forms_mining.htm. For more information contact the Nevada Division of Minerals, 400 West King Street, Suite 106, Carson City, NV, or call (775) 684-7040.

Nevada Commission on Tourism's Down and Dirty Adventure Guide (Tourism Commission)—An online guide to outdoor recreational opportunities and challenges in Nevada, this site contains links to Hiking, Biking, Climbing, Backcountry, Sandboarding, Off-road, Water, and Air sports activities. Each of these sites further provides one with the ability to choose the challenge, the area, the degree of difficulty (from novice to X-treme), and a keyword search. This site also contains a movie that can be downloaded and viewed. There is also a search area containing Resources, Did You Know, Top 10 Challenges, Ordering a Guidebook, a Nevada Map, Articles about Outdoor Activities, and a Tread Lightly section. It is a unique and interesting web site, certainly aimed at those wishing to explore more than the Nevada gaming. To view this web site go to http://www.travelnevada.com/adventure/. For more information contact the Nevada Commission on Tourism, 401 North Carson Street, Carson City, NV 89701, or call (800) NEVADA-8.

Plan of Goals, Strategies, and Recommendations for the Preservation and Protection of Wild Horses for the State of Nevada (Commission for the Preservation of Wild Horses)—This report was written by the commission with recommendations to the Nevada legislature on the best method to preserve and protect the wild horse populations residing in Nevada. A summary of the life history of wild horses, their geographic areas of inhabitance, and population trends are included. Some of the recommendations include a sale and adoption program, using wild horses in at-risk youth programs, and their promotion as a point of attraction for tourism. Also included are statistics gathered by the U.S. Bureau of Land Management. To obtain a copy of this report contact the Commission for the Preservation of Wild Horses, 123 West Nye Lane, Carson City, NV 89706-0818, or call (775) 687-1400.

NEVADA'S WORLD WIDE WEB HOME PAGE

Like other state home pages, Nevada's "Official State of Nevada Website," http://www.nv.gov/, offers itself as a portal to various links and windows to state government agency web sites. Although the page is accessible using Netscape, it seems to be designed to work better with Internet Explorer (IE). In some instances, the utilization of IE is necessary to delve into further layers of information on a state agency's home page.

One of the more interesting features is that the Nevada home page provides a direct link to Google, one of the Internet's better search engines. Google is also featured on many state agency web sites as well. The search engine can be used to search for information on that state agency or information on all of Google as it relates to that state agency and its services.

There are several main links from the home page. These links access information on State Agencies, Tourism, Public Safety, Online Services, Education, Social Services, Employment, and other topics. From each of these main links one is taken to more specific information or provided links to more detailed, subject-oriented web pages.

There are several banners at the top that provide links to specific cities in Nevada such as Reno, Carson City, Las Vegas, and others. Running down the right side of the web site are current press releases, mostly issued from the governor's office. While the subject content varies from day to day, the press releases are useful and informative. As of this writing, the state and citizens of Nevada have opposed the U.S. government's decision to utilize Yucca Mountain as a nuclear waste disposal site. As this challenge deepens, expect to view more press releases on this topic. Finally, the web site offers some brief weather data on major cities in Nevada. It's interesting to note the temperature variations between Reno and Las Vegas, for example.

Overall, this home page is useful, interesting, and informative. Its maintenance appears to occur on a daily basis; the links provided generally guide the novice or experienced researcher easily; and by offering Google directly from many web pages and sites, the Nevada home page provides a "twist" on information retrieval.

COMMERCIAL PUBLICATIONS AND WEB SITES

Nevada Atlas and Gazetteer: Topographical Maps of the Entire State, Public Lands and Back Roads (Yarmouth, ME: DeLorme Mapping Company, 2000, $19.95)—This fourth edition map provides topographical details of Nevada and is quite useful to those engaged in hiking, biking, or driving the public lands and back roads. To purchase contact the DeLorme Mapping Company, Two DeLorme Drive, P.O. Box 298, Yarmouth, ME 04096, or call (800) 581-5105.

Nevada Legislative Publications (Carson City, NV: Legislative Counsel Bureau.)—As mentioned earlier in the "Legal Publications" section, all of the Nevada legal and legislative publications are available for purchase. All are available in a paper format with the exception of the *Nevada Law Library* that is available on a CD-ROM ($325.00 if purchased separately or $200.00 when purchased with the *Official Nevada Revised Statutes with Annotations*). For example, the *Nevada Revised Statutes with Annotations* costs $575.00, the *Nevada Administrative Code* costs $350.00, and the *Nevada Administrative Code* costs $350.00 for a new set ($125.00 for the annual supplement). There are other legal publications also available from this agency. For purchase or more information contact Nevada Legislative Publications, Legislative Building, Room 1189, 401 South Carson Street, Carson City, NV 89701-4747, or call (775) 684-6835. An electronic order form is available at http://www.nevadalegislature.com/publications/Print/nrs.htm.

[Year] Municipal Directory Information (Carson City, NV: Nevada League of Cities and Municipalities, 2003, $20.00)—This directory provides contact and other information on members and affiliates of the league. Names, positions, and telephone numbers of municipal officials, hours of operation, council meeting dates and times, and regional and national leagues information can be obtained in the directory. Non-members may purchase a copy of the directory. Contact the Nevada League of Cities and Municipalities, 310 South Curry Street, Carson City, NV 89703, or call (775) 882-2121. You can also view its web page at http://www.nvleague.org/NVLeague/pub.htm.

SOURCES CONSULTED

Correspondence with Duncan Aldrich, University of Nevada-Reno; Teresa Wilt, Nevada Legislative Council.
Google, http://www.google.com.
Government Documents Round Table, American Library Association. *Directory of Government Document Collections & Librarians*, 7th ed. Bethesda, MD: Congressional Information Service, 1997.
Jobe, Janita. "State Publications." *Journal of Government Information*, 27 (2000): 733–768.
Numerous departmental web pages via the state's home page at http://www.nv.gov.
State and Local Government on the Net, http://www.piperinfo.com/state/index.cfm.
State Web Locator, http://www.infoctr.edu/swl/.
Survey response from Eileen Kessler, Nevada State Library, 2000.

New Hampshire

Eric W. Johnson

GOVERNMENT PUBLISHING AND THE DEPOSITORY SYSTEM

The New Hampshire State Depository Program was established in 1973 with the passage of the New Hampshire State Government Information Dissemination and Access Act, ensuring that citizens would have access to public documents to "allow increased citizen involvement in state policies and empower citizens to participate in state policy decision making" (*New Hampshire Revised Statutes Annotated*, Title XVI, Chapter 202-B, Section 1). The State Library was charged with the administration of the depository program, and the State Librarian authorized to designate no more than twenty-five public and academic libraries as state government information access libraries, taking into account geographic representation, population served, and the capability of the library to carry out the program. Currently, there are twenty-two depository libraries in the state (thirteen public, eight academic, one law) and the State Library.

Each state agency deposits twenty-five copies of its "tangible state government information products," with the exception of the State Reporter and any intra or interoffice publications and forms, with the State Librarian. The library provides cataloging and locator services for the material. In a 2001 revision of the act, the State Librarian was mandated to work with the various components of state government to preserve electronic information products and to increase the quality and quantity of state government information available in electronic format.

USEFUL ADDRESSES AND TELEPHONE NUMBERS

The most complete collections of New Hampshire state publications may be found at the following libraries:

New Hampshire State Library
Electronic and Government Information Resources Section

20 Park Street
Concord, NH 03301
Phone Number for New Hampshire Reference Questions: (603) 271-2144; (603) 271-2239
E-Mail Address for New Hampshire Reference Questions: mccormick@library.state.nh.us/
Library's Home Page: http://www.state.nh.us/nhsl/index.html
Depository Library Program Page: http://www.state.nh.us/nhsl/stdocs/index.html

University of New Hampshire Library
Milne Special Collections and Archives
18 Library Way
Durham, NH 03824-3592
Phone Number for New Hampshire Reference Questions: (603) 862-1919
E-Mail Link for New Hampshire Reference Questions: http://www.izaak.unh.edu/specoll/e-mailform.htm
Library's Home Page: http://www.library.unh.edu/

INDEXES TO NEW HAMPSHIRE STATE PUBLICATIONS

Each month, the State Library compiles a shipping list of publications received from state agencies and distributed to state depository libraries. Most shipping lists from January 1996 to the present are available online at the State Library's web site at http://www.state.nh.us/nhsl/shiplist/index.html. In addition, the 1991 and 1994 editions of the *Checklist of New Hampshire State Departments' Publications* are also online.

State publications may be located by searching the NHU-PAC, a union catalog that contains the holdings of the State Library as well as more than 300 public, school, and special libraries in the state. In most instances, the records in the NHU-PAC reflect only those titles acquired by a library since the mid-1980s. The NHU-PAC may be accessed via telnet at http://www.state.nh.us/nhsl/nhupac.html.

The web site of the Milne Special Collections and Archives at the University of New Hampshire includes lists of popular state documents arranged by subject at http://www.izaak.unh.edu/specoll/statedocs/sdcontents.htm.

ESSENTIAL STATE PUBLICATIONS

Directories

Businesses and Organizations in New Hampshire (State Library)—This online directory allows users to search for New Hampshire-based businesses and organizations that have a web site on the Internet. The database is searchable by keyword, name, town, county, region, or subject. The directory site includes a note that "links are provided to New Hampshire based businesses or organizations as a public service. The State of New Hampshire does not endorse the products, services or viewpoints contained on these outside links." The database is available on the web at http://sudoc.nhsl.lib.nh.us/buzurl/.

Manual for the General Court (Secretary of State)—This biennial publication, known familiarly as "The Red Book," is a compendium of facts and statistics about New Hampshire's cities and towns as well as a directory of state, city, and town government officials. The *Manual* is not available online. For information on obtaining a print copy, contact the Office of the Secretary of State, 107 North Main Street, Concord, NH 03301-4989, or call (603) 271-3242.

Education Directory (Department of Education)—This annual publication lists New Hampshire schools by type with addresses, telephone numbers, number of pupils, and names of principals or headmasters. It is available from the Department of Education at 101 Pleasant Street, Concord NH 03301-3860, or call (603) 271-3494. While this directory is not available online in its entirety, similar information about New Hampshire schools may be obtained at http://www.ed.state.nh.us/NHPublicSchools/nh1.htm.

State of New Hampshire Telephone Directory (Administrative Services)—This listing of state agencies and personnel provides employee name, agency, division or bureau, title, and contact information, including both telephone and fax numbers. The online version, available at http://admin.state.nh.us/directory/search_internet.asp, is searchable by department, individual listing, or topic. A print copy of the directory may be obtained by contacting the State House Visitor's Center, 107 North State Street, Room 119, Concord, NH 03301-4951, or calling (603) 271-2154, or via the order form online at http://www.gencourt.state.nh.us/visitorcenter/welcome.asp.

Financial/Budgetary Resources

Comprehensive Annual Financial Report (Department of Administrative Services, Division of Accounting Services)—This is an annual report mandated by federal law that shows the condition of the state's finances on the basis of Generally Accepted Accounting Principles (GAAP). The latest report and prior reports back to 1997 are available online at http://admin.state.nh.us/accounting/reports.htm. For a print version, contact the Division of Accounting Services, State House Annex—310, 25 Capitol Street, Concord, NH 03301-6312, or call (603) 271-6566.

Governor's Operating Budget, [Year]–[Year] Biennium (Department of Administrative Services, Budget Office)—The state's biennial budget is available online at http://admin.state.nh.us/budget/, and in its House Bill format at http://www.gencourt.state.nh.us/ie/. The budget is divided into the following sections: General Government, Administration of Justice and Public Protection, Resource Protection and Development, Transportation, Health and Social Services, Education, and State Total Summary. For information about print copies of the budget, contact the Budget Office, State House Annex, Room 120, 25 Capitol Street, Concord, NH 03301-6312, or call (603) 271-3204.

Legal Resources

New Hampshire Revised Statutes (Legislative Services)—The codified law of the state comprising 47 titles, contains the full text of the state's statutes in force through the latest legislative session. The statutes are available online at http://www.gencourt.state.nh.us/rsa/html/indexes/default.html. The full text may be searched by keyword or phrase, or titles may be browsed. A List of Sections Affected (LSA) identifies all changes made to the statutes during specific legislative sessions, which might not yet be reflected in the printed and online versions of the *Revised Statutes*. For information on the print version of the statutes, call the Office of Legislative Services at (603) 271-3435. The official version of the statutes is published by West Group and is listed below under "Commercial Publications and Web Sites."

New Hampshire State Constitution (Secretary of State)—The Constitution was established October 31, 1783 to take effect June 2, 1784, and subsequently amended and in force December 1990. It is divided into two major sections: a Bill of Rights, which details the rights and privileges of New Hampshire citizens; and Form of Government, which sets out the duties and boundaries of the various government offices, the House, and the Senate. The Constitution is available online at http://www.state.nh.us/constitution/constitution.html. Information about print copies may be obtained from the Office of the Secretary of State, 107 North Main Street, Concord, NH 03301-4989, or call (603) 271-3242.

House Journal (House of Representatives) —This is the daily record of proceedings of the state's House of Representatives. It is available online from the 1997 session to the present at http://www.gencourt.state.nh.us/hcaljourns/. Similarly, the *Senate Journal* (Senate), its counterpart for the State Senate, is available online from the 1999 session to the present at http://www.gencourt.state.nh.us/scaljourns/default.html. For information about print versions, contact the House Clerk's Office at (603) 271-2548 and the Senate Clerk's Office at (603) 271-3420.

Statistical Resources

Economic Conditions in New Hampshire (Employment Security Department, Economic and Labor Market Information Bureau)—This is a monthly publication which highlights economic development affecting the state, including: seasonally adjusted labor force, not seasonally adjusted labor force, non-farm wage and salary employment estimates, unemployment compensation claims data, and U.S. Consumer Price Index information. The publication is archived online back to the February 1999 issue.

Vital Signs—New Hampshire Economic and Social Indicators (Employment Security Department, Economic and Labor Market Information Bureau)—This is an annual publication that reviews the New Hampshire economy in seventeen categories. The previous four years are examined in tables comparing the statistics of that time period. A narrative of recent happenings within the category is augmented with charts and graphs. The publication is archived online back to the 1992–1995 edition, published in January 1997.

Both *Economic Conditions in New Hampshire* and *Vital Signs* are available online at http://www.nhes.state.nh.us/elmi/econanalys.htm. Print copies may be requested from the Economic and Labor Market Information Bureau, New Hampshire Employment Security, 32 South Main Street, Concord, NH 03301; by calling (603) 228-4124; or by e-mail at elmi@nhes.state.nh.us.

The Economic and Labor Market Information Bureau compiles a host of other employment and wage statistics and makes them available online at http://www.nhes.state.nh.us/elmi/econstat.htm. Here may also be found information on the Consumer Price Index and employment projections.

Electronic Statistical Reports (Department of Education)—Available online only at http://www.ed.state.nh.us/ReportsandStatistics/reports.htm, these reports contain statistical information on a variety of state educational topics such as test results, costs per pupil, enrollment and dropout, finances, state aid, teacher salaries, and youth risk behavior surveys.

New Hampshire Vital Statistics Report (Health and Human Services, Community and Public Health Office, Bureau of Health Statistics and Data Management)—This annual report summarizes the collection of data for New Hampshire residents including births, deaths, infant deaths, fetal deaths, marriages, and divorces occurring in New Hampshire and these events that occur out-of-state for New Hampshire residents. The 1998 figures were prepared in 2000 and published the following year; that report, along with other similar reports, is available online at http://www.dhhs.state.nh.us/DHHS/BHSDM/LIBRARY/Data-Statistical+Report/default.htm. Requests for print copies may be made to the New Hampshire Department of Health and Human Services, Office of Community and Public Health, Bureau of Health Statistics and Data Management, 6 Hazen Drive, Concord, NH 03301-6527; by calling (603) 271-4477 or (800) 852-3345, ext. 4477; or via e-mail at healthstats@dhhs.state.nh.us.

New Hampshire's Cities and Towns (State Library)—This is an online database used to locate information about all of New Hampshire's cities and towns, as well as unincorporated places. The information available includes postal contact information; elective districts; a link to its Community Profile; general links to school, library, and local sites; and the URLs of any web sites. The database may be searched at http://www.state.nh.us/municipal/index.html.

Other Resources

Books About New Hampshire (State Library)—This is a 1999 update by Donna V. Gilbreth of a list originally published in 1946, which was itself updated by a 1979 New Hampshire Department of Education publication, *New Hampshire-iana: Books of New Hampshire 1969–1979*, using information from a column on new books still being published in the State Library's own publication, *Granite State Libraries*. The guide is not intended to be a comprehensive bibliography, and excludes certain types of materials, including general and town histories, genealogies, travel guides, regimental histories, local cookbooks, and government documents. It is divided into the following subjects: Around the State: Natural Landscape and Guidebooks; Arts and Crafts; History; Legends and Folklore; New Hampshire Cooking; People of New Hampshire; Personal Views: Essays, Journals, etc.; Poetry and Drama; Politics and Government; Fiction; and Books for Children and Young Adults. A title index links to individual records, which provide author, title, publisher, and a brief summary of each book. The bibliography is available online at http://www.state.nh.us/nhsl/nhbooks/index.html.

The New Hampshire Almanac (State Library)—Compiled by the staff of the State Library, this is an online compendium of information about the state. Here are found fast facts, demographics and statistics, history, state symbols, and information about elections, flora and fauna, government, and people and places. The *Almanac* can be found at http://webster.state.nh.us/nhinfo/.

Official New Hampshire Guidebook (Division of Travel and Tourism)—This is an annual travel guide to the state, listing attractions, events, and accommodations. It is available from the State of New Hampshire Division of Travel and Tourism Development, 172 Pembroke Road, P.O. Box 1856, Concord, NH 03302-1856; by calling (800) FUN-IN-NH, ext. 169; by completing the online form at http://www.visitnh.gov/freeguidebook.html; or by e-mail at travel@ dred.state.nh.us. General tourist information is also available online at the division's web site, http://www.visitnh.gov/.

NEW HAMPSHIRE'S WORLD WIDE WEB HOME PAGE

The official state web site is *Welcome to New Hampshire: Your Online Portal to State Government*; its home page is located at http://www.state.nh.us/. The site is easily navigable and searchable, with links to the Governor and Executive, Legislative, Judicial, and E-Government pages on one side of the home page, and further links to Residents, Businesses, Visitors, Government, Laws and Rules, State Employees, and ShopNH on the other side. "Just for Kids" links to pages designed specifically with children in mind.

The web site is administered by the New Hampshire State Library. Comments about the project may be e-mailed to the State Library at webmaster@ webster.state.nh.us or mailed to Webster Project, New Hampshire State Library, 20 Park Street, Concord, NH 03301.

COMMERCIAL PUBLICATIONS AND WEB SITES

New Hampshire Register (Tower Publishing Company, 588 Saco Road, Standish, ME 04084)—Published in one form or another since 1768, the *New Hampshire Register* is a compendium of information on state, local, and federal government offices; town officials; 36,000 statewide business listings; schools, colleges, and universities; newspapers and magazines; population trends; elected officials; associations; tax rates; maps; and more. It can be ordered from the publisher at the above address or through the publisher's web site at http://towerpub.com/.

New Hampshire Revised Statutes Annotated (West Group, 610 Oppermann Drive, Eagan, MN 55123)—The commercial, official annotated version of the *New Hampshire Revised Statutes* includes extensive annotations and cross-references, detailed legislative history, references to relevant state and federal cases, comprehensive decision notes, and special indexes and tables. For more information, contact West Group at (800) 328-4880; ordering information is also found on the publisher's web site at http://west.thomson.com/.

SOURCES CONSULTED

New Hampshire State Library's web site, http://www.state.nh.us/nhsl/nhbooks/index.html.

Numerous departmental web pages via the state's web site, http://www.state.nh.us/.

New Jersey

Eric W. Johnson

GOVERNMENT PUBLISHING AND THE DEPOSITORY SYSTEM

The New Jersey State Library, affiliated with Thomas Edison State College, is the primary depository for official publications of the state government. State officers, departments, commissions, and committees are required by law to file at least seventy-five copies of any annual or special reports, "serial or other publications of a general information character . . . for permanent reference use and exchange purposes" (*New Jersey Revised Statutes*, Title 52, Chapter 14, Sections 14-25.1 and 25.2). The state mandated in 1957 that "the State Library shall . . . maintain as part of the State Library . . . a documents depository service" (NJRS, Title 18A, Section 73-35: 20(d)).

In keeping with this law, the State Library maintains three copies, one permanent and the others circulating, of state publications, and supplies copies of most current materials to fifty-one academic, public, and law libraries in New Jersey who agree to maintain the collection and make the materials available for at least five years. Shipments sent to depository libraries include a shipping list, with items grouped by issuing agency, and a title and call number provided. Catalog cards are included for new items for those libraries that have requested cards.

USEFUL ADDRESSES AND TELEPHONE NUMBERS

The most comprehensive collections of New Jersey state publications can be found at the following libraries:

State Library of New Jersey
State Government Information Services
P.O. Box 520
Trenton, NJ 08625-0520
Phone Number for New Jersey Reference Questions: (609) 292-6294
E-Mail Address for New Jersey Reference Questions: dmercer@njstatelib.org

Library's Home Page: http://www.njstatelib.org/
Government Publications Page: http://www.njstatelib.org/aboutus/SLIC/Libnjdoc
  .htm

Archibald S. Alexander Library
Rutgers, The State University of New Jersey
169 College Avenue, CAC
New Brunswick, NJ 08901-1163
Phone Number for New Jersey Reference Questions: (732) 932-7388
E-Mail Address for New Jersey Reference Questions: fetzer@rci.rutgers.edu
Library's Home Page: http://www.libraries.rutgers.edu/

A complete list of New Jersey State Depository Libraries can be found online
at http://www.njstatelib.org/aboutus/SLIC/libnjdep.htm.

INDEXES TO NEW JERSEY STATE PUBLICATIONS

New Jersey state publications were listed in the State Library's printed
Checklist of Official New Jersey Publications, produced from 1965 until 1996. Documents are included in the online catalog *JerseyCat*, which is accessible by New
Jersey libraries and residents, and in the online catalogs of other depository
libraries.

The State Library assigns call numbers using a library-designed system
based on the Dewey Decimal System number for New Jersey history. Three
types of materials are denoted: 974.90 is used for monographs, such as reports
or public hearings; 974.901 is used for annual publications, such as annual
reports or statistical publications; 974.905 is used for periodicals and serials.
The 974.90s are then subarranged by subject and year.

ESSENTIAL STATE PUBLICATIONS

Directories

New Jersey School Directory (Department of Education)—This online directory of school districts, public and non-public schools, and charter schools
provides names, addresses, and telephone numbers for superintendents, business administrators, board secretaries, principals, and schools throughout the
state. Links to "Report Card" provide statistical information (enrollment, attendance, instructors, and proficiency assessment), and additional links to
"Comparative Spending Guide" and "State Aid Summary" allow for comparisons between schools and school districts. The directory may be found online
at http://www.state.nj.us/njded/directory/index.shtml. For more information, contact the Department of Education, 100 River View Plaza, P.O. Box
500, Trenton, NJ 08625-0500, or call (609) 292-4041.

New Jersey State Agency Telephone Numbers (State)—This is an online direc-
tory of telephone numbers organized alphabetically by agency or department.
The directory is available at http://www.state.nj.us/infobank/orgphone.htm.
A similar index, *New Jersey Agency FAX Directory*, may be found at http://

www.state.nj.us/infobank/fax.htm. An *Employee Directory*, online at http://www.state.nj.us/infobank/phonform.htm, allows a name search; post office boxes are listed for many employees. For more information about the telephone directories, e-mail to feedback@state.nj.us.

Financial/Budgetary Resources

Comprehensive Annual Financial Report for the Fiscal Year Ended June 30, [Year] (Office of Management and Budget)—This annual report, which presents the financial position and operating results of the state under Generally Accepted Accounting Principles, is comprised of three sections: Introductory, Financial, and Statistical. Several recent editions of the report are available online at http://www.state.nj.us/treasury/omb/publications/archives.shtml.

FY [Year] Budget Bill (Office of Budget and Management)—The *Budget Bill* reflects legislative action on the proposed budget, and includes revenue certification, veto summary, veto, and the Appropriations Act presentation. The most recent bill is available online at http://www.state.nj.us/treasury/omb/publications/. Prior years' bills are archived at http://www.state.nj.us/treasury/omb/publications/archives.shtml, under "Appropriations Bill."

State of New Jersey Budget FY [Year] (Office of Management and Budget)—The governor's annual revenue and spending plan as presented to the state legislature contains the following sections: Governor's Message; Summaries of Appropriations, including the Budget in Brief and Budget Highlights; Summaries of Revenues, Expenditures and Fund Balances; Budget Recommendations (of Executive Departments); and Appendices. The most recent budget is available online at http://www.state.nj.us/treasury/omb/publications/; previous years' budgets may be found at http://www.state.nj.us/treasury/omb/publications/archives.shtml.

For information on print versions of any of these publications, contact the Office of Management and Budget, P.O. Box 0221, Trenton, NJ 08625-0221, or call (609) 292-6746.

Legal Resources

New Jersey Revised Statutes (Legislature)—This contains the text of the compilation of the laws of the state, comprised of fifty-nine titles and an appendix of emergency and temporary acts. There is a link to the online version of the Statutes (which are called *New Jersey Permanent Statutes*) from the legislature's home page at http://www.njleg.state.nj.us/. The official commercial set is published by West Group, and listed below.

New Jersey State Constitution 1947 Updated through Amendments Adopted in November, 2000 (Legislature)—The New Jersey State Constitution consists of eleven articles: Rights and Privileges; Elections and Suffrage; Distribution of the Powers of Government; Legislative; Executive; Judicial; Public Offices and Employees; Taxation and Finance; Amendments; General Provisions; and Schedule. It is available online in a searchable version at http://www.njleg.state.nj.us/lawsconstitution/constitution.asp. For information about a print version, contact the Office of Legislative Services at (800) 792-8630 or via e-mail at leginfo@njleg.org.

Statistical Resources

[*Educational Data*] (Department of Education)—This page on the Department of Education's web site provides links to statistics on state education, including *Vital Education Statistics* (enrollment, graduates, dropouts, certificated staff, and non-certificated staff); the *New Jersey School Report Card* (enrollment, class size, student disabilities, attendance, proficiency assessment for grades 4 and 8, personnel, salaries and benefits, revenues, per pupil expenditures, and school narratives); *New Jersey Statewide Assessment Reports*; *New Jersey Special Education Data*; *State Aid Summaries*; *Comparative Spending Guide*; and various surveys. Most reports are in PDF format. This statistics page is located online at http://www.state.nj.us/njded/data/. For further information, contact the Department of Education, 100 River View Plaza, P.O. Box 500, Trenton, NJ 08625-0500, or call (609) 292-4041.

New Jersey Department of Labor Statistical Review (Department of Labor, Office of Labor Planning and Analysis)—This biennial publication contains a variety of workload, financial, and administrative statistics relating to the operating areas of the department, including information on unemployment and disability insurance, employment and training services, vocational rehabilitation services, and workplace standards, but also some broad indicators of economic activity. The latest edition of the *Statistical Review* is available online at http://www.wnjpin.net/OneStopCareerCenter/LaborMarketInformation/lmi15/index.html. For more information, contact the Department of Labor, Labor Planning and Analysis, P.O. Box 388, Trenton, NJ 08625-0388, or call (609) 292-0982.

New Jersey Health Statistics (Department of Health and Senior Services, Center for Health Statistics)—This publication contains annual statistical data summaries for the state of New Jersey, its counties, and, in later years, selected municipalities on the following subjects: births, deaths, marriages, divorces, communicable diseases, and population. The publication is available online at http://www.state.nj.us/health/chs/hlthstat.htm. Inquiries about a print version should be directed to the Center for Health Statistics, P.O. Box 360, Trenton, NJ 08625-0360, or call (609) 984-6702, or via an online form at http://www.state.nj.us/health/feedback.htm

Other Resources

New Jersey Economic Indicators (Department of Labor, Division of Labor Market and Demographic Research)—*Economic Indicators* is a monthly (except February) publication providing an overview of the state's economy. Regular features include "New Jersey's Economy at a Glance," "The Economic Situation," and "Comparison of Economic Trends in New Jersey and the U.S." A few specific articles follow, and the bulk of the publication is devoted to economic statistics. The latest issue is available online by linking to "Monthly Economic Indicators" at http://www.wnjpin.net/OneStopCareerCenter/

LaborMarketInformation/lmilist.htm. The title is available at no charge from the Department of Labor, Publications Unit, P.O. Box 057, Trenton, NJ 08625-0057, or by calling (609) 292-7567.

Travel Guide New Jersey (New Jersey Commerce and Economic Growth Commission, Office of Travel and Tourism)—This annual travel guide divides the state into six regions, and provides tourist information (attractions, accommodations), general articles on history, beaches, sports, the arts, camping, and other topics, and a fold-out map and calendar of events. Much of the information contained in the publication is available on the Office of Travel and Tourism's web site at http://www.state.nj.us/travel/index.html. The *Guide* is available at no charge from the Office of Travel and Tourism, 20 West State Street, P.O. Box 820, Trenton, NJ 08625-0820, by calling (609) 777-0885, or (800) VISIT-NJ; or via an online order form at http://www.state.nj.us/travel/orderform.shtml.

NEW JERSEY'S WORLD WIDE WEB HOME PAGE

The State of New Jersey home page, on the Internet at http://www.state.nj.us/, provides a great many links to state information, agencies, and services. Across the top of the page are links to a "Calendar of Events," "Visit NJ," "NJ Commuter," "Lottery," "Legislative," and "Judiciary." Five major divisions appear along the left side: "My New Jersey," linking to a customizable informational page primarily for state residents; "New Jersey People," linking to general information about services, and FAQs; "New Jersey Open for Business," linking to sites of interest to the business community; "Government Information," linking to state directories and to local, state, and federal links; and an excellent "Hangout NJ for Kids," which provides younger browsers with information on everything from history, state symbols, facts, and famous firsts to articles on lighthouses, diners, and the early movie industry, along with games, cartoons, and coloring books.

Other links on the page include "In Focus," a current topic of interest; "Fiscal Response," budgetary and other financial information; "Education," and "Security." The latest news releases are listed, as are pull-down menus for online services, quick links, and departments and agencies. There is even a link to the New Jersey State Museum store.

The web page is under the direction of the Communications and Creative Services department of the New Jersey Office of Information Technology. For more information, contact the office at P.O. Box 212, Trenton, NJ 08625-0212, or via e-mail at feedback@state.nj.us, or call (609) 984-4082.

COMMERCIAL PUBLICATIONS AND WEB SITES

Municipal Directory (New Jersey State League of Municipalities, 407 West State Street, Trenton, NJ 08618)—This directory contains names and addresses of mayors, municipal clerks, engineers, attorneys, managers, and administrators of New Jersey municipalities. It is available from the League at the above address, or by calling (609) 695-3481, or via a printable form at the League's web site at http://www.njslom.org/.

New Jersey Statutes Annotated (West Group, 610 Opperman Drive, Eagan, MN 55123)—The commercial, official annotated version of the *New Jersey Revised Statutes* includes extensive annotations and cross-references, detailed legislative history, references to relevant state and federal cases, comprehensive decision notes, references to other research tools and relevant materials, and special indexes and tables. For more information, contact West Group at (800) 328-4880; ordering information is also found on its web site at http://west .thomson.com/.

SOURCES CONSULTED

E-mail response from Deborah Mercer, New Jersey State Library, August 2002.
New Jersey State Library's web site, http://www.njstatelib.org/.
Numerous departmental web pages via the state's official web site, http://www.state .nj.us/.
Survey response from Robert Lupp, New Jersey State Library, January 2001.

New Mexico

Daniel C. Barkley

GOVERNMENT PUBLISHING AND THE DEPOSITORY SYSTEM

In 1978 the New Mexico state legislature enacted legislation establishing a Depository Clearinghouse that required state agencies to submit copies of their publications to it (SRC 72-1, SRC 72-3, SRC 88-1). In 1995 the rules governing the clearinghouse that had established style and format standards and detailed statutory filing procedures were combined and replaced by 1 NMAC 3.4.10.1-3.4.10.6 (*New Mexico Annotated Code*). As originally mandated, state agencies must submit five copies of any publication to the State Records Center and Archives. State agencies must also provide the State Librarian with a minimum of twenty-five copies of each publication for further deposit into state depository libraries.

The State Publications Program is comprised of the State Depository Clearinghouse, located at the State Library, and twenty-four depository libraries located throughout the state. The intent of the depository program is to provide New Mexico residents with access to information compiled by state agencies through their reports, minutes, statistics, newsletters, bulletins, impact statements, and other studies published. The disposition of the thirty copies sent to the clearinghouse are as follows:

- The clearinghouse retains three copies for historical, research, and circulation purposes.
- The State Records and Archives Department retains one copy.
- The Library of Congress receives two copies.
- Remaining copies are distributed to state depository libraries that have been ranked according to size and location.

A state agency is defined as "any agency, authority, board, bureau, commission, committee, department, institution or officer of state government except the judicial and legislative branches" (1 NMAC 3.4.10.7). Each state agency is required to have a "publications officer" who is responsible for ensuring distribution of that agency's publications to the State Library. A state publication is defined as "any processed document or other information funded in whole or in part by the State Legislature or issued at the request of, or contracted out by, an agency regardless of physical format or characteristics" (1 NMAC 3.4.10.7.6). These publications include pamphlets, reports, directories, catalogs, bibliographies, brochures, or periodicals.

A Memorandum of Agreement must be contracted between the State Library and the requesting library before it can be designated as a depository. There are also certain publications that are exempt from depository distribution (1 NMAC 3.4.10.7.2). Libraries wishing to become depositories must agree to provide sufficient shelf space and provide trained staff to assist the public in accessing state publications. Other provisions include the need to provide access to state publications by author/agency, title and subject; provide appropriate technology for access to those publications, regardless of form or format; retain material for a minimum of five years; and accept all publications distributed.

USEFUL ADDRESSES AND TELEPHONE NUMBERS

The most complete collections of New Mexico state publications may be found at the following libraries:

New Mexico State Library
State Depository Clearinghouse
1209 Camino Carlos Rey
Santa Fe, NM 87507
Phone Number for New Mexico Reference Questions: (505) 476-9700
E-Mail Address for New Mexico Reference Questions: http://www.stlib.state.nm.us/ask/ask.html
State Library Home Page: http://www.stlib.state.nm.us/Default.htm
State Publications Program Page: http://www.stlib.state.nm.us/libraryservices/statepubs/stpubabout.html

New Mexico State University
Library, Branson Hall
P.O. Box 3475
Las Cruces, NM 88003-0006
Phone Number for New Mexico Reference Questions: (505) 646-7481
E-Mail Address for New Mexico Reference Questions: govdocs@lib.nmsu.edu
New Mexico State University Home Page: http://www.nmsu.edu

University of New Mexico
Zimmerman Library
Government Information Department
Albuquerque, NM 87131-1466
Phone Number for New Mexico Reference Questions: (505) 277-5441
E-Mail Address for New Mexico Reference Questions: govref@unm.edu
Government Information Department Home Page: http://elibrary.unm.edu/govinfo/

INDEXES TO NEW MEXICO STATE PUBLICATIONS

The State Library generates a list of "optional items" that are sent to depositories and have no retention requirements (1 NMAC 3.4.10.7.4). The State Library also generates a shipping list of publications that are sent to depository libraries (see http://www.stlib.state.nm.us/libraryservices/statepubs/ship.html). Shipping lists online date back to 1995, and they include the call number and the phrase "limited copies" if there are not sufficient copies for each depository library. There is no other index that exists, nor is one mandated by state law.

The State Library has developed a call number system based on the structure and hierarchy of the state government (see http://www.stlib.state.nm.us/libraryservices/statepubs/nmclassoutline.html). Depository libraries are encouraged to use this system but many opt for the Library of Congress classification numbers.

ESSENTIAL STATE PUBLICATIONS

Directories

New Mexico Cultural Resources Directory: The Complete Guide to Arts, History, and Community Events (Office of Cultural Affairs)—This is a compendium of New Mexico cultural resources providing contact information on state agencies, groups, and individuals involved in maintaining the rich cultural history of New Mexico. It is arranged alphabetically from Arts Associations through Performing Arts. Copies may be requested by contacting the New Mexico Office of Cultural Affairs, La Villa Rivera Building, 228 E. Palace Avenue, P.O. Box 2087, Santa Fe, NM 87504-2087, or call (505) 827-8233.

Prevention Services Directory, Fiscal Year 2002 (Department of Health)—This directory provides a comprehensive account of contracted services for the current fiscal year. It provides information on the amount of funding each contractor receives, the contract for each prevention contractor, contract requirements, and individualized prevention plans. Also included is a map with full contact information, community needs assessments, prevention initiatives, and technical support. New Mexico Department of Health, Behavioral Health Services Division, Harold Runnels Building, 1190 St. Francis Drive, Santa Fe, NM; call (505) 827-2601. The online directory can be located at http://www.health.state.nm.us.

State of New Mexico Telephone Directory (Governor's Office)—This directory consists of emergency, agency, and legislative phone numbers and Internet addresses of most state employees. It is arranged alphabetically by state agency and compiled by the Office of the Governor, State Capitol Building, Santa Fe, NM 87503. Call (505) 827-3000. The online version features the entire directory in a downloadable (309Kb) PDF file that is arranged by executive branch, or House and Senate chambers. Go to http://www.state.nm.us/category/phonebook/phone_idx.html for more information.

Financial/Budgetary Resources

Current Financial Statements and *Current Financial Summaries* (State Board of Finance)—Both of these databases provide detailed financial information on state government operations for the current and past fiscal years. The current year files are available in a PDF format. Financial statements date back to 1997 and are, in some cases, available in an HTML format. Also included on each database are links to other types of financial statistics oriented toward projected state revenues, economic growth, bond reports, and expenditures. Contact the New Mexico State Board of Finance, Bataan Memorial Building, Suite 181, 407 Galisteo Street, Santa Fe, NM 87501, or call (505) 827-4980. The financial statement database is located at http://nmsbof.state.nm.us/fr/fs and the summaries can be found at http://nmsbof.state.nm.us/gf/summary/.

Legislative Finance Committee Budget Recommendations for FY [Year] (Legislative Finance Committee)—This online resource provides details on the New Mexico legislature's budget request. The database is arranged by subject (e.g., Legislative, Public Safety, Higher Education) and provides insight into state agency operating requests for the upcoming fiscal year. The Legislative Finance Committee, a bipartisan group, has responsibility for working out the differences between what the governor proposes and the state legislature requests for each fiscal year budget. Currently, the budget must be approved in its entirety by the governor and the state legislature, as the governor does not now possess the power to veto the budget via line-item. The database is located at http://legis.state.nm.us/lfcpubli.asp and is maintained by the Legislative Finance Committee, 325 Don Gaspar, Suite 101, Santa Fe, NM 87501. Call (505) 986-4550; e-mail ifc@state.nm.us.

New Mexico State Budget (Department of Finance and Administration)—Compiled by the State Budget Division, this annual report provides the annual budget as requested by the governor and approved by the state legislature. The state budget is a performance-based operation as mandated by the *Accountability in Government Act* (NMSA 6-3A-1-8). There are also links to the next fiscal year's appropriation requests, budget operating instructions, capital projects, the budget preparation system, a staff directory and assignments, and an explanation of the performance-based program budgeting. Copies can be obtained by contacting the New Mexico Department of Finance and Administration, State Budget Division, Bataan Memorial Building, Suite 190, 407 Galisteo Street, Santa Fe, NM 87503, or call (505) 827-3640. The web page is http://www.state.nm.us/clients/dfa/indexBUD.htm.

Legal Resources

Constitution of the State of New Mexico (Secretary of State)—The New Mexico State Constitution is unique among others in the United States in that English and Spanish are both recognized as official languages. The 1997 edition is the latest version of the Constitution and it can be obtained by contacting the Office of the Secretary of State, State Capitol Annex, Suite 300, 325 Don Gaspar Avenue, Santa Fe, NM 87503, or call (505) 827-3600. There is a link to a commercial version of the state Constitution from the governor's home page. Go to http://www.governor.state.nm.us to view it online.

Legislative Handbook (Legislative Council Service)—This handbook, published annually, is one of the many services performed by staff members of the Legislative Council Service. The handbook is designed to help state legislators and their staff in the processes and procedures of drafting legislative bills and reports. There are a limited number of copies distributed to state depository libraries. The handbook is compiled by the New Mexico Legislative Council Service, Room 411, State Capitol Building, Santa Fe, NM 87501, call (505) 986-4600.

The New Mexico Administrative Code (Commission on Public Records)—This contains the codification of law and rule changes that have been enacted by the state legislature and that are now ready for agency implementation. The online version features an explanation of the *Code*, a browse compilation, and a search engine. The online resource is maintained by the New Mexico Commission on Public Records, 1205 Camino Carlos Rey Avenue, Santa Fe, NM 87507. Call (505) 476-7900, e-mail rules@rain.state.nm.us. The online resource can be found at http://www.nmcpr.state.nm.us/nmac/.

New Mexico Register (Commission on Public Records)—The official publication for all notices of rulemaking and filings of adopted, proposed, and emergency rules in New Mexico. By state law, all state agencies must publish notices of rulemaking and all adopted rules in the *Register*. Agencies may publish proposed rules and other materials that relate to administrative law at their discretion. It is published biweekly. The online version provides links to submittal deadlines and publication dates, subscription information, previous issues, the 2002 Cumulative Index and the 2001 Annual Index, and the *New Mexico Administrative Code*. Contact the New Mexico Commission on Public Records, 1205 Camino Carlos Rey Avenue, Santa Fe, NM 87507. Call (505) 476-7900, or fax (505) 476-7901; e-mail rules@rain.state.nm.us. It is available online at http://www.nmcpr.state.nm.us/nmregister/.

New Mexico State Courts Annual Report (Administrative Office of the Courts)—This annual report highlights the accomplishments and activities of the New Mexico judiciary in the past calendar year. The report includes information on court funding, caseloads, case dispositions, and other judicial activities. The report is available from the Administrative Office of the Courts, Annual Report Editor, 237 Don Gaspar, Santa Fe, NM 87501, or call (505) 827-4800. A statistical compendium can be located at http://www.nmcourts.com. E-mail crtlink@nmcourts.com to contact the court for questions or suggestions.

Statistical Resources

County Health Profiles (Department of Health)—Each report is a complete health profile for every county in New Mexico. The latest set is the third update of this series. A wealth of information on demographic, health, and other vital statistics can be found in these reports. Each report also includes data sets on alcohol-related deaths, accidents, and DWI arrests. To obtain these reports contact the New Mexico Department of Health, Public Health Division, Bureau of Vital Records and Health Statistics, 1105 St. Francis Drive, Santa

Fe, NM 87502-6110, or call (505) 827-2532. These reports are available in many state depository libraries and on the Internet at http://dohewbs2.health.state.nm.us/VitalRec/County%20Profiles/County%20Profiles.htm.

New Mexico Selected Health Statistics Annual Report (State Center for Health Statistics)—This annual report provides an overview of selected vital and health statistics for the past calendar year for New Mexico. Related data from earlier years are also included. Data sets are by place of residence. Death and births of New Mexico residents that occur elsewhere are also included in the tabulations. Primary sources include reportable certificates of birth and death and from federal and state reporting systems. It is compiled by the State Center for Health Statistics and Office of New Mexico Vital Records and Health Statistics, Public Health Division, Department of Health, 1105 St. Francis Drive, P.O. Box 26110, Santa Fe, NM 87502-6110. Call (505) 827-0121. See http://www.health.state.nm.us for more information. With appropriate attribution, permission is granted to quote from or reproduce materials from the report.

New Mexico Tribal Report 2002 (Department of Health)—This is a compendium of vital statistics on all Native American tribes and pueblos located in New Mexico. Birth data are obtained from the hospital based on information submitted by the parents. Information on deaths is obtained from death certificates filed by funeral directors or supplied by an informant acting on behalf of the family. This report also features separate sections on major New Mexico tribal groups: Apache, Navajo, and Pueblo. The report may be viewed on the web at http://dohewbs2.health.state.nm.us/VitalRec/; select "Publications." This report may be available from the State Center for Health Statistics, Office of New Mexico Vital Records and Health Statistics, 1105 South St. Francis Drive, Santa Fe, NM 87502-6110, or call (505) 827-2510.

Other Resources

Atlas of Primary Care Access in New Mexico (Department of Health)—The 2001 *Atlas* is a result of a two-year process of collaboration and research between the New Mexico Department of Health, PHD, Primary Care/Rural Health Bureau (PC/RH), and several other partners. The primary goal was to produce a document that would aid researchers in primary care access data. Data sets include information on births, demographics, facilities, health professionals, immunization, mortality statistics, and special health population services. Contact the New Mexico Department of Health, Primary Care/Rural Health Bureau, Health Systems Bureau, Public Health Division, 625 Silver SW, Suite 201, Albuquerque, NM 87102, or call (505) 841-5870. Another office is located at 1190 St. Francis Drive, Room N1055, Santa Fe, NM 87502.

Catalog of Local Assistance Programs, 2001 (Department of Finance Administration)—Similar in nature to the *Catalog of Federal Domestic Assistance*, this state version brings together into a single format all the various assistance programs administered by the state of New Mexico. It is designed to assist local governments, local representatives, and New Mexico citizens by providing information on the administration of local programs as well as how to apply for funds from these programs. Similar in arrangement to the *CFDA*, information is provided on the structure of the program, purpose, eligibility, use of funds, special conditions, funding availability, the application process, authorization, related programs, and information contacts. Contact the Department of Finance Administration, Local Government Division, Bataan Memorial Building, Suite 202, Santa Fe, NM 87503, or call (505) 827-4370. An online copy can be located at http://www.nmlocalgov.net/plan/plan_list .html (see Figure 13).

The Condition of Higher Education in New Mexico, 2001 (New Mexico Commission on Higher Education)—This report has been generated from the latest statistical information on students enrolled in New Mexico public and private colleges and universities as of March 12, 2002. Demographic information on students utilizing higher education, degree program completion, tuition and fees paid, financial aid received, and institutional expenses can be found in this report. Contact the New Mexico Commission on Higher Education, 1068 Cerrillos Road, Santa Fe, NM 87501, or call (505) 827-7383; e-mail highered@ che.state.nm.us. The online report can be found at http://www.nmche.org/ reports/index.html.

The Factbook (Economic Development Division)—The online version contains data links to Excel spreadsheets and links to other data web sites maintained by state agencies. Information includes chapters on business incentives in New Mexico, agriculture and natural resources, workforce and demographic statistics, education, technology, energy, taxes, transportation, geography, climate, history, culture, and international trade. Keyword searching is also available. Maintained by the New Mexico Economic Development Department, Economic Development Division, P.O. Box 20003, Joseph M. Montoya Building, 1100 St. Francis Drive, Santa Fe, NM. Call (800) 374-3061. The *Factbook* is available online at http://www.edd.state.nm.us/FACTBOOK/ index.html.

New Mexico Agriculture Statistics (Department of Agriculture)—This annual publication contains agriculture statistics for the past calendar year. Tables are arranged by crop and by county. This compilation provides much more detail than its companion volume produced by the U.S. Department of Agriculture. For more information contact the New Mexico Department of Agriculture, MSC 3189, P.O. Box 30005, Corner of Gregg and Espina, Las Cruces, NM 88003-8005, or call (505) 646-3007. A copy can be found online at http:// www.nass.usda.gov/nm/nmbulletin/bltntoc.htm.

New Mexico Blue Book, 1999–2000 (Secretary of State)—First issued in 1882 by the secretary of the territory, this millennium edition provides an overview of New Mexico history from different points of view and perspectives. It contains a register of state elected officials, economic information, state attractions, and a section on how to find and use state government resources. Included in this special edition is a set of trivia questions on the Land of Enchantment. Published by the Office of the Secretary of State, State Capitol Annex, Suite 300, 325 Don Gaspar Avenue, Santa Fe, NM 87503. Call (505) 827-3600, or outside New Mexico (800) 477-3632. To view the *Blue Book* online go to http://www.sos.state.nm.us/.

New Mexico's Natural Resources (Energy, Minerals and Natural Resources Department)—The Energy, Minerals and Natural Resources Department (EMNRD) was created in 1987 out of a merger, supported by state law, be-

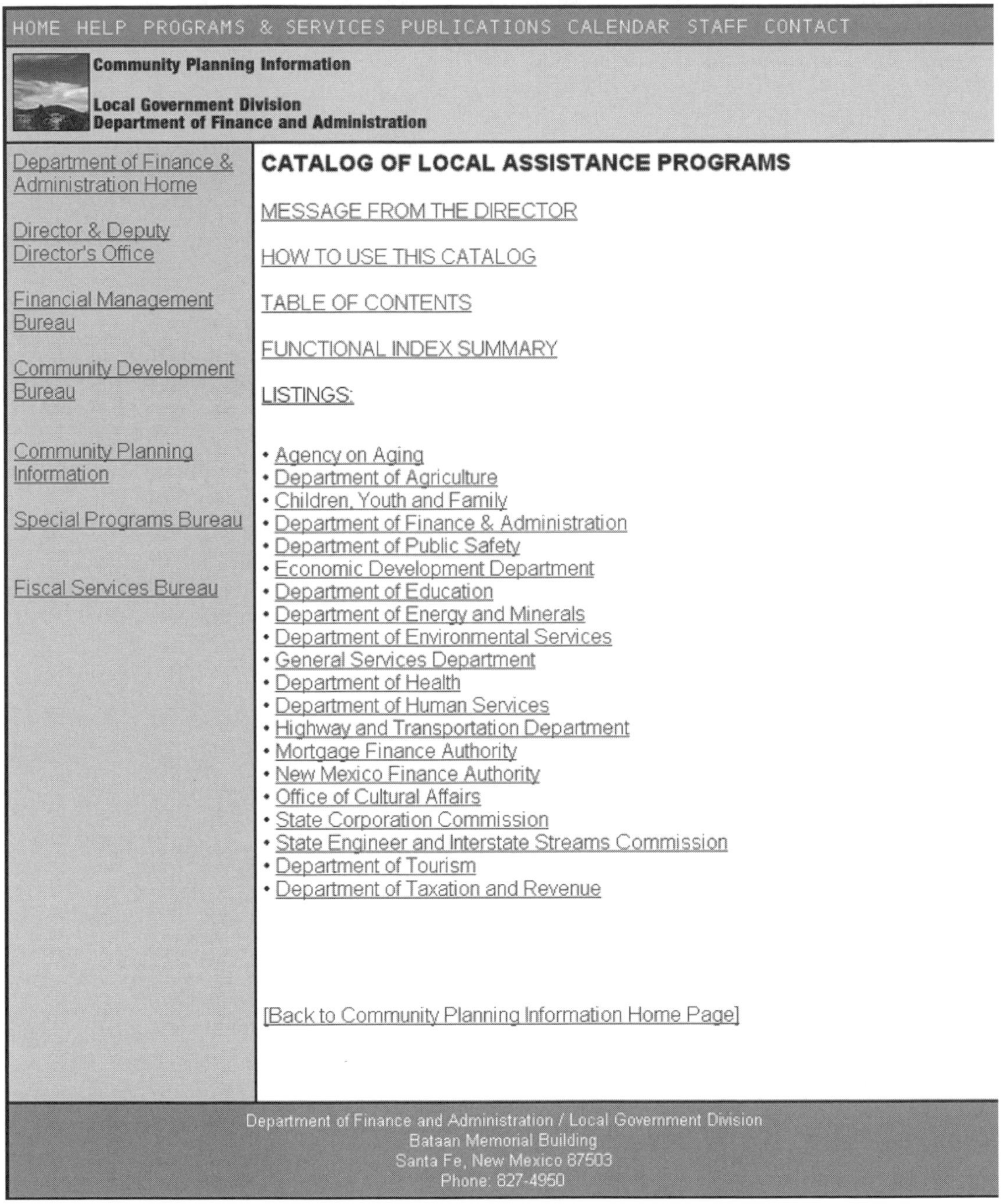

HOME   HELP   PROGRAMS & SERVICES   PUBLICATIONS   CALENDAR   STAFF   CONTACT

Community Planning Information

Local Government Division
Department of Finance and Administration

Department of Finance &
Administration Home

Director & Deputy
Director's Office

Financial Management
Bureau

Community Development
Bureau

Community Planning
Information

Special Programs Bureau

Fiscal Services Bureau

CATALOG OF LOCAL ASSISTANCE PROGRAMS

MESSAGE FROM THE DIRECTOR

HOW TO USE THIS CATALOG

TABLE OF CONTENTS

FUNCTIONAL INDEX SUMMARY

LISTINGS:

- Agency on Aging
- Department of Agriculture
- Children, Youth and Family
- Department of Finance & Administration
- Department of Public Safety
- Economic Development Department
- Department of Education
- Department of Energy and Minerals
- Department of Environmental Services
- General Services Department
- Department of Health
- Department of Human Services
- Highway and Transportation Department
- Mortgage Finance Authority
- New Mexico Finance Authority
- Office of Cultural Affairs
- State Corporation Commission
- State Engineer and Interstate Streams Commission
- Department of Tourism
- Department of Taxation and Revenue

[Back to Community Planning Information Home Page]

Department of Finance and Administration / Local Government Division
Bataan Memorial Building
Santa Fe, New Mexico 87503
Phone: 827-4950

Figure 13. Local governments, non-profit organizations, and other groups can often apply for grants from the state. This publication from New Mexico summarizes funds that are available. *Source*: http://www.nmlocalgov.net/plan/plan_list.html.

tween the Natural Resources Department and the Energy and Minerals Department. This annual report contains an overview of five EMNRD agencies: Energy Conservation and Management, Forestry, Mining and Minerals, Oil Conservation, and State Parks. Each section details a particular division's area of responsibility, history, main objectives and goals, and other pertinent operational information. The online version of the report is broken into five separate downloadable PDF files. Copies are available without charge. Contact the New Mexico Energy, Minerals and Natural Resources Department, 1220 S. St. Francis Drive, Santa Fe, NM 87505, or call (505) 476-3407. The report can also be found online at http://www.emnrd.state.nm.us.

Water Quality and Water Pollution Control in New Mexico (Water Quality Control Commission)—This 1998 report serves as a basic source of information on water quality and water pollution in New Mexico. The report was written to satisfy requirements mandated in the federal Water Pollution Control Act (33 U.S.C. 1288). The report is intended not only for the U.S. Congress, but also for those in the general public, interest groups, consultants, state legislators, government entities, and university or other educational officials concerned about water in New Mexico. The report provides an overview of progress in diminishing water pollution; an estimate of the environmental, social, and economic impact of pollution within the state; and a description of non-point source pollution and pollution control. Copies of the report are available by contacting the New Mexico Environment Department, Surface Water Quality Bureau, Harold Runnels Building, N2063, 1190 St. Francis Drive, Santa Fe, NM 87502, or call (505) 827-2928. The document can be viewed at http://www.nmenv.state.nm.us/.

NEW MEXICO'S WORLD WIDE WEB HOME PAGE

Welcome to New Mexico (http://www.state.nm.us/)—This is the official home page for New Mexico, and was developed as a portal to ensure easy access to the variety of information, government, and other resources now available online.

The site provides links to eight broad-subject-oriented pages (e.g., Living in New Mexico, Working in New Mexico, etc.). The page can also be searched by keyword or by popular site. There is also a site map, help screen, and contact information available. Whether searching for visitor information or relocating to New Mexico, the portal provides information for everyone regarding life, work, education, and health in New Mexico.

COMMERCIAL PUBLICATIONS AND WEB SITES

Health Care Coverage and Access in New Mexico: An Analysis of the 1999 Health Policy Commission Statewide Household Survey of Health Care Coverage (Albuquerque, NM: Bureau of Business and Economic Research, University of New Mexico, 2000)—This provides an analysis of health care coverage, access, and services available to the population in New Mexico. The report data were gathered by a random sample telephone survey of adults and children in approximately 3,900 households. This report updates and expands upon the original survey conducted in 1993. It was contracted to the Bureau of Business and Economic Research at the University of New Mexico by the New Mexico Health Policies Commission. Copies of the report were distributed to many state depository libraries. An online version can be found at http://hpc.state .nm.us/reports/. Contact the Bureau of Business and Economic Research, 1920 Lomas Boulevard NE, Albuquerque, NM 87131-6021, or call (505) 277-2216.

New Mexico Business—Current Economic Report (Albuquerque, NM: Bureau of Business and Economic Research)—This report, published ten times per year, is a comprehensive statistical report on the economy in New Mexico. It contains articles that summarize or address economic or demographic subjects. There are several pages of graphs illustrating changes in economic variables, sixty state economic indicators updated with each issue, key national variables, comparisons between the U.S. and New Mexico economies, and more. A one-year subscription is available for $25.00. A sample of the report, an Excel file from an article in the latest report, or an order form are available at http://www.unm.edu/~bber/pubs/pubs-con.htm. For further information contact the Bureau of Business and Economic Research, 1920 Lomas Boulevard NE, Albuquerque, NM 87131-6021, or call (505) 277-2216.

New Mexico Atlas and Gazetteer: Topo Maps of the Entire State: Public Lands, Back Roads, 4th ed. (Yarmouth, ME: DeLorme Mapping Company, 2000)—This latest edition provides a wealth of information on the backcountry of New Mexico. The topographical maps provide good detail of the backcountry, including roads, trails, and other access points, in New Mexico. Available from the DeLorme Mapping Company, Two Delorme Drive, P.O. Box 298, Yarmouth, ME 04096. Call (800) 581-5105.

New Mexico Register 2001; New Mexico Rules Annotated, 2002 edition; New Mexico Statutes Annotated (Charlottesville, VA: LexisNexis/Michie Co.)—Like many other states, New Mexico makes available online an "unofficial" version of its *Register*, *Rules Annotated*, and *Statutes Annotated*. The "official" versions of these publications can be found in several state agency or state depository library web sites (see, for example http://elibrary.unm.edu/govinfo/ newmexico.html). While these sites provide unfettered access to New Mexico citizens, those wishing to review copies must purchase them, either in paper or electronically, through the Michie Company. The *Register* is available for $270.00, the *Rules Annotated* for $95.00, and the *Statutes Annotated* for $800.00. See the LexisNexis home page at http://bookstore.lexis.com for further information.

2001 Directory of New Mexico Municipal Officials (Santa Fe: New Mexico Municipal League, 2001)—This annual publication contains the most current information on officials in New Mexico's cities, towns, and villages. It is available for $35.00 from the New Mexico Municipal League, P.O. Box 846, Santa Fe, NM 87504-0846. Call (505) 982-5573, or outside New Mexico (800) 432-2036. See http://www.nmml.org for more information.

SOURCES CONSULTED

The Albuquerque Journal: The Sunday Journal. May 12, 2002, Section F, page 6.
Correspondence with Laurie Canepa and Marci Smith, New Mexico State Library and Archives.

Google, http://www.google.com.

Government Documents Round Table, American Library Association. *Directory of Government Document Collections & Librarians,* 7th ed. Bethesda, MD: Congressional Information Service, 1997.

Jobe, Janita. "State Publications." *Journal of Government Information,* 27 (2000): 733–768.

Numerous department web pages via the state's home page, http://www.state.nm.us/.

State and Local Government on the Net, http://www.piperinfo.com/state/index.cfm.

State Web Locator, http://www.infoctr.edu/swl/.

Survey response from Clark McLean, University of New Mexico, 2000.

New York

Eric W. Johnson

GOVERNMENT PUBLISHING AND THE DEPOSITORY SYSTEM

In January 1989, the New York State Library redesigned its State Document Depository Program, which had been in existence since the passing of the *New York State Printing and Public Documents Law* in 1955, which charged the State Library with serving as the central repository for the distribution of all public documents. The State Library increased the number of depository libraries within New York from 89 to over 300, and created four levels of participation in the program, depending on the size, content, and scope of the collection. "Information and Access Centers" have the basic finding aids, and are expected to refer patrons to libraries with larger collections; "Reference Centers" have a core collection of reference tools; "Depository Libraries" have the largest and broadest collections; and "Research Depository Libraries" own an extensive collection of documents on microfiche.

The redesigned program was legally formalized in 1993 by the approval of Chapter 176, *Laws of 1993*, which stated that state agencies, departments, commissions, institutions, and boards must send thirty copies of any report to the State Library. The State Library keeps several copies, and microfilmed copies are sent to the Research Depository Libraries and paper copies to the Depository Libraries. Documents appearing in the *Checklist of Official Publications of the State of New York* have been scanned for online access since 1995.

The *New York State Printing and Public Documents Law* defines a "public document" as "any final annual, biennial, regular, statutorily mandated or other report, study or multi-year plan issued by a state agency in multiple copies, which has been distributed to the public." It excludes from the definition

items issued strictly for administrative or operational purposes, inter-agency and intra-agency memoranda, drafts of reports, public service announcements, written opinions rendered in cases determined in the court of appeals, appellate divisions of the supreme court or any other court of record and any public documents or portions thereof that are compiled for law enforcement purposes and which, if disclosed, would interfere with law enforcement investigations or judicial proceedings, deprive a person of the right to a fair trial or impartial adjudication, identify a confidential source or disclose confidential information relating to a criminal investigation or reveal criminal investigative techniques or procedures, other than routine techniques and procedures.

USEFUL ADDRESSES AND TELEPHONE NUMBERS

The most comprehensive collection of New York state publications can be found in the following library:

New York State Library
Documents Unit
Cultural Education Center
Empire State Plaza
Albany, NY 12230
Phone Number for New York Reference Questions: (518) 474-7492
E-Mail Address for New York Reference Questions: nysddp@mail.nysed.gov
Library's Home Page: http://www.nysl.nysed.gov/index.html
New York State Documents Page: http://www.nysl.nysed.gov/statedoc.htm

A complete list of New York State Depository Libraries can be found online at http://www.nysl.nysed.gov/edocs/education/chcktext.htm#lis. Those designated with a "D" would have the most comprehensive collections of state publications.

INDEXES TO NEW YORK STATE PUBLICATIONS

The basic index of New York state publications is the State Library's *Checklist of Official Publications of the State of New York*, published since 1947. This monthly compilation of New York state documents acquired by the New York State Library includes in its citation the New York State Document Classification System call number, issuing agency, title, date of publication, pagination, OCLC number, LC subject headings, and, if the item is a periodical, the holdings. The *Checklist* is available online in annual cumulations from June 1989 to the present in HTML format at http://www.nysl.nysed.gov/edocs/education/chcktext.htm. Other formats are also available for more recent years.

The New York State Library also produced the *Dictionary Catalog of Official Publications of the State of New York*. This publication, subtitled "Monographs cataloged or recataloged by the New York State Library," consisted of quarterly cumulative issues with an annual cumulative volume. Included in this catalog were official state agency publications as well as publications relating to New York State that might not be official state publications. The latest cumulative microform edition covered publications from December 18, 1973 to December 31, 1991. A Serial Supplement covered serial publications from 1979 through 1986.

State publications may be located through *Excelsior*, the State Library's online catalog, which also provides access to scanned documents. The library catalogs of the other libraries in the State Document Depository Program will also include state publications.

For a detailed if slightly dated overview of the State Document Depository Program, consult Nancy Macomber's *New York State Document Depository Manual*, produced by the State Library in 1989 and available online at http://www.nysl.nysed.gov/edocs/education/depos.htm.

ESSENTIAL STATE PUBLICATIONS

Directories

Corporation and Business Entity Database (Department of State, Division of Corporations, State Records, and Uniform Commercial Code)—This online database, searchable by entity name, includes businesses and not-for-profit corporations, limited partnerships, limited liability companies, and limited liability partnerships, as well as other miscellaneous businesses. Records include the current entity name, the initial DOS filing date and county where filed, the entity type, and current status. Names and addresses of DOS process, registered agent, and chairman or CEO, as well as the address of the principal executive office, are listed. The database is accessible from http://wdb.dos .state.ny.us/corp_public/corp_wdb.corp_search_inputs.show. For more information, contact the Division of Corporations, State Records, and Uniform Commercial Code, 41 State Street, Albany, NY 12231-0001, or call (518) 473-2492; or via e-mail at corporations@dos.state.ny.us

The Directory of Public and Non-Public Schools and Administrators for the State of New York (Education Department)—This online directory provides data from the annual BEDS (Basic Educational Data System) data collection effort. School district records include the chief school officer, usually a superintendent of schools, a mailing address, and a telephone number. Individual school records are comprised of the school code number, type, grade levels, principal/headmaster, address, and telephone number. This directory is updated frequently, and the information may be browsed or downloaded. It is available online at http://www.nysed.gov/admin/bedsdata.html.

OGS Telephone Directory (Office of General Services)—This is a directory of telephone listings for all New York state employees. The online version, available at http://www.ogs.state.ny.us/telecom/, has separate directories by organization, individual listing, and functional topic. The print version may be purchased from the NYS Office of General Services, Directory Sales, 27th Floor, Erastus Corning II Tower Building, Empire State Plaza, Albany, NY 12242, or call (518) 474-5987.

Financial/Budgetary Resources

Annual Information Statement (AIS) (Division of the Budget)—The *AIS* constitutes the official form for disclosure of state financial information required under federal securities law. It contains information on the Enacted Budget Financial Plan; actual operating results for the prior three fiscal years; economic and demographic data; debt and other capital financing information; state government organization, workforce, pension systems, and financial procedures; and other financial information. The *Annual Information Statements* from 1997/1998 to the present are available on the web at http://www .budget.state.ny.us/investor/ais/ais.html, as are any quarterly updates to the current *AIS*. A print version is available from the Division of the Budget, State Capitol, Room 145, Albany, NY 12224, or call (518) 473-8705.

Enacted Budget (Division of the Budget)—The *Enacted Budget* reflects action by the legislature on the governor's *Executive Budget*, and includes the Executive Budget Financial Plan, which forecasts receipts and disbursements for the fiscal year. It is available online at http://www.budget.state.ny.us/ pubs/enacted/enacted.html, along with the text of enacted budget bills.

Executive Budget (Division of the Budget)—The governor's annual revenue and spending plan as proposed to the legislature is comprised of a textual and statistical Overview and two appendices. The Overview includes the budget director's explanation of the governor's blueprint for the coming fiscal year, the Financial Plan, major initiatives proposed by the governor, the economic outlook for the nation and the state, and legislative proposals necessary to implement the budget. Appendix I details state agencies' operating, local aid, and capitol projects spending, and includes statements on agency mission and organization and staffing, as well as budget requests from the legislature and the judiciary. Appendix II summarizes the governor's *Executive Budget*, providing an overview of the Financial Plan, explaining the state's revenue sources, and discussing the state's capital plan. The text, along with accompanying appropriation bills and amendments, is available online at http:// www.budget.state.ny.us/pubs/executive/executive.html. Previous budgets, from 1997–1998 on, are also archived on the web site.

For information on print versions of budgetary materials, contact the Division of the Budget, Budget Services Unit, State Capitol, Albany, NY 12224, call (518) 473-0580, or check the division's web site at http://www.budget .state.ny.us/site/contact.html.

Legal Resources

The Constitution of the State of New York, As Revised, with Amendments Adopted by the Constitutional Convention of 1938 and Approved by vote of the People on November 8, 1938. As Amended and in Force January 1, 2002 (Assembly)—The text of the state Constitution is comprised of twenty articles: Bill of Rights, Suffrage, Legislature, Executive, Offices and Civil Departments, Judiciary, State Finances, Local Finances, Local Governments, Corporations, Education, Defense, Public Officers, Conservation, Canals, Taxation, Social Welfare, Housing, Amendment to Constitution, and When to Take Effect. The Constitution is available online at http://assembly.state.ny.us/leg/?co=1.

New York State Consolidated Laws and *New York State Unconsolidated Laws* (Assembly)—Unlike the other states, which have single standardized codes, two compilations comprise New York's statutes: *New York State Consolidated Laws* and *New York State Unconsolidated Laws*. The *Consolidated Laws* are arranged by topic, then further divided by chapter and title, and contain the text of acts passed by the State Assembly. The *Unconsolidated Laws* contain the text of acts, such as one dealing with rent control, that are legally binding but have not been consolidated. Both sets of laws are available online on the State Assembly's pages at http://assembly.state.ny.us/leg/?sl=0 and on the Senate's pages at http://public.leginfo.state.ny.us/menugetf.cgi. For information about print versions of the Constitution and the Laws, contact the Assembly Public Information Office at (518) 455-4218.

An official commercial version of the *Consolidated Laws* is published by West Group and described below.

Statistical Sources

Labor Market Information (Department of Labor)—This page in the Department of Labor's web site, located online at http://www.labor.state.ny.us/labor_market/LMI_business/LMI_business.html, provides links to information on wages, employment and unemployment, demographics, and occupational injuries and illnesses, as well as directories of labor unions/employee associations and local labor market analysts. For more information, contact the Department of Labor, State Office Building Campus, Room 500, Albany, NY 12240-0003, or call (518) 457-9000, or via e-mail at nysdol@labor.state.ny.us.

New York State Statistical Yearbook (Nelson A. Rockefeller Institute of Government)—This annual reference guide to New York State facts and figures includes information on population and vital statistics, business and economic indicators, employment and personal income, elections, state and local government finance and employment, banking insurance, public safety and the criminal justice system, housing, education, health and human services, energy and utilities, transportation, agriculture, and environmental conservation and recreation. County maps, information on Economic Development Regions, and a directory of state governmental agencies round out the volume. *The Statistical Yearbook*, whose twenty-sixth edition appeared in 2001, is available from the Nelson Rockefeller Institute of Government, 411 State Street, Albany, NY 12203-1003, or call (518) 443-5522; or may be ordered online at http://www.rockinst.org/publications/NYS_Statistical_Yearbook.html.

New York, the State of Learning (Education Department)—This annual report is mandated by a law requiring the Board of Regents and the State Education Department to publish statistics detailing enrollment trends, indicators of student achievement, graduation, attendance, employment rates, teacher preparation, turnover, in-service education, and performance. The report is divided into two parts. The first volume, subtitled *Statewide Profile of the Educational System*, analyzed the statewide data included in the report, with illustrative figures, charts, and tables. The second, *Statistical Profiles of Public School Districts*, is comprised of individual district profiles, with tabular presentations of these data arranged by school district within each county. The entire 2001 report is available online at http://www.emsc.nysed.gov/irts/ch655_2001/. A print copy may be obtained from Information, Reporting and Technology Services, New York State Education Department, Room 863 EBA, Albany, NY 12234, or call (518) 474-7965.

Vital Statistics of New York State (Department of Health)—This annual report contains technical notes and statistics on population, live births, spontaneous fetal deaths, induced abortion, pregnancies, mortality, marriages, dissolutions of marriage, and city and village profiles. The latest report, as well as those for recent years, is available online at http://www.health.state.ny.us/nys doh/vr/mainvs.htm. For information about a print version, contact the Department of Health, Corning Tower, Empire State Plaza, Albany, NY 12237, or call (518) 474-2071, or via e-mail at bio-info@health.state.ny.us.

Other Resources

Local Government Handbook (Department of State)—The *Local Government Handbook*, first published in 1975 and currently in its fifth edition (2000), is an authoritative source of information about the origins and operations of the Empire State, including a brief history and overview of federal, state, and local government and describing their evolving relationships, structures, and functions. It is available online as a PDF file at http://www.dos.state.ny.us/lgss/list9.html. Print and CD-ROM versions are available from Department of State, Division of Local Government, 41 State Street, Albany, NY 12231-0001, or call (518) 473-3355, or via e-mail at localgov@dos.state.ny.us.

The I Love New York Travel Guide (Division of Marketing, Advertising and Tourism)—This annual tourist guide contains information about attractions, accommodations, and vacation ideas. It is available by calling (800) CALL-NYS or by completing an online form at http://www.iloveny.com/info _center/contact_us.asp. Similar travel information is available on the "I Love NY" web site at http://www.iloveny.com/main.asp.

NEW YORK'S WORLD WIDE WEB HOME PAGE

New York State's portal page, online at http://www.state.ny.us/, was unveiled in March 2001 as part of the governor's e-Commerce/e-Government initiative. A common web banner provides visitors to all state web pages with easy access to information by topic, geographic location, word search, or state agency.

Across the top of the page are links labeled "Governor," "map-NY," "e-bizNYS," "Citizen Guide" (for government-related information and FAQs), and "Search." In a column along the left side of the page are links to information on "Doing Business," "Working," "Learning," "Outdoors," "Living," "Government," "Healthcare," "Visiting," and "Government Agencies." From the "Living" link, children can access the "Kids' Room," with state facts (history, symbols, governors, a crossword puzzle, etc.) and fire safety information. "Featured Links" along the right side of the page include the governor's press releases, the State of the State Address, the state Constitution, and lottery information.

The portal page was designed by American Management Systems in collaboration with the New York State Office for Technology. For more information, contact the Office for Technology, State Capitol, Empire State Plaza,

P.O. Box 2062, Albany, NY 12220, or contact Customer Relations at (518) 473-2658, or via e-mail at customer.relations@oft.state.ny.us.

COMMERCIAL PUBLICATIONS AND WEB SITES

Gould's New York Consolidated Laws Unannotated (Gould Publications, Inc., 1333 North U.S. Highway 17-92, Longwood, FL 32750)—This commercial version of the *New York Consolidated Laws*, without any annotations, is available as a looseleaf or softcover set and on CD-ROM. For ordering information, contact the publisher at (800) 717-7917 or via e-mail at info@gouldlaw.com, or visit the publisher's web site at http://www.gouldlaw.com/.

McKinney's Consolidated Laws of New York Annotated (West Group, 610 Opperman Drive, Eagan, MN 55123)—Over 200 hardbound volumes provide the full text of New York statutes and the New York Constitution, plus New York, federal district, and bankruptcy court orders and rules. The set includes extensive notes of decisions, legislative history, indexes, a table of popular names, and short titles. For more information, contact West Group at (800) 328-4880; ordering information is also found on its web site at http://west.thomson.com/.

SOURCES CONSULTED

Macomber, Nancy, ed. *New York State Document Depository Manual.* Albany, NY: New York State Library, Legislative and Governmental Services, 1989.

New York State Library's web site, http://www.nysl.nysed.gov/index.html.

Numerous departmental web pages via the state's official web site, http://www.state.ny.us.

North Carolina

Lori L. Smith

GOVERNMENT PUBLISHING AND THE DEPOSITORY SYSTEM

The North Carolina state documents depository system was established in 1987. The State Library, which is part of the Department of Cultural Resources, was designated as the official depository for state publications. The North Carolina State Publications Clearinghouse was created as a unit within the State Library to coordinate the program.

The clearinghouse requires state agencies to submit ten copies of each publication for the depository program. Agencies can send as few as five copies of publications that are sold on a cost-recovery basis. The State Library also has the authority to exclude materials from the depository program that it deems inappropriate. Of the number requested/received, two copies are sent to the Library of Congress and up to five are retained by the State Library. The others are distributed to depository libraries around the state. The clearinghouse is required by law to make at least one microfiche copy of print publications it receives. In most cases, depository copies are distributed in microfiche rather than print. The clearinghouse is required to create a checklist of the publications it receives. From 1980 to 1998, the checklist was distributed as a printed document, free of charge, to North Carolina libraries that requested it. Since January 1999, the checklist has been disseminated via the State Library's web site. The State Library is also responsible for designating depository libraries, entering into formal contracts with them, and establishing guidelines for the depositories to follow.

The head of each state agency is charged with appointing a "publications officer" to coordinate the agency's participation in the depository program.

Chapter 125, Article 1A of the *North Carolina General Statues* is where legislation regarding the depository program appears. In section 125-11.6(2), "document" is defined as "any printed document including any report, directory, statistical compendium, bibliography, map, regulation, newsletter, pamphlet, brochure, periodical, bulletin, compilation, or register, regardless of whether the printed document is in paper, film, tape, disk, or any other format." Section 125-11.6(4) further defines "state publication" to mean

any document prepared by a State agency or private organization, consultant, or research firm, under contract with or under the supervision of a State agency: Provided, however, the term "state publication" does not include administrative documents used only within the issuing agency, documents produced for instructional purposes that are not intended for sale or publication, appellate division reports and advance sheets distributed by the Administrative Office of the Courts, the S.B.I. Investigative "Bulletin", documents that will be reproduced in the Senate or House of Representatives Journals, or documents that are confidential pursuant to Article 17 of Chapter 120 of the General Statutes.

An interesting aspect of the depository program legislation is that section 125-11.13 requires state agencies to use acid-free paper for printing any publication determined by the State Librarian and the university librarian at the University of North Carolina at Chapel Hill to be of historic value. State agencies have up to one year to begin publishing on acid-free paper after they've been notified that their publication has been designated to have historic value.

In 2002, the State Library began a three-year "Access to State Government Information Initiative" to devise a method for ensuring public access to state publications that are "born digital." Phase one of the project, to be carried out in 2002–2003, will involve the creation of an advisory group of stakeholders who will gather information about "born digital" publications being produced in North Carolina, and about methods being used by other states to provide access to such publications. Phase two will involve the consideration of various solutions, and phase three will involve testing and implementing the solution chosen, as well as making any necessary changes to state legislation.

USEFUL ADDRESSES AND TELEPHONE NUMBERS

The most complete collections of North Carolina publications can be found at the following libraries:

State Library of North Carolina
Information Services Branch
4641 Mail Service Center
Raleigh, NC 27699-4641
Phone Number for North Carolina Reference Questions: (919) 733-3270
Fax Number for North Carolina Reference Questions: (919) 733-5679
E-Mail Link for North Carolina Reference Questions: http://statelibrary.dcr.state.nc
    .us/forms/Genref.htm
Library's Home Page: http://statelibrary.dcr.state.nc.us/
State Publications Clearinghouse Home Page: http://statelibrary.dcr.state.nc.us/tss/
    deposito.htm

North Carolina Collection
CB # 3930, Wilson Library
University of North Carolina
Chapel Hill, NC 27514-8890

Phone Number for North Carolina Reference Questions: (919) 962-1172
E-Mail Address for North Carolina Reference Questions: nccref@email.unc.edu
Library's Home Page: http://www.lib.unc.edu/wilson/
North Carolina Collection Home Page: http://www.lib.unc.edu/ncc/

INDEXES TO NORTH CAROLINA STATE PUBLICATIONS

From 1940 to 1947, the University of North Carolina Library (Chapel Hill) published *Monthly Checklist of Official North Carolina Publications*. From 1952 to 1957 it published *Checklist of Official North Carolina Publications Received by the University of North Carolina Library*. And finally, from 1957 to 1980 it published *North Carolina Publications, a Checklist of Official State Publications*. The last two titles were issued bimonthly. From 1980 to date the North Carolina State Library has published the bimonthly *Checklist of Official North Carolina State Publications*. The most recent editions of the *Checklist* are available online at http://statelibrary.dcr.state.nc.us/stdocs/cheklist.htm. Biweekly shipping lists for both paper and microfiche shipments are also available from the State Publications Clearinghouse web site.

The State Library assigns classification numbers to state publications based on the *Classification Scheme for North Carolina State Publications*. An explanation and outline of this scheme is available online at http://statelibrary.dcr.state.nc.us/stdocs/class/class.htm. In essence, the scheme arranges publications by agency and function. In some ways the system is similar to the SuDoc classification system commonly used with federal publications.

In addition to those indexes, the State Library's online catalog is an excellent tool for finding bibliographic information about North Carolina publications. It can be accessed at http://statelibrary.dcr.state.nc.us/catalog.htm. The telnet version of the catalog offers options to search state documents by keyword or by call number. There is also a section of "Selected Acquisitions Lists" that provides a list of recently received state documents. A web version of the catalog is also available.

Another way to find North Carolina government information is by searching the *Find NC* site at http://www.findnc.org/. This site, subtitled *The Central Gateway to NC Government Information*, is maintained by the State Library. The site essentially functions as a search engine. It searches a number of different data sources, including state government web pages and Government Information Locator Service (GILS) records created by state agencies to describe each of their electronic information resources. *Find NC* also includes records for the State Library's collection of North Carolina print documents. In the "Frequently Requested Information" section of the site there is an extensive list of links arranged by subject that, if printed, would be over twenty pages long. In the "Agriculture" subject section, for instance, there are links to state sites on: Agricultural Marketing; Agricultural Statistics; Aquaculture; Department of Agriculture and Consumer Services; Food Distribution; North Carolina Agriculture History and Overview; North Carolina State Fair; North Carolina State Fairgrounds Rental; Pest Control, Insecticides, Fungicides, Rodenticides; Standards, Weights and Measures; Veterinary Services.

ESSENTIAL STATE PUBLICATIONS

Directories

Directory of State and County Officials of North Carolina (Secretary of State)—NC Docs. Call Number—X1 4:year. Names, mailing addresses, phone numbers, fax numbers, and e-mail addresses for state and county officials are supplied in this annual directory. The publication is divided into five sections: U.S. Government Officials, State Government Officials by Branch and Agency, Officials in Higher Education, Soil and Water Conservation District Supervisors, and County Officials. The online edition, at http://www.secretary.state .nc.us/pubsweb/library.asp, is updated periodically and is annotated with the date it was last amended. A print edition can be ordered from the Department of the Secretary of State, Publications Division, P.O. Box 29622, Raleigh, NC 27626-0622, or call (919) 807-2149. The price for a copy of the 2000 edition, mailed to an address outside North Carolina, was $10.75.

Education Directory: Public Schools of North Carolina (State Board of Education, Department of Public Instruction)—NC Docs. Call Number—G5 15:year/year. In addition to providing addresses and phone numbers for all the state's public schools, this directory provides contact information for school superintendents and employees of the Department of Public Instruction. It also includes contact information for educational organizations, associations, and councils, and for suppliers of educational materials. Some statistics on school systems are provided as well. The most recent edition of the directory is available on the web at http://www.ncpublicschools.org/nceddirectory/. A print copy can be ordered by calling (800) 663-1250 or (919) 807-3470. The price for the 2001–2002 edition was $15.00. For more ordering information, click the "Publication Sales" link from the *Education Directory* site or e-mail publications@dpi.state .nc.us.

North Carolina State Capitol Telephone Directory (Office of the Governor, Information Technology Services)—NC Docs. Call Number—I3 15:T2. The online version of this directory, at http://www.state.nc.us/phone/, offers alphabetical and departmental lists of state employees and allows the user to search for a specific name. The departmental listing includes information about toll-free numbers. For more information call (919) 981-5555.

North Carolina Statewide Electronic Mail Directory (Office of the Governor, Information Technology Services)—This online database of state employee e-mail addresses is available at http://www.state.nc.us/email/. For more information call (919) 981-5555.

Financial/Budgetary Resources

Comprehensive Annual Financial Report for the Year Ended June 30, [Year] (Office of the State Controller)—NC Docs. Call Number—I2.6 1:year. The revenues and expenditures of specific agencies, and of the state government as a whole, are reported each year in this publication. The first section of the report includes an organization chart and a list of state officials. The second part presents detailed financial statements and the State Auditor's report. The final section provides both financial and general statistics. Many tables in the final section provide figures for a ten-year period. Several recent editions of the report can be accessed online from the Office of the State Controller's "Financial Reports" page at http://www.osc.state.nc.us/financial/. Print copies of the report can be requested by e-mailing a request to info@mail.osc.state.nc.us. The Controller's Office can also be contacted by phone at (919) 981-5454.

The North Carolina State Budget: Post Legislative Budget Summary (Office of State Budget and Management)—NC Docs. Call Number—I2 1:A65 year/year. The 2001–2003 edition of this report was organized into seven sections: Summary of State Budget, Economic Outlook for 2001–2003, General Fund, Transportation, Capital Improvements, Reserves/Debt Service and Other Adjustments, and Appendix. Sections have textual summaries of financial activity and detailed tables of figures. The appendix includes several tables of historic statistics, some of which cover years going back to 1968. The most recent edition is available online at http://www.osbm.state.nc.us/osbm/pubs.html. Some older editions are available at http://www.osbm.state.nc.us/osbm/pubs_archive.html. Those with questions can write to Office of the State Budget and Management, 20320 Mail Service Center, Raleigh, NC 27699-0320, or call (919) 733-7061.

Legal Resources

North Carolina General Statutes (General Assembly)—The official version of the statutes is a commercial publication, but an unofficial version is provided on the General Assembly web site at http://www.ncleg.net/Statutes/Statutes.asp. This online version of the state's laws can be browsed by chapter or searched by keyword. A "caveat" on the site warns that "The North Carolina General Assembly is offering access to the Statutes on the Internet as a service to the public. . . . Please refer legal questions elsewhere." Therefore, those with questions about the laws are encouraged to contact a lawyer. Those with technical questions about the site itself can e-mail the Webmanager via an online form at http://www.ncleg.net/Help/Help.html.

North Carolina Legislation: A Summary of Legislation in the General Assembly of Interest to North Carolina Public Officials (University of North Carolina at Chapel Hill, Institute of Government)—NC Docs. Call Number—G41 24/2:year. The Institute of Government at UNC–Chapel Hill coordinates the university's Master of Public Information Program and offers numerous conferences and workshops for government officials. This annual publication summarizes all the legislation enacted during a session of the General Assembly. Faculty members at the institute who specialize in particular subject areas write the summaries for those subjects. Selected chapters from the most recent editions are available online at http://ncinfo.iog.unc.edu/pubs/nclegis/. The print edition of this title for 2001 was 305 pages and sold for $40.00. Information about ordering a copy can be found on the institute's "Publications" site at https://iogpubs.iog.unc.edu/. A free copy of the institute's catalog can be requested by writing to Publications Office, Institute of Government, CD #3330, Knapp Building, UNC-CH, Chapel Hill, NC 27599-3330, or calling (919) 966-4119.

North Carolina Register (Office of Administrative Hearings)—NC Docs. Call Number—M21 7:R 33. Issues of this title are published twice a month. Issues contain rules that state regulatory agencies are proposing or which have been approved, executive orders from the governor, and a variety of public notices. Rules that have been approved are eventually incorporated into the *Official North Carolina Administrative Code*. The *Administrative Code* is a commercial publication. The *Register* is available online in both HTML and PDF formats at http://www.oah.state.nc.us/rules/register/. Those who wish to begin a print subscription can access an online order form from the web address for the *Register*. The cost for an out-of-state subscriber in 2002 was $195.00 per year. Those with questions can write to Office of Administrative Hearings, Rules Division, 6714 Mail Service Center, Raleigh, NC 27699-6714, or e-mail oah.postmaster@ncmail.net.

Statistical Resources

Agricultural Statistics Division (Department of Agriculture and Consumer Services, Agricultural Statistics Division)—The home page of the Agricultural Statistics Division provides access to a wide variety of county, state, and national statistics on crops and livestock. The division's site has its own site map that functions as a detailed table of contents. The address for the home page is http://www.ncagr.com/stats/index.htm. Those with questions can write to Department of Agriculture and Consumer Services, Agricultural Statistics Division, P.O. Box 27767, Raleigh, NC 27611, or call (919) 856-4394.

Crime in North Carolina (Department of Justice, State Bureau of Investigation, Division of Criminal Information)—NC Docs. Call Number—M6 7:year. Annual statistics on murder, manslaughter, rape, robbery, aggravated assault, burglary, larceny, motor vehicle theft, arson, and other criminal offenses are reported in this publication. Some demographic information is included about persons who committed the crimes. A summary report is available online as an easily printable PDF file at http://sbi2.jus.state.nc.us/crp/public/Default .htm. Additional information from several recent editions of the full report is available from the same site. Sections in the full report include: Agency Reporting Status, Offenses and Clearances by Agency, Crime Trends, Arrests and Clearances, Hate Crime, Index Offenses—Analysis, Offenses by Population Group, Stolen and Recovered Property, Law Enforcement Officers Killed and Assaulted, and Law Enforcement Personnel. Those with questions about the report can e-mail the State Bureau of Investigation at stats@mail.jus.state.nc .us, or call (888) 498-9429. The Division of Criminal Information can also be reached at 3320 Garner Road, Raleigh, NC 27626-0500, or call (919) 662-4500.

North Carolina Demographic and Statistical Data Sources on the Web (State Library)—This web page, created by the reference staff at the State Library, provides links to statistical sites arranged by subject. Links listed on the page are coded with a "Q" to indicate a site for obtaining quick facts, with an "NC" to indicate a North Carolina government source, or an "R" to indicate an in-depth research site. The address of the page is http://statelibrary.dcr.state.nc

.us/iss/ncdataresources.html. Those with questions can contact the State Library's North Carolina Information Center Reference Desk at (919) 733-3270, or by e-mail at Reference@library.dcr.state.nc.us.

North Carolina Public Schools Statistical Profile (State Board of Education, Department of Public Instruction)—NC Docs. Call Number—G1 102:S79. Published annually since 1975, this source provides statistics about the state's public elementary and secondary schools. The first section is a statewide summary of information on students, school personnel, transportation, and school finances. The second section provides county-level statistics, and the third covers charter schools. Several recent editions of the reports are available online at http://www.ncpublicschools.org/fbs/stats/. Print copies can be ordered by calling (800) 663-1250 or (919) 807-3470. The price for the 2001 edition was $22.00. For more ordering information, click the "Publication Sales" link from the *Statistical Profile* site or e-mail publications@dpi.state.nc.us.

North Carolina Vital Statistics (Department of Health and Human Services, Division of Public Health, State Center for Health Statistics)—NC Docs. Call Number—J2 401:year. This annual publication is issued in two volumes. Volume one provides statistics on live births, fetal and infant mortality, non-fetal deaths, marriages, divorces, and annulments. Statistics are given at the state, county, and perinatal care region level, and for fifty large cities. A map of perinatal care regions is provided. The only racial breakdown provided is white and minority. Volume two of the publication gives statistics on the leading causes of death in the state. Totals and rates are given at the state and county levels for specific causes of death. The introduction to the 2000 edition of volume two explains that several statistics are being reported in a new way due to their usage of the tenth revision of *International Classification of Diseases*. Both volumes of this publication, in addition to other statistical resources, can be accessed from http://www.schs.state.nc.us/SCHS/healthstats/index.html. Those with questions, or who would like to enquire about the availability of print copies, can write to State Center for Health Statistics, 1908 Mail Service Center, Raleigh, NC 27699-1908, or call (919) 733-4728. Questions can also be e-mailed to SCHS.Info@ncmail.net.

Statistical Abstract of Higher Education in North Carolina (University of North Carolina General Administration, Program Assessment and Public Service Division)—This report provides statistics for colleges and universities in North Carolina on topics such as enrollment, faculty, degrees conferred, library resources, admissions, and housing. A map of post-secondary institutions in the state is also provided. Parts of the most recent report are available online at http://www.ga.unc.edu/publications/abstract/. Several previous editions are available at http://www.ga.unc.edu/publications/abstract/supp.html. Those who would like to enquire about the availability of a print copy can e-mail the Program Assessment and Public Service Division at ProgAssess@ga.unc.edu, or call (919) 962-4549.

Other Resources

North Carolina Manual (Secretary of State)—NC Docs. Call Number—X1 3: year/year. The description of this book in the secretary of state's online catalog at http://www.secretary.state.nc.us/pubsweb/catalog/catalog2.htm says, "This 1,200 page book may tell you everything you need to know about state government in North Carolina . . . and more!" This manual has been published, with minor variations in title and issuing agency, since 1874. An online order form accessible from the web address above can be used to order a copy. The form must be printed and mailed along with a check or money order to the Department of the Secretary of State, Publications Division, P.O. Box 29622, Raleigh, NC 27626-0622. The price for a 1999–2000 edition mailed outside the state of North Carolina was $20.37.

North Carolina Transportation Map (Department of Transportation)—NC Docs. Call Number—K1 11:year. The map shows state highways and provides safety information. A free copy can be requested by calling (877) DOT-4YOU or (919) 733-3109. More information can be found on the department's publications web page at http://www.ncdot.org/public/publications.

Popular Government (University of North Carolina at Chapel Hill, Institute of Government)—NC Docs. Call Number—G41 7:volume#/issue#. This magazine, published quarterly by the Institute of Government, includes articles of interest both to persons working in government and to citizens concerned about public policy. Topics covered include taxation and budgeting, personnel management, education, criminal justice, environmental issues, and social services. Articles from several issues and a cumulative index covering issues back to summer 1990 are available online. From the Institute of Government's "Publications" site at https://iogpubs.iog.unc.edu/. Select "Periodicals and Bulletins," then select *Popular Government*. Individual issues are sold for $7.00, plus tax. A one-year subscription for North Carolina residents is $20.00, plus tax. The *Popular Government* page includes a link to an order form and additional ordering information. Those with questions can write to Publications Office, Institute of Government, CB #3330, Knapp Building, UNC-CH, Chapel Hill, NC 27599-3330, or call (919) 966-4119. Questions can be e-mailed to sales@iogmail.iog.unc.edu.

NORTH CAROLINA'S WORLD WIDE WEB HOME PAGE

The address of the *NC @ Your Service* web portal is http://www.ncgov.com/. The home page of the site offers sections of information tailored for citizens, businesses, and state employees. The page can be personalized through the "My NC" link. A link is provided to "NC Stores" which offers centralized access to state agency sites that sell books, apparel, and other products.

Other options on the home page lead to information on local government, government officials, state agencies, a calendar of events, and a kids' page. Weather information and links to newspapers and other media in the state are also provided. At the bottom of the page the State Library provides an interesting fact about the state in a section headed "Did you Know . . ." A search box on the upper left corner of the page provides answers to frequently asked questions and a link to an advanced search page. A site map is available.

COMMERCIAL PUBLICATIONS AND WEB SITES

General Statutes of North Carolina (LexisNexis/Michie Co., Charlottesville, VA)—This official version of North Carolina's laws is a 21-volume set. The 2001 softbound edition sold for $600.00. Additional information can be found on the LexisNexis Bookstore site at http://bookstore.lexis.com. Questions can be e-mailed to bookstore.support@lexisnexis.com. Those who wish to order a copy can call (800) 223-1940.

North Carolina Manufacturer's Directory (Harris InfoSource, 2057 E. Aurora Road, Twinsburg, OH 44087-1999)—This directory lists manufacturing firms located in North Carolina. Access is given by SIC code, geography, product category, and company name. The price for the 2003 edition, in print or on CD-ROM, was $139.00. Additional information can be found on the Harris InfoSource web site at http://www.harrisinfo.com. Those with questions can call (800) 888-5900.

Official North Carolina Administrative Code (West Group, 610 Opperman Drive, Eagan, MN 55123)—Rules that have been approved and adopted by North Carolina's regulatory agencies and licensing boards are compiled and indexed in this multivolume set. Pricing and ordering information can be found on West Group's web site at http://west.thomson.com/, or by calling (800) 328-4880. Questions can also be e-mailed to bookstore@westgroup.com.

SOURCES CONSULTED

Correspondence with Jan Reagan, Head of the Documents Branch, State Library of North Carolina, August 2002.

North Carolina General Statutes via the General Assembly web site, http://www.ncga.state.nc.us/Statutes/Statutes.html.

Numerous departmental web sites via *NC @ Your Service*, http://www.ncgov.com/.

North Dakota

Daniel D. Cornwall

GOVERNMENT PUBLISHING AND THE DEPOSITORY SYSTEM

The North Dakota depository system was established in 1965 by *North Dakota Century Code* 54-24-09. Today, seven libraries in North Dakota serve as depositories for North Dakota documents. Depository libraries are required to retain all documents for at least five years.

State agencies provide eight copies of each publication to State Documents Services at the North Dakota State Library. The state depository administrator catalogs and distributes the documents to the depository libraries. North Dakota catalogs its state documents according to the Library of Congress classification system.

The state depository law requires deposit of "all publications issued by all executive, legislative, and judicial agencies of state government intended for general public distribution." The law defines state publications as "any informational materials regardless of format, method of reproduction, or source, originating in or produced with the imprint of, by the authority of, or at the total or partial expense of, any state agency." Reports by private bodies under contract to state agencies are also included in the definition of state publication provided by *North Dakota Century Code* 54-24-09. Administrative material and training materials used only within the issuing agency are exempted from the program.

USEFUL ADDRESSES AND TELEPHONE NUMBERS

The most complete collection of North Dakota state publications may be found at the following library:

North Dakota State Library
State Documents Services
604 E. Boulevard Avenue, Dept. 250

Bismarck, ND 58505-0800
Phone Number for North Dakota Reference Questions: (701) 328-4622
E-Mail Address for State Reference Questions: None available
Library's Home Page: http://ndsl.lib.state.nd.us
Library's State Government Page: http://ndsl.lib.state.nd.us/StateGovernment.html

INDEXES TO NORTH DAKOTA STATE PUBLICATIONS

The main index to North Dakota state publications is called *Publications of North Dakota State Departments*, which has been issued by the North Dakota State Library since 1977. This publication is available on the Internet at http://ndsl.lib.state.nd.us/StateGovernment.html, and print copies may be requested by mail from the address for the North Dakota State Library listed above. All North Dakota state documents can be located through ODIN, the North Dakota State Library's online catalog, which can be accessed from a link on the library's home page at http://ndsl.lib.state.nd.us.

ESSENTIAL STATE PUBLICATIONS

Directories

Directory of Elected Officials (Secretary of State)—This web site, located at http://www.state.nd.us/sec/directoryofelectedofficials.htm, provides contact information for State Officials, Congressional Delegation, and the Legislative Assembly. The State Officials section contains addresses, phone numbers, and fax numbers for the Governor, Lieutenant Governor, Secretary of State, State Auditor, State Treasurer, Attorney General, Commissioner of Insurance, Commissioner of Agriculture, Tax Commissioner, Superintendent of Public Instruction, the Public Service Commissioners, and the Justices of the Supreme Court. The section on the Legislative Assembly includes election district maps.

North Dakota Library Directory (North Dakota State Library)—This Internet-only directory, available at http://ndsl.lib.state.nd.us/LibraryDirectory.html, provides contact information for public and school libraries in North Dakota. Arranged by city, each entry contains the names, addresses, and phone numbers of key staff of each library. Some entries also include notes.

North Dakota State Government Directory (North Dakota Information Technology Department)—Located at http://lnotes.state.nd.us/public/swdir.nsf, this Internet-only publication provides contact information for all departments, divisions, and employees of North Dakota. The directory has four sections: Agencies by Name, Agencies by City, Employees by Name, and Employees by Agency (see Figure 14.)

Financial/Budgetary Resources

Comprehensive Annual Financial Report (Office of Management and Budget)—In addition to the usual financial information, this report features a state government organizational chart, a list of principal state officials, and a statistical

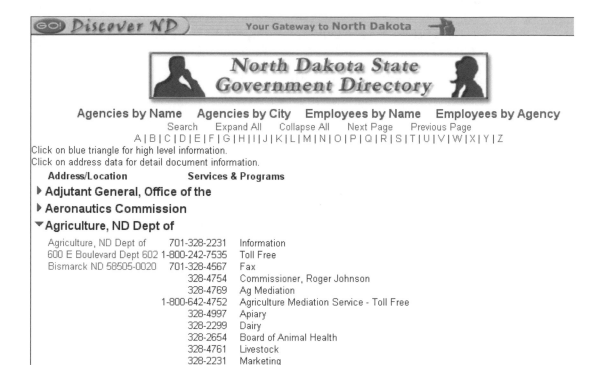

Figure 14. Some web sites, like the *North Dakota State Government Directory*, present information in lists that can be expanded and collapsed. *Source*: http://lnotes.state.nd.us/public/swdir.nsf.

section. The statistical section has tables listing population and employment, demographic statistics, public school enrollment and average cost per pupil, and other selected topics for the prior ten years. To obtain an official, printed copy of this report, or if you have questions about the content of the statements or the notes, please call the CAFR Project Coordinator at (701) 328-1666. Recent editions of the *Comprehensive Annual Financial Report* may be found on the Internet at http://www.state.nd.us/fiscal/pubindex.html.

Legislative Appropriations for the [Years] Biennium (Office of Management and Budget)—Published by the secretary of state, this document is the latest approved budget for the state of North Dakota. It is available on the web at http://www.state.nd.us/fiscal/pubindex.html.

Legal Resources

Attorney General Opinions (Office of the Attorney General)—Opinions going back to 1993 can be found on the Internet at http://www.ag.state.nd.us/

opinions/Opinions.htm. The North Dakota attorney general issues two classes of opinions—opinions requested by state officials and "open meetings" opinions, which can be requested by private citizens.

North Dakota Administrative Code (Secretary of State)—Published since 1978, the *Administrative Code* is the codification of all rules of state administrative agencies, as that term is defined by *North Dakota Century Code* Section 28-32-02. Many state agencies are not administrative agencies as defined by Section 28-32-02. The *Administrative Code* can be found on the Internet at http://www.state.nd.us/lr/information/rules/admincode.html.

North Dakota Century Code (Legislative Council)—The entire 65-title *North Dakota Century Code* is available on the Internet at http://www.state.nd.us/lr/information/statutes/cent-code.html. The numbering system for the *Century Code* is a three-part number, with each part separated by a hyphen. The first part refers to the title, the second to the chapter, and the third to the section. For example, Section 54-24-09 refers to the ninth section in Chapter 24 of Title 54. The official version of the *Century Code* is published by LexisNexis. The 23-volume set may be purchased for $650.00 at http://bookstore.lexis.com/bookstore/catalog.

Statistical Resources

North Dakota Agricultural Statistics (North Dakota State University)—This annual, 150-plus-page report is divided into seven sections: Introduction, Weather, Crops, Livestock, Economics, County Highlights, and Products and Services. Some of the information one can find in this publication includes: the number and size of North Dakota farms, the length of the growing season, North Dakota grain storage capacity, milk production, and farm assets and debts. The Products and Services section includes contact information for the North Dakota statistical field offices and information on finding historic estimates of farm statistics. The publication is available on the Internet at http://www.nass.usda.gov/nd/abindex.htm, or may be ordered in paper by sending payment (in 2002, $8.00) to North Dakota Agricultural Statistics Service, P.O. Box 3166, Fargo, ND 58108-3166. Make your check payable to: Agriculture Communication. For current prices, see the online order form at http://www.nass.usda.gov/nd/subscrib.htm.

North Dakota's Economic RoadMap (Job Service North Dakota)—The *RoadMap* is a review of many economic measures, including wages, employment, personal income, location quotient, population, and unemployment insurance claims. The measures are often compared to other areas of the nation. The information is reported on a statewide level, as well as for North Dakota's eight planning regions, fifty-three counties, and three metropolitan statistical areas (MSA). To order paper copies, call the Labor Market Information Center at Job Service North Dakota toll-free at (800) 732-9787 (TTY (800) 366-6888). The *RoadMap* is also available on the Internet at http://www.state.nd.us/jsnd/publications.htm?database=main.

Statistical Abstract of North Dakota (North Dakota State Library)—Funded by the North Dakota State Library, the North Dakota Librarians Association, the University of North Dakota College of Business and Public Administration, and the University of North Dakota Bureau of Economic and Business Research, the *Statistical Abstract of North Dakota* is available on the Internet at http://ndsl.lib.state.nd.us/Abstract.html. This annual publication is divided into chapters on: Population, Health and Vital Statistics, Climate, Income and Wealth, Labor Force, Employment and Earnings, Transportation, Agriculture, Energy and Related Mineral Activities, Construction and Housing, Banking, Finance, Manufacturing, Government Finances, Social Insurance and Welfare Services, Education, Government and Elections, Law Enforcement, Courts, and Prisons. Maps of North Dakota counties and planning regions are also included in this publication.

Other Resources

Face of North Dakota (North Dakota Geological Survey)—According to the Introduction, this volume is "not written as or intended to be a technical geologic report . . . rather, a generalized discussion of North Dakota's geology, meant to heighten people's awareness of our natural environment and surroundings and help them better understand the changes in rocks and landforms that can be seen across the state." This 200-plus-page report can be ordered online at http://www.state.nd.us/ndgs/Publication_List/geninfo_h .htm.

Governing North Dakota (University of North Dakota)—This is an explanatory text covering the North Dakota legislature, executive branch, judiciary, elections, and local governments including counties, cities, schools, townships, and other special districts. This publication may be ordered by contacting the North Dakota State Library at the address above.

North Dakota Blue Book (Secretary of State)—This biennial publication varies in format from edition to edition, but all include basic information on all three branches of North Dakota government, history, and economics. In 2002, the *Blue Book* cost $15.00 and could be ordered by contacting the Blue Book Order Department, North Dakota Heritage Center Museum Store, State Historical Society of North Dakota, 612 East Boulevard Avenue, Bismarck, ND 58505-0830, or by telephone at (701) 328-2666. Editions of the *Blue Book* back to 1995 can be found on the Internet at http://www.state.nd.us/sec/BlueBook/default.htm.

NORTH DAKOTA'S WORLD WIDE WEB HOME PAGE

Discover North Dakota—This is the state's web home page and can be found at http://discovernd.com/. Most of the front page is taken up with featured sites and highlighted services. The rest of *Discover North Dakota* is divided into ten sections: About, Business, Education, Employment, Government, e-Government, Health and Safety, Law, Living, and Visiting. The "About" menu contains links to state facts and symbols, as well as to sales of items sold by state agencies. The "Business" menu contains information on starting a business or nonprofit organization in North Dakota, as well as licensing information and specific information on agriculture. The "Education" menu provides links to schools, universities, and educational resources. The "Employment" menu provides links to employment posters, job listings, and professional licensing information. The "Government" menu includes links to federal, state, and local government web sites as well as listings of meetings and other governmental events. The "e-Government" menu is a listing of all available transactional state government services available on the Internet. Go here to buy maps, fishing licenses, or renew your vehicle registration. The "Health and Safety" menu includes information on accident statistics, long-term health care, hazardous waste materials, and more. The "Law" menu provides links to legal-related agencies in North Dakota. The "Living" menu includes information on housing, adoption, weather, and other information of interest to North Dakotans. The "Visiting" menu offers tourists a chance to order the official North Dakota vacation planner by writing North Dakota Tourism, 400 E. Broadway, Suite 50, Bismarck, ND 58501, or by calling (800) HELLO ND. Users can also find links to photographs, cultural events, and road and weather conditions. The *Discover North Dakota* web site is searchable by keyword, with an option to exclude legislative information from your search.

A helpful feature of *Discover North Dakota* is its Help and FAQ page. Selecting this link from the main page gives you links to: Index, Frequently Asked Questions, Search, and Contact Us. The "Index" is a list of subjects along with the responsible agency. Some of the direct links available through the index are: Abandoned Coal Mines, Child Support Resources, and a list of wanted offenders. Try using the index before the less useful Search function. The "FAQ" section provides popular links to regulations, public records, business, vacations, and education. This page can show you your tenant rights and how to properly display the state flag.

COMMERCIAL PUBLICATIONS AND WEB SITES

North Dakota Manufacturers Register (Manufacturers' News, Inc., Evanston, IL)—Published each June, this annual publication is divided into six sections: Buyers' Guide, Alphabetical by Company Name, Geographical by City, Standard Industrial Classification (SIC) code, Parent Company Alphabetical Listing, and County Marketing Breakdown Section. Each entry includes mailing and physical address, phone, fax, and toll-free numbers, e-mail and web addresses, annual sales, plant square footage, number of employees, distribution area, parent company information, and ISO certifications. More information is available for some entries. The *Register* can be ordered from the publisher's web site at http://mnistore.com/.

North Dakota Business Directory (American Business Directories, Omaha, NE)—This is an annual listing of North Dakota businesses by city and yellow page category, with a separate listing of major employers and of manufacturers by city and product. This volume can be ordered from the publisher's web site at http://www.directoriesusa.com/ or through major online booksellers such as Amazon.com.

SOURCES CONSULTED

North Dakota Century Code 54-24-09.
Numerous departmental pages from the state's home page, http://discovernd.com.
Survey response from Naomi Frantes, North Dakota State Library, 2000.

Ohio

J. Louise Malcomb

GOVERNMENT PUBLISHING AND THE DEPOSITORY SYSTEM

The Ohio State Library, the first library in the Northwest Territory, was established in 1817. It served as a depository for state records, maps, and laws and was open to state officials and members of the legislature. The State Library of Ohio collection of publications dates from the 1700s to the present. Older publications may not appear in the online catalog, but can be located by using appropriate indexes. The State Library Catalog is open to all users.

A government document is loosely defined as a

report, pamphlet, document, or other publication intended for general public use and distribution, which publication is reproduced by duplicating processes such as mimeograph, multigraph, planograph, rotaprint, or multilith, or printed internally or through a contract awarded to any person, company, or the state printing division of the department of administrative services.

The State Librarian is to "maintain a comprehensive collection of official documents and publications of this state and a library collection and reference service to meet the reference and information needs of officers, departments, agencies of state government, and other libraries." Conspicuously, Ohio residents are not specifically mentioned.

Distribution of Ohio government documents is included within *Ohio Revised Code Chapter 149: Documents, Reports, and Records*. A record is defined as "any document, device, or item, regardless of physical form or characteristic, created or received by or coming under the jurisdiction of any public office of the state or its political subdivisions, which serves to document the organization, functions, policies, decisions, procedures, operations, or other activities of the office."

Ohio Revised Code § 149.09 Distribution of pamphlet laws and ORC § 149.11 *Distribution of publications intended for general public use; schedules of record re-*

tention or destruction are mentioned as particularly relevant. A revision of the latter intending to update distribution and account for changing technologies is under consideration. The proposed revision and administrative code is available at http://winslo.state.oh.us/govinfo/149intro.html. Distribution and printing of other bills, acts, and typical legislative records are covered under other sections of *ORC § 149*.

The *Code* stipulates: "Each library receiving publications under this section or under section 149.09 of the Revised Code shall make these publications accessible to the public." Libraries must apply to the State Librarian to start or end state depository status. Ohio State Depository Libraries must accept all state publications. They cannot choose subjects. They may follow the federal guidelines for disposal of depository material, although no official guidelines exist for state disposal. The current policy of the Ohio State Library is to not discard any Ohio publications, although the State Librarian has the power to do so. Typically, 100 copies of specified state legislative documents go to the State Library of Ohio for distribution free of charge to other Ohio depository libraries.

The State Library of Ohio must retain two copies of all state publications,

send two copies to the document division of the library of congress; and send one copy to the Ohio historical society and to each public or college library in the state designated by the state library board to be a depository for state publications. In designating which libraries shall be depositories, the board shall select those libraries which can best preserve such publications and which are so located geographically as will make the publications conveniently accessible to residents in all areas of the state.

Ohio Depository Libraries for State Publications are listed by city at http://winslo.state.oh.us/govinfo/govt_a-b.html.

The Ohio Historical Society Archives/Library is the official archive for the state of Ohio (http://www.ohiohistory.org/resource/statearc/index.html). It collects and preserves documents pertaining to the operation of state and local governments. The Historical Society is a member of the State Depository Program. The Ohio Electronic Records Committee formulates policy of digital archives. Records scheduled for removal from the archive and the state guidelines for such are listed at http://www.ohiohistory.org/resource/statearc/.

USEFUL ADDRESSES AND TELEPHONE NUMBERS

The State Library manages and distributes information to other state depository libraries. Other branches of the State Library exist but are limited to government employees or regional member access. All state depository libraries receive all information. No listing was discovered that declared which depository libraries are the biggest. Currently, 105 libraries receive legislative publications.

State Library of Ohio Main Library
274 East First Avenue
Columbus, OH 43201

Phone Number for Ohio Reference Questions: (614) 644-7004
E-Mail Address for Ohio Reference Questions: refhelp@sloma.state.oh.us
State Library's Home Page: http://winslo.state.oh.us/index.html
Government Information Services Page: http://winslo.state.oh.us/govinfo/slogovt
  .html

Ohio Historical Society Archives/Library
1982 Velma Avenue
Columbus, OH 43211
Phone Number for Ohio Reference Questions: (614) 297-2510
Library's Home Page: http://www.ohiohistory.org/resource/archlib/

Those with questions about the Ohio State Depository Program may contact
Government Information Department of the State Library of Ohio at (614) 644-
7051, or e-mail govinfo@sloma.state.oh.us.

INDEXES TO OHIO STATE PUBLICATIONS

Ohio Documents: A List of Publications of State Departments (State Library of
Ohio)—This was first published in 1971, and lists all publications issued by
the state of Ohio received by the Ohio State Library. The *Ohio Documents List
Online* (http://winslo.state.oh.us/govinfo/govstdocs.html) covers documents
since 1997. Items are marked as depository items (*), available while supplies
last (+), and no extra copies (−). Periodicals are included only in the annual
cumulation. Items coded with a (+) are available to the public free of charge
with a written request to the Government Information Services clerk at the
State Library of Ohio. The *Manual of the State Library of Ohio* implies that there
is no all-inclusive bibliography of government publications. They learn of
missing items through the media, requests from patrons, and claims from
other depository libraries. Abstracts of some of the reports are available online
through *Ohioline* (http://ohioline.osu.edu) or as URLs in the *Ohio Documents
List Online*.
   Earlier titles vary. *The Union Bibliography of Ohio Printed State Documents,
1803–1970* (Ohio Historical Society) is used by State Library employees to find
older publications not indexed in its catalog. The *Checklist of Ohio Public Documents* (Ohio Secretary of State) was published from 1933 to 1937. The State
Library of Ohio published several variations of the *Ohio Documents* in the past.
Checklist of Publications of the State of Ohio covered 1803 to 1952. *Selected Publications of the State of Ohio, 1945–1970* includes documents issued by state agencies. *Ohio State Publications: Annual List of Periodicals, 1945–1967* lists selected
state periodicals. *Documents Concerning Ohio Governors at the State Library of
Ohio* may also help identify state publications. The Historical Records Survey
(U.S.) issued two publications that record historical documents: *Ohio Imprints,
1796–1805* and *Check List of Ohio Imprints, 1796–1820*. Additionally, Bowker's
*State Publications: A Provisional List of the Official Publications of the Several States
of the United States from their Organization* can be consulted for historical publications, pages 200–217.
   Ohio Documents Classification Scheme (State Library of Ohio)—This outlines

the cataloging rules of Ohio state publications. It was written in 1962 and last revised in 1997. It explains the assignment and interpretation of the Ohio call number system.

ESSENTIAL STATE PUBLICATIONS

Directories

Ohio Depository Libraries for State Publications (State Library of Ohio)—This link (http://winslo.state.oh.us/govinfo/govt_a-b.html) from the State Library web site lists libraries entitled to state information. It does not include any law libraries or libraries in other states that participate in the program.

Appendix C: Directory of Legislative Information from *A Guidebook for Ohio Legislators* (Ohio General Assembly, Legislative Service Commission)—Available online at http://www.lsc.state.oh.us/guidebook/index.html, this source provides addresses, telephone numbers, or online access points for legislative information of Ohio legislators. It includes a bibliography of books and other media resources and a *Directory of Media at the State House.*

The 124th Ohio General Assembly (General Assembly)—This allows searching for state legislators by name, district, or zip code. *Search for Legislative Information* also allows searching for Legislative Agents and Executive Agency Lobbyists registered in Ohio, and their employers. See http://www.legislature.state.oh.us/.

Ohio Government Agencies by Name—Part of the official state web site, this page lists state agencies by name only; it does not name the departments or other agencies subsumed within these agencies. See http://www.state.oh.us/ohio/agency.htm.

Official Roster of Federal, State and County Officers (Ohio Secretary of State)—The next edition will be available in the fall, and may be ordered from the Secretary of State, Publications, 180 E. Broad Street, 15th Floor, Columbus, OH 43215, or call (614) 466-3613; e-mail prequest@sos.state.oh.us.

Ohio Educational Directory (Ohio Department of Education)—Users can search for categories of educational centers or for specific institutions or districts at http://www.ode.state.oh.us/data/OEDdistbuild.asp. This provides an Excel file to print address labels for Superintendents, Treasurers, or Principals. Also available in print.

The Ohio Municipal, Township and School Board Roster (Ohio Secretary of State)—This directory of municipal and township officers and members of boards of education, as well as municipal judges and clerks, is available to download from http://www.state.oh.us/sos/pubAffairs. Print copies can be requested by writing to Ohio Secretary of State, Publications, 180 E. Broad Street, 15th Floor, Columbus, OH 43215, or calling (614) 466-3613; or e-mailing prequest@sos.state.oh.us.

Financial/Budgetary Resources

Comprehensive Annual Financial Report for the Fiscal Year (Ohio Office of Budget and Management, State Accounting Division, Financial)—This basically gives an overview of the state's financial situation including data on budgeted versus actual revenues and expenditures, financial trends, and general state economic and social indicators. Print copies, if still available, may be requested from the Office of Budget and Management, State Accounting Division, Financial Reporting Section, 30 E. Broad Street, 34th Floor, Columbus, OH 43266-0411. It is also available via the web site at http://www.state .oh.us/obm/.

The State of Ohio Budget (Legislative Service Commission)—This includes the Budget in Brief and in Detail, the "Compare Document," and the Redbooks of the Senate and some departments. See http://www.lbo.state.oh.us/ 123ga/ohiobudget/. The Office of Budget and Management provides access to the past and current annual budget reports at http://www.state.oh.us/ obm/Information/budget/OperBudgetinfo.asp.

The Legislative Service Commission Ohio Budget (Legislative Service Commission) (http://www.lbo.state.oh.us/123ga/ohiobudget/)—This includes under "Operating Budget; Analysis Documents" a search engine that provides Final Analysis, Redbook Analysis, Compare Document, Appropriation Spreadsheets, and the Catalog of Budget Line Item (COBLI) for the selected agency. It also provides estimates of economic growth, revenues, and public assistance expenditures. The Operating Budget, State Revenue, and Expenditure History are found here.

Legal Resources

Ohio Constitution (General Assembly)—It was first adopted in 1802. Ohio's second Constitution of 1851 with amendments is in use today. The General Assembly displays an online version current through November 2000, at http://www.legislature.state.oh.us/constitution.cfm.

Anderson's Ohio Online Docs (Anderson Publishing)—This web site, at http://onlinedocs.andersonpublishing.com/, provides access to several publications. *The Ohio Revised Code* online contains the codified sections of acts signed by the governor. It also includes the current text of the Constitution. *The Ohio Administrative Code* displays the full text of administrative rules once they are adopted.

The Register of Ohio (Legislative Service Commission) (http://www.reg isterofohio.state.oh.us/)—This site provides public notice and information about state agency rule-making proceedings. It is not available in print.

Senate Journals and *House Journals*—These are the only publications setting forth amendments as introduced and voted upon the floor. The *Journals* can be picked up at the LSC Document Distribution Room on the ground level of the State House. Contact the Legislative Service Commission at (614) 466-9745 for more information.

Ohio's Laws, Rules and Constitution (General Assembly and Department of Administrative Services) (http://www.state.oh.us/ohio/ohiolaws.htm)—This site includes the Constitution, the Laws, the *Ohio Revised Code* (ORC), the *Administrative Code*, and the Department of Administrative Services Directives. The ORC and the *Administrative Code* are provided by Anderson Publishing, a commercial vendor. Laws are covered here only through the 123rd General Assembly.

The General Assembly web site (http://www.legislature.state.oh.us/)—This site provides information through *Laws, Acts and Legislation*. This page, entitled *Ohio Legislation and Documents*, includes the official versions of Bill Analyses and the Status Report of Legislation (SRL), as well as the publications mentioned in the previous paragraph. Applied Virtual Vision (AVV) is an Internet development company that provides the Ohio Session Laws (http://Ohio Acts.avv.com/). The Ohio government pays for this service. Ohio Session Laws provide access to acts of the General Assembly before they have been incorporated into the *Ohio Revised Code*.

Ohio Legislative Service Commission (http://www.lsc.state.oh.us/)—The *Ohio Legislative Service Commission* (LSC) was created by statute in 1953 to provide technical and research services to members of the Ohio General Assembly. The site includes search capabilities for bills, session law, legislators, school funding, the *Ohio Revised Code*, the *Ohio Administrative Code*, the Ohio Constitution, Lobbyists, Legislative Office of Education Oversight (LOEO) Publications, and Joint Committee on Agency Rule Review (JCARR) Weekly Reports information. LSC publications are available at http://www.lsc.state.oh.us/publications.html and include *Legislative Information Sources Available to the Public* and *A Guidebook for Ohio Legislators* (http://www.lsc.state.oh.us/guidebook/index.html). Both are useful references for those interested in the legislative process. The guidebook is also available in print. *Navigating a Bill in Ten Easy Steps* (http://www.lsc.state.oh.us/navigatebill.html) provides an explanation of how to read a bill and what different abbreviations mean.

The Ohio Supreme Court Web Site (http://www.legislature.state.oh.us/judicial.cfm)—This site provides access to some online publications, such as the *Report of the Ohio Commission on Racial Fairness 1999* and *Family Law Reform: Minimizing Conflict, Maximizing Families 2001* as Adobe Acrobat files.

Statistical Resources

Statistical Abstract of Ohio (Ohio Department of Development, Office of Strategic Research) (http://www.odod.state.oh.us/research/)—Issued from 1969 until the mid-1990s, the *Statistical Abstract of Ohio* gave an overview of the state's demographic and socioeconomic status. Similar data are now updated continuously on the web site. The department's current *Product List* is available from the web site.

Report on Vital Statistics (Ohio Department of Health, Center for Vital and Health Statistics)—Statistics related to Ohio's births, deaths, marriages, and divorces are available on the *Data Warehouse* web site at http://dwhouse.odh.ohio.gov/. The primary focus is on Ohio resident live birth and death data as compiled from information collected by the Ohio Department of Health, Office of Vital Statistics. For print copies, contact the Ohio Department of Health, Center for Vital and Health Statistics, at (614) 728-2702.

Ohio County Profiles (Ohio Department of Development)—Demographic and socioeconomic statistics are given for Ohio and its counties in this biennial publication. Data are primarily from state and federal sources. It is available free on the Internet and in print or CD-ROM for $ 75.00 from Ohio Department of Development, Office of Strategic Research, P.O. Box 1001, Columbus, OH 43216-1001. See the department's web site at http://www.odod.state.oh.us/ for other publications.

Annual Report of the State Board of Education (Ohio Department of Education)—This annual provides an overview of public elementary/secondary education in Ohio, with statistics on finances, enrollment, and facilities, among others. Many of the statistics are available on the department's web site at http://www.ode.state.oh.us. Print copies of this report and others may be requested from the department. See the ODE Bookstore site at http://webapp1 .ode.state.oh.us/ed/pubs.asp, or call (614) 728-3471.

Ohio Traffic Crash Facts (Ohio Department of Public Safety)—Issued annually, this report gives statistics on fatalities, injuries, and property damage caused by traffic accidents in Ohio. It gives trends and data reporting accidents involving alcohol, insurance, child restraints, and motorcycle helmets. The report is available on the Internet (http://www.state.oh.us/odps/crash_re ports.htm) and in print, while supplies last, from Ohio Department of Public Safety, 1970 West Broad Street, Columbus, OH 43218-2081, or call (614) 466-2550.

Ohio Election Statistics (Ohio Office of the Secretary of State)—The Ohio Elections Commission provides past and current election data including voter turnout and some trends dating to 1803. Available on the Internet at http:// www.state.oh.us/sos/election_services.htm, the report, while available in print, may be requested from the Ohio Office of the Secretary of State, Elections Section, 180 E. Broad Street, 15th Floor, Columbus, OH 43215, or call (614) 466-2585; e-mail prequest@sos.state.oh.us.

Ohio Labor Market Review (Ohio Department of Job and Family Services, Labor Market Information Bureau)—This is a monthly report on Ohio employment, unemployment, hours, and earnings by industry and MSA. It is available on the web at http://lmi.state.oh.us/ces/lmr.htm. It is normally posted during the last week of the month following the month being reported. Those with questions can contact the Ohio Department of Job and Family Services, Labor Market Information Bureau, Labor Market Analysts, 4300 Kimberly Parkway, Columbus, OH 43232, or call (614) 466-1109.

Ohio Department of Agriculture Annual Report and Statistics (Ohio Department of Agriculture)—This is available for $5.00 from the National Agricultural Statistics Service, Room 5829, South Building, U.S. Department of Agriculture, Washington, DC 20250. It is available online at http://www.state.oh.us/agr/ Annual%20Report/ar-statsindex.htm.

Other Resources

The Fundamental Documents of Ohio (Ohio Historical Society Archives/ Library) (http://www.ohiohistory.org/resource/database/funddocs.html)— This site contains links and citations for many government documents from the 1700s and 1800s. For more information, contact the Historical Society at (614) 297-2300.

The Guide to Organizing a Business in Ohio (Secretary of State)—This guide offers advice on setting up a business in the state. It is based on the statutory provisions of the *Ohio Revised Code* in effect at the time of publication. The latest edition is at http://www.state.oh.us/sos/Gd%20to%20Org%20 Business.htm.

OHIO'S WORLD WIDE WEB HOME PAGE

The State of Ohio web site (http://www.state.oh.us/) features a nice search engine of the entire Ohio portal. Many of the sources mentioned in this chapter are available through this portal.

COMMERCIAL PUBLICATIONS AND WEB SITES

Anderson Publishing provides officially approved versions of Ohio legislative materials both in print and online. *Anderson's Ohio Online* (http://onlinedocs.andersonpublishing.com/) provides access to the *Administrative Code*, Ohio Constitution, *Revised Code*, Court Rules, and Session Law.

The West Group offers approved Ohio legislative information. The *Ohio Administrative Code* and *West's Ohio Digest* are two of their products. For more information on these titles, see the publisher's web site at http://west .thomson.com/, or call (800) 328-4880.

SOURCES CONSULTED

Anderson's Ohio Online. Anderson Publishing, http://onlinedocs.andersonpublishing .com/.

Dow, Susan L. *State Document Checklists: A Historical Bibliography*. Buffalo, NY: William S. Hein & Co., 1990.

Hall, Audrey. *Manual*. Columbus: State Library of Ohio, Government Information Services.

Lane, Margaret T. *State Publications and Depository Libraries: A Reference Handbook*. Westport, CT: Greenwood Press, 1981, 553–554.

Manz, William H. *Guide to State Legislative and Administrative Materials*. 2000 ed. Littleton, CO: Fred B. Rothman Publications, 2000.

The Ohio General Assembly Web Site, http://www.legislature.state.oh.us/.

OhioDocuments List. State Library of Ohio, 2000; http://winslo.state.oh.us/govinfo/ govstdocs.html, December 6, 2001.

Parrish, David W. *State Government Reference Publications: An Annotated Bibliography*, 2nd ed. Littleton, CO: Libraries Unlimited, 1981.

State Capital Universe. Bethesda, MD: LexisNexis, 2001; http://web.lexis-nexis.com/ stcapuniv, December 5, 2001. (Available to subscribers only.)

State Library of Ohio, http://winslo.state.oh.us/.index.html.

The State of Ohio Web Site, http://www.state.oh.us/.

Statistical Universe. Bethesda, MD: LexisNexis, 2001; http://web.lexis-nexis.com/ statuniv, December 5, 2001. (Available to subscribers only.)

U.S. Census Bureau. *Statistical Abstract, 2000 Edition*. "Appendix 1: Guide to State Statistical Abstracts." December 4, 2001; http://www.census.gov.

WorldCat. Columbus, OH: OCLC; http://www.oclc.com, October 4, 2001. (Available to subscribers only.)

Oklahoma

Daniel C. Barkley

GOVERNMENT PUBLISHING AND THE DEPOSITORY SYSTEM

The Oklahoma state depository system was established in 1978 by 65 OS 1991 Section 3-113-115 (see the *Oklahoma Statutes* at http://www.lsb.state.ok.us/tsrs/os_oc.htm). Currently, eighteen libraries participate in the program (see http://www.odl.state.ok.us/sginfo/depsys.htm for a list of participating libraries). 65 OS 1991, Section 3-113.1 established the Publications Clearinghouse, a unit of the Oklahoma Department of Libraries (ODL). The director of the ODL has statutory authority to adopt rules and regulations as necessary to perform the functions and duties of the clearinghouse.

Every agency (with the exception of higher education institutions) that issues publications is required to deposit a maximum of twenty-five copies with the clearinghouse. A state agency is defined as "any office, officer, department, division, unit, board, commission, authority, institution, substate planning district, or agency in any branch of the state government" (65 OS 1991 Section 3-113.2). A publication is defined as

any informational materials, regardless of format, method of reproduction, or source, which originate in or are produced with the imprint, by the authority, or at the total or partial expense of an agency supported wholly or in part by state funds and which are distributed to persons outside of the creating agency or are required by law. (65 OS 1991 Section 3-113.2)

USEFUL ADDRESSES AND TELEPHONE NUMBERS

The best collections of Oklahoma state publications can be located at the following libraries:

Northwestern Oklahoma State University
J. W. Martin Library

Government Documents Department
709 Oklahoma Boulevard
Alva, OK 73717
Phone Number for Oklahoma Reference Questions: (405) 327-8572
E-Mail for Oklahoma Reference Questions: vpgraybill@nwosu.edu
Martin Library Government Documents Department Home Page: http://www
    .nwalva.edu/library/GovDoc/index.html

Oklahoma Publications Clearinghouse
Oklahoma Department of Libraries
200 NE 18th Street
Oklahoma City, OK 73105-3298
Phone Number for Oklahoma Reference Questions: (405) 522-3505 or (800) 522-8116
Oklahoma Department Libraries Reference Desk Home Page: http://www.odl.state
    .ok.us/genref/index.htm
Oklahoma Publications Clearinghouse Page: http://www.odl.state.ok.us/sginfo/
    opchist.htm

Oklahoma State University
Edmon Low Library
Documents Department
Stillwater, OK 74078-1071
Phone Number for Oklahoma Reference Questions: (405) 744-6546
E-Mail for Edmon Low Library Reference Questions: lib-doc@okstate.edu
Edmon Low Library Government Documents Department Home Page: http://www
    .library.okstate.edu/govdocs/index.htm

Public Library of Enid and Garfield County
120 West Maine
P.O. Box 8002
Enid, OK 73702-8002
Phone Number for Oklahoma Reference Questions: (580) 234-6313
Public Library Home Page: http://www.enid.org/library.htm

INDEXES TO OKLAHOMA STATE PUBLICATIONS

One of the Publications Clearinghouse's many duties is to publish official lists of state publications and distribute these lists to all Oklahoma state depository libraries, other libraries within the state, and every Oklahoma state agency. To this end, *Oklahoma Government Publications: A Checklist* (see http://www.odl.state.ok.us/ship/shipsearch.asp) fulfills these requirements. The *Checklist* has been issued since 1977. In addition to this checklist the clearinghouse must compile and maintain a permanent record of state publications (65 OS 1991, Section 3-115).

When the clearinghouse receives state agency publications, it catalogs and classifies them and distributes copies to all depository libraries. One copy of each publication received is also sent to the Library of Congress and two copies are retained by the clearinghouse for archival purposes. The classification system utilized is based on issuing state agency.

ESSENTIAL STATE PUBLICATIONS

Directories

ABC: Oklahoma State Agencies, Boards, and Commissions (Oklahoma Department of Libraries)—This provides a complete listing of all Oklahoma state agencies, elected officials, cabinet members, the state legislature, high courts, and institutions. Each listing includes statutory citations, addresses, phone numbers, and sections on the agency's mission statement, history, and function. Published every November by the West Group, the directory is available at no charge at either the Wright or Cartwright libraries (branches of the Oklahoma Department of Libraries). To obtain a copy through the mail send $2.00 to the Oklahoma Department of Libraries, 200 NE 18th Street, Oklahoma City, OK 73105-3298, or call (405) 522-3576. The directory is available online at http://www.odl.state.ok.us/sginfo/abc/index.htm.

Directory of Oklahoma Public Libraries and Systems (Oklahoma Department of Libraries)—This is an online resource that provides access to addresses, phone/fax numbers, and hours of operation for libraries in the Oklahoma Public Library systems. Listings in the directory can be retrieved by city, by county, or by library system. A list of the libraries that have web sites is also available. Developed by the Office of Library Development and the Office of Public Information, Oklahoma Department of Libraries, 200 NE 18th Street, Oklahoma City, OK 73105-3298. Call (405) 522-3217 or fax (405) 525-7804. The directory is available online at http://www.odl.state.ok.us/go/pl.asp.

Resource Directory (Department of Commerce and Oklahoma State University)—This provides contact information for companies and agencies that can assist businesses in various endeavors. Separate sections of this directory give information on: Business Assistance Providers, Public Sector Financing, Regulatory Agencies, Information Sources, and Associations and Membership Groups. The directory is produced jointly by the Office of Business Development at the Department of Commerce and the Cooperative Extension Service's Home-Based and Micro Business Resource Office at Oklahoma State University. Copies can be requested from Oklahoma State University, Cooperative Extension Service, Home-Based and Micro Business Resource Office, 135 HES, Stillwater, OK 74078-6111, or call (405) 744-5776, or fax (405) 744-5506. E-mail enquiries can be sent to muske@okstate.edu. The directory is available on the web at http://fcs.okstate.edu/microbiz/resources.htm.

State of Oklahoma Telephone Directory (Office of State Finance)—This source provides phone numbers and addresses of state agency workers. It is arranged alphabetically by state agency. The directory is maintained by the Office of State Finance, Information Services, 2300 North Lincoln, Room 122, State Capitol Building, Oklahoma City, OK 73105-4801. Call (405) 521-2141. Contact this agency for more information about obtaining a copy of its directory.

Financial/Budgetary Resources

Oklahoma 2001: Comprehensive Annual Financial Report for the Fiscal Year Ended June 30th (Office of State Finance, Division of Central Accounting and Reporting)—This annual publication details the state of financial affairs within Oklahoma. There is an Introductory Section, a Financial Section, and a Statistical Section. The letter of transmittal on page seven of the 2001 edition summarizes the contents as follows:

The Introductory Section contains an overview of the State's economic performance, a review of current initiatives, and summary financial data. The Financial Section contains Management's Discussion and Analysis, Government Wide Financial Statements, Fund Financial Statements for Government Funds, Proprietary Funds, Fiduciary Funds and Similar Component Units, and for Major Component Units. . . . The Statistical Section contains selected financial and demographic information.

For more information contact the Oklahoma Office of State Finance, Division of Central Accounting and Reporting, 2300 North Lincoln Boulevard, Room 122, Oklahoma City, OK 73105-4801, or call (405) 521-2114. Several recent editions of the report are available online at http://www.osf.state.ok.us/comp -fr.html.

State of Oklahoma Executive Budget (Office of State Finance)—This 2-volume annual publication includes the governor's budget recommendations and historical data in detail for each state agency. Print copies of this publication may be available from the Oklahoma Office of State Finance, 2399 North Lincoln Boulevard, Oklahoma City, OK 73105-4801. Call (405) 521-2114. Editions back to fiscal year 1998 are available online at http://www.osf.state.ok.us/budget .html.

Legal Resources

Oklahoma House of Representative Legislative Manual, 5th Edition (Research, Legal and Fiscal Division, Oklahoma House of Representatives)—The *Legislative Manual* provides guidelines to new and veteran legislators and their staff on the legislative process, bill preparation and drafting, and other essential information on operational issues. Each piece of legislation introduced into the Oklahoma House must abide by and follow the guidelines established in the *Manual*. It is available for those affiliated with the Oklahoma House of Representatives, although copies are available in many Oklahoma depository libraries. The *Manual* is produced by the Oklahoma House of Representatives, Research, Legal and Fiscal Divisions, 2300 North Lincoln Boulevard, Oklahoma City, OK 73105. Call (800) 522-8502.

Oklahoma Legislature (Oklahoma Legislative Service Bureau)—This online resource provides information to the public on the Oklahoma House and Senate agendas, meeting notices, session highlights, and legislative summaries. The web page also provides links to the Oklahoma State Constitution and the Oklahoma Statutes, the text and status of measures, a text-search mechanism for measures, a map of the State Capitol complex, a glossary of legislative terms, and a search feature to find one's legislators. During a legislative session, the web page is updated daily to assist interested parties in tracking current and developing legislative matters. The House and Senate *Journals* appear in an RTF format. It was developed by the Oklahoma Legislative Service Bureau, Room B-30, State Capitol Building, Oklahoma City, OK 73105. Call (405) 521-4144. The most recent legislative session can be located on the web page at http://www.lsb.state.ok.us/newindex.html. Copies of measures can be obtained by contacting the Legislative Service Bureau, Bill Distribution, Room 310, 2300 North Lincoln Boulevard, State Capitol Building, Oklahoma City, OK 73105, or call (405) 521-5514. There is no charge. To view online go to http://www2.lsb.state.ok.us/billtext.html.

Oklahoma Public Legal Research System (Oklahoma Attorney General's Office)—This is designed to provide Oklahoma citizens online access to state statutes, cases, and other law-related information. Sponsored by the Oklahoma Attorney General's Office, the database contains links to Oklahoma Attorney General opinions, the state Constitution, state statutes, state court decisions, and state agency rules and decisions. On the web page all of the links can be searched by keyword. The state Constitution and agency rules also feature a browse capability. It is maintained by the Oklahoma Attorney General, 112 State Capitol Building, Oklahoma City, OK 73105. Call (405) 521-3921. The web page can be located at http://oklegal.onenet.net/.

Oklahoma Register and the *Oklahoma Administrative Code* (Office of Administrative Rules, Secretary of State)—Each of these publications is the official record for Oklahoma's rules and rule-making notices. Each publication also assists the approximately 150 regulatory agencies in Oklahoma by providing guidelines and templates on the design and publication of the rules and code. The *Code* contains a compilation of state agency rules and the governor's executive orders. It has been published on an annual basis since 1996 and is cumulative by its supplements. The 1999 edition consists of nine volumes. The *Register* is a semi-monthly publication that serves as the supplement to the *Code* between published supplements. The *Register* includes new rules, emergency rules, notices of proposed rules and the rule-making process, executive orders, and local project funding contract announcements.

The *Code* and the *Register* are available online at http://www.sos.state.ok .us/oar/oar_welcome.htm. Both publications can also be found in all state depository libraries as well as in all county clerk offices. The *Code* is available for $975.00 plus $500.00 for the 2000 Supplement. The *Register* is available for $500.00 for an annual subscription. For further information contact the Oklahoma Secretary of State, Office of Administrative Rules, State Capitol Building, 2300 North Lincoln Boulevard, Oklahoma City, OK 73105, or call (405) 421-4911.

State of Oklahoma Constitution (Legislative Service Bureau)—This is included in the Oklahoma Text Search and Retrieval System that is maintained by the Legislative Service Bureau. The online version can be searched by keyword or section number. Paper copies are available in all depository libraries and may be available by contacting the Oklahoma Legislative Service Bureau, Room B-30, State Capitol Building, Oklahoma City, OK 73105, or call (405) 521-4144. The Constitution can be accessed from http://www.lsb.state.ok.us/.

Who's Who in the Oklahoma Legislature (Oklahoma Department of Libraries)—This publication provides membership rosters of the Oklahoma House and Senate. Included are an address, phone number, e-mail, and a link to each member's brief biographical information. A paper copy can be obtained for

$4.00 from the Oklahoma Department of Libraries, Public Information Office, Oklahoma City, OK 73105-3298, or call (405) 522-3576. The online version is located at http://www.odl.state.ok.us/sginfo/whoiswho/index.htm.

Statistical Resources

Demographic State of the State: A Report to the Governor and Legislature on Population Trends for the State of Oklahoma (Office of Business Development, Department of Commerce)—This report is required by state statute 74 OS 1986, Section 5018. The report provides detailed information on population trends by city and county in the state of Oklahoma from 1970 to the present. Much of the statistical information is derived from U.S. Census Decennial Censuses and Population Estimates. Data are available at the state and county levels by age, race, and sex. It is developed and maintained by the Oklahoma Department of Commerce, Office of Business Development, Information Services Team, 900 North Stiles, Oklahoma City, OK 73126-0980. Call (405) 815-6552 or (800) 879-6552. A PDF version is available for viewing or downloading at http://busdev3.odoc5.odoc.state.ok.us/. Once you are on this web site, click the "Data and Statistics" button, then select "Publications and Lists."

Oklahoma Almanac (Oklahoma Department of Libraries)—The *Almanac* is the "Blue Book" of Oklahoma, containing information on Oklahoma's state agencies and the executive, judicial, and legislative branches of government. Also included are information on the state election results, county statistics, tourism, wildlife and nature, Oklahoma history, federal government contacts, a list of Oklahoma museums, statewide associations, and other pertinent and useful information. Copies are available for $15.00 for paperback and $25.00 for hardback from the Oklahoma Department of Libraries, 200 NE 18th Street, Oklahoma City, OK 73105-3298, or call (405) 348-2288. An online version can be found at http://www.odl.state.ok.us/almanac/index.htm.

Oklahoma Health Statistics (Oklahoma Department of Health)—This yearly report provides tabulated birth, death, marriage, and divorce data for Oklahoma. Data appear in table and graph form and are available on the state as a whole, by major metropolitan area, or by county or city with a population of over 2,500. The tables are arranged by gender, age, and race. The statistical information is gathered and collated by the Oklahoma State Department of Health, 1100 NE 10th Street, Oklahoma City, OK 73117. Call (405) 271-5600. Current and past reports (from 1993) are available at http://www.health .state.ok.us/program/phs/ohs/index.html.

ORIGINS (Oklahoma Department of Health)—This cooperative online resource, established by the Economic Development Act of 1987, is co-produced by the Oklahoma Department of Commerce, the University of Oklahoma, and Oklahoma State University. The *Oklahoma Resources Integration General Information Network Systems (ORIGINS)* is an electronic database providing economic, social, labor, and demographic statistical data. Aimed at community leaders, educators, businesses, government agencies, and decision makers, *ORIGINS* provides a comprehensive data source which is maintained and updated on a regular basis. There are also links to other state and federal data sources. All of the databases are keyword searchable. For further information contact the Oklahoma State Department of Health, 1100 NE 10th Street, Oklahoma City, OK 73117, or call (405) 815-5151 or (405) 325-2931. *ORIGINS* can be found at http://origins.ou.edu/front.htm.

Profiles: 2000 State Report: Oklahoma Educational Indicators Program (Office of Accountability, Education Oversight Board)—This report was developed in accordance with the Oklahoma Education Reform Act of 1990 for the purpose of assessing performances of public schools and school districts. The report presents a host of relevant educational statistics and community characteristics for the public to evaluate the academic effectiveness of a particular school district. Data are available in three major categories: Community Characteristics, District Education Programs, and Student Performance. Contact the Oklahoma Education Oversight Board, Office of Accountability, Oklahoma City, OK 73105 or call (405) 522-4578. E-mail contact@ed-stats.state.ok.us for a free paper copy. To view the report online go to http://schoolreportcard .org/downloadstaterpt.htm. This report may take up to twenty minutes to download, dependent on modem speed.

State of Oklahoma Uniform Crime Report/Crime in Oklahoma (State Bureau of Investigation)—This report contains compilations of statistics on adult and juvenile offenders that have been received from more than 302 sheriffs' offices and police departments within Oklahoma. Statistics are provided on seven types of crimes committed: murder, forcible rape, robbery, aggravated assault, burglary, larceny-theft, and motor vehicle theft. It has been published annually since 1974. Oklahoma State Bureau of Investigation, 600 North Harvey, Suite 300, Oklahoma City, OK 73116. Call (405) 848-6724 or (800) 522-8017. The report is available online at http://www.osbi.state.ok.us/Crime_Stats.htm. All annual reports are in a PDF format. The database contains reports from 1998 to the present.

Statistical Abstract of Oklahoma (University of Oklahoma's College of Business, Center for Economic and Management Research)—The *Statistical Abstract* is a comprehensive single reference source for a variety of economic and demographic statistical data on Oklahoma, one of the few "exempt" from depository library publications. This annual publication, issued since 1956, is available for $22.50 from the Oklahoma Department of Commence, 900 North Stiles, Oklahoma City, OK 73104, or call (405) 815-5151. It can also be obtained from the Center for Economic and Management Research, College of Business, University of Oklahoma, Norman, OK 73019, or call (405) 325-2931. An online copy of the report is located at http://origins.ou.edu/abstract/default.htm.

Other Resources

A Century to Remember: A Historical Perspective of the Oklahoma House of Representatives (Oklahoma House of Representatives)—This report provides a historical perspective and review on the early Oklahoma government. Published concurrently with dedication of the restored chamber of the Oklahoma House of Representatives, this work contains a history of the chamber as well as information about how the House currently operates and how technology has impacted and changed its operations. The information was gathered and written by George G. Humphreys, Oklahoma House of Representatives, 2300

North Lincoln, Oklahoma City, OK 73105. Call (405) 521-2711. Contact this address for further information about obtaining a copy.

Forty-Six Important Federal Publications About Oklahoma: The 46th State (Oklahoma Department of Libraries)—This is a bibliography listing forty-six federal government publications recognized by the compilers as important in the state's history. It excludes publications on the Indian Wars; items are listed chronologically. It was compiled by Adriana Edwards-Johnson (University of Central Oklahoma) and Steve Beleu (Oklahoma Department of Libraries) and issued by the Oklahoma Department of Libraries, 200 NE 18th Street, Oklahoma City, OK 73105-3298. Call (405) 348-2248. A limited number of copies were printed and distributed to Oklahoma state depository libraries. This publication can be located online at http://www.odl.state.ok.us/pubsonline/index.htm.

Is the Dust Bowl Returning? (Oklahoma Department of Libraries)—With severe drought conditions similar to those in the 1930s, the Oklahoma Department of Libraries' Steve Beleu has created a web page that provides maps, reports, and other information from the 1930s as well as today, reflecting past and current "dust bowl" conditions. Go to http://www.odl.state.ok.us/usinfo/dustbowl/index.htm to access this useful web page.

Oklahoma Documents for Small and Medium Libraries (Oklahoma Department of Libraries)—This annotated bibliography provides a suggested list of useful and informative state publications. It is arranged by major category (e.g., General Reference, Education) with each section containing brief annotations on publications that have been issued during the past two years. Also included in the bibliography is a list that compares federal and state legal materials along with represented state agencies and their street and web addresses. It was compiled by Vicki Sullivan and revised by Lauren Donaldson, Oklahoma Publications Clearinghouse, Oklahoma Department of Libraries, 200 NE 18th Street, Oklahoma City, OK 73105. Call (405) 522-3217. Contact the Clearinghouse for more information.

Oklahoma Today (Tourism and Recreation Department)—The official magazine of Oklahoma, *Oklahoma Today* presents topics on the people, places, history, and culture of Oklahoma (see Figure 15). Issued six times per year, an online or hard copy subscription is available for $17.95 per year from the Oklahoma Tourism and Recreation Department, P.O. Box 53384, Oklahoma City, OK 73152-3384, or call (405) 521-2496 in Oklahoma or toll free (800) 777-1793. The latest copy is available online at http://travelok.com/infocenter/oktoday.asp. It has been published since 1956.

The Road to Employment for People with Disabilities (Office of Handicapped Concerns)—This is a handbook that covers job strategies for persons with disabilities. Each section includes information on job search strategies, a directory of local employers, employment programs, community-based rehabilitation facilities, and information for the employer. This publication may be available from the Office of Handicapped Concerns, 2712 Villa Prom, Oklahoma City, OK 73107, or call (405) 521-3756.

OKLAHOMA'S WORLD WIDE WEB PAGE

There are two useful web pages that connect you to a variety of information on Oklahoma. The official state web page is called *Your Oklahoma* (see http://

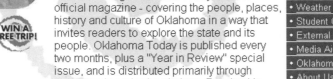

SITE SEARCH • TRAVEL PROFESSIONALS • TRIP PLANNER • SPECIAL OFFERS • VACATION IDEAS

INFORMATION CENTER
OKLAHOMA TODAY
MAGAZINE

Award-winning Oklahoma Today is the state's official magazine - covering the people, places, history and culture of Oklahoma in a way that invites readers to explore the state and its people. Oklahoma Today is published every two months, plus a "Year in Review" special issue, and is distributed primarily through newsstands and subscriptions. Readership exceeds 180,000.

Select A Category
* Brochures and Travel Guides
* OK Tourism Industry Info.
* Visitor Information
* FAQ, Fun Facts
* Weather
* Student Guide
* External Links
* Media Aids
* Oklahoma Today Magazine
* About Us
* Interactive State Maps

Visit the **Oklahoma Today Website**.

Every effort is made by the Oklahoma Tourism & Recreation Department to ensure correct information is presented. Please notify us in the case of incorrect or outdated information.

Our Events | Food & Lodging | Things to Do | Fun Stuff | Our Heritage | Information Center
Site Search | Travel Professionals | Trip Planner | Special Offers | Customer Service

Figure 15. State tourism departments not only publish colorful and informative materials, they sometimes give away free trips. Note the icon on the left side of this web page. *Source*: http://travelok .com/infocenter/oktoday.asp.

www.state.ok.us). The second has been designed by the Oklahoma Department of Libraries and is called *State Government Information* (see: http:// www.odl.state.ok.us/sginfo/index.htm).

Your Oklahoma provides multiple entry access to major topics, popular sites, new government features, new government agency publications, and other useful information. There are direct links to the state agency directory, state calendar of events, and popular sites that provide pertinent citizen information on such things as hunting and fishing, voter registration, marriage licenses, and tourism.

A pull-down menu on eight major subject areas that contain links to more information on that major subject is available. The ability to track legislation, review the latest state financial report or new state agency reports, and a keyword search that covers all state agencies is apparent.

State Government Information (SGI) provides a different means to search for state information. While its orientation is more toward the State Library in the sense that this web page has a direct link to the State Library electronic catalog, the Publications Clearinghouse, and Archives and Records, its page is nonetheless very useful for its information content and arrangement.

SGI provides access to the state web server. This web server contains information on the governor, lieutenant governor, agency directory, history fact sheet, and other topics of interest. SGI contains a feature called *Surf Oklahoma* that provides links to Oklahoma state agencies, boards, and commissions; selected agency hot topics; both chambers of the Oklahoma legislature; and to state government online.

Each web page is functional, useful, and easy to use. Each also provides links to pertinent information for citizen use. Neither should be ignored when performing searches for information on state agencies, tourism, "how-to" information, facts, and publications.

COMMERCIAL PUBLICATIONS AND WEB SITES

Book of Lists/Journal Record Book of Lists (Oklahoma City: The Journal Record Publishing Company, 1999)—This ranks businesses, industry, and services located within Oklahoma, and is available for $38.00 from the Journal Publishing Company, 222 North Robinson, Oklahoma City, OK 73102. Call (405) 235-3100; online at http://journalrecord.clickdata.com

Directory of Oklahoma's City and Town Officials (Oklahoma City: Oklahoma Municipal League, Annual)—This publication provides names and addresses of current officials within city and town governments, and is organized alphabetically by town. It also includes the *Municipal Blue Pages*. Oklahoma Municipal League, 201 NE 23rd Street, Oklahoma City, OK 73105. Call (405) 528-7515; online at http://www.oml.org.

Oklahoma Atlas & Gazetteer (Yarmouth, ME: DeLorme Mapping Company, 2000)—This contains topographical maps of Oklahoma, including back roads and outdoor recreation areas. A paper copy can be obtained for $19.95 from the DeLorme Mapping Company, P.O. Box 298, Yarmouth, ME 04096, or call (800) 581-5105. See http://www.delorme.com for further information.

The Oklahoma Business Directory (Omaha, NE: American Business Directories Company)—This includes information on approximately 154,000 businesses by city, a yellow page category, major employers, and manufacturers by city and product. A paper copy is available for $450.00. Contact the American Business Directories Company, 5711 South 86th Circle, Omaha, NE 68127, or call (402) 596-4600 or (800) 555-7124. See http://www.infoUSA.com.

Oklahoma Directory of Manufacturers and Processors (Department of Commerce and Harris InfoSource)—This annual publication (1996–) is produced through the joint efforts of the Department of Commerce and a commercial publisher, Harris InfoSource. The directory provides information on Oklahoma companies and manufacturers by name, city, county, product, and SIC Product Code. It also contains alphabetical and geographical sections. The geographical section is the most detailed in providing firm name, address, telephone number, year established, and market served. Oklahoma residents can order a print or CD-ROM copy from the Oklahoma Department of Commerce, 900 North Stiles, Oklahoma City, OK 73126-0980, or call (405) 815-5183 or (800) 879-6552. Persons outside Oklahoma can order copies from Harris InfoSource, 2057 E. Aurora Road, Twinsburg, OH 44087, or call (800) 888-5900. The directory may be found online in the "Developing Your Business" section of the Department of Commerce site at http://busdev3.odoc5.odoc.state.ok.us/. Registration is necessary in order to obtain a username and password to view the directory. See also the Harris InfoSource page at http://www.harrisinfo.com/.

Oklahoma Foundation Databook (Portland, OR: C and D Publishing, 2003)— This is a directory of over 1,000 grant-making foundations in Oklahoma. Included are comprehensive profiles of the largest foundations and a categorical listing of the over 7,774 grants awarded in the past year. Information provided also includes the name of the foundation, its address, phone number, date of establishment, grants issued, contact person, and so on. A print copy is available for $100, and a print copy plus a CD-ROM for $150. Contact C and D Publishing, 1017 SW Morrison #500, Portland, OR 97205, or call (877) 924-7468. An order form is available online at http://www.foundationdatabook .com/okorder.html.

Oklahoma Media Guide (Oklahoma City: Oklahoma Press Service, Inc., 2000)—This annual publication provides staff names, addresses, e-mail, fax, web sites, and other useful information. A paper copy is available for $25.00 from the Oklahoma Press Service, Inc., 3601 North Lincoln Boulevard, Oklahoma City, OK 73105, or call (405) 524-4421. See http://www.okpress .com for more information.

Oklahoma Place Names (George H. Shirk) (Norman, OK: University of Oklahoma Press, 1987)—This is an indispensable book containing information on the origin of name, date of founding, and other pertinent details of towns in Oklahoma. A paper copy is available for $14.95 from the University of Oklahoma Press, 1005 Asp Avenue, Norman, OK 73019-6051, or call (405) 325-2999 or (800) 364-5798.

Oklahoma Session Laws (Eagan, MN: West Group)—This is the "official" publication of the Oklahoma laws and resolutions enacted and approved by the Oklahoma legislature. The 2002 Supplement is available from the West Group for $92.00. See http://west.thomson.com/.

Oklahoma Statutes—(Eagan, MN: West Group, 1996)—This is a 6-volume set containing all laws of the state of Oklahoma, organized into eighty-five subject areas. The 2002 Supplement is available from the West Group for $292.00. See http://west.thomson.com/ for more information.

SOURCES CONSULTED

Correspondence with Steve Beleu, Oklahoma State Library; Suzanne Holcome, Oklahoma State University.

Google, http://www.google.com.

Government Documents Round Table, American Library Association. *Directory of Government Document Collection & Librarians*, 7th ed. Bethesda, MD: Congressional Information Service, 1997.

Jobe, Janita. "State Publications." *Journal of Government Information*, 27 (2000): 733–768.

Numerous departmental web pages via the state's home page, http://www.state.ok .us/.

State and Local Government on the Net, http://www.piperinfo.com/state/index.cfm.

State Web Locator, http://www.infoctr.edu/swl/.

Survey response from Donna Denniston, Oklahoma State Library.

Oregon

Daniel D. Cornwall

GOVERNMENT PUBLISHING AND THE DEPOSITORY SYSTEM

Oregon's state depository system was established in 1907 under *Oregon Revised Statutes* (ORS) 357.004, 357.090-357.105. Currently, twenty-nine depository libraries participate in the program. State agencies are required by statute to send the State Library fifteen or thirty copies of all their publications that fall into the definition of public documents. As defined by the depository law, "Public documents" are

informational matter produced for public distribution regardless of format, method of reproduction, source or copyright, originating in or produced with the imprint of, by the authority of or at the total or partial expense of any state agency. "Public document" includes informational matter produced on computer diskettes, CD-ROMs, computer tapes or other electronic storage media.

Another part of the depository law specifically exempts the State Board of Higher Education, the Oregon Supreme Court, the Oregon Court of Appeals, and the Oregon Tax Court from the depository program.

The State Library collects, catalogs, and classifies all public state documents; distributes them to Oregon Documents Depository Program libraries; and keeps Oregon documents in its collection permanently. Libraries in the Oregon Documents Depository Program catalog all depository documents in their online catalogs. Depository libraries are not required to use the Oregon documents call system, OrDocs, in their cataloging. The OrDocs classification system used by the State Library is similar to the Superintendent of Documents classification for federal documents and based on agency structure rather than subject structure. Those wishing to know more about the OrDocs classification system can consult an online guide at http://www.osl.state.or.us/home/techserv/catclass.html.

Two types of depository libraries are specified in *Oregon Administrative Rules*

543-70-000: full depository libraries that receive all public documents deposited with the State Library, and core depository libraries that receive only public documents identified by the State Librarian as those "for which members of the public have the most significant and frequent need." The current list of *Core Oregon Documents* is on the web at http://www.osl.state.or.us/home/techserv/cordocs.html. All depository libraries are required to make their Oregon documents accessible to the public free of charge. Full depositories must retain all depository documents for a minimum of five years. Core depositories must retain all depository documents for a minimum of three years.

USEFUL ADDRESSES AND TELEPHONE NUMBERS

The most complete collections of Oregon state publications may be found at the following libraries:

Oregon State Library
250 Winter Street NE
Salem, OR 97301-3950
Phone Number for Oregon Reference Questions: (503) 378-4198
Library's Home Page: http://www.osl.state.or.us/home/index.html
Oregon Document Depository Page: http://www.osl.state.or.us/home/techserv/
   ordocs.html

Knight Library
15th Avenue and Kincaid
1299 University of Oregon
Eugene, OR 97403-1299
Phone Number for Oregon Reference Questions: (541) 346-3060
E-Mail Address for Oregon Reference Questions: tstave@oregon.uoregon.edu
Library System Home Page: http://libweb.uoregon.edu/
Document Center Home Page: http://libweb.uoregon.edu/govdocs/

The Valley Library
Oregon State University
Corvallis, OR 97331
Phone Number for Oregon Reference Questions: (541) 737-7293
E-Mail Address for Oregon Reference Questions: valley.ref@orst.edu
Library's Home Page: http://osulibrary.orst.edu/
Government Information and Maps Page: http://osulibrary.orst.edu/research/
   govpubs.htm

INDEXES TO OREGON STATE PUBLICATIONS

While Oregon does not publish a formal index of publications distributed through the state depository program, it does post the shipping lists of items sent to depositories. The lists can be found at http://www.osl.state.or.us/home/techserv/shippingpage.html. Each entry in the shipping list contains the OrDocs number, publishing agency, and title of documents. Oregon core documents appear in red.

ESSENTIAL STATE PUBLICATIONS

Directories

Oregon Agricultural Resources Directory (Agriculture)—Oregon Documents Call Number—A.8Ag8/5. This directory includes contact information for the Oregon Department of Agriculture, other selected government agencies, Oregon Commodity Commissions, Oregon Farm Bureaus, Oregon Farmers' Markets, Soil and Water Conservation Districts, Oregon State University agricultural resources, and a wide variety of agricultural associations. There is a searchable database of the directory at http://oda.state.or.us/dbs/resource _guide/search.lasso. Available search fields for the database include: Type of Organization, Organization Title, Program Area, City, and State. The 2001 edition of the directory was over 140 pages. Paper copies can be ordered for $5.00 per copy by calling (503) 986-4550.

Oregon Directory of American Indian Resources (Commission on Indian Services)—Oregon Documents Call Number—L/In2/2.8Am3. This biennial listing of Native American resources can be found on the Internet at http://www .leg.state.or.us/cis/. This directory is divided into four chapters based on regions in Oregon, chapters for the state and federal governments, and listings of Native American commissions and organizations. Each of the regional chapters provides a listing of tribes, American Indian resources, Indian education resources, Title V Projects, Johnson O'Malley programs, and publications created by Native American entities. Other notable features include a map of Oregon Indian communities and population and other demographics for Oregon's nine federally recognized tribes. Paper copies of the directory can be obtained by writing the Legislative Commission on Indian Services, 900 Court Street NE, Room 167, Salem, OR 97301, or by calling (503) 986-1067.

Oregon School Directory (Education)—Oregon Documents Call Number— E.8Sch6. This annual listing has a number of helpful features. In addition to the school and district listings, there is an index to school personnel and a two-year school calendar. Each district entry includes contact information, a partial staff listing, and the student enrollment and staffing from the previous year. The directory also lists staff for the Oregon Department of Education and Oregon educational organizations. It is available on the Internet at http://www.ode.state.or.us/pubs/directory/index.htm, or may be obtained in paper by a prepaid order to Documents Sales Clerk, Oregon Department of Education, 255 Capitol Street NE, Salem, OR 97310-0203. The 2001–2002 directory sold for $10.00. The web site given above also provides a file of mailing labels for schools and districts in Oregon.

Financial/Budgetary Resources

Comprehensive Annual Financial Report (CAFR) (Administrative Services)— Oregon Documents Call Number—Ad/Ac2.1. Located on the Internet at http://scd.das.state.or.us/publications.htm, the CAFR is Oregon's report of audited revenues and expenses. The CAFR also contains the state of Oregon's organization chart and a listing of principal state officials. In addition, the CAFR contains eleven "statistical schedules" that include figures on per-capita debt for the prior ten years, a listing of the state's ten largest private employers, and several other tables comparing Oregon with the United States. Free paper copies of the CAFR going back to 1999 may be ordered by calling the State Controller's Division at (503) 373-7277. Academics and members of the investment community may write to the State Controller's Division, Department of Administrative Services, 155 Cottage Street NE, U50, Salem, OR 97301-3969. This annual report may also be ordered by e-mail at jean.l .gabriel@state.or.us.

State of Oregon Legislatively Adopted Budget (Office of the Governor)—Oregon Documents Call Number—Ad.3B85. Published since 1967, this biennial document contains the spending plan for Oregon as adopted by the legislature. Highlights from this documents are available online at http://www.leg.state .or.us/comm/lfo/home.htm. It is not available for purchase, but can be consulted at Oregon depository libraries. A summary of the *Legislatively Adopted Budget* can be obtained by writing the Legislative Fiscal Office, 900 Court Street NE, H-178 State Capitol, Salem, OR 97301, or by calling (503) 986-1828.

Governor's Budget (Administrative Services)—Oregon Documents Call Number—Ad.3B85/2. This biennial document lists Oregon's proposed spending by agency and by broad program areas such as public safety, economic and community development, natural resources, and transportation. Information on numbers of state employees and the expenditure of lottery revenues is also available in the budget document. The latest version of the *Governor's Budget* is available on the Internet at http://www.bam.das.state.or.us/pub/bam publications.htm.

Oregon Economic and Revenue Forecast (Administrative Services)—Oregon Documents Call Number—Ad.3Ec7. Located on the Internet at http://www .oea.das.state.or.us/economic.htm, each 100-plus-page issue provides an overview and outlook for the international, national, western regional, and Oregon economies. In addition, the *Forecast* presents outlooks for various fund sources. An appendix provides population projections by sex and age up to seven years in the future. The projections attempt to estimate the number of populations that might have an impact on state spending such as kindergartners, "at-risk" youth, and older workers. In addition to the forecasts and projections, the *Forecast* also provides selected historical information back to 1980. The report is published four times a year: March 1, June 1 (May 15 during legislative sessions), September 1, and December 1. A free paper subscription can be obtained by sending your name and mailing address to Oregon Economic and Revenue Forecast, Office of Economic Analysis, Department of Administrative Services, 155 Cottage Street NE U20, Salem, OR 97301-3966, or by calling (503) 378-3405.

Legal Resources

Civil Rights Laws Handbook (Bureau of Labor and Industries)—Oregon Documents Call Number—Lab.6C49. Published since 1996, this biennial publication lists state and federal civil rights laws protecting individuals from discrimination in the workplace, housing, and in public accommodations. The newly revised and updated 1998 *Civil Rights Laws Handbook* focuses on the employment aspects of Oregon law, defining protected classes, theories of discrimination, and outlining discrimination-free personnel practices. It contains expanded sections on complying with state and federal family leave laws and the new disability statute. Also included are discussions of sexual harassment, race and national origin discrimination, and reinstatement rights. Oregon revised statutes and administrative rules are included. It is not available on the Internet but may be ordered for $15 using the order form at http://www.boli.state.or.us/technical/tabooks.html. You may also either write Bureau of Labor and Industries, 800 N.E. Oregon Street, #32, Portland, OR 97232, or call (503) 731-4200, ext. 4, to order this publication.

Oregon Administrative Rules (Secretary of State)—Oregon Documents Call Number—S.6Ad6/2. Available on the Internet at http://arcweb.sos.state.or.us/banners/rules.htm, the *Rules* can be browsed either in chapter or agency order. A simple search using an Excite interface is available. In 2003, a subscription to the *Oregon Administrative Rules Compilation* and a one-year subscription to the *Oregon Bulletin* was $600.00. The *Oregon Bulletin* is the monthly update to the *Oregon Administrative Rules* and also contains proposed regulations. Both can be ordered from the web site above. Call (503) 373-0701, ext. 240, for more information.

Oregon Appellate Courts Reports: Advance Sheets and Bound Volumes (Supreme Court)—Oregon Documents Call Number—None. The Advance Sheets, printed in paperback form, are published bimonthly and contain all cases decided by the Supreme Court, Court of Appeals, and Tax Court. Recent opinions of these courts are posted on the Internet at http://www.publications.ojd.state.or.us/. As of July 2002, Advance Sheets subscriptions were $150.00/year and Bound Volumes were sold individually at $35.00/each. For more information contact the Oregon Judicial Department Publications Section, Supreme Court Building, 1163 State Street, Salem, OR 97301-2563, or call (503) 986-5656.

Oregon Revised Statutes (Legislature)—Oregon Documents Call Number—L/L52/4.6R32. Available on the Internet at http://landru.leg.state.or.us/ors/, the text appearing in this database was produced from material provided by the Legislative Counsel Committee of the Oregon Legislative Assembly. The official edition is the printed published copy of the *Oregon Revised Statutes*. The online statutes may be browsed by chapter or searched by keyword. The 19-volume paper set of the *Oregon Revised Statutes* can be ordered for $319.00 by using the order form at http://www.lc.state.or.us/. Up-to-the minute ordering information can be obtained by calling the Legislative Counsel Committee at (503) 986-1243.

Summary of Major Legislation (Legislature)—Oregon Documents Call Number—L/L52.6.6Su6. Located on the Internet at http://landru.leg.state.or.us/comm/commsrvs/ in the "Committee Services Publications" section, *Summary of Major Legislation* is a compilation of selected bills, memorials, and resolutions considered by the Oregon Legislative Assembly. Summaries contain background information, effects of enacted measures, and effective dates. Summaries of vetoed bills and text of the governor's veto messages are included. A helpful subject index and a chapter number conversion table for the latest Oregon slip laws may be found at the end of the *Summary*. Legislative measures covered by this publication are divided into five major sections: Economic Issues, Governmental Issues, Human Services Issues, Natural Resources Issues, and Judiciary Issues. Paper copies of this publication may be requested by writing Legislative Publications and Distribution, 900 Court Street NE, Room 49 State Capitol, Salem, OR 97301, or by calling (503) 986-1180.

Wage and Hour Laws (Bureau of Labor and Industries)—Oregon Documents Call Number—Lab.6W12. Last published in 1998, *Wage and Hour Laws* spells out the rules on worktime, paydays, meals, and lunch periods, and provides employers with basic information on minimum wage, overtime, minimum wage exemptions, and independent contractors. This book contains all applicable statutes and rules as well as text discussing such topics as when you can pay a volunteer, when you can pay less than minimum wage, and how the child labor laws work. It is not available on the Internet but may be ordered for $15.00 using the form at http://www.boli.state.or.us/technical/tabooks.html. You may also either write Bureau of Labor and Industries, 800 N.E. Oregon Street, #32, Portland, OR 97232, or call (503) 731-4200, ext. 4, to order this publication.

Statistical Resources

Oregon Benchmark Performance Report (Oregon Progress Board)—Oregon Documents Call Number—ED/P94.3B43. Located at http://www.econ.state.or.us/opb/sitemap.htm, this report has seven chapters that mark Oregon's progress in the areas of Economy, Education, Civic Engagement, Social Support, Public Safety, Community Development, and Environment. Each chapter begins with a narrative overview, then provides about ten to fifteen charts of performance measures. Some of the measures included are: Workers @ 150 percent or More of Poverty (Chapter 2), Voting (Chapter 4), and Marine Species at Risk (Chapter 8). Most performance measures have ten years worth of data. If you are looking for some sort of socioeconomic trend in Oregon, start here.

Oregon Health Trends (Health)—Oregon Documents Call Number—HR/H34.3H34. Located at http://www.ohd.hr.state.or.us/chs/oht.cfm, this is an occasional newsletter that carries useful health-related statistics. Recent issue topics included: Teen Pregnancy, Youth Suicide, and Weapons Use among the Young. Newsletters published from 1995 to the present are available on the web site.

Oregon Labor Trends (Employment Department)—Oregon Documents Call Number—Em.3L11/2. This monthly magazine provides information on employment trends and has in-depth coverage of economic and labor market topics. Each fifteen- to twenty-page issue comes packed with charts and graphs. Issues may be downloaded in PDF format from http://www.qualityinfo.org/ (select "Publications"), or you can sign up for a free subscription at http://www.qualityinfo.org/olmisj/PubOrder.

Oregon Vital Statistics Annual Report (Human Services)—Oregon Documents

Call Number—HR/H34.3V83. This two-volume annual report provides state-wide statistics on births, abortions, and teen pregnancy (volume 1), and deaths (all ages), perinatal deaths, and adolescent suicide attempts (volume 2). Some notable tables in this report include Table 2-23, births by county of occurrence, type of institution, and delivery attendant; Table 2-29, most popular baby names, Oregon occurrence (Number 1 in 1999—Jacob and Emily); Table 3-5, contraceptive use, number of previous abortions, and number of living children by age of patient; and Table 6-11, years of potential life lost before age 65 from the leading causes of death, by year, Oregon residents, 1985–2000. Reports back to 1995 are available on the Internet at http://www.ohd.hr .state.or.us/chs/annrep.cfm.

Oregon Vital Statistics County Data Book (Human Services)—Oregon Documents Call Number—HR/H34.7V83. The *County Data Book* is an annual compilation of vital statistics data by county, including Births, Abortions, Teen Pregnancy, Teen Suicide Attempts, and Deaths by County of Residence. Notable tables include Table 3, births to unmarried mothers; Table 8, prenatal care by mother's county of residence; and Table 17, suicide attempts by age and county of residence. The current edition and prior editions back to 1995 are available on the web at http://www.ohd.hr.state.or.us/chs/cdb.cfm.

Report of Criminal Offenses and Arrests (Oregon State Police)—Oregon Documents Call Number—PO/L41.3C86. This is an annual statistical summary of crime in Oregon; statistics are available for the state and county levels. Some of the statistics provided include tables of statewide offenses by day of week, statewide offenses by type of location, county five-year profile of crimes against property, and drug offenses by county and type. Reports back to 1995 are available on the Internet at http://www.leds.state.or.us/oucr/offense _report/crim_arrests.htm.

Other Resources

Oregon Blue Book (Secretary of State)—Oregon Documents Call Number— S.8B62. Published since 1934, the current issue of this extremely useful biennial publication is available on the web at http://bluebook.state.or.us/. The *Oregon Blue Book* is divided into seven major sections: State, Local, Facts, Cultural, Kids, National, and Education. Under these sections is a treasure house of material on Oregon. A sample of the things you can find here are legislator pictures (under State), city and county profiles (under Local), industry profiles and scenic images (under Facts), listings of newspapers and television stations (under Cultural), contact information for Oregon Indian tribes (under National), and special education resources. If you can afford only a single Oregon document, get the *Oregon Blue Book*! It can be ordered in paperback or hardcover by using the order form at http://bluebook.state.or.us/order.htm, or by sending a letter and check to Secretary of State, Attention: Oregon Blue Book, P.O. Box 3370, Portland, OR 97208-3370. Current prices can be obtained by calling the Office of the Secretary of State at (503) 986-2204.

Oregon Driver Manual (Driver and Motor Vehicle Services)—Oregon Documents Call Number—T/M85.8D83. The first edition of the *Oregon Driver Manual* was published in 1937. In keeping with modern times, Oregonians and others can find it on the Internet at http://www.odot.state.or.us/dmv/forms/manuals_forms.htm. It now contains 120 pages of information on defensive driving and Oregon's rules of the road. For more information call (503) 945-5000.

Oregon Voters' Pamphlet (Secretary of State)—Oregon Documents Call Numbers—Primary election: S.8V94; General election: S.8V94/2. Voters' pamphlets back to 1995 can be consulted on the Internet at http://www.sos.state.or.us/elections/Publications/vp.htm.

OREGON'S WORLD WIDE WEB HOME PAGE

Oregon's main web page is *Oregon.gov* at http://www.oregon.gov. At the top of the home page, there is a search box and a drop-down list of popular sites. For the casual user, the drop-down list may be all that's needed since it links to things like Oregon job listings, a state employee directory, Oregon laws and regulations, lottery results, and an unclaimed property list. For those whose needs are not served by the "popular" links, Oregon's portal is organized by broad topics. Unlike many states, Oregon's portal serves up information in Spanish in addition to English. Each of these areas can be reached by clicking on the left-hand menu. There is a "text-only" link, but you have to scroll down past the menu to find it.

Oregon's broad topics are Government, Living, Visiting, Working, Business, Education, Oregon Facts, OnLine Services, and Español, the Spanish portal pages. Each subject page has a helpful one- or two-paragraph introduction stating the types of information that can be found under that subject page. There are three subareas of *Oregon.gov* that merit special attention: Maps and Demographics (found under Oregon Facts), Citizen Services, and Business Services (both found under OnLine Services). Maps and Demographics provides links to maps of economically distressed areas; state, county, and city maps; geology maps; and even bicycling maps and touring info. Citizen Services is where people can go to: change their address with the department of motor vehicles, make sure their contractors have valid licenses, find a job, sign up for distance education, or look for a mortgage lender. Business Services allows businesses to: find links to various business resources and information, download corporate forms, download tax forms, locate licensing and regulatory information, and more.

The search function on *Oregon.gov's* front page is powered by a search engine provided by the Oregon State Library's Government Information Locator Service (GILS) project. It supports searches by keyword and phrase. Any results screen also provides links to the *Oregon Revised Statutes*, *Oregon Administrative Rules*, and the *Oregon Blue Book*. If your original query is not answered by your search results, an answer may well be found by browsing the *Oregon Blue Book*. A very nice touch and unsurprising that librarians thought of it!

COMMERCIAL PUBLICATIONS AND WEB SITES

Atlas of Oregon (University of Oregon Press, Eugene, OR)—Last published in 2001, the *Atlas of Oregon* maps the whole of the state from Oregon native cultures, exploration, politics, religion, and economic growth to landforms, volcanoes, lakes, place names, vegetation, and wildlife habitat. More than 700 maps, accompanied by hundreds of charts and diagrams, make this a valuable resource. The 2001 edition sold for $100.00 and can be ordered through the publisher's web site at https://millrace.uoregon.edu/uopress. Call (866) 672-8527 or (541) 346-5885 for more information.

Oregon Book: Information A to Z (Saddle Mountain Press, Newport, OR)—As the title implies, this work on Oregon covers nearly everything—places, weather, government, culture, history, transportation, economy, culture, and more, in an alphabetical format. The 1998 edition of this book sold for $29.95. Saddle Mountain Press is not on the Internet, but you can write them at Saddle Mountain Press, 1434 6 Street, Astoria, OR 97103.

Oregon Firsts (Pumpkin Ridge Productions, North Plains, OR)—Last published in 1994, *Oregon Firsts* describes over 1,500 chronological and other ranking firsts for Oregon, including the first mail order service in any American library. The 1994 edition sold for $24.95 plus $4.00 shipping per copy. Prepaid orders can be sent to Oregon Firsts Media, Pumpkin Ridge Productions, P.O. Box 33, North Plains, OR 97133-0033, or call (503) 647-0021.

Oregon Geographic Names (Oregon Historical Society Press, Portland, OR)— Last published in 1992, this nearly 1,000-page work explains the history behind nearly 5,000 Oregon place names. Each entry includes dates when places were first named and reasons for the choice of names. The sixth edition sold for $19.95 and can be ordered by completing the form at http://www.ohs .org/publications_old/oderform.htm. Print it out and mail it to Oregon Historical Society, 1200 SW Park Avenue, Portland, OR 97205-2483. You may enclose a check (made out to OHS), or use Mastercard or Visa. If you do use a credit card, you may fax your order to (503) 221-2035 or call OHS at (503) 306-5230.

SOURCES CONSULTED

Core Oregon Documents. Oregon State Library, http://www.osl.state.or.us/home/ techserv/cordocs.html.

Numerous departmental web pages via the state's home page, http://www.oregon .gov/.

Oregon Revised Statutes. Oregon State Legislature, 2000. (Via the web at http://landru .leg.state.or.us/ors/.)

Oregon State Publications home page, http://www.osl.state.or.us/home/techserv/ ordocs.html.

Survey response from Jey Wann, Oregon State Library, 2000.

Pennsylvania

Eric W. Johnson

GOVERNMENT PUBLISHING AND THE DEPOSITORY SYSTEM

The Pennsylvania State Library has served as the official depository for Pennsylvania state publications since the earliest days of its existence. In 1971, the General Assembly passed legislation setting up a formal Pennsylvania Depository Library Program (*Pennsylvania Code*, Title 22, Chapter 143), under the direction of the State Librarian.

The State Library receives up to 250 copies of state publications for its own collection and for distribution to other libraries. According to the *Code*, a publication is

any printed or otherwise reproduced item prepared for distribution to the public, or used within any state agency as a regulatory instrument, including but not limited to documents, pamphlets, studies, brochures, books, annual reports, codes, regulations, journals, periodicals or magazines printed by or for the Commonwealth, its legislature, its courts, its constitutional offices, or any authority, board, commission, or department or other State governmental agency or issued in conjunction with, or under contract with, the Federal government, local units of government, private individuals, institutions or corporations. (*Pennsylvania Code*, Title 22, Chapter 143.1)

Eligible depository libraries include state college and university libraries, district library centers, regional library resource centers, libraries of state-related universities and colleges, U.S. documents depository libraries, and other academic and public libraries under certain conditions.

USEFUL ADDRESSES AND TELEPHONE NUMBERS

The most complete collection of Pennsylvania state publications may be found at the following library:

State Library of Pennsylvania
Walnut Street and Commonwealth Avenue
Box 1601
Harrisburg, PA 17105-1601
Phone Number for Pennsylvania Reference Questions: (717) 787-3273
E-Mail Link for Pennsylvania Reference Questions: ra-reference@state.pa.us
Library's Home Page: http://www.statelibrary.state.pa.us/libraries/site/default.asp

INDEXES TO PENNSYLVANIA STATE PUBLICATIONS

To classify its Pennsylvania state documents, the State Library uses the Bordner scheme, similar to the Superintendent of Documents classification scheme. Publications are arranged by the issuing agency rather than by subject. The Bordner scheme is detailed in the *Revised Classification Scheme for Pennsylvania State Publications* (5th ed., edited by Ann L. Kemper, State Library of Pennsylvania, Harrisburg, PA, 2002), available online in a PDF file at http://www.statelibrary.state.pa.us/libraries/lib/libraries/Pa_Documents _Classification_June_2002.pdf.

The State Library issues a quarterly *Pennsylvania Documents Checklist*, which is cumulated annually. These checklists contain monographs and new serials received by the State Library of Pennsylvania, but are not intended to be complete records of publications issued by an agency. Checklists since 1998 are available online at http://www.statelibrary.state.pa.us/libraries/cwp/ view.asp?a=13&Q=43074. Checklists for 1998–2001 are arranged alphabetically by issuing agency as described by the agency itself. Beginning in 2002, Checklists are arranged by call number and include page numbers and hyperlinks to documents, if available. Each entry includes the call number, OCLC number, publication title, number of pages, issuing agency, and date.

State publications may also be located through two online catalogs: *PILOT*, the State Library's Keystone Library Network Catalog, online at http://pilot .sshe.edu:8020, and the *Access Pennsylvania* database, a large statewide union catalog, at http://205.247.101.10/. *Franklin*, the University of Pennsylvania Libraries' online catalog, accessible from the libraries' web site at http://www .library.upenn.edu/; and Pennsylvania State University Libraries' *The Cat*, accessible at http://cat.libraries.psu.edu/, also include many Pennsylvania state publications.

ESSENTIAL STATE PUBLICATIONS

Directories

Commonwealth Phone Directory (Department of General Services)—This online PDF file includes an alphabetical personnel listing as well as listings for the governor's office, other agencies and departments, the Senate and House, and miscellaneous information. This directory is available at http://www .dgs.state.pa.us/. For information about a print version, contact the Commonwealth Information Center, 402A Finance Building, Harrisburg, PA 17120; or call (717) 787-2121, or e-mail gs-cic@state.pa.us.

Corporations Searchable Database (Department of State, Corporations Bureau)—This is an online records repository of more than 1.5 million companies that do business in the Commonwealth. Corporations can be searched by general name, old name, or orphan name (non-profits), and the Uniform Commercial Code can also be searched for financing statement information. Basic entity information can include any of the following: entity number, type, consent, filed date, current name, original name, address, and purpose or description. The database may be found online at http://www.dos.state.pa.us/ CorpsApp/CorpsWeb/wfDefault.aspx. For more information, contact the Corporation Bureau at 206 North Office Building, Harrisburg, PA 17120; or call (717) 787-1057, or e-mail corps@pados.state.pa.us.

Pennsylvania Education Directory (Department of Education)—This annual publication contains a current complete listing of Pennsylvania schools, colleges, school districts, educational organizations; and names, addresses, administrators, and related information about the educational entities that the Department of Education serves. This directory is available online as EdNA (Education Names and Addresses) at http://edna.ed.state.pa.us/. The section on colleges and universities may be found online at http://www.pde highered.state.pa.us/higher/site/default.asp. A paper copy is available from Applied Arts Publishers, Box 479, Lebanon, PA 17042-0479; an order form may be found on the web at http://www.pdeinfo.state.pa.us/depart_edu/site/ default.asp. Select "PA Ed Dir Order Form" in the "Find Documents" section. For more information about education, contact the Pennsylvania Department of Education, 333 Market Street, Harrisburg, PA 17126, call (717) 783-6788, or visit its web site at http://www.pde.state.pa.us/pde_internet/site/default .asp.

The Pennsylvania Manual (Department of General Services)—This is the official guide to state government, personnel, and information. Published annually, it includes the Governor's Letter; Pennsylvania Past and Present; the text of the Constitution of Pennsylvania; sections on the General Assembly, the Executive and Judicial branches, Local Government, Elections, Federal Government; and an Appendix listing awards, state parks and forests, political party officials, institutions of higher education, and media and periodicals. The *Manual* is available online in a PDF format at http://www.dgs.state.pa .us/dgs/cwp/view.asp?a=3&Q=116280&dgsNav=|. A print copy may be ordered from the Pennsylvania Historic and Museum Commission, Keystone Building, 400 North Street, Harrisburg, PA 17120-0053, by telephone at (717) 787-5109, or via e-mail to tcarocci@phmc.state.pa.us.

Financial/Budgetary Resources

Comprehensive Annual Financial Report for the Fiscal Year Ended June 30, 20___ (Office of the Budget)—The *Comprehensive Annual Financial Report* includes the Commonwealth's independently audited general purpose financial statements as of and for a particular fiscal year, and is devised to provide the state government and citizens with information required to assess the Commonwealth's financial position, results of operations, and the management of its financial resources. The latest report, along with some prior reports, is available online at http://www.budget.state.pa.us/budget/site/default.asp. Select "Budget and Financial Rpts." An official print copy may be obtained from the Deputy Secretary for Comptroller Operations, Room 207, Finance Building, Harrisburg, PA 17120.

Financial Statistics (Department of Community and Economic Development)—This online database provides information on revenues, expenditures, and debt for Commonwealth municipalities and counties. The database may be accessed from the "Communities in Pennsylvania" page at http://www.inventpa.com/, by following the link to the "Governor's Center for Local Government Services," and then linking to "Electronic Filing and Municipal Statistics." For more information, contact the Department of Community and Economic Development, 4th Floor, Commonwealth Keystone Building, Harrisburg, PA 17120-0225, or visit its web site at http://www.inventpa.com/

Pennsylvania FY–FY Governor's Executive Budget (Office of the Budget)—The text of the governor's proposed budget as transmitted to the General Assembly. The *Budget* includes a Reader's Guide with background information; Overview and Summaries; Tax Expenditures; Departmental Presentations; Capital Budget; Public Dept; Other Special Funds; a summary of salaried Complement; and Statistical Data. The text of the most recent budget may be found online at http://www.budget.state.pa.us/budget/site/default.asp.

Pennsylvania FY–FY Budget in Brief (Office of the Budget)—This synopsis of the governor's proposed budget includes the total recommended budget, the governor's recommended budget, and narrative summaries of departmental funding. The text of the most recent *Budget in Brief* may be found online at http://www.budget.state.pa.us/budget/site/default.asp. Past *Budgets in Brief* are online at that site as well.

For print versions of budgetary material, contact the Office of the Budget, 7th Floor Bell Tower, 303 Walnut Street, Harrisburg, PA 17101-1808, or call (717) 787-2542.

Legal Resources

Constitution of Pennsylvania (Legislature) —The Constitution consists of a Preamble; eleven Articles: Declaration of Rights, The Legislature, Legislation, The Executive, The Judiciary, Public Officers, Elections, Taxation and Finance, Local Government, Private Corporations, and Amendments; Schedules to the Constitution of Pennsylvania; and an Appendix of supplementary provisions of constitutional amendments. The text, as included in the *Pennsylvania Manual*, is available online at http://www.dgs.state.pa.us/. A print copy may be ordered from the Office of the Chief Clerk, House of Representatives, Room 129, Main Capitol Building, Harrisburg, PA 17120-0028, or call (717) 787-2372.

The Pennsylvania Code (Legislative Reference Bureau)—A compilation of the laws of the Commonwealth of Pennsylvania, the *Code* is a looseleaf service consisting of 64 titles, updated regularly by the *Pennsylvania Code Reporter*. A subject arrangement is followed, and each title brings together administrative regulations, court rules, or other documents on related subjects. Within each title in descending order come parts, chapters, subchapters, and sections; in some chapters there are also subparts, articles, divisions, and subdivisions. A

searchable and browseable online version of the *Code* may be found at http://
www.pacode.com/. The print version of the *Code* is edited, printed, and distributed by Fry Communications, 800 West Church Road, Mechanicsburg, PA
17055-3198. Call (717) 766-0211, ext. 2340; or toll-free in Pennsylvania (800)
524-3232, ext. 2340; or toll-free outside the state (800) 334-1429, ext. 2340.

The Pennsylvania Bulletin (Legislative Reference Bureau)—This is the official
gazette for information and rule-making, and serves as a temporary supplement to the *Code*. The *Bulletin* contains an updated list of *Pennsylvania Code*
Chapters Affected and a quarterly Subject Index as finding aids. The online
version, located at http://www.pabulletin.com/, includes statewide and local
court rules; the Governor's Proclamations and Executive Orders; actions by
the General Assembly; rule-makings and proposed rule-makings by state
agencies; and state agency notices.

The print versions of the *Code* and the *Bulletin* are edited, printed, and distributed by Fry Communications, 800 West Church Road, Mechanicsburg, PA
17055-3198. Questions about the *Code* and the *Bulletin* should be addressed to
the Legislative Reference Bureau, 641 Main Capitol Building, Harrisburg, PA
17120-0033; questions about the print versions should go to Fry Communications at (717) 766-0211, ext. 2340 or (800) 334-1429, ext. 2340 (out of state),
or (800) 524-3232, ext. 2340 (in Pennsylvania).

Statistical Resources

County/Municipal Demographic Report (Department of Community and Economic Development)—This online database provides general information relating to counties and municipalities, including census population, land area,
Federal EIN, Home Rule (designation, name, year), form of government, number of full-time and part-time employees, and incorporation year. The database may be accessed at http://ctcoas01.state.pa.us/dced/MSS.dyn_mun
_demographics.show. For more information, contact the Department of Com-
munity and Economic Development, 4th Floor, Commonwealth Keystone
Building, Harrisburg, PA 17120-0225, or visit its web site at http://www
.inventpa.com/.

K–12 Schools Statistics (Department of Education)—This page in the Department of Education's web site contains links to a number of reports on enrollments, graduates, professional personnel, and home education, as well as
detailed tables on enrollment. Most reports provide information for the last
three or four years. See the page at http://www.pde.state.pa.us/k12sta
tistics/site/default.asp. For more information about educational statistics,
contact the Pennsylvania Department of Education, 333 Market Street, Harrisburg, PA 17126, call (717) 783-6788, or visit its web site at http://www.pde
.state.pa.us/.

Pennsylvania Labor Force (Department of Labor and Industry)—This periodical publication includes information on labor force, employment, and unemployment in Pennsylvania and major areas. Also provided is a count of
statewide and area non-agricultural wage and salary jobs by industry, as well
as number of hours and pay earned in selected manufacturing industries. The
publication, along with other labor statistical reports, is available online by

linking from http://www.dli.state.pa.us/ to "Publications," and then "Workforce Information and Statistics."

Pennsylvania Statistical Abstract (Pennsylvania State Data Center)—This annual publication contains data on the Commonwealth and its sixty-seven counties, collected from state and federal agencies as well as other sources. Topics include Population, Vital Statistics, Industrial Development, Banking, Employment, Education, Social Services, Taxes, Government, Crime, and Infrastructure. The *Abstract* is available in print or CD-ROM format from the State Data Center, Institute of State and Regional Affairs, Penn State Harrisburg, 777 West Harrisburg Pike, Middletown, PA 17057-4898. For more information, call the Data Center at (717) 948-6336, or visit the web site at http://pasdc.hbg.psu.edu/pasdc/Products_and_Services/Publications/pa _statistical_abstract.html.

Pennsylvania Vital Statistics (Department of Health)—Annual Commonwealth, county, and municipality data on births, deaths, population, induced abortions, and reported pregnancies, are reported in numerous ways. An online version is available at http://webserver.health.state.pa.us/health/. Select "Health Statistics and Vital Records." More detailed birth and death statistics may be found in the department's *Birth and Death Statistics*, available online at the same site. For more information on either publication, contact the Bureau of Health Statistics and Research at (717) 783-2548 or via e-mail at webmaster@health.state.pa.us.

Status Report on Education in Pennsylvania (Department of Education)—This online report includes current and trend data on all areas of elementary, secondary, post-secondary and vocational-technical education. Information is grouped under major areas of students, staff, finances, schools, and libraries. The report is available online as a PDF file at http://www.pde.state.pa.us/ k12statistics/site/default.asp. For information on obtaining a print version, contact the Pennsylvania Department of Education, 333 Market Street, Harrisburg, PA 17126, call (717) 783-6788, or visit the web site at http://www.pde .state.pa.us/.

Other Resources

ARIAS, the Archives Records Information Access System (Pennsylvania Historical and Museum Commission, Pennsylvania State Archives)—This database of digitized historical archival records currently includes about 200,000 of some 500,000 records from the Pennsylvania State Archives, with the remaining documents soon to be available. Content, sequence, and image quality vary among the record series, which include invaluable primary source material about the Revolution, Civil War, Spanish-American War, and World War I, among other topics. *ARIAS* is accessed at http://www.phmc.state.pa .us/bah/dam/overview.htm.

Another online archival project, *Doc Heritage* (Pennsylvania Historical and Museum Commission, Pennsylvania State Archives), provides a sampling of government records and historical manuscripts, from colonial times to the mid-1990s, from the Pennsylvania State Archives. Each document image is accompanied by textual historical background; documents include the 1681

Charter of King Charles to William Penn, Civil War photographs, and information on the Johnstown Flood. *Doc Heritage* is found online at http://www.docheritage.state.pa.us/. For more information on *ARIAS* and *Doc Heritage*, contact the State Archives, Pennsylvania State Archives, 350 North Street, Harrisburg, PA 17120-0090, or call (717) 783-3281.

Pennsylvania Travel Planner (Department of Community and Economic Development)—The annual guide to Pennsylvania's tourist attractions, sports, children's activities, resorts, and shopping also has sections on the Commonwealth's tourism regions, with accommodation information. The guide is published by Independence Publishers, 101 E. Darby Road, Havertown, PA 19083, or call (800) 852-2046. A free copy is available from the department's Pennsylvania Tourism, Film and Economic Development Marketing Office, 400 North Street, Fourth Floor, Harrisburg, PA 17120; by calling (717) 787-5453 or (800) 237-4363; or via e-mail at http://www.experiencepa.com/experiencepa/travelPlanner.do. Much of the information in the *Travel Planner* is available online at http://www.experiencepa.com/experiencepa/home.do.

Recreational Guide and Highway Map (Department of Conservation and Natural Resources)—The annual official transportation and tourism map includes information on state parks and forests. The map is available with the *Travel Planner* mentioned above.

PENNSYLVANIA'S WORLD WIDE WEB HOME PAGE

The Commonwealth of Pennsylvania's home page, *PA PowerPort*, is located online at http://www.state.pa.us/. The site was designed to allow users to customize features, and to move easily from one area to another.

Links on the left-hand side of the page take the user to pages on general information, business, government, education, living, technology, visiting, and working in Pennsylvania; to helpful tools and *PA PowerPort* tips; and a virtual newsstand, listing local newspapers and radio and television stations by region. The center of the page is devoted to top state government news. On the right are extensive links to "What's Hot," "Featured Websites," "Citizen Services" (which includes links to state agencies), "Government Happenings," and legislative information, along with weather, driving conditions, and lottery results. "Kids' Pages" are accessed from this page, and within the "Kids' Pages" may be found state symbols and emblems, facts and figures, and links to other "Kids' Pages" in the various state agencies' web sites.

PA PowerPort was developed with the assistance of Microsoft and Lancaster-based Peripherals Plus Technologies, Inc., and launched in October 2000, one of the first state government Internet portals in the nation. The site has received a number of awards for excellence. For more information, contact the web master at webmaster@state.pa.us.

COMMERCIAL PUBLICATIONS AND WEB SITES

Legislative Directory (Pennsylvania Chamber of Business and Industry, 417 Walnut Street, Harrisburg, PA 17101)—This is a complete pocket guide to Pennsylvania's General Assembly, providing name, office, location, and telephone number of all members and congresspersons from Pennsylvania. It is available online at http://www.pachamber.org/dir/LegislativeDirectory/main.asp. A print version is available by contacting the chamber at the address above; by calling (717) 720-5462 or (800) 225-7224; or via e-mail at info@pachamber.org.

SOURCES CONSULTED

Numerous departmental web pages via *PA PowerPort*, the state's official web site, http://www.state.pa.us.

Pennsylvania State Library's web site, http://www.statelibrary.state.pa.us/libraries/site/default.asp.

Rhode Island

Eric W. Johnson

GOVERNMENT PUBLISHING AND THE DEPOSITORY SYSTEM

In 1985, the Rhode Island State Publications Clearinghouse was established as a section of the Rhode Island State Library (*Rhode Island General Laws*, Title 29, Chapter 7), to maintain a complete and permanent collection of state publications. Section 29-7-2(4) of the law defines a state publication as "any publication regardless of physical form or characteristics produced, made available electronically, printed, purchased, or authorized for distribution by a state agency, except those determined by the issuing agency to be required for official use only for administrative or operational purposes." Publications required to be deposited include "technical papers, annual reports, financial reports, bulletins, special reports, newsletters, brochures, databases and other documents that would be of interest to the general public" (Section I:III, *Rules and Guidelines for the Rhode Island State Publications Clearinghouse*).

The State Librarian and the director of the clearinghouse are responsible for administering the system. A State Publications Clearinghouse Advisory Committee, consisting of eight members, advises the State Librarian and the clearinghouse director (who are ex-officio members) on the operations of the clearinghouse.

A minimum of twenty-five copies of each publication is deposited with the clearinghouse for distribution to depository libraries, prior to public release. There are eleven full and fourteen selective state depositories throughout Rhode Island. The State Library, Providence Public Library, and the University of Rhode Island Library retain all state documents permanently, while the other depository libraries are required to maintain only those publications produced in the last five years.

USEFUL ADDRESSES AND TELEPHONE NUMBERS

The most complete collections of Rhode Island state publications may be found at the following libraries:

Rhode Island State Library
State House, Room 208
Providence, RI 02903
Phone Number for Rhode Island Reference Questions: (401) 222-2473
E-Mail Address for Rhode Island Reference Questions: gfacincani@sec.state.ri.us.
Library's Home Page: http://www.state.ri.us/library/web.htm
State Publications Clearinghouse Page: http://www.state.ri.us/library/clear/CLEAR
   .htm

Providence Public Library
Rhode Island Collection
225 Washington Street
Providence, RI 02903
Phone Number for Rhode Island Reference Questions: (401) 455-8005
E-Mail Link for Rhode Island Reference Questions: http://www.provlib.org/
   elibrary/emailref/emailref.htm
Library's Home Page: http://www.provlib.org/index.htm

University of Rhode Island Library
Government Publications
Kingston, RI 02881
Phone Number for Rhode Island Reference Questions: (401) 874-4610
Library's Home Page: http://www.uri.edu/library/

INDEXES TO RHODE ISLAND STATE PUBLICATIONS

State publications are classified by the SWANK classification scheme spe-cifically developed for state documents, with Rhode Island assigned number 39 as a state designation. The clearinghouse inputs full original cataloging in MARC format into OCLC. A quarterly *Checklist of Rhode Island State Documents*, with annual cumulations, lists citations in alphabetical order by the name of the issuing agency. Citations include main entry (author), title, OCLC number, SWANK number, and receiving libraries. The *Checklists* from 1996 on are avail-able online at http://www.state.ri.us/library/clear/CHECK.HTM.

State publications may also be located through the online catalog of *HELIN* (Higher Education Library Information Network), a consortium of Rhode Is-land academic libraries which includes the University of Rhode Island, at http://131.128.70.2/search, and the online catalog of *CLAN* (Cooperating Li-braries Automated Network), a similar consortium of public libraries, includ-ing the Providence Public Library, at http://seq.clan.lib.ri.us/.

ESSENTIAL STATE PUBLICATIONS

Directories

The Rhode Island Government Owner's Manual (Secretary of State)—This an-nual factbook of Rhode Island state information includes the state Constitu-tion, biographies of legislators, rules of the State House and Senate, listings of city and town officials, lists of state agencies, and a host of historical and demographic facts. While the *Manual* is not available online in its entirety, pieces of it are scattered throughout the state's web site. A print copy may be requested from the Office of Public Information, Office of the Secretary of State, State House Room 217, Providence, RI 02903, or call (401) 222-2357. A CD-ROM version is offered free to all Rhode Island residents and at a cost to others; this may be ordered online at http://www.corps.state.ri.us/cdorder/order1.asp or by calling (401) 222-2357.

Directory of City-Town Officials (Department of Community Affairs)—This annual listing of Rhode Island's city and town officials provides names and addresses for all officials. A web version of this information, entitled "Find Your Officials," may be found online at http://www.muni-info.state.ri.us/indiv.htm.

School Directory (Department of Education)—This is a listing of elementary and secondary schools in Rhode Island, with names and addresses, principals, grade levels, e-mail addresses, and web sites. The directory is available from the Rhode Island Department of Education, 255 Westminster Street, Providence, RI 02903, or by calling (401) 222-4600, ext. 2459. Information on schools may be found online at http://www.ridoe.net/School_Directory/K12.htm.

The Rhode Island Corporations InfoLink (Secretary of State, Corporations Division)—This online corporate database provides information on entity status, registered agent and address, initial directors, date of incorporation, address of principal office, and all activity history for active and inactive business entities. The database is searchable by name, entity identification number, agent, officer, and words in the purpose statement. It is available online at http://www.corps.state.ri.us/. For more information about the database, contact the Corporations Division, 100 North Main Street, 1st Floor, Providence, RI 02903-1335, or call (401) 222-3040, or via e-mail at corporations@sec.state.ri.us.

Financial/Budgetary Resources

Comprehensive Annual Financial Report (Department of Administration, Office of Accounts and Controls)—The *Comprehensive Annual Financial Report* (CAFR) shows the status of the state's finances on the basis of Generally Accepted Accounting Principles (GAAP). Recent editions are available online at http://controller.doa.state.ri.us/FinRpts_x.htm. Call (401) 222-6731 for more information.

State Budget (Budget Office)—This consists of the Governor's Budget Message and the current fiscal year's budget, divided into Capital Budget, Executive Summary, Technical Appendix, Program Summary, and Personnel Supplement. The *State Budget* is available online at http://www.budget.state.ri.us/operating.htm. Information about the budget may be obtained from the Rhode Island State Budget Office by calling (401) 222-6300.

Legal Resources

Constitution of the State of Rhode Island and Providence Plantations (General Assembly)—The state's Constitution consists of fifteen Articles: Declaration of

Certain Constitutional Rights and Principles; Suffrage; Of Qualification for Office; Of Elections and Campaign Finance; Of the Distribution of Powers; Of the Legislative Power; Of the House of Representatives; Of the Senate; Of the Executive Power; Of the Judicial Power; Of Impeachments; Of Education; Home Rule for Cities and Towns; Constitutional Amendments and Revision; and General Transition. It is available on the web at http://www.rilin.state .ri.us/gen_assembly/RiConstitution/riconst.html.

State of Rhode Island General Laws (Law Revision Office)—This is the codified compilation of each successive edition of the *Public Laws* arranged alphabetically into titles. The eight volumes of the last major revision in 1956 have expanded to twenty-eight volumes, encompassing forty-seven titles. The online version, available at http://www.rilin.state.ri.us/Statutes/Statutes.html, is provided for information purposes only; the official record for the state is the print version. The online version is searchable by keyword; searching tips are provided. The Law Revision Office may be contacted by e-mail at cmassouda@rilin.state.ri.us.

Public Laws of Rhode Island and Providence Plantations (Law Revision Office)— This is published annually and consists of all acts passed by the General Assembly during the previous legislative session. The only exceptions to this are resolutions and acts of a local and private nature applying to a single person, organization, and community; these are compiled and published separately in an annual *Acts and Resolves* volume. Public laws from 1994 to the present, as well as acts and resolutions from 1996 to the present, are available online at http://www.rilin.state.ri.us/gen_assembly/genmenu.html and searchable by chapter number, bill number, or subject. Inquiries about print copies of *Public Laws* may be addressed to the Law Revision Office by e-mail at cmassouda@ rilin.state.ri.us.

Statistical Resources

Information Works! (Department of Education)—This is a comprehensive online statistical summary, by individual school, school district, and the entire state system, of reports on assessment and demographics, indicators and financial information, and school details and goals, presented in both statistical and graphical formats. Schools are searchable by district, school name, grade level, school code, or district name, or may be selected from a list of school districts. A report for the entire state includes assessments, demographics, property value per student, tax capacity and effort, and financial data. The 2002 reports may be found online at http://www.infoworks.ride.uri.edu/ 2002/reports/. Previous reports to 1998 may be accessed from the same web site. For more information, contact the Rhode Island Department of Education, 255 Westminster Street, Providence, RI 02903, or by calling (401) 222-4600.

Local Government (Rhode Island Economic Development Corporation)—This online city and town information page provides links to monographs on each of Rhode Island's thirty-nine cities and towns. In addition to a brief history, government information, community links, and places of importance, a series of economic indicators highlights resident labor force and unemployment, private sector employment, new construction, median house costs, population estimates, births, and deaths. The portal page is available online at http://www.riedc.com/mcds/rimcdrame.html. The corporation may be contacted at One West Exchange Street, Providence, RI 02903; or call (401) 222-2601, or e-mail at riedc@riedc.com.

Other Resources

The Rhode Island Economy (Rhode Island Economic Development Corporation)—This is an occasional publication highlighting state economic trends. It reviews goods and services, and provides graphs on population, labor force, and salaries and earnings. The latest edition, published in March 1999, is available online at http://www.riedc.com/pdfpubs/RI%20Economy.PDF. A print copy may be requested from the corporation through its web site at http://www.riedc.com/edcForm/requestForm.asp, or at One West Exchange Street, Providence, RI 02903. Call (401) 222-2601, or e-mail at riedc@riedc.com. General information about the state's economy may also be found online at http://www.riedc.com/aboutri/economy/econframe.html.

Rhode Island Official Travel Guide (Rhode Island Tourism Division)—This is an annual guide to places and events, accommodations, and attractions. The *Guide*, divided primarily into regions, includes many advertisements, suggestions for tours, and special sections on golf, the outdoors, and specific areas such as Newport. The *Guide* may be ordered online at http://visitrhodeisland.com/toolbar/contact.asp, or through the Rhode Island Tourism Division, One West Exchange Street, Providence, RI 02903; call (401) 222-2601 or (800) 556-2484, or e-mail at visitrhodeisland@riedc.com.

Rhode Island Facts and History (Rhode Island Tourism Division)—This is also found on the Tourism Division's web site at http://visitrhodeisland.com/history/index.html, providing a host of facts on history, famous Rhode Islanders, state symbols, and trivia. Similar historical information on the Rhode Island Constitution, early history, independence, the Royal Charter, and state emblems may be found online at *Rhode Island History*, a page of the secretary of state's web site, at http://www.state.ri.us/submenus/rihstlnk.htm.

RHODE ISLAND'S WORLD WIDE WEB HOME PAGE

The main Rhode Island government web page, located online at http://www.ri.gov/, provides links to "Government," "Living in RI," "Business," "Recreation and Travel," "Health and Public Safety," "Working in RI," "Education," and "RI Facts and History." Included also are lists of "Top RI Links," directing users to the governor, judiciary, General Assembly, secretary of state, and tourism; a "Find It" section with general information on everything from birth certificates to traffic reports and state lottery results; links to online state services; and Rhode Island government news.

RI.gov, designed as "Rhode Island's one-stop access to state government," is a collaboration between the state's Chief Information Officer and New England Interactive, a private web company. Users may contact *RI.gov* via an online form at http://www.ri.gov/help/contact.html. New England Interactive may be contacted at 3 Sunset Ridge, Lexington, MA 02421; call (781) 862-3180, or e-mail at Info@newenglandinteractive.com.

A second useful web site is that of the Rhode Island Secretary of State, located online at http://www.state.ri.us/. From this rather crowded page users may link to State Departments and Agencies, Public and General Laws, the State Library, Tourism Information, and other information, including on-line tax forms and a list of local officials. A "Kids' Page" links younger users to fun facts, state symbols, folk stories, and an online coloring book. Comments on this web site may be directed to the Office of the Secretary of State, State House Room 217, Providence, RI 02903; or call (401) 222-2357, or e-mail at comments@sec.state.ri.us.

COMMERCIAL PUBLICATIONS AND WEB SITES

Connecticut/Rhode Island Atlas and Gazelleer (Yarmouth, ME: Delorme Mapping Company)—This atlas, part of a series covering all fifty states, contains topographic maps of roads, elevation contours, lakes and streams, public recreation lands, land cover, campgrounds, and so on. For ordering and price information see the publisher's web site at http://www.delorme.com/ or call (800) 561-5105.

General Laws of Rhode Island (Charlottesville, VA: LexisNexis/Michie Co.)—This 29-volume version of the *State of Rhode Island General Laws* includes full annotations, a comprehensive index, and the *Rhode Island Court Rules*. Cumulative supplements are published annually. It is available in print or on CD-ROM. For price and ordering information see the publisher's web site at http://bookstore.lexis.com/bookstore/catalog or call (800) 223-1940.

SOURCES CONSULTED

Numerous state department and agency web pages via *RI.gov*, the state's official web site, http://www.ri.gov/.

Rhode Island State Library's web site, http://www.state.ri.us/library/web.htm.

South Carolina

Lori L. Smith

GOVERNMENT PUBLISHING AND THE DEPOSITORY SYSTEM

A depository system for South Carolina government publications was established by law in 1982. Agencies and departments in the state government, including state-supported colleges and universities, are required to send at least fifteen copies of their publications to the South Carolina State Library. The State Library is charged with gathering the publications from state agencies/departments, organizing them, providing bibliographic control for them, and distributing copies to the other depository libraries.

In title 60, chapter 2, part 10 (d) of the *Code of Laws of South Carolina, 1976,* a state publication is defined as

any document, compilation, register, book, pamphlet, report, map, leaflet, order, regulation, directory, periodical, magazine or other similar written material excluding interoffice and intraoffice communications issued in print by the State, any state agency or department or any state-supported college or university for the use or regulation of any person; it shall also include those publications that may or may not be financed by state funds but are released by private bodies such as research and consultant firms under contract with or supervision of any state agency.

In part 10 (e), print is clarified to mean "all forms of duplicating other than the use of carbon paper."

The State Library retains three of the legally required fifteen copies, one of which is designated as an archival copy. Of the remaining copies, one is sent to the Library of Congress and the other eleven to depository libraries in South Carolina.

USEFUL ADDRESSES AND TELEPHONE NUMBERS

The most complete collections of South Carolina documents can be found in following libraries:

South Carolina State Library
1500 Senate Street
P.O. Box 11469
Columbia, SC 29211
Phone Number for South Carolina Reference Questions: (803) 734-8666
E-Mail Link for South Carolina Reference Questions: http://www.state.sc.us/scsl/
    forms/refform.html.
Library's Home Page: http://www.state.sc.us/scsl/
Depository System Home Page: http://www.state.sc.us/scsl/doclibs2.html

Cooper Library
Clemson University Libraries
Campus Box 34-3001
Clemson, SC 29634-3001
Phone Number for South Carolina Reference Questions: (864) 656-5168 or toll free at
    (877) 886-2389
E-Mail Address for South Carolina Reference Questions: curef@clemson.edu
Library's Home Page: http://www.lib.clemson.edu
Documents Department Home Page: http://www.lib.clemson.edu/govdocs/SCDocs/
    scdocs.htm

INDEXES TO SOUTH CAROLINA STATE PUBLICATIONS

From 1951 to 1968 the Historical Commission of South Carolina (Department of Archives and History) issued *A Checklist of South Carolina State Publications*. The State Library published this title from 1970 to 1988.

There is no formal bibliography of recently issued South Carolina state publications, but monthly lists of the items sent to depository libraries are available online from August 2000 to the present at http://www.state.sc.us/scsl/doclibs2.html. South Carolina publications are also included in the online catalog of the State Library, *WebLION*. The address for *WebLION* is http://www.state.sc.us/scsl/scslweb/welcome.html.

The call numbers assigned to South Carolina publications by the State Library are similar to the SuDoc numbers commonly used with federal documents. Materials are arranged by issuing agency rather than by subject. A guide to the basic call number assigned to each state agency is available online at http://www.state.sc.us/scsl/authlist.html.

In September 2000, the Office of Information Resources of South Carolina's State Budget and Control Board submitted a report to the legislature that was entitled *Government Information Resources 2000*. The report presented the results of a survey of state agencies and colleges/universities that was done to gather data about the information products they created, and of those, which were sold and which were freely distributed to the public. The report provides detailed information about the publications produced by each agency/institution and gives contact information both for those that are sold and for those that are available free of charge. The full report is online at http://www.state.sc.us/irc/2000r/. The seventh section of the report provides an alphabetical list of sources with e-mail addresses and phone numbers of the persons to contact for more information.

ESSENTIAL STATE PUBLICATIONS

Directories

Directory of Exports from South Carolina (Department of Commerce)—SC Docs. Call Number—C736 8.E96. Exporting adds billions of dollars to South Carolina's economy each year, and this directory is one tool the state uses to encourage foreign trade. It provides product descriptions and contact information for over 1,500 South Carolina companies who are involved in international trade. In addition to the alphabetical section of company listings, indexes are included that provide product descriptions for the SIC codes used in the directory, and list companies by the SIC code of the products they sell. The directory is available online at http://www.callsouthcarolina.com/. Select "International Trade" from the top toolbar, then select "Exporter's Directory" from the menu on the left. Those who wish to enquire about the availability of print copies can write to South Carolina Department of Commerce, P.O. Box 927, Columbia, SC 29202, or call (803) 737-0400. Questions can be sent via e-mail by selecting "Contact Us" from the Department of Commerce web page at http://www.callsouthcarolina.com. Several other Department of Commerce publications are available online from the Team South Carolina site at http://www.teamsc.com/library.html.

Directory of Historical Records Repositories in South Carolina (Department of Archives and History, State Historical Records Advisory Board)—SC Docs. Call Number—H6295 8.H47. Libraries and other institutions that hold significant collections of historical materials, such as letters, diaries, and photographs, are listed in this directory. It is available on the web at http://www.state.sc.us/scdah/repository/repositories.htm. A typical entry in the directory includes the following elements: facility address, contact information for the individual in charge of the historical records program, dates covered by the collection, physical volume of the collection, scope and contents of the collection, operating hours of the facility, and the address of the institution's web site. Those interested in obtaining a print copy of the directory can contact Donna Millwood at (803) 896-6135, or via e-mail at millwood@scdah.state.sc.us. Those with questions about the directory can contact the Department of Archives and History at (803) 896-6112.

Directory of Schools (Department of Education)—SC Docs. Call Number—Ed8332 8.S24-3. The information in this directory is available on easily browseable web pages, or in a printer-friendly version that can be customized to include only those sections desired. The address to access both versions is http://www.myscschools.com/PublicInformation/schooldirectory.cfm. The directory provides the names and phone numbers of persons in state-level education offices, and the names, mailing addresses, and phone numbers of persons in school district offices. For each school, the name of the principal is given along with a mailing address and phone number. Those who wish to enquire about the availability of a printed edition can write to South Carolina Department of Education, 1429 Senate Street, Columbia, SC 29201, or call (803) 734-8500. Questions can also be e-mailed to the Office of Public Information at bethrog@sde.state.sc.us.

Phone Numbers for South Carolina State Government (State Telephone Directory) (State Budget and Control Board, Division of the State Chief Information Office)—This searchable database of state government employees and their telephone numbers is available online at http://www.state.sc.us/phone/. An agency can be selected from a pull-down menu to get a listing of employees by function. In addition to names and phone numbers, a mailing address for each office or division is also given in the functional listing. An alphabetical listing of employees by agency can be selected from another pull-down menu. The listing for a specific person can be found by searching for his/her first or last name. Information in the database is updated by the telephone coordinator of each agency, and the date the directory was last updated is given at the top of the web page. Those with questions can contact the Chief Information Office Help Desk at (803) 896-0001.

Financial/Budgetary Resources

Appropriation Bills and Acts (Budget and Control Board, Office of State Budget)—Links to all the documents and legislation that result from the budget process each year are gathered on one web page by the Office of State Budget. Items available include the *Governor's Executive Budget*, the appropriation bills approved by the House Ways and Means Committee, the full House, the Senate Finance Committee, the full Senate, the Conference Committee, and the final General Appropriation Act. If the governor vetoes any items in the act, his/her veto messages are available on the page as well. Pages for recent years can be accessed from http://www.state.sc.us/osb/appbills .htm. The legislature provides similar information for the most recent year on its "General Appropriations" page at http://www.scstatehouse.net/html -pages/budget.html.

Comprehensive Annual Financial Report for the Fiscal Year Ended June 30, __ (Office of the Comptroller General)—SC Docs. Call Number—C7395 1. The most recent editions of this report are available via a link on the comptroller general's home page at http://www.cg.state.sc.us/. The report provides a detailed overview of the state government's revenues and expenditures, and presents financial statements for numerous state funds. The introductory section of the report includes a listing of state officials and an organization chart. The statistical section at the end of the report includes tables of revenues by source, expenditures by function, as well as demographic and general statistics. The online version of the report contains all the financial information that appears in the print edition, but photographs and some other materials have been omitted. Those who wish to obtain a print copy can write to Office of the Comptroller General, P.O. Box 11228, Columbia, SC 29211, or call (803) 734-2121. Questions or requests can be faxed to (803) 734-2064, or e-mailed to cgoffice@cg.state.sc.us.

Governor's Executive Budget: Fiscal Year [Year] (Governor)—SC Docs. Call Number—G7461 3.B82. The governor's recommendations on funding for state agencies and departments, and for specific programs, are outlined in this publication. The first part of the budget is a textual description of the governor's goals in specific areas. The second part is a detailed, line-item presentation of the amount the governor recommends that the legislature appropriate for specific divisions or programs within each agency. The most recent edition of this publication should be available via the governor's home page at http://www.state.sc.us/governor/index.html. Those with questions can write to Office of the Governor, P.O. Box 12267, Columbia, SC 29211, or call (803) 734-2100. Messages can also be e-mailed to the governor at governor@govoepp.state.sc.us.

Legal Resources

South Carolina Code of Laws (General Assembly, Legislative Council)—SC Docs. Call Number—A3 6.976. The General Assembly makes a searchable version of the state's codified laws available on its web site at http://www.scstatehouse.net/html-pages/research.html. The full text of the laws can be searched by keyword, or the titles and chapters of the *Code* can be browsed. A copyright message and disclaimer on the site tells users the most recent session of the General Assembly for which laws have been included, and warns users that the state of South Carolina does not guarantee the accuracy of the online edition. A commercial edition of the *Code* is published by the West Group and is described below. Those with questions about the online edition can contact the Legislative Council at (803) 734-2145, or via e-mail at COU@scstatehouse.net.

South Carolina Code of Regulations (General Assembly, Legislative Council)—Like the laws, a searchable version of the state's regulations is made available on the General Assembly's web site at http://www.scstatehouse.net/html-pages/research.html. The regulations can also be searched by keyword or browsed by chapter. Each chapter presents all the regulations promulgated by one agency, division, or department. A copyright message/disclaimer on the site tells the user the most recent issue of the *South Carolina State Register* for which regulations have been incorporated into the *Code of Regulations*. As with the laws, the accuracy of the online edition is not guaranteed. Those who wish to enquire about the availability of a print edition can contact the Legislative Council at (803) 734-2145, or via e-mail at COU@scstatehouse.net.

South Carolina State Register (General Assembly, Legislative Council)—SC Docs. Call Number—A3L524 8.R33. The *Register* contains regulations being presented for public comment, and the finalized version of regulations that have been approved for implementation, as well as public notices and other documents. Finalized regulations will eventually be incorporated into the *South Carolina Code of Regulations*. Issues of the *Register* released between January 1997 and June 2002 are available online at http://www.scstatehouse.net/aregist.htm; however, a subscription is required to access online the issues published after June 30, 2002. The cost for either a print or online subscription for the 2002–2003 fiscal year was $95. An order form is available online via a link from the site mentioned above. Those with questions can write to South Carolina State Register, Lynn P. Bartlett, Editor, P.O. Box 11489, Columbia, SC 29211, or call (803) 734-2145.

[Year] Summary of Statewide Legislation (General Assembly, Legislative Council)—SC Docs. Call Number—A3L524 8.S85-2. This publication provides a

summary of all legislation passed during a specific session of the General Assembly that will be applied statewide. The report also provides a summary of local and temporary acts and joint resolutions that were passed, as well as a summary of regulations that were adopted. The report is available as a Word document from a link on the Legislative Council page at http://www .scstatehouse.net/html-pages/lcouncil.html. Those who wish to enquire about the availability of a print copy can write to South Carolina Legislative Council, P.O. Box 11489, Columbia, SC 29211, or call (803) 734-2145.

Statistical Resources

Crime in South Carolina (Law Enforcement Division, Uniform Crime Reports Department)—SC Docs. Call Number—L41066 3.C64. Like the Uniform Crime Reports (URC) publications issued by other states, this title from South Carolina gives statistics on murder, rape, robbery, aggravated assault, breaking or entering, larceny, and motor vehicle theft. However, since 1991, South Carolina has served as a test site for the proposed National Incident Based Reporting System (NIBRS). Due to its participation in this test, its crime figures are calculated somewhat differently than in other states. An explanation of the differences between the numbers reported under UCR guidelines and under NIBRS guidelines is given in the introduction to the publication. The most recent editions of the report are available online at http://www.sled.state.sc .us/SLED/. Those who wish to enquire about the availability of a print edition can write to South Carolina Law Enforcement Division, Uniform Crime Reports Department, P.O. Box 21398, Columbia, SC 29221, or call (803) 896-7016.

South Carolina Community Profiles (Budget and Control Board, United Way of South Carolina, Sisters of Charity Foundation of South Carolina)—This web site is the result of a grant-funded study that was done, according to the site, "to assess the well-being of South Carolina and its residents." The address is http://167.7.127.238/community/index.htm. For each of the state's counties, information is provided in the following areas: Demographics, Economics, Education, Health, Housing, Poverty, and Public Safety. For each topic, statistics are given in a combination of text, tables, and graphs. The site includes a glossary of the geographic and statistical terms used in the profiles. Those with questions can write to Laura Kelley, South Carolina Budget and Control Board, Office of Research and Statistics, 425 Dennis Building, 1000 Assembly Street, Columbia, SC 29201, or via e-mail at lkelley@drss.state.sc.us.

South Carolina Statistical Abstract (Budget and Control Board, Office of Research and Statistics)—SC Docs. Call Number—B8595Res 3.S71-2. The *Abstract* presents tables of statistics gathered from both state and federal sources on topics such as Agriculture, Banking and Finance, Criminal Justice, Education, Employment, Income, Population, Recreation and Tourism, and Transportation. A note at the bottom of each table tells the source(s) from which the statistics were taken. The online version, available at http://www.ors2.state .sc.us/abstract/index.html, also has a note at the bottom of each table that tells the last date the table was updated and by whom. The publication includes an inventory of the statistics kept by state agencies and departments. Copies of the 2001–2002 edition of the *Abstract* were sold for $40 either as a bound print edition or as CD-ROM. The price includes shipping and handling. An order form is available online at http://www.ors2.state.sc.us/abstract/order.pdf. Those with questions can write to Office of Research and Statistics, 1919 Blanding Street, Columbia, SC 29201, or call (803) 734-3793.

South Carolina Vital and Morbidity Statistics (Department of Health and Environmental Control, Division of Biostatistics)—SC Docs. Call Number— H3496 3.V47. This annual publication reports statistics on births, fetal deaths and abortions, deaths, marriages, divorces, and annulments. Demographic information, such as the age and marital status of women who gave birth, is also included. Many statistics are given at the county level, and some tables include statistics from several previous years. A table in the introductory section of the report lists the most popular first names given to children born during the year. (In 2000, William and Hannah were the names used most frequently.) The most recent editions of this report are available online at http://www.scdhec.net/co/phsis/biostatistics/. Select "Publications and Reports" from the menu that appears on the left side of the screen. Those interested in enquiring about the availability of print copies can write to South Carolina Department of Health and Environmental Control, Office of Public Health Statistics and Information Services, Division of Biostatistics, 2600 Bull Street, Columbia, SC 29201, or call (803) 898-3649. *South Carolina Vital and Morbidity Statistics* is also called *Volume I, Annual Vital Statistics Series*. It is supplemented by another publication, entitled *South Carolina Detailed Mortality Statistics*, which is also called *Volume II, Annual Vital Statistics Series*. Copies of this supplementary title are also available online at the address given above. It provides detailed information about deaths based on the categories outlined in the *International Classification of Diseases*.

Other Resources

DiscoverSouthCarolina.com (Department of Parks, Recreation, and Tourism)— The state's main tourist information site is http://www.discoversouth carolina.com. The site not only offers information about tourist destinations, but also about the tourism industry and its economic impact on the state. An online form on the site allows the user to request a free travel guide. A section of the site called "Virtual SC" has video clips on various activities or areas of the state that can be viewed with Windows Media Player software. The "Activities and Special Interests" section includes a searchable database of golf courses in the state. Those who would like more information can call (803) 734-1700.

South Carolina Hurricane Guide (Emergency Management Division)—SC Docs. Call Number—Ad495Em 8.H86-2. The most recent edition of this publication is available online at http://www.state.sc.us/emd/library/brochures/hurricaneguide02/index.html. The guide provides detailed information for South Carolina residents or visitors about preparing for, surviving, and recovering after a hurricane. It includes a map of emergency evacuation routes and a list of important web sites and phone numbers. Those who wish to enquire about the availability of print copies can write to South Carolina

Emergency Management Division, 1100 Fish Hatchery Road, West Columbia, SC 29172, or call (803) 737-8500.

South Carolina Wildlife (Department of Natural Resources, Conservation Education and Communication Division)—SC Docs. Call Number—N2197Co 3.S58. This glossy magazine is published bimonthly and includes articles on South Carolina's native wildlife and their habitats. The most recent edition is available online at http://www.scwildlife.com/ (or at http://www.dnr.state .sc.us/magazine/index.htm). That page also includes a link to an online form that can be used to subscribe to the magazine. A one-year subscription costs $10. Those who wish to subscribe can also call this toll-free number, (888) 664-WILD (9453).

SOUTH CAROLINA'S WORLD WIDE WEB HOME PAGE

The address of South Carolina's home page is http://www.myscgov.com. A ribbon icon at the top of the home page once led to an announcement that a 2002 study of state government home pages named South Carolina's site the sixth best in the nation. It is indeed well organized and easy to use.

Across the top of the home page are photos of the state's governor, official seal, state tree, state bird, and state flower. Beneath those is a toolbar with buttons leading to pages on the following topics: News, Government, Education, Business, Health, Public Safety, Environment, Tourism, and Online Services. Below that another toolbar offers buttons for home, site index, help, and personalize. Those toolbars appear on every page until the user follows a link to an agency-level site or resource.

Along the left side of the screen there is a pull-down list of frequently asked questions and a selection of "Quick Links." The center of the screen features news and announcements. The right side of the screen presents a site search box, weather information for various cities, and a search box to find weather information for a specific zip code.

The site is maintained by the Budget and Control Department's Division of the State Chief Information Office. Those with questions can e-mail the webmaster at webmgr@scs.state.sc.us.

COMMERCIAL PUBLICATIONS AND WEB SITES

Code of Laws of South Carolina, 1976, Annotated (West Group, 610 Opperman Drive, Eagan, MN 55123)—This commercial version of the state's codified laws is available as a 44-volume set which is updated by an annual cumulative supplement. The current price for the set can be found on the West Group's web site at http://west.thomson.com/. Those with questions can contact West Group's customer service department at (800) 328-4880.

SCIway, South Carolina's Information Highway (SCIway.Net, P.O. Box 13318, James Island, SC 29422)—According to information on the "About" page of this commercial web site, it was first created at The Citadel in 1996 as a public service project. In 1997 the site was taken over by a private company and it no longer receives any financial support from the government. The site, found at http://www.sciway.net, provides well-organized links to numerous government sources, as well as other commercial sources. Topic selections on the home page include, among others: Accommodations, Arts, Business Directory, Churches, Counties, Fast Facts and Firsts, Government/Politics, History, Jobs, Maps, Recreation, Sports, and Webcams. A link to "Shop *SCIway*" allows the user to search a catalog of South Carolina products available for sale. The link to "Zoom!" leads to an extensive alphabetical subject directory of the site. The site also has a site map and is searchable by keyword. Those who wish to receive news updates can sign up for the site's free e-mail newsletter. Those who wish to ask questions about South Carolina can use the site's online bulletin boards (registration is required). Those with questions about the site itself can call (843) 814-5885, or e-mail rod.welch@sciway.net.

SOURCES CONSULTED

Numerous departmental web pages via the state's home page, http://www.myscgov
.com.
South Carolina Code of Laws, http://www.scstatehouse.net/html-pages/research.html.
Survey response from Deborah Hotchkiss, South Carolina State Library, 2000.
WebLION (State Library's catalog), http://www.state.sc.us/scsl/scslweb/welcome
.html.

South Dakota

Daniel D. Cornwall

GOVERNMENT PUBLISHING AND THE DEPOSITORY SYSTEM

South Dakota's current depository system was created in 1974 by *South Dakota Codified Laws* (SDCL) 14-1A. At that time, the South Dakota State Library was designated at the administrator for the state publications distribution center and depository library system. Additionally, administrative regulations for the depository system were created by *Administrative Rules of South Dakota* (ARSD) 24:30:06. Nine libraries currently participate as full depositories in the South Dakota program. The depositories are located geographically throughout South Dakota, except for the Library of Congress. Local libraries are required to make these materials available to the public and to retain them for five years (unless superseded). By statute, the University of South Dakota Library is charged with permanently retaining one copy of each publication distributed.

State agencies supply thirteen copies of printed publications (two copies of audiovisual materials) to the State Publications Distribution Center at the South Dakota State Library. SDCL 14-1A-1(4) defines a state publication as

any document, compilation, journal, law, resolution, bluebook, statute, code, register, pamphlet, list, microphotographic form, tape or disk recording, compact disc, floppy diskette, book, proceedings, report, memorandum, hearing, legislative bill, leaflet, order, regulation, directory, periodical or magazine published, issued, in print, or purchased for distribution, by the state, the Legislature, constitutional officers, any state department, committee, or other state agency supported wholly or in part by public funds.

For each publication, the State Library assigns a South Dakota documents classification number and catalogs the item into OCLC, a national union catalog. Each month, the State Library sends the depositories a shipping of South Dakota government publications. A monthly checklist is provided with the classification and OCLC numbers created by the State Library.

South Dakota documents are classified according to a system similar to the Superintendent of Documents, based on agency organization. The South Dakota classification schedule is available at http://www.sdstatelibrary.com/govinfo/depositories.htm.

USEFUL ADDRESSES AND TELEPHONE NUMBERS

The most comprehensive collections of South Dakota state documents can be found at the following libraries:

I. D. Weeks Library
The University of South Dakota
414 East Clark Street
Vermillion, SD 57069
Phone Number for South Dakota Reference Questions: (605) 677-6085
E-Mail Address for South Dakota Reference Questions: weeksref@usd.edu
Library's Home Page: http://www.usd.edu/library/idweeks.cfm
Note: The University of South Dakota is the only library required to permanently retain South Dakota state documents.

South Dakota State Library
Mercedes MacKay Building
800 Governors Drive
Pierre, SD 57501-2294
Phone Number for South Dakota Reference Questions: (800) 423-6665 (in South Dakota) or (605) 773-3131
E-Mail Address for South Dakota Reference Questions: library@state.sd.us
Library's Home Page: http://www.sdstatelibrary.com/
Depository Library Program Home Page: http://www.sdstatelibrary.com/govinfo/depositories.htm

INDEXES TO SOUTH DAKOTA STATE PUBLICATIONS

Since 1975, the State Library has published the *Monthly Checklist of South Dakota Government Publications*. Issues for recent years are available on the web at http://www.sdstatelibrary.com/govinfo/depositories/checklists/. All newly received South Dakota government publications are cataloged in the South Dakota Library Network catalog at http://webpals.sdln.net/cgi-bin/pals-cgi?palsAction=newSearch&setWeb=SDSCAT. The State Library is beginning a retrospective cataloging project to provide better access to historical government publications.

ESSENTIAL STATE PUBLICATIONS

Directories

Directory of Arts Festivals and Powwows (South Dakota Arts Council)—South Dakota Documents Call Number—None. Arranged by month, this two-part directory lists arts festivals and powwows held in South Dakota. Each entry contains the festival name and location, its date, entry deadline, whether it is juried, contact information, estimated audience, number of allowed exhibitors, and admission fee. A must for persons planning to display arts and crafts in South Dakota. The directory is available on the web at http://www.state.sd .us/deca/sdarts/powwow.htm. Free paper copies can be obtained by contacting the South Dakota Arts Council, Office of Arts, 800 Governors Drive, Pierre, SD 57501-2294. The council may also be contacted by phone at (605) 773-3131, by fax at (605) 773-6962, or by e-mail at sdac@stlib.state.sd.us.

South Dakota Arts Directory (South Dakota Arts Council)—South Dakota Documents Call Number—ED 300: D 627/. This 40-page guide provides information on local, state, tribal, and nationwide arts organizations that have activities in South Dakota. Each organization entry contains organization name, contact person, address, phone number, and e-mail/web site information if available. Some entries have additional notes. Free paper copies of the directory can be obtained by contacting the South Dakota Arts Council, Office of Arts, 800 Governors Drive, Pierre, SD 57501-2294. The council may also be contacted by phone at (605) 773-3131, by fax at (605) 773-6962, or by e-mail at sdac@stlib.state.sd.us. This resource is also available on the web at http:// www.state.sd.us/deca/sdarts/sdadir.htm.

South Dakota Criminal Justice Directory (Division of Criminal Investigation)— South Dakota Documents Call Number—AT 150: D 63/. This 100-plus-page directory is an effort to provide contact information for every criminal justice entity in South Dakota, regardless of jurisdiction. The directory is divided by jurisdiction and each entry provides basic contact information along with a listing of key staff. The directory is available on the Internet at http://www .sddci.com/administration/sac/crimjusticedirectory.htm. For more information about the directory, please contact the Division of Criminal Investigation at 3444 E. Highway 34, Pierre, SD 57501-5070, by phone at (605) 773-3331, or by fax at (605) 773-4629.

South Dakota State Government Phone Book (Bureau of Administration)— South Dakota Documents Call Number—None. Located at http://purl.sdln .net/sds/12433476/1, this directory provides contact information for employees across South Dakota. The directory is searchable by employee name, agency, city, and phone number. The *Phone Book* is not available in paper.

South Dakota's Manufacturers and Processors Directory (Governor's Office of Economic Development)—South Dakota Documents Call Number—EC 150:M 319/Year. Available on the web at http://purl.sdln.net/sds/ec150-m319/1, this directory is searchable by business name, product type, and business city. Every entry contains contact information, including toll-free phone numbers and web sites if available, top officials, products produced, and the six-digit NAICS code. For more information about the directory, contact the Governor's Office of Economic Development at 711 East Wells Avenue, Pierre, SD 57501-3369. The department can also be contacted by phone at (800) 872-6190 or (605) 773-5032, by fax at (605) 773-3256, or by e-mail at goedinfo@state.sd.us.

Financial/Budgetary Resources

South Dakota Comprehensive Annual Financial Report (CAFR) (Bureau of Finance and Management)—South Dakota Documents Call Number—None. In addition to the expected financial statements of revenue sources and expenses, the CAFR contains several features of interest to the general researcher. The introductory section contains a list of key state officials and an explanation of state functions. The statistical section of the report contains tables on historical census counts and major employers in South Dakota, per capita income, unemployment by industry, and livestock production. The most recent version of the *South Dakota Comprehensive Annual Financial Report* is available on the Internet at http://www.state.sd.us/bfm/main.htm. For more information about the report, contact the Bureau of Finance and Management at 500 E. Capitol Avenue, Pierre, SD 57501, by phone at (605) 773-3411, or by fax at (605) 773-4711.

State of South Dakota Governor's Budget (Governor)—South Dakota Documents Call Number—EX 200: B 859/2/. This is the governor's proposal to the legislature for the annual spending plan. Organized by agency, it includes mission statements, number of employees, and budget data. It also includes agency performance indicators for the past three years. Available on the web at http://www.state.sd.us/bfm/main.htm.

Legal Resources

Administrative Rules of South Dakota (South Dakota Code Commission)—South Dakota Documents Call Number—LE 225: R 861/. Published since 1978, the *Administrative Rules* are the executive branch regulations for the state of South Dakota. An online version is located at http://legis.state.sd.us/rules/index.cfm, which can be browsed by title, or searched by keyword or rule number. The browseable section of the rules is arranged by rule number. The *Rules* are available either as HTML or Microsoft Word files. Paper copies of any rule may be requested either by using the order form at http://legis.state.sd.us/rules/index.cfm?FuseAction=PriceList, or by calling the agency at (605) 773-4935. In 2002, costs for individual rules varied from $.09 to $14.79. The entire set sold for $250.00.

Session Laws of South Dakota and Documents of the . . . Legislative Session (Legislature)—South Dakota Documents Call Number—None. Session laws back to 1997 are available on the Internet at http://legis.state.sd.us/index.cfm. Each individual year has its own table of contents, topical index, and keyword search. Session laws may also be retrieved individually by chapter number. Each session law contains a brief legislative history and all bill versions. Audio recordings of some committee hearings related to the session law are also available.

South Dakota Codified Laws (Legislature)—South Dakota Documents Call Number—LE 125: C 648/. Available on the Internet at http://legis.state.sd.us/statutes/index.cfm, the *South Dakota Codified Laws* may be browsed by title, searched by keyword, or retrieved one citation at a time. The keyword search may be filtered by chapter or section number. The 33-volume paper version of *South Dakota Codified Laws* is available from the LexisNexis bookstore web site at http://bookstore.lexis.com/bookstore/catalog/. In addition to laws, the LexisNexis set has annotations from state case law, Attorney General opinions, and results of state law reviews.

Supreme Court Opinions (South Dakota Unified Judicial System)—South Dakota Documents Call Number—None. Supreme Court opinions dating back to 1996 can be accessed at http://www.sdjudicial.com/index.asp?category =opinions&nav=53. Opinions may be browsed by date or may be searched at http://www.sdjudicial.com/index.asp?category=search&nav=5. This is a combined search with the court calendar and it is important to note that this screen defaults to searching the calendar, not the opinions. Make sure you have "opinions" selected from the drop box before you continue! Opinions may be searched by keyword, date, or case number. Unfortunately, the key-word option searches the full text of every opinion, so a party name search will retrieve many cases not directly related to your search. Another weakness is that there is no apparent order to the search results, which may not be sorted. For information on prior years' opinions, contact the Supreme Court Clerk's Office at 500 East Capitol Avenue, Pierre, SD 57501, by phone at (605) 773-3511, or by fax at (605) 773-6128.

Statistical Resources

Crime in South Dakota (Division of Criminal Investigation)—South Dakota Documents Call Number—AT 150:C 868/. *Crime in South Dakota* is the annual publication that presents compiled crime data voluntarily reported by South Dakota sheriffs and police departments. The report is divided into sections by offense and by contributing agency. Sections concerned with offenses begin with a legal definition of the offense, the number of offenses reported, the number of offenses cleared (closed), and the total number of people arrested for that offense. Victim and offender demographics are provided for each of-fense. Editions of *Crime in South Dakota* back to 1997 can be viewed at http://www.sddci.com/administration/sac/crimeinsd.htm.

South Dakota Community Abstract (South Dakota State Data Center)—South Dakota Documents Call Number—ED 380:Ab 89/YEAR. This annual publica-tion provides information on South Dakota, its sixty-six counties, and those cities with a population of 500 or more. Available tables include taxable sales, education, population, income, employment, vital statistics, and other impor-tant data. The complete publication is available for $45.00 (which includes postage and handling) or you may order one area for $5.00. This publication is not available on the Internet, although a sample page can be seen at http://www.usd.edu/brbinfo/sdc/publications.htm. To order a copy, call or write the South Dakota State Data Center at Business Research Bureau, USD Pat-terson Hall, Room 132, 414 E. Clark, Vermillion, SD 57069, by phone at (605) 677-5287, or by fax at (605) 677-5427.

South Dakota State and County Population Estimates (South Dakota State Data Center)—South Dakota Documents Call Number—ED 380:C 832/YEAR. This publication provides estimates of the resident population of South Dakota and counties by age, race, and gender. It is not available on the Internet, although a sample page can be seen at http://www.usd.edu/brbinfo/sdc/publi cations.htm. To order a copy, call or write the South Dakota State Data Center at Business Research Bureau, USD Patterson Hall, Room 132, 414 E. Clark, Vermillion, SD 57069, by phone at (605) 677-5287, or by fax at (605) 677-5427.

Vital Statistics and Health Status Report (Health)—South Dakota Documents Call Number—HE 125: V 83/. This annual report is divided into sections on Natality, Infant Mortality, Induced Abortion, Mortality, Marriage and Divorce, and Communicable Disease data. It is not available on the Internet but can be requested by sending an e-mail to DOH.info@state.sd.us with your name, mailing address, and name of the report you are requesting. Other reports related to vital statistics can be ordered, and some viewed at http://www.state.sd.us/doh/Stats/index.htm.

Other Resources

Environmental Permitting and Regulation Guide (Environment and Natural Resources)—South Dakota Documents Call Number—WA 200:P 41/1. This guide is divided into five sections. Sections I and II present the introduction and department organization. Section III is composed of a table that matches customer groups and environmental programs. Included in the table are both environmental permitting programs and environmental regulatory programs. Sections IV and V describe the department's environmental programs. Each description contains the rationale for the program and if applicable, a flowchart of the permitting process. The *Guide* is available on the Internet at http://www.state.sd.us/denr/Enviro/. If you would like to be added to the mailing list for the *Guide*, call the department at (605) 773-3153.

South Dakota Consumer Handbook (Attorney General)—South Dakota Documents Call Number—AT 130:H 191/. This helpful guide is divided into eight chapters: How to Protect Yourself, Consumer Protection Laws, Smart Shopping, New and Used Car Shopping, Senior Rights, Landlord-Tenant Relations, Credit Cards, and Federal Credit Laws. The back of the book contains a reference guide listing contact information for state and federal consumer protection agencies. Along the way to the back of the book, you will learn how to file a complaint and learn how to recognize scams like foreign lotteries and work-at-home scams. For questions on material contained in the *Handbook*, please contact the Division of Consumer Protection at 500 East Capitol, Pierre, SD 57501, by phone at (800) 300-1986 in-state, (605) 773-4400 outside SD, by fax at (605) 773-7163, or by e-mail at help@atg.state.sd.us.

South Dakota Facts and Stats: Reference Page (South Dakota State Library)—South Dakota Documents Call Number—None. Located at http://www.sdstatelibrary.com/sdfacts/index.htm, this web site is the perfect place to send students who are given South Dakota as "their" state. From here you can link to state signs and symbols, a chronology of South Dakota and its governors, even read history newsletters geared to a fourth-grade reading level. Adults can find things to interest them as well, with links to genealogy sites, supreme court opinions, and even a "literary map" of authors who "reflect something significant about the South Dakota identity."

SOUTH DAKOTA'S WORLD WIDE WEB HOME PAGE

South Dakota's main web page can be found at http://www.state.sd.us/. The site is lighter on graphics than other states and loads easily. The main page, which does require the visitor to scroll through several screens to see the entire page, is divided into three columns. On the left-hand side of the screen is a list of government-related links, including a link to Forms, to South Dakota Public Broadcasting, and a State Government Phone Book. The middle column carries "Government News," which in August 2002 included stories on the West Nile virus, the current drought, and wildfire updates. The right-hand column contains spotlighted state agency sites like the current budget and the governor's "cybersafe" initiative.

Across the top of South Dakota's web page is a navigation bar familiar to users of state web sites. This navigation bar takes you to seven main areas: Government, Business, Travel/Parks, Education, Employment, and Family/Health. Government provides links to government programs, elected officials, and state agencies. The Business menu provides access to business-related agencies and business start-up guides. The Travel/Parks menu allows you to find information on Mt. Rushmore, current cultural events, campsites, road conditions, and weather. The Education menu provides links to state signs and symbols in addition to the expected education agency links. The Employment menu is the route to take if you need to find a private or public sector job, get help with work-related disabilities, or for employers to report their new hires. Family/Health is where the visitor finds information on adoption, child care, food stamps, and medical licensing.

The South Dakota web site is searchable by keyword. Any search can be limited to a single agency—a handy feature! An "Ask-A-Librarian" link is available for the frustrated and perplexed. The "Ask-A-Librarian" page offers several helpful links including a page of "South Dakota Facts and Stats," statewide journal article databases, the library's catalog, as well as an e-mail address and a South Dakota–only toll-free number for asking further questions. People outside South Dakota can call the "Ask-a-Librarian" service at (605) 773-3131. The direct URL for the "Ask-a-Librarian" service is http://www.sdstatelibrary.com/askalibrarian.htm.

A hidden treasure of the South Dakota home page is a link found at the very bottom of the page labeled "Mailing Lists." Clicking on this link takes you to a list of electronic mailing lists (see Figure 16). Some of the lists worth noting are "Department of Education Writing Improvement" list, dedicated to sharing ideas for teaching writing to K–12 students; "Public Utilities Commission Filings Mailing List," which provides documents filed with the South Dakota Public Utilities Commission; and the "Department of Health Flu List," which provides news of current flu strains and availability of vaccine during the peak flu months of October through April. If you are planning a trip to South Dakota in the fall or winter, check the mailing list archives to avoid the flu bug's bite!

COMMERCIAL PUBLICATIONS AND WEB SITES

South Dakota Legal Research Guide (Hein Publishing, Buffalo, NY)—Last published in 1999, this text has illustrations and bibliographies to guide a layperson or law student through background information and many bibliographical sources. Research techniques are intertwined with South Dakota government

Association of Conservation Information Mailing List
An organization comprised of information officers from around the country with the Game, Fish and Parks being a member of this group.

Association For Instructional Resource Centers for the Visually Handicapped Mailing list.
Library rosource list for the visually handicapped.

Bureau of Information & Telecommunication Newsletter
A newsletter of whats new and changing in technology within South Dakota government.

Department of Education English as a Second Language Mailing List
A mailing list for teachers or anyone else teaching english as a secondary language to students in South Dakota.

Department of Education Literacy Mailing List
A mailing list for teachers or anyone else teaching literacy to students of any age in South Dakota.

Department of Education Writing Improvement
A mailing list for teachers or anyone else to provide K-12 teachers across the curriculum with ideas and information that can be used to improve the instruction of writing in South Dakota classrooms.

Department of Health Public Health Issues List
DOH distributes information about outbreaks, recalls, disease trends and other issues of public health significance.

Department of Health Flu List
The flu list is a seasonal mailing (October-April) that posts information on the influenza season, what types of virus are circulating, and availability of vaccine.

GREENSPACE Mailing List
The purpose of the Great Faces, Green Spaces list server is to provide an easy way to share information among those interested in community forestry.

GFP-NEWS Mailing List
The GFP-NEWS mailing list is being set up to distribute the weekly new releases of the Game, Fish and Parks Department to department employees, state and national media, and the public. Up to now, only employees and the media have been able to receive these news releases directly.

Public Utilities Commission Agendas Mailing List
A mailing list for distribution of PUC meeting Agendas.

Public Utilities Commission Minutes Mailing List
A mailing list for distribution of PUC meeting Minutes.

Public Utilities Commission Filings Mailing List
A mailing list for distribution of PUC Filings.

Public Utilities Commission Rules Mailing List
A mailing list for distribution of information regarding PUC Rules.

Public Utilities Commission News Releases Mailing List
A mailing list for distribution of PUC News Releases.

Figure 16. South Dakota's list of mailing lists. *Source*: http://www.state.sd.us/ maillist/index.htm.

and history, which aids research in the state's Constitution and statutory law. An entire chapter is devoted to electronic resources. This guide may be ordered from Hein Publishing's web site at http://www.wshein.com/.

South Dakota Leaders: From Pierre Chouteau, Jr., to Oscar Howe (University of South Dakota Press, Vermillion, SD)—Published to celebrate the 100th anniversary of the admission of South Dakota into the Union, this book profiles twenty-nine men and women whose achievements were notable in the history of the fortieth state. Persons profiled include Sitting Bull, Crazy Horse, George McGovern, and Laura Ingalls Wilder. The book is currently out of print.

SOURCES CONSULTED

Numerous departmental web pages via the state's home page, http://www.state.sd .us/.

South Dakota Codified Laws, via the web at http://legis.state.sd.us/statutes/index.cfm.

Survey response from Ann Eichinger, South Dakota State Library.

Tennessee

J. Louise Malcomb

GOVERNMENT PUBLISHING AND THE DEPOSITORY SYSTEM

The government of Tennessee recognized the need to distribute its documents to libraries in 1917 with the passage of chapter 42 of the Acts of 1917. One aspect of the early legislation concerned the care of depository publications, stating,

It is the duty of the librarian or other person in charge of each depository to give receipt for and carefully preserve all state documents and publications so received. One (1) of the two (2) copies shall be lendable on application, to the persons, if any, allowed to take other books from the library of the depository. The other copy shall not be allowed to be taken from the premises of the depository. *Tennessee Code Annotated* 12-612.

The *Code* further stipulates how libraries are selected to serve as depositories and recognizes the Tennessee State Library at Nashville, the library of the University of Tennessee at Knoxville, and the Cossitt Library at Memphis. Other libraries are designated depositories by executive order of the governor. The legislative library is also to receive all state documents and publications otherwise distributed to depository libraries for use by members of the general assembly.

Depositories are to receive, without charge, copies of bills and other legislative publications. By legislation enacted in 1999 (Chapter 150/1), depository libraries are to receive House and Senate *Journals* electronically rather than as bound volumes. For additional information about the depository program, refer to the web site of the Tennessee State Library at http://www.state.tn .us/sos/statelib or to the *Tennessee Annotated Code* at http://www.tennessee anytime.org/laws/laws.html.

Tennessee State Documents Classification Schedule (Tennessee Library Association, Advisory Committee on State Documents)—Eric Wedig and Stephen

Patrick compiled a guide to the Tennessee State Documents Classification Schedule in 1987. It was issued in looseleaf form for updating purposes.

USEFUL ADDRESSES AND TELEPHONE NUMBERS

The most complete collections of Tennessee documents may be found at the following libraries:

Tennessee State Library and Archives
Public Services Section
403 Seventh Avenue North
Nashville, TN 37243-0312
Phone Number for Tennessee Reference Questions (615) 741-2764; fax (615) 532-2472
E-Mail Link for Tennessee Reference Questions: reference@state.tn.us
Tennessee Documents Home Page: http://www.state.tn.us/sos/statelib/techsvs/tsp/
   tsphome.htm
Library's Home Page: http://www.state.tn.us/sos/statelib/tslahome.htm

University of Memphis
Ned R. McWherter Library
Memphis, TN 38152-3250
Phone Number for Tennessee Reference Questions: (901) 678-2208
E-mail Address for Tennessee Reference Questions: reflib@cc.memphis.edu
Government Publications Department Home Page: http://www.lib.memphis.edu/
   gpo/unclesam.htm
Library's Home Page: http://exlibris.memphis.edu

INDEXES TO TENNESSEE STATE PUBLICATIONS

A List of Tennessee State Publications (Tennessee State Library)—Published since 1954, this is now available online at http://www.state.tn.us/sos/ statelib/techsvs/tsp/tsphome.htm. The State Library describes this list as

a bibliography of documents received from Tennessee state agencies by the Tennessee State Library and Archives during a specified quarter. Records from county courthouses such as land and marriage records are not included in this listing. Listed materials are available for use at Tennessee State Library and Archives during business hours; however, Tennessee State Library and Archives does not provide copies of state publications. REQUESTS FOR PUBLICATIONS SHOULD BE MADE DIRECTLY TO THE ISSUING AGENCY.

Search also the online catalog of the Tennessee State Library at http://www .state.tn.us/sos/statelib/tslahome.htm.
Historical and Bibliographical Study of the Administrative Departments of the State of Tennessee (Columbia University)—In 1940, Frances N. Cheney published the study as an M.S. Thesis at Columbia University, including the bibliography of Tennessee documents. The Historical Records Survey completed the *Checklist of Tennessee Imprints* covering 1793–1850 and available as a Kraus reprint.
   For earlier documents, consult R.R. Bowker's *State Publications: A Provisional*

List of the Official Publications of the Several States of the United States from Their Organization, pages 885–910.

ESSENTIAL STATE PUBLICATIONS

Directories

Tennessee Blue Book (Tennessee Secretary of State)—Entitled *Tennessee Blue Book and Official Directory* from 1929–1930 to 1936 and *Tennessee Hand-Book and Official Directory* before 1929, the *Tennessee Blue Book* is the guide to Tennessee state government. Since 1999 it has been available online at http://www .state.tn.us/sos/blue.htm. It provides directory information about state agencies as well as general information about government services.

Historically, directory information has been included in the *Tennessee Blue Book*, but for online directory assistance use the *Tennesseeanytime* directory site at http://www.tennesseeanytime.org/directory/index.html.

Financial/Budgetary Resources

Tennessee Comprehensive Annual Financial Report for the Year Ended June 30, 2000 (Tennessee Department of Finance and Administration)—Issued annually, the *Comprehensive Annual Financial Report* gives an overview of the state's financial situation. Reports from 1997 to the present are available on the web from the Division of Accounts' web site, http://www.state.tn.us/ finance/act/accounts.html.

Tennessee State Budget, A Summary and 3-year Overview (Tennessee Department of Finance and Administration, Division of the Budget)—Prepared by the Governor's Office and the Department of Finance and Administration, the summary gives the basic overview of appropriations and expenditures and has been issued under this title since 1984, with various other titles prior to that date. Budget documents, including the current year's budget and an executive summary appear on the Division of Budget's web site, http://www .state.tn.us/finance/bud/budget.html. The web site also provides an excellent overview of the state's budget process at http://www.state.tn.us/finance/ bud/process.html.

Economic Report to the Governor of the State of Tennessee on the State's Economic Outlook (Center for Business and Economic Research, University of Tennessee, Knoxville)—Issued annually, the report focuses on the overall economic well-being of the state, including forecasts. Recent editions are available online at http://bus.utk.edu/cber/erglist.htm. Contact the Center for Business and Economic Research at (865) 974-5441 for more information.

Legal Resources

Check List of Acts and Codes of the State of Tennessee, 1792–1939 (Tennessee Historical Records Survey Project, Division of Professional and Service Projects, Work Projects Administration, Tennessee State Library)—This WPA bibliography is of historical importance for researching the early laws of the state of Tennessee. Current legislative activities are reported on the web page for the General Assembly of Tennessee at http://www.legislature.state.tn.us. It includes access to bills.

Public and Private Acts of the General Assembly (Tennessee General Assembly)—Since 1999 the *Public Acts* have been available online at http://www.state.tn.us/sos/acts/acts.htm. The OCLC record lists the title history of the official title as "Acts passed at the General Assembly of the State of Tennessee, 1803–1829; Public acts passed at the General Assembly of the State of Tennessee, 1831–1836; Private acts passed at the General Assembly of the State of Tennessee, 1831–1833; Public acts of the State of Tennessee passed at the General Assembly, 1857–1862; Public and private acts and resolutions passed by the General Assembly ..., 1897; Public acts of the State of Tennessee ..., 1911–1981; Private acts of the State of Tennessee ..., 1911–; Public acts and resolutions of the State of Tennessee ..., 1982–." Microfilm editions of historical sets are available from a variety of vendors, including LexisNexis and W. S. Hein. For current pricing and contact information see the LexisNexis site at http://www.lexisnexis.com/academic/solutions/, or the W. S. Hein site at http://www.wshein.com.

Tennessee Code Annotated: The Official Tennessee Code (Under supervision of the Tennessee Code Commission by LexisNexis/Michie Co., Charlottesville, VA)—The *Public Acts* are codified in the *Tennessee Code Annotated*, published officially since 1955 by Michie (earlier by Bobbs-Merrill). Now it is also available via the Internet at http://www.tennesseeanytime.org/laws/laws.html.

Tennessee Administrative Register (TAR) (Tennessee Department of State)—The *TAR* is compiled and published monthly by the Department of State pursuant to *Tennessee Code Annotated*, Title 4, Chapter 5. The *TAR* contains the following in their entirety or in summary form: (1) various announcements (e.g., the maximum effective rate of interest on home loans as set by the Department of Commerce and Insurance, formula rate of interest, and notices of review cycles); (2) emergency rules; (3) proposed rules; (4) public necessity rules; (5) notices of rule-making hearings, and (6) proclamations of the Wildlife Resources Commission. *TAR* is available on subscription for $50.00 per year. Contact the Division of Publications, 312 Eighth Avenue North, 8th Floor, William R. Snodgrass Tower, Nashville, TN 37243, or call (615) 741-2650. There are no restrictions on the reproduction of official documents appearing in the *Tennessee Administrative Register*. Recent issues are available online at http://www.state.tn.us/sos/pub/tar.htm.

Understanding Your Court System: A Guide to the Judicial Branch (Tennessee Supreme Court, Administrative Office of the Courts)—This 10-page booklet is a great place to begin exploration of the state court system and is available in PDF from the state courts' web site at http://www.tsc.state.tn.us/geninfo/Publications/publications.htm. The main web site at http://www.tennesseeanytime.org/laws/courts.html also links to the rules, various reports, and the "opinions" of both the Appellate and Supreme Courts, since 1995 (http://www.tsc.state.tn.us/geninfo/Courts/AppellateCourts.htm).

Reports of Cases Argued and Determined in the Supreme Court of Tennessee (Tennessee Supreme Court)—Historically this has been published by a variety of publishers in microform and print. Other excellent web sites with legal information include: Supreme Court and AOC at http://www.tsc.state.tn.us and the *FindLaw* site at http://www.findlaw.com/11stategov/tn/courts.html

Statistical Resources

Tennessee Statistical Abstract (University of Tennessee: Center for Business and Economic Research)—Published triennially since 1969, this it is available from the University of Tennessee, Center for Business and Economic Research, Glocker Building, Suite 100, Knoxville, TN 37996-4170, or call (865) 974-5441. The price for the 2003 edition was $46.00, plus $6.00 for shipping and handling. The most recent edition is available online at http://bus.utk.edu/cber/tsa.htm.

Tennessee Vital Statistics for the Year (Tennessee Department of Health, Office of Health Statistics and Research)—Published annually, *Tennessee Vital Statistics* reports information at the local level within Tennessee for births, deaths, marriages, and divorces. Recent issues are available online in the "Health Data" section at http://www2.state.tn.us/health/statistics/index.html. It can be purchased from the Office of Health Statistics and Research for $10.00 per year. Write to Health Statistics and Research, Tennessee Department of Health, Cordell Hull Building, 4th Floor, 425 5th Avenue North, Nashville, TN 37247-5262, or call (615) 741-1954.

Certification of Election Returns for the General Election (Tennessee Office of the Secretary of State, Elections Division)—Biennially produced to report official election statistics, this report is available free while supplies last, or on the web site at http://www.state.tn.us/sos/election/results/results.htm.

Report Card, 2000 (Tennessee Department of Education)—Available online at http://www.state.tn.us/education/rptcrd00/index.html, the *Report Card* has been issued since 1996 to provide the status of Tennessee's education system. The web site also provides copies of its annual report, the *Youth Risk Behavior Survey*, and other publications of interest in the field of education.

Other Resources

Tennessee Conservationist (Tennessee Department of Environment and Conservation)—Published six times a year, the *Tennessee Conservationist* focuses on the preservation, protection, and use of the state's natural and cultural resources. Subscribe for $15.00 per year; write to Tennessee Conservationist, Department of Environment and Conservation, Nashville, TN 37243-0440, or call (615) 532-0104. Additional information about environmental issues and natural resources is accessible at the department's web site at http://www.state.tn.us/environment/natural.htm.

Official Tennessee Highway Map (Tennessee Department of Transportation)—The Department of Transportation provides a number of important links on its web site including the one to the *Official Tennessee Highway Map* and how to order a print copy (http://www.tdot.state.tn.us/maps.htm). The web site also links to the department's *Strategic Plan* and the *Tennessee Rail Plan*.

TENNESSEE'S WORLD WIDE WEB HOME PAGE

Tennessee's home page can be found at http://www.state.tn.us, http://www.tennesseeanytime.org, or http://www.tennessee.gov. It is attractive and easy to navigate, offering a site map, a variety of directories, and a search engine for state pages, as well as city and county web sites.

COMMERCIAL PUBLICATIONS AND WEB SITES

Tennessee Administrative Register Deskbook (R. T. Associates)—This is an index to the official compilation of rules and regulations of the state of Tennessee. Request additional information from R. T. Associates, P.O. Box 36416, Baltimore, MD 21286.

Tennessee Librarian: Quarterly Journal of the Tennessee Library Association (Nashville: Tennessee Library Association, 1948–   )—Preceded by *Tennessee Libraries*, the *Tennessee Librarian* includes articles concerning state publications. Copies are sent to members of the Tennessee Library Association and to businesses that advertise in the journal. See the *Tennessee Librarian* page at http://www.tnla.org/tl.html for more information.

SOURCES CONSULTED

Dow, Susan L. *State Document Checklists: A Historical Bibliography*. Buffalo, NY: William S. Hein & Co., 1990.

Lane, Margaret T. *State Publications and Depository Libraries: A Reference Handbook*. Westport, CT: Greenwood Press, 1981.

Parrish, David W. *State Government Reference Publications: An Annotated Bibliography*, 2nd ed. Littleton, CO: Libraries Unlimited, 1981.

State Capital Universe. Bethesda, MD: LexisNexis, 2001; http://web.lexis-nexis.com/stcapuniv, September 23, 2001. (Available to subscribers only.)

Statistical Universe. Bethesda, MD: LexisNexis, 2001; http://web.lexis-nexis.com/statuniv, September 16, 2001. (Available to subscribers only.)

Tennessee Anytime. September 23, 2001, http://www.tennesseeanytime.org.

Tennessee Code Annotated 12-612.

Tennessee Supreme Court and Administrative Office of the Courts home page, http://www.tsc.state.tn.us, September 24, 2001.

Vile, John R., and Byrnes, Mark, eds. *Tennessee Government and Politics: Democracy in the Volunteer State*. Nashville: Vanderbilt University Press, 1998.

Texas

Daniel C. Barkley

GOVERNMENT PUBLISHING AND THE DEPOSITORY SYSTEM

The Texas state depository library system was established in 1963 (Vernon's *Texas Statutes and Code Annotated* 441.001–441.106 [VTSCA]). As directed, the Texas State Library and Archives Commission (TSLAC) has responsibility for the administration of the depository program (VTSCA 441.104). Currently, there are forty-eight libraries that participate in the state depository program. See http://www.tsl.state.tx.us/statepubs/depositories.html for a complete list of the participating libraries.

The depository system was established to collect, distribute, and preserve the various publications of the Texas state government and its agencies. It is also organized to promote use of state publications by its citizens. The TSLAC is the coordinator between state agencies, colleges, and universities that produce publications and the depository community that receives these materials.

Each state agency must designate one or more staff persons as agency liaisons and notify the TSLAC as to who those liaisons are. They are directed by law "to maintain a record of the agency's state publications and shall furnish to the Texas State Library a list of the agency's new state publications as they become available" (VTSCA 441.103[a]). The agency must also furnish a sufficient number of copies to the TSLAC if that publication appears in paper. If that item is in an electronic medium, the agency must provide the TSLAC either online access to the publication, a sufficient number of copies on an electronic external storage device, or if pubic access is being given, one free online connection.

A state agency is defined as "a state office, officer, department, division, bureau, board, commission, legislative committee, authority, institution, sub-state planning bureau, university system, institution of higher education as defined . . . or a subdivision of one of those entities" (VTSCA 441.101[3]). A state publication is defined as "information in any format that is produced by the authority of or at the total or partial expense of a state agency or is required to be distributed under law by the agency." Further definition provides that a state publication is

publicly distributed outside the agency by or for the agency; does not include information the distribution of which is limited to contractors with or grantees of the agency; persons within the agency or within other government agencies; and members of the public under a request made under the open records law.

These definitions were last updated in 1997 (VTSCA 441.101 [4]).

The duties of the TSLAC are to acquire, organize, and retain state publications as well as collect publications from state agencies and distribute them to depository libraries. The TSLAC must also establish a microform program for the preservation and management of the collection and make those microforms available to state depository libraries at a reasonable cost. A list of all state publications collected and cataloged must be distributed on a regular basis, regardless of form or format. The TSLAC must also provide online access to electronic-only publications (VTSCA 441.104).

USEFUL ADDRESSES AND TELEPHONE NUMBERS

The best collections of Texas state publications can be located at the following libraries:

Dallas Public Library
J. Erik Jonsson Central Library
Government Information Center
Publications Division
1515 Young Street
Dallas, TX 75201
Phone Number for Texas Reference Questions: (214) 670-1468
Government Information Center's Home Page: http://dallaslibrary.org/CGI/TEXAS/
    links.htm
Library's Home Page: http://dallaslibrary.org/home.htm

Houston Public Library
Texas Room
500 McKinney Avenue
Houston, TX 77002
Phone Number for Texas Reference Questions: (832) 393-1313
E-Mail Link for Texas Reference Questions: http://www.hpl.lib.tx.us/hpl/
    interactive/answers.html
Library's Home Page: http://www.hpl.lib.tx.us/hpl/hplhome.html

Texas Legislative Reference Library
Texas State Capitol Building
1100 Congress Avenue
Room 2N.3
Austin, TX 78701
Phone Number for Texas Reference Questions: (512) 463-1252

E-Mail Link for Texas Reference Questions: reference.desk@tsl.state.tx.us
Library's Home Page: http://www.lrl.state.tx.us

Texas State Library and Archives Commission
Texas State Library
P.O. Box 12927
Austin, TX 78711
Phone Number for Texas Reference Questions: (512) 463-5455
E-Mail Link for Texas Reference Questions: reference.desk@tsl.state.tx.us
Library's Home Page: http://www.tsl.state.tx.us
Texas Depository Program Home Page: http://www.tsl.state.tx.us/statepubs/index
  .html

Texas Tech University
Libraries
Information Services—Documents Section
18th and Boston
P.O. Box 40002
Lubbock, TX 74909-0002
Phone Number for Texas Reference Questions: (806) 742-2282
E-Mail Link for Texas Reference Questions: http://library.ttu.edu/ul/help/ask/
Library's Home Page: http://library.ttu.edu/ul/

University of North Texas
Willis Library
Government Documents Department
P.O. Box 305190
Denton, TX 76203-5190
Phone Number for Texas Reference Questions: (940) 565-2413
E-Mail Link for Texas Reference Questions: http://www.library.unt.edu/forms/ref/
  emailref.htm
Library's Home Page: http://www.library.unt.edu/default.htm
Government Information Connection Page: http://www.library.unt.edu/govinfo/
  default.asp

INDEXES TO TEXAS STATE PUBLICATIONS

The TSLAC is required to publish the *Texas State Publications Annual Index*. This index has been published under various titles since 1921. In 1978 the index was known as the *Texas State Documents Index*; since 1989 the *Index* has appeared under its current title and configuration; 1994 marked the introduction of an electronic version. Now issued exclusively in electronic format, the *Index* can be found at http://www.tsl.state.tx.us/statepubs/annualindex/index.html.

The TSLAC has the responsibility to acquire and catalog all agency publications. Upon receipt, catalogers create bibliographic records (see http://www.tsl.state.tx.us/statepubs/classmanual.html for a complete explanation of the *Texas Documents Cataloging Manual and Classification Scheme*) and send them to OCLC. Those records are also incorporated into the TSLAC's public access catalog. A monthly checklist providing brief bibliographic information along with a subject index is created from these cataloging records. This checklist is announced on the *Texas State Publications* online web site. It is then compiled on an annual basis.

ESSENTIAL STATE PUBLICATIONS

Directories

Ask Ted: Texas Education Directory (Education Agency)—This provides current directory and mailing information for Texas schools, school districts, regional educational service centers, and related educational organizations. A search can be performed by county, school district, or individual school. Another key feature is the ability to print mailing labels directly from the list being viewed. A CD-ROM or paper version of the directory can be purchased. For non-profits the cost of either is $20.00. For those in the private sector the cost is $35.00. Contact the Texas Education Agency, 1701 North Congress Avenue, Austin, TX 78701-1494, or call (512) 463-9734. The directory can be found online at http://AskTED.tea.state.tx.us.

Directory of Licensed Occupations and Apprenticeship Program Contacts in Texas (Occupational Information Coordinating Committee)—This directory provides resources for people seeking information about career opportunities or job requirements in Texas. It is prepared by the Information Services Division of the Texas State Library for the Texas State Occupational Information Coordinating Committee, 9001 IH 35 North, Suite 103-B, Austin, TX 78753. Call (512) 837-7487. Copies are available in depository libraries and may be available from the committee.

Texas Directory of Multinational Companies (Economic Development, Business and Industry Data Center)—The directory contains two sections that highlight multinational companies operating or located in Texas. The first part contains an alphabetical listing and contact information for 439 Texas companies with operations abroad. The second section, organized by country, contains contact information for 1,118 foreign companies with operations in Texas. This list also includes the parent company location. It is available for $25.00 from the Texas Economic Development, Business and Industry Data Center, 1700 North Congress Avenue, P.O. Box 12728, Austin, TX 78711-2728, or call (512) 936-0100. An order form can be found at http://www.bidc.state.tx.us/bookorder form.cfm.

Texas Economic Development Reference Book—A Guide to Information Sources and Contacts (Economic Development, Business and Industry Data Center)—This reference book provides approximately 1,000 phone numbers and web pages that are organized by subject. Other information includes Texas phone listings for regional councils, state agencies, county clerks, city halls, chambers of commerce, and public libraries. It is available for $25.00 from the Texas Economic Development, Business and Industry Data Center, 1700 North Congress Avenue, P.O. Box 12728, Austin, TX 78711-2728, or call (512) 936-0100. The order form can be found at http://www.bidc.state.tx.us/bookorderform.cfm.

Texas Judicial Directory Online (Office of Court Administration)—This online directory is the web page for Texas courts, agencies, and committees and provides links to related state government and federal court sites. The directory can be searched by court type, court name, county, or by a judge's last name. Designed and maintained by the Office of Court Administration, 205 West 14th Street, Suite 600, Austin, TX 78701. Call (512) 463-1624. The directory can be located at http://www.info.courts.state.tx.us/juddir/juddir.exe.

Texas State Capitol Complex Telephone Directory (General Services Commission)—This is an online directory containing the names and phone numbers of state employees. Divided into state agency sections, it is useful for contact information for all state agency employees. Compiled by the General Services Commission, 1711 San Jacinto, Austin, TX 78711-3047. Call (512) 463-3035, e-mail public.info@gsc.state.tx.us. The directory is online at http://www.gsc .state.tx.us/telcom/phonec.html.

Financial/Budgetary Resources

Budgeting Handbook for Texas Counties (Comptroller of Public Accounts)— This handbook serves as a guide for county officials in evaluating their budgets, including the preparation process. It provides suggestions and instructions for budget preparation tasks that must be completed, time frames, and ways to determine estimated receipts and expenditures. Developed by the Texas Comptroller of Public Accounts, P.O. Box 13528, Capitol Station, Austin, TX 78711-3528. Call (512) 463-4000. The *Handbook* can be found at http://www .window.state.tx.us/lga/budgetco/.

Comprehensive Annual Financial Report for Year Ending . . . (Comptroller of Public Accounts)—This report presents financial operations for Texas for a particular fiscal year (latest available as of this writing is 2002). The report provides information on the management of Texas' financial resources. A copy of this report may be available from the Texas Comptroller of Public Accounts, P.O. Box 13528, Capitol Station, Austin, TX 78711-3528. Call (512) 463-4000. The online reports are located at http://www.window.state.tx.us/comptrol/ san/financial/finrpt.html.

Texas Comptroller of Public Accounts (Comptroller of Public Accounts)—This web site provides detailed fiscal information on taxes, the economy and economic forecasts, fiscal management, school district performance reviews, and other topics of interest on state government fiscal operations. The site can be located at http://www.cpa.state.tx.us/.

Legal Resources

Chief Elected and Administrative Officials (Legislative Reference Library)—This online edition provides contact information on all elected officials at the state and federal levels. It also includes contact information on state legislative committees, legislative staff, and agency officials. Compiled and maintained by the Texas Legislative Reference Library, P.O. Box 12488, Austin, TX 78711-2488. Call (512) 463-1252. The information can be viewed online at http:// www.lrl.state.tx.us/citizenResources/ceo/lrlhome.cfm.

General and Special Laws of the State of Texas (Legislative Council)—The report contains the laws and all joint and concurrent resolutions enacted in a particular session of the Texas legislature. It also includes tables and indexes. Copies may be available from the Texas Legislative Council, P.O. Box 12128, Austin, TX 78711-2128. Call (512) 463-1144.

Guide to the Texas Legislative Council (Texas Legislative Council)—The Texas Legislative Council is a non-partisan service agency for the state legislature and legislative agencies. The *Guide* is designed to assist members of the legislature in understanding and making the best use of council services. The *Guide* includes names and telephone numbers of council personnel. Paper copies are available from the Texas Legislative Council, Research Division, Robert E. Johnson Building, Room B.324, 1501 North Congress Avenue, P.O. Box 12128, Austin, TX 78711-2128, or call (512) 463-1144; e-mail hdist@tlc.state.tx.us. A PDF version can be located at http://www.tlc.state.tx.us/research/pubs.htm.

Opinions of the Attorney General (Attorney General's Office)—All opinions of the various Texas attorneys general from 1939 to current are now available. All letter opinions issued since January 21, 1953 are located as are all open records decisions issued since July 20, 1973. Paper copies can be obtained from the Office of the Attorney General, P.O. Box 12548, Austin, TX 78711-2548, or call (512) 463-2007. The opinions and decisions can be found at http://www.oag.state.tx.us/opinopen/opinhome.shtml.

Texas Constitution (Texas Legislative Council)—This online version provides a zipped file of the entire Constitution for downloading, an index of all constitutional sections, a search mechanism, and a "Frequently Asked Questions" feature. Paper copies can be obtained for $10.00 plus tax from the House Documents Distribution, P.O. Box 12128, Austin, TX 78711, or call (512) 463-1144. See http://www.capitol.state.tx.us/txconst/toc.html.

Texas Legislative Council Drafting Manual (Legislative Council)—The *Manual* is available in paper or online (see http://www.tlc.state.tx.us/legal/dm/cover.htm). This manual has been designed to assist the drafting staff of the state Legislative Council. It is also intended for use by state legislators and their staffs, lobbyists, and others with an interest in legislation and the legislative process. The *Manual* is available in paper for $25.00 from the Texas Legislative Council, Research Division, P.O. Box 12128, Capitol Station, Austin, TX 78711-2128, or call (512) 463-1143; e-mail: hdist@tlc.state.tx.us.

Texas Register and the Texas Administrative Code (Secretary of State)—Both of these resources are the official versions of the administrative rules and regulations governing Texas state agencies. New rules, proposed changes to rules, adopted rules, open meeting announcements, and other executive meetings and actions are printed in the *Texas Register* (see http://www.sos.state.tx.us/texreg/index.shtml). Current rules that become codified will be published in the *Texas Administrative Code* (see http://www.sos.state.tx.us/tac/index.shtml). Both versions are available in paper from the West Group (see http://west.thomson.com). Subscriptions are also available from the Texas Secretary of State, Texas Register Section, P.O. Box 13824, Austin, TX 78711-3824. Call (512) 463-5561. The *Register* can be purchased for $200.00 per year. The *Code* is available for $.50 per individual section retrieved.

Statistical Resources

Economic Indicators: The Texas Economy (Comptroller of Public Accounts)—This resource provides five critical measures of the Texas economy: Non-farm Employment, Retail Sales, Texas Consumer Price Index, Leading Indicators, and Texas Industrial Production Index. Within each of these main categories is a wealth of statistical information, gathered on a monthly basis, that provides a detailed look at the Texas economy. This resource also provides comparative data with U.S. economic indicators. The database is maintained by the Texas Comptroller of Public Accounts, P.O. Box 13528, Capitol Station, Austin, TX 78711-3528. Call (512) 463-4000. The online information can be found at http://www.window.state.tx.us/ecodata/ecoind/ecoind.html.

Snapshot: School District Profiles (Education Agency)—Since 1989 this free publication has provided extensive information regarding Texas school districts. School enrollments, graduation rates, federal and state funding, and other pertinent statistical information can be found. Published by the Texas Education Agency, Department of Research and Information, 1701 North Congress Avenue, Austin, TX 78701-1494. Call (512) 463-9734. The information can also be viewed online at http://www.tea.state.tx.us/perfreport/snapshot.

Texas Annual Employment and Earnings (Workforce Commission)—This is a data series detailing employment, earnings, and other related information regarding selected economic activities in the state and substate areas. Published annually since 1996, it is produced by the Texas Workforce Commission, Labor Market Information, 101 East 15th Street, Austin, TX 78778-0001. Call (512) 491-4922; e-mail lmi@twc.state.tx.us for information on obtaining a paper copy of this report.

Texas Cancer Registry (TCR) (Health Department)—The TCR is a population-based registry that collects data on all cancer cases diagnosed in Texas. Developed by the Texas Department of Health, the TCR maintains a statewide cancer incidence reporting system, analyzes cancer incidence, disseminates cancer information, and is used to identify populations at increased risk of cancer. For more information contact the Texas Department of Health, Texas Cancer Registry, 1100 West 49th Street, Austin, TX 78756, or call (512) 458-7523 or (800) 252-8059. The *Registry* is available online at http://www.tdh .state.tx.us/tcr/publication.html.

Crime in Texas: The Texas Crime Report (Public Safety Department)—This is the Texas version of the Federal Bureau of Investigation's *Uniform Crime Report*. Published since 1978, this annual report is a compilation of statistical information related to crimes, criminals, and Texas law enforcement agencies. It is published by the Texas Department of Public Safety, Uniform Crime Reporting Section, Identification and Criminal Records Division, 5805 North Lamar Boulevard, Austin, TX 78752-4422. Call (512) 424-2000. The report can be located at the department's web page at http://www.txdps.state.tx.us/ crimereports.

Texas Labor Market Review (Workforce Commission)—This is a monthly periodical that provides current information and statistics on the Texas economy and labor force. Each issue contains a brief overview of the economy, an in-depth article, and employment figures. Go to http://www.tracer2.com/ and select "LMI Publications" to see the latest issue. The *Review* is not copyrighted; please credit the Texas Workforce Commission for any information used. A free paper subscription is available by contacting the Texas Workforce Commission, Labor Market Information, 101 East 15th Street, Suite 103.A.2, Austin, TX 78778-0001, or call (512) 491-4904.

Texas Vital Statistics (Health Department)—This publication contains data on natality, mortality, marriages, divorces, and other vital statistics for counties and cities in Texas. Paper copies from 1956 to the present are available free of charge. It is published by the Texas Department of Health, 1100 West 49th Street, Austin, TX 78756-3199. Call (512) 458-7111 or (888) 963-7111 (toll free outside of Texas). Statistics can be located at http://www.tdh.state.tx .us/bvs/reports.htm.

Other Resources

Electronic State Business Daily (Building and Procurement Commission)—A state version of the federal *Commerce Business Daily* publication, this online resource provides contract and procurement information on bids solicited by state agencies. An interested party can view the most recent postings, browse or search by agency, procurement opportunity, or requisition number, or search by keyword. Developed for the Texas Building and Procurement Commission, P.O. Box 13047, Austin, TX 78711-3047. Call (512) 463-3035; e-mail public.info@tbpc.state.tx.us. The online information is located at http://esbd .tbpc.state.tx.us/1380/sagency.cfm.

Endangered and Threatened Animals of Texas: Their Life History and Management (Wildlife Commission)—This publication contains numerous entries on Texas endangered and threatened animals. Also included are photos, descriptions of endangered animals, maps of their range, and reasons for their decline. Linda Campbell is the principal author of this report. Contact the Texas Parks and Wildlife Commission, Resource Protection Division, Endangered Resources Branch, 4200 Smith School Road, Austin, TX 78744, or call (512) 389-4800 or (800) 792-1112 (toll free outside of Texas).

From Isolation to Participation: A History of Disability in Texas, 1835–1999 (Governor's Committee on People with Disabilities)—This report was prepared in conjunction with the fiftieth anniversary of the creation of the Texas Governor's Committee on People with Disabilities. The publication contains highlights of contributions made by disabled Texans from the state's earliest settlers such as Deaf Smith, to modern-day leaders in the community. The report also provides information on the state's institutions from their inception as asylums to now state-of-the-art facilities and a timeline that records historic events from 1835 to 1998. Focuses on the significant role persons with disabilities have played in the history of Texas. The report is available from the Texas Governor's Committee on People with Disabilities, P.O. Box 12428, Austin, TX 78711, or call (512) 463-5739. The report can also be found at http:// www.governor.state.tx.us/divisions/disabilities/resources/history/history.

Official Guide to Texas State Parks (Parks and Wildlife Commission)—This is the official and complete guide to the state parks of Texas. The guide contains an extensive history of each state park and provides camping, lodging, recreational activities, addresses, and phone numbers. Also included are a number of color photos and locator maps. Copies of the 2001 edition could be purchased for $19.95. Contact the Texas Parks and Wildlife Commission, Resource Protection Division, Endangered Resources Branch, 4200 Smith School Road, Austin, TX 78744, or call (512) 389-4800 or (800) 792-1112 (toll free outside of Texas).

Texas County Highway Maps (U.S. and Texas Departments of Transportation)—These maps provide detailed highway information on each of the 254 counties in Texas, and were produced from USGS 7.5 minute quadrangles, highway construction plans, aerial photographs, official city maps, and field inventory data. Maps also display the limits of incorporated cities, the public road network, and generalized hydrology. These were prepared in cooperation with the U.S. Department of Transportation, Federal Highway Administration, and the Texas Department of Transportation, Division of Transportation Planning, 125 East 11th Street, Austin, TX 78701-2483. Call (512) 463-8585. Full-scale maps are available only in photocopy prints and are printed on demand. Half-scale and quarter-scale maps are available in color. Full-scale are 4" = 1 mile, half-scale are 2" = 1 mile, and quarter-scale are 1" = 4 miles. Costs vary depending on scale, number of sheets, shipping, and reproduction qualities. Also available are an official state map, traffic maps, and state outline maps. See http://txdot.lib.utexas.edu/ for information on reproducing online maps.

Texas Highways (Highway Department)—Since 1954 this publication has provided a pictorial magazine of places and events that can be found on and along Texas highways. A yearly subscription is available for $17.50. It is prepared by the Texas Highway Department, Division of Travel and Information, P.O. Box 149233, Austin, TX 78714-9233. Call (512) 486-5823. Current issue and subscription details are available online at http://www.texashighways.com/currentissue/index.php.

Texas Government on the Web (State Library and Archives Commission)—Produced for information specialists, this guide, arranged in four parts, is designed to help find extensive information on Texas state government and its operations. There are four parts that include information on basic Internet terminology; an overview of the three branches of state government; a list of government web sites by subject; and a number of appendices that include a glossary of government terms, contact information, a list of commonly used citations for government resources, subject index, and a bibliography. Contact Sue Polanka, Library Development Division, Texas State Library and Archives Commission, P.O. Box 12927, Austin, TX 78711-2927, or call (512) 463-5465. This guide is available online at http://www.tsl.state.tx.us/ld/pubs/govinfo/index.html.

TEXAS' WORLD WIDE WEB HOME PAGE

The official state web page is known as *Texas Online* (http://www.state.tx.us). Like most other states the Texas state government recognizes the importance and value of a well-constructed web page that provides information ranging from government operations to tourism and travel. The web page is available in English or Spanish and provides the user with a number of options to gain insight into and information about Texas.

Aside from the usual links that are common on web pages today, *Texas Online* has three other means of accessing state information. A keyword search box is available on the initial web page. Utilizing this function allows one to search the broad spectrum of information placed on the web by various Texas government entities, including departmental/or agency web pages, publications, contact information, and other useful resources.

The Texas State Library and Archives Commission has developed a link called *TRAIL* (Texas Records and Information Locator) (see Figure 17). This search tool provides keyword searching to over 150 state agency web servers. See http://www.tsl.state.tx.us/trail/index.html. The third means allows one to search exclusively for funding opportunities (see http://www.tsl.state.tx.us/trail/grantsearch).

There are also direct links to the governor's office, online services such as filing/paying state taxes, registering a motor vehicle, parking and traffic fines, and obtaining professional licenses. Other links found can provide information on how to: conduct business with the state, obtain a marriage license, or apply to a state university. There are also links to useful regional and community web pages.

COMMERCIAL PUBLICATIONS AND WEB SITES

Essentials of Texas Politics, 8th ed. (Richard H. Kraemer, Charldean Newell, and David F. Prindle, eds.) (Florence, KY: Wadsworth Publishing Company, 2001)—The eighth edition has been updated to include information on Texas politics through the Bush administration. It is a seminal publication that covers Texas and its political scene since it became a state. See the publisher's web site at http://www.wadsworth.com/ or call (800) 354-9706.

Guide to Texas State Agencies, 11th ed. (Austin, TX: Lyndon B. Johnson School of Public Affairs, University of Texas at Austin, 2001)—This is a unique reference book on Texas state government. The *Guide* provides detailed descriptions of Texas' major executive, legislative, and judicial agencies. It also includes information on agency programs, functions, and organizational structure. The eleventh edition incorporates information on all of the 1997 legislative reforms. It also contains information on the state's higher education institutions, river authorities and regional councils, court system, sunset review schedule, staffing and funding levels, government web sites, and other aspects of the state government. See http://www.utexas.edu/lbj/pubs/index.html for ordering information.

The Handbook of Texas Online (Austin, TX: Texas State Historical Association)—This 2002 edition is an online encyclopedia of Texas history, geography, and culture. Its 23,000 entries provide detailed information on people, places, events, historical themes, institutions, and other topical categories. Designed to provide readers with concise, authoritative, factual, and non-partisan accounts on all aspects of Texas history. See http://www.tsha.utexas.edu/handbook/online for ordering information. It is available from the Texas State

TRAIL: Texas Records and Information Locator
Texas State Library and Archives Commission

Texas State Library and Archives Commission home page

Welcome to TRAIL

Advanced Search

View subject listings

Publications by type

Texas state agencies

Search tips and help

About TRAIL

Send your comments

Submit information to TRAIL (authorized users)

TEXAS GRANTS

Search TRAIL * Help

Keyword: [   ]

Submit Search

Please enter search terms and click on Submit button.

TRAIL searches and locates information from over 150 Texas state agency web servers. Enter your search term and click on the Submit button. The following are two different example searches (highlighted terms) for topics:

Looking for retail sales tax information: **sales tax, retail and sales and tax**

Establishing a new business: **"starting a business", business start**

New legislation introduced : **2001 bills, 77th legislature**

If you don't get the results you are seeking in your first search, try another way to search. You can use **advanced search features** search as boolean, phrase, and truncation. You may also use the **enhanced search capabilities.** If you don't locate the resource you are searching, you can send email to **reference.desk@tsl.state.tx.us** for further assistance.

In addition to searching, TRAIL also provides basic information about state agencies including contact, legal, budgetary and background resources on our **agency locator pages**.

For additional assistance, see the **Search tips and help** page.

home   contact   site index   policies & disclaimers

This page updated 8.30.2002

Figure 17. The Texas State Library and Archives Commission provides this excellent locator and search engine that helps the user find state government information. *Source*: http://www.tsl.state.tx.us/trail/index.html.

Historical Association, 2.306 Sid Richardson Hall, University of Texas, Austin, TX 78712, or call (512) 232-1513.

Texas Almanac (Dallas, TX: Dallas Morning News Company, 2002)—The *Almanac* provides information on practically anything one would like to know about Texas. Included are topics on History, Government, Recreation, Environment, Education, Business, Arts, Science, Agriculture, and on the 254 counties in Texas. The *Almanac* is distributed by the Texas A&M University Press. Ordering information and forms can be found online at http://www.tamu.edu/upress/.

Texas Atlas and Gazetteer: Topo Maps of the Entire State, Public Lands and Back Roads (Yarmouth, ME: DeLorme Mapping Company, 2000)—Delorme Mapping produces detailed topographical maps for many states. These maps provide information on the public lands and back roads of Texas for those interested in hiking, biking, or other outdoor recreational pursuits. The map is available for $24.95. Contact DeLorme Mapping Company, Two DeLorme Drive, P.O. Box 298, Yarmouth, ME 04096, or call (800) 581-5105.

Texas State Directory (Austin, TX: Texas Publishing Company)—This directory provides information on state, county, city, and federal government operations. It also includes information on election filing deadlines and other election information, contact information for government officials at all levels, and other useful names and addresses. The directory can be purchased for $29.00. Contact the Texas State Directory Press, P.O. Box 12186, Austin, TX 78711-2186. Call (512) 477-5698 or (800) 388-8075 (toll free outside of Texas). Ordering information is also available at http://www.txdirectory.com/.

Vernon's Texas Codes Annotated (Eagan, MN: West Group)—This is the legal authority for Texas laws and administrative code rules. See http://west.thomson.com for further information.

SOURCES CONSULTED

Correspondence with Cathy Hartman, University of North Texas.
Government Documents Round Table, American Library Association. *Directory of Government Document Collections & Librarians*, 7th ed. Bethesda, MD: Congressional Information Service, 1997.
Jobe, Janita. "State Publications." *Journal of Government Information*, 27 (2000): 733–768.
Numerous departmental web pages via the state's home page, http://www.state.tx.us/.
State Government and Politics, http://www.lib.umich.edu/govdocs/state.html.
State Legal Resources on the Web, http://www.lib.umich/edu/govdocs/statelaw.html#A.
Survey response from Coby Condrey, Texas State Library and Archives, 2000.
U.S. State and Local Gateway, http://www.statelocal.gov/.

Utah

Daniel C. Barkley

GOVERNMENT PUBLISHING AND THE DEPOSITORY SYSTEM

The Utah state depository system was established in 1979 (*Utah Code* 9-7-207) and currently has seventeen state depository libraries (see http://library.utah .gov/depositories.html for a complete list). The depositories are a blend of public, private, and academic libraries. The State Library Division has responsibility for providing guidance and direction of the depository program and the State Librarian has administrative oversight responsibilities. Under *Utah Code* 9-7-203-1, the Library Division shall "establish, operate, and maintain a state publications collection, a bibliographic control system, and depositories." In Utah, state depository libraries may be complete or selective.

Utah Code 9-7-101-6-a defines a state publication as

any book, compilation, directory, document, contract or grant report, hearing memorandum, journal, law, legislative bill, magazine, map, monograph, order, ordinance, pamphlet, periodical, proceeding, public memorandum, resolution, register, rule, report, statute, audiovisual material, electronic publication, micrographic form and tape or disc recording regardless of format or method of reproduction, issued or published by any state agency or political subdivision for distribution.

State publications excluded may be "correspondence, internal confidential publications, office memoranda, university press publications, or publications of the state historical society" (*Utah Code* 9-7-101-6-b). Other publications not included in the depository system are advertising, registration information or programs, training manuals used in workshops, seminars and conferences, minutes of meetings, newspapers not intended for public consumption, new releases, drafts or updates of plans, grant proposals, fliers or posters, and programs of theater, music, sports, and other events.

A state agency is defined as "the state, any office, department, agency, authority, commission, board, institution, hospital, college, university, or other instrumentality of the state" (*Utah Code* 9-7-101-5). Each state agency is required to deposit a sufficient number of copies of each publication as specified by the State Librarian. The Library Division sends two copies of each state publication to the Library of Congress, one copy to the State Archivist, one copy to each Utah state depository library, and retains two copies. Political subdivisions are required to send one copy of any publication generated to the State Archivist and one copy to the Library Division. Some materials considered by the Library Division as not of interest to the public are listed but not included in the depository system. There are a few other rules that govern special types of state publications. (See *Utah Code* 9-7-207.) The sections of the *Utah Code* that govern the depository system can be found online at http://www.le.state.ut.us/~code/TITLE09/TITLE09.htm.

USEFUL ADDRESSES AND TELEPHONE NUMBERS

The best collections of Utah state publications can be found at the following libraries:

State Library of Utah
Utah State Library Division
250 North 1950 West, Suite A
Salt Lake City, UT 84116-7901
Phone Number for Utah Reference Questions: (801) 715-6776
Library Home Page: http://library.utah.gov/index.html
Depository Program Home Page: http://library.utah.gov/depositoryprogram.html

University of Utah
Marriott Library
Government Documents and Microforms
Salt Lake City, UT 84112-0860
Phone Number for Utah Reference Questions: (801) 581-8863
E-Mail Address for Utah Reference Questions: http://www.lib.utah.edu/services/
    asklibrarian/asklibrarianform.html
State Documents and Information Home Page: http://www.lib.utah.edu/govdoc/
    library/statedocs.htm
Library Home Page: http://www.lib.utah.edu/

Utah State University
Merrill Library—UMC30
Special Collections & Archives
Logan, UT 84322-3000
Phone Number for Utah Reference Questions: (810) 797-2663
Merrill Library Home Page: http://library.usu.edu/

INDEXES TO UTAH STATE PUBLICATIONS

The Library Division currently publishes a biweekly bibliography of newly received materials (see http://library.utah.gov/statepubs.html). Access is by agency, author, title, and subject. The list is distributed to state depositories, state agencies, state officers, members of the legislature, and other libraries designated by the State Librarian.

State documents that are submitted are cataloged by the Library Division and entered into their online catalog. A list of titles is compiled and distributed. The most recent six months of lists can be seen at the aforementioned web page. This page also provides links to the online catalog and the current Utah state depository libraries. The online catalog also integrates electronic publications issued from state agencies.

ESSENTIAL STATE PUBLICATIONS

Directories

Directories of Utah Libraries (Utah State Library Division)—This is an online directory of all public and academic libraries in Utah. Included are links to all directors of public libraries in Utah, an alphabetical or county directory for public libraries, and a link to the *Utah Academic Library Directory* (UALC). Information includes name, address, telephone and fax numbers, e-mail and web addresses. Maintained by the Utah State Library Division, 250 North 1950 West, Suite A, Salt Lake City, UT 84116-7901. Call (801) 715-6777. It is available online at http://library.utah.gov/directories.html.

Utah Education Network: Community Connections (Office of Education and Office of Higher Education)—This online directory provides access to public school institutions in Utah. Included are links to Applied Technology Colleges, Public Colleges and Universities, School Districts and Their Web Sites, the Utah Electronic College, and the Utah Electronic High School. This resource is a result of a partnership between the Utah State Office of Education and the Utah State Office of Higher Education. Both agencies share joint maintenance responsibilities. This online resource can be viewed at http://www.uen.org/community/html/schools.html. You may also e-mail resources@uen.org for comments or suggestions.

Utah Online Directory of Community Health and Human Services (Department of Workforces Services)—This online directory provides information on various health and human services available in Utah communities. Information can also be found on volunteer opportunities, and on organizations, agencies, or individuals providing health care services. The directory is operated and maintained by the Utah Department of Workforces Services, P.O. Box 45249, Salt Lake City, UT 84145-0249. Call (810) 526-9675. For further information e-mail www@dwsa.state.ut.us, or view the directory at https://secure.utah.gov/communityservices/css.

Utah School Directory (Office of Education)—This annual publication contains pertinent information on all aspects of public and private education within Utah. Directory information includes private and public schools and school districts, Utah educational organizations, regional service centers, and the Utah State Office of Rehabilitation. Hard copies are available for $10.00 from the Utah State Office of Education, Public Relations, 250 East 500 South, Salt Lake City, UT 84111. Call (801) 538-7782. The directory can also be viewed at http://www.usoe.k12.ut.us/.

Utah State Directory of Employees (Administrative Services Department)—This online directory provides alphabetical or phonetic search capabilities and includes phone numbers and street and e-mail addresses for Utah state employees. The directory is maintained by the Department of Administrative Services, Central Stores, Salt Lake City, UT 84111. It can be viewed at http://web.state.ut.us/phone.htm.

Utah Court Directory (Utah Judicial Council, Administrative Office of the Courts)—This online directory provides contact information for each court in the Utah state court system. There are links provided for each court level (e.g., district, juvenile). It is maintained by the Utah Judicial Council, Administrative Office of the Courts, 450 South State Street, Salt Lake City, UT 84114-0241. Call (801) 578-3828. The directory can be viewed at http://www.utcourts.gov/directory/.

Financial/Budgetary Resources

Financial and Statistical Data Files—Annual Financial Reports (Office of Education)—These data files, available at http://www.usoe.k12.ut.us/data/files.htm, provide detailed financial information on the forty Utah public school districts and their budgets. Also included are fall enrollments, property taxes collected, maintenance costs on school buildings, and revenue. The data are from 1991 through the present and are stored in zipped files. It is maintained by the Utah State Office of Education, 250 East 500 South, Salt Lake City, UT 84114-4200. Call (801) 538-7500.

The [Year] Economic Report to the Governor (Governor's Office of Planning and Budget)—This annual report contains economic data, research, and analysis on the Utah economy. Information can also be found on economic, demographic, and fiscal analysis, long-term economic projects, growth planning, and in the 2002 report, the Winter Olympics. Data can be downloaded into Excel files. The online report is available at http://www.governor.utah.gov/dea/Publications.html. A paper copy may be requested from the Governor's Office of Planning and Budget, Demographic and Economic Analysis, 116 State Capitol, Salt Lake City, UT 84114, or call (801) 538-1036

State of Utah Comprehensive Annual Financial Report for Fiscal Year [Year] (Department of Administrative Services)—This publication presents the state's financial position, results of financial operations, and some demographic and statistical information to assist in understanding the financial condition of Utah. Available in a PDF format, this report includes an introductory section containing a list of principal officials, a state organization chart, and an overview of state operations. Other sections provide general purpose financial statements, including the State Auditor's report, and a statistical section provides a historical perspective of financial information. Currently only the past two fiscal years are available at http://wwwfin.state.ut.us/reports/cafr.htm.

Utah GOPB—Budget and Policy Analysis (Governor's Office)—This online resource provides links to numerous budget documents developed by the Governor's Office of Planning and Budget, Budget and Policy Analysis Section. This office has responsibility for the analysis of public policy issues including state budgets as well as providing appropriate recommendations to the governor. Budgets from several recent years are available online, as are the governor's current budget recommendations. It is maintained by the Governor's Office of Planning and Budget, 116 State Capitol, Salt Lake City, UT 84114. Call (801) 538-1027. The budgets as well as other resources can be found at http://www.governor.state.ut.us/gopb/budget.html.

Legal Resources

Legislative Drafting Manual for the State of Utah (Office of Legislative Research and General Counsel)—This manual is the guide that legislators and their staff refer to as they craft bills which may become state law. Last revised and updated in 1998, the *Manual* includes the Utah Constitution, *Code Annotated*, Rules of the Legislature, Administrative Rules, and other resources needed to write a piece of legislation. The *Manual* is available online at http://le.utah .gov/Documents/publications.htm. Paper copies are available in state depository libraries. View the Internet site or contact the Office of Legislative Research and General Counsel, 436 State Capitol, Salt Lake City, UT 84114. Call (801) 538-1032.

Utah Administrative Code Annotated (Department of Administrative Rules)— While the authorized paper edition of the *Code Annotated* is available from LexisNexis (see http://www.lexisnexis.com for pricing information), this edition provides many useful features also found in the paper edition. History notes and case law are included as well as the full text of all the permanent administrative rules of Utah. The paper edition is a 10-volume set. Go to http://www.rules.utah.gov/publicat/code.htm to view the *Code* online.

Utah Code—Statutes and Constitution (Office of Legislative Research and General Counsel)—The unofficial versions of the Utah Statutes, and the state Constitution, can be found online at http://www.le.state.ut.us/~code/code.htm. Sections are coded in HTML format with links to zipped WordPerfect files. Searches can be performed by keyword or by title. Links are also provided to the State Home Page, the Legislative Home Page, and a technical index. It is updated irregularly.

Utah State Bulletin (Office of Administrative Rules)—This is the official publication of the executive branch of the Utah state government on administrative rule changes and notices. As laws are passed, rules enforcing those changes are published in the *Bulletin*. Also contained are notices of agency meetings, changes in procedures or policies, and other bureaucratic requirements. Paper copies are printed and distributed bimonthly, and yearly subscriptions are available. Produced by the Office of Administrative Rules, Office of Legislative Printing, P.O. Box 140107, State Capitol, Salt Lake City, UT 84114-0107. Call (801) 538-1103. The *Bulletin* is available online at http:// www.rules.utah.gov/publicat/bulletin.htm. For more information on subscriptions go to http://www.rules.utah.gov/publicat/paperpub.htm. It also includes an index to the full-text documents. An unzip program is needed to view earlier years.

Utah State Legislature Publications Page (Legislative Research Council)—This web page provides links to numerous publications and other information sites that pertain to Utah legislative matters. From this site one can link to the

House and Senate, find information about a particular Utah state legislator, view the calendars of each chamber, and go to the *Utah Code* and Constitution that appear either in an HTML format or a searchable database. There are also links to numerous important publications including bill summaries (1997–present), the House and Senate *Journals* (1992–present), legislative rules, and other legislative documents. It is maintained by the Legislative Research Council. Go to http://www.le.state.ut.us/Documents/publications.htm. The Legislative Research Council can also be contacted by phone at (801) 538-1032.

Statistical Resources

State and County Historical Economic Data (Governor's Office of Planning and Budget)—This is a database of economic historical data by either the state or county level. Dates vary depending on the subject area reviewed. For example, merchandise exports dates range from 1990 to 2000; non-agricultural payroll employment from 1950 to 2000. There are also links to a host of other types of demographic and economic data. Maintained by the Governor's Office of Planning and Budget, Demographic and Economic Analysis, the web site is at http://www.governor.utah.gov/dea/HistoricalData.html.

State of Utah Long Term Economic and Demographic Projections (Governor's Office of Planning and Budget)—This online service provides economic projections on employment, labor force, and labor force participation rates for Utah. The employment projections are at the state level by detailed industry from 1980 to 2030. The labor force and labor force participation rates are by age group, area, or gender. The service also provides links to demographic and economic statistics, tables that provide employment and population data, presentations generated by the staff, documentation to the data, and data downloads. It is maintained by the Governor's Office of Planning and Budget, Demographic and Economic Analysis; the database can be located at http:// governor.utah.gov/dea/LongTermProjections.html. Contact the OPB at 116 State Capitol, Salt Lake City, UT 84114, or call (801) 438-1036.

Utah Data Guide: A Newsletter for Data Users (Governor's Office of Planning and Budget)—This guide provides data users with analyses on statistical data derived from the U.S. Bureau of the Census. It contains information on new research related to a variety of demographic and economic interests. Data sets are available from 1999 to the present and can be easily retrieved for viewing or for downloading. This was compiled by the Governor's Office of Planning and Budget, 116 State Capitol, Salt Lake City, UT 84114. Call (801) 538-1027 or (801) 538-1036. It is available online at http://governor.utah.gov/dea/ DataGuide.html. Current and past paper issues are available free of charge. Contact the above address to obtain copies.

Utah Economic and Business Review (Bureau of Business and Economic Research)—The *Review* is published bimonthly and features articles on trends and developments relating to the Utah economy. The *Review* also includes selected monthly and year-to-date business statistics, and is free to subscribers within the United States. To view the latest and past years' issues go to http://www.business.utah.edu/BEBR/busreview.html. To order go to http:// www.business.utah.edu/BEBR/subscribe.html. For more information contact the Bureau of Economic and Business Research, David Eccles School of Business, University of Utah, 1645 East Campus Center Drive, Room 401, Salt Lake City, UT 84112-9302, or call (801) 581-6333.

Utah State Courts Caseload Summaries (Utah Judicial Council)—This web site offers statistical summaries of caseloads in the various Utah courts, and has an easy-to-use search engine that allows one to search by year (back to 1997), court type, and judicial district. Caseload analysis can be found for recent fiscal years. Go to http://www.utcourts.gov/stats/ to search the site. It is maintained by the Utah Judicial Council, Administrative Office of the Courts, 450 South State Street, Salt Lake City, UT 84114-0241. Call (801) 578-3828.

Utah's Vital Statistics, Births and Deaths (Department of Health)—The statistics are organized by data year in four reports: Births and Deaths, Mortality, Marriages and Divorces, and Abortions. The births and deaths and marriages and divorces reports were first published in 1953. The other two reports were added later. Detailed summary tables are archived and are culled from various statistical reports filed with the Office of Vital Records and Statistics. Special data requests can be made in writing to the Utah Department of Health, Office of Vital Records and Health Statistics, P.O. Box 141012, Salt Lake City, UT 84114-1012, or call (801) 538-6105. The data can be located online at http://health.utah.gov/vitalrecords/Stats/statistics.htm.

Other Resources

Big Game Information (Division of Wildlife Resources)—This web page provides links to a variety of hunting and fishing activities in Utah. Included are Proclamations, Maps, Permit Application Forms, Drawings, Statistics, Annual Reports, and other useful information for hunting and fishing enthusiasts. There are also previews of several publications that can be obtained free or for a small fee. To view the web site go to http://www.wildlife.utah.gov/hunting/biggame.html. For publication information contact the Utah Division of Wildlife Resources, 1594 West North Temple, Suite 2110, Salt Lake City, UT 84114-6301, or call (801) 538-4728.

Doing Business in Utah: A Guide to Business Information (Community and Economic Development Department)—This publication, a joint project between several Utah and federal agencies, provides information and instructions on starting a business. Included in this resource are state regulations which must be complied with, sources of assistance, and other information needed for the new business owner. The information included in this publication is as current as possible. The paper edition may be more outdated than the online version. Paper copies may be obtained by contacting the Department of Community and Economic Development, 324 South State Street, 5th Floor, Salt Lake City, UT 84111, or call (801) 488-3233. The online copy can be viewed at http://www.utah.gov/business.html.

Trendlines: Perspectives on Utah's Economy (Workforce Services Department)— This is a magazine-style newsletter published biweekly and featuring articles on Utah's economy. Contributors are drawn from the Workforce Services staff as well as from the Governor's Office of Planning and Budget. Files are in a PDF format. Back issues are available for $1.00 (see http://jobs.utah.gov/

wi/pubs/publicat.asp). Additional links from this web site include services for job seekers and employers, Department of Workforce Services information, and other job- or economic-related sites. For more information contact the Utah Department of Workforce Services, Workforce Information Division, 140 East 300 South, Salt Lake City, UT 84111, or call (801) 526-9786. Visit the web site at http://jobs.utah.gov./wi/pubs/trendlines/current/tl.asp.

Utah Facts 2001 (Community and Economic Development Department)— This is the "blue book" of Utah, providing a variety of up-to-date facts and statistics on major topics of interest. Topics include population, education, the labor market, transportation, government operations, public utilities, real estate, and quality of life in Utah. The electronic edition of *Utah Facts* has been adapted from the printed copy. It is available online at http://dced.utah .gov/Factbook/index.html. A printed copy can be obtained from the Utah Department of Community and Economic Development, 324 South State Street, Suite 500, Salt Lake City, UT 84111. Call (801) 538-8700.

UTAH'S WORLD WIDE WEB HOME PAGE

Utah.gov (http://www.utah.gov) is the official web site for Utah and is the state's gateway to a variety of interactive services. Designed and maintained by Utah Interactive, Inc. (68 South Main Street, #200, Salt Lake City, UT 84101-1525; phone (801) 983-0175) in partnership with the Utah state government, this portal provides citizens, businesses, government agencies, and state employees with the capability to access multiple interactive services.

Started in 1999 as *eUtah.gov* for citizens and other interested parties to gain access to state government information, the home page has grown to include twenty interactive services processing 300,000–400,000 transactions per month. Utah citizens can renew their driver's or professional licenses, file state income taxes, purchase hunting and fishing licenses, register their vehicles, or send an electronic postcard. Businesses can renew their licenses, search business names, and conduct business with state government agencies.

The web page is grouped into seven "life-event" areas to help simplify users' lives. Each area provides subject-specific services, news features, or other types of pertinent information. Also provided is information on government services, officials, state employees, and state legislators. Maps can be found, a pictorial review of the recently concluded Winter Olympics can be viewed, and communication between a government official and a citizen can be established.

This is certainly one of the more innovative and functional web pages in existence.

COMMERICAL PUBLICATIONS AND WEB SITES

Beehive History (Salt Lake City, UT: Utah State Historical Society)—Published annually since 1974, *Beehive History* contains short stories and photographs on the history of Utah. It is a rich source of information written by scholars and independent authors. Copies of current and back issues are available for $2.50 each. Contact the Utah State Historical Society, 300 South Rio Grande, Salt Lake City, UT 84101-1143, or call (801) 533-3500.

Grace and Grandeur: A History of Salt Lake City (Thomas G. Alexander) (Carlsbad; CA: Heritage Media Corp., 2001, $54.95)—This monograph provides a history of Salt Lake City from its days as a wilderness outpost to being the host of the 2002 Winter Olympics. To purchase a copy of this publication contact the Utah State Historical Society, 300 South Rio Grande, Salt Lake City, UT 84101-1143, or call (801) 533-3500. It is also available from the publisher; see its web site at http://www.bookofbusiness.com/new/store/catalog.lasso.

On Being Poor in Utah (Garth Mangum et al.) (Salt Lake City, UT: University of Utah Press, 1998, $24.95)—This book identifies Utah's poor from who they are to where they are, and includes discussions on the causes of poverty in Utah, income maintenance, health and nutrition, housing, and education for the poor. It is available from the University of Utah Press, 1795 East South Campus Drive, Suite 101, Salt Lake City, UT 84112-9402, or call (800) 773-6672.

Statistical Review of Government in Utah (Salt Lake City, UT: Utah Foundation, 2001)—This publication contains the latest data about the Utah economy, taxes, and public expenditures at all levels of government. The *Review* also includes detailed information on demographic and population data, and is the longest-running abstract in Utah with its publication dating back to 1958. To view the most recent edition online go to http://www.utahfoundation .org/stat.html. For more information and to order a paper edition contact the Utah Foundation, 5242 College Drive, Suite 390, Salt Lake City, UT 84123, or call (801) 228-1838.

Utah Atlas and Gazetteer: Topo Maps of the Entire State, Public Lands, and Back Roads (Yarmouth, ME: DeLorme Mapping Company, 2000)—This latest edition, available for $19.95, provides topographical maps of Utah. Particular attention is paid to the public lands and back roads that provide access to outdoor enthusiasts for Utah's natural beauty. It is available from DeLorme Mapping Company, Two DeLorme Drive, P.O. Box 298, Yarmouth, ME 04096. Call (800) 581-5105.

Utah Directory of Business and Industry CD-ROM (Salt Lake City, UT: Utah Division of Business and Economic Development)—This 1999 directory contains information on more than 50,999 businesses and 9,800 individual employers that can be sorted by SIC code. The information contained in the directory can also be used to generate mailing lists. The CD-ROM can be obtained for $50.00 from the Utah Division of Business and Economic Development, Department of Community and Economic Development, 324 South State, 5th Floor, Salt Lake City, UT 84111, or call (877) 488-3233. View the table of contents online at http://www.dced.state.ut.us/busdev/dbi/bizdir99.htm.

Utah History Suite (Salt Lake City, UT: Utah State Historical Society)—This is a CD-ROM containing issues of *Utah Historical Quarterly, Beehive History, History Blazer,* and county histories of Utah. It is a useful resource for researchers and others who have an interest in Utah state history. The CD-ROM can be purchased for $39.95 from the Utah State Historical Society, 300 South Rio Grande, Salt Lake City, UT 84101-1143, or call (801) 533-3525.

Utah Statistical Abstract (Salt Lake City, UT: University of Utah, Bureau of Economic and Business Research, 1996, $40.00)—The *Abstract* provides the most complete time series data on various economic and demographic data on Utah. The latest edition contains nineteen sections plus an index. The *Abstract* is published every three to four years. It is not currently available online. For ordering information go to http://www.business.utah.edu/BEBR/pub order.html. You can also contact the Bureau of Economic and Business Research, David Eccles School of Business, University of Utah, 1645 East Campus Center Drive, Room 401, Salt Lake City, UT 84112-9302, or call (801) 581-6333.

SOURCES CONSULTED

Correspondence with Jill Moriearty, University of Utah.

Google, http://www.google.com.

Government Documents Round Table, American Library Association. *Directory of Government Document Collections & Librarians*, 7th ed. Bethesda, MD: Congressional Information Service, 1997.

Jobe, Janita. "State Publications." *Journal of Government Information*, 27 (2000): 733–768.

Numerous departmental web pages via the state's home page, http://www.utah.gov.

State and Local Government on the Net, http://www.piperinfo.com/state/index.cfm.

State Web Locator, http://www.infoctr.edu/swl/.

Survey response from Patricia Montgomery, Utah State Library Division, 2000.

Vermont

Eric W. Johnson

GOVERNMENT PUBLICATIONS AND THE DEPOSITORY SYSTEM

The *Vermont Statutes Annotated* (V.S.A.) does not establish a formal depository system per se, as do the laws of the other New England states. Rather, it mandates that

> the state librarian shall distribute . . . the acts and resolves of the general assembly, the legislative directory, the Vermont Statutes Annotated, the Vermont key number digest, the journals of the senate and house of representatives, the Vermont reports and other official reports and documents. The state librarian shall maintain records of all documents which he or she distributes. (V.S.A., Title 22, Chapter 13, Section 601)

One hundred copies of each publication are to be deposited in the State Library, "except when [the state librarian] determines that a lesser number is required" (V.S.A., Title 29, Chapter 53, Section 1156). These copies are distributed to various state offices and officials, and, depending on the particular title, to academic, public, and law libraries, and, upon request, to high schools and academies. Four copies of the *Acts and Resolves* are furnished to the Library of Congress.

"Public documents" are defined as including "the acts and resolves and journals of the general assembly, the reports of state officers or of any commission, board or person authorized by law to make reports" (V.S.A., Title 29, Chapter 53, Section 1101).

USEFUL ADDRESSES AND TELEPHONE NUMBERS

The most complete collections of Vermont state publications may be found at the following libraries:

Vermont Department of Libraries
109 State Street

Montpelier, VT 05609-0601
Phone Number for Vermont Reference Questions: (802) 828-3268
Library's Home Page: http://dol.state.vt.us/

Bailey/Howe Library
Special Collections
University of Vermont
Montpelier, VT 05405
Phone Number for Vermont Reference Questions: (802) 656-2138
Library's Home Page: http://library.uvm.edu/

INDEXES TO VERMONT STATE PUBLICATIONS

Vermont state publications may be searched on the web in the catalog of the Vermont Department of Libraries at http://web2.dol.state.vt.us/, and in the University of Vermont Libraries catalog at http://voyager.uvm.edu/. They are also listed in the VALS/DOL catalog (Vermont Automated Libraries System), which includes the Department of Libraries, Middlebury College, Norwich University, St. Michael's College, Trinity College, the University of Vermont, Vermont state colleges, and selected Vermont archives and public libraries. VALS/DOL may be accessed through the Department of Libraries' link at http://dol.state.vt.us/www_root/000000/html/_dol.html.

ESSENTIAL STATE PUBLICATIONS

Directories

Directory of Approved and Recognized Independent Schools, Approved Tutorials and Distance Learning Schools, Pregnant and Parenting Programs and State Operated Facilities (Department of Education)—This is an online listing of the in-state schools known to satisfy the requirements of Vermont compulsory school attendance law. This directory provides school names, addresses, contacts, telephone numbers, grade levels, and a brief description of the school. It is available at http://www.state.vt.us/educ/new/html/maindirectories.html.

Directory of Vermont Public Schools (Department of Education)—This online directory lists Vermont public schools alphabetically by school name, and includes addresses, telephone numbers, grade levels, and principals/headmasters. It is available at http://www.state.vt.us/educ/new/html/maindirectories.html. For more information about education issues, contact the Department of Education at 120 State Street, Montpelier, VT 05620-2501, call (802) 828-3135, or e-mail edinfo@doe.state.vt.us.

Legislative Directory (Secretary of State)—This is an online directory of names, addresses, telephone numbers, and e-mail addresses for Vermont state senators and representatives. Included are lists of standing committees of the House and Senate, and a Departmental and Staff Directory. The *Legislative Directory* may be found at http://www.leg.state.vt.us/legdir/legdir2.htm.

State Employee E-mail and Phone Directory (Department of Buildings and General Services)—This online telephone and e-mail directory of state employees, searchable by employee name, is located at http://phonebook.cit.state.vt.us/.

Telephone Listings for State of Vermont Government Agencies and Departments (Department of Buildings and General Services)—This provides a listing of state employees arranged by department, including job title, telephone number, and fax number. An online version, searchable by word or phrase, is available at http://phonebook.cit.state.vt.us/department_search.php3. For a print version of the telephone directory, contact the Department of Buildings and General Services at 2 Governor Aiken Avenue, Drawer 33, Montpelier, VT 05633-5802, or call (802) 828-3314.

Vermont Business Registry (Department of Economic Development)—This is an online registry of businesses with at least one physical location in Vermont. The database is searchable by business name, city/town, product category, business attributes, NAICS code, and business size. The *Registry* may be found at http://www.vermontbusinessregistry.com/. For more information, contact the Department of Economic Development, National Life Building, Drawer 20, Montpelier, VT 05620-0501, or call (802) 828-3080, or e-mail info@think vermont.com. The department's web site is http://thinkvermont.com/index .cfm.

Financial/Budgetary Resources

Comprehensive Annual Financial Report for the Fiscal Year Ended June 30, [Year] (Department of Finance and Management)—This source is an annual state financial report of "general purpose combined financial statements" and "combining and individual fund financial statements." The report covers revenues, expenditures, and changes in fund balances, and is available online at http://www.state.vt.us/fin/Publications.htm.

FY Executive Budget Recommendations (Department of Finance and Management)—The annual budget recommendation of the governor consists of the governor's message, a narrative overview, departmental recommendations, balance sheets, and a departmental appropriation history. The document can be found online at http://www.state.vt.us/fin/Key_Budget_Documents.htm. The actual Appropriation Act containing the amounts approved by the legislature may also be found at the same URL.

For a print version or for more information on the state budget or the *Comprehensive Financial Annual Report*, contact the Department of Finance and Management, 109 State Street, Montpelier, VT 05609-0401, or call (802) 828-2376.

Legal Resources

Constitution of the State of Vermont (as established July 9, 1793, and amended through September 21, 1995) (General Assembly)—The text of the state's Constitution is divided into two sections: "A Declaration of the Rights of the Inhabitants of the State of Vermont," and "Plan or Frame of Government," with amendments through 1995. The state Constitution is available online at http://www.leg.state.vt.us/statutes/const2.htm; copies of the Vermont Constitution are available as a pamphlet or in a convenient pocket-sized version from the Secretary of State's Office, Redstone Building, 26 Terrace Street, Montpelier, VT 05609-1101, or by calling (802) 828-2363.

The Journal of the House (Legislature)—This is the daily record of all actions taken by the Vermont House of Representatives on bills, amendments, resolutions, and appointments. Similarly, *The Journal of the Senate* (Legislature) is the daily record of the Vermont Senate. The current day's journals are available online through the state's Legislative Service at http://www.leg.state.vt.us/docs/service2.cfm. The House and Senate *Journals* can be located online at http://www.leg.state.vt.us/docs/docs2.cfm.. The *Journals* are currently not searchable. For information on print copies, contact the Vermont Legislative Council, 115 State Street, Montpelier, VT 05633-5301, or call (802) 828-2231.

Vermont Statutes Annotated (Legislature)—This is the compiled laws of the state of Vermont, divided into thirty-three titles. The online version, *Vermont Statutes Online*, is the unofficial edition, not edited for publication, and available at http://www.leg.state.vt.us/statutes/statutes2.htm. The official online version is available on the LexisNexis web site at http://198.187.128.12/vermont/lpext.dll?f=templates&fn=fs-main.htm&2.0. Both online versions are searchable, or browseable by title. For information about the print version, contact the Vermont Legislative Council at the address noted above.

Statistical Resources

Community Profiles (Agency of Human Services)—This is an annual comprehensive listing of outcomes and indicators, reported at the community and county levels by the school Supervisory Union (SU), used to measure achievement toward healthy communities in Vermont. Data are presented at the SU, county, and state levels, and include statistics on community involvement, school success, family stability, healthy behaviors, crimes, injuries, welfare, employment, and poverty, among others. The *Profiles* are available online at http://www.ahs.state.vt.us/publs.htm.. For a print copy, contact the Agency of Human Services, 103 South Main Street, Waterbury, VT 05676, or call (802) 241-3102.

Economic Data (Department of Economic Development)—This web page, located at http://thinkvermont.com/economic/index.cfm, provides links to data sources on Vermont covering Industry Statistics; Economy; Labor Trade and Occupations; People and Places; Agriculture; General Statistics; Business and Research Resources; and Small Business Profiles. For more information, contact the Department of Economic Development, National Life Building, Drawer 20, Montpelier, VT 05620-0501, call (802) 828-3080, or e-mail info@thinkvermont.com.

State of Vermont [Year] Vital Statistics (Department of Health)—This very comprehensive annual report provides statistics on population, births, deaths, marriages, divorces, civil unions, and dissolutions. Statistics are presented for the entire state and by county and town. Additional information, such as most popular names given, is also provided. The reports from several recent years may be accessed online at http://www.healthyvermonters.info/pubs.shtml. Print copies are available from the Department of Health, 108 Cherry Street, P.O. Box 70, Burlington, VT 05402-0070, or by calling (802) 863-7200.

Vermont School Report (Department of Education)—The *Vermont School Report* is designed to be an easy-to-access information source for educators, parents, community members, school boards, and the business community, to use as part of a locally developed public engagement strategy to improve the quality of education. These data often allow for comparisons of one school to another school(s) or to a statewide average. Indicators are displayed in seven sections: General Information, listing school names, addresses, and telephone numbers, type of school, principal, teacher–pupil ratio, and so on; Program Information; Staff Information; Community Social Indicators; Financial Resources; Financial Expenditures; and Student Performance. The *School Report* is updated continuously; a "Complete Vermont Report" shows state averages and totals for up to four years of data. The *Vermont School Report* is available online-only at http://crs.uvm.edu/schlrpt/index.htm.

Other Resources

The State Papers of Vermont (Secretary of State)—The secretary of state is mandated by state law (V.S.A., Title 3, Chapter 5, Section 117) to preserve and publish pertinent archival material. The twenty-two volumes of *The State Papers of Vermont* range in publication date from 1918 to 1991, and include indexes to papers; town charters; petitions; laws; a guide to the papers of Vermont's governors; an index to legislative reports; and much information from the eighteenth century. Availability and prices for the volumes may be found online at http://www.vermont-archives.org/publicat/pubs.htm. Print copies of the *Papers* are available through the Vermont Department of Libraries, 109 State Street, Montpelier, VT 05609-0601. Questions may be referred to the Assistant State Archivist by e-mail at ccarter@sec.state.vt.us.

VermontVacation.com (Department of Tourism and Marketing)—This is the state's official tourism web site. It may be found at http://www.vermontvacation.com/. The site provides information on recreation, lodging, dining, arts and culture, nature, state products, and farms, and is maintained by the Department of Tourism and Marketing, 6 Baldwin Street, Drawer 33, Montpelier, VT 05633-1301. Call (802) 828-3676, or e-mail info@VermontVacation.com.

VERMONT'S WORLD WIDE WEB HOME PAGE

Vermont's state home page, revamped in 2003, is located at http://vermont.gov/. From this portal, the user can link to various state agencies and departments, a telephone/e-mail directory, a calendar of events, press releases, and a site map. There are major links at the top of the page to Access Government 24/7, Find the Facts, Living in Vermont, Doing Business in Vermont, Education, Health and Public Safety, Recreation and Travel, and Employment in Vermont. Several other groupings of links (How Do I?, Vermont Community, Online Government Service, Top Vermont Sites, and Vermont Government News) provide access to specific information as well.

The site, which is searchable, was developed and is maintained by New

England Interactive, P.O. Box 1381, Montpelier, VT 05602. Call (802) 279-8518, or submit comments/questions at http://vermont.gov/help/contactus.html.

A "Kids' Page" at http://vermont.gov/find-facts/kidspage.html includes links to state facts, and to information on state parks, government, agriculture, and natural resources. Links are also provided to a list of the "Top 25 Things for Vermont Kids" and to the secretary of state's kids' page, which includes information on government, geography, history, state emblems and symbols, and a photo gallery.

COMMERCIAL PUBLICATIONS AND WEB SITES

Official Vermont Attractions Map and Guide—This is available free of charge from the Vermont Attractions Association, Box 1284, Montpelier, VT 05601; call (802) 229-4581, or e-mail attractions@vtchamber.com. This annual Vermont road map includes a list of state tourist attractions.

Vermont Life (Montpelier, VT: Vermont Life)—This magazine, published quarterly since 1946, showcases Vermont's people, places, and heritage through articles and photographs. Articles are indexed on the publication's web site at http://www.vtlife.com/index.html. The site also previews the latest issue and provides a searchable calendar of events. Subscriptions are available from Vermont Life, 6 Baldwin Street, Montpelier, VT 05602, or call (802) 828-3241.

Vermont Traveler's Guidebook—This is available free of charge by calling the Vermont Chamber of Commerce, (802) 223-3443, or ordering online at http://www.vtchamber.com/. This annual illustrated guide in magazine format highlights lodging, restaurants, attractions, camping, and shopping, with numerous advertisements, top ten seasonal events, activities for children, and other tourist information. This guide is geared for spring, summer, and fall activities; a similar *Vermont Winter Guide* includes winter activities, accommodations, attractions, and information about Vermont. Much of the information from the guides is available online, at http://www.vtchamber.com/guide/index.html.

SOURCES CONSULTED

Numerous departmental web pages via the state's official web site, http://vermont.gov/.

Vermont Department of Libraries' web site, http://www.dol.state.vt.us/.

Virginia

Lori L. Smith

GOVERNMENT PUBLISHING AND THE DEPOSITORY SYSTEM

The depository library system in Virginia was established in 1981. It is coordinated by the Library of Virginia in Richmond, which serves the Commonwealth in the same capacity as a State Library. There are fourteen depositories in the system—thirteen in Virginia, and the Library of Congress.

There was a major revision to Virginia's depository law in 2001. Many provisions of the law that originally appeared in titles 2.1 and 2.2 of the *Code of Virginia*, which deals with "Administration of the Government," were transferred to title 42.1, which deals with "Libraries."

In essence, the depository law requires state agencies to send the Library of Virginia a sufficient number of their publications to meet the needs of the depository system. The library keeps two copies permanently and distributes the remainder to the depository libraries. The depositories are required to make the documents available to the public and to keep them for at least five years.

According to title 42.1, section 19.1 of the *Code of Virginia* (§ 42.1-19.1), which took effect in October 2001, "agency" is defined as "every agency, board, commission, office, department, division, institution or other entity of any branch of the state government." The same section of the law defines "publication" as

all written documents fixed in any tangible format which can be understood, reproduced, or otherwise communicated, either directly or with the aid of a machine or device, and issued by an agency of the Commonwealth in full or in part at state expense. Publication excludes those written documents that apply solely to the agency's administrative and internal operations.

USEFUL ADDRESSES AND TELEPHONE NUMBERS

The best collections of Virginia state documents are located in the following libraries:

Library of Virginia
800 E. Broad Street
Richmond, VA 23219
Phone Number for Virginia Reference Questions: (804) 692-3562
E-Mail Address for Virginia Reference Questions: mclark@lva.lib.va.us
Library's Home Page: http://www.lva.lib.va.us
Depository Program Home Page: http://www.lva.lib.va.us/whatwedo/statedocs/
    index.htm

Government Information Resources
University of Virginia Library
P.O. Box 400154
Charlottesville, VA 22904-4154
Phone Number for Virginia Reference Questions: (434) 924-3133
E-Mail Link for Virginia Reference Questions: http://www.lib.virginia.edu/govdocs/
    refform2.htm
Alderman Library, Government Information Resources Home Page: http://www.lib
    .virginia.edu/govdocs/

INDEXES TO VIRGINIA STATE PUBLICATIONS

The Librarian of Virginia is required, in § 42.1-19.3 of the *Code of Virginia*, to "prepare, publish and make available annually a catalog of publications printed by state agencies." The law requires the catalog to be indexed by subject, author, and issuing agency, and to include the date of publication, and when available, information about the price of the publication and how it may be purchased or obtained free of charge.

From 1927 to 1992 the catalog was published as the *Check-list of Virginia State Publications*. The current title of this catalog, which is compiled by the Documents Team in the Library of Virginia's Collection Management Division, is *Virginia State Documents*. It has been published under that title since 1993. The most recent edition can be found online at http://www.lva.lib.va.us/whatwehave/gov/vsd/index.htm.

ESSENTIAL STATE PUBLICATIONS

Directories

Report of the Secretary of the Commonwealth to the Governor and General Assembly of Virginia (Secretary of the Commonwealth)—This annual publication is the "Blue Book" for Virginia. It provides information about the purpose of each state government department, agency, board, and commission, and about the current officeholders or members. Contact information is given for each entity including, when available, a web site address. The *Report* also gives general information about the Commonwealth and its history. Print copies can be purchased from the Office of the Secretary of the Commonwealth, P.O. Box 2454, Richmond, VA 23218-2454, ATTN: Blue Book. The phone number is (804) 786-2441. The 2001–2002 edition was priced at $32 plus shipping. Further information about purchasing the publication, including information about beginning a subscription to the online version, is available on the web at http://www.commonwealth.state.va.us/SoC/report.cfm.

Virginia State Agencies, Quick Reference Telephone Directory (Department of Information Technology, Division of Telecommunications, Directory Assistance Section)—This directory provides phone numbers for state agencies and their subdivisions. Numbers are given by office or position title, but no names are provided for specific state government employees. This source is available as a PDF file at http://www.vipnet.org/cmsportal/government_881/government_957/index.html. That page, the "Contact Virgina Government" page, also provides access to searchable electronic directories of government employees and agencies.

Financial/Budgetary Resources

Commonwealth of Virginia, Executive Budget (Department of Planning and Budget)—Issued biennially, this publication provides details about the governor's proposed budget for state government agencies and programs. General overviews of the state's economy and projected revenues are provided, as well as information about proposed capital projects and aid the governor recommends be given to local governments or to programs administered locally. The most recent editions of the *Executive Budget*, plus other budgetary information, are available on the web at http://www.dpb.state.va.us/budget/budget.htm.

Report of the Comptroller to the Governor of Virginia, a Comprehensive Annual Financial Report (Department of Accounts, Comptroller)—The revenues, expenditures, and debts of the state are reported in this publication. The report includes state government organizational charts and presents a general overview of the state's finances and economy. Recent editions are available on the web at http://www.doa.state.va.us/docs/Publications/CAFR/cafr.htm. Requests for print copies can be addressed to Department of Accounts, P.O. Box 1971, Richmond, VA 23218. The telephone number is (804) 225-3038. A less complex and more easily understandable version of the report is also available. It is called *Virginia Financial Perspective: A Report to the Citizens of the Commonwealth for the Fiscal Year [Year]*, and it's found on the web at http://www.doa.state.va.us/docs/Publications/Popular/poprpt.htm. Print copies of either report can be requested via an online form at http://www.doa.state.va.us/docs/General/RequestForm.htm.

Legal Resources

Code of Virginia (General Assembly, Virginia Code Commission)—This is the codified, or subject-divided, version of Virginia's laws. The official edition is a commercial publication issued by Michie Company, a subdivision of LexisNexis. An unofficial edition of the *Code* is available online and can be accessed from the Virginia Code Commission page at http://leg1.state.va.us/000/src.htm or from the General Assembly page at http://legis.state.va.us/Laws/CodeofVa.htm.

Virginia Administrative Code (General Assembly, Virginia Code Commission)—This title pulls together the administrative rules and regulations of all the state's government agencies. West Group publishes the official, commercial edition. An unofficial edition is available on the web from the Virginia Code Commission page at http://leg1.state.va.us/000/srr.htm or from the General Assembly page at http://legis.state.va.us/Laws/AdminCode.htm.

The Virginia Register of Regulations (General Assembly, Virginia Code Commission)—Proposed regulations, proposed changes to existing regulations, and newly adopted final regulations are published in the *Virginia Register*, which is issued biweekly. Comments or objections made by the governor or members of the General Assembly during the adoption process will be published in the *Register* as well. Other types of information contained in the *Register* are emergency regulations, executive orders, tax bulletins, and notices of public hearings. A subscription to the *Virginia Register*, which includes quarterly indexes issued in January, April, July, and October, is $125 per year. Single issues, when available, are $5 each. Contact the Virginia Code Commission, General Assembly Building, Capitol Square, Richmond, VA 23219. The telephone number is (804) 786-3591. Issues from volume 14, number 20 to date are available online as PDF files at http://legis.state.va.us/code comm/register/issfiles.htm. Various issues in a variety of formats are available as a searchable database at http://legis.state.va.us/search/reg_query .htm.

Statistical Resources

Crime in Virginia (Department of State Police, Uniform Crime Reporting Section)—The Department of State Police collects incident-based statistics from law enforcement agencies throughout Virginia and publishes them in this annual report. The first section of the report provides a history of the Uniform Crime Reporting Program and Virginia's involvement in it. The second section defines and gives statistics on "Group A Offenses" such as homicide, robbery, and assault. The third section has statistics about the offenders and victims involved in Group A Offenses, and about the locations and times of the offenses. The fourth section deals with law enforcement officers who were killed or assaulted. The fifth section gives the value of property lost through criminal offenses, and the sixth section provides statistics on arrests made. Additional sections give statistics for cities and counties, and summaries for the agencies that submitted statistics. The most recent editions of the publication are available on the web at http://www.vsp.state.va.us/crimestatistics.htm. Print copies may be ordered from the Department of State Police, UCR Section, P.O. Box 27472, Richmond, VA 23261-7472. Enclose a check or money order for $5, payable to Department of State Police, with your request.

Northern Virginia Data Book (Northern Virginia Planning District Commission)—Virginia is divided into twenty-one Planning Districts. The local governments in each district work cooperatively with each other through a commission. Many of the commissions have produced informational reports that focus on their districts. The *Northern Virginia Data Book* is one such publication. The fourth edition of this title was issued in 1998. It provides statistical data on population, education, income, employment, economy, transportation, housing, and other topics for the towns, cities, and counties in the Northern Virginia Planning District. Data for the publication were obtained from federal, state, and local sources. One local source frequently cited is the Metropolitan Washington Council of Governments. Copies of the *Data Book* can be ordered from the Northern Virginia Planning District Commission, 7535 Little River Turnpike, Suite 100, Annandale, VA 22003. The phone number is (703) 642-0700. The price for the 1998 edition was $45. Further information about the publication is available on the web at http://www.novaregion.org/db98 .htm. Further information about Virginia's other Planning District Commissions is available at http://www.institute.virginia.edu/vapdc/.

Virginia Health Statistics Annual Report (Virginia Department of Health, Center for Health Statistics)—Vital statistics have been collected and reported annually in Virginia since 1913. The title of the report that publishes these statistics was changed from *Virginia Vital Statistics Annual Reports* to the current title in 1995. The report is now issued in three separate volumes. The first volume contains city and county data; the second contains statewide data; the third focuses on teenagers. All volumes use the same chapter divisions: Report Organization and Summary Data, Population Estimates and Projections, Resident Total and Teenage Pregnancies, Resident Live Births, Induced Terminations and Natural Fetal Deaths, Infant Deaths and Perinatal Deaths, Resident Deaths, and Communicable Diseases. Copies of the report may be ordered from the Virginia Center for Health Statistics, P.O. Box 1000, Richmond, VA 23218-1000. The phone number for requests is (804) 662-6276. The price for the 1999 edition was $20 per volume or $50 for the three-volume set. Many tables of statistics are also available online at http://www.vdh.state.va .us/stats/Stats.htm.

Virginia Statistical Abstract (Weldon Cooper Center for Public Service, University of Virginia, Charlottesville)—This biennial source includes statistics in twenty-three subject areas: Agriculture; Communications; Construction; Courts and Law Enforcement; Education; Finance, Insurance, and Real Estate; Forestry, Fisheries, and Minerals; Geography and Climate; Government and Elections; Government Employment; Government Finances; Income and Wealth; Labor Force and Employment; Manufacturing; Services; Population; Power and Energy; Social Insurance and Welfare; Taxes; Tourism and Recreation; Transportation; Vital Statistics; and Trade. A textual introduction at the beginning of each section describes the sources from which the statistics were obtained and provides definitions of terms. In addition, each table includes a source note. Special sections in the index lead to tables of county and city data, town data, and Metropolitan Statistical Area data. The *Virginia Statistical Abstract* is available online from a link at http://www.ccps.virginia.edu/ Demographics/. Many tables are available as both PDF files and as Microsoft Excel spreadsheets. Print copies of the publication can be ordered from the Weldon Cooper Center for Public Service, University of Virginia, P.O. Box 400206, Charlottesville, VA 22904-4206. The number for phone orders is (434) 982-5704 or TDD (804) 982-HEAR. Orders or requests for additional information can be e-mailed to cps-pubs@virginia.edu. The title is available for single-issue purchase or on a standing order. The price for the 2000 edition was $45 plus shipping and handling.

Other Resources

VaStat (Weldon Cooper Center for Public Service, University of Virginia, Charlottesville)—This web site provides links to a multitude of other sites that have statistical information about Virginia. The address is http://www .virginia.edu/coopercenter/vastat/.

VIRGINIA'S WORLD WIDE WEB HOME PAGE

My Virginia—The Official Commonwealth of Virginia Home Page—This can be found at http://www.myvirginia.org/ or http://www.vipnet.org/cms portal/. The site is administered by the Virginia Information Providers Network (VIPNet), which was established by state legislation passed in 1996. VIPNet contracts with a private firm, Virginia Interactive, Inc., who manages the *My Virginia* site and provides assistance to government agencies in creating web-based services and information resources. An eleven-member board of directors, six from the public sector and five from the private sector, is appointed by the governor to oversee VIPNet.

Unlike many state web sites, *My Virginia* is not state funded, but is instead supported by fees charged to the business community. According to the VIPNet "Overview" page, http://www.vipnet.org/vipnet/design/onlinecd/ overview.html, "VIPNet has been funded through online services for businesses, including enhanced data access, electronic filing, and licensing applications."

The *My Virginia* site is very well organized and user-friendly. The home page offers links such as "Find My Community," "Government," "State Web Site List," and "Business." A section of "Online Services" offers a choice between "Citizen Services," "Business Services," "PDA/Wireless Services," and "Premium Services." A search box allows keyword searching of the site, and a "Find it Fast" link takes the user to a scrolling list of popular government links. A special section leads to "Emergency Notifications" about weather conditions, terrorism threats, or other emergency situations. Users of the site are also able to create their own personalized version of the page. Those with sufficiently sophisticated web browsers can chat with support personnel online by clicking the "Live Help" link.

COMMERCIAL PUBLICATIONS AND WEB SITES

Michie's Code of Virginia (LexisNexis/Michie Co., Charlottesville, VA)—The *Code*, the official codified edition of Virginia's laws, is a 29-volume set which is updated by an annual cumulative supplement. As of May 2003, the price for the set was $500. Additional information about the set can be obtained at http://bookstore.lexis.com/bookstore/catalog.

Virginia Administrative Code (West Group, Eagan, MN)—This is the official edition of the state's administrative rules and regulations. The last complete revision was published in 1996. It is updated with semiannual, cumulative supplements. In May 2003, the 22-volume set was priced at $353.97. For current information see the publisher's web site at http://west.thomson.com/.

SOURCES CONSULTED

Check-List of Virginia State Publications 1989–90 Combined Edition. Cataloged, edited, and indexed by Dorothy Harrison, Rob Keeton, and Trudy McCarty. Richmond: Virginia State Library and Archives, 1992.

Code of Virginia, General Assembly, Virginia Code Commission, http://leg1.state.va .us/000/src.htm.

Numerous departmental web pages via *My Virginia*, http://www.myvirginia.org/.

Research assistance from Joy Suh, George Mason University, 2001.

Survey response from Mary S. Clark, Library of Virginia, 2000.

Washington

Daniel D. Cornwall

GOVERNMENT PUBLISHING AND THE DEPOSITORY SYSTEM

The Washington state publications depository program was begun in 1963. The State Library is responsible for the depository system, and the laws governing the program are outlined in sections 27.04.045 and 40.06.020 of the *Revised Code of Washington* (RCW). There are twelve full and twenty-three partial depositories in the Washington program that receive state publications. State publications are defined in chapters 40.06 and 40.07 RCW as "annual and biennial reports, special reports required by law, state agency newsletters, periodicals and magazines, and other printed informational material intended for general distribution to the public or to the Legislature." The law specifically excludes business forms, preliminary draft reports, working papers, typewritten correspondence, interoffice memoranda, staff memoranda, or news releases sent exclusively to the media.

State depository libraries are expected to house the collection, provide reference services, actively promote the collection with their parent institutions, and alert Washington State Library staff to the existence of fugitive state documents. (Fugitive documents are publications that should be distributed through the depository program but have not been.)

USEFUL ADDRESSES AND TELEPHONE NUMBERS

The most complete collection of Washington state publications may be found at the following library:

Washington State Library
State Documents
P.O. Box 42460
Olympia, WA 98504-2460
Phone Number for Washington Reference Questions: (360) 704-5221

E-Mail Link for Washington Reference Questions: http://www.statelib.wa.gov/ask
 .aspx
Washington State Library's Home Page: http://www.statelib.wa.gov/
Depository Program Home Page: http://www.statelib.wa.gov/gov_publications.aspx

The Washington State Library is the only permanent depository for Washington state documents. Those with questions about Washington's depository library system may contact the State Documents Coordinator at the address, phone number, or e-mail address given above for the State Library.

INDEXES TO WASHINGTON STATE PUBLICATIONS

No separate index or checklist is published for Washington state publications, but all state publications can be found through the Washington State Library's online catalog at http://www.statelib.wa.gov/catalog.aspx and through the national bibliographic database OCLC.

Washington state publications are classified according to a modified Dewey Decimal System. Every call number begins with WA, then a subject appropriate Dewey number, followed by a cutter number related to the issuing agency, followed by letters based on prominent words in the title.

ESSENTIAL STATE PUBLICATIONS

Directories

Pictorial Guide to the Washington State Legislature (Washington State Legislature)—Washington Documents Call Number—WA 328.3 L52was. This joint House/Senate publication provides pictures and contact information for House and Senate members.

State of Washington SCAN (State Controlled Area Network) Telephone Directory (Department of Information Services)—Washington Documents Call Number—WA 351.71 Ad6sta w4. This yearly directory contains telephone numbers for all executive branch departments. The directory can be purchased from Washington State Department of Information Services, P.O. Box 42445, Olympia, WA 98504-2445, or call (360) 407-4DIS (4347); or by e-mail at Tech Central@www.wa.gov. The 1999 directory sold for $4.50. State government telephone numbers may also be found online at http://dial.wa.gov/.

Washington Court Directory (Office of the Administrator of the Courts)—Washington Documents Call Number—WA 347 Ad65was c. The online version of the directory can be found at http://www.courts.wa.gov/court_dir/. The entire directory can be downloaded as either a PDF or Word 97 format file. All of the same information can be found in HTML format as well. In addition to phone numbers for the Washington court system, it has links to Washington tribal courts, courthouse facilitators, and dispute resolution centers. The site also features a courthouse locator that can produce maps and driving directions for most courts.

Financial/Budgetary Resources

Comprehensive Annual Financial Report (Office of Financial Management)—Washington Documents Call Number—WA 351.72 F52ann fin. In addition to the financial information on income and expenditures one expects to find in a financial report, there is a current organizational chart of Washington state government as well as pictures of all the current statewide elected officers. A hard copy of this report may be obtained by contacting the Office of Financial Management at (360) 664-7700 or the Telecommunications Device for the Deaf at (360) 664-3649. *The Comprehensive Annual Financial Report* is also available on the Internet at http://www.ofm.wa.gov/reports/reports.htm#C.

Economic and Revenue Forecast for Washington State (Office of the Forecast Council)—Washington Documents Call Number—WA 333.7 N211eco r. Issued quarterly, this publication has chapters on economic forecasts for the state of Washington and the nation, statistics on Washington business activities, and revenue forecasts for the state. There is often a "Special Report" included as well. In November 2001, this special report was about annual state personal income from 1970 to 2000. The forecasts can be found online under *Economic and Revenue Forecast* on the following page: http://www.wa.gov/ofc/home.htm.

Office of Financial Management Budget Site (Office of Financial Management)—This web page, at http://www.ofm.wa.gov/budget.htm, includes extensive executive branch budget information. In addition to current and past budget proposals, instructions and guides for budgets can be found here. This site also includes the *Agency Activity Inventory*, which summarizes the major activities of each budgeted agency within Washington state government. Entries address the nature of the services offered by the agency, what clients are involved, and how much the activity costs under the current budget.

Personnel Detail Report (Office of Financial Management)—Washington Documents Call Number—Paper: WA 351.72 F52sta wpd; CD-ROM: WA 351.72 F52sta w7 year. This amazing document is available in paper, on CD-ROM, and on the Internet at http://www.ofm.wa.gov/reports/reports.htm#P. The *Personnel Detail Report* offers a microscopic look at Washington state employees. Every single state employee is listed by department with his/her position title, salary, and hours scheduled per week. In addition to the personal detail, there are employee totals for every department, plus maximum salary limits. Interestingly, this publication covers the legislative and judicial branches as well as the executive branch. This is THE place to find answers to the how-many, how-much questions of Washington government employment.

Legal Resources

Bill Information (Washington State Legislature)—This site, located at http://www.leg.wa.gov/wsladm/bills.cfm, provides access to bills dating back to 1997. For the current biennial session, bills and committee reports are available. There is a daily status report, along with a separate key to make it comprehensible. Finally, and quite helpfully, there is a table that relates passed bills to the current *Revised Code of Washington*.

Criminal History Records (Washington State Patrol)—This web page at http://www.wa.gov/wsp/crime/crimhist.htm provides online access to individual criminal histories. It is a fee-based service and an account number or credit card number is required. The public may request print copies of records that include an individual's convictions, any offenses under one year old for which an arrest is pending, and whether or not the subject is a registered sex offender or kidnapper. More detailed information is available to law enforcement agencies and child care agencies. In 2002, record fees varied from $10 to $25, depending on how much identifying information is submitted. To open an account, request forms, or get more information, call (360) 705-5100, e-mail crimhis@wsp.wa.gov, or write to Identification and Criminal History Section, Washington State Patrol, P.O. Box 42633, Olympia, WA 98504-2633.

Legislative Manual (Washington State Legislature)—Washington Documents Call Number—WA 328.3 L52j. This biennial publication contains the rules of each body, joint rules, biographical, and other information about the legislature and state government. The House and Senate rules are available online via the legislature website at http://www.leg.wa.gov/. Print copies of the *Manual* are held by many libraries in Washington, and in other states.

Revised Code of Washington (RCW) (Office of the Code Revisor)—These are the codified laws of the state of Washington. The current version of the RCW is available on the web at http://www.leg.wa.gov/wsladm/rcw.cfm. The RCW is also issued as a multi-volume set, which is generally reprinted every other year. A supplement is issued for the year in which the RCW is not reprinted in its entirety. The most recent edition is the 2000 edition and the cost was $210 per set, plus 8 percent sales tax. It is also issued on CD-ROM at a cost of $50 plus 8 percent sales tax. To obtain copies, call (360) 786-6777, or write to Office of the Code Reviser, P.O. Box 40552, Olympia, WA 98507. The RCW has not been assigned a Washington Documents Call Number.

Washington Administrative Code (Office of the Code Reviser)—The *Washington Administrative Code* (WAC) is a compilation of the administrative laws and regulations of Washington state agencies. It is prepared by the Code Reviser from original rules filed by the various state agencies with the reviser's office. The web version, updated twice a month, is available at http://www.leg.wa .gov/wac/. Published in paper and CD-ROM format, it is available from Office of the Code Reviser, P.O. Box 40552, Olympia, WA 98507, or call (360) 786-6777. In 2002, the price of the multi-volume set was $370, plus 8 percent sales tax. The price for the 2000 CD-ROM (which came bundled with *Revised Code of Washington*) was $100 plus 8 percent sales tax. Copies may be obtained from the Office of the Code Reviser at the address or phone number given above. The WAC does not have a Washington Documents Call Number.

Washington State Register (Office of the Code Reviser)—Washington Documents Call Number—WA 347 St2 wsr. The *Washington State Register* contains the full text of proposed, emergency, and permanently adopted rules of state agencies, executive orders of the Governor, notices of state agency public meetings, rules of the state supreme court, summaries of Attorney General opinions, and juvenile disposition standards that have been filed in the Office of the Code Reviser before the closing date for that issue. Published on the first and third Wednesday of each month, a one-year subscription in either paper or electronic format is available from the Office of the Code Reviser, P.O. Box 40552, Olympia, WA 98507, or call (360) 786-6777. The subscription price for 2002 was $195 plus 8 percent sales tax. A free, searchable version is available online at http://slc.leg.wa.gov/wsr/register.htm.

Statistical Resources

LMI Review: Quarterly Review of Washington State Labor Market Information (Department of Employment Security)—Washington Documents Call Number—WA 331.13 Em71ab m. This quarterly publication presents an in-depth focus on labor market and economic conditions in Washington state; special articles on labor market, occupations, economic, and demographic subjects. Paper issues may be obtained by writing the agency at 212 Maple Park, Olympia, WA 98504-9046. *LMI Review* is also on the web at http://www.wa.gov/esd/lmea/pubs/lmirev/lmirmain.htm.

Population Trends (Office of Financial Management)—Washington Documents Call Number—WA 351.72 F52swp. According to the introduction,

Population Trends provides demographic data for the state, counties, cities, and towns. Population determinations contained in this document were developed by the Office of Financial Management (OFM) and represent the official state population figures. Annual population figures for Washington's cities, towns, and counties have been developed and released for over three decades. These estimates are cited in numerous statutes using population as criterion for fund allocations, program eligibility, or program operations and as criteria for participation in the Growth Management Act.

This annual publication is available on the web at http://www.ofm.wa.gov/pop/poptrends/index.htm.

Washington Agricultural Statistics (Department of Agriculture)—Washington Documents Call Number—WA 630 Ag8was. This composite publication, published annually in the fall, contains current and revised data for most reports released during the year. This publication also contains other data such as farm economics, planting and harvesting dates, county-level data, and detailed commodity information. The report is available on the web at http://www.nass.usda.gov/wa/homepage.htm.

Washington State Data Book (Office of Financial Management)—Washington Documents Call Number—WA 351.72 F52sta w3 years. According to the preface to the 1999 edition, the purpose of this biennial publication is to "present, in one reference document, a diversity of information on Washington, its people, economy and government. The information is obtained from state and federal agencies as well as private businesses." This publication is divided into sections on Population, Economy, State Government Finance, Human Services, Criminal Justice, Education, Natural Resources, Environment, Energy, Transportation, and Local Government and Special Districts. The *Data Book* also lists source publications, and addresses and phone numbers of contributing agencies. The *Data Book* is available on the Internet at http://www.ofm.wa.gov/databook/index.htm.

Washington State Vital Statistics (Department of Health)—Washington Documents Call Number—WA 360 H343ann ss. Issued annually, this publication contains information on births, deaths, fetal deaths, induced abortions, marriages, divorces, hospital admissions and finances, and information on the health habits and risk behaviors of Washingtonians. Paper copies may be requested by writing to the Washington Center for Health Statistics, 1112 SE Quince Street, P.O. Box 47814, Olympia, WA 98504-7814, or by e-mail at vrinfo@doh.wa.gov. Tables containing much of the same data can be found online at http://www.doh.wa.gov/EHSPHL/CHS/CHS-Data/main.htm.

Other Resources

Big Game Hunting Seasons and Rules (Department of Fish and Wildlife)—Washington Documents Call Number—WA 639.2 F62big g. This annual guide to hunting regulations is available on the web at http://www.wa.gov/wdfw/wlm/game/hunter/hunter.htm.

Index to Geologic and Geophysical Mapping of Washington, 1899-2003 (Department of Natural Resources)—Washington Documents Call Number—WA 333.7 G291 ope 92-8 1992. According to the introduction to the *Index*,

this work is a cumulated update to our previous indexes of geologic and geophysical mapping 1899 to 1983 (Manson, 1984) and 1984 to 1998 (Manson, 1999), and includes maps received in the Washington Division of Geology and Earth Resources (DGER) library to date. The index shows only pertinent and original mapping at scales from 1:480 through 1:580,000 as issued in published and open-filed reports.

This resource is available on the web at http://www.dnr.wa.gov/geology/mapindex.htm. The *Index* itself is a large PDF file (5.4 megabytes). Thankfully, the web site notes which Washington libraries are likely to have the maps found in the *Index*.

Quarterly Business Review (Department of Revenue)—Washington Documents Call Number—WA 336.2 R311qbr. The *Quarterly Business Review* is a compilation of statistics on gross income, taxable retail sales, and accrued tax liability reported by state excise taxpayers. Some of the tables available each quarter are "County Taxable Retail Sales," "Taxable Retail Sales for Selected Cities," and "Public Utility Tax." Figures are reported by industry according to Standard Industrial Classification Code. The *Review* is available on the web at http://www.dor.wa.gov/content/Statistical_Reports/stats_qbr.asp. The web site contains business data back to 1989.

Women in the Washington State Legislature—1913–2000 (Washington State Library)—Located at http://www.statelib.wa.gov/women/women.htm, this database contains information on women who have served in the Washington state legislature. Information given includes the number of the district they represented, the county or counties they represented, whether they served in the House or Senate (or both), the date of their first term, the number of terms they served, the years they served, and their ages when first elected. County information includes counties that were partially represented within the district at the time a legislator served. Some legislator entries contain biographical information.

WASHINGTON'S WORLD WIDE WEB HOME PAGE

The official web site of the state of Washington is called *Access Washington* and it is found at http://access.wa.gov. The state's Department of Information Services has maintained the site since 1998. *Access Washington*'s emphasis is on services for the public. The largest portion of the home page is a section called "At Your E-Service," which contains a small sampling of the services available to Washingtonians over the state's home page. When the page was accessed in January 2002, some of the services available were ordering birth, death, marriage, and divorce certificates; finding a licensed contractor; reserving a campsite; obtaining a criminal history; and finding jobs or employees. The "E-Service" section provides links to a full list of online services. Other prominent links on the *Access Washington* home page are "Consumer Help," "Local Resources," "Business," "Education," and "Traffic Watch."

The Washington State Library maintains two noteworthy web resources, *FindIt Washington* and *FindIt Consumer*, as part of its Government Information Locator Service (GILS) project.

FindIt Consumer is a web search engine that limits its spidering to the "Top 100 Consumer Web Sites." In addition to searching state and federal web sites, *FindIt Consumer* offers answers to frequently asked questions such as: How do I start a business in Washington? We're hiring a professional. How can I make sure they are licensed? Is there a program in Washington state for first-time homebuyers? How can I get a credit score for Insurance? You may even find answers to questions you were not asking, but should be.

FindIt Washington is also a search engine, but it spiders the entire state. An added value at *FindIt Washington* is a database of printed government publications. The records are brief, but do give holdings for libraries in Washington.

In general, if you are looking for a particular service, go to *Access Washington* at http://access.wa.gov. If you are not sure of what you are looking for, try *FindIt Washington* at http://find-it.wa.gov/. If you are looking for consumer information, you should go to *FindIt Consumer* at http://finditconsumer.wa .gov/.

COMMERCIAL PUBLICATIONS AND WEB SITES

Sine Die: A Guide to the Washington Legislative Process (University of Washington Press, Seattle, WA)—Published in 1997, this is a comprehensive guide to legislative structure, process, and history in the state of Washington. Separate chapters are also devoted to budgeting, relations with the governor, and the role of gender in the legislature. See the publisher's site at http://www .washington.edu/uwpress/index.html for further information.

Washington Almanac (West Winds Press, Portland, OR)—The *Almanac* is an A–Z guide to all things Washingtonian. It was compiled from a number of sources, including other publications, web sites, private businesses, and personal interviews with local, state, and federal government agencies. From this resource one may learn where in the state to find prisons and crabs, and historical information about petroglyphs and lighthouses. Brief to moderate length articles are presented on each subject. A section on further reading is provided as well. The most recent edition was published in 1999. West Winds Press is an imprint of the Graphic Arts Center Publishing Company. See the publisher's web site at http://www.gacpc.com/gacpc/index.htm for further information.

Washington State Almanac (Electronic Handbook Publishers, Sammamish, WA)—Published annually, this *Almanac* provides profiles for every Washington county, complete with locator map and information on the following topics: Population, Land Area, Personal Income, Businesses, Business Indicators, Property Assessments, and Employment. In addition, there are comparison tables between counties, and plenty of maps and charts for counties, municipalities, and the state. This almanac also has sections on sources and terminology. Copies may be ordered from Electronic Handbook Publishers, Inc., 24106 NE 6th Place, Sammamish, WA, or call (425) 836-0598.

Washington State Atlas and Databook (Public Sector Information, Eugene, OR)—Last published in 1998, this is still the best source for map-based information. The *Atlas* is divided into chapters on Geography, History, Evolution of State, Evolution of Counties, Population, Cities and Towns, State Government, Transportation, Economy, U.S. Government, and Weather. Whether you are looking for a map of court districts, a map of population density, or information on potato production, this is a good source. The publisher of this title is no longer in business, but copies are available in several libraries around the country.

Washington State Yearbook: The Evergreen State Government Directory (Electronic Handbook Publishers, Sammamish, WA)—This annual publication is produced in cooperation with the Washington Office of the Governor and the Office of the Secretary of State. It is primarily a directory of government officials in Washington state at the local, state, and federal levels. Entries for high-level officials such as the governor, legislators, and Supreme Court judges contain brief biographical sketches. Entries for agencies have short descriptions of their functions and list the numbers of employees working for a given agency. Other helpful features of the *Yearbook* include a list of publications about Washington (which was consulted for this chapter), a guide to pronouncing Washington place names, and lists of media sources, organizations, and parks and museums. Copies may be ordered from http://www .washingtonstateyearbook.com or by calling (425) 836-0598.

SOURCES CONSULTED

Numerous departmental web pages via the state's home page, http://access.wa.gov.
Revised Code of Washington. Olympia, WA: Office of the Code Reviser, 2001. (Via the web at http://www.leg.wa.gov/wsladm/rcw.cfm.)
State of Washington Publication Guidelines. Olympia, WA: Office of Financial Management, 1996.
Survey response from Shirley Dallas, Washington State Library.
Washington State Yearbook. Sammamish, WA: Electronic Handbook Publishers, 2001.

West Virginia

J. Louise Malcomb

GOVERNMENT PUBLISHING AND THE DEPOSITORY SYSTEM

In the section dedicated to West Virginia in her book *State Publications and Depository Libraries: A Reference Handbook*, Margaret T. Lane writes that with West Virginia's Act of 1905, the state's Department of Archives and History first became responsible for distributing state reports to other states. In Chapter 63 of the 1953 Acts of the Legislature, the Department of Archives and History became responsible for sending "two copies of all reports, etc. to state institutions of higher learning." In Senate Bill 207, which was passed in 1972, Lane further notes in her book, an amendment was provided to the *Code* that changed the 1953 Act's wording "so that it is more permissive than mandatory" to send copies of all reports to state institutions of higher learning.

The *West Virginia Code*, Chapter 10-1-18 (2001) gives the legal description of the state depository program, giving the responsibility for management of the program to the West Virginia Library Commission. The *Code* provides the following definitions important for understanding the program and its coverage:

As used in this section, the following terms have the following meanings:

(1) "Public document" means any document, report, directive, bibliography, rule, newsletter, pamphlet, brochure, periodical, request for proposal, or other publication, whether in print or an unprinted format, that is paid for, in whole or in part, by funds appropriated by the Legislature and may be subject to distribution to the public;

(2) "Depository library" means a library designated to collect, catalog, maintain and make available all or particular selected state publications to the general public; and

(3) "State agency" means any state office, whether legislative, executive or judicial, including, but not limited to, any constitutional officer, department, division, bureau, board, commission or other agency which expends state appropriated funds.

A member of the State Library staff, who must hold a graduate degree in library science, is assigned oversight of the "state publications clearinghouse."

The primary responsibility of the program is to receive and distribute "all state public documents to depository libraries around the state." Certain libraries are designated as "complete depository libraries" and receive two copies of all public documents. These include the West Virginia University library, the Marshall University library, and the state department of archives. Other depository libraries are designated by the clearinghouse with consideration given for geographic coverage and complimentary to the existing federal depository library program.

While the clearinghouse oversees the receipt and distribution of documents to depository libraries, state agencies also are given the responsibility to have a "documents officer." These officers are required to "deposit with the clearinghouse a minimum of fifteen copies as required to meet the needs of the library system. If fewer than forty copies of a public document are produced, no more than two such copies are required to be deposited with the clearinghouse."

The West Virginia University Libraries' "West Virginia Federal Depository Libraries" web page is a very useful source of information about West Virginia's depository libraries. It is available at http://www.libraries.wvu.edu/government/westvirginia/wvfedlibraries.htm and provides the name, address, telephone number, depository number, designation date, and congressional district of each library, as well as the name of each library's documents librarian; gives details about each library's collection and organization and the services each library provides; and specifies each library's hours and available equipment. It does not, however, provide information about holdings of state government publications.

USEFUL ADDRESSES AND TELEPHONE NUMBERS

The most complete collections of West Virginia state documents may be found in the following libraries:

Archives and History Library
The Cultural Center
1900 Kanawha Boulevard East
Charleston, WV 25305
Phone Number for West Virginia Reference Questions: (304) 558-0230, ext. 168
Library's Home Page: http://www.wvculture.org/history/index.html

Downtown Campus Library
P.O. Box 6069
West Virginia University
1549 University Avenue
Morgantown, WV 26506-6069
Phone Number for West Virginia Reference Questions: (304) 293-4040, ext. 4040
Web Form for West Virginia Reference Questions: http://www.libraries.wvu.edu/
    ask/form.htm
Library's Home Page: http://www.libraries.wvu.edu/downtown/index.htm
Government Information Services Home Page: http://www.libraries.wvu.edu/
    government/index.htm

James E. Morrow Library
One John Marshall Drive
Marshall University
Huntington, WV 25755
Phone Number for West Virginia Reference Questions: (304) 696-2342
Web Form for West Virginia Reference Questions: http://www.marshall.edu/
    library/ask.htm
Library's Home Page: http://www.marshall.edu/library
Government Documents Department Home Page: http://www.marshall.edu/library/
    govdocs/index.html

West Virginia Library Commission (State Library)
Cultural Center
1900 Kanawha Boulevard East
Charleston, WV 25305
Phone Number for West Virginia Reference Questions: (304) 558-2045 or (800) 642-
    9021 (toll-free in West Virginia)
Library's Home Page: http://librarycommission.lib.wv.us/

INDEXES TO WEST VIRGINIA STATE PUBLICATIONS

The *West Virginia State Publications Checklist* has been published under various titles since 1942 by the state's Department of Archives and History (agency name varied 1980–1982). It is available online at http://www.wv culture.org/history/statedocs.html.

In 1939 the department included a retrospective list of publications in its Biennial Report for 1936/38. Part II of *A Bibliography of West Virginia* lists titles of official documents of the state from 1861 to 1939, including bibliographic information about the documents relevant to the establishment of the state.

The West Virginia Archives and History web site at http://www .wvculture.org/history/index.html also provides a link to the West Virginia union catalog, lists numerous links to genealogical resources, and includes a link to the State Archives, which includes information about accessions, civil war medals, guides to collections, and staff research guides.

Additionally, Bowker's *State Publications: A Provisional List of the Official Publications of the Several States of the United States from their Organization* can be consulted for historical publications, pages 719-734.

ESSENTIAL STATE PUBLICATIONS

Directories

The State Government Phone Book (accessible from http://www.state.wv.us)— This allows the searcher to enter a person's name and limit the search to a particular agency. The generated results include the person's phone number, agency, and mailing and e-mail addresses.

The West Virginia Legislature Capitol Mailing Addresses (Legislative Reference and Information Center)—This provides the names, addresses, and capitol telephone numbers of West Virginia's Senate and House members. Each congressperson's district is also provided. The directory is available at http://www.legis.state.wv.us/.

The West Virginia School Directory (Department of Education)—This lists the state's public and private elementary and high schools, providing each school's address, telephone and fax numbers, total enrollment, grades taught, and web page address, if the school has one. The directory may be found at http://wvde.state.wv.us/ed_directory.

The West Virginia Library Directory (West Virginia Library Commission)— This is an alphabetical listing of every public, private, and school library in the state. Each library name offers a link to the library's address and telephone number and a link to the library's web site, if one exists. The directory may be found at http://wvlc.lib.wv.us/vtls40/english/alphcode.html.

Financial/Budgetary Resources

West Virginia Comprehensive Annual Financial Report for the Fiscal Year (West Virginia Department of Administration)—Similar to reports in almost every state, the West Virginia Department of Administration, Finance Division, Financial Accounting and Reporting Section issues an annual overview of its financial situation. The print report can be obtained free of charge while available from the West Virginia Department of Administration, Finance Division, Financial Accounting and Reporting Section, 208 7th Avenue, South Charleston, WV 25303. Consult the web site at http://www.state.wv.us/admin/finance/cafrgap.htm for current reports and summary statistics. The governor's current budget is available from the State Budget Office web site at http://www.state.wv.us/admin/finance/budget/. For previous editions of the budget contact West Virginia State Budget Office, Building 1, Room 127-E Capitol Building, Charleston, WV 25305; call (304) 558-0040; fax (304) 558-1588; or e-mail budget@state.wv.us.

Legal Resources

West Virginia State Code (West Virginia Legislative Reference and Information Center)—General information about the Senate, House, and committees, as well as the code, current acts, bills, and bill tracking are available at http://www.legis.state.wv.us/State_Code/finishedData/toc2.html. The *Constitution of West Virginia* is available as a full-text, HTML document from a link on the *State Code*'s web page. Additional information can be requested and comments can be made by calling (877) 565-3447, or specific contacts are listed at http://www.legis.state.wv.us/legishp.html.

Code of State Rules (CSR) (West Virginia Secretary of State)—Although the web site, http://www.wvsos.com/csr/, does not explain what the CSR includes, it does provide a nice table of contents, a search engine, and the Index to the CSR. Also available from the secretary of state's web site is the *West Virginia Register*, which contains meeting notices and details of current proposed rules, and provides a chronological weekly index of the rules. The address for the online version is http://www.wvsos.com/adlaw/register/register.htm. It currently provides copies of the weekly register from the current year and previous year as downloadable PDF files. For details and prices for ordering single issues, specific titles, and subscriptions cost, see the "Services" section at http://www.wvsos.com/adlaw/adlawpages.htm#services, or call (304) 558-6000.

West Virginia Legislature—This web site, http://www.legis.state.wv.us, includes Senate member pages, House member pages, a listing of the names of West Virginia governmental positions, and the individuals currently holding these positions; links to the legislature's joint committee and court of claims; an ability to search the *West Virginia State Code*; acts of the legislature for the past three years; bill tracking for the past two years; a kids' page providing basic information about the state's history, symbols, and famous residents; downloadable brochures; a listing of internship opportunities and search engines; links to the West Virginia Congressional Delegation and other state legislatures; and the ability to e-mail the site.

Statistical Resources

State of West Virginia Official Returns of the General Election (Office of the Secretary of State, Elections Division)—This contains statistics that report on a biennial basis how the populace voted for state and local offices. The report is available from the division's web site at http://www.wvsos.com/elections/main.htm. For additional information contact the West Virginia Office of the Secretary of State, Elections Division, Building One, Suite 157-K, 1900 Kanawha Boulevard East, Charleston, WV 25305-0770.

Annual Report: Vital Health Statistics of West Virginia (West Virginia Department of Health and Human Resources, Public Health Bureau, Epidemiology and Health Promotion Office)—Issued under various titles since the early 1900s, this reports data on births, deaths, marriages, and divorces for the counties and cities of West Virginia. While available, the print reports may be requested free from the Epidemiology and Health Promotion Office, 350 Capitol Street, Room 165, Charleston, WV 25301-3701. The center also publishes the *West Virginia Health Status Atlas* and many other health-related publications. All are listed on its publications web site at http://www.wvdhhr.org/bph/oehp/hsc/vr/publicat.htm.

West Virginia Educational Statistical Summary (West Virginia Department of Education, Office of Technology and Information Systems)—This annual publication tracks the progress of educational programs. It is available for no cost from the department, 1900 Kanawha Boulevard East, Building 6, Room B-346, Charleston, WV 25305-0330. See also the department's web site at http://wvde.state.wv.us/data.

West Virginia Annual Planning Information (Bureau of Employment Programs, Research, Information, and Analysis)—This is an annual report on employment programs and status and is free upon request from the bureau, 112 California Avenue, Charleston, WV 25305-0112; http://www.state.wv.us/bep/LMI/default.htm.

West Virginia Agricultural Statistics (West Virginia Department of Agriculture)—This contains statistical data, much of which is available on the department's web site at http://www.nass.usda.gov/wv/. A print report is available for $5.00 from the Agricultural Statistics Board Publications, South Building, Room 5829, U.S. Department of Agriculture, Washington, DC 20250.

Crime in West Virginia (West Virginia State Police)—Similar to the FBI's report for the nation, this source compiles and publishes a report for the state and its localities. The print report is available from the Uniform Crime Reporting Section, 725 Jefferson Road, South Charleston, WV 25309-1698, at no cost. Many editions are available online at http://www.wvstatepolice.com/ucr/ucr.htm.

Other Resources

Annual Report and *Enviro Factsheets* (West Virginia Department of Environmental Protection)—These are provided by the Public Information Office of the department at http://www.dep.state.wv.us/item.cfm?ssid=24. Both sources cover the various aspects of concern about the environment in West Virginia, from mountaintop mining to urban runoff.

Official West Virginia State Highway Map (West Virginia Department of Transportation)—This tourist map is available free of charge by calling (800) CALL WVA. The Department of Transportation also produces the *State General Highway Map* that is available for $2.50 plus postage and handling. It identifies all main highways and important county roads, mileage between intersections, mileage diagram of the state, and major streams; http://www.wvdot.com/7_tourists/7d1_availablemaps.htm. For other spatial information consult the Governor's Office of Technology at http://www.state.wv.us/got/itparcmap.htm or the West Virginia State GIS Technical Center Data at http://wvgis.wvu.edu/data/data.php. The GIS Technical Center Data allows browsing by subject and offers the option of downloading the entire data catalog as an Excel document. It also has sections for Interactive Mapping and Index and Status Maps.

Wonderful West Virginia (West Virginia Division of Natural Resources)—This is a full color magazine about the state. Subscriptions are available for three years for $40.00, two years for $28.00, and one year for $15.00 from the West Virginia Division of Natural Resources, Capitol Complex, Building 3, Room 662, 1900 Kanawha Boulevard East, Charleston, WV 25305. Subscriptions may also be placed by telephone at (800) CALL WVA, or submit on online form: comments@wonderfulwv.com.

WEST VIRGINIA'S WORLD WIDE WEB HOME PAGE

The state's home page is located at http://www.state.wv.us. It currently does not provide a specific link to libraries, but a short list of local public libraries and the West Virginia Library Commission is included, along with a link to the state schools, under the "Education" link that is available from the main page. The home page provides links to officials' and state agencies' web sites, to information about government jobs, to tax forms for businesses and individuals, and to information and addresses for local departments of motor vehicles and regional recycling centers. The home page also offers information on school closings, current road conditions and work zones, and the latest lottery numbers.

COMMERCIAL PUBLICATIONS AND WEB SITES

The Business and Economic Review Archive (West Virginia University College of Business and Economics)—This is a free quarterly publication that focuses on business issues within West Virginia. Additionally, the West Virginia University College of Business and Economics offers its Bureau of Business and Economic Research web site at http://www.bber.wvu.edu. Its physical address is P.O. Box 6025, Morgantown, WV 26506-6025 and its telephone number is (304) 293-7831. The bureau states its focus as West Virginia and includes in its mission statement the goal to "Disseminate information, research findings, and data products to the private and public sectors." The bureau also sells publications that provide profiles of different areas and industries within the state, such as the *Annual West Virginia County Data Profiles* series which "provides the latest business and economic information about every county and metropolitan statistical area in the State of West Virginia and now includes data through 1997 as well as information on the state and nation."

West Virginia Research League Statistical Handbook—This terrific resource gives a quick overview of the state, including statistics on socioeconomic and demographic characteristics for the state's geographic areas. Data are taken from federal and state reports. For $15.00 plus tax and postage, the print edition is available from the West Virginia Research League, P.O. Box 11176, Charleston, WV 25339-1176. For other specific information consult the Research League's web site at http://www.wvrl.org/.

SOURCES CONSULTED

Dow, Susan L. *State Document Checklists: A Historical Bibliography*. Buffalo, NY: William S. Hein & Co., 1990.

Lane, Margaret T. *State Publications and Depository Libraries: A Reference Handbook*. Westport, CT: Greenwood Press, 1981, 553–554.

Parrish, David W. *State Government Reference Publications: An Annotated Bibliography*, 2nd ed. Littleton, CO: Libraries Unlimited, 1981.

State Capital Universe. Bethesda, MD: LexisNexis, 2001; http://web.lexis-nexis.com/stcapuniv, December 5, 2001. (Available to subscribers only).

Statistical Universe. Bethesda, MD: LexisNexis, 2001; http://web.lexis-nexis.com/statuniv, December 5, 2001. (Available to subscribers only).

U.S. Census Bureau. *Statistical Abstract, 2000 Edition*. "Appendix 1: Guide to State Statistical Abstracts." December 4, 2001, http://www.census.gov.

West Virginia Division of Culture and History, Archives and History Section. *West Virginia State Publications Checklist*. Charleston, WV: Archives and History Section, January–June 2000.

West Virginia Federal Depository Libraries. West Virginia University Libraries. December 5, 2001, http://www.libraries.wvu.edu/government/westvirginia/wvfedlibraries.htm.

West Virginia State Code, Chapter 10. "Establishment of state publications clearinghouse;

definitions; powers of West Virginia library commission; designations by state agencies." Available at http://www.legis.state.wv.us/State_Code/finished Data/toc2.html, December 6, 2001.

West Virginia State Home Page. December 2, 2001, http://www.state.wv.us.

Wisconsin

J. Louise Malcomb

GOVERNMENT PUBLISHING AND THE DEPOSITORY SYSTEM

In 1991, Wisconsin passed Act 285, amending earlier statutes and requiring state government agencies to forward copies of publications to Wisconsin's Reference and Loan Library for distribution to depository libraries. More information about the depository program can be found at http://www.dpi .state.wi.us/dltcl/rll/depgen.html.

The Wisconsin Reference and Loan Library is the manager of the state government depository program. Its responsibilities include distribution of the state government publications to the depository libraries; coordinating, planning, and developing procedures; and evaluating services.

The two other main state depository libraries are the State Historical Society Library and the Legislative Reference Bureau Library. These two libraries maintain document collections for archival purposes and have fairly complete collections. The Legislative Reference Bureau Library's patron base is the members of the legislature, and it does not lend items from its collection. According to its web page at http://www.wisconsinhistory.org/library/ govpub/wiscan.html, the State Historical Society Library "serves as the permanent collection for all Wisconsin state government publications." It receives two copies of all publications distributed through the state depository program, one of which gets put out for circulation to the public; the other becomes part of the archival collection. It is geared toward serving the public, and can lend documents via interlibrary loan.

According to the Legislative Reference Bureau's web page at http://www .legis.state.wi.us/lrb/Library/index.htm, its "library collection contains over 85,000 items related to the lawmaking process and public policy issues, including clippings, classified by subject, which often provide comprehensive information not available from other sources; Wisconsin state documents; basic reference sources; and drafting records since 1927."

Wisconsin statute 35.82(3) notes that state document depository libraries shall be chosen on the basis of which libraries agree to receive state documents, are adequately staffed, and are capable of ensuring access to those state documents. The statute dictates that "regional" state government depositories will receive all state documents possible (approximately three-quarters of all documents) while "selective" depositories maintain partial collections (about two-thirds). There can be no more than ten regional state government depositories and not more than thirty-five selective state depositories. The regional depositories are: Milwaukee Public Library, University of Wisconsin–Stevens Point, Fond du Lac Public Library, University of Wisconsin–Eau Claire, La Crosse Public Library, University of Wisconsin–Platteville, University of Wisconsin–Green Bay, Superior Public Library, and University of Wisconsin–River Falls. There are thirty-five selective state depository libraries. Wisconsin state government documents are also deposited, according to Wisconsin Statute 35.82(2), at the Library of Congress in Washington, DC, and at the Council of State Governments in Lexington, Kentucky.

Statute 35.82(5) states that "each state document depository library shall make freely available to inhabitants of the state all state documents retained by the library, shall keep state documents readily accessible for use and shall render assistance in their use to such inhabitants without charge." See the complete text of these statutes at http://www.legis.state.wi.us/rsb/stats.html.

USEFUL ADDRESSES AND TELEPHONE NUMBERS

The most complete collections of Wisconsin publications can be found at the following libraries:

Government Publications Section
State Historical Society Library
816 State Street, 2nd Floor
Madison, WI 53706
Phone Number for Wisconsin Reference Questions: (608) 264-6535, fax (608) 264-6520
Library's Home Page: http://www.wisconsinhistory.org/library/index.html
Government Publications Section Home Page: http://www.wisconsinhistory.org/
    library/govpub/index.html

Dr. H. Rupert Theobald Legislative Library
Wisconsin Legislative Reference Bureau
100 North Hamilton Street
Madison, WI 53701-2037
Phone Number for Wisconsin Reference Questions: (608) 266-0341, fax (608) 266-5648
Library's Home Page: http://www.legis.state.wi.us/lrb/Library/index.htm

Wisconsin Reference and Loan Library
2109 South Stoughton Road
Madison, WI 53716-2899
Phone Number for Wisconsin Reference Questions: (608) 224-6165, toll-free number
    (888) 542-5543

Library's Home Page: http://www.dpi.state.wi.us/dltcl/rll/
Depository Program Home Page: http://www.dpi.state.wi.us/dltcl/rll/inddep.html

INDEXES TO WISCONSIN PUBLICATIONS

Wisconsin Public Documents was published by the State Historical Society Library from 1917 to 1998 under various titles. This guide is a checklist of publications issued by Wisconsin state government agencies and received by the society as depository items. The guide also has an annual periodicals supplement and indexes for author, title, and subject. Once published monthly, the checklist was published on a quarterly basis from 1990 to 1998, when it ceased.

The Wisconsin Reference and Loan Library publishes its state "Document Depository Shipping Lists" on the web at http://www.dpi.state.wi.us/dpi/dlcl/rll/indship.html. Links to the items that are also available online are included.

Dow lists several bibliographic resources of historical importance because they provide a record of documents issued by the state of Wisconsin:

Check List of the Journals and Public Documents of Wisconsin. Wisconsin Free Library Commission. 1787–1903.

A Check List of Wisconsin Imprints. Wisconsin Historical Records Survey. 1833–1869.

Wisconsin State Publications. Wisconsin Free Library Commission. 1902–1903.

Wisconsin Library Bulletin. Division of Library Services. 1905–1942.

Additionally, Bowker's *State Publications: A Provisional List of the Official Publications of the Several States of the United States from their Organization* should be consulted for historical publications, pages 265–285.

ESSENTIAL STATE PUBLICATIONS

Directories

Wisconsin Blue Book (Legislative Reference Bureau)—This has been published since 1853 and is available online beginning with the 1997–1998 edition. Visit the web site at http://www.legis.state.wi.us/nav/bb.htm. This is a superb example of a state manual, providing both a comprehensive look at Wisconsin state government organization and a statistical overview. It is well indexed. The Wisconsin state legislature's web site at http://www.legis.state.wi.us/index.htm links to the home pages of individual representatives and senators, listings of committees, and e-mail lists, as well as the *Wisconsin Blue Book* (see Figure 18).

The Wisconsin state government web site has a link to several general directories for state information at its Directories portal, entitled: "Index to Wisconsin Government and University Directories." Directories included on this site are: Local Court Directory, Public Transit Providers Directory, State of Wisconsin Departmental Directory, State of Wisconsin Employee Telephone

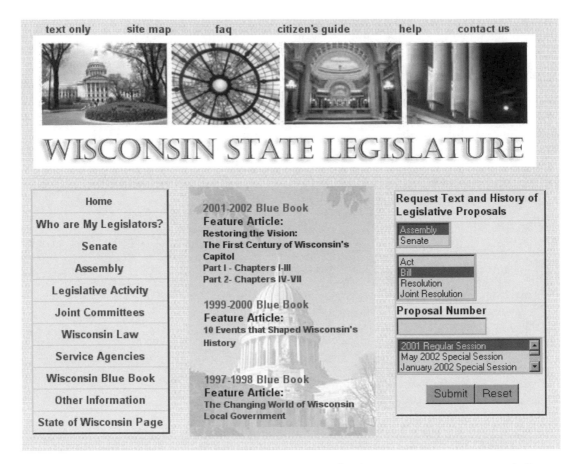

Figure 18. The Wisconsin *Blue Book* is an excellent example of a state government manual. *Source*: http://www.legis.state.wi.us/nav/bb.htm.

Directory, State Park Directory, Court of Appeals Directory, and University of Wisconsin Directories. Select "Directories" from the site map at http://www.wisconsin.gov/state/core/site_map.html.

Wisconsin State Officers (Legislative Reference Bureau)—Issued biennially and now part of the *Wisconsin Brief* series, this publication lists constitutional officers and members of the Wisconsin delegation to Congress and the Wisconsin legislature. The bureau has from time to time also issued biographical information about state officials, usually written by Gary Watchke and entitled *Brief Biographies. . . . Wisconsin Officials*. The Legislative Reference Bureau also published *State Officers as Appointed by the Governor as Required by Statute* in 1989 and 1994.

Directory of State Agencies' Legislative Liaisons (Wisconsin Ethics Board)—The Wisconsin Ethics Board maintains a web site specifically about lobbying, providing this directory of state agencies' legislative liaisons, and also a listing of "Organizations Employing Lobbyists." Look for the "Who" column on the Lobbying site at http://ethics.state.wi.us/LobbyingRegistrationReports/LobbyingOverview.htm.

Wisconsin Public School Directory (Wisconsin Department of Public Instruction)—Published under a variety of titles and with some agency name changes, this directory lists all schools within Wisconsin and other agencies related to the education mission. Directories are available for Wisconsin public and private schools from the Department of Public Instruction's web site at http://www.dpi.state.wi.us/index.html. Directories to institutions of higher education, libraries, and the University of Wisconsin System are given on the Education portal of the Wisconsin web site at http://www.wisconsin.gov/state/core/education.html.

Financial/Budgetary Resources

Wisconsin State Budget (Wisconsin State Budget Office)—The most recent state budget as well as related documents are available online at http://www.doa.state.wi.us/debf/index.asp. For earlier budgets, the record for the title in the Wisconsin Historical Society Archives catalog, *Arcat*, states,

Printed budgets showing the current budget, actual receipts and expenditures of the previous three years, and estimated budget for the coming biennium. The major division of the budget is by operation, maintenance, and capital accounts, and by state agencies; included are many detailed charts and tables. The first volume, 1915, and volumes for 1935 to the present, can be found in the public documents section of the State Historical Society Library

and gives specifics about earlier and later title changes.

Executive Budget Bills Enacted by the Wisconsin Legislature (Legislative Reference Bureau)—This annual publication has been issued in print since 1931 and online from 1994 to the present at http://www.legis.state.wi.us/lrb/pubs/pubsub/budget.htm.. A biennial publication from the Legislative Fiscal Bureau is the *Comparative Summary of Wisconsin State Budget*. The Legislative Fiscal Bureau has also biennially published the series *State Budget Process* (Informational Paper 65) since 1979. Those titles are available online at http://www.legis.state.wi.us/lfb/index.html; select "Publications."

Comprehensive Annual Financial Report for the Fiscal Year (State Controller's Office)—The comprehensive state annual financial reports from the fiscal year ending June 30, 1995 to the present are available in PDF format on the web at http://www.doa.state.wi.us/debf/cafr/CAFR.htm. The report provides details of the revenues and expenditures of the state. The print version of this report is published annually by the Wisconsin Department of Administration but has limited distribution. Contact the Department of Administration, State Controller's Office, P.O. Box 7932, Madison, WI 53707-7932; or call (608) 266-3628.

Wisconsin Tax Bulletin (Wisconsin Department of Revenue)—This quarterly newsletter has articles on "tax laws, administrative rules, and return filing requirements . . . interpretations of Wisconsin tax laws" and reports on current litigation. The *Bulletin* is available by subscription for $7.00 a year or free on its web site at http://www.dor.state.wi.us/ise/wtb/index.html. The Department of Revenue web site at http://www.dor.state.wi.us/html/taxpubs.html links to a variety of other tax publications in PDF format.

Legal Resources

The Wisconsin legislature web site, http://www.legis.state.wi.us/nav/wislaw.htm, has a link to the Wisconsin Acts from 1995–1996 to the present. Acts from sessions earlier than 1995 can be found in the publications *Executive Agencies, Boards, Councils, and Commissions Created, Abolished or Altered by the 1991 Legislature (Acts 1–323)* and *Executive Agencies, Boards, Councils, and Commissions Created, Abolished or Altered by the 1993 Legislature (Acts 1–497)*.

Wisconsin State Constitution (Revisor of Statutes Bureau)—This is available in PDF format at http://www.legis.state.wi.us/rsb/2wiscon.html. Other titles produced by the Revisor of Statutes Bureau include *Wisconsin Administrative Code*, which is searchable by code number or keyword, and *Administrative Register*. Both are available in PDF format at http://www.legis.state.wi.us/rsb/code/index.html.

Wisconsin Statutes and Annotations, which is searchable by statute or keyword, is available at http://www.legis.state.wi.us/rsb/stats.html. The Revisor of Statutes Bureau publishes a print edition of *Wisconsin Statutes and Annotations* biennially. For information about obtaining print copies of these titles contact the Department of Administration's Document Sales and Distribution Section at (800) 362-7253 or (608) 264-9419.

Links off the Wisconsin state government page include: Supreme Court of Wisconsin http://www.courts.state.wi.us/supreme/, and the Court of Appeals http://www.courts.state.wi.us/appeals/.

Statistical Resources

Wisconsin Blue Book (Legislative Reference Bureau)—The most recent edition available online at http://www.legis.state.wi.us/lrb/bb/index.html, is perhaps the best place to begin to search for statistics about the state of Wisconsin. It is available from the department for $9.45 plus tax, although state residents can request a free copy. It includes statistics on elections (see also Wisconsin Election Statistics page at http://elections.state.wi.us/sebpage4.html), education, state finance, and the population. Call (800) 362-7253 or (608) 264-9419 to request or order a copy.

Wisconsin Statistical Abstract (Bureau of Planning and Budget)—Issued irregularly, this databook has not been updated since 1979.

Wisconsin Agricultural Statistics (Department of Agriculture, Trade and Consumer Protection)—This provides statistical information about the state of agriculture in Wisconsin. Most data are at the state and/or county level. The report is available from the Agricultural Statistics Service, P.O. Box 8934, Madison, WI 53708-8934, for $5.00. Call (800) 789-9277 or (608) 224-4848; or e-mail nass-wi@nass.usda.gov.

Wisconsin Marriages and Divorces (Wisconsin Department of Health and Family Services, Bureau of Health Information, Division of Health Care Financing)—Wisconsin's Department of Health and Family Services issues separate reports instead of one "vital statistics report." The report on marriages and divorces provides county/state-level data on brides and grooms, and marriages and divorces/annulments for a variety of breakdowns. Other titles include: *Wisconsin Deaths* and *Wisconsin Births and Infant Deaths*. Print copies of all the reports may be requested from the department, P.O. Box 309, Room 133, Madison, WI 53701-0309, usually at no cost. Call (608) 266-2838. Consult the department's web site for current data at http://www.dhfs.state.wi.us. The department also sells birth, death, marriage, and divorce records from the state of Wisconsin on microfiche. If all the records were purchased together, it would cost $294.80. Call (608) 266-1371 or (608) 266-1373 to enquire about vital records. Most of the records are post-1907. Pre-1907 records are also available for viewing at the Wisconsin Historical Society, http://www.wisconsin history.org/genealogy/vitalrecords/index.html.

Wisconsin Economic Indicators (Wisconsin Department of Workforce Development)—Most workforce statistics are now available via the department's web site, but this monthly report remains the historical record for reporting labor force and economic conditions for the state. While supplies last, the report is available from the department at no cost: P.O. Box 7944, Madison, WI 53707-7944, or call (608) 266-0851. See the current information on the Web at http://www.dwd.state.wi.us/lmi/wi_econ_indicators.htm.

Wisconsin Crime and Arrests (Wisconsin Office of Justice Assistance, Statistical Analysis Center)—Available from the Statistical Analysis Center, 131 W. Wilson Street, Suite 202, Madison, WI 53702-0001, this free annual gives statistics on crime and arrests for the state and local areas. Call (608) 266-3323 to request information or see the most recent editions of the report on the web at http://oja.state.wi.us/asx/crimereports.asp.

Basic Facts About Wisconsin's Elementary and Secondary Schools (Wisconsin Department of Public Instruction)—Staff, expenditures, enrollments, pupils, by state, county, and district are given in this annual report. It may be requested from the department at Publication Sales, Drawer 179, Milwaukee, WI 53293-0179. Call (800) 243-8782 or (608) 266-2188; e-mail pubsales@dpi .state.wi.us. See the report online at http://www.dpi.state.wi.us/dpi/dfm/ sfms/basicpdf.html

Annual Small Business Report (Wisconsin Department of Administration)—This brief report has been issued under various titles since 1992. Other business statistics are available at the Wisconsin Department of Commerce site, http://www.commerce.state.wi.us/MT/MT-COM-3999.html. Information on this site includes: Metro Areas Forecast, Wisconsin Small Business Profile, and Major Wisconsin Industry Profiles.

Population Trends in Wisconsin: 1970–2000 (Wisconsin Department of Administration)—The Demographic Services Center web site publishes this overview of the state online in PDF format. From the department's home page at http://www.doa.state.wi.us/index.asp, select "Public Service," then "Census and Population Information." An earlier publication, *Population Trends in Wisconsin 1950–1975*, was published by the University of Wisconsin–Madison web site. Other statistics available on the Demographic Services Center site include: *Population Trends in Wisconsin 1990–2000* and *County Estimates of Total Housing Units*.

Other Resources

The State Historical Society Library maintains an archives page that describes its holdings http://www.wisconsinhistory.org/archives/descrip.html. The library's archived state government holdings include:

the records of the governor's office; records of state agencies that contain formal minutes of governing boards, committees, commissions and task forces; legal opinions; administrative rulemaking and legislative files; policy records; selected case files; narrative and statistical reports; special study records; and selected visual, audio, graphic, cartographic and electronic records. (http://www.wisconsinhistory.org/archives/readroom/staterec.html)

The State Historical Society Library also has a digital book that may be of interest to genealogists, the *Roster of Wisconsin Volunteers, War of the Rebellion, 1861–1865*, http://www.wisconsinhistory.org/roster/index.html. This book can be searched by soldiers' last names (alphabetical), by regiment, or can just be browsed generally.

The Wisconsin Department of Natural Resources, who are "dedicated to the preservation, protection, effective management, and maintenance of Wisconsin's natural resources" (http://www.dnr.state.wi.us/aboutdnr/), publishes the bimonthly magazine *Natural Resources Magazine* at http://www.wnrmag.com/. Current issues, as well as all issues from 1996 to date, are available from this site, with full-color photos included. Subscriptions to the magazine for anyone in the United States are $8.97 a year (6 issues).

The Wisconsin Department of Commerce sells a variety of publications with a charge for shipping and handling, such as *Going into Business in Wisconsin: An Entrepreneur's Guide* ($5.00); *Directory of Local Development Partners* ($4.00); and *Wisconsin's 2000–2001 Minority Owned Business Directory* ($15.00). Consult its web site at http://www.commerce.state.wi.us/MT/MT-FAX-0606.html.

WISCONSIN'S WORLD WIDE WEB HOME PAGE

The Wisconsin state web page, http://www.wisconsin.gov/state/home, has links to government, business, education, and statistical sites. Links include: the Governor's Office, State and Local Agencies, Vital Records, Business Statistics, State Legislature, and the Federal Government.

The purpose of the site is "to provide a free service, enabling the global community to easily and rapidly search Wisconsin State Government information that has been posted on the Internet" (http://www.wisconsin.gov/state/core/faq_portal.html). Many of the government documents found through this site are in PDF format, so users will need Adobe Acrobat software (downloadable free off the site).

COMMERCIAL PUBLICATIONS AND WEB SITES

The Metropolitan Milwaukee Association of Commerce publishes a number of books about the Milwaukee and Wisconsin business and political climate, including the *Metro Milwaukee Economic Factbook*, which costs $80.00 for non-members, and the *Metro Milwaukee Market Profile* ($15.00 non-members) (http://www.mmac.org/living/bizfacts/subs/pubs.jsp). The group provides a free listing of local and state government officials; however, it has a *really long* download time: http://www.mmac.org/mmac/about/subs/publica tions.jsp.

West's Wisconsin Statutes Annotated (Eagan, MN: West Group)—This set of hardbound books includes the full text of Wisconsin's statutes, as well as the Constitution and the state's court rules. See the West Group's web site at http://west.thomson.com/ or call customer service at (800) 328-4880 for ordering information. Unlike most states, this commercial version is unofficial. The official version of the statutes, *Wisconsin Statutes and Annotations*, is produced by the Wisconsin Revisor of Statutes Bureau.

Wisconsin's Past and Present: A Historical Atlas (Madison: University of Wisconsin Press, 1998)—This book provides 144 pages of historical maps, photographs, and charts that show Wisconsin's development as a state. It covers both natural and cultural history. See the University of Wisconsin Press web site at http://www.wisc.edu/wisconsinpress/index.html, or call (773) 568-1550.

SOURCES CONSULTED

Dow, Susan L. *State Document Checklists: A Historical Bibliography*. Buffalo, NY: William S. Hein & Co., 1990.

Lane, Margaret T. *State Publications and Depository Libraries: A Reference Handbook*. Westport, CT: Greenwood Press, 1981.

Parrish, David W. *State Government Reference Publications: An Annotated Bibliography*, 2nd ed. Littleton, CO: Libraries Unlimited, 1981.

Peters, John. A. "Government Publications: Only a Library Away." *Wisconsin Library Bulletin* (Fall 1983): 108–109.

Revisor of Statutes Bureau. "1999–2000 Wisconsin Statutes and Annotations," http://www.legis.state.wi.us/rsb/stats.html, December 31, 2001.

State Historical Society of Wisconsin, http://www.wisconsinhistory.org/, December 31, 2001.

State Historical Society of Wisconsin. "State Government Records," http://www.wisconsinhistory.org/archives/readroom/staterec.html.

State Historical Society of Wisconsin Library. "Government Publications Collections of the State Historical Society of Wisconsin," http://www.wisconsinhistory.org/library/govpub/collect.html, December 31, 2001.

Statistical Universe, http://web.lexis-nexis.com/statuniv.

"2000–2001 Wisconsin Acts," http://www.legis.state.wi.us/2001/data/acts/, December 31, 2001.

U.S. Census Bureau. "Appendix 1: Guide to State Statistical Abstracts." *Statistical Abstract of the United States 2000*. Washington DC: Department of Commerce, 2000, 902–905.

Wisconsin. Department of Public Instruction. "The Wisconsin Document Depository Program," http://www.dpi.state.wi.us/dltcl/rll/depgen.html, December 31, 2001.

Wisconsin. Legislative Reference Bureau. "1999–2000 Wisconsin Blue Book," http://www.legis.state.wi.us/lrb/bb/index.html.

Wisconsin. "Portal Home," http://www.wisconsin.gov/state/home, December 31, 2001.

Wisconsin Public Documents, 1942–. Madison: State Historical Society of Wisconsin, 1998.

Wyoming

Daniel D. Cornwall

GOVERNMENT PUBLISHING AND THE DEPOSITORY SYSTEM

The Wyoming state publications depository program was established in 1941 by Wyoming Statute 9-2-1026.6 and is administered by the Wyoming State Library. Currently, the State Library collects seven copies of each publication "issued by a state officer, commission, commissioner or board of a state institution" and distributes them to the State Library's collection, the University of Wyoming, the Library of Congress, and the Council of State Governments. These depositories were established by statute and there is no mechanism for creating new ones. The term "publication" is not defined by the statute.

The State Government Information Coordinator sends semi-yearly reminders to all state government entities regarding statutory deposit requirements. As new publications come to the coordinator's attention, she contacts the publishing entity to acquire copies.

Wyoming state publications are classified according to a system similar to Superintendent of Documents numbers, called WyDocs. All WyDoc numbers begin with a two- or three-letter prefix based on the name of the issuing agency. The basic WyDocs structure is as follows:

XX(X)   Agency class letters

1.   Departmental/administrative office

1a-1   Its advisory body

1a-2, etc.   Other advisory bodies of the department

2.   Departmental division

2a-1   Its advisory body (if applicable)

2a-2, etc.   Other advisory bodies of the division

2b-2, etc.   Sections, units, programs of the division

2c-2, etc.   Institutions tied to the division

Much more detailed information can be found in *WyDocs: The Wyoming State Documents Classification System*, Wyoming Documents Number AD 12.2:3/993. Copies may be obtained by writing the State Library at the address below.

USEFUL ADDRESSES AND TELEPHONE NUMBERS

The most complete collections of state publications may be found at the following libraries:

Wyoming State Library
Statewide Information Services
2301 Capitol Avenue
Cheyenne, WY 82002-0060
Phone Number for Wyoming Reference Questions: (307) 777-6333
E-Mail Address for Wyoming Reference Questions: Wslref@swyld.state.wy.us
Wyoming State Library's Home Page: http://will.state.wy.us/
Depository Program Home Page: http://will.state.wy.us/sis/wydocs/index.html

Coe Library
University of Wyoming
P.O. Box 3334
Laramie, WY 82071
Phone Number for Wyoming Reference Questions: (307) 766-4114
E-Mail Address for State Reference Questions: CoeRef@uwyo.edu
Library Home Page: http://www-lib.uwyo.edu/LibCoe/coe.htm

Those with questions about the state's depository library system may contact the State Documents Coordinator at the address, phone number, or e-mail address given above for the State Library.

INDEXES TO WYOMING STATE PUBLICATIONS

The Wyoming State Library catalogs all state publications received. All state publications may be looked up in the statewide catalog database *WyldCat*, which is available at http://wyldweb.state.wy.us. Be sure to select "Wyoming State Library" as your starting catalog. The Wyoming State Library does not produce a publications checklist.

ESSENTIAL STATE PUBLICATIONS

Directories

Catalog of Wyoming State Grant Programs (Wyoming State Library)—WyDocs Call Number—AD 12.4/3. This is a compilation of data gathered from state agencies that disburse or award grants on a selective, competitive, or discretionary basis. The web version of the directory is at http://cowgirl.state.wy .us/grantscat/. Paper copies may be obtained by contacting the State Library Publications office at (307) 777-5915.

Wyoming Blue Book (Department of State Parks and Cultural Resources)—

WyDocs Call Number—AM 1.2:27/. A comprehensive guide to Wyoming state government; this contains listings of all past governors, elected officials, and other information regarding state agencies. Copies may be obtained by contacting the Wyoming State Archives at Blue Books, State Archives, Department of State Parks and Cultural Resources, Barrett Building, Cheyenne, WY 82002, by phone at (307) 777-7826, or by e-mail at wyarchive@state.wy .us. At the time of this writing, the full 5-volume set sold for $87.47. The *Blue Book* is not available on the Internet.

Wyoming Foundations Directory (Laramie County Community College)— WyDocs Call Number—CK 5.4/2. Compiled and edited by M. Ann Miller, this is a print guide to public and private foundations with interest in the state of Wyoming. Describing itself as "primarily a guide to public and private foundations with interest in the state of Wyoming," the seventh edition (1999) contains information drawn from 990-PF forms, mail and telephone contacts with foundation representatives, and the Foundation Center's FC Search database. Listings are broken down into two sections: grantmakers based in Wyoming, and out-of-state foundations that designate Wyoming as an area of focus for giving. Entries generally provide contact information; application deadlines and procedures; names of officers and directors; areas of interest; and sample grants. At a minimum, contact information and some suggestions as to area of interest are provided. Copies may be ordered for $5.00 from Laramie County Community College Library, Instructional Resources Center, 1400 E. College Drive, Cheyenne, WY 82007, or call (307) 778-1206.

Wyoming State Government Directory (Secretary of State)—WyDocs Call Number—SA 1.8. This annual directory provides a listing of all U.S., state, county, and local officials; state agency personnel, boards, and commissions, and judicial branch members. The directory also contains a listing of Wyoming government addresses, alphabetized by agency. Paper copies can be obtained for $5.00 by contacting the Wyoming Secretary of State at State Capitol Building, Cheyenne, WY 82002-0020, or by calling (307) 777-5333. This directory is available on the Internet at http://soswy.state.wy.us/director/dir-toc.htm.

Financial/Budgetary Resources

A and I Budget Division Web Site (Department of Administration and Information)—This site is on the Internet at http://ai.state.wy.us/budget/index .asp. Everything you need to know about Wyoming's current budget can be found here. In addition to the executive branch budget requests, you can find budget instructions, a directory of departmental specialists, and a financial profile of the state.

Comprehensive Annual Financial Report (State Auditor's Office)—This report provides detailed summaries of the state's financial activities for a given fiscal year. The most recent edition is available online as a series of PDF files at http://sao.state.wy.us/download.htm. Look for the "Accounting" section. For more information, contact the Wyoming State Auditor's Office, 200 West 24th Street, Cheyenne, WY 82002, or call (307) 777-7831.

Wyoming State Government Annual Report (Department of Administration and Information)—WyDocs Call Number—AD 1.4/2. This report includes budget and program information from the five elected officials, cabinet-level agencies, and the separate operating agencies, along with licensing boards and commissions. All of the program entries highlight the outcomes of the goals and objectives from their respective strategic plans. The *Annual Report* is on the web at http://www-wsl.state.wy.us/slpub/reports/. Printed copies are available for $15.00. To order a copy, contact Department of Administration and Information, State Library Division, Publications and Marketing Office, Supreme Court/State Library Building, Room G-12, Cheyenne, WY 82002-0060, or call (307) 777-5915.

Legal Resources

Bill Information (Legislature)—Located at http://legisweb.state.wy.us/sessions/legsess.htm, this site is a gateway to legislative information. Wyoming's legislature alternates between regular sessions and budget sessions. A two-thirds vote is required to introduce a non-budget bill during a budget session. To get to a bill status, first click on the session you are interested in. Then click on "Bill Information." The bill information page offers the following lists of bills for both House and Senate: Introduced Bills, Bill Titles, Resolutions, Bills by Sponsor Name, Bills by Subject, Daily Bill Status, Adopted/Failed Amendments, Engrossed Bills Enrolled Acts, and Chapter Bills. All of these lists are in PDF format. There is no separate search for bills.

State Agencies Rules and Regulations (Secretary of State)—This is located on the web at http://soswy.state.wy.us/rules/rules.htm. It is not published in paper as a separate publication, but copies of individual rules are available from Rules Officer, Wyoming Secretary of State's Office, The Capitol Building, Room B-10, 200 West 24th Street, Cheyenne, WY 82002-0020; call (307) 777-5407; fax: (307) 777-7640, or e-mail rules@state.wy.us.

Wyoming *State Constitution* (Legislature)—The Constitution is on the web at http://legisweb.state.wy.us/statutes/titles/title97.htm. It is not really title 97 of the statutes, but is numbered that way so it can be displayed through the legislative database.

Wyoming State Law Library Database of Supreme Court Decisions (State Law Library)—The Wyoming State Law Library is working in conjunction with the Oklahoma Court Network to create a free, searchable database of Wyoming case law. The goal of the project is to include every case from 1870 to the present. As of this writing, the database includes cases from 1996 to 2003. It is available online at http://courts.state.wy.us/state_law_library.htm. Those with questions about the database can call (307) 777-7509.

Wyoming Statutes (Legislature)—Only the most current version is available on the web at http://legisweb.state.wy.us/statutes/statutes.htm. Wyoming statutes are browseable and searchable. The search page also searches the current year's bill file. The only available search is a full-text search. The page rather unhelpfully includes a search of the entire Internet as well. A user is better off with the browse feature. The paper edition of the statutes is published by LexisNexis.

Statistical Resources

Equality State Almanac (Department of Administration and Information)—WyDocs Call Number—AD1.4/1. This source contains demographic and economic data. The *Almanac* is available on the web at http://eadiv.state.wy.us/almanac/almanac.asp. Copies may also be obtained upon request by contacting the Division of Economic Analysis at (307) 777-7504, or by e-mail at ead@missc.state.wy.us. The *Almanac* is also available at all county libraries, community college and university libraries, and the State Library.

Statistical Report Series (Department of Education, Data and Technology Unit)—This series of reports is available online at http://www.k12.wy.us/DATATECH/statseries.html. Report number one deals with assessed school values and tax levies, report number two provides information about enrollment and staffing, and report number three gives financial data for school districts. Other statistical reports are available on the Data and Technology Unit home page at http://www.k12.wy.us/DATAandTECH.HTM. Those with questions can call the Department of Education at (307) 777-7675.

Wyoming Vital Statistics (Department of Health)—WyDocs Call Number—HE 5.4/1. This annual report includes data on births, deaths, marriages, and divorces. It is available on the web at http://wdhfs.state.wy.us/vital_records/. Paper copies can be obtained by contacting Vital Records Service, Wyoming Department of Health, Preventive Health and Safety Division, Hathaway Building, Cheyenne, WY 82002, or by e-mail at ddrisc@state.wy.us.

Other Resources

Annals of Wyoming (Wyoming State Historical Society)—WyDocs Call Number—UW 41.9/2. This quarterly print journal is available as a benefit of membership in the Wyoming State Historical Society. Membership is open to anyone interested in Wyoming and western history. In addition to the *Annals*, membership dues include receipt of the *Wyoming History Journal* (published quarterly), and ten issues of the society newsletter, the *Wyoming History News*. The membership rates are: $20.00 for individuals, $30.00 for dual membership (two people at one address), $15.00 for students under the age of 21, and $40.00 for institutional memberships. To join the society, or for more information about the organization, write to Judy West, Membership Coordinator, Wyoming State Historical Society, PMB#184, 1740H Dell Range Road, Cheyenne, WY 82009. The most recent table of contents for the *Annals* may be viewed on the Internet at http://wyshs.org/annals.htm.

Wyoming Corporations Search (Secretary of State)—Located at http://soswy.state.wy.us/corporat/webtips.htm, this site provides extensive, if cryptic information about Wyoming-based corporations. Print the page at the URL above before searching the corporations databases because it (1) gives detailed search help and (2) provides an explanation of the fields found in each record. Unfortunately, you can search only by name of corporation. If you are so inclined and have appropriate database software, you may download the entire 20MB corporations database in a "zipped, XBASE" format. The file is approximately 184 MB when unzipped.

WYOMING'S WORLD WIDE WEB HOME PAGE

Wyoming's web page has been around since 1995 and is administered by the Department of Administration and Information, Division of Information Technology. The home page for the state of Wyoming is found at http://www.state.wy.us, and has its main navigation bar at the left of the page. Be sure to scroll down to the bottom of the page to find all of the news and announcements on the home page! There are about three screens' worth of page, and lower parts of the page are easy to miss. In addition to the navigation buttons discussed below, the home page has three major sections—an unannotated list of "Featured Links," a piece of "Interesting Wyoming Trivia," and a list of upcoming educational/cultural events around the state. Unfortunately, the design of the home page makes this event list easy to miss.

The major links from the home page are Governor's Office, About Wyoming, Business, Government, Tourism, Kids' Page, News, Moving, and Virtual Tour.

- *Governor's Office*—Provides links to Wyoming boards and commissions, gubernatorial proclamations and executive orders, and a RealAudio archive of events and announcements.
- *About Wyoming*—This site (http://www.state.wy.us/about.asp) is *the* place to go for student reports about Wyoming. This page has links to state symbols and history. It also contains a link to the Wyoming's Geographic Information Systems initiative, which contains a wealth of advanced geospatial data that might not be useful to students until they hit college!
- *Business*—A list of unannotated links to departments and resources that the web page author felt might be helpful to businesses. A more helpful page can be found by clicking on the phrase "Wyoming is open for business," which takes you to a page of different links sorted by subject and also contains the Wyoming Business Directory.
- *Government*—Links you to local and federal agencies as well as state agencies.
- *Tourism*—This link takes you to an attractive page that offers photogenic sites, an events calendar, and road construction information.
- *Kids*—Takes you to child-oriented games and information.
- *News*—This page is a hidden treat. In addition to the expected list of agency press releases, the News page links you to the home pages of Wyoming magazines, newspapers, and radio and television stations. A great place to find local Wyoming news.
- *Moving*—Contains relocation resources including links to Wyoming job banks and cost-of-living information.
- *Virtual Tour*—This page is actually a list of county profiles. Each page contains general information about the county, local business and industry, recreational opportunities, and current weather and road conditions.

The search page for Wyoming is powered by Inktomi and supports AND, OR, and phrase searches.

COMMERCIAL PUBLICATIONS AND WEB SITES

Wyoming: A Source Book (University Press of Colorado, Niwot, CO, 1996)—This source book contains topics ranging from water, environmental, and land-use issues to statistics on population, wildlife, agriculture, crime, American Indians, politics, social services, and more. It includes a variety of maps, charts, and graphs. The material in this volume was gathered from state and federal agencies. It is available from the publisher's web site at http://www.upcolorado.com/index.asp. Call (720) 406-8849 for more information.

Wyoming Place Names (Mountain Press Publishing Co., Missoula, MT, 1998)—This is a guide to the origin of place names in Wyoming with an emphasis on state history. This 240-page book was compiled from information in books, newspapers, private letters, pamphlets, and interviews. See the publisher's web site at http://www.mtnpress.com/, or call (800) 234-5308.

SOURCES CONSULTED

Numerous departmental web pages via the state's home page, http://www.state.wy.us/.

Survey response from Emily Sieger, State Government Information Coordinator, Wyoming State Library.

WyDocs: The Wyoming State Documents Classification System. Wyoming Documents Number AD 12.2:3/993.

Appendix: Quick Reference Guide to Depository Laws and Coordinating Agencies

State	Depository Law Citation and Web Address for Free Edition of State Laws	Depository Program Coordinating Agency
Alabama	*Alabama Code*, sects. 41-8-40 to 41-8-48 http://alisdb.legislature.state.al.us/acas/alisonstart.asp (select "Visit *ALISON*" then click the "*Code of Alabama*" tab on the left side of the screen)	Program not funded.
Alaska	*Alaska Statutes*, sects. 14.56.90 to 14.56.180 http://www.legis.state.ak.us/folhome.htm	Alaska State Library Government Publications P.O. Box 110571 Juneau, AK 99811-0571 (907) 465-2927 http://library. state. ak.us/asp/asp.html
Arizona	*Arizona Revised Statutes*, sect. 41-1335 http://www.azleg.state.az.us/ars/ars.htm	Arizona State Library, Archives and Public Records Research Division 1700 West Washington Phoenix, AZ 85007 (602) 542-3701 http://www.lib.az.us/is/index.html
Arkansas	*Arkansas Code of 1987 Annotated*, sects. 13-2-201 to 13-2-214 http://www.arkleg.state.ar.us/data/resources.asp	Arkansas State Library One Capitol Mall Little Rock, AR 72201 (501) 682-2053 http://www.asl.lib.ar.us/

State	Depository Law Citation and Web Address for Free Edition of State Laws	Depository Program Coordinating Agency
California	*California Government Code*, sects. 14900 to 14912 http://www.leginfo.ca.gov/calaw.html	California State Library Government Publications Section Room 304 Sacramento, CA 95814 (916) 654-0069 http://www.library.ca.gov/html/ gps.cfm
Colorado	*Colorado Revised Statutes*, sects. 24-90-201 to 24-90-208 http://www.colorado.gov/ government.htm (select *Colorado Revised Statutes* in the "Colorado Constitution and Statutes" section)	Colorado State Library State Publications Library 201 E. Colfax Room 314 Denver, CO 80203 (303) 866-6725 http://www.cde.state.co.us/ stateinfo/index.htm
Connecticut	*General Statutes of Connecticut*, sects. 11-9b to 11-9d http://www.cga.state.ct.us/lco/ Statute_Web_ Site_LCO.htm	Connecticut State Library 231 Capitol Avenue Hartford, CT 06106 (860) 757-6570 http://www.cslib.org/gis.htm
Delaware	*Delaware Code Annotated*, title 29, part VIII, chapter 87, sect. 8731 http://www.michie.com/resources1.asp (select Delaware in the "Legal Resources" section)	Delaware Public Archives 121 Duke of York Street Dover, DE 19901 (302) 744-5000 http://www.state.de.us/sos/dpa/
Florida	*Florida Statutes*, chap. 257.05 http://www.leg.state.fl.us/Statutes/ index.cfm	State Library of Florida Florida Collection R. A. Gray Building 500 S. Bronough Street Tallahassee, FL 32399-0250 (850) 245-6600 http://dlis.dos.state.fl.us/stlib/flcoll. html
Georgia	*Official Code of Georgia Annotated*, title 20, chap. 5, sect. 2 http://www.legis.state.ga.us/ (select "GA Code")	Government Documents Department University of Georgia Libraries Athens, GA 30602-1645 (706) 542-3251 http://www.libs.uga.edu/govdocs/ collections/georgia.html

State	Depository Law Citation and Web Address for Free Edition of State Laws	Depository Program Coordinating Agency
Hawaii	*Hawaii Revised Statutes*, chap. 93, parts 1 to 2 http://www.capitol.hawaii.gov/default. asp (select "Bill Status and Docs")	Hawaii State Library Hawaii and Pacific Section 478 South King Street Honolulu, HI 96813-2901 (808) 586-3535 http://www.hawaii.gov/hidocs/ hp_main.html
Idaho	*Idaho Statutes*, title 33, chap. 25, sect. 2505 http://www3.state.id.us/idstat/TOC/ idstTOC. html	Idaho State Library State Documents 325 W. State Street Boise, ID 83702 (208) 334-2150 http://www.lili.org/statedocs/
Illinois	*Illinois Administrative Code*, title 23, subtitle B, chap. 1, part 3020 http://www.cyberdriveillinois.com/ library/isl/depos/ildeposrules.html (*Code* not full text, this section only)	Illinois State Library 300 S. 2nd Street Springfield, IL 62701-1696 (217) 782-7596 http://www.sos.state.il.us/library/ isl/depos/depos.html
Indiana	*Indiana Code*, title 4, article 23, chap. 7.1, sects. 25 to 28 http://www.in.gov/legislative/ic/code/	Indiana Division, Indiana State Library 140 North Senate Avenue Indianapolis, IN 46204 (317) 232-3670 http://www.statelib.lib.in.us/www/ isl/whoweare/indiana.html
Iowa	*Iowa Code*, title 7, chap. 256, subchap. 4, part 1, sects. 256.50 to 256.56 http://www.legis.state.ia.us/Code.html	State Library of Iowa State Documents Center 1112 East Grand Avenue Des Moines, IA 50319 (515) 281-4102 http://www.silo.lib.ia.us/for-state-govt/state-documents-center/ index.html
Kansas	*Kansas Statutes*, chap. 75, article 25, sects. 2566 to 2568 http://www.kslegislature.org/cgi-bin/ statutes/index.cgi	Kansas State Library 300 S.W. 10th Avenue, Room 343-N Topeka, KS 66612 (785) 296-3296 http://kslib.info/ref/

State	Depository Law Citation and Web Address for Free Edition of State Laws	Depository Program Coordinating Agency
Kentucky	*Kentucky Revised Statutes*, title 14, chap. 171, sect. 500 http://www.lrc.state.ky.us/statrev/frontpg.htm	State Publications Program Department for Libraries and Archives 300 Coffee Tree Road P.O. Box 537 Frankfort, KY 40602-0537 (502) 564-8300, ext. 248 http://www.kdla.net/arch/statpub.htm
Louisiana	*Louisiana Revised Statutes*, title 25, sects. 121 to 124.1 http://www.legis.state.la.us/tsrs/search.htm	State Library of Louisiana P.O. Box 131 Baton Rouge, LA 70821 (225) 342-4914 http://www.state.lib.la.us/Dept/UserServ/recorder.htm
Maine	*Maine Revised Statutes*, title 1, chap. 13, subchap. 3, sects. 501 to 505 http://janus.state.me.us/legis/statutes/	Maine State Library Documents Office State House Station #64 Augusta, ME 04333 (207) 287-5600 http://www.state.me.us/msl/about/msldocs. htm
Maryland	*Maryland Code*, Education vol., title 23, subtitle 3, sects. 301 to 304 http://www.michie.com/resources1.asp (select Maryland in the "Legal Resources" section)	Enoch Pratt Free Library 400 Cathedral Street Baltimore, MD 21201 (410) 396-5430 http://www.epfl.net/index.html (this library coordinated the program until it was recently discontinued due to lack of funding)
Massachusetts	*Massachusetts General Laws*, title II, chap. 6, sects. 39 to 39B http://www.state.ma.us/legis/laws/mgl/	George Fingold Library State House Room 341 Boston, MA 02133 (617) 727-6279 http://www.state.ma.us/lib/government/govt.htm
Michigan	*Michigan Compiled Laws*, chap. 397, Act 540 of 1982, sect. 397.19 http://michiganlegislature.org (select "Law Info")	Library of Michigan 717 West Allegan Street P.O. Box 30007 Lansing, MI 48909-7507 (517) 373-1300 http://www.michigan.gov/hal/0,1607,7-160-17449_18637-57845--,00.html

State	Depository Law Citation and Web Address for Free Edition of State Laws	Depository Program Coordinating Agency
Minnesota	*Minnesota Statutes*, chap. 3, sect. 3.302 http://www.leg.state.mn.us/leg/statutes.asp	Minnesota Legislative Reference Library 645 State Office Building St. Paul, MN 55155-1050 (651) 296-8338 http://www.leg.state.mn.us/lrl/mndocs/mndocs.asp
Mississippi	*Mississippi Code of 1972*, title 25, chap. 51, sects. 1 to 7 http://www.michie.com/resources1.asp (select Mississippi in the "Legal Resources" section)	Mississippi Library Commission Government Services Department 1221 Ellis Avenue Jackson, MS 39209-7328 (601) 961-4119 http://www.mlc.lib.ms.us/reference/state-docs/index.htm
Missouri	*Missouri Revised Statutes*, title 11, chap. 181, sects. 100 to 130 http://www.moga.state.mo.us/homestat.asp	Missouri State Library P.O. Box 387 or 600 N. Main Jefferson City, MO 65102-0387 (573) 751-3615 http://www.sos.mo.gov/library/reference/statedocs/stdocs.asp
Montana	*Montana Code Annotated*, title 22, chap. 1, part 2, sects. 211 to 218 http://leg.state.mt.us/css/mtcode_const/laws.asp	State Publications Center Montana State Library 1515 East 6th Avenue P.O. Box 201800 Helena, MT 59620-1800 (406) 444-5351 http://msl.state.mt.us/lisd/spc/index. htm
Nebraska	*Nebraska Revised Statutes*, chap. 51, sects. 411 to 418 http://statutes.unicam.state.ne.us/default. asp	Nebraska Library Commission The Atrium 1200 N Street, Suite 120 Lincoln, NE 68508-2023 (402) 471-4016 http://www.nlc.state.ne.us/docs/stclear. html
Nevada	*Nevada Revised Statutes*, title 33, chap. 378, sects. 150 to 210 http://www.leg.state.nv.us/law1.cfm	Nevada State Library and Archives 100 North Stewart Street Carson City, NV 89701-4285 (775) 684-3320 http://dmla.clan.lib.nv.us/docs/nsla/stpubs/stpubs.htm

State	Depository Law Citation and Web Address for Free Edition of State Laws	Depository Program Coordinating Agency
New Hampshire	*New Hampshire Revised Statutes*, title XVI, chap. 202-B, sects. 1 to 5 http://www.gencourt.state.nh.us/rsa/html/indexes/default.html	New Hampshire State Library Electronic and Government Information Resources Section 20 Park Street Concord, NH 03301 (603) 271-2143 http://www.state.nh.us/nhsl/stdocs/index.html
New Jersey	*New Jersey Revised Statutes*, title 52, chap. 14, sects. 24 to 25.1 http://www.njleg.state.nj.us/ (look for link in "Laws and Constitution")	State Library of New Jersey State Government Information Services P.O. Box 520 Trenton, NJ 08625-0520 (609) 292-6294 http://www.njstatelib.org/aboutus/SLIC/Libnjdoc.htm
New Mexico	*New Mexico Statutes Annotated*, chap. 18, article 2, sects. 18-2-4 to 18-2-4.1, sect. 18-2-7.1 http://www.michie.com/resources1.asp (select New Mexico in the "Legal Resources" section)	New Mexico State Library State Depository Clearinghouse 1209 Camino Carlos Rey Santa Fe, NM 87507 (505) 476-9716 http://www.stlib.state.nm.us/libraryservices/statepubs/stpubabout.html
New York	*Consolidated Laws of New York*, PPD, *New York State Printing and Public Documents*, articles 1 to 4 http://assembly.state.ny.us/leg/ (select "New York State Laws")	New York State Library Documents Unit Cultural Education Center Empire State Plaza Albany, NY 12230 (518) 474-7492 http://www.nysl.nysed.gov/statedoc.htm
North Carolina	*North Carolina General Statutes*, chap. 125, article 1A, sects. 125-11.5 to 125-11.13 http://www.ncleg.net/Statutes/Statutes.asp	State Library of North Carolina Information Services Branch 4641 Mail Service Center Raleigh, NC 27699-4641 (919) 733-3270 http://statelibrary.dcr.state.nc.us/tss/deposito.htm
North Dakota	*North Dakota Century Code*, title 54, chap. 24, sect. 9 http://www.state.nd.us/lr/information/statutes/cent-code.html	North Dakota State Library State Documents Services 604 E. Boulevard Avenue, Dept. 250 Bismarck, ND 58505-0800 (701) 328-4622 http://ndsl.lib.state.nd.us/StateGovernment.html

State	Depository Law Citation and Web Address for Free Edition of State Laws	Depository Program Coordinating Agency
Ohio	*Ohio Revised Code*, title 1, chap. 149, sects. 149.09, 149.11, 149.12, and others http://onlinedocs.andersonpublishing.com/revisedcode/	State Library of Ohio Main Library 274 East First Avenue Columbus, OH 43201 (614) 644-7004 http://winslo.state.oh.us/govinfo/slogovt.html
Oklahoma	*Oklahoma Statutes*, title 65, chap. 3, sect. 113.3 http://www.lsb.state.ok.us/tsrs/os_oc.htm	Oklahoma Publications Clearinghouse Oklahoma Department of Libraries 200 NE 18th Street Oklahoma City, OK 73105-3298 (405) 522-3505 http://www.odl.state.ok.us/sginfo/opchist.htm
Oregon	*Oregon Revised Statutes*, chap. 357, sects. 357.001 to 357.006, and 357.090 to 357.105 http://landru.leg.state.or.us/ors/	Oregon State Library 250 Winter Street NE Salem, OR 97301-3950 (503) 378-4198 http://www.osl.state.or.us/home/techserv/ordocs.html
Pennsylvania	*Pennsylvania Code*, title 22, chap. 143, sects. 143.1 to 143.8 http://www.pacode.com/ (These are regulations. PA laws and statutes are not freely available online.)	State Library of Pennsylvania Walnut Street and Commonwealth Avenue Box 1601 Harrisburg, PA 17105-1601 (717) 787-3273 http://www.statelibrary.state.pa.us/libraries/site/default.asp
Rhode Island	*Rhode Island General Laws*, title 29, chap. 7, sects. 29-7-1 to 29-7-8 http://www.rilin.state.ri.us/Statutes/Statutes.html	Rhode Island State Library State House, Room 208 Providence, RI 02903 (401) 222-2473 http://www.state.ri.us/library/clear/CLEAR.htm
South Carolina	*Code of Laws of South Carolina*, title 60, chap. 2, sects. 60-2-10 to 60-2-30, and others http://www.scstatehouse.net/html-pages/research.html	South Carolina State Library 1500 Senate Street P.O. Box 11469 Columbia, SC 29211 (803) 734-8666 http://www.state.sc.us/scsl/doclibs2.html

State	Depository Law Citation and Web Address for Free Edition of State Laws	Depository Program Coordinating Agency
South Dakota	*South Dakota Codified Laws*, title 14, chap. 1A, sects. 14-1A-1 to 14-1A-9 http://legis.state.sd.us/statutes/index.cfm	South Dakota State Library Mercedes MacKay Building 800 Governors Drive Pierre, SD 57501-2294 (605) 773-3131 http://www.sdstatelibrary.com/govinfo/depositories.htm
Tennessee	*Tennessee Code*, title 12, chap. 6, sects. 12-6-107 to 12-6-110, 12-6-112, and others http://www.michie.com/resources1.asp (select Tennessee in the "Legal Resources" section)	Tennessee State Library and Archives Public Services Section 403 Seventh Avenue North Nashville, TN 37243-0312 (615) 471-2764 http://www.state.tn.us/sos/statelib/techsvs/tsp/tsphome. htm
Texas	*Texas Statutes*, Government Code, title 4, chap. 441, sects. 441-101 to 441-106 http://www.capitol.state.tx.us/statutes/statutes. html	Texas State Library and Archives Commission P.O. Box 12927 Austin, TX 78711 (512) 463-5455 http://www.tsl.state.tx.us/statepubs/index.html
Utah	*Utah Code*, title 9, chap. 7, sects. 9-7-101 to 9-7-203, 9-7-207 to 9-7-209, and others http://www.le.state.ut.us/Documents/code_const.htm	State Library of Utah Utah State Library Division 250 North 1950 West, Suite A Salt Lake City, UT 84116-7901 (801) 715-6776 http://library.utah.gov/depositoryprogram.html
Vermont	*Vermont Statutes Annotated*, title 22, chap. 13, sect. 601; title 29, chap. 53, sect. 1101, and others http://www.leg.state.vt.us/statutes/statutes2.htm	Vermont Department of Libraries 109 State Street Montpelier, VT 05609-0601 (802) 828-3268 http://dol.state.vt.us/
Virginia	*Code of Virginia*, title 42.1, chap. 1, sects. 42.1-19 to 42.1-19.4 http://leg1.state.va.us/000/src.htm	Library of Virginia 800 E. Broad Street Richmond, VA 23219 (804) 692-3562 http://www.lva.lib.va.us/whatwedo/statedocs/index. htm

State	Depository Law Citation and Web Address for Free Edition of State Laws	Depository Program Coordinating Agency
Washington	*Revised Code of Washington*, title 27, chap. 27.04, sect. 27.04.045; title 40, chap. 40.06, sects. 40.06.10 to 40.06.900, and others http://www.leg.wa.gov/rcw/index.cfm	Washington State Library State Documents P.O. Box 42460 Olympia, WA 98504-2460 (360) 704-5221 http://www.statelib.wa.gov/ gov_publications.aspx
West Virginia	*West Virginia Code*, chap. 10, article 1, sect. 10-1-18a http://www.legis.state.wv.us/ State_Code/finishedData/toc2.html	West Virginia Library Commission Cultural Center 1900 Kanawha Boulevard East Charleston, WV 25305 (304) 558-2045 http://librarycommission.lib.wv.us/ index.htm
Wisconsin	*Wisconsin Statutes*, chap. 35, subchap. 2, sects. 35.78 to 35.91 http://www.legis.state.wi.us/rsb/ stats.html	Wisconsin Reference and Loan Library 2109 South Stoughton Road Madison, WI 53716-2899 (608) 224-6174 http://www.dpi.state.wi.us/dltcl/rll/ inddep.html
Wyoming	*Wyoming Statutes*, title 9, chap. 2, article 10, sect. 9-2-1026.6(c) http://legisweb.state.wy.us/statutes/ statutes.htm	Wyoming State Library Statewide Information Services 2301 Capitol Avenue Cheyenne, WY 82002-0060 (307) 777-6333 http://will.state.wy.us/sis/wydocs/ index.html

Index

About the Authors

LORI L. SMITH began her career in 1987 as the coordinator of the Missouri documents collection at St. Louis Public Library. She became the head of the government documents department at Southeastern Louisiana University's Sims Memorial Library in 1991. Shortly thereafter, she was appointed by the state librarian to serve on a task force charged with drafting bylaws for the Louisiana Advisory Council for the State Documents Depository Program. She has served as a member of the council since its inception.

DANIEL C. BARKLEY is Coordinator of Government Information/Periodicals/Microforms at the University of New Mexico, Albuquerque. He has served as Chair of the American Library Association's Government Documents Round Table (GODORT) and is incoming Chair of the U.S. Public Printer's Depository Library Council. He is also the Chair of the New Mexico Depository Library Council.

DANIEL D. CORNWALL is the administrator of the Alaska State Publications Program as well as the technical services librarian for the Alaska State Library.

ERIC W. JOHNSON is the Interim Library Director at the Sims Memorial Library, Southeastern Louisiana University, Hammond, Louisiana.

J. LOUISE MALCOMB teaches Government Information: Resources and Organization for Indiana University's School of Library and Information Science, Bloomington, Indiana. She has also served there as Head of Undergraduate Library Services and as Head and Librarian for Geography and Maps.